# Lecture Notes in Computer Science 2745

Edited by G. Goos, J. Hartmanis, and J. van Leeuwen

T0226142

**Springer**
*Berlin*
*Heidelberg*
*New York*
*Hong Kong*
*London*
*Milan*
*Paris*
*Tokyo*

Minyi Guo   Laurence Tianruo Yang (Eds.)

# Parallel and Distributed Processing and Applications

International Symposium, ISPA 2003
Aizu-Wakamatsu, Japan, July 2-4, 2003
Proceedings

 Springer

Series Editors

Gerhard Goos, Karlsruhe University, Germany
Juris Hartmanis, Cornell University, NY, USA
Jan van Leeuwen, Utrecht University, The Netherlands

Volume Editors

Minyi Guo
The University of Aizu, Department of Computer Software
Aizu-Wakamatsu City, Fukushima 965-8580, Japan
E-mail: minyi@u-aizu.ac.jp

Laurence Tianruo Yang
St. Francis Xavier University, Department of Computer Science
Antigonish, NS, B2G 2W5, Canada
E-mail: lyang@stfx.ca

Cataloging-in-Publication Data applied for

Bibliographic information published by Die Deutsche Bibliothek
Die Deutsche Bibliothek lists this publication in the Deutsche Nationalbibliografie;
detailed bibliographic data is available in the Internet at <http://dnb.ddb.de>.

CR Subject Classification (1998): F.1, F.2, D.1, D.2, D.4, C.2, C.4, K.6, H.2, H.4

ISSN 0302-9743
ISBN 3-540-xxx Springer-Verlag Berlin Heidelberg New York

Springer-Verlag Berlin Heidelberg New York
a member of BertelsmannSpringer Science+Business Media GmbH

http://www.springer.de

© Springer-Verlag Berlin Heidelberg 2003
Printed in Germany

Typesetting: Camera-ready by author, data conversion by PTP-Berlin GmbH
Printed on acid-free paper     SPIN: 10929261     06/3142     5 4 3 2 1 0

# Preface

Welcome to the proceedings of the 2003 International Symposium on Parallel
and Distributed Processing and Applications (ISPA 2003) which was held in
Aizu-Wakamatsu City, Japan, July 2–4, 2003.

Parallel and distributed processing has become a key technology which will
play an important part in determining, or at least shaping, future research and
development activities in many academic and industrial branches. This international symposium ISPA 2003 brought together computer scientists and engineers,
applied mathematicians and researchers to present, discuss and exchange ideas,
results, work in progress and experience of research in the area of parallel and
distributed computing for problems in science and engineering applications.

There were very many paper submissions from 13 countries and regions, including not only Asia and the Pacific, but also Europe and North America. All
submissions were reviewed by at least three program or technical committee
members or external reviewers. It was extremely difficult to select the presentations for the symposium because there were so many excellent and interesting
ones. In order to allocate as many papers as possible and keep the high quality
of the conference, we finally decided to accept 39 papers (30 long papers and
9 short papers) for oral technical presentations. We believe all of these papers
and topics will not only provide novel ideas, new results, work in progress and
state-of-the-art techniques in this field, but will also stimulate future research
activities in the area of parallel and distributed processing with applications.

The exciting program for this symposium was the result of the hard and
excellent work of many people, such as external reviewers and program or technical committee members. We would like to express our sincere appreciation to
all authors for their valuable contributions and to all program or technical committee members and external reviewers for their cooperation in completing the
program under a very tight schedule.

April 2003

Minyi Guo
Laurence Tianruo Yang

# Organization

ISPA 2003 is organized mainly by the Department of Computer Software, University of Aizu, Japan.

## Executive Committee

| | |
|---|---|
| Honorary General Chair: | Tetsuhiko Ikegami, University of Aizu, Japan |
| Steering Committee: | Li Xie, Nanjing University, China |
| | Nikolay N. Mirenkov, University of Aizu, Japan |
| | Damin Wei, University of Aizu, Japan |
| Program Chair: | Minyi Guo, University of Aizu, Japan |
| Program Vice-Chair: | Laurence Tianruo Yang |
| | St. Francis Xavier University, Canada |
| Publication Chair: | Wenxi Chen, University of Aizu, Japan |
| Local Organization Chair: | Hirokuni Kurokawa, University of Aizu, Japan |

## Sponsoring Institutions

Association for Computing Machinery
The Information Processing Society of Japan
Lecture Notes in Computer Science (LNCS), Springer-Verlag, Heidelberg

# Program/Technical Committee

| | |
|---|---|
| S. Akl | Queen's University, Canada |
| H.R. Arabnia | University of Georgia, USA |
| D.A. Bader | University of New Mexico, USA |
| A. Bourgeois | Georgia State University, USA |
| R. Buyya | Monash University, Australia |
| W. Cai | Nanyang Technological University, Singapore |
| J. Cao | Hong Kong Polytechnic University, China |
| W.-L. Chang | Southern Taiwan University of Technology |
| V. Chaudhary | Wayne State University, USA |
| H.-C. Chen | Clark Atlanta University, USA |
| D. Chen | Nanjing University, China |
| W. Chen | University of Aizu, Japan |
| Z. Cheng | University of Aizu, Japan |
| X. He | University of Sydney, Australia |
| C.-H. Hsu | Chung Hua University, Taiwan |
| Z.Y. Huang | University of Otago, New Zealand |
| Q. Jin | University of Aizu, Japan |
| H. Kato | Shonan Institute of Technology, Japan |
| H. Kurokawa | University of Aizu, Japan |
| Z. Liu | Nagasaki Institute of Applied Science, Japan |
| S. Olariu | Old Dominion University, USA |
| T. Rauber | University of Bayreuth, Germany |
| H. Shen | JAIST, Japan |
| E. Sha | University of Texas at Dallas, USA |
| S.G. Sedukhin | University of Aizu, Japan |
| S. Sekiguchi | AIST, Japan |
| I. Stojmenovic | University of Ottawa, Canada |
| N.-C. Wang, | Chaoyang University of Technology, Taiwan |
| G. Wu | University of Shanghai, China |
| Z. Wu | Bond University, Australia |
| C. Xu, | Wayne State University, USA |
| C.-S. Yang | National Sun Yat-Sen University, Taiwan |
| L.T. Yang | St. Francis Xavier University, Canada |
| J. Zhang | University of Alabama, USA |
| W. Zhang | University of Shanghai, China |
| W. Zhou | Deakin University, Australia |
| A.Y. Zomaya | University of Sydney, Australia |

# Table of Contents

## Session 2A: Network Routing

## Session 2B: Performance Evaluation of Parallel Systems

## Session 3A: Wireless Communication and Mobile Computing

## Session 3B: Parallel Algorithms (I)

## Session 4A: Parallel Architecture and Network Topology

## Session 4B: Data Mining and Evolutionary Computing

## Session 5A: Image Processing and Modelling

## Session 5B: Parallel Algorithms (II)

## Session 6A: Network Security

## Session 6B: Database and Multimedia Systems

## Author Index

# Localized Algorithms and Their Applications in Ad Hoc Wireless Networks

Jie Wu

Department of Computer Science and Engineering
Florida Atlantic University
Boca Raton, FL 33431
jie@cse.fau.edu
http://www.cse.fau.edu/jie

**Abstract.** An ad hoc wireless network is a special type of wireless multi-hop network without infrastructure or centralized administration. As a result of the mobility of their nodes, ad hoc wireless networks are characterized by dynamically changing topologies. A localized algorithm is a special distributed algorithm where each node performs an exceedingly simple task based on local information, with no information sequentially propagated globally in the network. The importance of localized algorithms is their scalability in mobile environments. Decisions made based on localized algorithms are adjustable to the change (such as a topological one) due to the mobile node. We discuss a generic framework that can capture many existing localized broadcast algorithms in ad hoc wireless networks. The framework can easily integrate other objectives such as energy-efficient design and reliability that ensures broadcast coverage. In addition, the framework is extensible to cover other collective communication, which includes one-to-many (multicasting), all-to-one (reduction or aggregation), and all-to-all (gossiping).

An ad hoc wireless network [15], or simply ad hoc network, is a special type of wireless multi-hop network without infrastructure or centralized administration. Unlike cellular networks where nodes interact through a centralized base station, nodes in an ad hoc network interact in a peer-to-peer fashion. As a result of the mobility of their nodes, ad hoc networks are characterized by dynamically changing topologies. The applications of ad hoc networks range from civilian (e.g., distributed computing, sensor networks) to disaster recovery (search-and-rescue), and military (battlefield).

*Collective communication* represents a set of important communication functions that involve multiple senders and receivers. Four basic types of collective communication services include: *one-to-many communication* (also called multicasting), *one-to-all communication* (broadcasting), *all-to-one communication* (reduction or aggregation), and *all-to-all communication*. In ad hoc networks, broadcasting a message to the entire network is a basic operation and has extensive applications. For example, broadcasting is used in the route discovery process in several reactive routing protocols ([8], [12], [14]), when advising an

M. Guo and L.T.Yang (Eds.): ISPA 2003, LNCS 2745, pp. 1–5, 2003.

error message to erase invalid routes from the routing table [11]. Operations that rely on broadcasting include naming, addressing, and dense-mode multicasting. The aggregation process is frequently used in sensor netw orks [6], where information captured at each sensor is gathered and sent to the base station. In the reduction process, different messages from different senders are combined to form a single message for the receiv er. Although collective communication has been extensively studied in wired netw orks and multicomputers [5], it is not well studied in ad hoc networks. All solutions in wired netw orks and multicomputers are based on constructing and maintaining global information/infrastructure. Due to the dynamic nature of ad hoc netw orks, global information/infrastructures, obtained through global information exchanges, are no longer suitable.

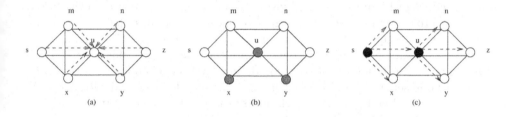

**Fig. 1.** (a) Broadcast storm problem. (b) Forward node set without routing history (static). (c) F orw ard node set with routing history (dynamic). Blac nodes are visited nodes and gray nodes are forward nodes.

*Blind flooding* is a simple approach to perform broadcasting without using an y global information/infrastructure, where a broadcast message is forwarded by every node in the netw ork exactly once. Due to the broadcast nature of wireless communication (i.e., when a source sends a message, all its neighbors will hear it), blind flooding may generate excessive redundant transmission. Redundant transmission may cause a serious problem, referred to as the *broadc ast storm problem* [19], in which redundant messages cause communication contention and collision. Figure 1 (c) shows an example of a broadcasting initiated from source *s* in an ad hoc netw ork, represented by a unit disk graph model [3] where node connectivity is determined by geographical distance betw een nodes. Only node *u* needs to forward the message to ensure the cov erage based on the broadcast nature of the communication. When all nodes forward the message once, serious con tention and collision may occur at node *u* (see Figure 1 (a)).

The follo wing approach is normally used to address the broadcast storm problem: only a subset of nodes is used to perform message forwarding. Such nodes are called *forward no des* Ideally, a small set of forward nodes should be selected to minimize message conten tion and collision and, at the same time, to ensure broadcast cov erage. Both deterministic and probabilistic approaches can be used to find a forward node set. The probabilistic approach ([7], [19]) offers a simple scheme in which each node, upon receiving a broadcast message, forwards the message with probability $p$. The value $p$ is determined by relevan t information gathered at each node. How ev er, the probabilistic approals cannot guarantee broadcast coverage and will not be considered further. In the deterministic approach, the forward node set can be selected statically (independent of an y broadcast process) or dynamically (during a particular broadcast process).

In static approaches, the forward node status of eac h node is determined based on network topology only and it is independant of any particular broadcasting. Figure 1 (b) shows such a forward node set (not a minimum one). The source node may or may not belong to the set, but it will forward the broadcast message. In dynamic approaches, the forward node status of each node is also dependent on the *location of the source and the progress of the broadcast process* F orward nodes that have relay ed the broadcast message are called *visited nodes* (blac k nodes in Figure 1 (c)), and visited node information can be piggybacked with the broadcast message. The status of eac h node can be determined right after the first receipt of the broadcast message or after a backoff delay (so more copies of the same message may arrive before the decision). In this way, the status can be better decided with visited node information. Therefore, the resultant forward node set in general is smaller than the one derived statically. In addition, the forward node status of each node can be determined by itself or by its neighbors. The forward node set also forms a *connected dominating set* (CDS). A dominating set is a subset of nodes in the netw ork where every node is either in the subset or a neighbor of a node in the subset. It has been prov ed that finding the smallest set of forward nodes with global netw ork information/infrastructure is NP-hard.

A localized algorithm [6] is a special distributed algorithm where each node performs an exceedingly simple task based on local information, with no information sequentially propagated globally in the net w ork.The importance of localized algorithms is their scalability in mobile environments. Decisions made based on localized algorithms are adjustable to the change (such as a topological one) due to the mobile node. Many broadcast algorithms ([1], [2], [4], [9], [10], [13], [16], [17], [18], [20], [21], [24]) ha v ebeen proposed in ad hoc netw orksto address the broadcast storm problem. Some of them are based on global information/infrastructure. Some others are built on distributed algorithms that are not localized; that is, ones that exhibit sequential information propagation with long dela y and costly maintenance, making them less applicable in ad hoc netw orks. Among existing localized broadcast schemes, some are either ineffective in redundancy reduction or are too specialized to integrate other desirable objectives. Different assumptions and models have been used, but lack a generic framework that provides in-depth understanding of the underlying mechanisms. In addition, there is no systematic approach to integrate other objectives suc h as energy-efficient design and reliability that ensures broadcast cov erage. The challenge in energy-efficient design is to dynamically adjust transmission range to achieve the objectives of reducing con ten tionand minimizing energy consumption in both communication and computation. The traditional reliabilit y approach through redundancy conflicts with reducing contention by av oiding excessive redundancy.

The ACK/NACK approach suffers from possible two problems; either another form of broadcast storm problem when excessive ACK messages are sent back to the sender or, excessive memory used to hold unstable messages in the NACK approach since the broadcast message cannot be ensured of delivery without an ACK message.

We first present our preliminary results of a generic framework [22] that covers many deterministic and localized broadcast schemes, where each node determines its own forwarding/non-forwarding status based on local information. *The framework is built on the theory that global c over age and onnectivity c an b e achieved through local c over age and connectivity b ased on the notion of local view.* Specifically, this local approach is based on $k$-hop neighborhood information (for a small $k$) and $h$-hop routing history information (for a small $h$) piggybacked with the broadcast message. The choice of $k$ and $h$ is adjustable without compromising broadcast coverage based on host mobility and cost-effectiveness trade-offs. The forward node set is determined on demand without resorting to any pre-defined infrastructure. Then, a more generic framework [23] is discussed that covers all deterministic and localized broadcasting schemes where the status of each node is either determined by itself or by its neighbors. Our generic framework aims at balancing cost (in collecting net w ork information andin decision making) and effectiveness (in deriving a small forward node set). This generic framework can potentially be used to implement other t ypes of collective communication, such as one-to-all, all-to-one, and all-to-all. We also present ideas to extend the generic framework by including energy-efficiency design, with the objective of reducing both contention and power usage at the same time. Finally, w e will discuss thoughts on extending the framework to address the coverage issue by making a sensible trade-off between minimizing forward node set and maintaining a certain degree of redundancy for reliability without solely relying on ACK/NACK.

# References

1. K. M. Alzoubi, P . J. Wan, and O. Frieder. Distributed heuristics for connected dominating sets in wireless ad hoc networks. *Journal of Communications and Networks.* 4, (1), Mar. 2002, 22-29.
2. S. Butenko, X. Cheng, D. Z. Du, and P. Pardalos. On the construction of virtual backbone for ad hoc wireless netw orks. *Pr oc. of the 2nd Confeence on Cooperative Control and Optimization*, 2002, 43-54.
3. B. N. Clark, C. J. Colbourn, and D. S. Johnson. Unit disk graphs. *Discr ete Mathematics.* 86, 1990, 165-177.
4. F. Dai and J. Wu. Distributed dominant pruning in ad hoc wireless net w orks. T echnical report. accepted to appear in *Proc. of ICC'03*, 2003.
5. J. Duato, S. Yalamanchili, and L. Ni. *Interc onne ctionNetworks: An Engineering Approach.* IEEE Computer Society Press. 1997.
6. D. Estrin, R. Govindan, J. Heidemann, and S. Kumar. Next century c hallenges: Scalable coordination in sensor net w orks. *Proc. of A CM MOBICOM'99.* 1999, 263-270.
7. Z. J. Haas, J. Y. Halpern, and L. Li. Gossip-based ad hoc routing. *Pr oc. of IEEE INFOCOM'02.* 3, 2002, 1707-1716.

8. D. B. Johnson and D. A. Malts. Dynamic source routing in ad-hoc wireless net-w orks. In T. Imielinski, H. Korth, editor, *Mobile Computing.* Kluw er Academic Publishers. 1996, 153-181.

9. H. Lim and C. Kim. Flooding in wireless ad hoc networks. *Computer Communications Journal.* 24, (3-4), 2001, 353-363.

10. W. Lou and J. Wu. On reducing broadcast redundancy in ad hoc wireless netw orks. *IEEE Transactions on Mobile Computing.* 1, (2), April-June 2002, 111-122.

11. V. D. Park and M. S. Corson. T emporally-ordered routing algorithm (TORA) version 1: Functional specification. *Internet Draft,* 1997.

12. M. R. Pearlman and Z. J. Haas. Determining the optimal configuration of the zone routing protocol. *IEEE Journal on Selected A reas in Communications.* 17, (8), F eb. 1999, 1395-1414.

13. W. Peng and X. Lu. On the reduction of broadcast redundancy in mobile ad hoc net w orks. *Proc. of ACM MOBIHOC'00.* 2000, 129-130.

14. C. Perkins and E. M. Roy er. Ad-hoc on-demand distance vector routing. *Proc. of the 2nd IEEE WMCSA.* 1999, 90-100.

15. C. E. Perkins. *Ad Hoc Networks.* Addison Wesley, 2001.

16. A. Qayyum, L. Viennot, and A. Laouiti. Multipoint relaying for flooding broadcast message in mobile wireless netw orks. *Pr oc. of the 35th Hawaii International Conferenc e on System Sciene (HICSS-35).* 2002, (CD-ROM).

17. I. Stojmenovic, S. Seddigh, and J. Zunic. Dominating sets and neighbor elimination based broadcasting algorithms in wireless networks. *IEEE Transactions on Parallel and Distributed Systems.* 13, (1), Jan. 2002, 14-25.

18. J. Sucec and I. Marsic. An efficient distributed network-wide broadcast algorithm for mobile ad hoc netw orks. CAIP Technical Report 248, Rutgers University, Sept. 2000.

19. Y. C. Tseng, S. Y. Ni, Y. S. Chen, and J. P. Sheu. The broadcast storm problem in a mobile ad hoc netw ork. *Wireless Networks.* 8, (2-3), Mar.-May 2002, 153-167.

20. J. E. Wieselthier, G. D. Nguyen, and A. Ephremides. On constructing minimum spanning trees in $k$-dimensional spaces and related problems. *Pr oc. of IEEE IN-F OCOM'00* 2000, 585-594.

21. B. Williams and T. Camp. Comparison of broadcasting techniques for mobile ad hoc netw orks. *Pr œ. of ACM MOBIHOC'02.* 2002, 194-205.

22. J. Wu and F. Dai. Broadcasting in ad hoc netw orks based on self-pruning. *Proc. of IEEE INFOCOM'03,* 2003.

23. J. Wu and F. Dai. A generic distributed broadcast scheme in ad hoc wireless networks. accepted to appear in *Proc. of IEEE Int'l Conf. on Distributed Computing Systems (ICDCS),* 2003.

24. J. Wu and H. Li. On calculating connected dominating set for efficient routing in ad hoc wireless netw orks. *Proc. of the 3r d International Workshop on Discrete A lgorithms and Methds for Mobile Computing and Communications (DIALM'99).* 1999, 7-14.

# Towards a Single System Image for High-Performance Java

Francis C.M. Lau

Department of Computer Science and Information Systems
The University of Hong Kong
Pokfulam Road, Hong Kong, P.R. China
fcmlau@csis.hku.hk

Multithreaded programming in Java is an attraction to programmers writing high-performance code if their programs can exploit the multiplicity of resources in a cluster environment. Unfortunately, the common platforms today have not made it possible to allow a single Java program to span multiple computing nodes, let alone dynamically to cling on to additional nodes or migrate some of its executing code from one node to another for load balancing reasons during runtime. As a result, programmers resort to parallel Java programming using such devices as MPI. Ideally, a "Single System Image" (SSI) offered by the cluster is all that is needed. But the purist's idea of SSI is not at all easy to achieve if indeed it can be achieved. A workable SSI solution will likely require a major concerted effort by designers on all fronts, from those of the hardware and OS to those looking after the upper or middleware layers. In the meantime, partial SSI implementations offer limited but useful capabilities and help clear the way for more complete SSI implementations in the future. We present in this talk our brave attempts to provide partial SSI in a cluster for the concurrent Java programmers, and discuss how the design of the Java Virtual Machine (JVM) has made it possible (or has given us some of the troubles). At the core of our present design are a thread migration mechanism that works for Java threads compiled in Just-In-Time (JIT) mode, and an efficient global object space that enables cross-machine access of Java objects. We close with some thoughts on what can be done next to popularize our or similar approaches. The following gives an overview of the system we have implemented[1] which will serve as a major guiding example for our discussion.

SSI can be implemented at different layers such as the hardware, the OS, or as a middleware. We choose to implement SSI as a middleware by extending the JVM, resulting is a "distributed JVM" (DJVM). Our DJVM supports the scheduling of Java threads on cluster nodes and provides locality transparency to object accesses and I/O operations. The semantics of a thread's execution on the DJVM will be preserved as if it were executed in a single node.

The DJVM needs to extend the three main building blocks of the single-node JVM: the execution engine, the thread scheduler, and the heap. Similar to the single-node JVM runtime implementation, the execution engine can be classified into four types: interpreter-based engine, JIT compiler-based engine,

---

[1] A joint work with W.Z. Zhu and C.L. Wang.

M. Guo and L.T.Yang (Eds.): ISPA 2003, LNCS 2745, pp. 6–7, 2003.

mixed-mode execution engine, and static compiler-based engine. There are two modes of thread scheduling that can be found in current DJVM prototypes: static thread distribution and dynamic thread migration. The heap in the DJVM needs to provide a shared memory space for all the Java threads scattered in various cluster nodes, and there are two main approaches: realizing a heap by adopting a distributed shared memory system or by extending the heap.

Our proposed DJVM [1] exploits the power of the JIT compiler to achieve the best possible performance. We introduce a new cluster-aware Java execution engine to support the execution of distributed Java threads in JIT compiler mode. The results we obtained show a major improvement in performance over the old interpreter-based implementation [2]. A dynamic thread migration mechanism is implemented to support the flexible distribution of Java threads so that Java threads can be migrated from one node to another during execution.

Among the many challenges in realizing a migration mechanism for Java threads, the transferring of thread contexts between cluster nodes requires the most careful and meticulous design. In a JIT-enabled JVM, the JVM stack of a Java thread becomes a native stack and no longer remains bytecode oriented. We solve the problem of transformation of native Java thread context directly inside the JIT compiler. We extend the heap in the JVM to a Global Object Space (GOS) that creates an SSI view for all Java threads inside an application. The GOS support enables location transparent access not only to data objects but also to I/O objects. As the GOS is built inside JVM, we exploit the JVM runtime components such as the JIT compiler and the threaded I/O functions to minimize the remote object access overheads in a distributed environment.

As the execution speed in JIT mode is typically much faster than that in interpreter mode, the cost to access an object in a JIT compiler enabled DJVM becomes relatively high, which in turn puts pressure on the efficiency of the heap implementation. To reduce the communication overheads, optimizing caching protocols are used in our design. We employ an "adaptive object home migration protocol" to address the problem of frequent write accesses to a remote object, and a timestamp-based fetching protocol to prevent the redundant fetching of remote objects, among other optimization tricks.

# References

1. W.Z. Zhu, C.L. Wang and F.C.M.Lau, "JESSICA2: A Distributed Java Virtual Machine with Transparent Thread Migration Support", *IEEE 4th International Conference on Cluster Computing (CLUSTER 2002)*, Chicago, USA, September 2002, 381–388.
2. M.J.M. Ma, C.L. Wang, and F.C.M. Lau, "JESSICA: Java-Enabled Single-System-Image Computing Architecture", *Journal of Parallel and Distributed Computing*, Vol. 60, No. 10, October 2000, 1194–1222.

# The Earth Simulator

Ken'ichi Itakura

The Earth Simulator Center, Japan Marine Science and Technology Center,
3173-25 Showa-cho, Kanazawa-ku, Yokohama-city, Kanagawa Pref.
236-0001 Japan, itakura@es.jamstec.go.jp

The Earth Simulator is a high speed parallel computer developed for research on global environment change. Target sustained performance of the Earth Simulator is set to 1,000 times higher than that of the most frequently used supercomputers around 1996 in the climate research field. The Earth Simulator is the fastest supercomputer in the world today.

An attempt to understand large scale phenomena on the earth such as global warming and EL Niño events by numerical simulations is very important and challenging. The Earth Simulator project has been started by the Science and Technology Agency of Japan (STA) in 1997 aiming to understand and predict global environment change of the earth.

The Earth Simulator Research and Development Center (ESRDC) was a joint team established by National Space Development Agency of Japan (NASDA), Japan Atomic Energy Research Institute (JAERI) and Japan Marine Science and Technology Center (JAMSTEC). ESRDC engaged in the development of the Earth Simulator that is the main resource for the project. The Earth Simulator contributes not only to the promotion of research on global environment change, but also to the promotion of computational science and engineering.

Between July 2002 and March 2003, there were only five whole system failures. Twice were problems of Interconnection Network Nodes and three times were troubles with job scheduling operation software. The Earth Simulator consists of 640 processor nodes and it has an enormous number of parts; 5120 vector processors, 1 million memory chips, 20,000 memory controller chips, 160,000 serial-parallel translate chips and so on. The storage system consists of RAID5 disk arrays which helps to save user data from disk troubles. Some small errors are happen every day. However, practically every error is recovered by using correcting system or retrying by hardware and software. We check the diagnosis reports and do preventive maintenance on nodes in which some recoverable errors were happened.

Now, one of the most important problems is how to store and move massive amount of user data. This problem has two sides. One is how to provide processing nodes with data from permanent storage systems. Another is how to retrieve data from the Earth Simulator. The Earth Simulator has such high performance that the product data becomes enormous size. We have a tape cartridge system which provides peta byte class storage. However, the accessibility of the tape system is not so convenient which creates problems form users and wastes system resources. We plan to replace this with a hierarchy storage system, consisting of disks and tapes.

M. Guo and L.T.Yang (Eds.): ISPA 2003, LNCS 2745, p. 8, 2003.
© Springer-Verlag Berlin Heidelberg 2003

# Computing on the Restricted LARPBS Model

Yi Pan

Georgia State University, Atlanta, GA 30303,
pan@cs.gsu.edu,
http://www.cs.gsu.edu/pan

**Abstract.** Many algorithms have been designed on models using pipelined optical buses by several research groups. Linear array with a reconfigurable pipelined bus system (LARPBS) is one such model. The results in the literature show that most of the basic operations can be executed in $O(1)$ bus cycles on the LARPBS model. However, since a bus cycle time is proportional to the number of processors attached to it, a bus cycle is not really a constant time when the number of processors is large. In this paper, a more realistic model called restricted-LARPBS (RLARPBS) model is proposed, where a bus cycle can only accommodate a limited number of messages. We use a parameter to characterize this feature. Under the new model, we propose several basic data movement operations. Their time complexities are also analyzed.

## 1   Introduction

A lot of models have been proposed based on pipelined transmission of optical technology. The preliminary work indicates that arrays with pipelined buses are very efficient for parallel computation due to the high bandwidth within a pipelined bus system [3,1,2,4,5,6,9]. On the other hand, a lot of research has been done on reconfigurable systems. In an array with reconfigurable buses, messages can be transmitted concurrently when the bus is partitioned into many segments, and the diameter problem in a point-to-point network disappears when all segments are reconfigured as a single global bus. Based on the research in reconfigurable meshes and pipelined optical buses, a model called linear arrays with a reconfigurable pipelined bus system (LARPBS) has been proposed and studied by Pan, Hamdi and Li [10,11,12].

An LARPBS is a distributed memory system, which consists of processors linearly connected by a reconfigurable pipelined optical bus system. Each processor can perform ordinary arithmetic and logic computations, and interprocessor communication. All computations and communications are synchronized by bus cycles, which is similar to an SIMD machine. However, due to reconfigurability, an LARPBS can be divided into subsystems, and these subsystems can operate independently to solve different subproblems, which results in an MIMD machine. Input/output can be handled in a way similar to an ordinary SIMD/MIMD machine; further discussion on this issue is beyond the scope of the paper, since we are mainly interested in algorithm development and analysis.

M. Guo and L.T.Yang (Eds.): ISPA 2003, LNCS 2745, pp. 9–13, 2003.

Since then, many algorithms have been designed for the model, including inversion number computation, neural network computation, various matrix operations, selection, and sorting algorithms. In all the analysis of the algorithms, the time complexity includes the number of computation steps and communication steps where a communication step is equal to a bus cycle [5,6,10,12,13, 14,16,17]. Apparently, this assumption is not realistic for a system with large number of processors. As indicated in the literature [12,16], the bus cycle time is proportional to the number of processors attached to the bus, and hence is not a constant. To capture the major features of optical buses and have a fair and accurate time analysis, in this paper, we introduce a new model called Restricted LARPBS (RLARPBS) model. In the new model, we assume that only $m$ messages can be transmitted concurrently in a pipelined fashion, where $m < N$, the number of processors, and is dependent on optical technology. Under the new model, several fundamental data movement operations are proposed and analyzed. In particular, one-to-one permutation, broadcast, multicast, binary prefix sum, compression, split, are presented and analyzed.

## 2    One-to-One Communication

Since we can transfer $m$ messages each bus cycle, we need $N/m$ bus cycles to complete a one-to-one communication step on the RLARPBS model. To avoid message conflicts, we may schedule these messages which are $N/m$ apart to transmit their messages in the same bus cycle. Thus, in the first bus cycle, processors $0$, $N/m$, $2N/m$, etc send their own messages. By proper adjusting of select pulse and reference pulse in their addresses, the intended destination processors can receive the messages correctly. In the second bus cycle, processors $1$, $N/m+1$, $2N/m+1$, etc send their own messages. Clearly, we need $N/m$ bus cycles to complete this operation on the RLARPBS model.

## 3    Broadcast

For broadcast operation, the operation on the RLARPBS model will be the same as the one on the LARPBS model [12] since the operation involves only one message transmission, and hence the restriction will not affect it. Therefore, the total time remains to be $O(1)$ bus cycles on the RLARPBS model.

## 4    Multicast

Multicast is a one-to-many communication operation. Each processor may send a message to a group of processors in the system. Each processor receives only one message from a source processor during a multicast operation. If the sources are spread out evenly over the bus, this operation can be carried out in $S/m$ bus cycles, where $S$ is the number of sources in the operation. When the sources are crowded in a segment, this may increase the number of bus cycles used tremendously. Fortunately, most multicast operations in many applications are regular and the sources are spread out evenly over the optical bus [5,6]. For example, if a $N^{1/2} \times N^{1/2}$ matrix is mapped onto a $N$ RLARPBS in row-major fashion, and the first elements of each row need to be broadcast to all processors in the same row, the operation can be performed in $N^{1/2}/m$ bus cycles. If the matrix is mapped in column-major fashion, we can transpose the matrix and then perform the multicast operation. Since the transpose operation is a one-to-one communication operation, it can be done in $O(N/m)$ bus cycles. In this case, the multicast operation takes $O(N/m)$ bus cycles on the RLARPBS model. For irregular multicast operations, we need to analyze them case by case.

## 5   Binary Sum

Let us review this basic operation on the LARPBS model citePan4. First, processor $i$ sets its switch on the transmitting segment to *straight* if $a_i = 1$, and *cross* if $a_i = 0$. Second, processor 0 injects a reference pulse and a select pulse on the reference bus and the select bus, respectively, at the beginning of a bus cycle. Note that all other processors do not put any pulse or message on the three waveguides. If processor $j$ is selected (i.e., processor $j$ detects the coincidence of the reference pulse and the select pulse), the sum of the $N$ binary numbers is equal to $j$. The basic idea is to delay the select pulse whenever it passes a processor with a 0. When all processors have a value of 0, all switches on the bus are set to *cross* and thus introduce $N - 1$ unit delays. As a result, the two pulses will coincide at processor 0. When $j$ processors have a value of 1, $j$ switches on the bus are set to *straight* and thus introduce $(N - j - 1)$ unit delays in the transmitting segments of the select waveguides. Since there are always $(N - j - 1)$ unit delays on the receiving segments of the reference waveguides for processor $j$, the two pulses will coincide at processor $j$. As we can see from the above description, the address frame length can be very short (in fact a constant, not $N$ bits on the LARPBS model). Hence, the restriction on the new model will not affect the performance of this operation. Therefore, the time of this operation is $O(1)$ bus cycles on the RLARPBS model.

## 6   Binary Prefix Sum

Consider a LARPBS with $N$ processors and $N$ binary values $v_i$, $0 \leq i \leq N - 1$. The binary prefix sum requires the computation of $psum_i = v_0 + v_1 + ... + v_{i-1}$, for all $0 \leq i \leq N - 1$. This operation can be divided into a few phases. Similar to one-to-one communication, in order to avoid message conflicts, we first schedule the binary prefix sums among those processors which are $N/m$ apart. After such $N/m$ phases, each group will have its binary prefix sums. Then within each segment of $N/m$ processors, they can use a tree emulation to perform the prefix sum, which takes $O(\log(N/m))$ bus cycles. Hence, the total time is $O(N/m + \log(N/m))$ bus cycles on the RLARPBS model.

## 7   Integer Sum

The above binary prefix sum operation can be generalized to calculate the prefix sums of $N$ integers. Suppose that each integer has $d$ bits, the general prefix sums can be calculated in $O(dN/m + \log(N/m))$ bus cycles on the RLARPBS model.

## 8   Compression

Assume an array of $N$ data elements with each processor having one data element. Also, assume that the number of active data elements in the array is $s$. Active elements are labeled based upon certain values of their local variables. A processor with an active element is referred to as an active processor. The compression algorithm moves these active data elements to processors $N - s - 1$, $N - s$, ..., $N - 1$. In other words, the compression algorithm moves all active data items to the right side of the array. This algorithm is very important in many applications such as sorting. Using an analysis similar to that for the binary prefix sum operation, we can perform the operation in $O(N/m + \log(N/m))$ bus cycles on the RLARPBS model.

## 9   Split

In a split operation, it is desired to separate the active set from the inactive set. In other words, all data elements $D(i), 0 \leq i \leq N - 1$, whose $X(i) = 1$ are moved to the upper part of the array PE(N-s), PE(N-s+1), ... , PE(N-1), and all data elements $D(i), 0 \leq i \leq N - 1$, whose $X(i) = 0$ are moved to the lower part of the array PE(0), PE(1), ... , PE(N-s-1), where $s$ is the number of elements in the active set. In other words, $D(i)$ is moved to $D(j)$ where $j = N - 1 - \sum_{k=i+1}^{N-1} B(k)$ if $X(i) = 1$, and $D(i)$ is moved to $D(j)$ where $j = \sum_{k=0}^{i-1} \overline{X(k)}$ if $X(i) = 0$. This operation can also be performed in $O(N/m + \log(N/m))$ bus cycles on the RLARPBS model using a few compression and one-to-one communication operations [12].

## 10   Conclusions

A new computational model is proposed in this paper and several basic operations are designed and analyzed. These operations can be used as building blocks for many parallel algorithms on the RLARPBS model. We hope that the new model can realistically reflect both the high bandwidth of optical bus technology and its limitations. Future research includes improving the above basic operations and design new parallel algorithms on the new RLARPBS model.

# References

1. Z. Guo, R. Melhem, R. Hall, D. Chiarulli, and S. Levitan. Pipelined communication in optically interconnected arrays. *Journal of Parallel and Distributed Computing*, Vol. 12, No. 3, 269–282(1991).
2. Z. Guo. Optically interconnected processor arrays with switching capacity. *Journal of Parallel and Distributed Computing*, Vol. 23, pp. 314–329(1994).
3. Y. Han, Y. Pan and H. Shen, "Sublogarithmic Deterministic Selection on Arrays with a Reconfigurable Optical Bus," *IEEE Transactions on Computers,* Vol. 51, No. 6, pp. 702–707, June 2002.
4. S. Levitan, D. Chiarulli, and R. Melhem. Coincident pulse techniques for multiprocessor interconnection structures. *Applied Optics*, Vol. 29, No. 14, 2024–2039(1990).
5. K. Li, Y. Pan and S. Q. Zheng. Fast and processor efficient parallel matrix multiplication algorithms on a linear array with reconfigurable pipelined bus system. *IEEE Transactions on Parallel and Distributed Systems*, Vol. 9, No. 8, August 1998, pp. 705–720.
6. K. Li, Y. Pan, and S. Q. Zheng. Parallel matrix computations using a reconfigurable pipelined optical bus. *Journal of Parallel and Distributed Computing*, vol. 59, no. 1, pp. 13–30, October 1999.
7. K. Li, Y. Pan, and S.-Q. Zheng. Efficient Deterministic and Probabilistic Simulations of PRAMs on Linear Arrays with Reconfigurable Pipelined Bus Systems. *The Journal of Supercomputing,* vol. 15, no. 2, pp. 163–181, February 2000.
8. Y. Li, Y. Pan and S.Q. Zheng, "Pipelined time-division multiplexing optical bus with conditional delays," *Optical Engineering,* Vol. 36, No. 9, pp. 2417–2424, September 1997.
9. R. Melhem, D. Chiarulli, and S. Levitan. Space multiplexing of waveguides in optically interconnected multiprocessor systems. *The Computer Journal*, Vol. 32, No. 4, 362–369(1989)
10. Y. Pan and M. Hamdi. Quicksort on a linear array with a reconfigurable pipelined bus system. *Proc. of IEEE International Symposium on Parallel Architectures, Algorithms, and Networks*, pp. 313–319, June 12–14, 1996.
11. Y. Pan and K. Li. Linear array with a reconfigurable pipelined bus system - concepts and applications, *Information Sciences,* Vol. 106, No. 3/4, May 1998, pp. 237–258.
12. Y. Pan. "Basic data movement operations on the LARPBS model," in *Parallel Computing Using Optical Interconnections*, K. Li, Y. Pan, and S. Q. Zheng, eds., Kluwer Academic Publishers, Boston, USA, 1998.
13. S. Pavel and S. G. Akl. Matrix operations using arrays with reconfigurable optical buses. *Parallel Algorithms and Applications*, Vol. 11, pp. 223–242, 1996.
14. S. Pavel and S. G. Akl. Integer sorting and routing in arrays with reconfigurable optical bus. *Proc. 1996 International Conf. on Parallel Processing*, Vol. III, pp. 90–94, August 1996.
15. C. Qiao, R. Melhem, D. Chiarulli, and S. Levitan. Optical multicasting in linear arrays. *International Journal of Optical Computing*, Vol. 2, No. 1, 31–48(1991).
16. S. Sahni. Models and algorithms for optical and optoelectronic parallel computers. *Proceedings of the Fourth IEEE International Symposium on Parallel Architectures, Algorithms, and Networks*, June 23–25, 1999, Fremantle, Australia, pp. 2–7.
17. J. L. Trahan, A. G. Bourgeois, Y. Pan, and R. Vaidyanathan. An Optimal and Scalable Algorithm for Permutation Routing on Reconfigurable Linear Arrays with Optically Pipelined Buses. *Journal of Parallel and Distributed Computing*, Vol. 60, No. 9, Sept. 2000, pp. 1125–1136.

# Reliability of a Distributed Search Engine for Fresh Information Retrieval in Large-Scale Intranet

Nobuyoshi Sato[1], Minoru Udagawa[1], Minoru Uehara[1], and Yoshifumi Sakai[2]

[1] Department of Information and Computer Sciences, Toyo University
2100 Kujirai, Kawagoe City, Saitama 350-8585 Japan
{jju,ti980039}@ds.cs.toyo.ac.jp, uehara@cs.toyo.ac.jp
[2] Graduate School of Agricultural Science, Tohoku University
1-1 Tsutsumidori-Amamiyamachi, Aoba-ku, Sendai City, Miyagi 981-8555 Japan
sakai@biochem.tohoku.ac.jp

**Abstract.** We have developed distributed search engine, called Cooperative Search Engine (CSE), in order to retrieve fresh information. In CSE, a local search engine located in each Web server makes an index of local pages. And, a meta search server integrates these local search engines in order to realize a global search engine. However, in such a way, the communication delay occurs at retrieval time. So, it is thought to be difficult to search fast. However, we have developed several speedup techniques in order to realize real time retrieval. By the way, distributed search engines such as CSE are essentially fault tolerant. However, the meta server is single point of failure in CSE. So, we propose redundancy of meta search servers in order to increase availability of CSE. In this paper, we describe reliability of CSE and their evaluations.

## 1 Introduction

Search engines are very important for Web page retrieval. Typical search engines employ centralized architecture. In such a centralized search engine, a robot collects Web pages and an indexer makes an index of these pages to search fast. Now the update interval is defined as the period that a page is published but cannot be searched yet. In this case, centralized architecture has a problem that the update interval is very long. For an example, Google used to waste 2 to 3 months[1], currently 2 to 3 weeks[2]. So, we have developed a distributed search engine, Cooperative Search Engine (CSE)[3][4] in order to reduce the update interval.

In CSE, a local search engine located in each Web server makes an index of local pages. Furthermore, a meta search engine integrates these local search engines in order to realize a global search engine. By such a mechanism, though the update interval is reduced, communication overhead is increased. As this result, early CSE is suited for intranet information retrieval in small-scale networks that consist of less than 100 servers. However, international enterprises often have more than 100 servers in their domains.

M. Guo and L.T.Yang (Eds.): ISPA 2003, LNCS 2745, pp. 14–27, 2003.

In order to solve the scalability of CSE, we have developed several techniques such as Score based Site Selection (SbSS)[8], Persistent Cache[10]. In SbSS, when second or later page is retrieved in "Next 10" search, a client sends a query to at most top 10 sites by holding maximum score of each server. As this result, CSE realizes the scalability on retrieving second or later page. Persistent Cache keeps valid data after updating and it realizes the scalability on retrieving first page searched once.

A centralized search engine also has another problem, single point of failure. In such a search engine, the whole system stops when a server stops. On the other hand, in a distributed search engine, the whole system can continue to provide the service even if a few server stop. In this sense, distributed search engines are more reliable than centralized search engines.

In CSE, a local native search engine is running on each web server. And they are integrated by single meta search server, which is called location server. The location server selects suited sites by using Forward Knowledge. Queries are sent to selected sites. There is only one location server in CSE. Therefore, if the location server stops, then we cannot search documents. So, in this paper, we propose reliable architecture of CSE based on increasing redundancy of location servers.

The remainder of this paper is organized as follows: We describe about the overview of CSE and its behaviors in Sect. 2. We propose reliable architecture in Sect. 3, and evaluate it in Sect. 4. In Sect. 5, we survey the related works on distributed information retrieval. Finally, we summarize conclusions and future works.

## 2   Cooperative Search Engine

First, we explain a basic idea of CSE. In order to minimize the update interval, every web site basically makes indices via a local indexer. However, these sites are not cooperative yet. Each site sends the information about what (i.e. which words) it knows to the manager. This information is called Forward Knowledge (FK), and is Meta knowledge indicating what each site knows. FK is the same as FI of Ingrid. When searching, the manager tells which site has documents including any word in the query to the client, and then the client sends the query to all of those sites. In this way, since CSE needs two-pass communication at searching, the retrieval time of CSE becomes longer than that of a centralized search engine.

CSE consists of the following components (see Fig. 1).

**Location Server (LS):** LS manages FK exclusively. Using FK, LS performs Query based Site Selection described later. LS also has Site selection Cache (SC) which caches results of site selection.

**Cache Server (CS):** CS caches FK and retrieval results. LS can be thought of as the top-level CS. It realizes "Next 10" searches by caching retrieval results. Furthermore, it realizes a parallel search by calling LMSE mentioned later in parallel.

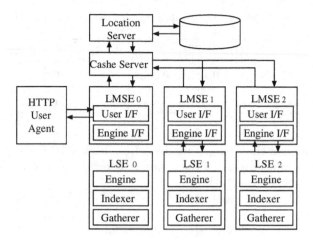

**Fig. 1.** The Overview of CSE

**Local Meta Search Engine (LMSE):** LMSE receives queries from a user, sends it to CS (User I/F in Fig. 1), and does local search process by calling LSE mentioned later (Engine I/F in Fig. 1). It works as the Meta search engine that abstracts the difference between LSEs.

**Local Search Engine (LSE):** LSE gathers documents locally (Gatherer in Fig. 1), makes a local index (Indexer in Fig. 1), and retrieves documents by using the index (Engine in Fig. 1). In CSE, Namazu[5] can be used as a LSE. Furthermore we are developing an original indexer designed to realize high-level search functions such as parallel search and phrase search.

Namazu has widely used as the search services on various Japanese sites.

Next, we explain how the update process is done. In CSE, Update I/F of LSE carries out the update process periodically. The algorithm for the update process in CSE is as follows.

1. Gatherer of LSE gathers all the documents (Web pages) in the target Web sites using direct access (i.e. via NFS) if available, using archived access (i.e. via CGI) if it is available but direct access is not available, and using HTTP access otherwise.

   Here, we explain archived access in detail. In archived access, a special CGI program that provides mobile agent place functions is used. A mobile agent is sent to that place. The agent archives local files, compresses them and sends back to the gatherer.

2. Indexer of LSE makes an index for gathered documents by parallel processing based on Boss-Worker model.

3. Update phase 1: Each $LMSE_i$ updates as follows.

   a) Engine I/F of $LMSE_i$ obtains from the corresponding LSE the total number $N_i$ of all the documents, the set $K_i$ of all the words appearing in some documents, and the number $n_{k,i}$ of all the documents including word $k$, and sends to CS all of them together with its own URL.

**Table 1.** The Evaluation of Update Times

|  | Gathering | Indexing | Transfer Index | Total |
|---|---|---|---|---|
| Namazu full | 0:25:50 | 0:20:32 | 0:00:00 | 0:46:22 |
| Namazu | 0:19:51 | 0:01:27 | 0:00:00 | 0:21:18 |
| CSE | 0:00:09 | 0:01:27 | 0:00:18 | 0:01:54 |
| Parallel CSE | 0:00:02 | 0:00:37 | 0:00:11 | 0:00:50 |

  b) CS sends all the contents received from each $LMSE_i$ to the upper-level
     CS. The transmission of the contents is terminated when they reach the
     top-level CS (namely, LS).
  c) LS calculates the value of $idf(k) = \log(\sum N_i / \sum n_{k,i})$ from $N_{k,i}$ and $N_i$
     for each word $k$.
4. Update phase 2: Each $LMSE_i$ updates as follows
  a) $LMSE_i$ receives the set of Boolean queries $Q$ which has been searched
     and the set of idf values from LS.
  b) Engine I/F of $LMSE_i$ obtains from the corresponding LSE the highest
     score $\max_{d \in D} S_i(d, q)$ for each $q \in \{Q, K_i\}$, $S_i(d, k)$ is a score of document
     $d$ containing $k$, $D$ is the set of all the documents in the site, and sends
     to CS all of them together with its own URL.
  c) CS sends all the contents received from each $LMSE_i$ to the upper-level
     CS. The transmission of the contents is terminated when they reach the
     top-level CS (namely, LS).

Note that the data transferred between each module are mainly used for distributed calculation to obtain the score based on the $tf \cdot idf$ method. We call this method the distributed $tf \cdot idf$ method. The score based on the distributed $tf \cdot idf$ method is calculated at the search process. So we will give the detail about the score when we explain the search process in CSE.

As an experiment, homepages (8000 files, 12MB) of about 2000 users were moved from a server of computer center of our school to a PC (Celeron 300MHz, 128MB of memory, FreeBSD), and parallel processing is performed with two PCs (A PC same as above and Celeron 400MHz dual, 128MB of memory, FreeBSD). The result of this experiment is shown in Table 1, where following 4 cases are used for comparisons: Full update with wget and Namazu, Simple update with wget and Namazu, CSE without parallel processing and CSE with parallel processing. As a result, simple update greatly shortens the index update time compared with full update, direct access greatly shortens the document collection time compared with HTTP access, and the parallel processing reduces the total updating time to about a half.

For the good performance of the update process, the performance of the search process is sacrificed in CSE. Here we explain how the search process in CSE is done.

1. When $LMSE_0$ receives a query from a user, it sends the query to CS.
2. CS obtains from LS all the LMSEs expected to have documents satisfying
   the query.

3. CS sends the query to each of all LMSEs obtained.
4. Each LMSE searches documents satisfying the query by using LSE, and returns the result to CS.
5. CS combines with all the results received from LMSEs, and returns it to $LMSE_0$.
6. $LMSE_0$ displays the search result to the user.

Here, we describe the design of scalable architecture for the distributed search engine, CSE.

In CSE, at searching time, there is the problem that communication delay occurs. Such a problem is solved by using following techniques.

**Query based Site Selection (QbSS).** [6] CSE supports Boolean search based on Boolean formula. In Boolean search of CSE, the operations "and," "or," and "not" are available, where "not" does not mean the negation but means the binary operation that represents the difference between two objects. Let $S_A$ and $S_B$ be the set of target sites for search queries $A$ and $B$, respectively. Then, the set of target sites for queries "$A$ and $B$," "$A$ or $B$," and "$A$ not $B$" are $S_A \cap S_B$, $S_A \cup S_B$, and $S_A$, respectively. By this selection of the target sites, the number of messages in search process is saved.

**Look Ahead Cache in "Next 10" Search.** [7] To shorten the delay on search process, CS prepares the next result for the "Next 10" search. That is, the search result is divided into page units, and each page unit is cached in advance by background process without increasing the response time.

**Score based Site Selection (SbSS).** [8] In the "Next 10" search, the score of the next ranked document in each site is gathered in advance, and the requests to the sites with low-ranked documents are suppressed. By this suppression, the network traffic does not increase unnecessarily. For example, there are more than 100,000 domain sites in Japan. However, by using this technique, about ten sites are sufficient to requests on each continuous search.

**Global Shared Cache (GSC).** [9] A LMSE sends a query to the nearest CS. Many CS may send same requests to LMSEs. So, we proposed Global Shared Cache (GSC) in order to globally share cached retrieval results among CSs. In this method, LS memories the authority $CS_a$ of each query and tells CSs $CS_a$ instead of LMSEs. CS caches the cached contents of $CS_a$.

**Persistent Cache.** [10] There is at least one CS in CSE in order to improve the response time of retrieval. However, the cache becomes invalid soon because the update interval is very short in CSE. Valuable first page is also lost. Therefore, we need persistent cache, which holds valid cache data before and after updating.

These techniques are applied to the following cases.

```
if it's the first page of ''Next 10" search
   if its query contains operators ''and" or ''not"
      if it has been searched once
         if searched before update
```

**Table 2.** The Response Time of Global Shared Cache

|  | without GSC | | GSC |
| --- | --- | --- | --- |
|  | Hit | No Hit |  |
| Response Time | 0.45s | 4.67s | 0.66s |

```
      Persistent Cache
    else // searched after update
      Global Shared Cache
    fi
  else // it has not been searched yet
    QbSS
  fi
  else // query does not contain ''and" or ''not"
    SbSS
  fi
else // 2nd or later page
  LAC
fi
```

QbSS can reduce a set of LMSEs to 40% theoretically, and to less than theoretical value if documents are not balanced among LMSEs. In our experiments, QbSS has reduced it to about 10%.

Next, we describe about the efficiency of score based site selection. We evaluated the performance of score based site selection with three PCs (Pentium3 1GHz, 256MB of memory PC for CS and LMSEs, Pentium3 933MHz dual, 1GB of memory PC and Pentium3 1.13GHz dual, 1GB of memory PCs for LMSEs. FreeBSD is installed into all PCs.). The result of this evaluation is shown in Fig. 2. In Fig. 2, there are 4 lines as follows; the retrieval time of 1st page without score based site selection, the retrieval time of second or later page without score based site selection, the retrieval time of first page with score based site selection, and the retrieval time of second or later page with score based site selection. Here, note that these retrieval times are normally hidden seemingly because CS retrieves in background, in order words, during users brows previous retrieval results. As shown at Fig. 2, score based site selection is effective when retrieving second and later pages.

Next, we evaluate the effect of Global Shared Cache (GSC). Table 2 shows the response times of GSC and without GSC. In case of without GSC, the response time is shortest if hit, however, the response time is longest if not hit. In case of GSC, if GSC is introduced by a LS, the response time is much shorter than the longest one.

Then, we describe the evaluation of persistent cache. To compare the retrieval times between before update and after update, we compared the retrieval times between normal cache and persistent cache in case of 20 sites of LMSEs. Here, "$A$ and $B$" is used as a conjunctive query, QbSS could not select sites since all sites have documents which contain keyword $A$ and $B$. Furthermore, since the

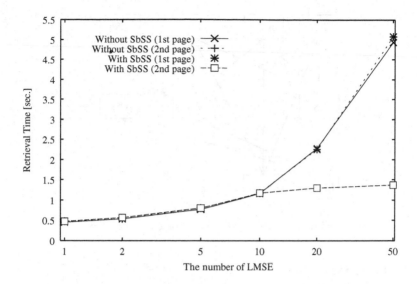

**Fig. 2.** The Evaluation of Score Based Site Selection

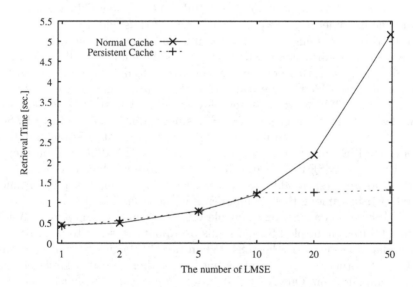

**Fig. 3.** The Scalability of Normal Cache vs. Persistent Cache at Retrieval

highest score of $A$ and $B$ is the same in these 20 sites, SbSS could not select these sites. In addition, assume that the number of retrieval results in a page is 10. It means that the request is sent to only 10 sites in persistent cache. In normal cache, however, the request must be sent to all 20 sites. Fig. 3 shows the scalability of normal cache and persistent cache. If the number of sites is increased to 50, normal cache spends more than 5 seconds. However, persistent cache spends only the same time as the case of 10 sites.

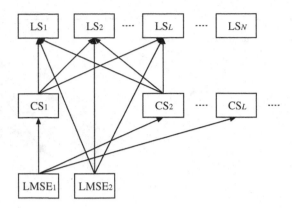

**Fig. 4.** The Relationship among Components

## 3 Reliability

Here, we describe the design of reliable architecture. First, we define types of faults as silent failures of both nodes and links in this paper. These failures occur at run time. If something is repaired, it is regarded as adding new one.

In distributed systems, a link fault cannot be different from delay caused by a node fault. If a failed link exists, though a node is not actually failed, it may seem failed. However, there may be another route to deliver messages. In such a situation, it is possible to increase reliability by forwarding messages. As such a system, there is P2P network. We employ basic mechanism of P2P network.

As described in previous section, LS is single point of failure in CSE. So, LS must be redundant. CS need not be redundant because at least one unfailed CS is needed. LMSE cannot be redundant because LMSE is depended on each Web server. Even if a LMSE has failed, CSE does not stop searching documents except a part of documents. In addition, a reference to LS group must be redundant. The relationship among these components is shown as Fig. 4.

A LMSE selects a CS from multiple CSs and sends a query to it. A LMSE selects a LS from multiple LSs and sends an update message to it. A LS broadcasts update messages to other LSs. When new LS begins to run, its reference is notified to other LSs by broadcasting. Here, there are two kinds of reliable group communication. One is anycast in which a message is sent to one of multiple servers. Another is broadcast (or multicast) in which a message is sent to all servers.

Anycast is realized as repeating unicasts until a message is sent successfully.

The way of broadcasting is dependent on the number of LSs, topology (i.e. rank, the number of links), routing and so on. There are two kinds of routing methods: breadth first routing and depth first routing. Furthermore, breadth first routing is dependent on TTL (Time-To-Live).

**Depth First Routing (DF).** In DF, a node receives a message including the list of visited nodes, and adds itself to the list, and forwards that modified

message to unvisited nodes. Therefore, DF is suited when there are few
nodes.

**Breadth First Routing with $TTL = 0$ (BF0).** In BF0, a node sends a
message to other nodes directly. BF0 is the best way when there is no link
fault.

**Breadth First Routing with $TTL = L$ (BFL).** In BFL, when a node has
received a message with TTL = $L$, a node broadcasts a message with TTL =
$L-1$ to all neighbor nodes if TTL > 0. BFL is available even if there are many
nodes. However, in BFL, the number of messages exponentially increases.

Link faults may cause to divide a network into some sub networks. In disconnected networks, meta index can be shared by using broadcast. In order to solve
this problem, we employ the following way. At updating time, a LMSE sends
meta index to a CS. A CS sends meta index, which is received from multiple
LMSEs, to a LS at once. A LS forwards meta index to other LSs by broadcasting. A LS replies the list of LSs that have received meta index to the CS. The
CS searches a CS which can deliver a message to undelivered LSs, and delegates
that CS to deliver a message to undelivered LSs. Since the number of CSs is
larger than the number of LSs, the possibility that a message is delivered to all
LSs is thought to be high.

## 4    Evaluations

First, we discuss only node fault.

When the number of LSs $N$ is equivalent to the number of links $L$, the system
does not stop while either at least one LS is running or at least one CS is running.
Therefore, system fault rate $F$ is defined as follow:

$$F = f^N + f^M - f^{N+M}$$

where $f$ is fault rate of elements (LS or CS), $N$ and $M$ are the number of LS
and CS respectively.

We show the relationship of system fault rate to fault rate of nodes in case
of $M = 2N$ as Fig. 5. Since this relationship is independent on routing, the
relationships of DF, BF0, and BF32 are equivalent to Fig. 3. If $N$ is greater
than or equal to 32, then system fault rate is less than 0.1. Therefore, the scale
of system is enough when $N = 32$.

Next, we discuss only link fault. We show the relationship of reachability to
fault rate of links in case of $N = 32$ as Fig. 6. Here, we define the reachability
as the rate of nodes which have received a broadcast message. In BF0, there are
many nodes which cannot receive a message. Next, we show the relationship of
the number of messages to fault rate of links in case of $N = 32$ as Fig. 7. The
number of messages in DF is nearly equal to the number of messages in BF0,
and it is very smaller than the number of messages in BF32. Therefore, DF is
the best.

Next, we discuss both node fault and link fault. We show the relationship
of system fault rate to fault rate of elements (nodes and links) as Fig. 8. In

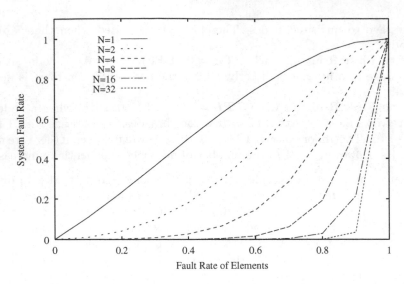

**Fig. 5.** The Relationship of System Fault Rate to Fault Rate of Nodes in Case of $M = 2N$

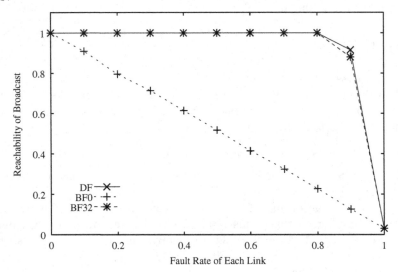

**Fig. 6.** The Relationship of Reachability to Link Faults

case of $N = 32$, if fault rate of each element is less than 0.9, then system fault rate is also less than 0.25. This result is worse than Fig. 3 because link faults prevent CS from communicating with LS. Although we can think the way that CS communicates with LS through other CSs, it is impossible because CS must communicates with LS in order to communicate with other CSs. Therefore, when both nodes and links are failed, CSE can search documents if and only if there is at least one pair of CS and LS, which can communicate with each other.

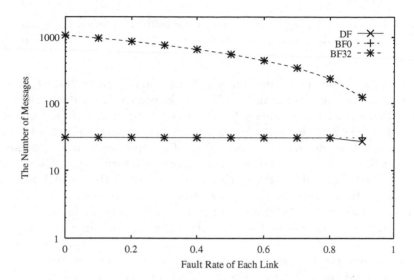

**Fig. 7.** The Relationship of the Number of Messages to Link Faults

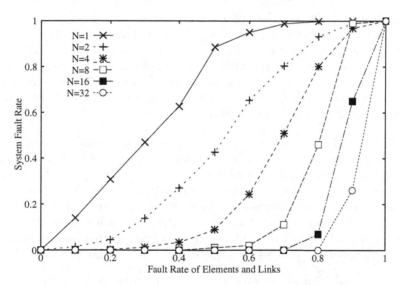

**Fig. 8.** The Relationship of Node and Link Faults to System Fault Rate

## 5 Related Works

Many researchers have already studied on distributed information retrieval and they have developed the following systems, Archie, WAIS, Whois++, and so on. These are not search engines for Web pages. However, Forward Knowledge (FK), which is introduced by Whois++, is a basic idea for distributed information retrieval. Several FK-based distributed Web page retrieval systems such as Harvest, Ingrid, and so on, are developed.

In Whois++[11], FKs are grouped as a centroid, each server transfers queries by using FK if it does not know their destinations. This is known as query routing.

Most famous research on distributed information retrieval will be Harvest[12]. Harvest consists of Gatherer and Broker. A Gatherer collects documents, summarizes them as SOIF (Summary Object Interchange Format), and transfer is to a Broker. SOIF is the summary of a document, which consists of author's name, title, key words and so on. Actually, a Gatherer needs to send almost full texts of collected documents to a Broker, because the full text of a document must be included in SOIF in Harvest's full text search. A Broker makes an index internally. A Broker accepts a query and retrieves by cooperating with other Brokers. In Harvest, both Glimpse and Nebula are employed as search engines, which really make indexes and search. The index size of Glimpse is very small and Nebula can search documents very fast. In Harvest, Gatherer itself can access documents directly. However, because Gatherer does not make an index, it needs to send the index to a Broker. Therefore, Harvest cannot reduce the update interval than CSE.

Ingrid[13] is the information infrastructure developed by NTT, which aims to realize topic-level retrieval. Ingrid links collected resources each other and makes an original topology. Forward Information (FI) servers manage this topology. Ingrid navigator communicates with FI servers in order to search the way to a resource. Ingrid is flexible but its communication latency is long because the way is sequentially searched. In CSE, only LS searches the way, so it may become bottleneck but its communication latency is short.

In distributed systems, there are two kinds of faults. One is fail-silent fault, another is Byzantine fault. In case of Byzantine fault, it is well known that 1-fault tolerant algorithm does not exist theoretically[14]. However, if semantics of correctness of algorithm is redefined, several algorithms such as Perry's global coin toss[15] and so on are available. Unfortunately, these methods are not suited for CSE because they are not scalable. Another approach is fault avoidance by voting outputs of redundant modules[16]. However, in this approach, we need more than 3 tasks that process the same work. Resources are not used efficiently.

In group communication, ISIS[17] is famous. ISIS supports several atomic broadcast communication methods: ABCAST, CBCAST and so on. However, in these methods, the slowest site becomes bottleneck. We do not employ group communication because such a bottleneck is intolerable for CSE.

P2P networks also realize fault tolerant communication. Napster, Freenet[18], gnutella, JXTA[19] and so on are known as P2P systems. Especially, gnutella is a pure decentralized file sharing system. However, such P2P systems are not efficient because the number of messages is very large. Furthermore, in P2P, consistency is not always guaranteed because the reachable area of a message is eliminated with TTL.

## 6   Conclusions

In this paper, we describe scalability and reliability of CSE. In order to increase scalability, we employ several techniques, especially SbSS and persistent cache. SbSS realizes scalable retrieval of second or later pages. The persistent cache realizes scalable retrieval of first page after updating once. Furthermore, in order to increase reliability, we employ redundant location servers, depth first message routing, multiple links of LS in both CS and LMSE in order to increase availability of CSE. As this result, for an instance, when the system consists of 32 LSs with their fault rate 90%, fault rate of the whole system is about 25%. Therefore, we conclude that our method realizes enough availability.

**Acknowledgment.** This research was cooperatively performed as a part of "Mobile Agent based Web Robot" project in Toyo University and a part of "Scalable Distributed Search Engine for Fresh Information Retrieval (14780242)" in Grant-in-Aid for Scientific Research promoted by Japan Society for the Promotion of Science (JSPS). The INOUE ENRYO Memorial Foundation for Promoting Sciences in Toyo University gave the support to this project. Finally, we thank the office of the Foundation in Toyo University.

## References

1. Yamana, H., Kondo, H., "Search Engine Google," IPSJ MAGAZINE, Vol.42, No.8, pp.775–780 (2001)
2. Google, "Google Information for Webmasters," http://www.google.com/webmasters/
3. Sato, N., Uehara, M., Sakai, Y., Mori, H., "Distributed Information Retrieval by using Cooperative Meta Search Engines," in proc. of the 21st IEEE International Conference on Distributed Computing Systems Workshops (Multimedia Network Systems, MNS2001), pp.345–350, (2001)
4. Sato, N., Uehara, M., Sakai, Y., Mori, H., "Fresh Information Retrieval using Cooperative Meta Search Engines," in proc. of the 16th International Conference on Information Networking (ICOIN-16), Vol.2, 7A-2, pp.1–7, (2002)
5. The Namazu Project, "Namazu," http://www.namazu.org/
6. Sakai, Y., Sato, N., Uehara, M., Mori, H., "The Optimal Monotonization for Search Queries in Cooperative Search Engine," in proc. of DICOMO2001, IPSJ Symposium Series, Vol.2001, No.7, pp.453–458 (2001) (in Japanese)
7. Sato, N., Uehara, M., Sakai, M., Mori, H., "Fresh Information Retrieval in Cooperative Search Engine," in proc. of 2nd International Conference on Software Engineering, Artificial Intelligence, Networking & Parallel/Distributed Computing 2001 (SNPD'01), pp.104–111, Nagoya Japan (2001)
8. Sato, N., Uehara, N., Sakai, Y., Mori, H., "Score Based Site Selection in Cooperative Search Engine," in proc. of DICOMO'2001 IPSJ Symposium Series, Vol.2001, No.7, pp.465–470 (2001) (in Japanese)
9. Sato, N., Uehara, M., Sakai, Y., Mori, H., "Global Shared Cache in Cooperative Search Engine," in proc. of DPSWS 2001, IPSJ Symposium Series, Vol.2001, No.13, pp.219–224 (2001) (in Japanese)

10. Sato, N., Uehara, M., Sakai, Y., Mori, H., "Persistent Cache in Cooperative Search Engine," MNSA'02 (to appear)
11. Weider. C., Fullton, J., Spero, S., "Architecture of the Whois++ Index Service", RFC1913 (1996)
12. Bowman, C.M., Danzig, P.B., Hardy, D.R., Manber, U., Schwartz, M.F., "The Harvest Information Discovery and Access System," 2nd WWW Conference, http://www.ncsa.uiuc.edu/SDG/IT94/Proceedings/Searching/schwartz.harvest/schwartz.harvest.html
13. Nippon Telegraph and Telephone Corp., "Ingrid", http://www.ingrid.org/
14. Fischer, M.J., Lynch, N.A., and Paterson, M.S., "Impossibility of distributed consensus with one fault process," Journal of ACM Vol.32, No.2, pp.3740–382 (1985)
15. Perry, K.J., "Randomized Byzantine agreements," IEEE Transaction of Software Engineering SE-11, No.6, pp.539–546 (1985)
16. Uehara, M., Mori, H., "Fault Tolerant Computing in Computational Field Model," in proc. of IEEE Conf. ECBS'97, pp.34–37 (1997)
17. Birman, K.P. "The Process Group Approach to Reliable Distributed Computing," Commun. of the ACM, vol.36, pp.36–53, Dec. (1993)
18. Clarke, I., Miller, S.G, Theodore W. Hong, Oskar Sandberg, Brandon Wiley, "Protecting Free Expression Online with Freenet," IEEE Internet Computing, Jan./Feb. pp.40–49 (2002)
19. Project JXTA, "JXTA," http://www.jxta.org/

# Self-Projecting Time Series Forecast – An Online Stock Trend Forecast System

Ke Deng[1] and Hong Shen[2]

[1]School of Computing and Information Technology
Griffith University, Nathan, QLD 4111, Australia

[2] Graduate School of Information Science
Japan Advanced Institute of Science & Technology
Tasunokuchi, Ishikawa, 923-1292 Japan
shen@jaist.ac.jp

**Abstract.** This paper explores the applicability of time series analysis for stock trend forecast and presents the Self-projecting Time Series Forecasting (STSF) System we have developed. The basic idea behind this system is online discovery of mathematical formulas that can approximately generate historical patterns from given time series. SPTF offers a set of combined prediction functions for stocks including Point Forecast and Confidence Interval Forecast, where the latter could be considered as a subsidiary index of the former in the process of decision-making. We propose a new approach to determine the support line and resistance line that are essential for market assessment. Empirical tests have shown that the hit-rate of the prediction is impressively high if the model were properly selected, indicating a good accuracy and efficiency of this approach. The numerical forecast result of STSF is superior to normal descriptive investment recommendation offered by most Web brokers. Furthermore, SPTF is an online system and investors and analysts can upload their real-time data to get the forecast result on the Web.

**Keywords:** Self-projecting, forecast, Box-Jenkins methodology, ARIMA, time series, linear transfer function.

## 1 Introduction

The increased complexity in stock market has suggested investors to utilize highly sophisticated mathematical techniques in order to analyze and predict price behaviors in the stock market. From the economists' point of view, the process of investment concerns financial decision-making about where to place wealth for best future returns, and also involves how to assess risks associated with future returns. Two kinds of analysis methods were employed in this process: fundamental analysis and technical analysis.

Fundamental analysis involves evaluation of some "intrinsic" value, comparison of this with the current market value of the share and finally investment decision-making. Implementation of fundamental analysis requires a series of point forecasts to. Technical analysis as an alternative uses various techniques and rules to identify trends and intervals in stock prices and trading volumes to place buy or sell orders. It

M. Guo and L.T.Yang (Eds.): ISPA 2003, LNCS 2745, pp. 28–43, 2003.

has been studied extensively for decades from the origin of Dow Theory to Elliot Wave Theory. A variety of software designed for technical analysts is currently being used in the stock market globally, but little has been developed for fundamental analysis. For this reason, we put our emphasis on the design of a forecast system, which can provide both point forecast and confidence interval forecast. Moreover, since most Web brokers currently offer merely qualitative forecast on market trends, investors are seeking an instructional tool for better investment decision-making in the quantitative sense. Another current trend is that investors are turning to the online investment and development of an online forecast tool is therefore of increasing significance. These reasons have inspired us to develop a quantitative online stock forecast system with the following properties.

- forecast using scientific method on both share price and volume.
- numerical prediction of price resistance line and support line.
- offer of online forecast services.
- use of powerful Perl script and platform independent JAVA languages.

In the rest part of this paper, we will overview the existing forecast methodology and theory, present the design and implementation of STSF system, and demonstrate our empirical test results and their analysis.

## 2  Theories and Methods for Forecast

Since last century, various theories and methods have been developed for forecast purpose, such as Multiple Regression Analysis, Nonlinear Regression, Trend Analysis, Moving average analysis, Hodrik-Prescott Filter, Exponential Smoothing [Hossein Arsham (2001)] and methodology by Neural network [C. P. Li]. In generating forecasts of events that will occur in the future, forecasters rely on the information concerning events that have occurred in the past. That is, in order to prepare a forecast, the forecaster must analyze past data and base the forecast on the results of this analysis. Below is an overview on some popular methods used for forecast:

*Neural network* is a widely used method for forecast. It first establishes an initial neural network for a certain application. Then, using the historical data to train this model, the neural network learns the pattern between input and output data. Finally, forecast can be made using the trained neural network. *Spectral analysis* is a signal processing method that characterizes the frequency of a measured signal by Fourier transform and statistics [Bruce L &.Richard T (1993), S. Lawrence (1987)]. *Regression model* uses historical data to build mathematical equations that represent the patterns of that data [Peter J & Pichard A (1996), Bruce L &Richard T (1979)]. *Time series analysis* is concerned with data which are not independent, but serially correlated, and where the relations between consecutive observations are of interest [Peter J (1996)]. As an application of time series analysis, *Box-Jenkins' modeling strategy* selects the forecast model from a group of candidates that best fits the particular set of time series data [O. D Anderson (1976), Alan Pankartz (1991), C.Chatfield (1975)]. There are several difficulties to use Box-Jenkins model for online forecast. First, its high computational complexity discourages application of the model. Secondly, it suits mainly for short-range (i.e. daily, weekly or monthly) forecast. Last, it usually needs to be re-built completely when new data is added to the system.

For the purpose of forecast, past time series data is used in the following way. First, it is analyzed in order to identify a pattern that can be used to describe it. Then this pattern is extrapolated, or extended, in order to prepare a forecast with the assumption that the same pattern will continue in the future. It should be noted that a forecast technique may not give accurate predictions unless this assumption is valid. Normally, we consider two types of forecasts. One is point forecast and the other is confidence interval forecast. Point forecast produces a number that represents our best prediction of the value of the variable of interest at a given point in time. It is essentially our 'best guess" for the future value of the variable being forecast. The accuracy of point forecast is supplied by confidence interval forecast which is an interval or range of values that is calculated so that we are "quite sure", say with 95 percent confidence, that the actual value of the variable being forecast will be contained in that interval. This interval is called "95 percent confidence interval". Although a confidence interval can be constructed with any desirable level of confidence, it is customary at 95 percent confidence.

# 3 Design of SPTF with Box-Jenkins Modeling Strategy

Single-equation regression modeling is one of the most widely used statistical forecast tools. Autoregression Integrated Moving Average (ARIMA) modeling as a Box-Jenkins' modeling category is a way of describing how a time series variable is related to its past value and has been discussed extensively in the literature [O.D Anderson (1976), Alan Pankartz (1991), John C. (1996), Helmut Lutkepohl (1993)]. A more general form of ARIMA is Dynamic Regression that shows how output $y_t$ of a time series variable is linearly related to the current and past values of one or more variables $(x_{1,t}, x_{2,t}, ...)$. In theory, if we have a correct model, ARIMA can give the best forecast in the sense that the mean of the squared forecast errors is minimized. In many cases the ARIMA model may fit data better than the more complex DR model.

Box-Jenkin modeling strategy is to build first an ARIMA model on each input as the base and then a DR model to forecast $y_t$ on inputs $(x_{1,t}, x_{2,t}, ...)$. Often an ARIMA model is able to produce reasonable forecast on a single input conveniently. Finally, these ARIMA models for stochastic inputs are used to perform diagnostic checks of the DR model's adequacy and to estimate the standard error ratio of the DR model forecasts.

## 3.1 Model Building

Our modeling process consists of three parts: model identification, model estimation and model checking. If a satisfied model has been established we may forecast and monitor the model. In addition, parsimony is an important principle during the modeling process in. Parsimony means that the satisfactory model containing the fewest coefficients needs to adequately explain the behavior of the observed data. A parsimonious model makes good use of the limited number of samples and tends to give more accurate forecasts. One noteworthy aspect is if a tentative model is found inadequate the whole procedure must stop as shown in Fig. 1. The information from the diagnostic check gives a valuable clue for model rebuilding.

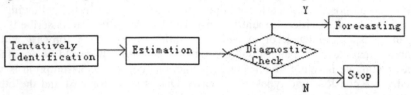

**Fig. 1.** Four steps of Box-Jenkins' Modeling Strategy

The four steps in Figure 1 are described as follows:

**Step 1 - Tentative Identification**: This step assumes stationary variance and mean and other conditions that are essential to process time series data by ARIMA. A stationary process in the weak sense is one whose mean, variance, and autocorrelation function are constant on time. Its strong form requires that the entire probability distribution function for the process is independent of time. If the random shock $a_t$ is normally distributed, then the two forms are identical. To identify a tentative model, we need to compute the sample ACF (autocorrelation function) and sample PACF (partial autocorrelation function) and compare them with the theoretical ACFs and PACFs. If the process mean is constant, we can use all n sample observations to estimate it. If the observed data series is not stationary, we can first modify the data to produce a stationary series, and later reverse them so that the resulting forecasts are comparable to the original data. We consider methods first for achieving a stationary variance and then for achieving a stationary mean.

For time series data we are often interested in autocorrelation patterns that measure how values of a series $(z_t)$ are related to its own future values $(z_{t+1}, z_{t+2, ...})$, or, equivalently, to its own past values $(z_{t-1, } z_{t-2}, ...)$, and provide the direction (positive or negative) and strength of the relationship among observations within a single time series $z_t$. When the observations are separated by k time periods, for k=1, 2, ..., k, we treat series $z_t$ and series $z_{t+k}$ as two random variables. We then consider the correlation coefficients for the two random variables $z_k$ and $z_{t+k}$ in the same way as for two random variables $X_i$ and $Y_i$. A study of autocorrelation patterns in a data series can often lead us to identify an ARIMA model for that series.

From sample data we can compute the population autocorrelation coefficients at various lags

$$k = 1, 2, ..., K \text{ as } \rho_k = \text{cov } (z_t z_{t+k}) / \sigma_z^2.$$

where the population variance $\sigma_z^2$ is defined to be the expected value $\sigma_z^2 = E(z_t - \mu_z)^2$; $\mu_z$ is the expected value (population mean) of the random variable $z_t$, $\mu_z = E(z)$; and cov$(z_t, z_{t+k})$ is defined as the expected value cov$(z_t, z_{t+k}) = E[(z_t - \mu_z) (z_{t+k} - \mu_z)]$. For a stationary series, cov$(z_t, z_{t+k})$, and thereoofore $\rho_k$, are independent of t; they depend only on k, the number of time periods separating $z_t$ and $z_{t+k}$.

The sample autocorrelation coefficient providing estimate of $\rho_k$ is usually expressed by $r_k = \sum_{t=1}^{n-k}(z_t - z_{t+k})(z_{t+k} - z)/ \sum_{t=1}^{n}(z_{t+k} - z)^2$. Jenkins and Watts (1968) discussed this and other formulas for $r_k$. The resulting set of values follows a sample autocorrelation function SACF. The importance of this strategy can be seen by comparing it with its standard errors. An approximate standard error for $r_k$ due to Bartlett (1946), is $s(r_k) = (1 + 2 \sum_{j=1}^{k-1} r_j^2)^{1/2} n^{-1/2}$.

To test for a linear association in the populations between $z_t$ and $z_{t+k}$, we test the null hypothesis, $H_0$: $\rho_k = 0$, against the alternate $H_a$: $\rho_k \neq 0$. We then compute the approximate t statistic, $t = (r_k - \rho_k) / s(r_k)$.

Note that t is the ratio of the statistic $r_k$ to its standard error $s(r_k)$ since $\rho_k$ is hypothesized to be zero. This t-value is considered significant if it is greater than 5% since then the interval confidence shall fall below the critical value of 95%.

Another useful measure of autocorrelation for stationarity is the partial autocorrelation coefficient. One way to think of this coefficient is to consider the set of K regression equations:

$$z_t = C_1 + \Phi_{11}z_{t-1} + e_{1,t}, \; z_t = C_2 + \Phi_{21}z_{t-1} + \Phi_{22}z_{t-2} + e_{2,t},$$

$$z_t = C_k + \Phi_{k1}z_{t-1} + \Phi_{k2}z_{t-1} + \dots + \Phi_{kk}z_{t-1} + e_{k,t}$$

The population coefficient of partial autocorrelation at lag k = 1, 2, …, K is the last coefficient ($\Phi_{kk}$) in each equation. Each population coefficient is estimated for a given data set by its sample counterpart $\Phi_{kk}$. The resulting set of values follows the sample partial autocorrelation function SPACF. Recall that when computing $r_k$ we considered only two random variables $z_t$ and $z_{t+k}$, and ignored the intervening random variables $z_{t+k-1}, z_{t+k-2}, \dots, z_{t+1}$. But for computing $\Phi_{kk}$ we need to take into account of all these intervening random variables simultaneously, as seen in the above equations. Computationally efficient formulas for computing $\Phi_{kk}$ values are available. The estimate of $\Phi_{kk}$ namely sample partial autocorrelation at lag k, is denoted by the symbol $r_{kk}$ and given by the formula

$$r_{11} = r_1, r_{kk} = (r_k - \sum_{j=1}^{k-1} r_{k-1, j} r_{k-j}) / (1 - \sum_{j=1}^{k-1} r_{k-1, j} r_j) \text{ for } k = 2, 3, \dots$$

where

$$r_{kj} = r_{k-1,j} - r_{kk} r_{k-1,k-j} \text{ for } j = 1, 2, \dots, k-1.$$

We can gauge the significance of each $\Phi_{kk}$ by computing it with its standard error, $S(\Phi_{kk}) = n^{-1/2}$.

An ARIMA model is built on the available data; its theoretical counterpart is an ARIMA process. Each ARIMA process has a theoretical autocorrelation function (ACF) and partial autocorrelation function (PACF) associated with it. To identify an ARIMA model in practice we first construct the SACF and SPACF for a given data series. Then we compare the SACF and SPACF with some common theoretical ACFs and PACFs. Upon finding a reasonable match, we choose the ARIMA associated with the matching theoretical ACF and PACF as a tentative ARIMA model for the data.

After a tentative model is identified, we estimate the initial values for its parameters. For an assumed AR process of order 1 or 2, initial estimates for $\Phi_1$ and $\Phi_2$ can be calculated by substituting estimates $r_j$ with the theoretical autocorrelations $\rho_j$ in the formula, for AR(1): $\Phi_1 = \rho_1$ for AR(1); $\Phi_1 = \rho_1 (1 - \rho_2) / (1 - \rho_2^2)$, $\Phi_2 = (\rho_2 - \rho_1^2) / (1 - \rho_2^2)$ for AR(2).

For an assumed MA process of order 1 or 2 the situation is little different. Initial estimates for $\Phi_1$ and $\Phi_2$ can be calculated by substituting estimates $r_j$ with the theoretical autocorrelations $\rho_1$ in the formula, for MA(1): $\rho_1 = -\theta_1 / (1 + \theta_1^2)$, and for MA(2): $\rho_1 = (-\theta_1(1 - \theta_2))/(1 + \theta_1^2 + \theta_2^2)$ and $\rho_2 = (-\theta_2)/(1 + \theta_1^2 + \theta_2^2)$.

Since the initial parameter must meet the requirement of invertibility, for the assumed ARMA(1,1) process the approximate values for the parameters are obtained by substituting the estimate $r_1$ and $r_2$ with $\rho_1$ and $\rho_2$ in the expression: $\rho_1 = (1 - \theta_1 \Phi_1)(\theta_1 - \Phi_1)/(1 + \theta_1^2 - 2\theta_1 \Phi_1)$ and $\rho_2 = \rho_1 \Phi_1$

A more general method for obtaining initial estimates of the parameters for a mixed autoregressive-moving average process was presented in (Anderson 1976).

**Step 2 – Estimation**: After identification of the tentative model, its parameters are estimated. Three principal algorithms used by popular statistical packages to estimate model parameters are unconditional least squares, conditional least squares, and maximum likelihood estimation. SPTF adopts the maximum likelihood estimation that is based on the least squares estimation: $S(\Phi, \theta) = \Sigma_{t=-\infty}^{n} [a_t \mid \Phi, \theta, w]^2 = \Sigma_{t=-\infty}^{n} [a_t]^2$

A minimum, and in practice infinite, sum can be replaced by a manageable finite sum to show the behavior of the autocorrelation function for the dth difference of an ARIMA process of order (p, d, q).

Now we show how, by iterative application of linear least squares, estimates may be obtained for an ARIMA model. We use $\beta$ as a general symbol for $k = p + q$ parameters $(\theta, \Phi)$. We need, then, to minimize $\Sigma_{t=1-Q}^{n} [at \mid w, \beta]^2 = \Sigma_{t=1-Q}^{n} [at]^2$

Expanding $[a_t]$ in a Taylor series about its value corresponding to some guessed set of parameter values $\beta_0' = (\beta_{1,0}, \beta_{2,0}, \ldots \beta_{k,0})$, we have approximately $[a_t] = [a_{t,0}] - \Sigma_{i=1}^{k} (\beta_i - \beta_{i,0}) x_{i,t}$, where $[a_{t,0}] = [a_0 \mid w, \beta_0]$ and $x_{i,t} = (-\partial [a_t] / \partial [\beta_t]) \mid \beta = \beta_0$.

Now, if $X$ is the $(n + Q) \times k$ matrix $\{x_{i,t}\}$, the $n + Q$ equations (1) may be expressed as $[a_0] = X(\beta - \beta_0) + [a]$, where $[a_0]$ and $[a]$ are column vectors with $n + Q$ elements.

The adjustments $\beta - \beta_0$, which minimize $S(\beta) = S(\Phi, \theta) = [a]'[a]$, may now be obtained by linear least squares, i.e. by :regressing" the $[a_0]$'s onto the $x$'s. Because the $[a_t]$'s will not be exactly linear in the parameter $\beta$, a single adjustment will not immediately produce least squares values. Instead, the adjusted values are substituted as new guesses and the process repeated until convergence occurs.

The derivatives $x_{i,t}$ may be obtained directly. However, for machine computation, a general nonlinear squares routine has been found very satisfactory, in which the derivatives are obtained numerically. This is done by perturbing the parameters "one at a time." Thus, for a given model, the values $[a_t \mid w, \beta_{1,0}, \beta_{2,0}, \ldots, \beta_{k,0}]$ for $t = 1 - Q$, ..., n are calculated recursively, using whatever preliminary "back forecasts" may need. The calculation is then repeated for $[a_t \mid w, \beta_{1,0} + \delta_1, \beta_{2,0}, \ldots, \beta_{k,0}]$, then for $[a_t \mid w, \beta_{1,0}, \beta_{2,0} + \delta_2, \ldots, \beta_{k,0}]$, and so on. The negative of the required derivative is then given to sufficient accuracy using

$$x_{i,t} = \{[a_t \mid w, \beta_{1,0}, \beta_{2,0}, \ldots, \beta_{k,0}] - [a_t \mid w, \beta_{1,0}, \beta_{2,0}, \ldots, \beta_{2,0} + \delta_i, \ldots, \beta_{k,0}]\}/\delta_i$$

The above method for obtaining derivatives has the advantage of universal applicability and requires us to program only the calculation of the $[a_t]$'s, not their derivatives. For detailed discussion of the estimation, see Box and Jenkins (1970).

For this step we use back forecast to obtain $[a_0]$. This is done by setting $[e_k] = 0$ and using back recursion $[e_t] = [w_t] + \theta[e_{t+1}]$ (model ARIMA(0,1,1)). Higher accuracy would be achieved by beginning the back recursion further on in the series. Values of $[a_t]$ obtained by successive use of $[a_t] = \theta[a_{t-1}] - [w_t]$.

To obtain a first adjustment for $\theta$, we regress the $[a_0]$'s onto the x's. Notice that we need to choose step $\delta$ properly to avoid overshoot and speed up convergence.

**Step 3 - Diagnostic Checking:** The diagnostic check is used to check the adequacy of the tentative model with the parameter obtained from the previous step. If the model is an adequate ARIMA representation of the autocorrelation patterns in the available data, then there should be no further significant autocorrelation patterns left in the residual series $a_t$. We construct the SACF of the residual series. If the residual SACF shows that each residual autocorrelation is relatively small to its standard error (not far away from of its two standard error limits, it suggests that model adequately represents the autocorrelation patterns in the data. Another check is to perform a joint test with null hypothesis $\mathbf{H_0 : \rho_1(a) = \rho_2(a) = \ldots = \rho_K(a) = 0.}$ If $H_0$ is true, then the following statistic $\mathbf{Q^* = n\ (n + 2)\ \sum_{k=1}^{K} (n - k)^{-1}\ r_k^{\ 2}\ (a)}$ is approximately $\chi^2$ distributed with $K - m$ degrees of freedom (m is the number of coefficients estimated in the model ). For a detailed discussion of the properties of this statistic, see Ljung and Box (1978). We calculate the $Q^*$ and compare it with the $\chi^2$ value of critical points for relevant freedom degree. If the $Q^*$ is less than the 5% of the critical $\chi^2$ value for the relevant freedom degree, we don't reject $H_0$.

Here we also need to introduce two useful graphical ways to check the normality of the residual $a_t$. Because a standard assumption is that the random shocks $(a_t)$ are distributed normally, we can perform t tests on coefficient significance. One way to check for normality is to examine a histogram of the residuals. Another is to plot the model residuals in a normal probability plot. They are very helpful for practical normality test. To create the normal probability plot, the standardized residuals are ordered from lowest to highest. These values are then plotted against a set of theoretically ordered normal values. If the residuals are normally distributed, the resulting plot is a straight line.

**Step 4 – Forecast:** Forecast requires a decision to be made at current time t and the optimal decision depends on the expected future value of a random variable, $y_{t+h}$, being predicted. The number of time points forecast into the future forecast horizon is called the lead time, denoted by h. The value of the random variable for such a forecast is the value of $y_{t+h}$. A forecaster wishes to obtain a prediction as close as possible to the actual value of the variable from the current or future temporal point of interest. When the model is built, it is desirable to minimize the difference between the forecasts and the observed values. This difference is known as the forecast error, $e_t$. One criterion for measuring the precision of forecast is the sum of squared forecast errors. A more commonly used criterion is the mean square forecast error (MSFE). This MSFE can be used as an overall measure of accuracy for these forecasts.

$$- \quad \mathbf{MSFE = \sqrt{(\sum_{t=n+1}^{n+m} (\breve{y}_t - y_t)^2 / m)}}$$

Here we are considering m forecasts $(\breve{y}_t)$ for periods from $n + 1$ through $n + m$, and m future observed values $(y_t)$ that are unknown when we forecast from time t originally equal to n.

To perform point forecast, we input relevant historical data into the model and set some unknown values to be zero. We also need forecast confidence intervals. The formula of forecast interval is: $\breve{y}_t = y_t + t_{(1-\alpha/2,\,df)}\ \sqrt{(1 + \sum_{i=1}^{h-1} \psi_i^{\ 2})}\ \sigma^2$, where $t_{(1-\alpha/2,\,df)}$ means $(1 - \alpha/2)$th percentile of a distribution with $df$ degrees of freedom. The forecasts may be updated with the assistance of the $\psi$ weights. As the lead time gets greater, the interval generally becomes larger, although the exact pattern depends on the $\psi$. Different forecast functions have different error structures, and possess therefore different forecast error variances. The forecast intervals clearly depend on the type of forecast error and its variance. Hence, different processes have different forecast profiles.

❑  **Forecast Profile for the AR Process**
AR(p) forecast profiles are recognizable by spreading forecast intervals as well. The spread exponentially declines until it phases out. The rate of this declination is a function of the magnitude of the autoregressive parameters. The forecast error for AR(1) is computed by the expanding forecast interval of AR(1) process: $E(e_1^2) = \sigma_e^2$, $E(e_2^2) = (1 + \varphi_1^2) \sigma_e^2$, $E(e_3^2) = (1 + \varphi_1^2 + \varphi_1^4) \sigma_e^2$ and $E(e_h^2) = (1 + \varphi_1^2 + \varphi_1^4 + ... + \varphi_1^{(2h-2)}) \sigma_e^2$.

Second and higher order autoregressive processes, such as $Y_t = C + \varphi_1 Y_{t-1} - \varphi_2 Y_{t-2} + e$ may be characterized by oscillation if the second-order autoregressive parameter, $\varphi_2$, is not of the same sign as the first-order autoregressive coefficient.

❑  **Forecast Profile for the MA Process**
The point forecast of an MA(1) process is derived from the formula from the MA model. The expectation of $e_{t+1}$ through $e_{t+h}$ equals 0. Therefore, as the forecast function is extended, the forecast function rapidly converges to $e_h$ series mean. A stationary MA(1) e-process is a short, one-period ahead, the best forecast is the mean of the series. The forecast variance of such an MA series around mean can also be computed as $E(e_{t+h}^2) = (1 + \theta_1^2)\sigma_e^2$.

Owing to the short, one-period memory of this process, the value of the error variance remains the same after the initial shock. The forecast interval is merely the point forecast plus or minus 1.96 times the square root of the forecast error variance. For detailed discussion about the forecast confidence interval, see the Box and Jenkins (1976).
The result of forecast with confidence interval can be found in Figure 2.


## 3.2  Interpretation of the Model

Two general interpretations of the forecasts from an ARIMA model are the weighted average forecasts and the exponentially moving average (EWMA) forecast. Consider the one-step ahead forecast from origin t=n from a stationary AR(1) model: $z_{n+1} = C + \Phi_1 z_n$.

We can rewrite the this model as $z_{n+1} = \mu(1 - \Phi_1) + \Phi_1 z_n$ where $\mu$ is the average of z. The first term gives a weight of $(1 - \Phi_1)/n$ to each observation and the sum of the weights given to the observed $z_t$ values is 1.0. Thus the ARIMA forecast of $z_{n+1}$ is a weighted average of the n available values. A similar result can be shown for multi-step ahead forecasts from the AR(1) and forecasts from other ARIMA models.

ARIMA (0,1,1) models have a special interpretation: They are exponentially weighted moving averages on the available data. To show this we begin by writing the ARIMA (0,1,1) in back shift (B) form where, and C=0 for simplicity: $(1-B) z_t = (1-\theta_1 B) a_t$.

After Taylor series expansion, we may write the above as
$$(1 + \theta_1 B + \theta_1^2 B^2 + \theta_1^3 B^3 + ...)(1-B)z_t = a_t$$

$B^i$ is defined as follows: When $B^i$ multiplies any time-subscripted variable, the time subscript is shifted back by I time periods. We can derive the following formula from it.

$$z_{n+1} = (1 - \theta_1)z_n + \theta_1 (1 - \theta_1)z_{n-1} + \theta_1^2 (1 - \theta_1)z_{n-2} + \ldots$$

The implied weights given to the past z's in the one-step ahead forecast from the above equations are $\theta_1^{k-1}(1 - \theta_1)$, where k=1,2,3… is the number of past time periods. When $|\theta_1|<1$, these weights decline exponentially as k increases.

## 4   Implementation of SPTF

Now we present the implementation of SPTF. We implement SPTF as a Web server application running in server/client environment. The (Web) server runs under UNIX and also supports CGI for building up interaction with the client that can be any Web browser running on PC and java applet.

To maintain functionality and flexibility at the same time, we implement some steps (such as Identification) as one-way process and other steps as repeatable process (such as Forecasting). To help users follow the correct steps, clear and meaningful tips were added in the application. In addition, to make the application strong, the reset function must be added in the operation process.

We use java to implement the SPTF function and Perl script to implement data flow transaction between server and client. The Forecasting part and some part of File Management were written by JAVA (compressed as JAR file). The File Management part as CGI file is written by Perl script. Using CGI we can upload specific data file from browser to server as the input series. The web page is created using Dreamweaver.

## 5   Empirical Tests

Fifteen listed companies were randomly selected for empirical test by using their one-year historical price. We use twenty latest prices as "unknown future" and use the rest prices to build up the models for each company. We found that six shares are approximately suitable to be tentatively identified as MA(1) model (implemented completely). Among these six, there are four shares whose one-month prices average falls in the 95% forecast confidence interval and five shares whose one-month price average falls in the 99% forecast confidence interval. This shows that if the model is chosen properly the prediction hit-rate is impressively high. The hit rate in this experiment is 66.6% for 95% confidence interval and 80% for 99% confidence interval.

### 5.1   Test Outcome

We present the identification process, 95% confidence interval forecast and 99% confidence interval forecast result for six listed companies. They are National Australia Bank Limited (NAB), Channel E Limited (CEL), H-G Ventures Limited (HVG), SPC Limited (SPC), FFI Holdings Limited (FFI) and RM Williams Holdings

Limited (RMW). We chose the data from 24 July 2000 to 23 July 2001. The original price data is collected from  http://www.tradingroom.com.au/quotes_charts/index.jsp.

The following figures show the process and result of the tests.

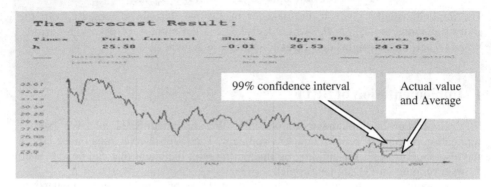

(a) 99% confidence forecast interval and true prices

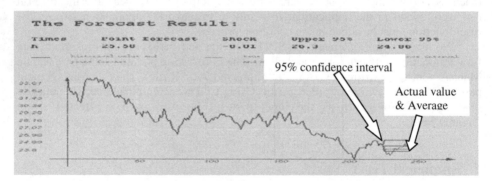

(b) 95% confidence forecast interval and true prices

**Fig. 2.** Identification and forecast of company NAB

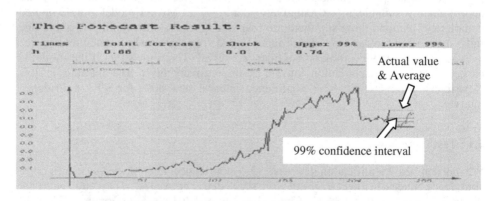

(a) 99% confidence forecast interval and true prices

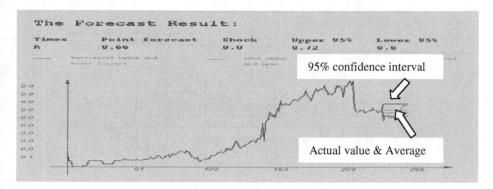

(b) 95% confidence forecast interval and true prices

**Fig. 3.** Identification and forecast of company CEL

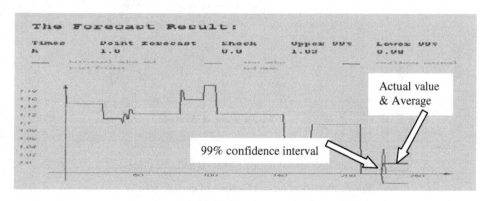

(a) 99% confidence forecast interval and true prices

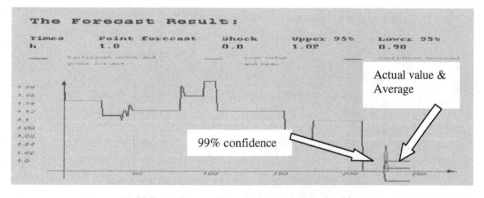

(b) 95% confidence forecast interval and true prices

**Fig. 4.** Identification and forecast of company FFI

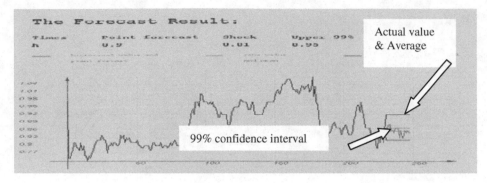

(a)   99% confidence forecast interval and true prices

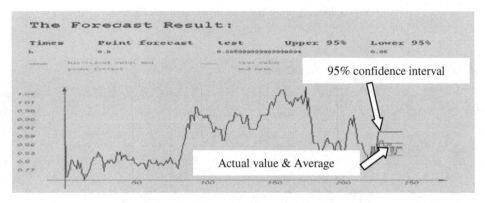

(b) 95% confidence forecast interval and true prices

**Fig. 5.** Identification and forecast of company HGV

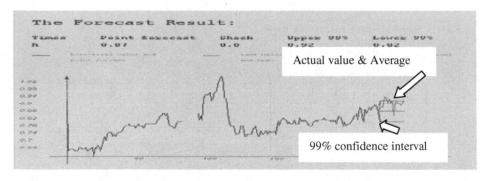

(a)   99% confidence forecast interval and true prices

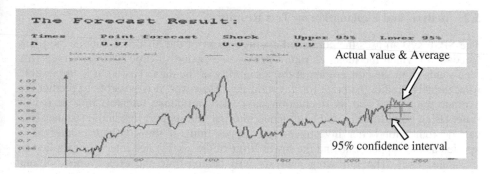

(b) 95% confidence forecast interval and true prices

**Fig. 6.** Identification and forecast of company SPC

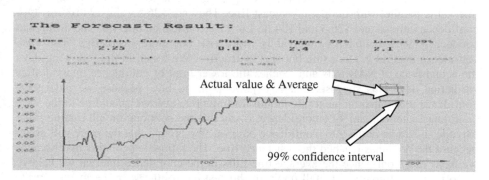

(a) 99% confidence forecast interval and true prices

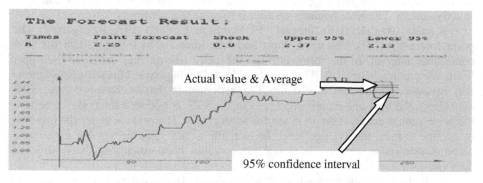

(b) 95% confidence forecast interval and true prices

**Fig. 7.** Identification and forecast of company RMW

## 5.2   Analysis and Explanation on Test Results

The SPSF system uses the computed average mean of the historical data as the point forecast, to which the mean of future prices in a period of time will converge. This idea stems from the concern about the variability of the data. That is, it is impossible to accurately predict the price for a certain day. However, it is possible to predict the average price level and its fluctuation interval (Confidence Interval) in a period of time. Using point forecast and confidence interval, the support line and resistance line can be found for better investment (the upper limit of the confidence interval is applied as the support line and the lower limit of the confidence interval is applied as resistance line). The following analysis will demonstrate the effectiveness of our approach.

Let us look at National Australia Bank (NAB) as the first example. From Figure 2 the point forecast for the next day is \$25.58. Because the model identified is MA(1) $(z_t = \theta_1 a_{t-1} + a_t)$, the following forecasts converge to the computed mean of the available data after one step forecast. The upper limit and lower limit of confidence interval is parallel with the point-forecast line. They are \$26.53 and \$24.63 for 99% confidence interval and \$26.3 and \$24.86 for 95% confidence interval. The difference between is 95% confidence interval is more risk but more instructive. The 99% confidence interval is more safe but less instructive. We found in the following days the actual price of NAB falls and reaches the lower limit of confidence interval after prediction day. This suggests that is a good point to buy, because we have 95% confidence to say that the next one-month trading price average should be in the 95% confidence interval, and 99% confidence to say that the next one-month trading price average should be in the 99% confidence interval. We predict that the price will go up because the price has reached the resistance line. The rationale behind is that because we have 95% confidence the average line falls in the confidence interval we believe the price cannot continue to fall down in the rest days, otherwise the average price must be out of the confidence interval. Obviously the 99% confidence limit gives a stronger signal for a buying point. The true value trend proves this suggestion is exactly correct. The price bounces up after it reaches the low limit.

Another example is to forecast FFI Holdings Limited (FFI) in Figure 4. The point forecast is \$1.0. The upper limit and low limit are \$1.02 and \$0.98 for 99% confidence interval. In the following day the price rise quickly and over the upper limit. We predict the price will fall down in the following days. This strongly suggests that investors should sell this share. The rationale is that because we have 99% confidence the next one-month average is in the 99% confidence interval, we believe the price cannot continue go up in the following days. The price is under the pressure to decline to meet the average level. In fact, the actual value proves our investment recommendation is correct. The actual price comes back quickly to the confidence interval.

In the Figure 7, the forecast for RWM is given. The actual price rises up quickly after prediction day. We predict the price will go back in next days. This is a good point to sell the shares because we have 95% and 99% confidence that the price average will falls in the confidence interval. The price really goes down in the rest days. But in fact from Figure 6 we can see the true price average in next one-month is out of the confidence interval. Two possible reasons cause this problem. One is the model is not proper to represent the time series observation. We should study the diagnostic check result to tentatively identify a new model or improve the current model. Another reason is that it belongs to the Type II error. Usually, we cannot get a recommend from such situations. We found the test average does not fall in the 95% and 99% confidence interval. From this example our prediction is still valuable to the investment.

# 6 Conclusion

We have presented a new stock trend prediction system – Self-projecting Time Series Forecast system (STSF). SRTF works by finding out the pattern of historical data of individual share and forecasting its future trends. SPTF avoid the miscellaneous financial methodology and theories. The basic idea behind SPTF is to find a mathematical formula that will approximately generate the historical patterns in a time series by self-projecting time series forecast models. Such forecast can be considered as the best-weighted average of the past value observation.

We have shown how time series analysis and Box-Jenkins' modeling strategy can be applied to financial time series forecast. We have proposed a new method for determining the support line and resistance line for better investment. Also, we designed SPTF as an online system to meet the rapid growth of online investment. Moreover, SPTF is different from Conventional web brokers who normally offer the investment recommendation with descriptive language. SPTF prediction result incorporate both Forecast and Confidence Interval Forecast, where the latter one could be considered as a subsidiary index of the former one in decision-making.

The empirical test give a hit-rate is 66.6% for 95% confidence interval prediction and 80% for 99% confidence interval prediction respectively. This is a remarkable result considering the variability of stock trends.

The current version of SPTF System possesses only basic functions to implement modeling and forecast. Many powerful functions are yet to be added, which remains to be our future work. Particularly, the following functionalities will be explored:
- Stabilization of variance based on Box-Cox transformation.
- Estimation by using any of the principal algorithms.
- Diagnostic checks to reveal hidden information for modeling.

# References

O.D. Anderson, *Time Series Analysis and Forecasting*, The Box-Jenkins Approach, Butterworth & Co. Ltd (1976)

T. W. Andersson, *The Statistical Analysis of Time Series*, John Wiley & Sons, Inc (1971)

C. Chatfield, *The Analysis of Times Series: Theory and Practice*, Chapman & Hall Ltd. (1975)

Hossein Arsham, *Time Series Analysis and Forecasting Technique*,

George E.P. Box & Gwilym M. Jenkins, *Time series Analysis Forecasting and control*, Resivised Edition, Holden-Day, Inc. (1976)

Bruce L. Bowerman & Richard T. O'Connell, *Time Series and Forecasting,* Wadsworth, Inc. (1979)

Bruce L. Bowerman & Richard T. O'Connell, *Forecasting and Time Series an Applied Approach*, Wadsworth, Inc. (1993)

Peter J. Brockwell & Pichard A. Davis, *Introduction to Time Series and Forecasting*, Springer-Verlag New York, Inc. (1996)

Paul B. Farrell, *Expert Investing on the Net*, John Wiley & Sons, Inc. (1996)

Douglas Gerlach, *The Complete Idiot's Guide to Online Investing*, Que Corporation, (1998)

Warren Gilchrist, *Statistical Forecasting*, John Wiley &Sons, Ltd. (1976)

James D. Hamilton, *Time Series Analysis*, Princeton University Press (1994)

John C. Handley, "Department of Accounting and Finance", *Research Paper* 96–15, The University of Melbourne (1996)

E. J. Hannan, *Multiple Time Series*, John Wiley & Sons, Inc (1970)

C. P. Li, *Stock Market Prediction Using Neural Networks*

Helmut Lutkepohl, *Introduction to Multiple Time Series Analysis*, Second Edition, Springer Verlag Berlin . Heidelberg (1993)

S. Lawrence Marple Jr., *Digital Spectral Analysis with Application*, Prentice Hall PTR A Simon & Schuster Company, (1987)

Alan Pankartz, *Forecasting with Dynamic Regression Model*, John Wiley & Sons, Inc. (1991)

T. Subba Rao (ed.), *Development in Time Series Analysis*, Champman & Hall (1993)

Robert A. Yaffee & Monnie McGee, *Introduction to Time Series Analysis and Forecasting with Application of SAS and SPSS*, Academic Press, Inc. (2000)

http://www.elliottwave.com/eduation (20 Jun. 2001)

http://imagine.gsfc.nasa.gov/docs/science/how_l1/spectral.html (12 Jun. 2001)

http://www.stsci.edu/stsci/meetings/adassVII/sturme.html (5 Jun. 2001)

http://www.ipac.caltech.edu/iso/isap/isap.html (24 May. 2001)

http://www-stat.stanford.edu/~hastie/mrc.html (11 Apr. 2001)

http://www.spss.com/spss10/regression/regression.htm (11 Apr. 2001)

http://help.sap.com/saphelp_45b/helpdat...24b52060634e10000009b38f9b9/content.htm (2 Apr. 2001)

http://www.bun.kyoto-u.ac.jp/~suchii/chi-square.html (12 May 2001)

http://www.nuhertz.com/statmat/distributions.html (10 May 2001)

http://www.marymt.edu/~psychol/exper/Chap12.html (2 May 2001)

http://ubmail.ubalt.edu/~harsham/stat-data/opre330Forecast.htm

http://members.nbci.com/_xxmc/joe_li/honex.html

# A Web-Based Graphical Interface for General-Purpose High-Performance Computing Clusters

Bing Bing Zhou[1], B. McKenzie[2], and Andrew Hodgson[2]

[1] School of Information Technologies, University of Sydney,
NSW 2006, Australia
[2] School of Information Technology, Deakin University,
Geelong, VIC 3217, Australia

**Abstract.** In this paper we present our work on the development of a Web-based graphical interface for users to remotely log into high-performance computing clusters. We show that the conventional thin-client Web technology has limitations for applications with complex user interface requirements and the rich-client technology such as the Curl is the preferred technology for our graphical interface development. The Curl technology takes the advantage of the processing power of clients to transfer some of the server's jobs to the client. Therefore, it can significantly ease the processing burden on the server and reduce the network traffic. More importantly, adopting the Curl technology we are able to establish a system which can provide just-in-time service delivery to remote users.

## 1 Introduction

Access to high performance computing resources from remote locations can be complex. This is because computational environments of different systems may differ and user interfaces to different resources vary. Currently, a lot of attention has been attracted to the development of Web-based portals to allow users to have access to resources of high-performance computing systems via an integrated and easy-to-use Web page interface. With such Web-based systems, users can have access to remotely located computing resources from anywhere there is a Web browser available.

Currently, most Web systems are developed based on the so called thin-client technology. With such technology, the server does most of the processing and clients only act as dumb terminals mainly for entering inputs and displaying the results of server-side operations. Each time when a client sends a request to the server, the server will act accordingly and send a new Web page back to the client for display. As Web development increasingly focuses on applications, the limitations of this conventional technology are becoming more and more apparent. In this paper we shall show that an alternative technology, that is, the rich-client technology is preferred for the development of systems with

M. Guo and L.T.Yang (Eds.): ISPA 2003, LNCS 2745, pp. 44–52, 2003.

complex user interface requirements, such as the Web-based graphical interface for remotely accessing our general-purpose high-performance computing cluster.

One of the characteristics of our general-purpose PC cluster is that users can freely log into any PC in the cluster. Conventionally, to access a remote computer is via Telnet, rlogin, or SSH client tool. However, with these tools, users can only obtain a text-based, command-line interface for interaction with the remote machine. For general users, such a command-line interface is not convenient to use and a more intuitive and easy-to-use graphical interface is preferred. Thus, the design and development of a powerful and user-friendly graphical interface for remotely accessing such high-performance computer system is critical to fully exploit the capability of the system. A Web-based graphical interface is thus developed for users to remotely log into our cluster. With this Web-based interface, the user can access the system from anywhere there is a Web browser available, and more importantly, good features of other Web-based portals for remotely accessing high-performance computing resources can be easily integrated to make our system very powerful and user-friendly for various types of real high-performance computing applications.

The thin-client technology is not suitable for our system. This is simply because, after logging into our cluster, the user may want to store data, create and edit files, compile, execute, and debug their programs, and so on. The user may frequently ask for these services, which may lead to frequent changes in the graphical interface. Using the thin-client technology, even a small change, such as creating/deleting a file, will request the server to generate a new Web page and send it back to the client for display. For a multi-user system the server can be overloaded and become a bottleneck. Fortunately, most computers used by remote users are not dumb terminals nowadays and the processing power of these computers can then be utilized to significantly reduce the processing load on the server. The rich-client technology we have finally decided to use is called Curl [8]. This advanced technology not only takes the advantage of the processing power of clients to transfer some of the server's jobs to the client, but also significantly reduces communication traffic between the client and server. More importantly, its very powerful client-side processing capability can provide just-in-time service delivery to remote users.

The paper is organised as follows. We first discuss some related work in Section 2. The system design is described in Section 3. The system implementation and its advantages in comparison with a system using the thin-client technology are presented in Section 4. The conclusions are given in Section 5.

## 2   Related Work

A Web-based portal is based on the Web, security and distributed computing technologies to provide secure, interactive services for users to access remote high-performance computing hardware and software from anywhere via a simple and easy-to-use Web browser. The existing Web-based portals for access to high performance computing resources can be divided into two categories. The first category is called user portals. The goal of this kind of portals is to allow users to have the ability to interact with the Grid [7] computing environment for authentication, simple job submission and tracking, file management and resource selection. Examples of the successful projects in this category are the NPACI Hot Page [15], designed to provide a Web interface for using Globus which provides application programmers with general tools required to access and use globally distributed high-performance computing resources [6], and the IPG Launch Pad [12], developed to allow users to easily submit and monitor jobs among various NASA Information Power Grid (IPG) resources.

The second category of the Web-based portals is developed for scientific problem solving and called science portals. This type of portals is designed to provide computational scientists with an application-specific environment for solving complex tasks involving remote high-performance computing resources. For example, the ECCE/ELN [5] project is designed for computational chemical scientists to simulate and model chemical engineering processes, the Cactus/ASC Portal [3] is for astrophysics simulations, and the JiPang [18,19] is to provide a Web-based interface to Ninf [1] and NetSolve [2,4] for high-performance computing using remotely located numerical computing libraries.

Several portal construction tools are now also available to aid in the development of Web-based portals on computational Grids. The well-known tools are the SDSC GridPort Toolkit [17], the NLANR Grid Portal Development Kit [9] and the Commodity Grid Toolkits, or CoG Kits [20].

Most existing Web portals are developed using the thin-client technology and are application-specific. In the development of our general-purpose high-performance computing cluster we shall integrate good features of these Web portals into our system to make it more powerful and capable of handling various types of applications. However, for remote login the user's graphical interface may need to be changed frequently. It is not desirable for the server to generate a new Web page and then send to the client for display every time a small change is required at the client side. Thus more advanced rich-client technologies have to be considered and one such technology is Curl.

Curl was created in 1995 by the Curl Corporation; a small Massachusetts company headed up by some of the leading computing specialists at MIT. It is a new Web-building technology that takes away much of the processing burden of the server and transfers it to the client. This allows powerful desktop PCs, which are fairly common today, to take a more active role in delivering rich content over the Web [21]. The Curl content language provides powerful client-side processing and is one language that incorporates text, graphics, markup, scripting, applets and systems programming. Also, Curl coexists with existing technologies such as HTML, JavaScript, Java, CGI, or Macromedia Flash [8].

When a Curl page is requested, it is delivered as raw data to the Web browser, as opposed to a fully rendered page. The raw data are then processed in real-time on the client. When the client make a request, therefore, only a small amount of data, that is, the direct result of business logic such as the results of back-end queries, needed by the client to update the interface is sent from the server. This eliminates the need to reload a whole Web page every time a new piece of data is requested. Curl leaves the server to focus on executing business logic while the client focuses on the presentation and formatting of information, as well as user interaction. In brief, Curl dramatically reduces the network bandwidth requirements and eases the server burden, and significantly increases user interactivity and client-side capabilities to match Windows-style applications for the Web [8,16,21].

Web sites written in Curl can be viewed using Surge Runtime Environment (RTE), that can be downloaded free of charge from the Curl website. Currently, the Surge RTE works with both Internet Explorer and Netscape Navigator, but it is only available for Microsoft Windows. However, RTE for the Mac OS X and Linux are being developed.

## 3   The System

The system of our Web-based graphical interface for remote login is made up of three major components, a client, a Web server and the general-purpose high-performance computing cluster. The client is a Web browser for users to gain access to the remote machine. All communication between the client and the remote machine must first go through the Web server, as shown in Fig. 1.

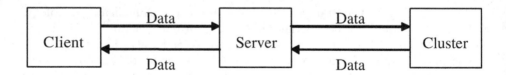

**Fig. 1.** The system overview

With Curl technology, the formatting, presentation and manipulation of data is accomplished exclusively on the client. Just-in-time service delivery is achievable and end-users will feel like they are interacting with a local application.

The major role of the Web server is to run a "server program". This "server program" is an application written in Java 2 that continually runs on the Web server. It accepts connection requests from clients and creates a thread to service each client. The Java thread is responsible for creating a Telnet connection to a PC in the cluster based on the information sent to it by the client. The thread also accepts requests from the client, translates the requests into commands that the remote machine understands and then sends the commands using the Telnet connection.

The flow of data among each of the major components within the system is shown in Fig. 2. Initially, the client Web browser requests a Curl applet from the Web server. The Curl applet is then transmitted as text, compiled and

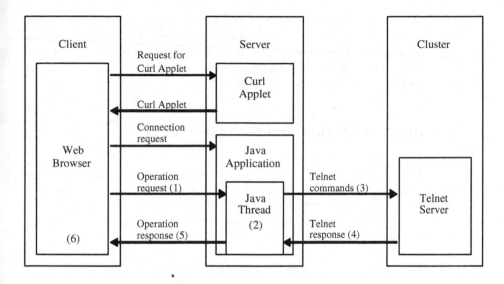

**Fig. 2.** Data flow among major system components

executed on the client machine using the Surge Runtime Environment. Upon loading, the client requests a socket connection to a "server program", a Java application running on the Web server. Once the server application has received this request, it creates a thread that will deal exclusively with the client. Each client that connects to the server is assigned its own thread. The thread first establishes a Telnet connection with a remote machine and then waits to receive requests and perform corresponding operations. When the client requires data from the remote computer, it sends a request to its thread indicating what operation to perform. The thread then executes the appropriate function to generate a Telnet command, sends it to the remote computer and waits for a response. Upon receiving the output of that command, the thread sends the resulting information back to the client, where it is processed and the interface is appropriately updated.

In the following we show an example of how the system performs a directory listing operation. The steps involved in this operation are shown in Fig. 2. Once the user double-clicks a directory icon, the client will send a message to its thread on the server indicating that it wants to display the contents in a particular directory (the operation request (1) in Fig. 2). The thread translates the request into a Telnet command (2) and sends that command to the remote machine through a Telnet connection (3). After the response comes back from the remote machine (4), the thread will forward it to the client (5). (For certain operations the server may do some simple operations and send a simplified result to the client.) Based the received result, the client will either produce and display the contents of that directory if the execution of the directory listing command on the remote machine is successful, or an error message if failed (6).

Note that, since the Curl content language provides very powerful client-side processing capabilities, all graphics manipulation and most of the data processing can be handled by the client. There is no need for the server to generate a new Web page for the interface updating every time a change is made. This will significantly enhance the system performance.

## 4    The Implementation and Comparison

The Curl content language is a very powerful programming language which encompasses the strengths of many traditional object-oriented programming, scripting, and markup languages. This enables us to create an effective and easy-to-use graphical interface (similar to those popular and user familiar desktop file managers) for users to manipulate their files located on remote machines, the general-purpose high-performance computing cluster in our particular case. Using the Curl technology our system can now successfully perform many functions such as logging in to, and logging out from a PC in the cluster; listing, creating, renaming, deleting, copying and moving files/directions; checking and changing file permissions; opening and editing text files. Programs have also been written for features such as multiple windows; different file-display styles; drag-and-drop files to different directories. In the near future we shall add more functions and features to the system to make the system more powerful and user- friendly. The technical issues of the current implementation are described in [10].

In the following we briefly describe our early system which used the thin-client Web technology and compare it with our new system using the rich-client Curl technology.

In our early system development the thin-client technology was adopted [13]. The major differences from our new system using Curl technology are as follows. Firstly, in our early attempt the server plays almost all the processing tasks, that is, to interpret requests from client and translate them into a format that the remote machine will understand, and also to generate a new Web page based on responses from the remote machine for each request. Secondly, the interactive communication between client and server is only through the use of HTML forms, a common practice in the current thin-client Web technology.

To request a service from the remote machine in our early system, the client first sends a HTML form to the server; the server then passes the form contents to a Java Servlet which is running on the server; the Servlet interprets the request to determine the required operation and then sends the operation information to a Java thread which is also running on the server; the Java thread processes the information, translates it into a Telnet command and sends it to the remote machine. After the command is executed on the remote machine, the result will be sent back to the Java thread. The Java thread calculates to see if the operation is successful and then passes the result to the Servlet. Based on the result of the performed operation the Servlet will dynamically generate a new Web page, which will be sent to the client and displayed to the user.

We can see from the above description that the server must generate a new Web page dynamically for each client's request. In the following example we show that to generate a new Web page the server may need to contact the remote machine more than once. Fig. 3(a) depicts how the system operates for a user request to create a new directory.

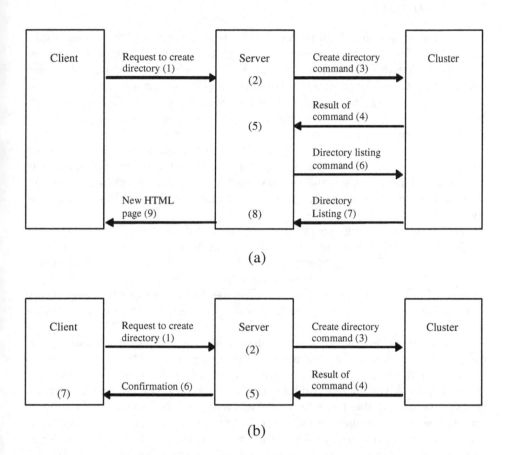

(a)

(b)

**Fig. 3.** Steps for the operation of directory creation (a) using the thin-client technology and (b) using the Curl technology

To create a new directory, the client first sends a request to the server (step (1) in Fig. 3(a)) and the server then translates it into a Telnet command (2) and sends the command to the remote machine (3). After the result is sent back (4), the server will check if the command is successfully executed on the remote machine (5). If the directory is created successfully, the server must send another command to the server again (6) to obtain the directory listing in order to produce a new Web page (8) for the client to update the current interface.

When the Curl technology is applied, the client is responsible for updating the interface. As indicated in Fig. 3(b), only a confirmation message is returned to the client. This message is much smaller than a full Web page that is graphically intensive due to the nature of the system.

## 5    Conclusions

In this paper we presented our project on the development of a Web-based graphical interface for users to remotely access high-performance computing clusters. We showed that the conventional thin-client Web technology has limitations for systems with complex user interface requirements. To overcome the problem the rich-client technology has to be seriously considered and the Curl is one such preferred technology for our graphical interface as it can significantly ease the processing burden on the server and reduce the communication traffic between client and server. Since the Curl content language is much more powerful than popular markup and scripting languages such as HTML and JavaScript and has all of the programming capabilities needed for advanced programming, we are able to develop a user-friendly graphical interface similar to those of familiar desktop file managers.

The Curl content language provides very powerful client-side processing capabilities. To take this advantage, in the near future we shall deal with the problem of network connection breakdown. When the network connection is broken, the client should still be able to perform tasks locally if there is no need for additional resources from the server or the remote machine. Final work can be saved locally and transferred to the remote machine when the network connection becomes available.

To make our cluster more general-purpose and easy to use by ordinary users, we need to coordinate the research and development in system resource management, computing packages for various kinds of applications, and graphical user interface. A Web-based graphical interface should be an appropriate service delivery mechanism due to its pervasiveness and platform neutrality. We expect that in the future ordinary users can effectively make use of the system hardware and software resources, with just a few clicks, to solve their hard problems, and more importantly to meet the performance requirement of each individual application.

## References

1. K. Aida, A. Takefusa, H. Ogawa, O. Tatebe, H. Nakada, H. Takagi, Y. Tanaka, S. Matsuoka, M. Sato, S. Sekiguchi, U. Nagashima, Ninf Project, *Proceedings of Asia-Pacific Advanced Network Conference*, Beijing, China, Aug. 2000.
2. D. C. Arnold and J. Dongarra, The NetSolve Environment: Progressing Towards the Seamless Grid, *Proceedings of 2000 International Conference on Parallel Processing*, Toronto, Canada, 2000.
3. Astrophysics Simulation Collaboratory, http://www.ascportal.org/project/goals.html, last visited on 23/6/2002.

4. H. Casanova and J. Dongarra, NetSolve: A Network Server for Solving Computational Science Problems, *The International Journal of Supercomputer Applications and High Performance Computing*, Volume 11, Number 3, pp 212–223, Fall 1997.
5. ECCE/ELN, http://www.pnl.gov/cpse/products.stm, last accessed on 23/6/2002.
6. I. Foster, C. Kesselman, Globus: A Metacomputing Infrastructure Toolkit, *Intl J. Supercomputer Applications*, 11(2):115–128, 1997.
7. I. Foster and C. Kesselman, The GRID: Blueprint for a New Computing Infrastructure, Morgan Kaufmann Publishers, Inc, 1999.
8. M. Gordon, J. Joly, D. Kranz, D. Maharry, P. J. Metzger and C. Ullman, Early Adopter Curl, Wrox Press Ltd, 2001.
9. The Grid Portal Development Kit, http://doesciencegrid.org//projects/GPDK/, last accessed on 23/6/2002.
10. A. Hodgson, A web based, graphical interface for remote accessing of high performance computer systems, Honours Thesis, Deakin University, Australia, 2002.
11. N. H. Kapadia, R. J. O. Figueiredo, and J. A. B. Fortes, PUNCH: a Portal to Running Tools, special issue on *Computer Architecture Education of IEEE MICRO*, Volume 20, Number 3, pp.38-47, May/June 2000.
12. G. Myers et al. NASA IPG Launch Pad Portal, http://www.ipg.nasa.gov/, last visited 23/6/2002.
13. B. Mckenzie, Efficient, secure and reliable remote accessing of high performance computer systems: towards a unified graphical interface, Honours Thesis, Deakin University, Australia, 2001.
14. P. Naughton and H. Schildt, The Complete Reference Java 2, Osborne/McGraw-Hill, 1999.
15. NPACI HotPage, https://hotpage.npaci.edu/about/about.html, last accessed on 23/6/2002.
16. J. Rosenberg, White Paper: Eliminating the submit button Web, Curl Corporation, 2002.
17. M. Thomas, S. Mock, J. Boisseau, M. Dahan, K. Mueller, D. Sutton, The Grid-Port Toolkit Architecture for Building Grid Portals, *Proceedings of the 10th IEEE International Symposium on High Performance and Distributed Computing*, Aug. 2001
18. T. Suzumura, S. Matsuoka, H. Nakad, A Jini-based Computing Portal System, *Proceedings of SC2001*, Denver, Colorado, Nov., 2001.
19. T. Suzumura, H. Nakada, M. Saito, S. Matsuoka, Y. Tanaka and S. Sekiguchi, The Ninf Portal: An Automatic Generation Tool for the Grid Portals, *Proceeding of ACM Java Grande 2002*, Seattle, Washington, November, 2002.
20. G. von Laszewski, I. Foster, J. Gawor, W. Smith, and S. Tuecke, CoG Kits: A Bridge between Commodity Distributed Computing and High-Performance Grids. *Proceedings of ACM Java Grande 2000 Conference*, pp 97–106, San Francisco, CA, June 2000.
21. White Paper: Consuming Web services on the client, Curl Corporation, 2001

# A Compressed Diagonals Remapping Technique for Dynamic Data Redistribution on Banded Sparse Matrix[1]

Ching-Hsien Hsu and Kun-Ming Yu

Department of Computer Science and Information Engineering
Chung Hua University, Hsinchu, Taiwan 300, ROC
Tel : 886-3-5186410
Fax: 886-3-5186416
{chh, yu}@chu.edu.tw

**Abstract.** In this paper, we present a new method, Compressed Diagonals Remapping (CDR) technique aims to the efficiency of data redistribution on banded sparse matrices. The main idea of the proposed technique is first to compress the source matrix into a Compressed Diagonal Matrix (CDM) form. Based on the compressed diagonal matrix, a one-dimensional local and global index transformation can be carried out to perform data redistribution on the compressed diagonal matrix, which is identical to redistribute data in the banded sparse matrix. The CDR technique uses an efficient one-dimensional indexing scheme to perform data redistribution on banded sparse matrix. A significant improvement of this approach is that a processor does not need to determine the complicated sending or receiving data sets for dynamic data redistribution. The indexing cost is reduced significantly. The second advantage of the present techniques is the achievement of optimal packing/unpacking stages consequent upon the consecutive attribute of column elements in a compressed diagonal matrix. Another contribution of our methods is the ability to handle sparse matrix redistribution under two disjoint processor grids in the source and destination phases. A theoretical model to analyze the performance of the proposed technique is also presented in this paper. To evaluate the performance of our methods, we have implemented the present techniques on an IBM SP2 parallel machine along with the v2m algorithm and a dense redistribution strategy. The experimental results show that our technique provides significant improvement for runtime data redistribution of banded sparse matrices in most test samples.

## 1   Introduction

The data-parallel programming model has become a widely accepted paradigm for programming distributed-memory parallel programs. To efficiently execute a data-parallel program on distributed memory multicomputers, appropriate data distribution is critical to the performance. Appropriate distribution can balance the computational load, increase data locality, and reduce interprocessor communication. Many data parallel programming languages such as High Performance Fortran (HPF), Fortran D, Vienna Fortran, and High Performance C (HPC) provide compiler directives for programmers to specify data distribution. Regular distributions provided by these languages, in general, have three types, BLOCK, CYCLIC, and BLOCK-CYCLIC(c). Dongarra *et al* [4] have shown that, these types of distribution are essential for many matrix algorithms design in distributed memory machines.

---

[1]This work was partially supported by the NSC of ROC under contract NSC91-2213-E-252-001.

M. Guo and L.T.Yang (Eds.): ISPA 2003, LNCS 2745, pp. 53–64, 2003.

Many methods were proposed to address the problems of the communication sets identification for array statements with BLOCK-CYCLIC($c$) distribution. [3, 6]    In [3], Chatterjee *et al.* enumerated the local memory access sequence of communication sets for array statements with BLOCK-CYCLIC($c$) distribution based on a finite-state machine.    In this approach, the local memory access sequence can be characterized by FSM at most $c$ states.    Gupta *et al.* [6] derived closed form expressions to efficiently determine the send/receive processor/data sets.    In many scientific applications, a distribution that is well suited for one phase may not be good for a subsequent phase in terms of performance.    Data redistribution is required for those algorithms during runtime.

Techniques for dynamic data redistribution of dense arrays are discussed in many researches [3-4, 8-9, 11-15, 17-18].    A detailed expatiation of these techniques was described in [8].    When data redistribution is carried out on sparse matrices, these algorithms become inapplicable since large amount of memory and data transmission costs will be wasted.    Another difficulty of redistributing data on sparse matrices is because nonzero elements are scattered unevenly, the coordinates of nonzero elements should be calculated at runtime.    The different structures of compressed representation and multiple levels of indirection access for nonzero elements also lead to the difficulty on determining the communication sets for a redistribution process. Therefore, data redistribution should be performed upon the nonzero structure to achieve better performance.    In order to provide efficient access of nonzero structures for sparse computation, many storage schemes were proposed [1, 16, 19]. One of the most famous structures is named CRS format, which is well suit for block-cyclic data redistribution of sparse matrices since the block-cyclic distribution is defined either by row or column.    Zapata *et al.* [2] proposed parallel sparse redistribution code for BLOCK-CYCLIC(x, *) to BLOCK-CYCLIC(y, *) data redistribution based on CRS structure. A previous work farther discussing these optimizations was presented in [10].

Instead of discussing method on general sparse matrix, this paper presents a different technique for data redistribution on banded sparse matrices.    To efficiently perform the redistribution of distributed bended sparse matrices, we first reconstruct the source matrix into a compressed diagonal matrix format.    The compressed diagonal matrix is structural similar to the CDS (Compressed Diagonal Scheme) representation.    For the efficiency of redistribution process, the upper diagonals and lower diagonals are compressed inversely to the CDS format.    Using a one-dimensional local and global index transformation method, data redistribution can be carried out on the compressed diagonal matrix.    Such process is identical to redistribute data in the original sparse matrix upon a matrix transposition phase.    An extension of present techniques is the ability to handle BLOCK-CYCLIC data redistribution on banded sparse matrix with non-symmetric lower and upper bandwidth.    One significant improvement of this approach is that a processor does not need to determine the complicated sending or receiving data sets for dynamic data redistribution.    The indexing cost is significantly reduced.    The second advantage of the present techniques is the achievement of optimal packing/unpacking stages consequent upon the consecutive attribute of column elements in a compressed diagonal matrix.    Another contribution of our methods is the ability to handle sparse matrix redistribution under two disjoint processor grids in the source and destination phases.

## 2  Preliminaries

In this section, we describe some notations and terminology used in this paper.

<u>Definition 1</u>: Given a sparse matrix $M_{n0 \times n1}$, a *sparse vector* is defined as the set of elements in a row of $M_{n0 \times n1}$. We define $M[0, 0:n_1-1]$ as sparse vector $v_0$ of $M_{n0 \times n1}$, $M[1, 0:n_1-1]$ as sparse vector $v_1$ of $M_{n0 \times n1}$, and so on.

<u>Definition 2</u>: Given a BLOCK-CYCLIC($x$, $*$) over $P$ processors to BLOCK-CYCLIC($y$, $*$) over $Q$ processors redistribution on sparse matrix $M_{n0 \times n1}$, the *Source Local Matrix* of processor $P_i$ denoted by $SLM_i$, is defined as the set of sparse vectors that are distributed to processor $P_i$ in the source distribution. The *Destination Local Matrix* of processor $Q_j$, denoted by $DLM_j$, is defined as the set of sparse vectors that are distributed to processor $Q_j$ in the destination distribution, where $0 \le i \le P-1, 0 \le j \le Q-1$.

<u>Definition 3</u>: Given a BLOCK-CYCLIC($x$, $*$) over $P$ processors to BLOCK-CYCLIC($y$, $*$) over $Q$ processors redistribution on sparse matrix $M_{n \times n}$, a *Basic Vector Cycle* (BVC) is defined as $BVC=lcm(x \times P, y \times Q)$. We define $\{v_0, v_1, ..., v_{BVC-1}\}$ is the first *BVC* of matrix $M_{n \times n}$, $\{v_{BVC}, v_{BVC+1}, ..., v_{2BVC-1}\}$ as the second *BVC* of matrix $M_{n \times n}$, and so on.

<u>Definition 4</u>: Given a sparse matrix $M_{n \times n}$, matrix $M$ is said to be bended when all its nonzero elements are confined within a band formed by diagonals parallel to the main diagonal.

<u>Definition 5</u>: Given a banded sparse matrix $M_{n \times n}$, the bandwidth of matrix $M$, $\beta$, is the number of total nonvoid diagonals; the lower bandwidth, $\beta_l$, of matrix $M$ is the largest $|i-j|$ such that $i > j$ and $M_{ij}$ is nonzero; the upper bandwidth, $\beta_u$, of a matrix $M$ is the largest $|i-j|$ such that $i < j$ and $M_{ij}$ is nonzero; therefore $\beta = \beta_l + \beta_u + 1$.

<u>Definition 6</u>: Given a banded sparse matrix $M_{n \times n}$, we use $d_0$ to represent the main diagonal of matrix $M$; $d_1$ and $d_{-1}$ represent the diagonals with distance 1 to the main diagonal $d_0$ in upper and lower triangle, respectively, and so on.

<u>Definition 7</u>: Given a banded sparse matrix $M_{n \times n}$ with bandwidth $\beta$, a *Compressed Diagonal Matrix* (CDM), denoted by $M_{CD}$, is a $\beta$ by $n$ matrix with $\beta$ rows and $n$ columns; we define $M_{CD}[0, 0:n-1]$ is the set of elements $d_{\beta u}$ with $\beta_u$ zero-entries; $M_{CD}[1, 0:n-1]$ is the set of elements $d_{\beta u-1}$ with $\beta_u-1$ zero-entries;...; $M_{CD}[\beta_u-1, 0:n-1]$ is the set of elements $d_1$ with one zero-entry; $M_{CD}[\beta_u, 0:n-1]$ is the set of elements $d_0$; $M_{CD}[\beta_u+1, 0:n-1]$ is the set of elements of one zero-entry with $d_{-1}$; ...; $M_{CD}[\beta-1, 0:n-1]$ is the set of elements of $\beta_l$ zero-entries with $d_{-\beta l}$. A generalized form to represent row $i$ of $M_{CD}$ can be expressed as $M_{CD}[i, 0:n-1]=\{0_h, M_{x,y}, M_{x+1,y+1}, ..., M_{x+\delta, y+\delta}, 0_t\}$, where $0_h$ and $0_t$ are two set of $x$ and $y$ zero-entries, respectively and $0 \le i \le \beta-1$, $x = \max\{i-\beta_u, 0\}$, $y = \max\{\beta_u-i, 0\}$, $\delta = \min\{n-i+\beta_u, n-\beta_u+i\}$. The paradigm of compressed diagonal matrix is shown in Fig. 1.

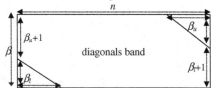

**Fig. 1.** Compressed Diagonal Matrix Paradigm

We use an example to clarify the above definitions.    Fig. 2(a) shows an example of banded sparse matrix $M_{24\times24}$.    According to definition 1, there are 24 sparse vectors of matrix $M_{24\times24}$, $v_0 = M[0, 0:23]$, $v_1 = M[1, 0:23]$, ..., $v_{23} = M[23, 0:23]$. According to definition 5, lower ($\beta_l$) and upper ($\beta_u$) bandwidth of $M$ is equal to 6 and 3, respectively; the bandwidth ($\beta$) of $M$ is 10.    From definitions 5 and 6, there are three upper diagonals $d_1$, $d_2$, $d_3$ and six lower diagonals $d_{-1}$, $d_{-2}$, $d_{-3}$, $d_{-4}$, $d_{-5}$, $d_{-6}$ of matrix $M$.    The corresponding compressed diagonal matrix is shown in Fig. 2(b). The shadow blocks in $M_{CD}$ are represented as dummy tail and dummy head in each diagonal.    Upon a BLOCK-CYCLIC(2,*) over 6 source processors to BLOCK-CYCLIC(3,*) over 4 destination processors redistribution, the size of *Basic Vector Cycle (BVC)* is equal to 12.    Therefore, there are two *BVCs* in matrix $M_{24\times24}$, $\{v_0, v_1, ..., v_{11}\}$ and $\{v_{12}, v_{13}, ..., v_{23}\}$.    By transposing the compressed diagonal matrix, we can also have two *BVCs* in $M_{CD}$.    $\{M_{CD}[0:9, 0], M_{CD}[0:9, 1], ..., M_{CD}[0:9, 11]\}$ and $\{M_{CD}[0:9, 12], M_{CD}[0:9, 13], ..., M_{CD}[0:9, 23]\}$ in column-wise.

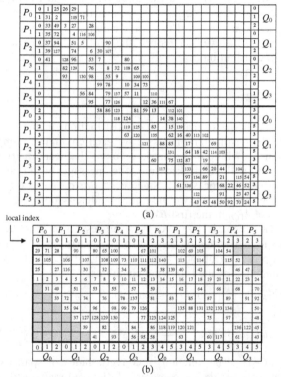

**Fig. 2.** BLOCK-CYCLIC data redistribution on a 24×24 banded sparse matrix and its compressed diagonal matrix (a) source and destination distribution of matrix $M$. (b) source and destination distribution of compressed diagonal matrix

# 3   Compressed Diagonals Remapping Technique

This section presents the Compressed Diagonals Remapping technique for performing BLOCK-CYCLIC(x, *) to BLOCK-CYCLIC(y, *) data redistribution on banded sparse matrix.   An example of BLOCK-CYCLIC(2,*) over six source processor to BLOCK-CYCLIC(3,*) over four destination processor redistribution represented by partitioning a banded sparse matrix $M_{24 \times 24}$ and the compressed diagonal matrix was shown in Fig. 2.   Fig. 2(a) shows the distribution shape of $SLM_s$ (LHS) and $DLM_s$ (RHS) in both source and destination phases for the global matrix.   To simplify the presentation, we plot the distribution shape for corresponding compressed diagonal matrix in Fig. 2(b).   In the following discussion, we assume that the index of local sparse matrix and compressed diagonal matrix starts from zero.   We also assume the compressed diagonal matrix of local sparse matrix is stored in each processor at program execution.

According to definition 7, we convert an $n \times n$ sparse matrix redistribution to a $\beta \times n$ compressed diagonal matrix.   By the transposition point of view, the sparse vectors of matrix $M$ can be regarded as matrix columns in $M_{CD}$.   For example, $M[0, 0:3] = M_{CD}[3:0, 0]$, $M[6, 0:9] = M_{CD}[9:0, 6]$, $M[23, 17:20] = M_{CD}[9:3, 23]$, etc.. Hereby, a BLOCK-CYCLIC(x, *) distribution on matrix $M$ can be transferred to the other pattern, that is BLOCK-CYCLIC(*, x) distribution on matrix $M_{CD}$.   Since a sparse vector of matrix $M$ (identical to matrix column of $M_{CD}$) will be distributed to the same computing node, we can reduce the problem further to one-dimensional BLOCK-CYCLIC redistribution case.

### 3.1 The Sending Stage

To perform the banded sparse matrix data redistribution, in the sending phase, one needs to calculate the destination processor for each column of compressed diagonal matrix $M_{CD}$.   Elements within those matrix columns that were distributed to the same destination processor will be packed into one message buffer and be sent to its corresponding destination processor.   Since each *Basic Vector Cycle* (BVC) has the same communication pattern [8], we only need to determine the communication sets for matrix columns of $M_{CD}$ in the first *BVC*.

Given a BLOCK-CYCLIC(x, *) over $P$ processors to BLOCK-CYCLIC(y, *) over $Q$ processors redistribution on banded sparse matrix $M_{n \times n}$, for a source processor $P_i$, the destination processor of local sparse vector $v_k$ of $SLM_i$ (or matrix column $c_k$ of $SLM_{iCD}$) can be computed by the following equations,

$$sg(k) = \left\lfloor \frac{k}{x} \right\rfloor \cdot x \cdot P + i \cdot x + mod(k, x) \tag{1}$$

$$dp(sg(k)) = mod\left( \left\lfloor \frac{sg(k)}{y} \right\rfloor, Q \right) \tag{2}$$

where $k$ = 0 to $BVC-1$.   The function $sg$ converts index of sparse vector (or matrix column) in source local matrix (or compressed diagonal matrix) to its corresponding global matrix index, i.e., $SLM_i[k, 0:n-1] = M[sg(k), 0:n-1]$.   The function $dp$ is used to determine the destination processor of a sparse vector $v_{sg(k)}$ in global matrix $M$.

Let us apply the example in Fig. 2 to explain the method described above.   The compressed diagonal matrix of $SLM$ in each source processor is shown in Fig. 3. Considering the source local matrix $SLM_4$ in Fig. 2(a) and $SLM_{4CD}$ in Fig. 3, for source processor $P_4$, according to equations 1 and 2, the destination processor of local sparse vectors, $v_0$ and $v_1$ are $Q_2$ and $Q_3$, respectively.   Since each *Basic Vector Cycle* (BVC) has the same communication set, it only needs to know the communication pattern in the first *BVC*.   Using the information obtained above, the matrix columns $c_0$ and $c_2$ in the first and the second *BVC* of $SLM_{4CD}$ will be packed to the message for destination processor $Q_2$; the matrix columns $c_1$ and $c_3$ in the first and the second *BVC* of $SLM_{4CD}$ will be packed to the message for destination processor $Q_3$.   An abbreviation form of the messages can be represented as $msg_{P4 \Rightarrow Q2}$: [(100, 109, -, 9, 55, -, 98, 130, -, 93), (54, 115, -, 21, -, 89, 134, 97, -, -)] and $msg_{P4 \Rightarrow Q3}$: [(-, 73, 34, 10, -, 78, 99, -, -, -), (-, 52, 46, 22, 68, -, -, -, 136, 61)].

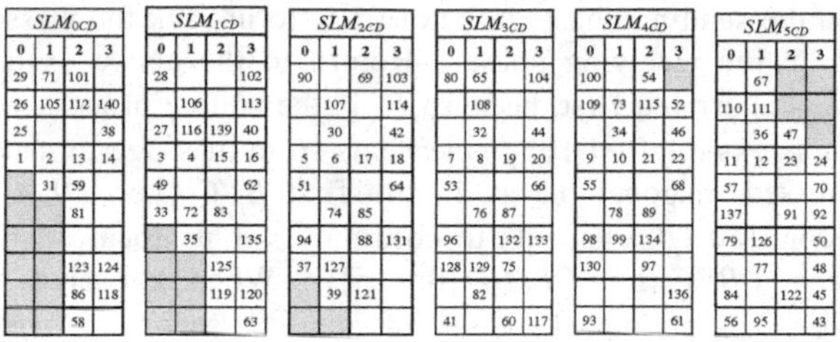

| SLM₀CD | | | | SLM₁CD | | | | SLM₂CD | | | | SLM₃CD | | | | SLM₄CD | | | | SLM₅CD | | | |
|---|---|---|---|---|---|---|---|---|---|---|---|---|---|---|---|---|---|---|---|---|---|---|---|
| 0 | 1 | 2 | 3 | 0 | 1 | 2 | 3 | 0 | 1 | 2 | 3 | 0 | 1 | 2 | 3 | 0 | 1 | 2 | 3 | 0 | 1 | 2 | 3 |
| 29 | 71 | 101 | | 28 | | | 102 | 90 | | 69 | 103 | 80 | 65 | | 104 | 100 | | 54 | | | 67 | | |
| 26 | 105 | 112 | 140 | | 106 | | 113 | | | 107 | 114 | 108 | | | | 109 | 73 | 115 | 52 | 110 | 111 | | |
| 25 | | | 38 | 27 | 116 | 139 | 40 | | 30 | | 42 | 32 | | 44 | | | 34 | | 46 | | 36 | 47 | |
| 1 | 2 | 13 | 14 | 3 | 4 | 15 | 16 | 5 | 6 | 17 | 18 | 7 | 8 | 19 | 20 | 9 | 10 | 21 | 22 | 11 | 12 | 23 | 24 |
| 31 | 59 | | | 49 | | | 62 | 51 | | | 64 | 53 | | | 66 | 55 | | | 68 | 57 | | | 70 |
| | 81 | | | 33 | 72 | 83 | | | 74 | 85 | | | 76 | 87 | | | 78 | 89 | | 137 | | 91 | 92 |
| | | 123 | 124 | | 35 | | 135 | 94 | | 88 | 131 | 96 | | 132 | 133 | 98 | 99 | 134 | | 79 | 126 | | |
| | 86 | 118 | | | 125 | | | 37 | 127 | | | 128 | 129 | 75 | | 130 | | 97 | | | 77 | | 48 |
| 58 | | | | | | 119 | 120 | 39 | 121 | | | | 82 | | | | | | 136 | 84 | | 122 | 45 |
| | | | | | | | 63 | | | | | 41 | | 60 | 117 | 93 | | | 61 | 56 | 95 | | 43 |

**Fig. 3.** Compressed diagonal matrices of $SLM_0$ to $SLM_5$

On constructing messages, the message for each destination processor is produced independently.   As an individual message established, another packing process will be carried out follows the previous message was sent.   The construction of messages and message passing are performed alternatively.   Such approach is mentioned asynchronous scheme.   As the asynchronous communication manner and non-blocking message passing mode in MPI library were applied to our implementation; advantages of these adoption improve the algorithm performance are twofold: one is because the message is constructed independently, the computation and communication overheads can be overlapped; the other one is memory requirement could be reduced by using single sending buffer.

### 3.2   The Receiving Stage

To construct local compressed diagonal matrix, in the receiving phase, a destination processor has to know the corresponding source processor for each sparse vector of its *DLM* (or matrix column of its local compressed diagonal matrix).   While a destination processor receives a message, it can extract data elements with a fixed size (the bandwidth $\beta$ of sparse matrix) section by section.   According to the communication pattern information obtained above, it then put those elements onto correct matrix columns in $DLM_{CD}$.

Given a BLOCK-CYCLIC($x$, *) over $P$ processors to BLOCK-CYCLIC($y$, *) over $Q$ processors redistribution on banded sparse matrix $M_{n \times n}$, for a destination processor $Q_j$, the source processor of local sparse vector $v_k$ of $DLM_j$ (or matrix column $c_k$ of $DLM_{jCD}$) can be computed by the following equations,

$$dg(k)=\lfloor k/y \rfloor \times y \times Q + j \times y + mod(k, y) \tag{3}$$

$$sp(dg(k)) = mod(\lfloor dg(k)/x \rfloor, P) \tag{4}$$

where $k = 0$ to $BVC-1$.   The function $dg$ converts index of sparse vector (or matrix column) in destination local matrix (or compressed diagonal matrix) to its corresponding global matrix index, i.e., $DLM_j[k, 0:n-1] = M[dg(k), 0:n-1]$.   The function $sp$ is used to determine the source processor of a sparse vector $v_{dg(k)}$ in global matrix $M$.

To clarify the method described above in the receiving phase, in Fig. 2(a), for destination processor $Q_2$, according to equations 3 and 4, source processors of sparse vectors $v_0$, $v_1$, $v_2$, are $P_3$, $P_3$, and $P_4$, respectively. Destination processor $Q_2$ will receive two messages from source processors $P_3$ and $P_4$. In this stage, one does not need to consider the arriving order of different messages. By the compressed diagonal remapping technique, a destination processor unpacks each coming message independently upon arbitrary receiving order and constructs the local destination compressed diagonal matrix. Because the matrix columns are packed sequentially by column-index in the sending phase, it is normally to unpack the message according to the index order in the receiving phase. Return to the above example, assume the message $msg_{P4\Rightarrow Q2}$ is arrived first, because $P_4$ is the source processor of sparse vector $v_2$ in $DLM_2$, it unpacks the first 10 ($\beta$) elements from message to matrix column $c_2$ of its local compressed diagonal matrix in the first $BVC$ (i.e., $DLM_{2CD}[0:9, 2]$); and unpacks the second 10 ($\beta$) elements to column $c_5$ of its local compressed diagonal matrix in the second $BVC$ (i.e., $DLM_{2CD}[0:9, 5]$). When it receives the message sent by $P_3$ (i.e., $msg_{P3\Rightarrow Q2}$), it unpacks the first and the second 10 ($\beta$) elements from message to columns $c_0$ and $c_1$ of its local compressed diagonal matrix in the first $BVC$ (i.e., $DLM_{2CD}[0:9, 0]$ and $DLM_{2CD}[0:9, 1]$); and unpacks the third and the fourth 10 ($\beta$) elements to columns $c_3$ and $c_4$ of its local compressed diagonal matrix in the second $BVC$ (i.e., $DLM_{2CD}[0:9, 3]$ and $DLM_{2CD}[0:9, 4]$).

The proposed unpacking technique in the receiving phase allows a destination processor to disassemble each received message one time and in arbitrary receiving order. The construction of local compressed diagonal matrix and message passing can be performed alternatively. One benefit of this approach is the computation and communication overheads can be overlapped via the asynchronous communication scheme and non-blocking message passing manner of MPI implementation. Another advantage is the destination local compressed diagonal matrix can be generated directly. It is unnecessary to perform sparse matrix to compressed structure transformation for subsequence phase of matrix computations in a parallel program.

## 4  Performance Evaluation and Experimental Results

### 4.1  Theoretical Analysis

Based on [9], a dense redistribution approach that exchange data elements of entire matrix through a redistribution is implemented to compare with the method presented in this paper. The algorithms proposed in [10] are also selected to study the efficiency of this work. To simplify the presentation, we use $CDR$, $Dense$ and $V2M$ to represent the proposed technique, the dense redistribution approach and the algorithms in [10], respectively, in the following discussion.

The numerical analysis proceeds with the definition of data transmission cost, which is defined as the amount of data exchanged between processors through a redistribution phase. Since the nonzero elements are distributed irregularly, to evaluate actual number of nonzero entries in a specific local sparse matrix is difficult. The global measurement is an alternative strategy to obtain legitimate performance analysis. Given a BLOCK-CYCLIC($x$, *) over $P$ processors to BLOCK-CYCLIC($y$, *) over $Q$ processors redistribution on banded sparse matrix $M_{n\times n}$ with bandwidth $\beta$, the total communication cost of the $CDR$ method can be defined as follows,

$$T_{comm}(CDR) = O(\beta \times n), \tag{5}$$

The *Dense* redistribution algorithm processes the entire matrix, we can have

$$T_{comm}(Dense) = O(n \times n), \tag{6}$$

By [10], a message is composed by numbers of meta-streams, the amount of data movement is approximately to two times of total nonzero elements plus the number of local sparse vectors in each *SLM*. Hence, the communication overheads of the *V2M* method can be defined as follows,

$$T_{comm}(V2M) = O(2 \times \alpha + n) = O(2 \times \theta \times n^2 + n), \tag{7}$$

Where, $\alpha$ is the number of nonzero elements in matrix $M_{n \times n}$, $\theta$ is the sparsity of $M_{n \times n}$.

According to equations 5 and 7, we can have the following equation,

$$T_{comm}(CDR) < T_{comm}(V2M) \Leftrightarrow \beta \times n < 2 \times \theta \times n^2 + n. \tag{8}$$

After reduction of the above inequality, we can have

$$T_{comm}(CDR) < T_{comm}(V2M) \Leftrightarrow \beta < 2\theta n, \tag{9}$$

The compressed diagonal remapping technique achieve lower communication overheads if $\beta < 2\theta n$. Therefore, we can predict that the *CDR* technique will have better performance than the *V2M* algorithm when a banded sparse matrix has smaller bandwidth or higher sparsity and matrix size.

The other term for evaluating the efficiency of a redistribution algorithm is transiting cost, which is defined as time complexity of an algorithm to perform data packing and unpacking. For *CDR* technique, by transposing the local compressed diagonal matrix, elements of a matrix column in $SLM_{CD}$ (or $DLM_{CD}$) will have consecutive memory addresses in row-major manner. To put these elements into message or extract them from message to local compressed diagonal matrix, by grouping the consecutive elements into a data section, only one memory movement operation is required. Therefore, to construct messages for corresponding destination processors in the sending phase and unpack received messages to generate local compressed diagonal matrix in the receiving phase, for a computation node, the transiting cost of *CDR* technique can be summarized as follows,

$$T_{tran}(CDR) = O(\frac{n}{P}) + O(\frac{n}{Q}), \tag{10}$$

For the *Dense* redistribution algorithm, entire local sparse matrix is scanned once in both sending and receiving phase in order to pack sending messages and construct local destination sparse matrix. For a computation node, the transiting cost of *Dense* method is defined as follows,

$$T_{tran}(Dense) = O((\frac{n}{P})^2 + (\frac{n}{Q})^2) \tag{11}$$

For the *V2M* method, each nonzero entry in CRS/CCS vectors is scanned exactly once and then packed into a message in the sending phase; a message is also scanned once to construct the destination matrix in the receiving phase. Hence, the transiting cost is direct proportion to the size of CRS/CCS vectors. For a computation node, the transiting cost of the *V2M* technique can be modeled as follows,

$$T_{tran}(V2M) = O(\frac{2\alpha + n}{P}) + O(\frac{2\alpha + n}{Q}), \tag{12}$$

## 4.2    Experimental Results

We have implemented the *CDR*, *Dense*, and *V2M* methods.    All of the three methods were written in the single program multiple data (*SPMD*) programming paradigm with C+MPI codes and executed on an IBM SP2 parallel machine.    Six matrices selecting from Harwell-Boeing Sparse Matrix Collection as shown in Table 2 were used for the test.    We use $\theta$, $n$, $\alpha$ and $\beta$ to represent sparsity, matrix size, total nonzero entries and bandwidth of the matrices, respectively.

**Table 1.** Test Matrices from Harwell-Boeing Sparse Matrix Collection

| name | JPWH991 | MCCA | MHD3200A | RW5151 | BCSSTM13 | BCSSTK16 |
|------|---------|------|----------|--------|----------|----------|
| $\theta$ | 0.6137% | 8.1164% | 0.6643% | 0.07613% | 0.52794% | 0.6189% |
| $n$ | 991x991 | 180x180 | 3200x3200 | 5151x5151 | 2003x2003 | 4884x4884 |
| $\alpha$ | 6027 | 2659 | 68026 | 20199 | 21181 | 147631 |
| $\beta$ | 395 | 108 | 59 | 202 | 1045 | 281 |

Fig.    4.    shows    the    performance    of    three    different    methods    to    execute    a BLOCK-CYCLIC(block, *) to BLOCK-CYCLIC(cyclic,*) redistribution on those sparse matrices.    A speedup study of *CDR* and *V2M* techniques to the *Dense* method is also figured on the upside of the performance chart.    From Fig. 4, we observed that the execution time of the *CDR*, *V2M*, and *Dense* algorithms has the order $T(V2M) < T(CDR) < T(Dense)$ for matrices *JPWH991*, *RW5151* and *BCSSTM13*; for matrices *MCCA*, *MHD3200A* and *BCSSTK16*, we have $T(CDR) < T(V2M) < T(Dense)$.    Lower    sparsity    is    the    reason    for    *V2M*    algorithm    to    have    better performance while smaller bandwidth is the reason for *CDR* technique to have better performance.    We also obtained some phenomenon from these experiments.

First, the *CDR* and *V2M* methods achieve higher speedup on performing the dynamic data redistribution of sparse matrices when matrix size is large (e.g. *RW5151*, *BCSSTK16*, *MHD3200A* and *BCSSTM13*).    Second, a *BN*-value is defined as the ratio of bandwidth($\beta$) to matrix size($n$), the *CDR* technique and *V2M* algorithm has higher speedup to the *Dense* method when *BN*-value is small (e.g. *MHD3200A*, *RW5151*, *BCSSTK16*) and lower matrix sparsity($\theta$) (e.g. *RW5151*, *BCSSTM13*, *BCSSTK16* and *MHD3200A*), respectively.    Third, considering matrices *JPWH991* and *BCSSTM13*, the *BN*-value of *JPWH991*($395/991 \cong 0.4$) is smaller than that of *BCSSTM13* ($1045/2003 \cong 0.52$), according to equation 5, speedup of the *CDR* technique to the *Dense* algorithm for *JPWH991* ($56.58/43.14 \cong 1.3$) will higher than that for *BCSSTM13*($140/795 \cong 1.47$).    Contrarily, the *CDR* method has higher speedup on *BCSSTM13* matrix.    This is because the *BCSSTM13* matrix has larger matrix size than *JPWH991*.    The communication cost of *CDR* method is reduced more significantly on *BCSSTM13*.

For matrices *JPWH991*, *RW5151* and *BCSSTM13*, larger bandwidth and lower sparsity are two major reasons for *V2M* algorithm to have better performance than *CDR* technique.    However, according to the analysis in section 4.1, the *CDR* technique has smaller transiting cost than that of the *V2M* algorithm.    Consequently, the *CDR* technique outperforms the *V2M* algorithm even on the matrix has small sparsity but with large size (e.g. *MHD3200A*, *BCSSTK16*).    For matrices *MCCA*,

*MHD3200A* and *BCSSTK16*, smaller bandwidth and higher sparsity are the most reasons for *CDR* technique to have better performance than *V2M* algorithm.

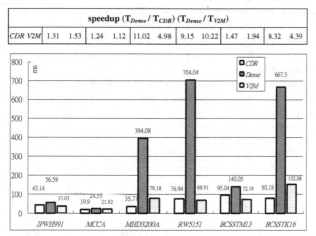

| speedup ($T_{Dense}$ / $T_{CDR}$) ($T_{Dense}$ / $T_{V2M}$) | | | | | | | | | | | |
|---|---|---|---|---|---|---|---|---|---|---|---|
| CDR V2M | 1.31 | 1.53 | 1.24 | 1.12 | 11.02 | 4.98 | 9.15 | 10.22 | 1.47 | 1.94 | 8.32 | 4.39 |

**Fig. 4.** Performance of the *CDR*, *Dense* and *V2M* methods to execute `BLOCK-CYCLIC(block,*)` to `BLOCK-CYCLIC(cyclic,*)` redistribution of different test matrices on a 64-node SP2

The other examination is made to compare the execution time of the *CDR*, *Dense* and *V2M* methods to perform `BLOCK-CYCLIC(2,*)` over 64 processors to `BLOCK-CYCLIC(4,*)` over 32 processors redistribution on those test matrices as shown in Fig. 5. We have similar observations as those described in Fig. 4. For *JPWH991*, *RW5151* and *BCSSTM13*, the execution time of the *CDR*, *V2M*, and *Dense* algorithms has the order $T(V2M) < T(CDR) < T(Dense)$; for *MCCA*, *MHD3200A* and *BCSSTK16*, the execution time of the *CDR*, *V2M*, and *Dense* algorithms has the order $T(CDR) < T(V2M) < T(Dense)$. The *CDR* technique performs very well when matrices have smaller bandwidth and higher sparsity. One another observation from this study is that when number of destination processors decreased in the receiving phase, the message startup cost for each source node is relative small. On the contrary, the size of each passing message becomes large. Therefore, the data transmission and memory transiting costs for local data packing and unpacking will become large as well. For the *Dense* and the *CDR* methods, the transiting cost is directly proportional to $n^2$ and $\beta n$, respectively. (i.e., $T_{tran}(Dense) \propto n^2$ and $T_{tran}(CDR) \propto \beta n$) When number of processing nodes reduced, if the matrix size is large, it will largely lead to higher communication and memory transiting overheads for *Dense* redistribution approach. On the other hand, the execution time of *CDR* technique grows gradually since the bandwidth of a matrix does not change. The test matrices *MHD3200A* and *RW5151* are two obvious examples for this phenomenon. The *CDR* technique provides speedup ($394/36\cong11$) and ($707/77\cong9.15$) to the Dense method for a `BLOCK-CYCLIC(block,*)` to `BLOCK-CYCLIC(cyclic,*)` redistribution over 64 nodes on *MHD3200A* and *RW5151*, respectively. However, from Fig. 5, the *CDR* technique achieves speedup ($540.84/42.32\cong12.78$) and ($863/85.91\cong10$) to the *Dense* method for data redistribution over 32 destination nodes on *MHD3200A* and *RW5151*, respectively.

We summarize the above theoretical analysis and experimental observations as following remarks.

*Remark* 1: Performance of the compressed diagonals remapping technique mostly depends on the size of matrix bandwidth. The *CDR* technique performs very well when matrix size is large and bandwidth is small.

*Remark* 2: Performance of the *V2M* algorithm depends on the total number of nonzero entries of a sparse matrix. The *V2M* algorithm performs well when matrix size is large and sparsity is small.

*Remark* 3: For banded sparse matrix with fixed bandwidth, the higher sparsity of the matrix, the higher efficiency of *CDR* technique when performing data redistribution on that banded sparse matrix.

| speedup ($T_{Dense}$ / $T_{CDR}$) ($T_{Dense}$ / $T_{V2M}$) | | | | | | | | | | | | |
|---|---|---|---|---|---|---|---|---|---|---|---|---|
| *CDR V2M* | 1.27 | 1.5 | 1.24 | 1.14 | 12.78 | 6.17 | 10.05 | 11.79 | 1.5 | 1.68 | 7.78 | 4.16 |

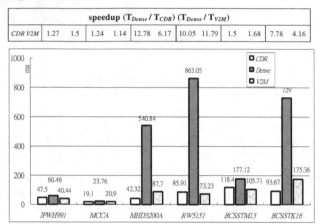

**Fig. 5.** Performance of the *CDR*, *Dense* and *V2M* methods to execute data redistribution of BLOCK-CYCLIC(2,*) over 64 nodes to BLOCK-CYCLIC(4,*) over 32 nodes on different test matrices

## 5  Conclusions

Dynamic block-cyclic data redistribution of sparse matrix is used to enhance the performance of SPMD programs in many scientific applications. In this paper, we have presented a new method to efficiently perform block-cyclic data redistribution on banded sparse matrix. An extension of present techniques is the ability to handle BLOCK-CYCLIC(x, *) to BLOCK-CYCLIC(y, *) data redistribution on banded sparse matrix with non-symmetric lower and upper bandwidth. Another contribution of this work is that a destination compressed diagonal matrix can be generated directly through a redistribution phase. A local sparse matrix to compressed structure transformation can be avoided during program execution. A significant improvement on algorithm performance is also presented via the asynchronous communication scheme applied to overlap communication and computation costs. The proposed technique can handle redistribution of sparse matrix with two disjoint processor grid. Experimental results show that our technique provides superior performance over a wide range of banded sparse matrix redistribution. When bandwidth of the matrix is small and the matrix size is large, the Compressed Diagonals Remapping technique performs very well for BLOCK-CYCLIC(x, *) to BLOCK-CYCLIC(y, *) data redistribution.

## References

1.  R. Asenjo, L. F. Romero, M. Ujaldon and E. L. Zapata, "Sparse Block and Cyclic Data Distributions for Matrix Computations", Proceedings of Adv. Workshop in High Performance Computing: Technology, Methods and Applications, pp. 359-377, June 1994.
2.  G. Bandera and E.L. Zapata, "Sparse Matrix Block-Cyclic Redistribution," In *Proceeding of IEEE Int'l. Parallel Processing Symposium* (IPPS'99), San Juan, Puerto Rico, April, 1999.
3.  S. Chatterjee, J. R. Gilbert, F. J. E. Long, R. Schreiber, and S.-H. Teng, "Generating Local Address and Communication Sets for Data Parallel Programs," *Journal of Parallel and Distributed Computing* , Vol. 26, pp. 72-84, 1995.
4.  Frederic Desprez, Jack Dongarra, and Antoine Petitet," Scheduling Block-Cyclic Data redistribution," *IEEE Trans. on PDS*, vol. 9, no. 2, pp. 192-205, Feb. 1998.
5.  I. Duff, R. Grimes, and J. Lewis," *Sparse matrix test problems," ACM Trans. Math. Soft.*, 15, pp. 1-14, 1989.
6.  S. K. S. Gupta, S. D. Kaushik, C.-H. Huang, and P. Sadayappan, "On Compiling Array Expressions for Efficient Execution on Distributed-Memory Machines," *JPDC,* Vol. 32, pp. 155-172, 1996.
7.  S. Hiranandani, K. Kennedy, J. Mellor-Crammey, and A. Sethi," Compilation technique for block-cyclic distribution," In *Proc. ACM ICS*, pp. 392-403, 1994.
8.  C.-H Hsu, S.-W Bai, Y.-C Chung, C.-S Yang, "A Generalized Basic-Cycle Calculation Method for Efficient Array Redistribution," *IEEE Trans. on PDS*, Vol. 11, No. 12, pp. 1201-1216, Dec. 2000.
9.  C.-H Hsu, Y.-C Chung and C.-R Dow, "Efficient Methods for Multidimensional Array Redistribution," *The Journal of Supercomputing*, Vol. 17, No. 1, 2000.
10. Ching-Hsien Hsu, "Optimization of sparse matrix redistribution on Multicomputers", Proceedings of *ICPP Workshops on Compiler and Runtime Techniques for Parallel Computing*, Aug. 2002.
11. Edgar T. Kalns, and Lionel M. Ni, "Processor Mapping Technique Toward Efficient Data Redistribution," *IEEE Trans. on PDS*, vol. 6, no. 12, Dec. 1995.
12. S. D. Kaushik, C. H. Huang, J. Ramanujam and P. Sadayappan, "Multiphase data redistribution: Modeling and evaluation," *Proceeding of IPPS'*95, pp. 441-445.
13. Neungsoo Park, Viktor K. Prasanna, Cauligi S. Raghavendra, "Efficient Algorithms for Block-Cyclic Data redistribution Between Processor Sets," *IEEE Trans. on PDS*, vol. 10, No. 12, pp.1217-1240, Dec. 1999.
14. Antoine P. Petitet, Jack J. Dongarra, "Algorithmic Redistribution Methods for Block-Cyclic Decompositions," *IEEE Trans. on PDS*, vol. 10, no. 12, 1999.
15. L. Prylli and B. Tourancheau, "Fast runtime block cyclic data redistribution on multiprocessors," *JPDC,* vol. 45, pp. 63-72, Aug. 1997.
16. L. F. Romero and E. L. Zapata, "Data Distributions for Sparse Matrix Vector Multiplication", Parallel Computing, vol. 21, no. 4, pp. 583-605, April 1995.
17. S. Ramaswamy, B. Simons, and P. Banerjee, "Optimization for Efficient Data redistribution on Distributed Memory Multicomputers," *JPDC,* Vol. 38, 1996.
18. Rajeev. Thakur, Alok. Choudhary, and J. Ramanujam, "Efficient Algorithms for Data redistribution, " *IEEE Trans. on PDS*, vol. 7, no. 6, June 1996.
19. M. Ujaldón, E.L. Zapata, S.D. Sharma and J. Saltz, "Parallelization Techniques for Sparse Matrix Applications," *JPDC*, vol. 38, no. 2, pp. 256-266, Nov. 1996.

# Scheduling Parallel Tasks onto NUMA Multiprocessors with Inter-processor Communication Overhead

Guan-Joe Lai[1], Jywe-Fei Fang[2], Pei-Shan Sung[1], and Der-Lin Pean[3]

[1] National Taichung Teachers College, Taichung, Taiwan, R.O.C.,
gjlai@ieee.org
[2] Tung Nan Institute of Technology, Taipei, Taiwan, R.O.C.,
jffang@mail.cc.tnit.edu.tw
[3] Silicon Integrated Systems Corp., Hsin-Chu, Taiwan, R.O.C.,
dlpean@sis.com.tw

**Abstract.** This paper addresses the problem of scheduling tasks onto Non-Uniform Memory Access (NUMA) multiprocessors with a bounded number of processors. An algorithm is proposed to schedule tasks by considering intertask communication overhead. The proposed algorithm exploits the schedule-holes in schedules; therefore, it could produce better schedules than that produced by existing algorithms. The proposed algorithm ensures performance within a factor of two times of the optimum for general directed acyclic task graphs. Experimental results demonstrate the superiority of the proposed algorithm over that presented in literature. A sharper bound on the multiprocessor scheduling problem by considering communication delay is also shown.

## 1  Introduction

Shared-memory multiprocessors are emerging as attractive platforms for parallel applications. Examples of such architectures include the Data General nuSMP, HP/Convex Exemplar, Sequent STiNG, and SGI Origin 2000. In such a paradigm, programmers could write parallel programs easier, but still require substantial tuning effort to reduce the impact of long-latency memory accesses. The difficulty lies in the fact that both data and programs must be partitioned and then distributed onto processors for efficient parallel execution, resulting in communication overhead[6], [11]. Additionally, access contention by several processors for shared communication media (e.g., switches, memory modules) could further exacerbate communication times. Therefore, to exploit the potential of parallel processing, scheduling algorithms must be developed. Such algorithms allocate tasks to processors and determine the execution order to attain a minimum completion time. This is usually considered as the multiprocessor scheduling problem. However, it is recognized that certain relaxed or simplified cases of scheduling problems still fall into the class of NP-hard problems[6]. Consequently, previous efforts have focused on finding heuristics for obtaining satisfactory solutions in a reasonable time complexity.

M. Guo and L.T.Yang (Eds.): ISPA 2003, LNCS 2745, pp. 65–75, 2003.

Several researchers have studied the scheduling problem. For instance, MCP [9] algorithm and Hwang's ETF algorithm[6] schedule tasks under the assumption that the number of processors is limited. Kwok and Ahmad proposed two algorithms, DCP[14] and FASTEST[5], under the condition that the number of processors is unlimited; Yang and Gerasoulis also presented DSC[12] in the same assumption. Dynamic Level Scheduling(DLS)[2] and MH[3] algorithms were introduced for arbitrary processor network architecture. In addition, MJD[8] and CPFD[4] algorithms are task duplication based algorithms.

However, none of the above works considered the impact of communication contention. They schedule tasks on the macro-dataflow[10] model. The assumption that there is no contention among communication channels on this model is not reasonable[13]. Selvakumar and Siva[11] presented an algorithm for scheduling tasks by considering intertask communications and the contentions in communication channels. However, the disadvantages of their approach are that a) the time complexity is apparently of a high order, and b) additional space is needed for keeping free time slot lists.

An algorithm referred to as the Task Scheduling with Communication Contentions (TSCC) algorithm is presented here. This algorithm exploits the schedule-holes[11] in schedules. It schedules tasks by considering non-negligible intertask communication and takes account of the communication contentions created by data exchange. Communication contentions arise from the communication medium having insufficient capacity to serve all transmissions, thereby causing significant contention delays. The experimental results reveal the superiority of our algorithm over that compared. In this paper, a sharper bound on the multiprocessor scheduling problem with the consideration of communication overhead is also shown. It is meaningful not only theoretically but also practically to give a better lower bound for evaluating the accuracy of the resultant heuristic solution more precisely.

The rest of this paper is organized as follows. Section 2 introduces the preliminaries and related work. Section 3 presents the proposed algorithm, and section 4 shows the lower performance bound. Experimental results are provided in section 5. Concluding remarks are finally made.

## 2      Preliminaries and Related Work

This section opens with the description of the program model, called the Shared Communication Resource (SCR) model[7], which enlarges the macro-dataflow program description to allow employment of scheduling heuristics on NUMA systems. The SCR model is formally described as follows.

A program is represented as a directed acyclic graph (DAG) based on the SCR model. The DAG is defined by a quintuple $G=(N_t, N_s, E, C, T)$, where $N_t$ is the set of tasks, $N_s$ is the set of SCR nodes, $C$ is the set of communication volumes, $T$ is the set of computation costs, and $E$ is the set of communication edges which define a partial order or precedence constraints on $N_t \cup N_s$. There is no communication edge between $n_i$ and $n_j$ when $n_i, n_j \in N_t$ or $n_i, n_j \in N_s$.

The value of $c_{ij} \in C$ is the communication volume occurring along the edge $e_{ij} \in E$, either $n_i \in N_t$, $n_j \in N_s$ or $n_i \in N_s$, $n_j \in N_t$. The value $\tau_i \in T$ is the computation time for node $n_i \in N_t$, and $\tau_i{=}0$ for all $n_i \in N_s$. When there is data dependence between tasks $n_i$ and $n_j$, where $n_i$, $n_j \in N_t$, there exists a node $n_s \in N_s$ so that $e_{is}$, $e_{sj} \in E$.

In SCR model, a task is an indivisible unit of computation; once task execution begins, it must continue to completion without interruption. Only one task at a time can access data from one SCR node. Two independent tasks must therefore access data from the same SCR node in sequence, making resource contention issue. Task execution is triggered by satisfying precedence constraints and by removing resource contentions. Precedence constraints occur when the execution of one task must be postponed until the arrival of all necessary data. The two kinds of resource contentions are that (a) execution of a task must be deferred until the completion of all the tasks scheduled before it within the same processor, and (b) a communication contention, in which data are received sequentially from the same communication channel; that is, a task cannot receive data from all its predecessors simultaneously. Experimental results[7] show that the adoption of the SCR model could achieve more realistic outcomes for the clustering/scheduling problem on NUMA systems.

Suppose next that a NUMA system is homogeneous, and that communications is half-duplex. Each processor has a co-processor to deal with communications, which allows computations and communications that are independent of each other to be overlapped. Formally, let P={$p_i$| i=1,..., |P|}, |P| $< \infty$, be the set of processors. Let $P(n_i)$ be the processor allocated by $n_i$, and $\eta(p_i,p_j)$ denote the latency required to transfer a message unit from $p_i$ to $p_j$, where $p_i, p_j \in$P.

Given a DAG and a system as described above, this problem is to obtain a non-preemptive schedule with a minimal completion time. To avoid high complexity, only the non-backtracking approach is considered here. Aiming to simplify it, only two kinds of communication latencies are considered. Let M = {$L_l,L_r$} be the set of latencies, where $L_l{=}\eta(p_i, p_i)$, $p_i \in$P, is the intraprocessor latency; and $L_r{=}\eta(p_i,p_j)$, where $p_i, p_j \in$P, and i$\neq$j, is the interprocessor latency.

Formally, let $N = N_t \cup N_s$, and $pred(n_i)$ be the set of predecessors of $n_i$. After satisfying the precedence constraints and removing communication contentions, the earliest starting time of node $n_j$, $est(n_j)$, is the earliest time that node $n_j$ can start execution. $\forall n_i \in pred(n_j)$, the earliest completion time of node $n_i$ is defined to be $ect(n_i) = est(n_i) + \tau_i$. Let $succ(n_i)$ be the set of immediate successors of $n_i$ and $lmt(P(n_i))$ be the last message time of the processor, which $n_i$ is allocated. Consequently, the earliest starting transmission time of edge $e_{ij}$ is defined to be $estt(e_{ij}) = max(ect(n_i), lmt(P(n_i)))$. For node $n_j$, we claim that a chain of communication edges can be found as $X_j{:}e_{1j} \to e_{2j} \to ... \to e_{qj}$, such that $estt(e_{1j}) \leq estt(e_{2j}) \leq ... \leq estt(e_{qj})$, where $n_1, n_2,..., n_q \in pred(n_j)$. Let $icti(e_{kj},e_{ij})$ denote the idle communication time interval between two communication edges, $e_{kj}$ and $e_{ij}$, in the chain $X_j$, $1 \leq k< i \leq q$; mathematically,

$$icti(e_{kj}, e_{ij}) = \begin{cases} 0, & \text{if } estt(e_{ij}) \leq estt(e_{kj}) + c_{kj} \times \eta(P(n_k), P(n_j)), \\ estt(e_{ij}) - estt(e_{kj}) - c_{kj} \times \eta(P(n_k), P(n_j)), & \text{otherwise.} \end{cases}$$

The idle communication time before the communication edge $e_{ij}$ is defined to be $\Omega(e_{ij})=min(icti(e_{kj},e_{ij}))$, $1\leq k < i$. Thus, for every $n_i \in pred(n_j)$,

$$est(n_j) = max \left\{ \begin{array}{l} min\{estt(e_{ij})\} + \sum (c_{ij} \times \eta(P(n_i), P(n_j)) + \Omega(e_{ij})), \\ max\{estt(e_{ij}) + c_{ij} \times \eta(P(n_i), P(n_j))\} \end{array} \right\}.$$

The longest completion time of node $n_i$, $lct(n_i)$, is the longest execution time from this node to the sink node. Formally, $\forall n_i \in N, lct(n_i)=max(c_{ij} \times L_l+\tau_j+lct(n_j))$, $\forall n_j \in succ(n_i)$. Initially, $\forall n_i \in N$ and $pred(n_i) = \emptyset$, let $est(n_i)=0$.

## 3   TSCC Algorithm

The TSCC algorithm exploits the schedule-holes in schedules by considering communication overhead. The schedule-holes are primarily due to that a task is scheduled after some tasks with higher priorities; however, it could be scheduled before these tasks and does not affect the earliest starting times of these tasks. Existing algorithms do not consider the conditions of exploiting schedule-holes. Therefore, the properties of exploiting schedule-holes are defined to ensure that the completion time of a DAG will be strictly curtailed after applying TSCC.

*Property 1.* The task $n_a$ could be scheduled onto $P(n_a)$ before $n_b$, if the scheduling operation at step i-1, which schedules $n_a$ onto processor $P(n_a)$ to minimize $est(n_a)$, does not affect the strict reduction of $est(n_b)$ at some future step j, i≤j, where $est(n_a) < est(n_b)$, $\tau_a+lct(n_a)-est(n_a) < \tau_b+lct(n_b)-est(n_b)$, and $P(n_a) = P(n_b)$.

*Property 2.* The operation, which schedules $n_a$ to minimize $est(n_a)$ at step i-1, should not affect the strict reduction of $est(n_b)$ at some future step j, i≤j, where $n_b$ is along the dominant sequence[12] which is the longest path of the scheduled DAG.

The reason of adopting the priority, $max(\tau_i+lct(n_i)-est(n_i))$, to select candicates is described as follows. When two nodes are ready and their least completion times are equal, the node that could be issued earlier should be scheduled first. When the two ready nodes have the same earliest starting time, the one which has the larger least completion time should also be scheduled first. If we mix these two situations, the priority function will be $max(\tau_i+lct(n_i)-est(n_i))$.

The TSCC algorithm initially finds the $lct$ for each node bottom-up, and then pre-schedules DAGs by a list scheduling that schedules tasks according to the priority, $max(\tau_i+lct(n_i)-est(n_i))$. Nodes with no predecessors are selected first. A candidate with $max(\tau_i+lct(n_i)-est(n_i))$ is allocated to a schedule by considering the properties 1 and 2; the chosen candidate node is then examined. The algorithm repeats this procedure until all nodes have been examined.

The time complexity of pre-scheduling is $O(|N|(|N| + |E|))$ and the time complexity for calculating $lct$ is $O(|N| + |E|)$, where $|N| = |N_t| + |N_s|$. The while loop is executed $O(|N|)$. The time complexity of finding the node, $n_i$, with $max(\tau_i + lct(n_i) - est(n_i))$ is $O(|N|)$. Checking the properties 1 and 2 is executed $O(|N||P|(|N| + |E|))$ times. The time complexity of TSCC algorithm then is $O(|P||N|^2(|N| + |E|))$. Consequently, in practical applications, the complexity of the TSCC algorithm is reasonable, because in[11] the corresponding complexity is $O(|N|^3|P||E|\log^2|P|)$.

1. Algorithm TSCC
2. Input: a NUMA system M, and a DAG G.
3. Output: a schedule with min. parallel completion time.
4. Begin
5. Initialization.
6. Finding $lct(n_i)$, $\forall n_i \in N_t \cup N_s$.
7. Pre-scheduling.
8. $unexam \leftarrow N_t \cup N_s$, $ready \leftarrow \emptyset$.
9. While $unexam \neq \emptyset \{$
10.     $ready \leftarrow ready \cup n_i$, $\forall n_i \in unexam$ and $pred(n_i) \cap unexam = \emptyset$.
11.     Finding $n_i$ with $max(\tau_i + lct(n_i) - est(n_i))$, $\forall n_i \in ready$.
12.     $n_s \leftarrow n_i$    /*$n_s$ is the selected candidate node*/
13.     If there is $n_k \in ready$, $n_k \neq n_s$, which satisfies properties 1 and 2
14.         $n_s \leftarrow n_k$.
15.     Scheduling $n_s$ to its corresponding processor.
16.     $unexam \leftarrow unexam - n_s$, and $ready \leftarrow ready - n_s$.
17. $\}$
18. End

## 4  Performance Bounds

This section introduces a sharper bound for the scheduling problem. The properties 3 and 4 describe the two kinds of resource contention as follows.

*Property 3.* For a communication $e_{ij}$ in a schedule, only one of the following three cases should be considered. Case 1: Only one task and one communication have resource contention relationships with $e_{ij}$. Case 2: Only one task has a resource contention relationship with $e_{ij}$. Case 3: Only one communication has a resource contention relationship with $e_{ij}$.

*Property 4.* For a task $n_i$ in a schedule, only one of the following three cases should be considered. Case 1: Only one task and one communication have resource contention relationships with $n_i$. Case 2: Only one task has a resource contention relationship with $n_i$. Case 3: Only one communication has a resource contention relationship with $n_i$.

**Theorem 1.** *For any DAG $G = (N_t, N_s, E, C, T)$ to be scheduled on a NUMA system, the schedule length, $\omega$, obtained by TSCC always satisfies*

$$\omega \leq \left(2 - \frac{1}{|P|}\right) \times \omega_{opt} + \sum_{i=1}^{x-1} c_{i,i+1} \times \left((\eta_{max} - \eta_{min}) + \frac{1}{|P|}\eta_{min}\right),$$

*where $\omega_{opt}$ is the length of the optimal schedule, $\eta_{max}=max(\eta(p_i,p_j))$ and $\eta_{min} = min(\eta(p_i,p_j))$, $\forall$ any pair $p_i$, $p_j \in P$.*

*Proof.* The set of all points of time in $(0, \omega)$ could be partitioned into two sets A and B. A is defined as the set of all points of times for which all processors are executing some tasks, and B is defined as the set of all points of time for which at least one processor is idle. If B is empty, all processors complete their last assignment at $\omega$ and no idle interval can be found within $(0, \omega)$. The TSCC schedule is indeed optimal and, thus, the theorem holds obviously. Therefore, we assume that B is non-empty. Moreover, we also assume that B is the disjoint union of $q$ open intervals as below: B=$(I_{l1},I_{r1})\cup(I_{l2},I_{r2})\cup...\cup(I_{lq},I_{rq})$, where $I_{l1} < I_{r1} < I_{l2} < I_{r2} <...< I_{lq} < I_{rq}$. Without loss of generality, we claim that a chain of tasks can be found, i.e., $X: n_1 \rightarrow n_2 \rightarrow... \rightarrow n_x$, so that

$$\sum_{i=1}^{q}(I_{r,i} - I_{l,i}) \leq \sum_{k=1}^{x}\tau_k + \sum_{k=1}^{x-1}c_{k,k+1} \times \eta(P(n_k), P(n_{k+1})). \qquad (1)$$

Let $n_x$ denote the task that finishes in the TSCC schedule at time $\omega$. Let $st(n_x)$ denote the stating time scheduled by TSCC for $n_x$. Three possibilities regarding the starting time of $n_x$ are

(a) $st(n_x) \leq I_{l1}$.

(b) $st(n_x) \in B$, i.e., there exists an integer $h$, $h \leq q$, so that $I_{lh} < st(n_x) < I_{rh}$.

(c) $st(n_x) \in A$ but $st(n_x) > I_{l1}$, i.e., there exists an integer $h$, $h \leq q$-1, so that $I_{rh} \leq st(n_x) \leq I_{l,h+1}$ or $I_{r,q} \leq st(n_x)$.

If the first possibility occurs, the task $n_x$ by itself constitutes a chain that satisfies our claim.

The second possibility is next considered. Suppose that $h$ is the index satisfying (b). Then, $n_x$ covers part of B from its right end to somewhere in between $I_{lh}$ and $I_{rh}$. An attempt is made to add the second task, $n_{x-1}$, to the chain. According to the properties 3 and 4, there is some task $n_g$ or some $e_{gx}$ that has a resource contention relationship with $n_x$. Therefore, let $n_{x-1} = n_g$, and add $n_{x-1}$ to the chain, $X$. The cycle can be repeated until the starting time of the last added task satisfies (a) or (c).

The third possibility is considered as follows. Suppose that $h$ is the index statisfying (c). By the properties 3 and 4, there is some task $n_g$ or some $e_{gx}$ that has a resource contention relationship with $n_x$. Therefore, let $n_{x-1} = n_g$, and add $n_{x-1}$ to the chain, $X$. The cycle can be repeated until the starting time of the last added task satisfies (a) or (b).

The whole process is repeated by considering the above mentioned three possibilities until $st(n_1) \leq I_{l1}$ is satisfied. Finally, a chain satisfying our claim (see Eq. 1) is constructed. Consequently, $\sum_{\varepsilon \in \Phi} (\tau_\varepsilon) \leq (|P| - 1) \sum_{k=1}^{x} \tau_k + |P| \sum_{k=1}^{x-1} c_{k,k+1} \times \eta_{\max}$, where $\Phi$ is the set of processor idle time intervals and $\tau_\varepsilon$ is the processor idle time interval (i.e., the left-hand sum is over all idle time intervals for processors). The chain, $X$, takes at least $\sum_{k=1}^{x} \tau_k + \sum_{k=1}^{x-1} c_{k,k+1} \times \eta_{\min}$ to finish all tasks in any schedule, i.e., $\omega_{opt} \geq \sum_{k=1}^{x} \tau_k + \sum_{k=1}^{x-1} c_{k,k+1} \times \eta_{\min}$. The following inequality is obvious, $\sum_{n_i \in N} \tau_i \leq |P| \times \omega_{opt}$. Consequently,

$$\omega = \tfrac{1}{|P|} \left( \sum_{n_i \in N} \tau_i + \sum_{\varepsilon \in \Phi} \tau_\varepsilon \right)$$
$$\leq \tfrac{1}{|P|} \left( |P| \times \omega_{opt} + (|P| - 1) \times \omega_{opt} + \sum_{i=1}^{x-1} c_{i,i+1} \times (|P|(\eta_{\max} - \eta_{\min}) + \eta_{\min}) \right)$$
$$\leq \left( 2 - \tfrac{1}{|P|} \right) \times \omega_{opt} + \sum_{i=1}^{x-1} c_{i,i+1} \times \left( (\eta_{\max} - \eta_{\min}) + \tfrac{1}{|P|} \eta_{\min} \right). \qquad \square$$

When the number of processors approaches infinite, the performance bound of the TSCC algorithm is within a factor of two times of the optimum for general DAGs. When $\eta_{min}=0$, our performance bound is reduced to the sum of Graham's bound for list scheduling[1]. When $\eta_{min} >0$, our performance bound is sharper than that in literature.

## 5   Experimental Results

This section presents experimental results to verify the preceding claims. The feasibility of the proposed algorithm was assessed by evaluating practical applications, such as the FFT, Laplace equation, Fork-trees, Join-trees and 160 randomly generated program graphs, whose graph sizes vary from a minimum of 364 nodes with 363 edges to a maximum of 365 nodes with 606 edges.

We have implemented an evaluation environment that takes SISAL[10] programs as input and evaluates their performance. The optimizing SISAL compiler translates programs to IF1 intermediate files based on the macro-dataflow model. The evaluation environment modifies these IF1 codes based on the paradigm for SCR model. The transformed intermediate files are scheduled by our proposed algorithms and evaluated their performance. The transformation progress does not modify any syntax of IF1; therefore, IF1 could be used as the intermediate code for the SCR model and SISAL compiler could generate executable machine code from it.

Let $L_l$ be 2 cycles/byte, and $L_r$ vary from 4, 8, and 16 to 32 cycles/byte. The average communication overhead associated with each edge varies from 32, 64, and 128 to 256 bytes. The cost required for each task varies randomly from 1 to 512 cycles. The processor number varies from 2, 4, 8, and 16 to 32. The speedup for a scheduling algorithm is defined as *Speedup = Sequential Completion Time / Parallel Completion Time*. Two algorithms are implemented for comparison. The first, a list scheduling algorithm schedules tasks according to the priority, $est(n_i)+\tau_i+lct(n_i)$. The task with $max(est(n_i)+\tau_i+lct(n_i))$ is scheduled onto a corresponding processor until there is no un-scheduled task. The second one, SCH[11] exploits schedule-holes to produce more adequate schedules.

Fig. 1 shows the experimental results of 160 fork trees, where "SCH" denotes the SCH algorithm, "List" the list scheduling and "TSCC" the TSCC algorithm. These results indicate that TSCC performs better than the others. As the number of processors increases, the difference in speedup between SCH and TSCC also increases. The main explanation is that the little possibility of causing the schedule-holes is due to the structures of fork trees. Fig. 1(b) confirms the superiority of TSCC in time complexity over the SCH algorithm.

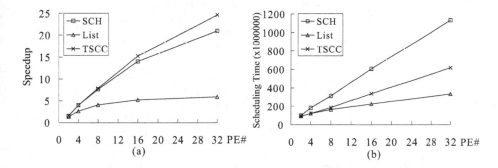

**Fig. 1.** (a)Speedup, (b)Scheduling time vs. number of processors for fork trees.

Fig. 2 shows the experimental results of 160 join trees. These results indicate that SCH performs better than the others. However, the average difference in speedup between SCH and TSCC is only about 0.744%, and the time complexity of SCH algorithm was apparently of a high order. The main explanation is that the great possibility of causing the schedule-holes is due to the structures of join trees. Fig. 2(b) also confirms the superiority of TSCC in time complexity over other algorithms.

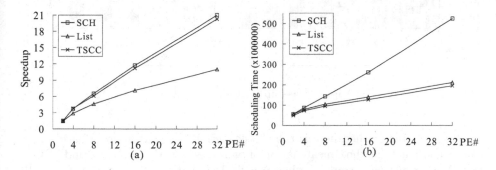

**Fig. 2.** (a)Speedup, (b)Scheduling time vs. number of processors for join trees.

Fig. 3 shows the experimental results of 160 random generated DAGs. Fig. 3(a) confirms that the speedups increase when the number of processors increases, which corresponds with findings in previous literature. These results also indicate that the performance gain of applying SCH is similar to that of applying TSCC; in fact, the average difference in speedup between SCH and TSCC is only 0.414%. However, the scheduling time of applying TSCC surpasses that of applying the SCH, as shown in Fig. 3(b). The main reason for the superiority of TSCC in time complexity is that SCH finds the earliest starting time by searching the list of free time slots in each processor.

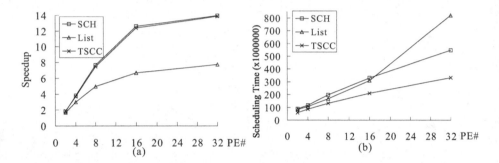

**Fig. 3.** (a)Speedup, (b)Scheduling vs. number of processors for random DAGs.

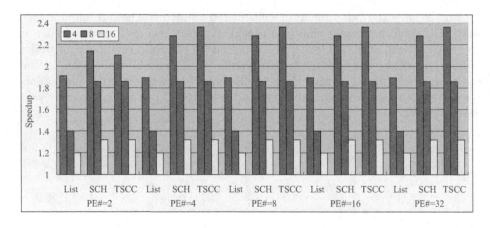

**Fig. 4.** Speedup for FFT algorithm.

The example applied here is the classical FFT. The task dependence graph can be considered as the concatenation of two trees: the MERGE tree and SPLIT tree. We execute this example when $n=2^{16}$. Fig. 4 shows the speedup for FFT. When the number of processors is 2, the SCH performs better than TSCC.

When the number of processors is greater than 2, TSCC is always superior to SCH, as shown in Fig. 4. These experimental results show that the TSCC algorithm has better performance than that of SCH when the join-degree is equal to the fork-degree within applications. Because TSCC also tries to balance the tradeoff between resource utilization and speedup, the optimal parallelism exploitation may not be achieved. The situation is also shown in Fig. 3. According to the comparison between Fig. 3 and 4, the minor superiority of SCH in Fig. 3 maybe result from that the number of join-structures is larger than that of fork-structures when we generate the random task graphs.

Finally, to show that TSCC is superior in resource utilization to others, the Laplace Partial-Differential Equation algorithm is evaluated. In such applications, a region is discretized and an iterative method is used to approximate function values within this region. The experimental results for Laplace partial-differential equation are similar to that of FFT. The difference of the performance between TSCC and SCH is very little. As the interprocessor communication latency increases, the difference of the performance between TSCC and SCH increases. However, the resource usage of TSCC is better than that of SCH. In Table 1, TSCC is always superior in the resource usage to SCH. This is because that TSCC also tries to balance the tradeoff between the resource utilization and speedup; the optimal parallelism exploitation may not be achieved. The situation is also shown in previous experimental results. In Table 1, the resource usage of applying TSCC is better than that of applying SCH.

**Table 1.** Processor Usage of Different Scheduling Algorithms

| | $L_r=40/L_l=4$ | | | $L_r=80/L_l=8$ | | | $L_r=160/L_l=16$ | | |
|---|---|---|---|---|---|---|---|---|---|
| PE# | SCH | List | TSCC | SCH | List | TSCC | SCH | List | TSCC |
| 2 | 2 | 2 | 2 | 2 | 2 | 2 | 2 | 2 | 2 |
| 4 | 4 | 4 | 4 | 4 | 4 | 4 | 4 | 3 | 4 |
| 8 | 8 | 8 | 7 | 8 | 8 | 4 | 8 | 8 | 3 | 8 |
| 16 | 16 | 16 | 7 | 15 | 16 | 4 | 15 | 13 | 3 | 8 |
| 32 | 16 | 16 | 7 | 15 | 16 | 4 | 15 | 13 | 3 | 8 |

# 6   Concluding Remarks

This work has examined the impact of scheduling tasks onto multiprocessor systems by exploiting schedule-holes in schedules with the consideration of non-negligible intertask communications and communication contentions. TSCC ensures performance within a factor of two times of the optimum for general DAGs. We demonstrate the performance of our algorithm by evaluating some practical application benchmarks and some random generated task graphs. Experimental results demonstrate the superiority of the proposed TSCC algorithm. The scheduling performance depends on the size of problem, the degree of parallelism and the task graph granularity. The above experiments show that the TSCC can obtain a good performance, if a proper task partitioning is provided. Since exact weight estimation may not be feasible in practice, the experiments show that as long as the task graph is coarse grain, the performance variations are small. Thus, coarse grain partitions with sufficient parallelism are commended.

**Acknowledgements.** This work was sponsored by National Science Council, No. NSC 89-2233-E-142-002

# References

1. E. G. Coffman and P. J. Denning, Eds.: Operating Systems Theory. Englewood Cliffs, NJ: Prentice-Hall, (1973)
2. G.C. Sih and L.A. Lee: A Compile-Time Scheduling Heuristic for Interconnection-Constrained Heterogeneous Processor Architectures. IEEE Trans. Parallel and Distributed Systems, **4(2)**, (1993)75–87.
3. H. El-Rewini, H.H. Ali, and T.G. Lewis: Task Scheduling in Multiprocessing Systems. Computer, (1995)27–37.
4. I. Ahmad and Y.-K. Kwok: On Exploiting Task Duplication in Parallel Program Scheduling. IEEE Trans. Parallel and Distributed Systems, **9(9)**, (1998)872–892.
5. I. Ahmad and Y.-K. Kwok: On Parallelizing the Multiprocessor Scheduling. IEEE Trans. Parallel and Distributed Systems, **10(4)**, (1999)414–432.
6. J.-J. Hwang, Y.-C. Chow, F. D. Anger and C.-Y. Lee: Scheduling Precedence Graphs in Systems with Interprocessor Communication Times. SIAM Journal of Comput., **18(2)**, (1989)244–257.
7. Lai, G.-J. and Chen, C.: Scheduling Parallel Program Tasks with Non-negligible Intertask Communications onto NUMA Multiprocessor Systems. Journal of Parallel Algorithms and Applications, **12**, (1997)165–184.
8. M.A. Palis, J.-C. Liou, and D.S.L. Wei: Task Clustering and Scheduling for Distributed Memory Parallel Architectures. IEEE Trans. Parallel and Distributed Systems, **7(1)**, (1996)46–55.
9. M.-Y Wu and D.D. Gajski: Hypertool: A Programming Aid for Message-Passing Systems. IEEE Trans. Parallel and Distributed Systems, **1(3)**, (1990)330–343.
10. Sarkar, V.: Partitioning and Scheduling Parallel Programs for Multiprocessors. The MIT Press, Cambridge, MA, (1989).
11. Selvakumar, S. and Siva Ram Murthy, C.: Scheduling Precedence Constrained Task Graphs with Non-Negligible Intertask Communication onto Multiprocessors. IEEE Trans. Parallel and Distributed Systems, **5(3)**, (1994)328–336.
12. T. Yang and A. Gerasoulis: DSC: Scheduling Parallel Tasks on an Unbounded Number of Processors. IEEE Trans. Parallel and Distributed Systems, **5(9)**, (1994)951–967.
13. Wolski, R. M. and Feo, J. T.: Program Partitioning for NUMA Multiprocessor Computer Systems. J. of Parallel and Distributed Computing, **19**, (1993)203–218.
14. Y-K. Kwok and I. Ahmad: Dynamic Critical-Path Scheduling: An Effective Technique for Allocating Task Graphs onto Multi-Processors. IEEE Trans. Parallel and Distributed Systems, **7(5)**, (1996)506–521.

# An Efficient Algorithm for Irregular Redistributions in Parallelizing Compilers

Hui Wang[1], Minyi Guo[1], Sushil K. Prasad[2], Yi Pan[2], and Wenxi Chen[1]

[1] Department of Computer Software,
University of Aizu, Aizu-Wakamatsu, Fukushima 965-8580, Japan
{hwang,minyi,wenxi}@u-aizu.ac.jp
[2] Department of Computer Science,
Georgia State University, Atlanta, GA 30303, USA
{sprasad,pan}@cs.gsu.edu

**Abstract.** High Performance FORTRAN version 2 (HPF-2) provides irregular distributions such as GEN_BLOCK and INDIRECT for load balancing and irregular problems. The irregular block redistribution problem is different from regular block-cyclic redistribution. This paper is devoted to develop an efficient algorithm that attempt to obtain near optimal scheduling while satisfying the minimal size of total steps condition and the minimal step condition for irregular array redistribution. Our algorithm is developed independently. It has comparable performance with a relocation algorithm developed previously.

## 1 Introduction

Parallelizing compiler, the core of automatic data parallel programming, is a recent approach to overcome the difficulties of programming in using message passing library, and the difficulties of designing and writing a large number of different interacting tasks to solve a single problem. In data parallel programming, the parallelizing compilation system performs all the low-level bookkeeping and takes part with the roles for communication among processors. Absence of a global address space in the distributed memory communication environment, the programmer needs to decompose the program data among the available processors and manage the communication.

When considering how data are distributed onto local processors in the distributed memory communication environment, access to local data is much faster than access to remote data located at any of the other nodes because the remote access incurs expensive inter-processor communication overhead. Therefore, for efficiency it is important to partition the program and data so as to try to (1) to minimize communications and (2) to maximize potential parallelism.

Among data parallel programming languages, High Performance FORTRAN version 2 (HPF-2) [1], is an informal standard for extensions to FORTRAN 95 to assist its implementation on parallel architectures. HPF-2 provides compiler directives for programmers to specify data mapping, such as array distribution.

M. Guo and L.T.Yang (Eds.): ISPA 2003, LNCS 2745, pp. 76–87, 2003.

As a generalized block distribution, GEN_BLOCK allows unequal-sized consecutive segments of an array to be mapped onto consecutive processors [1]. Many applications need data redistribution during computation since different phases there require different data mapping in order to execute loops efficiently without data dependencies [2].

```
        PARAMETER (S = /3, 5, 9, 4, 13, 4, 2/)
!HPF$ PROCESSORS P(7)
        REAL A(40), B(40), new(7)
!HPF$ DISTRIBUTE A( GEN_BLOCK (S) ) ONTO P
!HPF$ DYNAMIC B
        new = /2, 5, 3, 6, 8, 6, 10/
!HPF$ REDISTRIBUTE A( GEN_BLOCK(new) )
```

Above is an example of GEN_BLOCK and the redistribution in HPF-2. Given the above specification, array elements $A(1:3)$ are mapped on $P_1$, $A(4:8)$ are mapped on $P_2$, $A(9:17)$ are mapped on $P_3$, $A(18:21)$ are mapped on $P_4$, $A(22:34)$ are mapped on $P_5$, $A(35:38)$ are mapped on $P_6$, and $A(39:40)$ are mapped on $P_7$. Then $A$ is redistributed based on the *new* array.

In many scientific and engineering applications, the distribution of an array in a program can't remain fixed throughout the program. It is very often to change the distribution of the array at run-time. At that time, each processor is required to know which local elements of the array should be sent to the specified processor, and which elements of the array should be received from the specified processor. So an efficient algorithm is needed to relocate the elements of the array among different processors and perform the necessary communication among different processors.

Recent work on array redistribution has been divided into two areas: regular redistribution and irregular redistribution. Guo *et al.*[5] developed techniques to reduce overheads in both index computation and inter-node communication. They [6] presented an efficient index computation method and generate a schedule that minimizes the number of communication steps and eliminates node contention in each communication step.

There are relative little papers on irregular array redistribution. Leair *et al.* [7] have implemented the GEN_BLOCK data distribution in PGHPF, a High Performance Fortran compiler [8]. Yook and Park [9] proposed an algorithm for the redistribution of one-dimensional arrays in GEN_BLOCK. The algorithm attempts to obtain near optimal scheduling by trying to minimize the size of communication step and the number of steps. Lee *et al.* [10] focused on reducing the communication cost in GEN_BLOCK redistribution using a logical processor reordering method.

## 2    GEN_BLOCK Redistribution Communication Models

As a generalized block distribution, GEN_BLOCK allows possibly unequal-sized consecutive segments of an array to be mapped onto consecutive processors [1].

A redistribution $R$ is a set of routines that transfer all the elements in a set of source processors $SP$ to a set of target processors $TP$. Generally, the sending and receiving phases indicate that the array redistribution problem comprises the following two sub-problems:

(1) **Message generation**: The array to be redistributed should be efficiently scanned or processed in order to build all the messages that are to be exchanged between processors.

(2) **Communication schedule**: All messages must be efficiently scheduled so as to minimize communication overhead. Each processor typically has general massages to send to all other processors. The sizes of the messages are specified by values of a user-defined integer for array mapping from source processor to target processor.

To develop a communication schedule, we can use either blocking scheduling algorithms or non-blocking scheduling algorithms. The blocking scheduling algorithms are based on blocking communication primitives, while the non-blocking scheduling algorithms are based on non-blocking communication primitives. In general, because the non-blocking scheduling algorithms avoid excessive synchronization overhead, they are faster than the blocking scheduling algorithms. However, the non-blocking communication primitives need as much buffering as the data being redistributed [3,4]. It makes non-blocking scheduling algorithm much expensive in some situations. In this paper, we will propose some scheduling algorithms for GEN_BLOCK redistribution using blocking communication primitives.

In distributed memory parallel computing, the inter-processor communication overheads can be represented using an analytical model of typical distributed memory machines. To represent the communication time of a message passing operation, the model introduces two parameters: the start-up time $T_s$ and the unit data transmission time $T_m$.

Based on the one-step communication time in Equation (1), Equation (2) provides the total communication time of collective message passing delivered in multiple communication steps.

$$T_{step} = T_s + m \times T_m, \tag{1}$$

$$T_{total} = \sum T_{step}. \tag{2}$$

Since it is illegal to have node contention at the source processor and the target processor, a processor can only receive at most one message from one other processor in each communication step. Similarly, a processor can only send at most one message to one other processor in each communication step. It is also illegal to consider the contention at switches within the interconnection network. Thus the GEN_BLOCK redistribution has the following properties:

(1) Unlike regular redistribution, it has not a cyclic message-passing pattern.

(2) If $SP_i$ must send message to $TP_{j-1}$ and $TP_{j+1}$, therefore it must also send to $TP_j$, vice versa.

Figure 1 shows the redistribution communication of the example given above and describes the sending and receiving messages inside GEN_BLOCK in details. In this example, there are 7 source processors and 7 target processors, respectively. Source processor $SP_0$ has 3 unit data, and target processor $TP_0$ has 2 unit data. After the messages distribution in source and target processors, we can figure out how many messages each source processor should send out, to which target processors it should be sent, and how many unit data it should be sent to the specific processor. Clearly, in this example, $SP_0$ sends 2 unit data message to $TP_0$, and 1 unit data message to $TP_1$. etc.

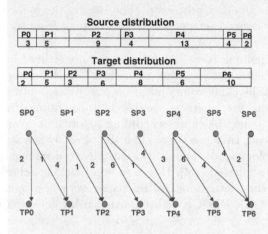

**Source distribution**

| P0 | P1 | P2 | P3 | P4 | P5 | P6 |
|----|----|----|----|----|----|----|
| 3  | 5  | 9  | 4  | 13 | 4  | 2  |

**Target distribution**

| P0 | P1 | P2 | P3 | P4 | P5 | P6 |
|----|----|----|----|----|----|----|
| 2  | 5  | 3  | 6  | 8  | 6  | 10 |

**Fig. 1.** A redistribution example

When implementing the redistribution problem as a matrix problem, we regard a message sent from source processor $SP_i$ to target processor $TP_j$ as an element $m_{i,j}$ of a matrix. $m_{i,j}$ also represents the size of the message.

A neighbor message set $(NMS)$ can be defined as a set of the messages that be sent from same processor or be received by same processor. According the label of source processor $SP_i$ or target processor $TP_j$, we can label each neighbor message set as $NMS_{2i}$ or $NMS_{2j+1}$, respectively. To avoid these $NMS$s that have only one element, we omit them and then reorder the remaining $NMS$s accordingly. If an $NMS_k$ can't be scheduled in the same communication step with another $NMS_{k'}$, there is a conflict tuple $(NMS_k, NMS_{k'})$. A link message defined as $NMS_k \cap NMS_{k'}(k \neq k')$, is the message that belongs to two different neighbor $NMS$s.

According to the definitions given above, neighbor message set in matrix implementation is a set of elements in the same row or column. If elements in row or column can't be scheduled in the same communication step with other row or column, there is a conflict tuple. A link message is the element that has both not-zero row-neighbor and not-zero column-neighbor.

With these assumptions, work on designing the scheduling algorithms should be concentrated on how to organize the order of each message so that the costs for GEN_BLOCK redistribution can be minimized. Clearly, the aims for the GEN_BLOCK redistribution:

(1) **Minimal Communication Step**: The minimum number of communication steps is the maximum number of fan-out (fan-in) arrows of the processor nodes. It indicates that minimum number of communication steps is the maximum cardinality of neighbor message sets.

Since the messages in the same neighbor message set cannot be scheduled in the same communication step, the size of total communication step should be equal to or larger than the maximum cardinality of neighbor message sets. Each neighbor message set may have at most two link messages, which are defined as the messages that must belong to two different neighbor message sets.

(2) **Minimal the Size of the Total Steps**: The total communication time is a linear function of the size of the total steps. In order to reduce the total communication time, the efficient way is to minimize the size of the total steps.

As a matrix problem, the GEN_BLOCK redistribution has the following features:

(1) The total number of the neighbors of an element $N_{i,j}$, $N_{Total} = B_{left} + B_{right} + B_{up} + B_{down} \leq 2$, where $B$ is 1 if $N_{i,j}$ has an neighbor in that direction, or is 0 if hasn't.

(2) The total number of non-zero elements in a matrix, or the total number of messages, $k$ satisfies with $max(m,n) \leq k \leq m + n - 1$, where $m$ and $n$ are the lengths of matrix column and row, respectively.

**Proof.** It is reasonable to eliminate a column or a row if all the elements in that column or row are zero. We assume there is at least one element in a column or a row. So the total number of messages $k \leq max(m,n)$. Suppose totally there are at least $m + n$ messages, we can find at least a cyclic message passing pattern, $\{m_{i,j}, m_{j,i}\}$, or at least a conflict, $\{m_{i,j}, m_{i,j'}, m_{i',j}, m_{i',j'}\}$.

(3) Elements in the same row or column can't be scheduled in the same time step. Clearly, elements in the same row or column represent messages sent to same processor or received from same processor.

Figure 2 shows the matrix implementation of the above example. The row and column represent the index of source processors and target processors, respectively. In Figure 2, $SP_0$ sends 2 unit data to $TP_0$, and sends one unit data to $TP_1$. $SP_1$ sends 4 unit data to $TP_1$, and sends one unit data to $TP_2$, and so on. The zero-value elements are ignored.

# 3   Our Algorithm

In the following discussion, we concentrate on two-dimensional array redistribution. Our algorithm can be generalized to that of higher dimensions.

Our redistribution algorithm contains two parts: (1) break the problem into a set of sub-problems that are similar to the original problems with smaller size, (2) solve these sub-problems recursively, and then create the solution to original problem by combining these solutions to sub-problems.

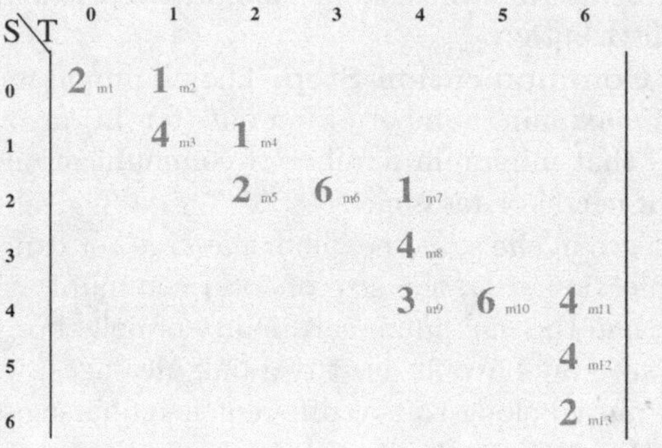

**Fig. 2.** The matrix implementation of the above example. The order of the message is labelled in a smaller font.

The algorithm is close to the divide-and-conquer algorithm that has been widely used in binary searching, Fast Fourier Transformation, matrix inversion, etc.

When breaking the problem into smaller units, we first separate the problem into a set of sub-problems where each sub-problem can be scheduled independently. That means there is no link message between each sub-problem. After obtaining the solutions to the sub-problems, we combine them together automatically to form the solution to the original problem. The main routine including

(1) Separating the neighbor message sets. Here we treat an $NMS$ as the smallest unit.

(2) After dividing into the smallest units, we group each pair of $NMS$, such as $\{NMS_1, NMS_2\}, \cdots, \{NMS_{2i+1}, NMS_{2i+2}\}, \cdots$. From matrix implementation, each pair contains one row and one column of the matrix.

Figure 3 shows the separating and grouping processes for the above example. In the example, there are totally 8 $NMS$s, and they are grouped into 4 pairs: $\{NMS_1, NMS_2\}, \{NMS_3, NMS_4\}, \{NMS_5, NMS_6\}, \{NMS_7, NMS_8\}$. Figure 3 indicates that all separations are taken place at link messages. Only link messages are divided and separated. It is reasonable since the link message is belong to both related row and related column, which makes conflicts happen.

After obtaining the pairs of $NMS$, we begin the merging processes to produce the scheduling. The principles for merging are

(1) Merging recursively. In phase 0, we generate the scheduling table for each $NMS$ pair. There are total $k$ pairs, while each pair forms a group. In phase 1, scheduling tables for the group of $\{NMS_1, NMS_2, NMS_3, NMS_4\}, \cdots$, the $i$-th group of $\{NMS_{4i+1}, NMS_{4i+2}, NMS_{4i+3}, NMS_{4i+4}\}, \cdots$, are merging together. Recursively, in phase $j$, scheduling tables for the $i$-th group of $\{NMS_{j\times(i+1)}, NMS_{j\times(i+1)+1}, \cdots, NMS_{j\times(i+j)}\}$ are merging together.

(2) Generating the scheduling tables for each group. The generating processes are quite same for each group in any phases. First, we detect the conflict information, and kick out the link message and those messages scheduled with

82      H. Wang et al.

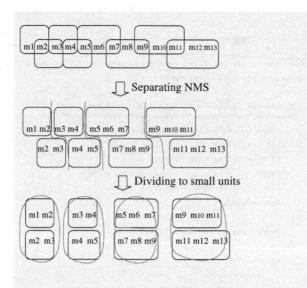

Fig. 3. Dividing the problem recursively into the smallest units for the above example.

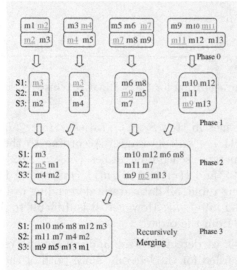

Fig. 4. Merging the smallest units to form the solution to the original problem recursively for the above example.

it. Then sort the remaining messages to make an optimal solution. If a message has more possible position in scheduling table, it stands with its closest ceiling. Finally, the link message together with those scheduled messages, are added into the scheduling table.

Figure 4 shows the merging processes from the smallest units to generate the scheduling tables recursively for the above example. In Figure 4, we assume

```
Algorithm 1:
  input M(x,y): Messages, x: source processor y: target processor
  output S(x,y): Scheduling table
  {
1    Divide the problem into independent sub-problems
2    Separate the Neighbor Message Sets: NMS1,NMS2, _ NMS2k;

3    // First phase: separation and group
4    for (i = 0; i < k; i++) {
5        Kick left-down link message out;
6        tmpMax(i) = Join(row in Mi, column in Mi);
7        Add left-down link message to tmpMax(i);
8        Update S(x,y);
9    }
10   // Second phase: recursively merge
11   while (j < k) {
12       for (i = j; i < k; i = i + 2 * j) {
13           if (Order(i, 0) != Order(i, 1)) {
14               Merge(sub-matrix from M(i-j) to M(i+j));
15           }
16       }
17       j = 2 * j;
28   }
  }
```

**Fig. 5.** Our algorithm for GEN_BLOCK redistribution.

the length of total messages in step $S_i$, $L_{Si}$, satisfies $L_{Si} \leq L_{S(i+1)}$. In phase 0, $m2$, $m4$, $m7$, and $m11$ are link messages. According to the length of messages, the algorithm generates scheduling tables $\{m3, m1, m2\}$, $\{m3, m5, m4\}$, $\{(m6, m8), (m9, m5), m7\}$, and $\{(m10, m12), m11, (m9, m13)\}$ for each pair, respectively. In a scheduling table, all data are in descending order. For example, here $m3 \leq m1 \leq m2$, and $m6 \leq m8$. However, it is difficult to determine which is larger, $m8$ or $m5$ just from the order.

In phase 1 of Figure 4, we detect that $m3$ and $m9$ are link messages. Further merging is straight forwarded for the left pair since both of them have the link message $m3$ in the same scheduling step. Since the link message $m9$ is in different scheduling step, we rearrange $m9$ and its related messages to perform optimal scheduling results. Similar situation happens in phase 2. Finally we obtain the scheduling table for the whole redistribution problem.

Our algorithm can generate sub-optimal communication scheduling table. It satisfies minimal size condition (higher priority) and minimal step condition. From the algorithm described in Figure 5 and Figure 6, we can estimate the time complexity of Divide-and-Conquer Algorithm is $O(n^2 log_2 n)$, where $n$ is the number of link messages, because sorting message needs $O(n^2)$, and merging needs $O(log_2 n)$ steps totally.

```
Algorithm 2: subroutine Merge
  range: sub-matrix from M(i-j) to M(i+j))
  location: link message i
  {
1   while (tmpNum != -1) {
2       tmpNum=total number of message in link message i's
3           row or column with order tmpOrder, if it is larger
4           than link message i, increase 1;
5       if (tmpOrder == Max(number of messages in i's row,
6                           number of messages in i's column) {
7           S[x[i]][y[i]] = tmpOrder;
8           update tmpMax;
9       } else if (tmpNum == 0) {
10          S[x[i]][y[i]] = tmpOrder;
11          update tmpMax;
12      } else if (tmpNum == 1) {
13          S[x[i]][y[i]] = tmpOrder;
14          exchange order;
15          update S(x,y) in sub-matrix from M(i-j) to M(i+j)
16          update tmpMax;
17      }
18  }
  }
```

**Fig. 6.** Merging sub-problems in our algorithm for GEN_BLOCK redistribution.

## 4   Performance and Discussion

To evaluate our algorithm, we implement it into codes and compare with the relocation algorithm. The simulation program generates a set of random numbers in the range of 0 to 100 as the size of message. Here we suppose that the number of source processors equals to the number of target processors. However, it is possible that some processors do not contain any elements. To keep the balance between source processors and target processor, we also suppose the total size of messages in both source processors and target processors are equal.

Inputs of the program are two arrays: a set of source processor and a set of target processors. According to these arrays, a message communication matrix can be generated. Then the algorithm presents a scheduling table of communication, which contains the time step for each message.

Before comparing results with a relocation algorithm developed previously, we briefly introduce the relocation algorithm [9]. Relocation algorithm is a scheduling algorithm that generates a suboptimal communication schedule. The algorithm satisfies minimal step condition and minimal size condition.

Relocation algorithm consists of two phases. In the first phase, called list scheduling, it sorts all messages in descending order. According to this list, it allocates the messages one by one. Each message shall occupy the smaller order. If there are conflict message in the smaller order, it shall move to next order without violating the minimal step condition. When it cannot allocate a message within the minimal step condition, it goes to the relocation phase.

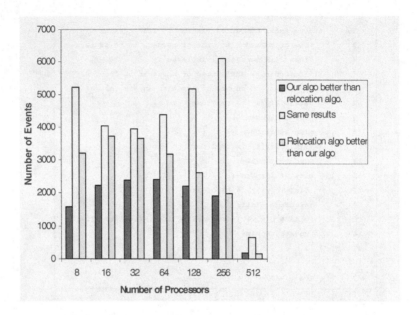

**Fig. 7.** The results of both our algorithm and a relocation algorithm

In order to allocate the new message in the relocation phase, the algorithm must relocate some already allocated messages. In this case, the new message must be a link message. That means the new message belongs to two different neighbor message sets. Since the situation is that the new message can't be allocated at this time, there must be one message should be relocated to other order so that new message take its order. Then keep relocating some messages until there are no conflicts any more. It indicates that there are to ways: one is to relocate the left side messages, and another is to relocate the right side messages. There are no changes to the right side messages when relocating the left side messages.

So the schedule is divided into two sub-message sets: left set and right set. The left set and the right set are kinds of GEN_BLOCK redistributions and can be seen as an input of the relocation scheduling algorithm, recursively. We may discard one of them because one of them does not satisfy the minimal size of total communication steps condition.

Figure 7 shows the simulation results of both our algorithm and the relocation algorithm. For each different number of processors, we plot one column for divide-and-conquer algorithm has better performance than relocation algorithm, one column for relocation algorithm has better performance than divide-

and-conquer algorithm, and one column for the same performance of them. The results indicate that both relocation algorithm and our algorithm have good performance.

Comparing with the relocation Algorithm, the disadvantage of our algorithm is too many *bad* link messages generated when merging the sub-problems. Bad link messages make the scheduling quite inefficient. It indicates the list scheduling is an efficient algorithm for GEN_BLOCK redistribution. So it is possible to develop a better algorithm if the new algorithm can include the excellent points from both of them.

## 5   Conclusion

In an HPF-2 compiler, GEN_BLOCK array redistribution makes unequal-sized blocks mapping possible. In this paper, we describe the communication models for GEN_BLOCK array redistribution and present three different implementations: regular implementation, matrix implementation, and interval graph implementation. In the regular implementation, we define related concepts and show both minimal step condition and minimal size of total steps condition for optimizing the GEN_BLOCK array redistribution.

A GEN_BLOCK algorithm is developed to achieve sub-optimal solutions. Our redistribution algorithm first breaks the problem into a set of sub-problems, and then solves these sub-problems recursively and creates the solution to original problem by combining these solutions to sub-problems.

Results from our algorithm are compared with these from a relocation algorithm. The results indicate that both of them have good performance on GEN_BLOCK redistribution.

Multi-dimensional GEN_BLOCK array redistribution are extended versions of one-dimensional array redistribution. Thus, the minimal step condition and the minimal size condition are also important in multi-dimensional GEN_BLOCK redistribution scheduling. Multi-dimensional GEN_BLOCK array redistribution scheduling can be performed by extending our algorithm.

## References

1. High Performance Fortran Forum, *High Performance Fortran Language Specification version 2.0*, Rice University, Houston, Texas, January 1997.
2. Y. Pan and J. Shang, Efficient and Scalable Parallelization of Time-Dependent Maxwell Equations Solver Using High Performance Fortran, *The 4th IEEE International Conference on Algorithms & Architectures for Parallel Processing,* Hong Kong, December 11-13, 2000, pp. 520–531.
3. S. D. Kaushik, C.-H. Huang, and P. Sadayappan. Efficient index set generation for compiling HPF array statements on distributed-memory machines. *Journal of Parallel and Distributed Computing* , 38(2):237–247, 1996.
4. R. Thakur, A. Choudhary, and G. Fox. Runtime array redistribution in HPF programs. *In Proceedings Scalable High Performance Computing Conference*, May 1994, pp. 309–316.

5. M. Guo, I. Nakata, A Framework for Efficient Data Redistribution on Distributed Memory Multicomputers, *The Journal of Supercomputing*, vol.20, no.3, pp.243–265, Nov., 2001.
6. M. Guo, I. Nakata, and Y. Yamashita, Contention-Free Communication Scheduling for Array Redistribution, *Proceedings of the International Conference on Parallel and Distributed Systems*, pp.658–667, December 1998.
7. M. Leair, D. Miles, V. Schuster, and M. Wolfe, *Euro-Par'99 Parallel Processing 5th International Euro-Par Conference*, Toulouse, France, Aug. 31–Sep. 3, 1999, Proceedings, Springer Verlag LNCS 1999.
8. PGHPF, a High Performance Fortran compiler, *http://www.pgroup.com/products/pghpfindex.htm.*
9. H. Yook and M. Park, Scheduling GEN_BLOCK Array Redistribution, *Proceedings of the IASTED International Conference Parallel and Distributed Computing and Systems*, November 3–6, 1999, MIT, Boston, USA.
10. S. Lee, H. Yook, M. Koo, M. Park, Processor reordering algorithms toward efficient GEN_BLOCK redistribution. *Proceedings of the 2001 ACM symposium on Applied computing*, 2001, Las Vegas, Nevada, USA, 2001: 539–543.

# Balancing Traffic in Meshes by Dynamic Channel Selection

Po-Jen Chuang and Yue-Tsuen Jiang

Department of Electrical Engineering, Tamkang University
Tamsui, Taipei Hsien, Taiwan 25137, R. O. C.
pjchuang@ee.tku.edu.tw

**Abstract.** This paper presents an idea of dynamic channel selection to balance traffic for a mesh network. The key idea is to maintain the history of channel utilization in each node and based on the recorded information the node router can predict the current load of the network and route packets through less trafficked or more appropriate channels to avoid congestion. Three dynamic channel selection policies, DCS-I, DCS-II and DCS-III, have been designed, each with specific advantages, to fit different situations. Performance of six established adaptive routing algorithms with five channel selection policies are evaluated through simulation. The results exhibit that when network traffic gets heavy, the proposed DCS-II and DCS-III yield constantly better performance in terms of *throughput* and *communication latency* than the other selection policies. DCS-II and DCS-III are also shown to bring about more even *buffer utilization* — manifesting the important link between balanced network traffic and desired performance.

## 1 Introduction

Wormhole routing is a popular switching technique in direct networks [1]. In wormhole routing, packets are transmitted by a cut-through approach which divides a packet into a number of flits and the flits are usually transmitted in parallel between routers. The efficiency of wormhole routing lies in low communication latency and small buffer sizes. Communication latency can be further reduced when adaptive routing algorithms are engaged to minimize channel contention. An adaptive routing algorithm is able to provide multiple paths between the source and destination nodes. As messages can be routed through more alternative paths, packet routing will be activated in a more flexible way. But when the network load becomes heavier, uneven traffic often results, that is, traffic tends to concentrate in a certain area of the network, causing early saturation of that area and hence degrading the overall network performance. To improve the situation, virtual channels [2,3] have been adopted by the wormhole routing algorithm to add up routing adaptivity in the mesh-connected network. By dividing a network into multiple disjoint logical networks to facilitate routing and avoid deadlocks, virtual channels may help postpone network saturation time, but congestion due to heavy traffic in the most congested area can still happen.

M. Guo and L.T.Yang (Eds.): ISPA 2003, LNCS 2745, pp. 88–99, 2003.

To avoid congestion in a mesh-connected network, a *restricted area* concept is proposed in [4]. The restricted area is defined to be the area of a network where buffer utilization concentrates. Such a highly active area can be observed following the characteristics of the employed routing algorithm and the concept of *the region of adaptivity* [5]. Based on this concept, the region with the most concentrated network traffic is marked off and set as the restricted area. Transmission inside the area will be "restricted" in such a way that messages will avoid entering the area as much as possible or get through it as fast as possible. The restricted area concept is indeed a *static* channel selection approach: It needs to obtain the adaptive region of the employed routing algorithm first to determine the location and size of the restricted area (which is fixed during the system-on period), requires routing headers to carry information of the restricted area, and involves additional computation for routing purpose.

To conduct channel selection in a more active and effective way, an idea of *dynamic channel selection* is proposed in this paper. The key point of the idea is to maintain the history of channel utilization in each node so that the node router can predict the current load of the network based on the recorded information and route the incoming packets through less trafficked (or more appropriate) channels to avoid traffic congestion. To serve this purpose, we add a counter to either end of a channel to record the frequency of packet routing. The counter values are taken as a proper indication of the channel utilization history and will be consulted to select appropriate routing channels for an incoming packet. Thus with dynamic channel selection, routing channels can be selected dynamically during routing according to the current traffic load. Three dynamic channel selection policies, DCS-I, DCS-II and DCS-III with different initial channel counter values, are introduced in the paper to show their varied performance. Extensive simulation runs are conducted to evaluate the performance of six routing algorithms [5-8] under five channel selection policies.

## 2    The Proposed Dynamic Channel Selection (DCS)

### 2.1    The Idea of Dynamic Channel Selection

The idea of dynamic channel selection is to maintain the history of channel utilization in each node so that the node router can predict the current load of the network based on the recorded information and then route packets through less trafficked or appropriate channels, to avoid overcrowded traffic. To serve this purpose, we add a counter to either end of a channel to record the frequency of packet routing. The counter values are taken as a proper indication of the channel utilization history of the network and will be consulted to set up priorities for selecting appropriate routing channels for an incoming packet. The advantage of this design is that routing channels can be selected dynamically during routing according to current traffic predicted based on the channel utilization history. For example, suppose a packet is about to travel from node A to node B. When the header flit of the packet proceeds from node A to node B, the counters at both ends of the channel that connects the two nodes will add 1 respectively. That is, whenever a packet is routed from a node to another, the counters on both sides of the connecting channel will each add 1. In this way the counter values at both ends of a channel will equal to each other. In the above case, the counter value on node A will equal to that on node B for the same channel. Based on this synchronized computation, a node will learn about the corresponding counter values of its four immediate neighboring nodes and thus catch the history of the surrounding network loads. When an incoming packet arrives, the node will be able to check the current traffic condition and go ahead selecting a less trafficked or more appropriate channel for routing. (Note that in order to predict the location of the congested areas, a channel counter records the frequency the channel is used by packets, not by flits. That is, the channel counter is used to record the frequency of channel utilization, not the period of channel occupancy.) As counter values increase with ongoing network traffic, they need to be reset after a fixed period of time to avoid counter overflow. With the aid of simple register shifts, reset can be realized by dividing the counter values over a certain value at a fixed time interval.

Fig. 1 illustrates the idea of dynamic channel selection and its effect in balancing channel utilization. (The thickness of lines indicates the size of the current network load: the thicker the line, the heavier the load.) To route a packet from source S1 to destination D1, as shown here, the dynamic channel selection policy will choose with higher priority the channels along the two arrowed paths — because they exhibit lower counter values — to avoid the heavily loaded area. A similar channel selection can be expected for packet routing from S2 to D2 in the same figure.

As mentioned, in balancing channel utilization for the mesh-connected network, routing algorithms with the restricted area concept [4] require packets to carry the needed extra information along the way, but routing algorithms with the proposed dynamic channel selection policy compares only the history of channel utilization indicated in channel counters — an apparently more dynamic and efficient practice.

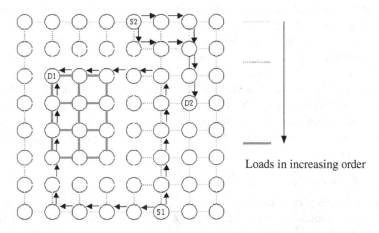

Loads in increasing order

**Fig. 1.** An illustration of the idea of dynamic channel selection.

## 2.2   The Dynamic Channel Selection (DCS) Strategy

As the dynamic channel selection strategy predicts network loads according to the values of channel counters, it is therefore essential to decide on initial counter values in the first place. Three initial counter values are proposed in the following to show their different operation and performance.

### 2.2.1   DCS-I: The Initial Counter Values Are Set to Be Zero

This is the simplest way to set the initial counter values, but with all counter values being set to 0, the dynamic channel selection strategy may work only for certain routing algorithms. In fact, DCS-I improves channel utilization only for routing algorithms with more even network traffic, such as the 3P algorithm. For routing algorithms with uneven traffic loads, i.e., with distinctive traffic imbalance between the adaptive and non-adaptive regions, DCS-I cannot balance the routing behaviors between the two regions — because it can distribute only the traffic in the adaptive region or the traffic in the non-adaptive region individually. The problem is, when all counter values are initially set to 0, the network traffic will distribute in a similar trend as that of the original routing algorithm. That is, routings in the adaptive region may be distributed more symmetrically over the area but they will remain in the area as no restrictions are imposed to prevent packets from entering it. Uneven channel utilization between the adaptive and non-adaptive regions thus persists.

### 2.2.2   DCS-II: The Initial Counter Values Are Set Based on the Adaptive
### Regions

The fact that DCS-I can not prevent packets from entering the congested area and thus fails to balance channel utilization for certain routing algorithms prompts us to bring in the restricted area concept. In the design of DCS-II, a Max_count value — the maximum value for the predetermined counter size — is set to some channel counters in the congested area, i.e., the restricted area, of the network. When a packet is to be routed, the Max_count counter values will keep it away from the restricted area and direct it to travel across regions with lighter traffic loads. To facilitate such a practice, the adaptive region and its bordering half of the non-adaptive region of a routing algorithm will be specified as the restricted area for DCS-II in which the values of certain channel counters will be set with the Max_count values to turn routing away to the non-restricted area. The setting of the restricted area and the choosing of channel counters to receive the Max_count values are provided next for different routing algorithms.

#### 2.2.2.1   The West-First Routing Algorithm

Due to the routing characteristics of the west-first routing algorithm, packet routing occurs more frequently in the east half of the mesh network. The east half of the network thus becomes the adaptive region for the algorithm while the west half the non-adaptive region. In practicing DCS-II, the whole adaptive region and its neighboring half of the non-adaptive region will be taken as the restricted area to facilitate traffic distribution. Counters of all eastbound channels in the area will be set with the Max_count values and all of the other channel counters in the network will be set with the value 0. Now, if a packet is to route towards its destination in the northeast of the restricted area, routing will be first kept away from entering the area by the Max_count counter values of the eastbound channels (in that area) and be directed to travel through channels with counter value 0. In this way, packet routing can be distributed as much as possible to the non-restricted area to secure more balanced buffer utilization for the network. On the other hand, if the packet is traveling to its destination in the southwest of the network, it will route following the policy of DCS-I because the channels to be taken are all with counter value 0.

### 2.2.2.2    The North-Last Routing Algorithm

For the north-last routing algorithm, the lower half of the network becomes the adaptive region and the upper half is the non-adaptive region. The restricted area for running DCS-II includes the whole adaptive region and its bordering half of the non-adaptive region, and the counters of all southbound channels in the area are set with the Max_count values (the other counter values of the network are 0). Routing is conducted in the same way as in the west-first routing algorithm.

### 2.2.2.3    The Negative-First Routing Algorithm

The routing characteristics of the negative-first routing algorithm turn the first and third quadrants of a network into the adaptive region, and the second and fourth quadrants the non-adaptive region. The restricted area for practicing DCS-II includes the vertical central half of the network, and the Max_count counter values are set to all the northbound and southbound channels in the area.

### 2.2.2.4    The 3P Routing Algorithm

The entire network can be taken as the adaptive region for the 3P routing algorithm because the algorithm distributes traffic quite proportionally over the network.

### 2.2.2.5    The Mesh_Route Routing Algorithm

The routing characteristics of the mesh_route routing algorithm make the third quadrant of the network its adaptive region. The restricted area thus covers the adaptive region and its surrounding half of the non-adaptive region. The Max_count counter values are set to all westbound and southbound channels in the area.

### 2.2.2.6    The PFNF Routing Algorithm

The PFNF routing algorithm employs the positive-first routing algorithm and the negative-first routing algorithm respectively in its two virtual networks. The restricted area is thus located in the vertical central half of the entire network, and its northbound and southbound channels are set with the Max_count counter values.

### 2.2.3    DCS-III: The Initial Counter Values Are Set Based on the Network Load

To practice DCS-II, as mentioned, we need to follow the routing characteristics of the employed routing algorithm in the first place to locate the restricted area and then to initialize counter values for channels. To simplify the operation, we move on to consider a new approach able to activate the idea of dynamic channel selection effectively and yet without involving the complexity of DCS-II. Based on channel utilization obtained from experimental evaluation, we detect a similar routing trend for all routing algorithms: Traffic in the heavily loaded area tends to get more hectic with time, while traffic in the lightly loaded area shows a diminishing tendency. Such a routing trend enables us to predict the current traffic distribution of the network and to come up with a new approach, DCS-III, which initializes counter values based on network traffic loads.

When the system runs after a specified length of time into a steady state and the current network load can be predicted based on the history of channel utilization, DCS-III will set the Max_count counter values to the two most used channel counters of each node and 0 to the other two (less frequented) counters. Thus, packet routing will choose to travel through the two counters with value 0, instead of the two with the Max_count values, to balance buffer utilization and avoid traffic congestion. Such a channel selection design proves more dynamic and adaptive as the "restricted area" (to set up the Max_count values) will be obtained according to current traffic loads and can be adaptively changed corresponding to the ever changing network traffic during the system-on period.

## 3    Performance Evaluation

In two-dimensional meshes, packets are transmitted in four directions: east, west, south and north, and the characteristics of packet transmission can be observed and analyzed by using turn models [6]. Extensive simulation runs have been conducted to evaluate the effect of dynamic channel selection. Specifically, the performance of six adaptive routing algorithms (including three turn models — the west-first, north-last and negative-first, and three algorithms with virtual channels — 3P, mesh_route and PFNF) with various channel selection policies — normal, RA, DCS-I, DCS-II and DCS-III are evaluated and compared. (Note that Normal refers to the original routing algorithm — routing with "random" channel selection; RA represents routing with the concept of restricted area — routing with "static" channel selection.)

### 3.1    The Simulation Model

The simulation is conducted in a 16×16 mesh. A pair of unidirectional links connects each pair of neighboring routers, and each router connects to its local processor through a pair of unidirectional links.   Input buffering is assumed, i.e., buffers are partitioned into flits and are associated with each input channel from neighboring routers. A flit may contain a predetermined number of bits. Thus, without loss of generality, we assume only a flit is involved at each "pipeline stage" in the wormhole routing. Under this assumption, it is clear that the buffer size for each input channel to be used is no bigger than one flit and it is therefore enough to show the general result with the buffer size being assumed to be one flit in each input channel. The processor generates messages (assumed to have 20 flits per packet) at time intervals chosen from an exponential distribution. Messages that are blocked from immediately entering the network are queued up at the source processor, and those arriving at a destination processor are immediately consumed. To get steady state results, the simulation is carried out for 140,000 packets with the results of the first 40,000 packets being excluded.

Communication latency, throughput [9] and the average buffer utilization are the three performance parameters of interest in our simulation. *Communication latency* is measured from the time a packet is generated at the source node until the tail flit reaches the destination. *Throughput* is the average number of flits that complete transmission per unit time. The *average buffer utilization* refers to the average buffer utilization at each node, and is a clear indicator of the entire network traffic distribution. Note that the network traffic load is defined to be the ratio of the average traffic generated by a node to the average bandwidth available per node (i.e., the average flit generation rate per node), also denoted as the referenced index of workload degrees in the figures. The selection policies include the random input selection and the no-turn output selection [10].

## 3.2 Simulation Results

Simulation results for the west-first, north-last, negative-first, 3P, mesh_route and PFNF routing algorithms with the five channel selection policies are collected under five traffic patterns, uniform, matrix transpose, hotspot, bit reversal and perfect shuffle. (Due to limited space, only part of the results is presented in the following figures to assist discussion.) The results depicted in Fig. 2 are the performance of the six algorithms collected under the uniform traffic pattern. As the results indicate, performance of each algorithm with different channel selection policies turns out quite consistent at lower traffic loads but becomes dividing when traffic loads increase. Take Fig. 2 (a) as an example. Performance of the west-first algorithm appears nearly the same for all channel selection policies when network traffic is light, but roughly starting from traffic load 10 performance begins to diversify withdifferent channel selection policies and the difference grows more distinctively after load 15. Simulation results collected under the other four traffic patterns all demonstrate such a performance trend. The trend reveals that when the traffic load is heavy, proper channel selection policies are important in maintaining and improving network performance. According to our simulation results, of the five channel selection policies, RA, DCS-II and DCS-III turn over constantly better performance – larger throughput and lower communication latency – in heavily loaded networks.

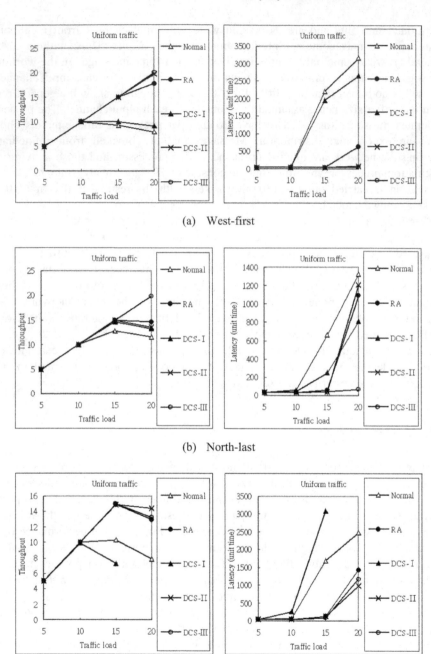

**Fig. 2.** Network performance for various routing algorithms with different channel selection policies under uniform traffic.

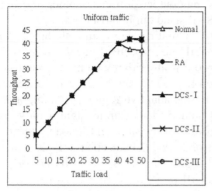
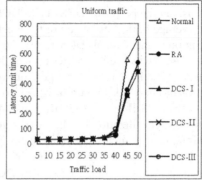

(d)    3P

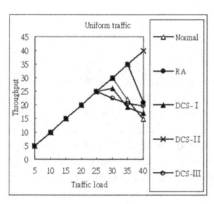
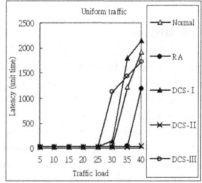

(e)    Mesh_route

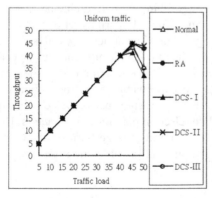
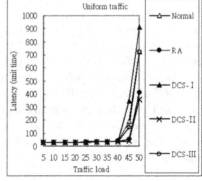

(f)    PFNF

**Fig. 2.** (continued)

The three leading channel selection policies may outperform one another in different situations, but the proposed DCS-II and DCS-III stand out in most cases.

The average buffer utilization of the west-first routing algorithm with three channel selection policies, Normal, DCS-II and DCS-III, are respectively depicted in Figs. 3-5. From Fig. 3 which gives buffer utilization of the algorithm with its original routing pattern at traffic load 15, we see quite uneven buffer utilization as traffic concentrates in part of the network (which turns out to be the adaptive region of the algorithm). Then with DCS-II and DCS-III, Figs. 4 and 5 demonstrate significantly more balanced buffer utilization for the same algorithm at the same traffic load. Indeed, we find through experimental evaluation that proper channel selection policies can help balance the average buffer utilization of an algorithm and boost up its performance accordingly. Among them, DCS-II and DCS-III prove to work better than the other employed channel selection policies in balancing network traffic distribution under all algorithms.

# 4   Conclusion

To balance buffer utilization in a more active and efficient way, an idea of dynamic channel selection has been proposed in this paper. To activate the idea, we add a counter to either end of a routing channel to record routing frequency of that channel. The counter values of all routing channels are then taken as the channel utilization history of the network and will be consulted to find less trafficked or more appropriate routing channels for the incoming packets. Three dynamic channel selection policies with different initial counter values are presented: DCS-I sets the initial counter values of all channels to 0, DCS-II sets counter values based on the adaptive regions, while DCS-III sets counter values according to the current network load.

The performance of six adaptive routing algorithms with five channel selection policies are evaluated and compared through simulation. Experimental results exhibit a similar performance trend for all routing algorithms: When network traffic is light, performance appears nearly the same for an algorithm with any channel selection policies; when traffic grows heavier, performance of an algorithm diversifies with different channel selection policies. Among the five channel selection policies, the proposed DCS-II and DCS-III are shown to give better performance — larger throughput and lower latency — than the other selection policies in most cases. DCS-II and DCS-III are also shown to yield more balanced average buffer utilization — manifesting the significant interaction between buffer utilization and network performance.

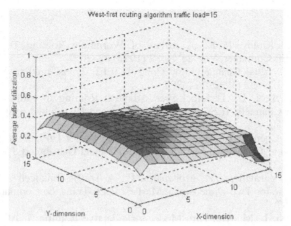

**Fig. 3.** Average buffer utilization for the west-first routing algorithm.

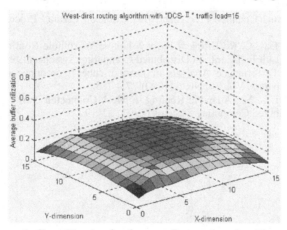

**Fig. 4.** Average buffer utilization for the west-first routing algorithm with DCS-II.

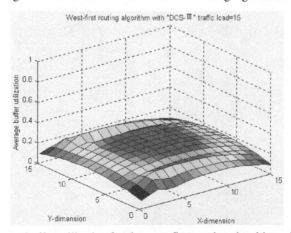

**Fig. 5.** Average buffer utilization for the west-first routing algorithm with DCS-III.

# References

1.  Ni, L. M., McKinley, P. K.: A survey of Wormhole Routing Techniques in Direct Networks. IEEE Computer, Vol. 26, No. 2 (1993) 62–76.
2.  Dally, W. J.: Virtual Channel Flow Control. IEEE Trans. on Parallel and Distributed Systems, Vol. 3, No. 3 (1992) 194–205.
3.  Dally, W. J., Akoi, H.: Deadlock-Free Adaptive Routing in Multicomputer Networks Using Virtual Channels. IEEE Trans. on Parallel and Distributed Systems, Vol. 4, No. 4 (1993) 466–475.
4.  Chuang, P.-J., Chen, J.-T., Jiang, Y.-T.: Balancing Buffer Utilization in Meshes Using a "Restricted Area" Concept. IEEE Trans. on Parallel and Distributed Systems, Vol. 13, No. 8 (2002) 814–827.
5.  Upadhyay, J., Varavithya, V., Mohapatra, P.: A Traffic-Balanced Adaptive Wormhole Routing Scheme for Two-Dimensional Meshes. IEEE Trans. on Computers, Vol. 46, No. 2 (1997) 190–197.
6.  Glass, C. J., Ni, L. M.: The Turn Model for Adaptive Routing. J. ACM, Vol. 41, No. 5 (1994) 874–902.
7.  Su, C.-C., Shin, K. G.: Adaptive Deadlock-Free Routing in Multicomputers Using Only One Extra Virtual Channel. Proc. 22nd Int'l Conf. on Parallel Processing, Vol. I (1993) 227–231.
8.  Boura, Y. M., Das, C. R.: Efficient Fully Adaptive Wormhole Routing in $n$-Dimensional Meshes. Proc. 14th Int'l Conf. on Distributed Computing Systems (1994) 589–596.
9.  Dally, W. J.: Performance Analysis of $k$-ary $n$-cube Interconnection Networks. IEEE Trans. on Computers, Vol. 39, No. 6 (1990) 775–785.
10. Glass, C. J., Ni, L. M.: Adaptive Routing in Mesh-Connected Networks. Proc. 1992 Int'l Conf. on Distributed Computing Systems (1992) 12–19

# An Ad Hoc On-Demand Routing Protocol with Alternate Routes

Hsi-Shu Wang and Chiu-Kuo Liang

Department of Computer Science and Information Engineering
Chung Hua University
Hsinchu, Taiwan 30067, Republic of China
ckliang@chu.edu.tw

**Abstract.** Because of node mobility and power limitations, the network topology changes frequently. Routing protocols plays an important role in the ad hoc network. A recent trend in ad hoc network routing is the reactive on-demand philosophy where routes are established only when required. In this paper, we propose a scheme to improve existing on-demand routing protocols by creating a mesh and multiple alternate routes by overhearing the data packet transmission. Our scheme establishes the mesh and alternate routes without transmitting any extra control message. We apply our scheme to the Ad-hoc On-Demand Distance Vector (AODV) protocol and evaluate the performance improvements by ns-2 simulations.

## 1   Introduction

A "mobile ad hoc network" (MANET) [1] is an autonomous system of mobile routers (and associated hosts) connected by wireless links. Ad hoc networks consist of hosts communicating one another with portable radios. These networks can be deployed impromptly without any wired base station or infrastructure support. In ad hoc mobile networks, routes are mainly multihop because of the limited radio propagation range, and topology changes frequently and unpredictably since each network host moves randomly. Therefore, routing is an integral part of ad hoc communications, and has received interests from many researchers. The key challenge here is to be able to route with low overheads even in dynamic conditions. Overhead here is defined in terms of the routing protocol control messages which consume both channel bandwidth as well as the battery power of nodes for communication.

On-demand routing protocols build and maintain only needed routes to reduce routing overheads. Examples include Ad Hoc On-Demand Distance Vector (AODV) [2, 3], Dynamic Source Routing (DSR) [4, 5], and Temporally Ordered Routing Algorithm (TORA) [6]. This is in contrast to proactive protocols (e.g., Destination Sequenced Distance Vector (DSDV) [7]) that maintain routes between all node pairs all the time. In on-demand protocols, a route discovery process (typically via a network-wide flood) is initiated whenever a route is needed. Each node in on-demand routing does not need periodic route table update exchange and does not have a full topological view of the network. Network hosts maintain route table entries only to destinations that they communicate with.

In this paper, we propose an algorithm that utilizes a mesh structure to provide multiple alternate paths to the Ad Hoc On-Demand Distance Vector (AODV) protocol

M. Guo and L.T.Yang (Eds.): ISPA 2003, LNCS 2745, pp. 100–111, 2003.
© Springer-Verlag Berlin Heidelberg 2003

that is one of the on-demand routing algorithms. We construct the mesh structure without producing additional control messages by overhearing the data packet transmission. Since an ad hoc network has limited bandwidth and shared wireless medium, it is critical to minimize the number of packet transmissions. It is beneficial to have multiple alternate paths in MANET due to the wireless networks are prone to route breaks resulting from node mobility, fading environment, single interference, high error rate, and packet collisions.

The rest of the paper is organized as follows. In Section 2, we review the AODV protocol. Section 3 illustrates the protocol operation in detail. Performance evaluation using the ns-2 simulator is presented in Section 4 and concluding remarks are made in Section 5.

## 2  Ad Hoc On-Demand Distance Vector Routing

The Ad Hoc On-Demand Distance Vector (AODV) routing protocol described in [2, 3] is built on the DSDV [7] algorithm previously described. AODV is an improvement on DSDV because it typically minimizes the number of required broadcasts by creating routes on a demand basis, as opposed to maintaining a complete list of routes in the DSDV algorithm. The authors of AODV classify it as a pure on-demand route acquisition system, since nodes that are not on a selected path do not maintain routing information or participate in routing table exchanges.

### 2.1  Construction of AODV

When a source node desires to send a message to a destination node and does not already have a valid route to that destination, it initiates a path discovery process to locate the destination node. It broadcasts a route request (RREQ) packet to its neighbors, which then forward the request to their neighbor, and so on, until either the destination or an intermediate node with a "fresh enough" route to the destination is located. AODV utilizes destination sequence numbers to ensure all routes are loop-free and contain the most recent route information. Each node maintains its own sequence number, as well as a broadcast ID. The broadcast ID is incremented for every RREQ initiated by the node, and together with the node's IP address to uniquely identify an RREQ. Intermediate nodes can reply to the RREQ only if they have a route to the destination whose corresponding destination sequence number is greater than or equal to that contained in the RREQ.

During the process of forwarding the RREQ, intermediate nodes record in their route tables the address of the neighbor from which the first copy of the broadcast packet is received which can be used in establishing a reverse path. If additional copies of the same RREQ are later received, these packets are discarded. Once the RREQ reaches the destination or an intermediate node with a fresh enough route, the destination/intermediate node responds by unicasting a route reply (RREP) packet back to the neighbors from which it first received the RREQ. As the RREP is routed back along the reverse path, the nodes along this path will set up the forward route entries in the route tables, which are pointing to the node from which the RREP came. These forward route entries indicate the active forward route. Associated with each route entry a route timer is set up in order to delete the entry if it is not used within the specified lifetime. Since the RREP is forwarded along the path established by the RREQ, AODV only supports the use of symmetric links. Figure 1 shows the process of AODV route discovery.

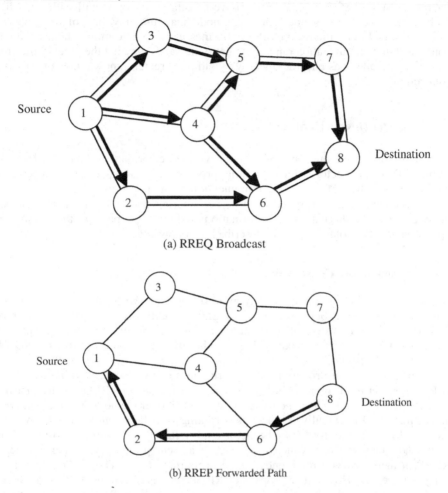

(a) RREQ Broadcast

(b) RREP Forwarded Path

**Fig. 1.** AODV route discovery

## 2.2   Maintenance

Routes are maintained as follows. If a source node moves, it is able to reinitiate the route discovery protocol in order to find a new route to the destination. If a node along the route moves, its upstream neighbor will notice the move and propagate a link failure notification message to each of its active upstream neighbors to inform them of the erasure of that part of the route [18]. These nodes in turn propagate the link failure notification to their upstream neighbors, and so on until the source node is reached. The source node may then choose to reinitiate route discovery for that destination if a route is still desired.

An additional aspect of the protocol is the use of hello messages, periodic local broadcasts by a node to inform each mobile node of other nodes in its neighborhood. Hello messages can be used to maintain the local connectivity of a node. Nodes listen for retransmission of data packets to ensure that the next hop is still within reach. If such a retransmission is not heard, the node may use any one of a number of techniques, including the reception of hello messages, to determine whether the next hop is within communication range. The hello messages may list the other nodes from which a mobile has heard, thereby yielding greater knowledge of network connectivity.

# 3    The Proposed Protocol

The main purpose of our study is to improve the performance of the Ad Hoc On-Demand Distance Vector (AODV) routing protocol. Therefore, we take advantage of the broadcast nature of wireless communications; a node promiscuously "overhears" data packets that are transmitted by their neighboring nodes. From these packets, a node can obtain alternate path information and become part of the mesh. The operation details of our scheme are described as follows.

## 3.1    Primary Route Construction

Our algorithm does not require any modification to the AODV's route request propagation process, but instead we slightly modify the AODV's route reply procedure. We add a value called the number of *hops to destination* (HTD), which is a loose upper bound of the maximal hops to the given destination, into each *ROUTE REPLY* (RREP) packet.

At the beginning of primary route construction, source $S$ sends *ROUTE REQUEST* (RREQ) packet to all its neighbors. Every host that receives RREQ for the first time does the same as well. Thus, the RREQ will flood all over the network, and will arrive at destination $D$ eventually (if there is a routing path between $S$ and $D$). When $D$ receives REEQ packet for the first time, it sends a RREP back with a zero-value HTD to the host (say $P$) from which the RREQ was sent previously. When $P$ receives RREP, it then creates a route entry for $D$ in its route table. The HTD value of that entry is increased. Host $P$ then propagates RREP, with HTD, to the host from which $P$ receives RREQ for the first time. Every other host receiving RREP will do the same thing as $P$ does. Figure 2 shows the process of primary route construction.

## 3.2    Alternate Route Construction

The alternate routes are established during the route data delivery phase. We slightly modify data delivery phase to accomplish the task. Taking advantage of the broadcast nature of wireless communications, a node promiscuously "overhears" packets that transmitted by their neighboring nodes. In data delivery phase, we insert a HTD field into common header of data packet. The field can help us to establish a right direction of the alternate route. From these packets, a node obtains alternate path information and becomes part of the mesh as follows. When a node that is not part of the primary

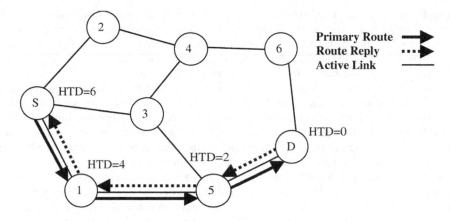

**Fig. 2.** Primary route construction

route overhears a data packet not directed to it transmitted by a neighbor on the primary route, it does the update alternate route procedure. If there is no alternate route entry or the HTD of data packet is smaller than route entry than it record that neighbor as the next hop to the destination and the HTD in its alternate route entry. By the update alternate route procedure, the nodes that overhear the data packets sending from the nodes on the primary route can choose the smallest HTD among them to update. Nodes that have an entry to the destination in their alternate route table are part of the mesh. The primary route and alternate route together establish a mesh structure (see Figure 3).

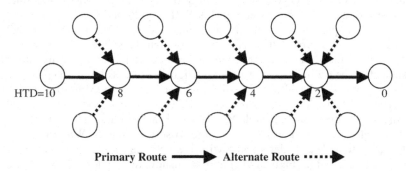

**Fig. 3.** Structure of primary route and alternate route

### 3.3    Route Maintenance

When a node detects a link break, it changes the common header of data packet to make it forward by the mesh node that not on the primary route. After that the node performs a one-hop data broadcast to its immediate neighbors. Neighbor nodes that receive this data packet unicast the data packet to their next hop node only if they have an entry for the destination in their alternate route tables and the HTD in it is smaller than that in the data packet. By this way, data packets can be delivered through one or more alternate routes and will not be dropped when route breaks occur. In order to prevent packet from tracing a loop, every mesh node will forward the data packet only if the packet is not a duplicate and they have the alternate route entry with a smaller HTD than that in the data packet. When a node of the primary route receives the data packet from alternate routes, it operates normally and forwards the packet to its next hop when the packet is not a duplicate. The node that detected the link break also sends a ROUTE ERROR (RERR) packet to the source to initiate a route rediscovery. Due to the purpose of our goal is to build a fresh and optimal route that reflects the current network situation and topology; we reconstruct a new route instead of continuously using the alternate paths. This is also the reason why we choose to overhear the data packet to construct the alternate routes.

A route is timed out when it is not used and updated for certain duration of time in AODV routing protocol. We apply the same technique in our scheme to purge the alternate routes. Nodes that can overhear data packet transmitted through the primary route add or update the alternate route and set up or update it's expire time. If an alternate route is not updated its expired time during the timeout interval, the node removes the path from the alternate route table. In AODV, each RREQ packet has a unique identifier so that nodes can detect and drop duplicate RREQ packets. Our protocol uses this method to help nodes drop duplicate data packets.

## 3.4 Example

We use Figure 4 as an example to show how the mesh and alternate routes are constructed by overhear technique and used in data delivery. When the RREQ reaches the destination node D, the primary route Ⓢ–①–②–③–Ⓓ is selected. Figure 4(a) show that the destination D set its HTD value to 0 and sends a RREP with increased HTD value 2 to node 3. After receiving this RREP, only node 3 relays the packet to node 2 since it is part of the route. Node 3 also increases the HTD value before it relays the packet. See Figure 4(b). The other node on the select primary route do the same thing until the RREP packet reach the source node S. Figure 4(c) shows the HTD state after the primary route was build. Figures 4(d), 4(e) and 4(f) show how the nodes 4 and 5 build the alternate while the data packet transmitting through the primary route. When node S sends the data packet to node 1, nodes 4 and 5, who are within the propagation range of node S, will overhear the data packet but do nothing, since it is useless to record an alternate route to source node S. While node 1 relays the data packet to node 2, nodes 4 and 5 will overhear the packet and add an entry into their alternate route table. Figures 4(g) and 4(h) show that nodes 6 and 7 will add an entry when node 2 forwards the data packet to node 3. Figure 4(i) and 4(j) illustrate that nodes 6 and 7 update their route entry since node 3 has a smaller HTD value than their alternate route entries. Besides, nodes 8 and 9 will insert a route entry in their alternate route table. It seems that the alternate route in nodes 8 and 9 is useless. Figure 4(k) explains the usage of the alternate routes record in nodes 8 and 9. If the link between nodes 2 and 3 is broken and nodes 6 and 7 are moved out of the propagation range of node 3, node 8 will be moved into the propagation range of node 2 and node 3. We can find an alternate route to salvage the data packets, which is shown in Figure 4(l). Notice that the alternate route will be updated when any data packet transmission can be overheard. It makes our alternate route reflects the current network situation and topology.

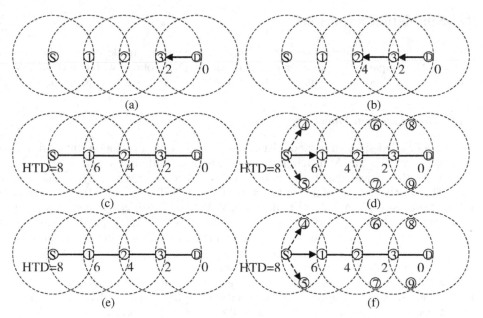

**Fig. 4.** (a)-(f)

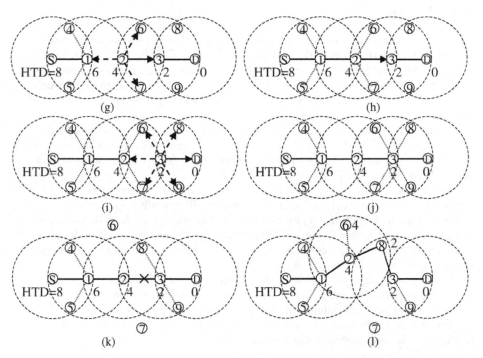

**Fig. 4.** (g)-(l)

# 4    Simulation Experiments

In this section, we evaluate the performance improvements made by our alternate routing. We compare the simulation results of the AODV protocol with that of AODV protocol that applied our scheme as AODV-AR (AODV with Alternate Routes).

## 4.1    The Simulation Model

We use a detailed simulation model based on ns-2[8] in our evaluation. In the recent papers[9, 12, 13], the Monarch research simulation multihop wireless networks complete with physical, data link, and medium access control (MAC) layer models on ns-2. The Distributed Coordination Function (DCF) of IEEE 802.11 [10] for wireless LANs is used as the MAC layer protocol. The radio model uses characteristics similar to a commercial radio interface, such as Lucent's WaveLAN [11]. WaveLAN is modeled as a shared-media radio with a nominal bit rate of 2Mb/s and a nominal radio range of 250m. A detailed description of the simulation environment and the models is available in [8, 9] and will not be discussed here.

The RREQ packets are treated as broadcast packets in the MAC. RREP and data packets are all unicast packets with a specified neighbor as the MAC destination. RERR packets are treated broadcast in AODV. Detect link breaks using feedback from the MAC layer. A signal is sent to the routing layer when the MAC layer fails to deliver an unicast packet to the next hop. No additional network layer mechanism such as hello messages [2] is used.

Both protocols maintain a send buffer of 64 packets. It contains all data packets waiting for a route, such as packets for which route discovery has started, but no reply has arrived yet. All packets (both data and routing) sent by the routing layer are queued at the interface queue until the MAC layer can transmit them. The interface queue has a maximum size of 50 packets and is maintained as a priority queue with two priorities each served in FIFO order. Routing packets get higher priority than data packets.

We use traffic and mobility models similar to those previously reported using the same simulator [9, 12, 13]. A traffic generator was developed to simulate continuous bit rate (CBR) sources. The source-destination pairs are spread randomly over the network. The size of data payload was 512-byte.

We use two mobility models, which use the random waypoint model [9] in a rectangular field. In the first experiment model, 50 mobile nodes move around a rectangle region of 1500 meters by 300 meters. The second model, 100 mobile nodes move around a rectangle region of 2200 meters by 600 meters. Each node randomly selects a location, and moves toward that location with a speed uniformly distributed between 0-20 m/s.

Once the location is reached, another random location is targeted after a pause. We vary the pause time, which affects the relative speeds of the mobiles. Simulations are run for 100 s. Each data point represents an average of 100 runs with identical traffic models, but different randomly generated mobility scenarios. Identical mobility and traffic scenarios are used across protocols.

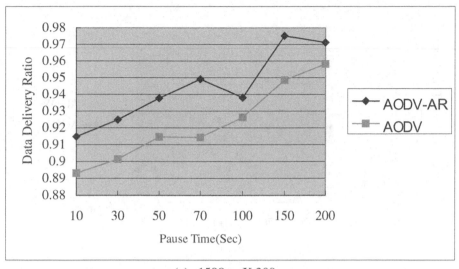

(a)  1500 m X 300 m

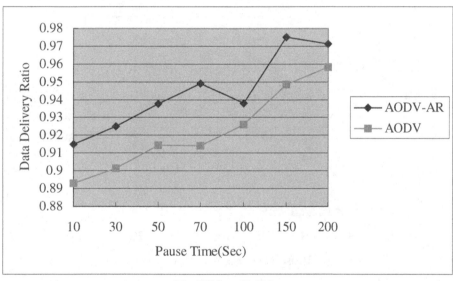

(b)  2200 m X 600 m

**Fig. 5.** Data packet delivery rate

## 4.2    Performance Results

Figure 5 shows the throughput in packet delivery ratio. The ratio of the data packets delivered to the destination to this generated by the CBR source. Our scheme improves the throughput performance of AODV. We use seven different pause times

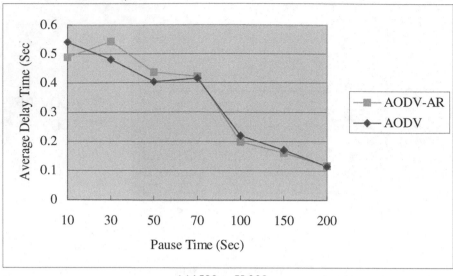

(a)1500 m X 300 m

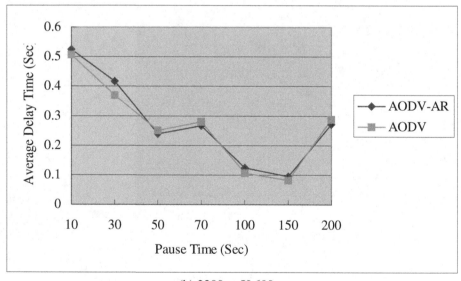

(b) 2200 m X 600 m

**Fig. 6.** Average Delay time

from 10 sec to 200 sec to measure the influence of mobility. As the pause time gets shorter, the performance gain by alternate routes becomes more significant. Our protocol is able to deliver more packets to the destination than AODV. AODV try to repair the primary route by send RREQ packet while the node is closer to destination node than source node. After a period of time if the node don't get RREP packet the node will drop the data packet. Alternate paths may be broken as well as the primary route because of mobility. Moreover, packets can be lost because of collisions and contention problems.

Average end-to-end delay of data packets – This includes all possible delays caused by buffering during route discovery latency, queuing at the interface queue, retransmission delays at the MAC, and propagation and transfer times. Fig.6 shows the simulation result. We can find out that at some time AODV-AR has smaller average delay time than AODV. The reason is that AODV try to recover the primary route at the node that near destination, it will cost the time to wait the RREP packet to be sent back from the destination. If our protocol salvages the data packet successfully and AODV fails to recovery the primary route, then the packet's delay time of our protocol will be less than that of AODV.

## 5    Conclusion

We presented a scheme take advantage of the broadcast nature of wireless communications to build alternate route without any yield any extra overhead. Our scheme can be incorporated into any ad hoc on-demand unicast routing protocol to improve reliable packet delivery in the face of node movements and route breaks.

In the future, we may try to repair the primary route with alternate route which we build by overhear. In this thesis, the node of main route goes through another node of main route by using backup route only one hop. If we can increase it to two hops or more, then the backup route should be more reliable.

## References

1.    J. Macker and S. Corson, "Mobile Ad Hoc Networks (MANET)," IETF WG Charter., http://www.ietf.org/html.charters/manet-charter.htm, 1997.
2.    C. E. Perkins and E. M. Royer, "Ad Hoc On-demand Distance Vector Routing," Proc. 2nd IEEE Wksp. Mobile Comp. Sys. And Apps., Feb.1999, pp.90–100.
3.    C. E. Perkins, E. M. Royer and S. R. Das, "Ad Hoc On-demand Distance Vector (AODV) Routing," IETF, Internet Draft, draft-ietf-manet-aodv-11.txt , June. 2002.
4.    D. Johnson and D. Maltz, "Dynamic Source Routing in Ad Hoc Wireless Networks," T. lmielinski and H. Korth, Eds. Mobile Computing, Ch. 5, Kluwer, 1996.
5.    D. Johnson, Dave Maltz, Y Hu, Jorjeta Jetcheva, "The Dynamic Source Routing Protocol for Mobile Ad Hoc Networks (DSR)," IETF, Internet Draft, draft-ietf-manet-dsr-07.txt, February. 2002.
6.    M. S. Corson and V. D. Park, "Temporally Ordered Routing Algorithm (TORA) version 1: Functional specification," Internet-Draft, draft-ietf-manet-tora-spec-00.txt, Nov.1997.
7.    C. E. Perkins and P. Bhagwat, "Highly Dynamic Destination-Sequenced Distance-Vector Routing (DSDV) for Mobile Computers," *ACM SIGCOMM '94*, pp. 234–244.
8.    Kevin Fall and Kannan Varadhan, editors. ns notes and documentation, The VINT Project, UC Berkeley, LBL, USC/ISI, and Xerox PARC, November 1999. Available from http://www-mash.cs.berkeley.edu/ns/.
9.    J. Broch et al., "A Performance Comparison of Multihop Wireless Ad Hoc Network Routing Protocols," Proc. IEEE/ACM MOBICOM '98, Oct. 1998, pp.85–97.
10.   IEEE, "Wireless LAN Medium Access Control (MAC) and Physical Layer (PHY) Specifications," IEEE Std. 802.11-1997, 1997.
11.   B. Tuch, "Development of WaveLAN, an ISM Band Wireless LAN," *AT&T Tech.* J., vol. 72, no. 4, July/Aug 1993. pp. 27–33.

12. E. M. Royer and C-K Toh, "A Review of Current Routing Protocols for Ad Hoc Mobile Wireless Networks," *IEEE Personal Communication*, pp. 46–55, 1999.
13. C. E. Perkins, E. M. Royer, S. R. Das, and M. K. Marina, "Performance Comparison of Two On-Demand Routing Protocols for Ad Hoc Networks," *IEEE Personal Communications*, Feb. 2001.
14. S. Murthy and J. J. Garcia-Luna-Aceves, "A routing protocol for packet radio networks, " *ACM MOBICOM*, 1995, pp. 86–94.
15. S. Corson and J. Macker, "Mobile Ad hoc Networking (MANET):Routing Protocol Performance Issues and Evaluation Considerations," IETF, Internet Draft,http://www.ietf.org/rfc/rfc2501.txt, Jan. 1999

# Design of a Viable Fault-Tolerant Routing Strategy for Optical-Based Grids

Peter K.K. Loh and W.J. Hsu

School of Computer Engineering
Nanyang Technological University
Nanyang Avenue, Singapore 639798
{askkloh,hsu}@ntu.edu.sg

**Abstract.** This paper proposes and analyses a cost-effective fault-tolerant routing strategy for optical-based grid networks. We present the design of a fully adaptive, fault-tolerant routing strategy for multi-hop grid networks based on wavelength-division multiplexing. The routing strategy is both deadlock-free and livelock-free. Regardless of the number and type of faults and size of the grid network, only three buffer sets and two routing tables of size $O(d)$ are required at each node, where $d$ is the grid dimension. In the absence of faults, minimal paths with the least congestion are chosen to minimise latency. In the presence of faults or congestion, misrouting is selectively constrained to prevent livelock. The routing strategy requires only local fault information at each node, and does not require component redundancy or the isolation of healthy nodes and channels.

**Keywords:** Fault-tolerant routing, wavelength-division multiplexing, grid networks, deadlock-freedom, livelock-freedom

## 1 Introduction

In recent years, there has been increased interest in fault tolerance issues in optical-based parallel processing systems [1,5-6,8,10-11,18]. Optical-based parallel processing systems are networked multiprocessor systems with communication channels that may be implemented with optical technology. Current optical technology constrains the number of available wavelengths and tunability of optical transceivers, making it difficult to establish a completely optical communications path between every possible pair of communicating nodes in a large-scale, single-hop *all-optical networks* (*AONs*) [3,7,9,16-17]. In multi-hop networks, a more practical approach therefore incorporates wavelength conversion/amplification at intermediate nodes along a communication path [18]. Technological advances in the past decade have since made available physically smaller devices with increased optoelectronic conversion efficiency and lower power consumption [17]. A few interesting fault-tolerant routing strategies have recently been proposed for multi-hop networks using Wavelength Division Multiplexing (*WDM*) [1,5,10-11,18]. In *WDM* systems, communications on different optical wavelengths may be multiplexed onto an optical fiber. Corresponding de-multiplexing is then performed at the receiving node.

In Bandyopadhyay et al. [1], a fault-tolerant routing scheme is proposed for multi-hop networks. Here, each source-destination path is pre-computed to ensure that final

M. Guo and L.T.Yang (Eds.): ISPA 2003, LNCS 2745, pp. 112–126, 2003.
© Springer-Verlag Berlin Heidelberg 2003

delivery of the message is guaranteed in the presence of faults. All established paths are thus deadlock-free and livelock-free. To minimise communication overheads, an upper bound for the path setup time is specified, exceeding which the communication is considered blocked. Dynamic faults that occur during path establishment can be tolerated. In this strategy, it is required that each fault-free node and its associated router know the routing path to every other node when the network is fault-free. This may result in a node maintaining complex routing tables that are not cost-effective with increase in network size. Additionally, each fault-free router also maintains a queue of messages received over a control channel. The control channel is used for path establishment and transmission of fault information. This inevitably necessitates a consideration of fault tolerance issues for the control channel.

Fault-tolerant routing for optical-based, ring networks has been proposed by Gerstel et al. [5], in which a single fault can be tolerated and alternate routing may be determined statically. When routing is blocked in a specified direction, rerouting is simply invoked in the opposite direction. In more complex networks, however, a set of heuristics to provide some adaptivity is required to cope with faults.

Lalwaney and Koren [10-11] have proposed a fault-tolerant scheme that tolerates faulty links. The fault model here assumes that a link failure is caused by an optical transmitter and/or receiver failure. In this scheme, it is assumed that every node has at least one fault-free tunable transmitter and receiver that can tune to the transmitting and receiving wavelengths of all channels of that node. In the event of a transmitter failure, the fault-free tunable transmitter alternately switches between its normal operating frequency to that of the failed transmitter. Both communication streams are time-multiplexed onto a given link. Using tunable transmitters and receivers essentially enables logical reconfiguration of the network topology to bypass the link faults. However, contemporary transmitters have limited tuning range that restricts the types of logical topologies that can be supported [3, 17].

In Shen et al. [18], a fault-tolerant routing strategy has been proposed for multi-hop, optoelectronic *WDM*-networks of node connectivity $(f + 1)$. Up to $f$ channel faults may be tolerated provided faults occur before path establishment. This routing model uses a combination of circuit switching to reserve communication paths and packet switching to physically transmit the messages along these paths. The fault-tolerant routing strategy can handle both optical channel and wavelength conversion faults. Faults that are known before the routing stage, after finding the communication path or after path establishment but before transmission, can be tolerated. However, the strategy requires preprocessing to locate alternate paths during path finding, which increases communication overheads. Despite this, dynamic faults that occur during message transmission are not tolerated as in [12]. Finally, there are no specified mechanisms to tolerate node (processor) failures.

The challenge then is to design a fault-tolerant optical-based routing strategy with the following desired properties:

- For reliability, the strategy should tolerate component (both node and link) faults that may occur not only before but also during message transmission.
- For efficiency, minimal or no preprocessing should be employed. Alternate paths for rerouting should, preferably, be computed "on the fly".
- For cost-effectiveness, existing optical transmitters/receivers should be exploited during the absence and presence of faults with no component redundancy. Local (nearest neighbour) fault information should be used with low complexity routing

information that scale slowly with network size. Towards these objectives, the use of communication- and space-efficient schemes [4,14] becomes an important consideration.

In this section, we propose a fault-tolerant routing strategy for multi-hop *WDM*-based 3-dimensional grid networks, such as [13,15,19], with the following properties:

- Adaptive and tolerant to both node and link faults
- Fault detection and handling are performed locally at each node
- Routing strategy is both deadlock-free and livelock-free
- A node maintains 3 buffer sets and 2 size $O(d)$ routing tables, $d$ is node degree
- Spare optical transmitters/receivers are not required
- No computation/broadcast of additional information for table updates is needed

The rest of the paper is organised as follows. Section 2 introduces the terminology and notations used in subsequent sections. The design of the routing model is discussed in Section 3 while section 4 details the proofs for routing properties. Section 5 evaluates and compares its performance. Section 6 concludes the paper.

## 2   Preliminaries

A 3-dimensional multi-hop grid (3-D grid) is an $m_0$ by $m_1$ by $m_2$ network containing $N = \prod_{i=0}^{2} m_i$ nodes. Each node, with coordinates $(x, y, z)$, may be addressed as $i = (z* m_0* m_1 + x* m_1 + y)$, where $0 \leq i < N$. Each node along a dimension $d$ of the grid, may represent a system that comprises a sub-network, and is interfaced to a bi-directional optical link (fiber). Each optical link along a dimension $d$ may be viewed directionally. If the optical link is interfaced to any two nodes along dimension $d$, $V_a = (a_2, a_1, a_0)$ and $V_b = (b_2, b_1, b_0)$, we denote the direction along dimension $d$ as $F_d$, when $b_d > a_d$ or as $B_d$, when $a_d > b_d$. Finally, each optical link is comprised of multiple channels, with each channel supporting transmission at a unique frequency optical $\lambda$. Contemporary technology enables support for 128 different optical frequencies per fiber [3].

## 3   Design of the Routing Strategy

In this section, we discuss the design of the routing strategy. We start off with the design of a set of space-efficient routing tables [12]. These tables make use of a variation of the compact labelling scheme known as interval labelling [20].

### 3.1 Node and Link Labelling Schemes

Nodes and associated links of regular networks like grids can be labelled based on a modified interval labelling scheme for adaptive routing. In an interval labelling scheme (*ILS*), the links of each node may be labelled with an interval, such that the collections of interval sets at any node are disjoint. Messages can only be routed over the link associated with an interval containing the destination address. That is, a link labelled with the interval $[a, b)$ can be used to route messages to destination nodes $\{a, a+1, a+2, \ldots, b\text{-}1\}$. To illustrate the modified ILS for adaptive routing, we exemplify the approach with a 4 by 3 by 2 grid, as shown in Figure 1. Table 1 shows the ILS A for the 3-D grid, where $B_d$ and $F_d$ $(d = 0, 1, 2)$ represent the backward and forward directions, respectively, along dimension $d$ of the grid and $\setminus$ is the modulus operator.

Assume that the message at node $i$ is destined for node $v$. Then, $f(v) = v \setminus m_0$ is computed and the interval associated with a $B_0$ or $F_0$ link is first determined. Depending on which interval $f(v)$ falls within, the message is then routed via $B_0$ or $F_0$ to the correct dim1-dim2 plane. If $f(v)$ does not fall into an interval, then $v$ is in the same dim1-dim2 plane as the source node. In the second phase, $g(v) = v \setminus (m_0 m_1)$ is computed and compared to intervals assigned to links in dimensions 1 and 2. The message destined for $v$ will be routed along the $B_1$ or $F_1$ channel until it reaches the correct row of the destination. Finally, $v$ is compared and the message is routed along $B_2$ or $F_2$ to reach the destination node. The bold arrows in Figure 1 show the message path taken from source node 0 to destination node 23 using the ILS A.

**Table 1.** ILS A for 3-D Grids

| Direction | Interval |
|:---:|:---|
| $B_0$ | $[0, i \setminus m_0)$ |
| $F_0$ | $[(i + 1) \setminus m_0, m_0)$ |
| $B_1$ | $[0, m_0 * \lfloor i / m_0 \rfloor)$ |
| $F_1$ | $[m_0 + m_0 * \lfloor (i \setminus m_0 m_1) / m_0 \rfloor, m_0 m_1)$ |
| $B_2$ | $[0, \lfloor i / m_0 m_1 \rfloor * m_0 m_1)$ |
| $F_2$ | $[\lfloor i / m_0 m_1 \rfloor * m_0 m_1 + m_0 m_1, m_0 m_1 m_2)$ |

ILS A defines a minimal path between any two clusters and the routing is in increasing dimension order. Hence, the routing is minimal, deadlock-free and livelock-free in the absence of faults and congestion [2]. In a grid, however, routing can be either in increasing or decreasing dimension order. ILS A, which defines increasing dimension-order routing, determines one path for routing. To handle component faults and congestion, the routing strategy must be able to exploit alternative paths. An alternative ILS B for decreasing dimension-order routing is defined in Table 2 for the grid in Figure 1.

ILS B is used in a similar way to ILS A. If the source and destination nodes are not on the same plane, the message is first routed along $B_2$ or $F_2$ towards the correct dim0-dim1 destination plane. On the destination plane, the destination address $v$ is compared to the intervals assigned to links in dimensions 1 and 0. Once the message has arrived at the same row as its destination via $B_1$ or $F_1$, the message is routed to its destination via $B_0$ or $F_0$. ILS B thus defines decreasing dimension-order routing. An example applying *ILS B* is shown in Figure 1. Dotted arrows represent the message path.

**Table 2.** ILS B for 3-D Grids

| Direction | Interval |
|---|---|
| $B_0$ | $[m_0 * \lfloor i/m_0 \rfloor, i)$ |
| $F_0$ | $[i+1, m_0 + m_0 * \lfloor i/m_0 \rfloor)$ |
| $B_1$ | $[\lfloor i/m_0 m_1 \rfloor * m_0 m_1, m_0 * \lfloor i/m_0 \rfloor)$ |
| $F_1$ | $[m_0 + m_0 * \lfloor i/m_0 \rfloor, \lfloor i/m_0 m_1 \rfloor * m_0 m_1 + m_0 m_1)$ |
| $B_2$ | $[0, \lfloor i/m_0 m_1 \rfloor * m_0 m_1)$ |
| $F_2$ | $[\lfloor i/m_0 m_1 \rfloor * m_0 m_1 + m_0 m_1, m_0 m_1 m_2)$ |

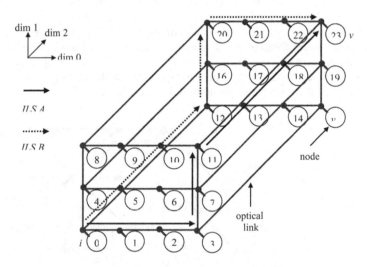

**Fig. 1.** Paths determined by ILS A & B

### 3.2 Wavelength Allocation Scheme

In this section, we describe the wavelength allocation scheme that assigns optical frequencies for reception to each node. That is, a node assigned with an optical frequency of $\lambda$ receives data destined for it on this frequency. To minimise the number of frequencies to be allocated and indirectly the amount of optical fibre, we cyclically shift the allocated frequencies. In this way, each group of nodes are allocated "unique" frequencies for data reception along a given network dimension. This scheme is adapted from a similar one used by Louri et al [15] for hypercubes. Specifically, the number of unique optical frequencies to be assigned is $W = \max (m_0, m_1, m_2)$ for an $m_0$ by $m_1$ by $m_2$ grid network. Assign optical frequencies $\{\lambda_0, \lambda_1, \ldots, \lambda_{W-1}\}$

to nodes of row 0 of dimension $d$, $\{v_0, v_1, ..., v_{W-1}\}$ respectively, where $d$ is the grid dimension with $W$ nodes. Subsequently, assign $\{\lambda_1, \lambda_2, ..., \lambda_{W-1}, \lambda_0\}$ to nodes of the next row of dimension $d$, and so on. For the next plane of nodes along an orthogonal dimension, assign optical frequencies $\{\lambda_1, \lambda_2, ..., \lambda_{W-1}, \lambda_0\}$ to nodes of row 0, and $\{\lambda_2, \lambda_3, ..., \lambda_{W-1}, \lambda_0, \lambda_1\}$ to nodes of the next row, and so on. Figure 2 illustrates the wavelength assignment for the $4 \times 3 \times 2$ grid network. Since ILS A or B routes messages along an optical link in dimension order, the optical reception frequency of an intermediate node along each dimension must be determined before routing takes place along that dimension. Consider source node, $u$, at location $(a, b, c)$ and destination node, $v$, at location $(x, y, z)$. The optical reception frequency index at $v$ can be computed from the source frequency index $\phi(u)$ by function $F$ as follows:

$$F : \phi(u) \rightarrow \phi(v),$$

where

$$F(\phi(u)) = (\phi(u) + (x - a) + (y - b) + (z - c)) \bmod W$$

Note that the wavelength allocation scheme is independent of the routing scheme used. The same optical frequency assignment would apply to the network regardless of whether the routing is based on *ILS A* or *ILS B*. It will become apparent later that the wavelength allocation scheme is also independent of the fault pattern. In the next section, we present the buffer allocation model at each node.

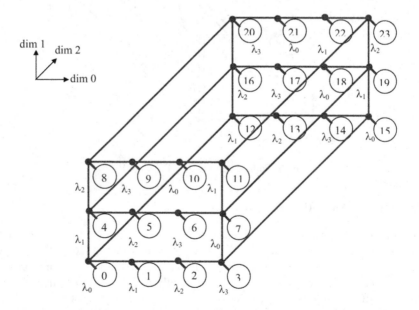

**Fig. 2.** Wavelength Allocation for 4 x 3 x 2 Grid

### 3.3 The Buffer Allocation Model

In this section, we present the buffer allocation model at each node. For a 3-D grid, there are a maximum of 6 input and output ports at each node as illustrated in Figure 3. Each input port comprises an optical demultiplexer that channels incoming optical frequencies into the $W$ opto-electronic receivers. Each receiver is tuned to a specific frequency and converts that frequency into a corresponding electronic signal. Each output port comprises $W$ opto-electronic transmitters, each of which converts an input electronic signal into a specified optical frequency. A transmitter may be tuned to transmit at more than one frequency. An optical multiplexer then combines up to $W$ different optical frequencies for transmission on the associated optical fiber. The electronic switch between the IO ports is responsible for the routing function, $R_{xy}$, where $x$ and $y$ denote input and output ports, respectively.

Figure 3 shows that there are three input buffers ($IB_{0i}$, $IB_{1i}$, and $IB_{2i}$) associated with each input port $i$ and three output buffers ($OB_{0j}$, $OB_{1j}$, and $OB_{2j}$) associated with each output port $j$. The number of buffer sets allocated is always three and is independent of the size and dimension of the grid network. Each buffer set supports communications in a specified direction. Messages in buffer set 0 have the most flexibility, being able to bi-directionally traverse a route along any grid dimension. Messages in buffer set 0 can also switch over to either buffer sets 1 or 2 when certain network or traffic conditions arise. Messages in buffer sets 1 and 2, however, are constrained to route in specified directions. In addition, messages in buffer set 1 are prohibited from using buffer set 2 and vice versa. These constraints are necessary to permit full adaptivity and prevent deadlock as will be proven in the next section. Finally, the injection buffer, $INJB$, holds new packets generated by the local CPU and the delivery buffer, $DB$, holds packets for consumption by the local CPU.

With this design, we are effectively dividing the physical interconnection network into three logical networks, $L_0, L_1$ and $L_2$ as illustrated in Figure 4. $L_0$ is connected with $L_1$ and $L_2$ through logical links whereas $L_1$ and $L_2$ are disconnected. There are at most three logical links for each bi-directional optical link (fiber). The logical links share the bandwidth of the fiber.

### 3.4 The Fault-Tolerant Routing Algorithm

Here, we present the fault-tolerant routing algorithm, **FTRoute**, in two parts: **AdaptiveRoute** and **LogicalRoute**. Let the locations of the source, current and destination nodes to be at $(x_s, y_s, z_s)$, $(x_c, y_c, z_c)$, and $(x_d, y_d, z_d)$, respectively. For a buffer $B$, $size(B)$ is the total number of places in the buffer and $hold(B)$ denotes the number of places that are currently occupied by a message. At each node, given the input port and buffer, and the message's destination node, the routing function $R$ specifies the output buffer and port to which the message may be moved. The routing function is defined as $R_{ij} : (i, p) \rightarrow (j, q)$ where $i$ and $j$ are the input and output ports, respectively, $0 \leq i, j < 6$ (for a 3-D grid), $p$ and $q$ are the buffer indices at the previous and current nodes, respectively, with $p, q \in \{0, 1, 2\}$. We assume fail-stop faults. The failure of an optical receiver may be assumed to be detected at the sending opto-electronic transmitter [11,18]. Thus, a faulty receiver may be treated as a faulty transmitter for analysis purposes (see Section 4).

***Definition of Dimension Reversal, DR*** **:** The dimension reversal number, *DR*, of a message is the number of times a message has been routed from a dimension $m$ to a neighbouring node in a lower dimension, $n < m$. Essentially, *DR* is used to control the extent of misrouting or non-minimal routing that the message undergoes. *DR* is assigned to each message header as follows:

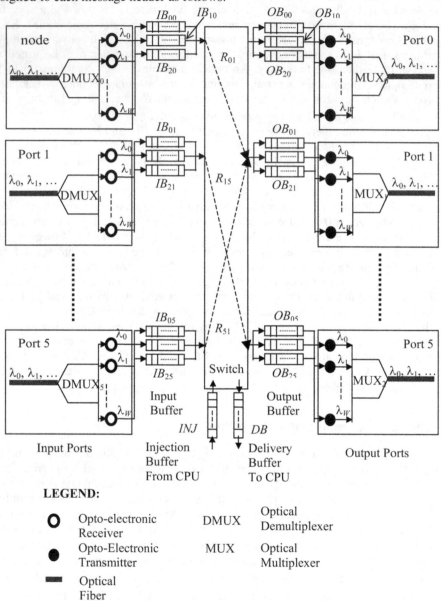

**Fig. 3.** Buffer Allocation Model at a Node

1) Every new message is initialized with a *DR* of 0.
2) Each time message is misrouted from an input buffer $IB_{mi}$ in any node to an output buffer $OB_{nj}$ in the same node, the *DR* of the message is incremented if $m > n$.
3) If a message is routed along a minimal path, the *DR* is not incremented.

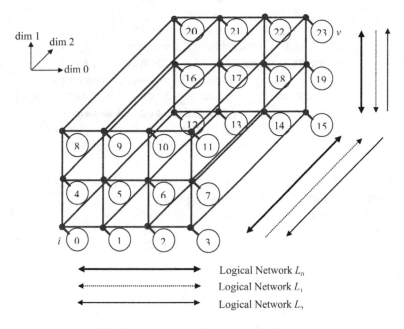

**Fig. 4.** Logical Networks (a) $L_0$ (b) $L_1$ (c) $L_2$

When *DR* reaches a specified limit, messages in $L_0$ are switched to $L_1$ or $L_2$. A message travelling in $L_1$ cannot switch to $L_2$ and vice versa. Algorithm *FTRoute* is as follows:

```
AdaptiveRoute
INPUT message from port i , where 0 ≤ i < 6
GET source buffer index p and dest addr v from msg
hdr
GET  dimension  reversal  count,  DR,  from  message
header
IF destination v reached
     STOP
ELSE
    RESET bit i in mask vector
    IF(p = 1 or 2)call LogicalRoute(p,message)//L₁ or L₂ //
    ELSE // message in L₀ //
       IF (dimension reversals DR < reversal limit RL)
          Select primary output port s based on ILS A
```

```
            Select alt. output port t based on ILS B
       IF hold(OB_{0s}<size(OB_{0s}) OR hold(OB_{0t})<size(OB_{0t})
            select(OB_{0j}) = min(hold(OB_{0s}), hold(O_{0t}))
       ELSE //fault encountered or traffic congestion//
            IF first(hold(OB_{0k}<size(OB_{0k})),0≤k<6 and k≠s,t
                 select(OB_{0j}) = OB_{0k}
                 IF (k < i) increment DR
                 ELSE discard and reTx message <EXIT>
            ELSE IF ((y_d<y_c) AND (z_d≥z_c)) OR ((y_d≤y_c) AND (z_d>z_c))
                      call LogicalRoute(1, message)
                 ELSE IF((y_d>y_c) AND (z_d≤z_c) OR ((y_d≥y_c) AND (z_d<z_c))
                      call LogicalRoute(2, message)
                      ELSE discard and reTx msg <EXIT>
R_{ij} : (i, p) → (j, q) // establish switched links //
GET local node's reception wavelength φ(c)
COMPUTE φ(v)=F(φ(c)) //compute dest node recept^n freq //
IF NON-FAULTY(transmitter(φ(v))
     send(message, φ(v))
 ELSE send(message, g(v))
```

```
LogicalRoute(p, message)
IF      (x_d < x_c)                  // In logical network, L_1 //
       IF (y_d = y_c) AND (z_d = z_c) select(OB_{1j}) = OB_{10}
       ELSE IF(y_d < y_c) AND (z_d = z_c)
             select(OB_{1j}) = min(hold(OB_{10}), hold(OB_{12}))
       ELSE IF(y_d = y_c) AND (z_d > z_c)
             select(OB_{1j}) = min(hold(OB_{10}), hold(OB_{15}))
       ELSE IF(y_d < y_c) AND (z_d > z_c)
       select(OB_{1j})=min(hold(OB_{10},hold(OB_{12}, hold(OB_{15}))
       ELSE    IF (x_d > x_c)
                   IF (y_d = y_c) AND (z_d = z_c)
                       select(OB_{1j}) = OB_{11}
                   ELSE IF (y_d < y_c) AND (z_d = z_c)
                       select(OB_{1j})=min(hold(OB_{11}),hold(OB_{12}))
                   ELSE IF (y_d = y_c) AND (z_d > z_c)
                       select(OB_{1j}) = min(hold(OB_{11}), hold(OB_{15}))
                   ELSE IF (y_d < y_c) AND (z_d > z_c)
                       select(OB_{1j})=min(hold(OB_{11}),hold(OB_{12}),hold(OB_{15}))
IF      (x_d < x_c)              // In logical network, L_2 //
       IF      (y_d = y_c) AND (z_d = z_c)
             select(OB_{2j}) = OB_{20}
```

**ELSE IF** $(y_d > y_c)$ AND $(z_d = z_c)$
$select(OB_{2j}) = min(hold(OB_{20}), hold(OB_{23}))$
**ELSE IF** $(y_d = y_c)$ AND $(z_d < z_c)$
$select(OB_{2j}) = min(hold(OB_{20}), hold(OB_{24}))$
**ELSE IF** $(y_d > y_c)$ AND $(z_d < z_c)$
$select(OB_{2j}) = min(hold(OB_{20}), hold(OB_{23}), hold(OB_{24}))$
**ELSE    IF** $(x_d > x_c)$
    **IF** $(y_d = y_c)$ AND $(z_d = z_c)$
        $select(OB_{2j}) = OB_{21}$
    **ELSE IF** $(y_d > y_c)$ AND $(z_d = z_c)$
        $select(OB_{2j}) = min(hold(OB_{21}), hold(OB_{23}))$
    **ELSE IF** $(y_d = y_c)$ AND $(z_d < z_c)$
        $select(OB_{2j}) = min(hold(OB_{21}), hold(OB_{24}))$
    **ELSE IF** $(y_d < y_c)$ AND $(z_d < z_c)$
$select(OB_{2j}) = min(hold(OB_{21}), hold(OB_{23}), hold(OB_{24}))$

## 4   Proofs of Routing Properties

In this section, we present the development of proofs for the fault-tolerant routing strategy. In order to achieve deadlock-free routing based on ILS A and ILS B, the following routing rules must be satisfied:

1. A new message enters the network if and only if there exists an *OB*, such that *hold(OB)*< (*size(OB)* - 1). This leaves at least one space for transit messages.
2. A transit message has higher priority than a new (entry) message.
3. Messages arriving at the same time are handled in a round robin fashion to ensure fairness and avoid channel starvation.
4. If *hold(DELB)* = *size(DELB)*, then *select(OB)* = *min(hold(OB$_{jq}$)*, where $0 \le j < 2d$ and $q \in \{0,1,2\}$. Message is re-injected into the network when the delivery buffer is full.
5. If *hold(OB$_{iq}$)* = *size(OB$_{iq}$)*, *select(OB$_{jq}$)* = *min(hold(OB$_{jq}$)*, $0 \le j < 2d$, $q \in \{0,1,2\}$ and $j \ne i$). When $\|select(OB)\| > 1$, one is chosen randomly.
6. Rate of message consumption exceeds rate of message injection [2].

**Lemma 1:**
Routing with *FTRoute* is minimal and adaptive.

**Proof:**
Routing using either ILS A or ILS B is deterministic, dimension-ordered and the corresponding route produced for any source-destination node cluster pair is the shortest. At any node, either ILS A or ILS B may be used.   ∎

**Lemma 2:**
Routing with ILS A and ILS B alone is not deadlock-free.

**Proof:**
Use of ILS A and ILS B alone creates a communications cycle. Consider the 2 by 2 by 2 grid in Figure 5. At cluster 0, a message destined for cluster 7 is routed over the path determined by ILS A. At cluster 3, a message intended for cluster 6 is routed over a path determined by ILS B. Cluster 7 sends to cluster 2 via ILS A. Finally, at cluster 6, a message destined for cluster 1, is routed along the path determined by ILS B. Since there is a cycle of communication requests, deadlock can arise.    ■

Prevention of deadlock requires adherence to the above specified routing rules as well as the routing directions specified by the logical networks. To prove deadlock-freedom in *FTRoute*, we must prove deadlock-freedom in *AdaptiveRoute* as well as in *LogicalRoute*.

**Theorem 1:**
Routing phase *AdaptiveRoute* is deadlock-free.

**Proof:**
We will prove this by contradiction. Assuming *AdaptiveRoute* is not deadlock-free with source and destination clusters $u$ and $v$, respectively. Then, a cycle of full IO buffers will exist, ($R_{ij}$ such that $hold(OB_{pi}) = size(OB_{pi})$ and $hold(OB_{qj}) = size(OB_{qj})$), at all nodes, inclusive of $u$ and $w$, in the communication path. Assume that $w$ is a neighbouring node of $v$ in the communication path. This implies that either Rule 6 ($v$ is not receiving the message) or Rule 1 is violated. If $hold(OB_{qk}) = (size(OB_{qk}) - 1)$, no new message can be injected but transit messages are not prohibited. A transit message then moves towards $v$ in the opposite direction to the movement of the empty buffer place. In either case, a deadlock cannot exist.    ■

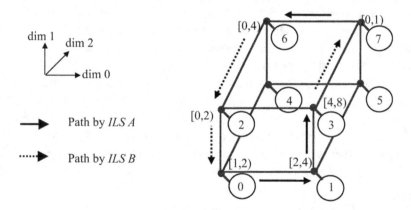

**Fig. 5.** Communications cycle exists with ILS A & B

**Lemma 3:**
Routing phase *AdaptiveRoute* is fully adaptive.

**Proof:**
Messages first attempt to follow the minimal paths defined by ILS A or ILS B. Misrouting is used when these minimal paths are congested or faulty. This is evident

from the routing algorithm where any *OB* can be used at some point. Specifically, a message may be routed in $L_0$ starting with any dimension and in any direction along a specified dimension. ∎

**Theorem 2:**
Routing phase *AdaptiveRoute* is not livelock-free in an *d*-D grid.

**Proof:**
By Lemma 3, *AdaptiveRoute* is fully adaptive. There exist clusters such that $hold(OB_{qj}) = size(OB_{qj})$ for $j = 0, 1, ..., d - 1$ (minimal paths) and $hold(OB_{qj}) < size(OB_{qj})$ for $j = d, d + 1, ..., 2d - 1$ (non-minimal paths). In such a situation, misrouted messages follow other paths that never reach their destinations. ∎

Although routing phase, *AdaptiveRoute*, achieves deadlock-freedom and adaptivity, livelock may occur. To prevent livelock, we make use of *Dimension Reversal*, *DR*, defined previously. After a new message enters the network, it is first routed in $L_0$. The message is initialized with *DR* of 0. *DR* is used to constrain misrouting and prevent livelock. Once *DR* reaches *RL*, the reversal limit, the message must use minimal routing by invoking *LogicalRoute*. In a $m_0$ by $m_1$ by $m_2$ grid, we let $RL = max\{m_0, m_1, m_2\}$. For increased misrouting, *RL* may be set higher. In *LogicalRoute*, however, misrouting is not allowed. When minimal paths are congested or faulty, messages have to wait instead of being routed along other paths. Here, messages are routed in either $L_1$ or $L_2$. The message in $L_1$ or $L_2$ cannot be switched back to $L_0$. Since $L_1$ and $L_2$ are disconnected, messages cannot switch between $L_1$ and $L_2$.

**Theorem 3:**
Routing phase *LogicalRoute* is deadlock-free and livelock-free.

**Proof:**
Since logical networks, $L_1$ and $L_2$, are disconnected, routing in the physical network is deadlock-free if routing in each logical network is deadlock-free. From Figure 4, it is evident that the permissible routing directions defined for the $L_1$ logical network do not contain any cycles and is deadlock-free. A message from any cluster in the dim0-dim2 plane, traversing dimension 1, can not return since the defined message paths are unidirectional in dimension 1. Since dimension 2 message paths are also unidirectional, no cycles of buffer requests can develop in the dim0-dim2 plane as well. Deadlock-freedom in the $L_2$ logical network can be proven similarly (see Figure 4). In either $L_1$ or $L_2$, routing is minimal and every step taken by a message is closer to its destination. This is evident from the routing algorithm, *LogicalRoute*. Hence, it is livelock-free. ∎

**Theorem 4:**
*FTRoute* is fully adaptive, deadlock-free and livelock-free.

**Proof:**
*DR* does not restrict the use of any particular set of output buffers and by Lemma 3, routing phase one, *AdaptiveRoute*, is fully adaptive. Routing phases one and two of *FTRoute* are deadlock-free by Theorems 1 and 3, respectively. In phase one, when

$DR$ constrains misrouting and when its value reaches the upper bound $RL$, a message is switched to either $L_1$ or $L_2$. The routes used in $L_1$ or $L_2$ are minimal. Phase two of *FTRoute* is livelock-free by Theorem 3. Hence, *FTRoute* is livelock-free.    ∎

**Theorem 5:**
*FTRoute* guarantees message delivery in a connected $d$-dimensional grid only if the number of faulty opto-electronic transmitters are upper bounded by $(W-1)(RL+d)$.

**Proof:**
In the worst case, in a connected $d$-dimensional grid, there is only one surviving input and output port at each node on the path. At each output port, up to $(W-1)$ opto-electronic transmitters can be faulty. The longest path involves up to $RL$ misroutes (see algorithm *AdaptiveRoute* and definition of $DR$). In either $L_1$ or $L_2$, *LogicalRoute* prohibits misrouting (by Theorem 3) and the message may be successfully delivered in a maximum of $d$ hops (where $d$ is the dimension of the grid). Hence, the length of the longest message path traverses $(RL+d)$ nodes before reaching the destination and the claim follows.    ∎

# 5   Conclusion

In this paper we have presented a fully adaptive, deadlock-free and livelock-free fault-tolerant routing strategy for low-dimensional opto-electronic grids. Our strategy is cost-effective and supports fault-tolerant routing with moderate amounts of resources. Only three logical networks, $L_0$, $L_1$ and $L_2$, and two routing tables of size $O(d)$ are needed ($d$ is the maximum degree of a processor) regardless of network size. Future work will proceed to extend the routing model to other regular networks.

**Acknowledgements.** This research is supported in part by the Academic Research Fund administered by the Ministry of Education and Nanyang Technological University, Singapore.

# References

1. S. Bandyopadhyay, A. Sengupta, and A. Jaekel, "Fault-tolerant routing scheme for all-optical networks", *Proc. SPIE – All-Optical Networking: Architecture, Control and Management Issues*, Vol. 3531, Nov. 1998, pp 420–431.
2. W.J. Dally and C.L. Seitz, "Deadlock-free Packet Routing in Multiprocessor Interconnection Networks", *IEEE Transactions on Computer*, Vol. 36, No. 5, May 1987, pp.547–553.
3. C. DeCusatis, E. Maass, D.P. Clement, and R.C. Lasky (Editors), *Handbook of Fiber Optic Data Communication, Academic Press*, 1998.
4. G.N. Frederickson and R. Janardan, "Space-Efficient and Fault-Tolerant Message Routing in Outerplanar Networks", *IEEE Transactions on Computers*, Vol. 37, No. 12, December 1988, pp 1529–1540.
5. O. Gerstel, R.S. Ramaswami, and H. Galen, "Fault tolerant multiwavelength optical rings with limited wavelength conversion", *IEEE Journal on Selected Areas in Communications*, Vol. 16, No. 7, Sep 1998, pp. 1166–1178.

6.  M. Guizani, M. A. Memon, and S. Ghanta, "Optical Design of a Fault-Tolerant Self-Routing Switch for Massively Parallel Processing Networks", *Proc. of 2<sup>nd</sup> International Conf. On Massively Parallel Processing Using Optical Interconnections (MMPOI'95)*, 1995, pp 246–253.
7.  O. Kibar, P. J. Marchand, and S. C. Esener, "High-Speed CMOS Switch Designs for Free-Space Optoelectronic MIN's", *IEEE Transactions on VLSI Systems*, Vol. 6, No. 3, Sept. 1998, pp 372–386.
8.  H. Kirkham and E. Hsu, "AbNET, a fault-tolerant fiber optic communication system", *Proc. of the IEEE International Workshop on Factory Communication Systems (WFCS'95)*, 1995, pp 175–181.
9.  W.S. Lacy, J.L. Cruz-Rivera, and D.S. Wills, "The Offset Cube: A Three-Dimensional Multicomputer Network Topology Using Through-Wafer Optics", *IEEE Transactions on Parallel and Distributed Systems*, Vol. 9, No. 9, September 1998, pp 893–908.
10. P. Lalwaney and I. Koren, "Fault tolerance in optically interconnected multiprocessor networks", *Proc. of Conf. On Fault-Tolerant Parallel and Distributed Systems*, 1995, pp 91–98.
11. P. Lalwaney and I. Koren, "Fault tolerance schemes for WDM-based multiprocessor networks", *Proc. of 2<sup>nd</sup> International Conf. On Massively Parallel Processing Using Optical Interconnections (MMPOI'95)*, 1995, pp 90–97.
12. P.K.K. Loh and W.J. Hsu, "Performance Analysis of Fault-Tolerant Interval Routing", *11<sup>th</sup> International Conference on Parallel and Distributed Computing Systems*, Chicago, Illinois, USA, 4<sup>th</sup> September 1998.
13. P. K.K. Loh and W.J. Hsu, "A Viable Optical Bus-Based Interconnection Network", *2<sup>nd</sup> International Conference on Information, Communications & Signal Processing*, December 1999.
14. P. K.K. Loh and V. Hsu, "A Genetics-Based Fault-Tolerant Routing Strategy for Multiprocessor Networks", *Future Generation Computer Systems*, Vol. 17, No. 4, 2001, pp 415–423.
15. A. Louri, B. Weech, C. Neocleous, "A Spanning Multichannel Linked Hypercube: A Gradually Scalable Optical Interconnection Network for Massively Parallel Computing", *IEEE Transactions on Parallel and Distributed Systems*, Vol. 9, No. 5, May 1998, pp 497–512.
16. G.C. Marsden, P.J. Marchand, P. Harvey, and S.C. Esener, "Optical Transpose Interconnection System Architectures", *Optics Letters*, Vol. 18, No. 13, pp 1083–1085, July 1993.
17. R. Ramaswami and K.N. Sivarajan, *Optical Networks: A Practical Perspective*, Morgan Kaufmann Publishers, 1998.
18. H. Shen, F. Chin, and Y. Pan, "Efficient Fault-Tolerant Routing in Multihop Optical WDM Networks", *IEEE Transactions on Parallel and Distributed Systems*, Vol. 10, No. 10, October 1999, pp 1012–1025.
19. T. Szymanski, "Hypergrids: Optical Interconnection Networks for Parallel Computing", *Journal of Parallel and Distributed Computing*, Vol. 26, pp 1–23, 1995.
20. J. van Leeuwen and R.B. Tan, "Interval Routing", *The Computer Journal*, Vol.30, No.4, 1987, pp 298–307.

# Direct Execution Simulation of Mobile Agent Algorithms

Jiannong Cao[1], Xuhui Li[1,2], Sou King[1], and Yanxiang He[2]

[1] Internet and Mobile Computing Lab, Department of Computing,
Hong Kong Polytechnic University, Hung Hom, Kowloon, Hong Kong
{csjcao,csxhli}@comp.polyu.edu.hk
[2] Parallel and Distributed Computing Lab, Computer School, Computer School,
Wuhan University, Wuhan, Hubei, China
{lixuhui,yxhe}@whu.edu.cn

**Abstract.** Mobile agent has been applied to develop the solutions for various kinds of parallel and distributed computing problems. However, performance evaluation of mobile agent algorithms remains a difficult task, mainly due to the characteristics of mobile agents such as distributed and asynchronous execution, autonomy and mobility. This paper proposes a general approach based on direct execution simulation for evaluating the performance of mobile agent algorithms by collecting and analyzing the information about the agents during their execution. We describe the proposed generic simulation model, named MADES, the architecture of a software environment based on MADES, and a prototype implementation. A mobile agent-based distributed load balancing algorithm is used for experiments with the prototype.

## 1 Introduction

Mobile agent, as a new network computing technology, has been applied to solve various parallel and distributed computing problems, including parallel processing [19], information searching and retrieval [12], network management [16], and distributed coordination and synchronization [3]. Mobile agent exhibits new characteristics such as mobility and autonomy, while retaining the features of conventional parallel and distributed computing techniques. Different from conventional distributed programs which are bounded to the nodes in the system where they execute, mobile agents can migrate autonomously from one node to another during its execution. They can choose the migration route according to the runtime condition, providing a new model of computation in which the use of the resources and the integration of the services are remarkably different from the conventional models [7]. Therefore, in the past decade, many mobile agent-based solutions have been proposed for problems that have been solved using conventional distributed methods, taking the advantages of the mobile agent technology to improve performance in circumstances where the systems exhibit heavy network traffic, large amount of transferring data, and unbalanced workload among nodes.

To develop mobile agent applications, algorithms for mobile agent operation and interaction need to be designed. Performance evaluation of mobile agent algorithms therefore becomes essential because it can help discover the performance and scalability bottlenecks, and thus optimizes mobile agent application design. However,

M. Guo and L.T.Yang (Eds.): ISPA 2003, LNCS 2745, pp. 127–138, 2003.
© Springer-Verlag Berlin Heidelberg 2003

it remains a complex task mainly due to the characteristics of mobile agents such as distributed and asynchronous execution, autonomy and mobility.

Ad hoc approaches have been taken, including writing application-specific simulation from scratch, constructing and reasoning about an analytic model of the algorithm, or deploying live code across the real environment. Each approach has a number of limitations. Theoretical analysis, as in evaluating conventional parallel and distributed algorithms, involves using mathematical techniques which tends to simplify the underlying operating environment characteristics and is limited to relatively static and small systems. The difficulty of constructing the analytical model increases tremendously when it is applied to mobile agent algorithms where the variety of the circumstances and the features such as reactivity, autonomy, and mobility of the agent should be considered. Live deployment provides the most realistic evaluation environment but there are significant challenges in cost and feasibility to deploying and evaluating mobile agent code in a wide-area system.

Alternatively, simulation has been proposed as a valuable method for analyzing the complex nature of the dynamic aspects of parallel and distributed systems. However, in existing works on simulating mobile agent algorithms, people often build custom simulations under different system and network environments [13, 20]. Such simulations are specific to the particular mobile agent algorithms. Furthermore, new simulation programs need to be developed whenever a new mobile agent algorithm is to be evaluated whereas many parts of the simulation are often repetitious.

In this paper, we describe a generic simulation model, called MADES, for evaluating the Mobile Agent algorithms based on Directly Executing Simulation. The repeated and tedious work on building simulations can be reduced by providing a generic simulation model, which allows us to develop a general purpose system for simulating certain kinds of mobile agent algorithms [2]. In such a generic simulation system, basic and common features and structures of simulations can be abstracted into well designed modules and architecture, and thus the designer of the algorithm to be simulated need not worry about the low-level details governing the simulation implementation.

Direct execution simulation [1, 4] adds realism in the simulation by allowing the evaluation of real code and meanwhile, provides a controllable environment for collecting and processing execution information. Live mobile agent code running in the system generates various events which are monitored by the simulation system. Since the code of the simulated algorithm is directly executed, the simulation model employs real execution system in itself so that the parallelism and mobility embedded in algorithms under simulation can be exploited in a natural way. It can also be designed to accurately model the performance metrics and offer the potential for accurate prediction of program performance on real systems. The simulation system is responsible of generating various simulation parameters, such as topology, delay, network bandwidth, and execution time on a host. It also monitors and tracks the effects of various system conditions and network conditions, so the performance of the mobile agents under can be evaluated based on the information collected by the simulation system.

The rest of the paper is organized as follows. In Section 2, we describe related works on performance evaluation and simulation of distributed systems, and mobile agent systems in particular. In Section 3, the model and the environment of MADES are presented. A prototype implementation of MADES is described in Section 4. A mobile agent based distributed load balancing algorithm is used as to experiment with the prototype. Finally, Section 5 concludes the paper and discusses our future works on it.

## 2  Background and Related Works

Since mobile agent programs are parallel and distributed ones in nature, performance evaluation methods that have been successfully used in conventional parallel and distributed systems can be adopted to evaluate the performance of mobile agent algorithms. Three major approaches have been used to evaluate a parallel/distributed algorithm: constructing and reasoning about an analytic model of the algorithm, building and deploying a real implementation, and performing a simulation of the algorithm.

In analytic studies, performance of parallel and distributed algorithms are often measured using some mathematical models, such as queuing models and Markov chain models to describe the metrics of the performance such as execution time, speedup, and throughput [8, 9]. This approach has also been adopted for the analysis of mobile agent system performance. Works include the use of canonical stochastic analysis to develop a performance model and derive the optimal number of mobile agents required for report generating [11], and the use of Petri nets with the application of probability distributions to model parameters of a data retrieval application, such as request size, time for searching data in a server, processing time, size of replies and queries, code size of migrating agents, and throughput [18]. Though these theoretical analyses can relatively accurately describe the relationship between the performance metrics and their factors, it often requires a lot of effort to derive the mathematical models and sometimes it is even harder to make comparison between two algorithms which may have the similar complexity. Furthermore, the continual need for the derivation and solving of new models whenever changes are made to either the algorithm or the underlying environment is a hindrance to the algorithm designer.

In the implementation and deployment approach, the algorithm is implemented using a programming language and deployed in a real system environment for execution. When the code is executed, a monitoring program running in the distributed environment collects the real-time data of the distributed application for performance evaluation [14, 15]. The cost incurred by this approach is too high because the system needs to be reserved for running the algorithm code in order to obtain accurate performance results, the code needs to be executed over a long period of time to produce data for analysis, and the collection of information may contaminate the results. We have not seen any work in this category for evaluating mobile agent applications.

Simulation allows an algorithm to be analyzed and tested in a controllable environment before an actual implementation is built. The difference between simulation and the real implementation is that, in the simulation approach, the execution of the algorithm is under the control of a simulator which can embody most major characteristics of the real operating environment such as the underlying network. Works can be found in literature on simulating mobile agent applications [13, 20]. However, these works are efforts devoted to evaluating different, application-specific mobile agent programs under different system assumptions. There has been no general purpose simulation system for mobile agent algorithms.

Besides the approaches described above, there have been some other studies on the performance evaluation of mobile agent systems [10] and performance comparison between the mobile agent technology and other parallel and distributed mechanisms such as RPC and REV [18]. Some studies also propose the approaches for the steps of doing performance analysis of mobile agent systems and application, e.g. in [5, 6] the authors gauge the performance characteristics of different mobile agent platforms and applications by using a hierarchical framework of benchmarks designed to isolate performance properties of interest. The studies provide a lot of original data and feasible means which can be utilized in developing our direct execution simulation environment for mobile agent algorithms.

## 3   The MADES Model and Environment

### 3.1   The MADES Model

Conventionally, discrete-event simulation has been used for simulating parallel and distributed algorithms, which is driven with either traces [21] or executables [4, 17]. For mobile agent applications, execution-driven simulation is more applicable, because the interaction between events of different agents during the simulation can affect the course of the simulated execution. This allows more accurate modeling of the effects of contention and synchronization in simulations of multiple mobile agents.

The generic MADES simulation model is based on direct execution simulation. As shown in Fig.1, it comprises three layers, namely *Task layer*, *Simulation layer*, and *Execution layer*. The components in the three layers cooperate to simulate the mobile agent algorithm by directly executing the algorithm code. Here, the execution of the mobile agent algorithm and the simulation is completely interleaved. The mobile agent code is instrumented at appropriate points so as to generate events for the simulation. When the simulation is in action, it processes the event and then returns control to the mobile agent code. This method facilitates feedback from the simulation to guide the execution of the mobile agent code.

In Task layer, mobile agent algorithms are implemented by a set of mobile agents representing the task to be performed. MA Servers and Network Simulation in the Simulation layer are responsible for the simulation of the operations of the system nodes and the interconnection network. As a simulation platform for running mobile agents, MA Server simulates the local processing environment on a node such as the service time, workload, and so on. It also instantiates a concrete mobile agent system for hosting mobile agents. Network component is responsible for simulating the network environment. MA Servers communicate with each other under the assistance of Network, which, for example, allows us to simulate the execution of the mobile agent algorithm in the Internet environment by running the agents in a LAN or in a single host. The mobile agents are simulated by direct execution. The concrete work of executing the mobile agents is the task of Execution layer which is composed of a set of mobile agent systems managed by MA Servers.

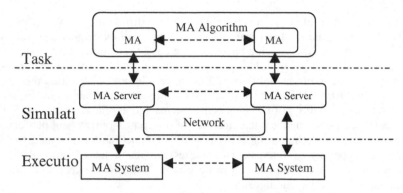

**Fig. 1.** The overview of MADES

Mobile agents have some common behaviors including creation, communication, clone, migration and dispose. Fig. 2 shows the workflow of the mobile agents, being traced by the major behaviors, which can be classified into following stages:

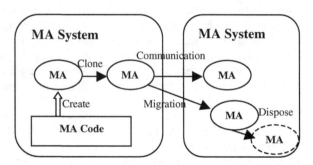

**Fig. 2.** The behaviors of mobile agents

- MA server creates a new MA or clones an existing MA for doing jobs.
- The MA communicates with other MA for retrieving information. Then it decides whether to migrate, clone or take any other actions based on the MA algorithms and incoming information.
- The MA migrates to other host.
- The MA is disposed when its job is finished.

One of the main tasks that MADES performs is to provide the information of agent's execution for performance evaluation. Generally, performance of a mobile agent can be characterized by execution time, number and delivery time of messages, migration delay, and number of migrations. Performance regarding communication and migration in terms of the network traffic and latency should also be concerned. Therefore, the work of MADES concentrates on capturing the event of these behaviors and collecting the state of execution when they occur.

## 3.2  A Software Environment for MADES

Based on the MADES model, we have designed a software environment to simulate
and evaluate mobile agent algorithms. As shown in Figure 3, the architecture of the
software environment consists of three modules: *User Interface*, *Simulation Control*
and *Simulation System*. The details of each component in these modules are presented
in the rest of this section.

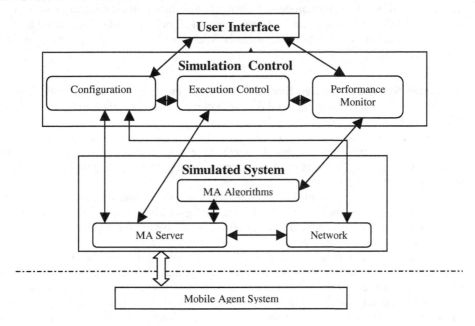

**Fig. 3.** Architecture of software environment for MADES

**User Interface.** User Interface enables the user to set the necessary parameters used
by the other components in the simulation. The parameters include simulated hosts,
network topology, bandwidth and so on. Certainly, User Interface is also the interface
for the user to monitor the execution condition of the whole system and to show the
information of the performance evaluation of the mobile agents.

**Simulation Control.** The Simulation Control module is composed of Configuration,
Execution Control and Performance Monitor. Configuration can retrieve and save the
information of simulation configuration. Simulation configuration consists of MA
server configuration and network configuration. The former is about the system
environment configuration such as the number of the MA Servers and the conditions
of the workload and throughput, the latter focuses on the simulation of underlying
network which includes the network speed, bandwidth and topology.

Execution Control is responsible for initializing, controlling and terminating the
simulation execution. It provides an interface and uses events to drive the simulation.
Users can initialize or stop the simulation system by corresponding mechanisms

provided by the User Interface. It controls the initialization and termination of mobile agents, MA server and Performance Monitor.

Performance Monitor gathers and processes performance information of mobile agents in the simulation. Each mobile agent is associated with a performance object which collects the information of the mobile agent's execution and transforms them into the data that the performance monitor need to evaluate the performance of the agent and the whole algorithm. Performance Monitor gathers the original data from the performance objects and processes them to form the evaluation information of the agent algorithm. The performance of mobile agent algorithm is often measured by the execution time in each host, the number and cost of migrations, and cost of communication.

**Simulated System.** Simulated System is the implementation of the MADES model described in the last subsection. And the three components have the same functions as they are in the model.

Mobile agent server is used to encapsulate the entities that combine the concept of mobile agent system. It simulates the work of a host containing the mobile agent system. As direct execution is used, a concrete agent system is used and managed by this component.

Network involves the simulation of network topology and communication cost. The network topology and the bandwidth are configured by the user, and the real-time communication cost is generated by certain network simulation algorithm according to the configuration.

Mobile agent algorithm implemented by mobile agents is the target of the evaluation. In the environment, each agent is associated with a performance object whose task is to record the information when the actions are taken and send the data to the Performance Monitor when the work is finished. As a part of the agent being transparent to the user, the performance object is created with its owner agent and accompany with the agent during its whole lifetime. Thus the behaviors of the agent can all be recorded and Performance Monitor can get the details of the execution of every agent in the MA algorithm to evaluate the performance.

# 4   A Prototype

## 4.1   The Implementation of the Prototype

We built a prototype of MADES according to the system environment model described in the last section. The prototype is implemented with Java Development Kit 1.3, and built on IBM Aglets 2.0. Here the concrete agent system is the Aglets server named Tahiti, provided by the release of Aglets.

In the prototype, User Interface is implemented by MainWindow class. When the environment is started, a MainWindow object is initialized and waiting for the user to set the necessary parameters, as shown in Figure 4. MainWindow implements an interface called DataInterface which can provide the facilities to set and get the parameters of configuration. The parameters include port numbers of Tahiti Server, network topology, and bandwidth of each network links. It also provides an interface for users to start up the control of the simulation and an interface for Performance Monitor to show the performance information of algorithm.

Execution Control is implemented by the ExecControl class, which acts as an event listener of the user interface. When the user starts the simulation after having input necessary parameters, the parameters and control are passed to ExecControl. Then ExecControl would create a simulation environment based on the parameters, create several MA Server objects and a Performance Monitor object.

Performance Monitor is implemented by PerfMonitor class and is embedded into the user interface. When PerfMonitor is created, it would initialize a server socket for listening to the connections from the agents' performance objects and create a socket for exchanging data with the performance objects as the connection is established. The performance object associated with each agent is implemented by PerfObj class. During the execution of the mobile agent, PerfObj keeps on sending the data to PerfMonitor. PerfMonitor then gathers the performance information of the mobile agent and displays them in the user interface.

The Configuration component in the environment model is implemented by Configuration class. It would load and save the parameters of simulation in configuration file, and provide the configuration data to MainWindow through DataInterface.

In its initialization, RunTahiti, the implementation of MA Server, instantiates a Tahiti object. To simulate the network environment in execution simulation, the communication between Tahiti servers is encapsulated by RunTahiti objects, and the delay for the data transmission would be calculated according to the information of network bandwidth and traffic provided by Network component.

Aglets implementing a mobile agent algorithm are started on the Tahiti servers under the control from RunTahiti objects. In the prototype, each mobile agent extends a class named MAglet rather than Aglet. MAglet is a direct subclass of Aglet. It has a PerfObj object which is an aglet event listener. MAglet encapsulates the work of connecting to PerfMonitor and reporting the current state of the aglet generated by PerfObj when the event of interest occurs. PerfObj records the state of MAglets including the execution time, migration and communication condition, which may not be enough for the circumstances where the states specific to the algorithms are required. Therefore, PerfObj contains a list of log objects which is exposed to the subclass of MAglets to enable it to log the data required for further specific evaluation. After the simulation, PerfMonitor processes the data from the PerfObj objects and evaluates the performance of the algorithms.

Network is implemented by three classes, Network, VertixSet and Cost class. Initially, upon invoked by the Configuration component, the Network cooperates with VertixSet and Cost classes to generate a simulated network topology and cost between adjacent nodes based on the parameter including network topology type, bandwidth and numbers of simulated nodes. After that, the costs between nodes are re-computed for finding the shortest path between nodes.

During simulation, Network is responsible for simulating the network communication environment for agent migration and communication. After random generation of the network topology, checking is performed to see whether the topology graph is connected, and then shortest paths between node are generated. This is done by using Dijkstra's Shortest Path algorithm.

## 4.2 An Experiment with the Prototype

To demonstrate the functionality of the prototype, we have implemented the simulation of a mobile agent-based, dynamic load balancing algorithm. Dynamic load balancing is a classical distributed problem in the distributed system. The major objective of dynamic load balancing is to equalize system workload among participated hosts to achieve an improvement of overall system performance, such as increasing system throughput. In this example, mobile agents are used to implement distributed dynamic load balancing as an alternative to traditional message passing scheme.

The simulation of dynamic load balancing is implemented by using the cooperation of a collection of mobile agents. The detail of the algorithm can be found in [3]. With the help of PerfObj and the code in the aglets to record the state into PerfObj, the general and specific data about the performance of the mobile agent program is captured by PerfMonitor and displayed on the console in User Interface. Users can choose the mobile agent in Mobile Agent List to know its information in detail. Fig.4 shows that the information of mobile agents is displayed in User Interface.

After the simulation, the original information of agent's execution is collected and processed by the PerfMonitor, and the problem specific information in the execution is also logged by PerfObjs and PerfMonitor. The data would be further processed to get the final performance of the algorithm. In this simulation example, two metrics representing the performance of the algorithm are calculated, and they are:

- System throughput: It is represented by the sum of all jobs' base execution time executed in a particular host.
- Average Queue Length: It is represented by the average load information (represented as waiting time in queue length) of a particular host.
- Based on the information provided by the direct execution simulation prototype, we evaluate the performance of Load balancing using mobile agents and get the results as shown in Figure 5.

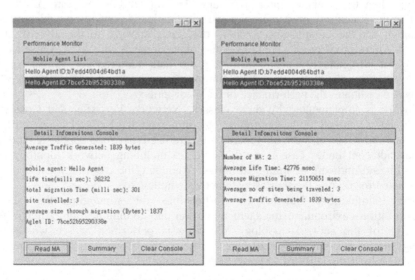

**Fig. 4.** Performance Monitor of Simulator

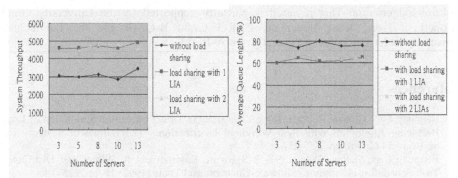

**Fig. 5.** The performance of the algorithm based on the data from the simulation model

The simulation results generated from the prototype of MADES matches with the one that the simulation programs we built specifically for the algorithms. From this example, we can see that our MADES simulation model can actually be applied to the simulation and performance evaluation of the mobile agent application and algorithms.

# 5 Conclusion and Future Works

In this project, we have described MADES, a generic simulation model, and the software environment based on MADES for evaluating the performance of mobile agent algorithms. MADES adopts the direct execution simulation approach in which the mobile agent application can be directly executed, while at the same time, the information about the performance of the application is collected and processed by the simulation system. A prototype of the MADES model has been implemented using Java and the IBM Aglets mobile agent platform. A mobile agent-based, dynamic load balancing algorithm has been simulated on the prototype which demonstrated the capabilities and features of the simulation system.

The main idea of developing MADES is to build framework addressing the need for having a general purpose simulation environment that allows various mobile agent algorithms to be modeled and simulated in different systems. With such a simulation system, users can easily build simulations of their mobile agent algorithms without worrying about many details governing the simulation's implementation.

There are much more work to carry out for enhancing the functionality of the prototype simulation system. First, the system can be improved with the addition of a tracing mechanism for real time monitoring and visualization of the agent execution. Second, the current prototype was built using the Tahiti server provided by the Aglets. It was relatively easy to implement, but the information of the agent that can be collected during the run time is limited. Much more work can be done in the layer underlying the mobile agent platform to insert the components for collecting the data into the system so as to obtain more information. Third, the scale of the simulation could be expanded to include the simulation of the system load of the hosts, which can make the simulation of the agents' execution be used in the circumstance where the load varies from time to time.

**Acknowledgements.** This research is partially supported by the University Grant Council of Hong Kong under the CERG Grant B-Q518 and the Polytechnic University under HK PolyU Research Grant A-PD54.

# References

1. Jiannong Cao, Graeme Bennett, Kang Zhang. 2000. Direct Execution Simulation of Load Balancing Algorithms with Real Workload Distribution. The Journal of Systems and Software 54 (2000), pp. 227–237.
2. Jiannong Cao, Mathew Pole. 1997. A Software Environment for Simulating Distributed Task-Scheduling algorithms. Software-Concepts and Tools (1997) 18, pp. 125–136.
3. Jiannong Cao, Xianbing Wang, Sajal K. Das, "A Framework of Using Cooperating Mobile Agents to Achieve Load Balancing in Distributed Web Server Groups", Proc. 5th International Conference on Algorithms and Architectures for Parallel Processing (ICA3PP2002) (IEEE Computer Society Press), Oct. 2002.
4. Phillips M. Dickens, Philip Heidelberger, David M. Nicol. Parallelized Direct Execution Simulation of Messasge-Passing Parallel Programs. IEEE Transactions on Parallel and Distributed Systems. 7 (10), 1996. pp. 1090–1105.
5. Marios D. Dikaiakos, George Samaras. Quantitative Performance Analysis of Mobile Agent Systems: A Hierarchical Approach. Technical Report TR-00-02, Department of Comuter Science, University of Cyprus, June 2000.
6. Marios D.Dikaiakos, George Samaras. Performance Evaluation of Mobile Agents: Issues and Approaches. Performance Engineering, LNCS 2047, pp. 148–166,2001.
7. Oren Etzioni, Daniel S. Weld. Intelligent Agents on the Internet: Fact, Fiction, and Forecast. IEEE Expert, Vol.10, No.3, pp. 44–49, 1995.
8. Greg Franks, Shikharesh Majumdar, John Neilson, Dornia Petriu. Performance Analysis of Distributed Server Systems. Proc. of The 6-th International Conference on Software Quality, pp. 15–26, October 1996.
9. Anshul Gupta, Vipin Kumar. Performance Properties of Large Scale Parallel Systems. Journal of Parallel and Distributed Computing Vol.19, No.3, 1993, pp. 234-244.
10. Leila Ismail, Daniel Hagimont. A Performance Evaluation of the Mobile Agent Paradigm. Conference on Object-Oriented, pp. 306–313, 1999.
11. Seong-Hwan Kim, Thmas G.Robertazzi. Mobile Agent Modeling. Technical Report, University at Stony Brook, College of Engineering and Applied Science, No. 786, November 2000
12. O. de Kretser, A. Moffat, T. Shimmin, and J. Zobel. Methodologies for distributed information retrieval. Proc. of the Eighteenth Int'l Conference on Distributed Computing Systems, pp. 26–29, May 1998.
13. Anselm Lingnau, Oswald Drobink. Simulating Mobile Agent Systems with Swarm. First International Symposium on Agent Systems and Applications Third International Symposium on Mobile Agents, October, 1999.
14. Bernd Mohr. SIMPLE: a Performance Evaluation Tool Environment for Parallel and Distributed Systems. 2nd European Conference, EDMCC2, pp. 80–89, April 1991. Springer, Berlin, LNCS 487.
15. B.Meyer, M.Heineken, C.Popien. Performance Analysis of Distributed Applications with ANSAmon. International Conference on Open Distributed Processing (ICODP '95), pp. 293–304
16. B. Pagurek, Y. Wang, and T. White. Integration of mobile agents with SNMP: Why and how. NOMS'2000, 2000
17. Vijay S. Pai, Parthasarathy Ranganathan, and Sarita V. Adve, RSIM: An Execution-Driven Simulator for ILP-Based Shared-Memory Multiprocessors and Uniprocessors, IEEE TCCA Nesletter, Oct. 1997.

18. A.Puliafito, S.Riccobene, M.Scarpa. An Analytical Comparison of the Client-server, Remote Evaluation and Mobile Agents Paradigms. First International Symposium on Agent Systems and Applications Third International Symposium on Mobile Agents, October 1999, pp. 278.
19. Luís Moura Silva, Victor Batista, Paulo Martins, Guilherme Soares. Using Mobile Agents for Parallel Processing. International Symposium on Distributed Objects and Applications, September, 1999
20. Adelinde M. Uhrmacher, Petra Tyschler, Dirk Tyschler. Modeling and Simulation of Mobile Agents. Future Generation Computer Systems , 2000. pp. 107–118
21. Songnian Zhou. A Trace-Driven Simulation Study of Dynamic Load Balancing. IEEE Transaction on Software Engineering, Vol.14, No.9, 1988. pp. 1327–1341.

# MPI-2 Support in Heterogeneous Computing Environment Using an SCore Cluster System

Yuichi Tsujita[1]*, Toshiyuki Imamura[1] **, Nobuhiro Yamagishi[1],
and Hiroshi Takemiya[2]

[1] Center for Promotion of Computational Science and Engineering,
Japan Atomic Energy Research Institute
6-9-3 Higashi-Ueno, Taito-ku, Tokyo 110-0015, Japan
`tsujita@hiro.kindai.ac.jp`
`imamura@im.uec.ac.jp`
[2] Hitachi East Japan Solutions, Ltd.
2-16-10 Honcho, Aoba-ku, Sendai, Miyagi 980-0014, Japan

**Abstract.** An MPI library for heterogeneous computing environment,
Stampi, has been implemented on an SCore cluster system to enable
dynamic process creation defined in MPI-2 and MPI communication
among multiple clusters. Objective of this implementation is realization
of heterogeneous computing environment with an SCore PC cluster
and other machines. Through performance measurement, sufficient
performance has been achieved and effectiveness of our flexible implementation has been confirmed.

**Keywords:** MPI, SCore, MPICH-SCore, dynamic process creation,
router process

## 1   Introduction

MPI [1,2] communication among multiple platforms is one of key methods to
realize heterogeneous parallel computation. An MPI library named Stampi [3]
was developed to realize such communication. In intra-machine MPI communication, a vendor-supplied high performance MPI library is used. On the other
hand, TCP/IP is used in inter-machine MPI communication. In addition, router
processes on IP-reachable nodes were implemented to realize inter-machine MPI
communication when computation nodes can not communicate outside directly.

Recently, a PC cluster is focused to get huge scale of computational resources
without much cost. To provide flat computing environment on a PC cluster, an

---

\* Corresponding author, Present address: Department of Electronic Engineering and
Computer Science, Faculty of Engineering, Kinki University, 1 Takaya-Umenobe,
Higashi-Hiroshima, Hiroshima 739-2116, Japan.
\*\* Present address: Department of Computer Science, The University of Electro-
Communications, 1-5-1 Chofugaoka, Chofu-shi, Tokyo, 182-8585 Japan.

M. Guo and L.T.Yang (Eds.): ISPA 2003, LNCS 2745, pp. 139–144, 2003.
© Springer-Verlag Berlin Heidelberg 2003

SCore cluster system [4] was developed. MPICH-SCore [4] is an MPICH [5] library on an SCore cluster system. Although it realizes intra-machine MPI communication, dynamic process creation to other platforms including an SCore PC cluster and inter-machine MPI communication are not available.

Parallel computation with an SCore PC cluster and other machines such as a parallel computer or a graphic server machine is effective in huge scale of parallel computation. To realize such computation, we implemented Stampi on an SCore cluster system. Stampi uses an MPICH-SCore library in intra-machine MPI communication and TCP/IP in inter-machine MPI communication. In this paper, outline, architecture and preliminary results of Stampi on an SCore cluster system are described.

## 2    Implementation of Stampi on an SCore Cluster System

### 2.1    Architectural Mechanism

High performance intra-machine MPI communication is available with MPICH-SCore in an SCore cluster system. But inter-machine MPI communication and dynamic process creation are not available. Stampi was implemented on an SCore cluster system to realize such mechanism. Architectural view of Stampi is shown in Fig 1. As shown in this figure, intra-machine MPI communication is available using the same MPICH-SCore library as an SCore cluster system uses. In addition, inter-machine MPI communication is available using TCP/IP socket connections. Once a program has started, Stampi selects the most efficient communication method possible between any two processes flexibly. When each computation node can not communicate outside directly, router process is invoked on a server node which can communicate outside. Then inter-machine MPI communication is carried out through the router process. Besides, users can select the number of router processes for high performance inter-machine MPI communication.

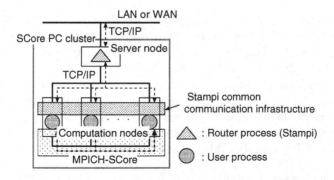

**Fig. 1.** Architecture of Stampi on an SCore cluster system.

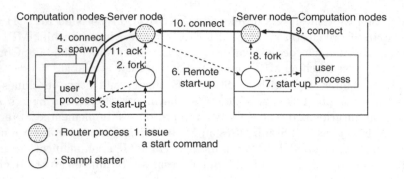

**Fig. 2.** Execution mechanism of Stampi on an SCore cluster system.

## 2.2    Execution Mechanism

In inter-machine MPI communication among two SCore PC clusters using Stampi, user processes are invoked and network connection among those user processes and router processes is established using execution mechanism which is shown in Fig. 2. Firstly, user processes are initiated by a Stampi start-up command (starter). When those user processes issues a spawn function (`MPI_Comm_spawn` or `MPI_Comm_spawn_multiple`), an additional starter process is invoked on a remote machine. Then the starter on the remote machine invokes additional user processes and a router process if it is required. After network connection has been established among user processes and router processes on both machines, message data from user processes are transfered to user processes on a destination host.

## 2.3    Execution Method

In the execution of a Stampi application, the following command;

```
% jmpirun -node 2,network=myrinet2k -group scoregrp1 program
```

initiates an executable named "program". Original options of an SCore cluster system such as "-node", "-group" and "network=" are available in options of the command. If a spawn function is used in a program, dynamic process creation based on MPI-2 (dynamic mode) is realized.

Stampi also supports static process creation mode based on MPI-1 (static mode) among two computers. We implemented additional communication mechanism to support the static mode among computers on the dynamic process creation mechanism. Let us assume that there are two SCore PC clusters; computers A (comp-a) and B (comp-b). When the following command;

```
% jmpirun -node 1 -group half0 program : -host comp-b \
  -node 1 -group half1 program
```

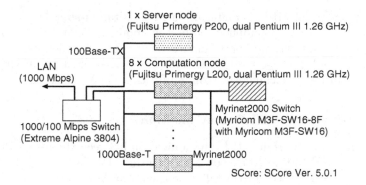

**Fig. 3.** Schematic diagram of an SCore PC cluster which was used in performance measurement.

is issued on a computer A, a single user process is initiated on each computer and a single `MPI_COMM_WORLD` is established among those computers. Here, character "\" means that the following line is continued without carriage return.

## 3   Performance Measurement of Stampi on an SCore Cluster System

We measured performance of intra-machine and inter-machine MPI communications of Stampi using an SCore PC cluster which is shown in Fig. 3. Network connections among computation nodes were established with Gigabit Ethernet(1 Gbps, full duplex mode) and Myrinet2000(2 Gbps). A server node was connected to a Gigabit Ethernet switch with 100 Mbps bandwidth and full duplex mode. Network connections from computation nodes to local area network (LAN) were established with 1 Gbps bandwidth.

In performance measurement, we calculated transfer rate as (message data size)/(RTT/2), where RTT is round trip time for ping-pong MPI communication between user processes. In addition, we defined that latency is RTT/2 of 0 Byte message data with a packet header in TCP/IP communication.

### 3.1   Intra-machine MPI Communication

In SCore-supplied method, a user process directly calls an MPICH-SCore library, while in Stampi-supplied method, an MPICH-SCore library is called by a user process through a Stampi common communication library.

We measured performance of intra-machine MPI communication in both methods to check whether performance degradation by implementing Stampi was significant or not. We observed that performance results of MPI communication via Gigabit Ethernet in SCore-supplied and Stampi-supplied methods were 104.3 MB/s and 103.7 MB/s for 1 MByte message data, respectively. Thus, performance ratio of MPI communication in the Stampi-supplied method relative to that in the SCore-supplied method is about 99 % ($103.7/104.3 \times 100$). Therefore, we consider that performance degradation in the Stampi-supplied method is negligible. We also observed that there was no significant performance degradation in intra-machine MPI communication via Myrinet2000.

## 3.2   Inter-machine MPI Communication

We measured inter-machine MPI communication between the SCore PC cluster and a Linux workstation (dual 600 MHz Pentium III CPU node, Linux SMP kernel 2.4.17). Stampi was also installed on the Linux workstation. The SCore PC cluster was connected to the Linux workstation with Gigabit Ethernet via two Gigabit Ethernet switches (NetGear GS524T). In this test, user processes on the SCore PC cluster communicated with user processes on the Linux workstation without a router process.

Firstly, we measured performance of inter-machine communication using raw TCP socket connections between a computation node in the SCore PC cluster and the Linux workstation. Performance results are shown in Table 1.

**Table 1.** Latencies and transfer rates of raw TCP socket connections between a computation node in an SCore PC cluster and a Linux PC via Gigabit Ethernet. Unit of numbers in this table is MB/s.

| Latency | Message data size (Byte) | | | | |
|---|---|---|---|---|---|
| | 64 K | 1 M | 8 M | 64 M | 256 M |
| 61 $\mu$s | 30.1 | 37.2 | 37.3 | 36.9 | 36.8 |

Secondly, we measured performance of inter-machine MPI communication in the dynamic mode and the static mode. In the dynamic mode, a single user process is initiated on the SCore PC cluster and an another user process is invoked on the Linux workstation. On the other hand, we initiated a single user process on a computation node in the SCore PC cluster and the Linux workstation each in the static mode. Performance results are shown in Table 2. From these results, we consider that the performance in both modes achieves almost the same value of raw TCP socket connections.

## 4   Related Works

There are several MPI libraries such as MPICH or PACX-MPI [6]. In MPICH, inter-machine MPI communication is established by direct connection between computers. Although PACX-MPI uses router process mechanism for inter-machine MPI communication, the number of router processes is fixed. In Stampi, router process is dynamically created according to communication mechanism of

**Table 2.** Latencies and transfer rates of inter-machine MPI communication between an SCore PC cluster and a Linux workstation. In this table, **dynamic** and **static** denotes dynamic and static process creation modes, respectively. In this table, **np(SCore)** and **np(Linux)** are the numbers of processes on the SCore PC cluster and the Linux workstation, respectively. Unit of numbers in this table is MB/s.

| | np(SCore) | np(Linux) | Latency | Message data size (Byte) | | | | |
|---|---|---|---|---|---|---|---|---|
| | | | | 64 K | 1 M | 8 M | 64 M | 256 M |
| dynamic | 1 | 1 | 57.0 $\mu$s | 19.5 | 33.9 | 34.6 | 34.9 | 35.0 |
| static | 1 | 1 | 106.5 $\mu$s | 18.9 | 33.7 | 35.0 | 35.3 | 35.4 |

computers or user's explicit configuration requests. In addition, users can select the number of router processes.

## 5    Summary

We have implemented a Stampi library on an SCore cluster system. Stampi uses a high performance MPICH-SCore library and TCP/IP socket connections in intra-machine and inter-machine MPI communications, respectively. Stampi also supports dynamic process creation based on MPI-2 among computers.

Through performance measurement, we observed that there was no significant degradation in performance of intra-machine MPI communication in the Stampi-supplied method compared with that in the SCore-supplied method. In inter-machine MPI communication, performance results in dynamic and static process creation modes were almost the same as those of raw TCP socket connections. Using this mechanism, users can execute an MPI program in both modes between an SCore PC cluster and other computer without awareness of network communication mechanism of each computer.

## References

1. Message Passing Interface Forum, "MPI: A Message-Passing Interface Standard", June 1995.
2. Message Passing Interface Forum, "MPI-2: Extensions to the Message-Passing Interface Standard", July 1997.
3. T. Imamura, Y. Tsujita, H. Koide and H. Takemiya, "An Architecture of Stampi: MPI Library on a Cluster of Parallel Computers", LNCS 1908, Recent Advances in Parallel Virtual Machine and Message Passing Interface, Springer, 2000, pp. 200–207.
4. PC Cluster Consortium, http://www.pccluster.org/.
5. W. Gropp, E. Lusk, N. Doss and A. Skjellum, "A high-performance, portable implementation of the MPI Message-Passing Interface standard", *Parallel Computing*, 22(6), pp. 789–828, 1996.
6. E. Gabriel, M. Resch, T. Beisel and R. Keller, "Distributed Computing in a Heterogeneous Computing Environment", LNCS 1497, Recent Advances in Parallel Virtual Machine and Message Passing Interface, Springer, 1998, pp. 180–188.

# Internet Traffic Congestion Modelling and Parallel Distributed Analysis

M. Isreb[1*] and A.I. Khan[2]

[1] School of Engineering, Monash University,
Gippsland Campus,
Churchill, Victoria, 3842
Australia
Mustafa.Isreb@eng.monash.edu.au
http://www.gippsland.monash.edu.au/gse/isreb.htm

[2] School of Network Computing, Monash University,
Peninsula Campus,
Frankston, 3199
Australia
Asad.Khan@infotech.monash.edu.au

**Abstract.** The level of complexity for modelling Internet traffic is equivalent to that of modelling highly non-linear natural systems. A network is essentially made up of a large number of queues. The effects of traffic volumes on service time and waiting time are discussed using a simplified form of the queuing theory. The key attributes that influence network traffic are identified. A numerical optimisation based approach is suggested to analyse the existing Internet architecture for future developments. The increase in the routing table sizes with the increase in the number of networked devices is discussed. A parallel-distributed routing approach is identified for devising a scalable routing architecture.

## 1  Introduction

The distributed nature of Internet and variety of underlying networks and protocols present a formidable challenge for modeling Internet traffic. The level of complexity is equivalent to that of modeling highly non-linear natural systems. The paper looks at the factors that would influence future Internet developments in light of the existing protocols and data transport mechanisms.

Internet traffic is prone to unexpected delays caused by transient network traffic congestions. Congestion may be defined as occurring in a network device when packets (data) arrive faster than they can be forwarded. With the growing reliance on critical services being delivered through the Internet; it's becoming increasingly important that factors affecting congestion be studied and effectively managed. Hence computational models, based upon these factors, are required to accurately analyse Internet traffic patterns and behaviors.

---

* Corresponding Author

M. Guo and L.T.Yang (Eds.): ISPA 2003, LNCS 2745, pp. 145–151, 2003.
© Springer-Verlag Berlin Heidelberg 2003

## 2 Congestion Control

Congestion can be brought about by several factors. If all of a sudden a stream of packets starts arriving at the recipient node then a queue would begin to form. If there were insufficient memory to hold these queued packets then packets would be lost. Having more memory may help to a point but Nagle (1987) discovered that congestion got worse if routers were equipped with an infinite amount of memory. The reason being by the time packets get to the front of the queue, they have already timed out (repeatedly), and duplicates have been already resent. With all these packets being forwarded to the next router, compounds the traffic flow and adds to the congestion. Slow processors and slow links can also cause congestion. Congestion tends to feed upon itself and become worse, [1].

## 3 Loss and Delay

A network is essentially made up of a large number of queues. Hence using the queuing theory most effectively does the analysis of networks, [2].
The main form of diagnosis within networks is to determine which link within a network is broken, [3-6].

Firstly a clear idea is required of what we need to analyse within a network for performance considerations. The time it takes for a data packet to be received at the destination address varies and is dependent upon the level of congestion present in the network. The level of congestion in other words determines the extent of delay to be expected in data packet transmissions. Delay may be perceived in terms of:

- Average delay
- Worst case delay
- Distribution of delay
- Delay between a pair of specific nodes

Also to be able to ascertain the performance of a network we need to be able to estimate the load on the network, to do this we need to know the number and length of messages entering the network, this is hard to determine.   We can make assumptions about the network in order to determine the number and length of messages, but in doing this we have to be careful that we do not develop a model, which is not applicable to the real world.

## 4 Network Design Attributes

The level of complexity involved in efficiently managing the network traffic over the Internet may be assessed from the probabilistic systems discussed in the previous sections. Hence the key factors, or attributes, which affect the performance and the cost of a network, need to be identified before any attempt is made at modelling such systems. These attributes may be summarised as follows.

## 4.1  Link Utilisation

All links must make full use of the available bandwidth capacity of the transmission media. However the time for servicing each transmission packet tends to increase as the link utilisation increases. Hence a balance must be reached where an acceptable level of link utilisation is made while $T_s$ remains within acceptable limits of service requirements.

## 4.2  Packet Length

It can be shown that the waiting time, $T_w$, is substantially reduced when constant length packets are used. This factor is exploited within the ATM protocols for achieving the higher throughput. However using fixed length data packets may introduce overheads for applications requiring different packet sizes for optimal communications and the addressing requirements.

## 4.3  Error Control

Generally the data packet is resent whenever there is a packet loss or a packet corruption. The resending of data packets could be done at the network level or at the application level. The network-level error control allows faster resends however there is no provision to skip non-essential data packets; e.g. in the case of voice and video. An application-level error control makes this distinction, albeit at a slower pace.

## 4.4  Flow Control

Network-level flow control would be more responsive to the network states as compared to an application-level flow control mechanism. However the application-level flow control would have simpler mechanisms for managing flow control for different types of service requirements (e.g. sending key strokes versus audio).

## 4.5  Congestion Control

Congestion control mechanisms may generally be divided into two groups: open loop and closed loop. Open loop solutions attempt to solve the problem by good design, in essence, to make sure it does not occur in the first place. Decisions relating to the management of traffic are made without regard to the state of the network. Alternatively, closed loop solutions are based upon the concept of a feedback loop. Open loop mechanisms do not add to the existing network traffic, but take no note of the state of the network. The closed loop solutions generally require additional packet transmissions to convey the state of the network, but do take into account the network states. Hence appropriate use of these solutions is essential for managing traffic congestion conditions effectively.

## 4.6  Connectionless versus Connection Oriented Services

Connectionless services are based upon the best try concept. The packets are not guaranteed to arrive in the same order as these are sent in or for that matter follow the same route. This introduces an assembly overhead at the network and the application levels. Higher throughputs are possible provided the error rate remains low. Connection-oriented services incur a connection set up overhead; however there are lesser overheads on the application side for error and flow control.

## 5  Limitations of the Existing Internet Architecture

Internet is made up of a number of separately managed and run internets; each internet is treated as an Autonomous System (AS).

The existing routing methods are based upon the use of lookup tables. Routing devices (routers) are used to manage efficient data paths within the AS or to send data to another AS. The routers manage copies of the shortest/most efficient paths to other destinations. These entries are known as lookup tables. The routing methodology used for routing data traffic within an AS is termed as Interior Gateway Protocol (IGP) and the routing of data traffic to other systems or to the core network is termed as exterior gateway protocol (EGP).

One of the commonly used EGP is the Border Gateway Protocol (BGP), developed by Lougheed and Rekhter [7] and later updated to BGP-4 by Rekhter and Li [8].

The Internet is approaching a crisis, and the optical networking coupled with Internet Protocol (IP) version 6 may accelerate its arrival. The problem relates to BGP routing tables. With the increase in the number of devices being attached to the Internet is increasing the size of the routing tables. The number of entries has increased by an order of the magnitude since the past six years. It is expected that the number of entries could reach the one million mark in the near future. This would have a crippling effect on the existing routing hardware by placing a very high demand on memory and processing resources within the routers. The queuing models discussed in Section 3 assume no significant overheads on account of the routing overheads. Hence the problem may be stated as follows. The increase in the number of devices would result in higher data traffic leading to classical queuing delays and the slow down in the processing capabilities of the gateway routers on account of the increase in their lookup table sizes.

In this paper we propose a two-pronged approach where the traffic modelling is separated from the limitation of BGP. In other word, the problem with the BGP table sizes needs to be addressed before the networks are re modelled for a very high number of networked devices.

## 6  Revised Computational Scheme for Very Large Routing Tables

The routing tables are the representation of the graph and its shortest paths to various destinations. The routing protocols dynamically construct and update these shortest paths depending upon the network loss-delay metrics. The networks and hosts on the Internet may be viewed as nodes on a connected graph. The process of computing the shortest paths and the process of searching for these shortest paths may be distributed and parallelised among the routers within an AS or even extended to the hosts within the AS. The revised computational model would eliminate the need for constantly adding to the hardware resources, at the routers level, with the increase in networked devices - the increased number of networked devices would implicitly provide the additional resources required to meet with the routing requirements.

In this paper we would not go to the exact mechanics of implementation, as it would require an extensive amount of space. We will however list the following parallel shortest search algorithms, already available in the literature [9], as potential areas of application.

## 6.1 Dijkstra's Algorithm

Dijkstra's *single-source* shortest-path algorithm computes all shortest paths from a single vertex, $v_s$. It can also be used for the all-pairs shortest-path problem, by the simple expedient of applying it $N$ times–once to each vertex, $v_0,...,v_{N-1}$.

Dijkstra's sequential single-source algorithm is given below. It maintains as $T$ the set of vertices for which shortest paths have not been found, and as $d_i$ the shortest known path from $v_s$ to vertex $v_i$. Initially, $T=V$ and all $d_i = \infty$. At each step of the algorithm, the vertex $v_m$ in $T$ with the smallest $d$ value is removed from $T$. Each neighbor of $v_m$ in $T$ is examined to see whether a path through $v_m$ would be shorter than the currently best-known path.

> procedure sequential_dijkstra
> begin
> $d_s = 0$
> $d_i = \infty, \text{for } i \neq s$
> $\text{for } i = 0 \text{ to } N - 1$
> $\quad \text{find } v_m \in T \text{ with minimum } d_m$
> $\quad \text{for each edge} (v_m, v_t) \text{ with } v_t \in T$
> $\quad\quad \text{if } (d_t > d_m + \text{length}((v_m, v_t))) \text{ then } d_t = d_m + length(v_m, v_t))$
> $\quad \text{endfor}$
> $\quad T = T - v_m$
> $\text{endfor}$
> end

An all-pairs algorithm executes the sequential algorithm $N$ times, once for each vertex. This involves $O(N^3)$ comparisons and takes time $N^3 t_c F$, where $t_c$ is the cost of a single comparison in Floyd's algorithm and $F$ is a constant. Empirical studies show that $F \approx 1.6$; that is, Dijkstra's algorithm is slightly more expensive than Floyd's algorithm.

*Parallel Dijkstra 1:* The first parallel Dijkstra algorithm replicates the graph in each of $P$ tasks. Each task executes the sequential algorithm for $N/P$ vertices. This algorithm requires no communication but can utilize at most $N$ processors. Because the sequential Dijkstra algorithm is $F$ times slower than the sequential Floyd algorithm, the parallel algorithm's execution time is

$$T_{Dijkstra1} = t_c F \frac{N^3}{P}$$

*Parallel Dijkstra 2:* The second parallel Dijkstra algorithm allows for the case when $P>N$. We define $N$ sets of $P/N$ tasks. Each set of tasks is given the entire graph and is responsible for computing shortest paths for a single vertex within each set of tasks; the vertices of the graph are partitioned. Hence, the operation Find $v_m \in T$ with minimum $d_m$ requires first a local computation to find the local vertex with minimum $d$ and second a reduction involving all $P/N$ tasks in the same set in order to determine the globally minimum $d_m$. The reduction can be achieved by using the butterfly communication structure [9] in $\log\left(\dfrac{P}{N}\right)$ steps. Hence, as the reduction is performed $N$ times and involves two values, the total cost of this algorithm is

$$T_{Dijkstra2} = t_c F \frac{N^3}{P} + N \log \frac{P}{N} (t_s + 2t_w)$$

## 7   Discussion and Concluding Remarks

The key factors that affect the data transmissions within the Internet may be summarised as follows:

1. Data traffic congestion
2. Loss and delay
3. Routing overheads

Items (1) and (2) are dependent upon various network design attributes such as

1. Link utilization considerations.
2. Packet lengths required within heterogeneous networks and protocols.
3. Error ad flow control mechanisms available.
4. Congestion control techniques available within different networking protocols.
5. Connectionless versus connection-oriented services.

It is envisaged that a macro-level network traffic model would need to be analyzed to assess the efficacy of the contemporary internetworking architectures. A possible way forward would be to formulate a series of optimisation problems that superimpose the requirements and the constraints, set within the attributes, on the probabilistic queuing models. The resultant models may then be contrasted with the existing internetworks for concentrating the re-engineering efforts.

The problem of increase in the routing overheads with the increase in the number of devices would require a fundamental change in the contemporary routing mechanism. The route processing calculations would need to be parallelised and distributed among the participating routing nodes within an AS. In fact this model may be extended to the level of individual workstations where each workstation connected to the network performs a portion of the total routing processing computations for the AS. The downside of distributing the processing loads at the workstation level would be seen as assigning load to the workstation, which has traditionally been in the domain of the dedicated routers. However the distributed model will have the advantage of being capable of forming self-organising networks that would automatically scale up the routing capacities as the number of workstations increases on the network.

# References

[1] Tanenbaum A S, Computer Networks, 3$^{rd}$ edition, Prentice-Hall Inc, Upper Saddle River, New Jersey, 1996.
[2] Kershenbaum A, Telecommunications Network Design Algorithms, McGraw-Hill computer science series, 1993.
[3] Parente V R, Switch Back to Routers, http://www.bcr.com/bcrmag/08/98p33.html, Business Communications Review, Volume 28, Number 8, pp. 33–36, August 1998.
[4] Kung H T, Traffic Management for High Speed Networks, Naval Studies Board, 1997
[5] Yang Q, Reddy, Alpati V S, A Taxonomy for Congestion Control Algorithms in Packet Switching Networks, IEEE Network Magazine, Volume 9, Number 5, July/August 1995.
[6] Verma D, Supporting Service Level Agreements on IP Networks, MacMillan Technical Publishing, 1999.
[7] Lougheed K, Rekhter Y, RFC 1267: A Border Gateway Protocol 3 (BGP-3), IETF, Networking Group, 1991
[8] Rekhter Y, Li T, *RFC 1771: A Border Gateway Protocol 4 (BGP-4)*, IETF, Networking Group, March 1995
[9] Foster I, *Designing and Building Parallel Programs*, Addison-Wesley, 1995, http://www-unix.mcs.anl.gov/dbpp/, retrieved on April 2003.

# Hierarchical Grown Bluetrees (HGB) – An Effective Topology for Bluetooth Scatternets

Tsung-Chuan Huang[1], Chu-Sing Yang[2], Chao-Chieh Huang[1], and Shen-Wen Bai[2]

[1] Department of Electrical Engineering
tch@mail.nsysu.edu.tw
[2] Department of Computer Science and Engineering,
National Sun Yat-sen University, Kaohsiung, Taiwan

**Abstract.** Bluetooth is a promising technology for short-range wireless communication and networking, mainly used as a replacement for connected cables. The specification defines how to build a piconet and there are several existing solutions to construct a scatternet from the piconets. The process to construct a scatternet is called *scatternet formation*. We find that a tree shape scatternet called *bluetree* has three defects: First, it lacks efficiency in routing because the bluetree may form a skewed tree, not a balanced tree, resulting in longer routing paths. Second, the parent nodes in bluetree are very likely to become the bottlenecks of communication. Third, it lacks reliability. When a parent node is lost, it could cause several separated subtrees. In this paper we introduce an algorithm to generate the bluetree hierarchically; namely, the algorithm grows nodes in the bluetree level by level. This resolves the foregoing defects in scatternet formation. We construct the bluetree , keeping it balanced, to achieve the shorter routing paths, and establish the connection pairs between the siblings to provide another path to route. As a result, the traffic load at parent nodes can be greatly improved. Besides, once a parent node is lost, only two separated parts will be caused. A better reliability is therefore obtained.

## 1 Introduction

Bluetooth is a fast growing technology for short-range wireless networks and wireless personal area networks (WPAN) in recent years. It aims at supporting wireless connectivity among mobile devices such as cellular phones, headsets, PDAs (Personal Digital Assistants), digital cameras, laptop and computer peripheries, etc. The Bluetooth technology enables the design of low-cost, low-power, small-size radios that can be embedded in the existing portable devices. For instance, three-in-one phone is the GSM (Global System for Mobile Communications) cellular phone in which Bluetooth module is embedded. That is, it is a GSM cellular phone outdoors, but becomes a Walkie-talkie indoors. When two three-in-one phones are in the range of communication, they can communicate with each other free charged. When connecting to PSTN (Public Switched Telephone Network) adapter indoors, the three-in-one phones can be used for fixed line communication and are charged based on the fixed line communication rate. This is the advantage and convenience of devices embedded with Bluetooh module.

M. Guo and L.T.Yang (Eds.): ISPA 2003, LNCS 2745, pp. 152–164, 2003.
© Springer-Verlag Berlin Heidelberg 2003

According to the Bluetooth specification [1], Bluetooth devices operate in the globally available 2.4GHz band that is reserved for Industrial, Scientific, and Medical (ISM) applications. This band with 83.5MHz is divided into 79 1MHz-spaced *channels* except the guard band. It uses the technique of frequency hopping spread spectrum (FHSS), called *frequency hopping sequences* (FHS), to define these channels, which co-exist in this wide band without interfering with each other. When two Bluetooth devices come into each other's communication range, a connection between them is established through the *inquiry* and *page* procedures defined in the Bluetooth specification. The inquiry procedure is used to discover other devices and the page procedure is used to establish actual link. The "sender" device which broadcasts inquiry message becomes *master* and the "receiver" device that always keeps listening becomes *slave*. After establishing the connection, time division duplex (TDD) is used for communicating between the master and the slaves. Each of 79 channels mentioned above is divided into 625-msec intervals, called *slots*. Different slots use different hop frequencies. The master transmits in even-numbered slots while the slave in odd-numbered slots. A group of devices sharing a common channel is called a *piconet*. Each piconet can only have one master which decides the frequency hopping sequence for the piconet and controls the access to the channel. There is no limit on the maximum number of connected slaves to the master, but the number of *active* slaves at one time can be at most 7. If a master has more than 7 active slaves, some slaves must be *parked*. Parked devices cannot operate in its piconet until it is unparked. The network constructed from connecting the piconets is called the *scatternet*. The process to construct a scatternet is called *scatternet formation*.

In [3, 4, 8], a tree-based scatternet called *bluetree* was proposed, in which the scatternet is formed using the topology of tree shape, the parent node being the *master* and the children as the *slaves*. These bluetrees will be called the *general bluetree* (GB) through the rest of this paper. The general bluetree has three defects. First, it is inefficient in routing. When the bluetree is a skewed tree, rather than a balanced tree, a longer routing path will be induced. Second, the parent nodes of bluetree are likely to become the bottlenecks of communication and result in heavy traffic load. Third, it is unreliable. When a parent node is lost, it may cause several separated parts: the subtrees of the losing node and the remaining part of the bluetree. This will lead to a time-consuming process for rebuilding the entire scatternet in order to maintain the connectivity.

In this paper we improve the structure of general bluetree and propose the formation methods to cope with these problems. The bluetree that we propose is called Hierarchical Grown Bluetree(HGB), which grows level by level and remains balanced during the process of scatternet formation. Compared to the skewed bluetree, HGB bluetree have a shorter routing path. In addition, a message can be sent via the connection between the siblings (refer to section 3 for details) instead of having to pass through the parent node. As a result, the communication bottlenecks at parent nodes can be greatly improved. Besides, once a parent node is lost, only two separated parts will be caused. One is the connected part below the lost node. The other is the remaining part of the bluetree. A better reliability can be achieved.

The remainder of this paper is organized as follows. Section 2 describes the relevant researches on Bluetooth scatternets. Section 3 presents our improving scheme of tree-based scatternet, HGB. Section 4 shows the experimental results. Finally, we conclude this paper in Section 5.

## 2  Related Work

Several methods for scatternet formation have been proposed [2, 3, 4, 5, 6, 7, 8]. In [2], the protocol-BTCP(Bluetooth Topology Construction Protocol) consists of two phases. In the first phase, all nodes join the link formation protocol. When two nodes establish a link, the one with smaller address becomes the winner and owns the other's address and clock information. The winners join in the link formation again until one with the smallest address is determined. This node becomes the leader to have the address and clock information of all nodes. In the second phase, the leader constructs the scatternet using the address and clock information of all nodes.

In [3], Zaruba *et al.* introduced "*Bluetrees*" as a practical protocol for forming connected scatternets, which has two variations: *Blueroot Grown Bluetree* and *Distributed Bluetree*. The former builds a scatternet starting from some specified node called *Blueroot*; the latter speeds up the scatternet formation process by selecting more than one root for tree formation and then merge the trees generated by each root. In [4], Tan *et al.* proposed a *TSF* scattenet formation protocol to construct a tree-based scatternet. The protocol is self-healing such that it allows node to join or remove at any time. In [5], Law *et al.* presented a randomized distributed algorithm for constructing the scatternet. The algorithm guarantees that any device can be a member of at most two piconets and the number of piconets is close to minimal. The Bluenet scheme in [6] tries to reduce as much bridge overhead as possible while maintaining a reasonable degree of connectivity in the resulting scatternet.

In [7], the generated topology is a connected mesh with multiple paths between any pair of nodes to achieve fault-tolerance. It contains three phases: neighbors discovery, isolated piconets formation, and piconets interconnection. In [8], Sun *et al.* presented a method to embed b-trees scheme into a scatternet which enables such a network to be self-routing. It requires only small fix-sized information and needs no routing table at each node regardless of the size of the scatternet. In [9], Bhagwat *et al.* provided a method for routing in the Bluetooth network. It uses on-demand routing protocols in which a node wishing to send a message broadcasts the network a query to learn the route to the destination before sending a message.

## 3  Hierarchical Grown Bluetree

In this section we describe our scatternet formation method and routing protocols in detail. The following statements are the definitions associated with node $x$ in the bluetree, which will be used throughout the rest of this paper:

- dev_info($x$) contains the address, clock and level of node $x$ in the bluetree.
- bd_addr($x$) is the Bluetooth MAC address of node $x$ as defined in the Bluetooth specification.
- level($x$) denotes the level of node $x$ in the bluetree.
- struc_array is a one-dimensional array recording the nodes in the bluetree, each node associated with 5 children. Table 1 is an example of array representation for the bluetree in Figure 1. Each node has a corresponding array index. The position of index 0 stores the root node 35. The positions from indices 1 to 5 record the children of node 35, i.e., 70, 21, 15, 39 and 33, respectively. Since node 70 has only one child, the position of index 6 stores

node 36 while the positions from indices 7 to 10 are set to 0. In this way, we reserved 5 array elements for recording the children of each node.

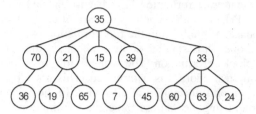

**Fig. 1.** An example of bluetree.

**Table 1.** struc_array for the bluetree in Fig. 1.

| Index | 0 | 1 | 2 | 3 | 4 | 5 | 6 | ... | 11 | 12 | ... | 21 | 22 | ... | 26 | 27 | 28 | 29 | 30 |
|---|---|---|---|---|---|---|---|---|---|---|---|---|---|---|---|---|---|---|---|
| Node | 35 | 70 | 21 | 15 | 39 | 33 | 36 | 0 | 19 | 65 | 0 | 7 | 45 | 0 | 60 | 63 | 24 | 0 | 0 |

- When a node is added or deleted, the parent will send an *update* message to the blueroot to update struc_array.
- When 5 children have been established, the parent will send a *complete* message with its level to the blueroot.
- When the bluetree has been a full tree with degree 5, the blueroot sends a *permit_inq* message to all of the leaf nodes.

## 3.1 Construction Protocol

In the Bluetooth specification [1], a node can be in one of several states. They are *inquiry* state, *inquiry scan* state, *page* state, *page scan* state and *connection* state. A node switches between these states according to the specific condition it met in the network. In scatternet formation, Zaruba *et al.* proposed a method in which an arbitrary node is initially designated as the *blueroot* [3]. This strategy is also applied in our method. An node is selected as the root of our bluetree. Using Figure 1 as an example, let us see the scatternet formation process in our method. Suppose that at the outset node 35 is selected as the blueroot. Node 35 accordingly enters into the inquiry state by broadcasting inquiry messages to discover other devices. All of the isolated nodes are in the inquiry scan state. Assume that node 70 receives the inquiry message and responses to node 35 with dev_info(70) message which contains the address, clock and level information of node 70.Node 35 now locks itself to deny the insertion of other nodes. It then switches to the page state to page node 70 and set up a link using the information in dev_info(70). At present, node 35 is the master and node 70 is its slave. After this, node 35 reenters into the inquiry state again. This process repeats again until the children of node 35 grow up to 5. To relieve the traffic load at the parent node, we improve the general bluetree topology by establishing extra connections between the siblings. In the bluetree scheme, the parent node acts as the master and the children nodes as the slaves. Because the Bluetooth specification only allows a master to have 7 slaves, we permit the parent nodes to have 5 children nodes at most, reserving two links for the connections between the siblings. In Fig.1, while node 35 is only with nodes 70 and 21 as its children, the master and slave connection between the siblings will be like in Fig 2 (a). The arrow tail represents the master while the arrowhead represents the slave. When the number of children increases from 3 to 5, the connections between the siblings will be as illustrated in Fig 2 (b) to (d), respectively. Take a look at node 33, when it acts as a master, the slaves will include the children nodes 60, 63, 24 and the sibling nodes 70, 21.

To see the traffic load at the parent node can be efficiently improved by our bluetree scheme, suppose that node 36 will communicate with node 60. In the general bluetree topology the message must be sent up to node 35 then down to node 60. Because any message from the source node must be sent to the common parent node then to the destination node, the common parent node incurs a heavy communication load. In our scheme, the message from node 36 can take the way from node 70 to node 33 then to node 60, rather than having to pass through node 35, because of the link from node 70 to 33. It effectively avoids the communication congestion at the common parent node (node 35 in this example).

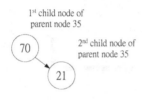

**Fig. 2.(a)** 2 children case.

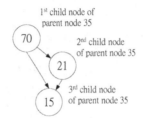

**Fig. 2.(b)** 2 children case.

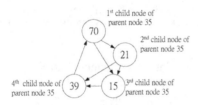

**Fig. 2.(c)** 4 children case.

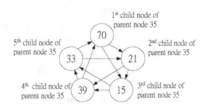

**Fig. 2(d)** 5 children case.

Once the blueroot has 5 children, all of the nodes in level 2 can enter into the inquiry state simultaneously by broadcasting inquiry messages to discover other devices. The nodes in level 3 can not enter into the inquiry state until all of the nodes in level 2 already grew up to 5 children. In other words the leaf nodes in $h$ level can enter into the inquiry state and concurrently build their own piconet only if they already had $5^{h-1}$ nodes. In this way our bluetree always keeps balanced in the scattenet formation process.

In the following we describe the procedures for each state. For clarity, the state transition diagram is illustrated in Fig. 3. The dash lines represent the access message and the solid lines indicate the state transition. When sending an access message, the node in the inquiry state and page state is the sender, while the nodes in the inquiry scan and page scan state are the receivers. The sender sends an access message. The receiver can respond to the access message. In the following procedure, $x$ implicitly denotes a sender and $y$ a receiver.

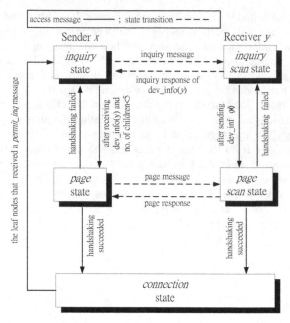

**Fig. 3.** The transition diagram

- The *inquiry state* procedure.

  Node $x$ in the inquiry state broadcasts inquiry messages periodically and keeps listening all the time. When it receives a response message from some node $y$, i.e., dev_info($y$), it locks itself and switches to the page state if its children is less than 5.
- The *inquiry scan* state procedure.

  All of the nodes in the inquiry scan state keep listening to the inquiry message. When a node $y$ receives the inquiry message from $x$, it responds dev_info($y$) to $x$ and switches to the page scan state.
- The *page state* procedure.

  Node $x$ in the page state handshakes with node $y$ that responded to the inquiry message. If the handshaking succeeded (the connection between $x$ and $y$ is established), node $x$ switches to the connection state otherwise $x$ unlocks itself and returns to the inquiry state.
- The *page scan* state procedure.

  Node $y$ in the page scan state handshakes with node $x$ that it sent response message to. If the handshaking succeeded (the connection between $x$ and $y$ is established), node $y$ switches to the connection state otherwise returns to the inquiry scan state.
- The *connection state* procedure.

  If the node in the connection state is switched from the page state (i.e., it is a master or parent node), it unlocks itself. If this node is the blueroot as well, it updates struc_array directly otherwise sends *update* message to the blueroot. The blueroot updates struc_array to reflect the successful connection in the page state. If 5 children have been established, the parent node sent a *complete* message to the blueroot. The blueroot broadcasts a *permit_inq* message to all of the leaf nodes if it receives a *complete* message and the maximum level is achieved. If the node is switched from the page scan state (i.e., it is a slave or leaf node), it records its level and just keeps listening. When a leaf node receives a *permit_inq* message, it switches to the inquiry state.

The detailed construction protocol is shown as bellow. All nodes execute this protocol in constructing the scatternet.

---

**Hierarchical Grown Bluetree Construction protocol**
// $x$ denotes a node in the inquiry or page state (i.e.,it is a sender); $y$ is a node in the inquiry scan or page scan state (i.e.,it is a receiver).
  **inquiry state:**
  broadcast inquiry messages periodically
    **on** receiving an inquiry response of dev_info($y$)
      **if** ||child($x$)|| < 5
        lock $x$
        switch to page state to add $y$ as its child
      **end if**
  **inquiry scan state:**
    listen to the inquiry messages
    **on** receiving the inquiry message from $x$
      send dev_info($y$) to $x$ and switch to page scan state
  **page state:**
    $x$ handshakes with $y$
    **if** handshaking succeeded  /* the connection is established */
      switch to connection state
    **else**
      unlock itself
      return to inquiry state
    **end if**
  **page scan state:**
    $y$ handshakes with $x$
    **if** handshaking succeeded /* the connection is established */
      switch to connection state
    **else**
      return to inquiry scan state
    **end if**
  **connection state:**
  // let $z$ be a node in the connection state
    **if** $z$ is a parent node
    unlock $z$
      **if** $z$ is the blueroot
        update the struc_array
      **else**
        send an *update* message to the blueroot
      **end if**
    // establish (master, slave) link between the siblings

```
    switch the number of z'children
      case 5:
        establish the links (4th child, 5th child), (3rd
        child, 5th child), (5th child, 1st child), (5th
        child, 2nd child) between the siblings
        if z is the blueroot
          send permit_inq message to its children
        else    /* z is not the blueroot */
          send a complete message to the blueroot

        end if

      case 4:
        establish the links (3rd child, 4st child), (2nd
        child, 4th child), (4th child, 1st child)
        between the siblings
      case 3:
        establish the links (2nd child, 3rd child), (1st child, 3rd
        child) between the siblings
      case 2:
        establish the (1st child, 2nd child) between the
        siblings
      end switch
    else
      record node z in the bluetree
    end if
    on receiving a permit_inq message
      if z is a leaf node
        switch to the inquiry state
      end if
    on receiving a complete message
      if z is the blueroot and the maximum level is
    achieved
          send a permit_inq message to all of the leaf
        nodes
      end if
    on receiving a update message
      if z is the blueroot
        update the struc_array
      end if
```

## 3.2 Routing Protocol

When a node wants to send a message to another node, it polls blueroot to get the routing path *rp*. The routing path *rp* contains the hops that the message will pass. The blueroot uses the following routing protocol to calculate the routing path.

**Hierarchical Grown Bluetree routing protocol**
// When node $s$ wants to send a packet $m$ to node $d$, it polls root to get the routing
//path.

```
  search struc_array for s & d
  if d is not found
    respond that d does not exist
  else
    s=0; d=0
```

    **while** $idx_s \neq idx_d$   /* $idx_s$ is the index of node $s$ and $idx_d$ is the index of node $d$ */

        **if** $idx_s > idx_d$

           `add` $idx_s$ `to the routing path` $rp$

$$idx_s = \left\lfloor \frac{idx_s - 1}{5} \right\rfloor$$

          $s=s+1$

        **else if** $idx_s < idx_d$

                `add` $idx_d$ `to the routing path` $rp$

$$idx_d = \left\lfloor \frac{idx_d - 1}{5} \right\rfloor$$

             $d=d+1$

           **end if**

       **end while**

       **if** $s=0$

          `add` $index(s)$ `to the routing path` $rp$

       **else if** $d=0$

             `add` $index(d)$ `to the routing path` $rp$

          **end if**

       **end if**

      `return the routing path` $rp$ `to node` $s$

   **end if**

Take Fig. 4 as an example and assume that node 36 wants to send a message to node 6. According to struc_array the blueroot finds the index of node 36 to be 6 and the index of node 6 is 131. Because 6<131, the blueroot appends 131 into $rp$ (i.e., $rp$=(131)). The parent of node 6 is node 60 whose index is 26. Because 6<26, index 26 is appended into $rp$. The $rp$ becomes (26, 131). Continuously, the parent of node 60 is node 33 whose index is 5. Because 6>5, index 6 is appended into $rp$. The $rp$ yields (6, 26, 131). Now, the parent of node 36 is computed to be node 70 and the index of node 70 is 1. Because 1<5, index 5 is appended into $rp$. The $rp$ becomes (6, 5, 26, 131). The parent of node33 is computed to be node 35 whose index is 0. Because 1<0, index 1 is appended into $rp$. The $rp$ is now (6,1, 5, 26, 131). The parent of node 33 is computed to be node 35 whose index is 0. Now since the common root of the source node and destination node is found, the routing path is obtained to be $rp$=(6,1, 5, 26, 131).

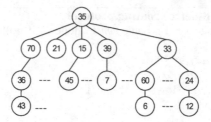

**Fig. 4.** A routing example in the bluetree.

**Table 2.** struc_array for the bluetree in Fig. 4.

| Index | 0 | 1 | 2 | 3 | 4 | 5 | 6 | ... | 16 | 21 | 26 | 30 | 31 | ... | 131 | ... | 141 | ... |
|-------|---|---|---|---|---|---|---|-----|----|----|----|----|----|-----|-----|-----|-----|-----|
| Node | 35 | 70 | 21 | 15 | 39 | 33 | 36 | 0 | 45 | 7 | 60 | 24 | 43 | 0 | 6 | ... | 12 | ... |

## 4  Experimental Results

Three values are measured to evaluate the performance of proposed protocol: Average
Routing Path (ARP), Destination Reachable Ratio (DRR) and Throughput. *ARP* is the
average number of hops counted from the source node to the destination node. *DRR* is
defined as the ratio of total reachable nodes from each node to the number of nodes in
the network when a node was lost. *Throughput* is the data amount that the destination
node can receive per second [10]. We compare the three values of general bluetree
(GB) to that of Hierarchical Grown Bluetree (HGB) by simulation.

### 4.1  ARP Evaluation

Since ARP represents the average routing path length of the bluetree, it will be the
smaller the better. To simplify the comparison, the node (except the leaf) degree of
the general bluetree is assumed to be 7 (i.e., the GB is balanced at the best case). Two
recursive functions for computing the path length from the source node with array $idx_s$
to the destination node with array index $idx_d$ in GB and HGB, respectively, are shown
as follows.

$$PL_{GB}(idx_s, idx_d) = \begin{cases} PL_{GB}(\left\lfloor \dfrac{idx_s - 1}{5} \right\rfloor, idx_d) + 1, & \text{if } idx_s > idx_d \\[2mm] PL_{GB}(idx_s, \left\lfloor \dfrac{idx_d - 1}{5} \right\rfloor) + 1, & \text{if } idx_s < idx_d \\[2mm] 0 & , \text{if } idx_s = idx_d \end{cases}$$

$$PL_{HGB}(idx_s, idx_d) = \begin{cases} PL_{HGB}\left(\left\lfloor \dfrac{idx_s-1}{5} \right\rfloor, idx_d\right)+1, \, s = s+1, \, \text{ if } idx_s > idx_d \\[2ex] PL_{HGB}\left(idx_s, \left\lfloor \dfrac{idx_d-1}{5} \right\rfloor\right)+1, \, d = d+1, \, \text{ if } idx_s < idx_d \\[2ex] 0, \, \text{ if } (idx_s = idx_d) \text{ and source node and destination nodeare} \\ \qquad \text{with the relationship of ancestor and descendant} \\[2ex] -1 \, \text{ otherwise} \end{cases}$$

Figure 5 shows the results with the number of nodes in the network varying from 5 to 500. We find that the ARP of HGB is consistently smaller than that of GB in each case. Since the GB in our experiment is assumed to be in the best case, the ARP of GB in the real situation will be larger than that we have obtained. This implies that the average routing path in HGB is shorter than that in GB.

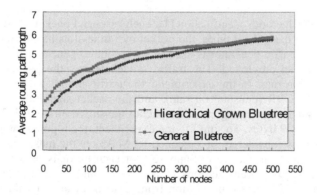

**Fig. 5.** ARP Comparison between GB and HGB.

## 4.2 DRR Evaluation

When a node was lost or failed for some reasons, the impacts on GB and HGB are different. In GB, the subtrees of the lost node becomes 7 separated parts at most, but the subtrees of the lost node are still connected in HGB because of the sibling connection. We use a 5-level full tree with degree 5 for GB and HGB to compare their DRR when one node is lost. The levels of lost node from 1 to 5 are examined. Figure 6 shows the DRR results. When the blueroot is lost, the DRR of GB is rather low (the number of reachable nodes is greatly reduced) because the GB is seriously splitted but the DRR of HGB is still 1 (the number of reachable nodes remains unchanged) because the HGB is connected. Since the subtrees of lower level contains less nodes than the higher level, the DRR goes higher on both GB and HGB when the level of lost node goes up (from 2 to 5). However, HGB is still a little bit better than GB because the subtrees of the lost node in GB is disconnected but are connected in HGB.

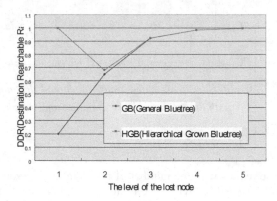

**Fig.6.** DRR comparison between GB and HGB varying the level of lost node from 1 to 5.

## 4.3 Throughput Evaluation

According to the Bluetooth specification [1], each baseband packet can cover 1, 3 or 5 time-slots. Among these three types, the packet of 5 time-slots has the largest payload size, 339bytes. A traffic generator is used in each node to generate the packets based on the traffic model employed. The traffic model defines the packet size and the packet transmission rate. In the experiment, the traffic model with constant packet transmission rate, CBR (constant bit rate), and the packet size with 5 time-slots are employed to evaluate the throughput. The packet transmissionrate is 433.9 Kbit/s and the packet size is 339 bytes. To simplify the experiment, the topology with two levels, namely a piconet, is considered. In a piconet, let M denote the master and $S_1$, $S_2$, $S_3$, $S_4$ and $S_5$ be the slaves, respectively. Suppose that each slave is either in sending or receiving mode. The data transmissions are assumed from $S_1$ to $S_3$, $S_4$ to $S_2$, M to $S_1$, $S_3$ to $S_4$ and $S_2$ to M. The data transmission from $S_1$ to $S_3$ means that the data are sent from a node in $S_1$'s subtree to that in $S_3$'s subtree.

The measured throughputs are shown in Figure 7. The results reveal that HGB outperforms GB. When the bluetree is large and the amount of transmission data is heavy, the congestion occurring at parent node in GB will be more serious. But the complete connections between the siblings in HGB, which provides multiple paths to route, will greatly improve the problem.

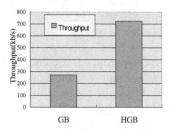

**Fig. 7.** Throughputs of GB and HGB

# 5 Conclusions

In this paper, a Hierarchical Grown Bluetree (HGB) topology and the construction protocol are proposed. The balance property of HGB makes its routing path shorter than GB's. The congestion problem occurring at the parent node in GB is improved by the complete connections between the siblings. On the other hand, the complete connections between the siblings causes only two separated parts when a parent node is lost: the connected part below the lost node and the remaining part of the bluetree. In our experiment, ARP evaluation shows that even the GB is balanced (namely in the best case) the HGB still has a shorter routing path. In the throughput evaluation, HGB has better throughput because no heavy congestion occurrs at the parent node. In DRR evaluation, if the blueroot is lost, serious splitting happens in GB but HGB is still connected. The reliability of GB is poor. When a node is lost, at most 8 parts (when the degree of the lost node is 7) will be caused in GB but only two separated parts happen in our scheme. It is time-consuming to recover a disconnected scatternet. From this point of view, HGB is also better than GB.

# References

[1]   Bluetooth Core Specification, http://www.bluetooth.com
[2]   Theodoros Salonidis, Pravin Bhagwat, Leandros Tassiulas, Richard LaMaire, "Distributed Topology Construction of Bluetooth Personal Area Networks," IEEE INFOCOM 2001, Anchorage, Alaska, April 2001.
[3]   G.V. Zaruba, S. Basagni, I. Chlamtac, "Bluetrees - scatternet formation to enable Bluetooth-based ad hoc networks," IEEE International Conference on Communications (ICC) 2001, pp. 273–277.
[4]   Godfrey Tan, Allen Miu, John Guttag and Hari Balakrishnan, "Forming Scatternets from Bluetooth Personal Area Networks," MIT Technical Report, MIT-LCS-TR-826, October 2001.
[5]   Ching Law and Kai-Yeung Siu, "A Bluetooth scatternet formation algorithm," Proceedings of the IEEE Symposium on Ad Hoc Wireless Networks 2001, San Antonio, Texas, USA, November 2001.
[6]   Z. Wang, R.J. Thomas, and Z.J. Haas, "Bluenet - a New Scatternet Formation Scheme," 35th Hawaii International Conference on System Science (HICSS-35), Big Island, Hawaii, January 7–10, 2002.
[7]   S. Basagni, C. Petrioli, "A Scatternet Formation Protocol for Ad Hoc Networks of Bluetooth Devices," IEEE Vehicular Technology Conference Spring 2002, Vol. 1, pp. 424–428.
[8]   M. Sun, C.K. Chang and T.H. Lai, "A Self-Routing Topology for Bluetooth Scatternets," Proc. I-SPAN 2002, Manila, Philippines, May 2002.
[9]   P. Bhagwat, A. Segall, "A routing vector method (RVM) for routing in bluetooth scatternets," Proc. IEEE International Workshop MoMuC, pp. 375–379. Nov. 1999.
[10]  Abhishek Das, Abhishek Ghose, Ashu Razdan, Huzur Saran, and Rajeev Shorey, "Enhancing Performance of Asynchronous Data Traffic over the Bluetooth Wireless Ad-hoc Network," Proceedings of IEEE INFOCOM '2001, Alaska, USA, April 2001.

# A Comparative Investigation into Optimum-Time Synchronization Protocols for a Large Scale of One-Dimensional Cellular Automata

Hiroshi Umeo[1], Masaya Hisaoka[1], and Takashi Sogabe[2]

[1] Univ. of Osaka Electro-Communication,
Neyagawa-shi, Hastu-cho, 18-8,Osaka, 572-8530, Japan
[2] Internet Initiative Japan Inc.,
Chiyoda-ku Kanda, Nishiki-cho, 3-13, Tokyo, 101-0054, Japan
{umeo,masaya,sogabe}@umeolab.osakac.ac.jp

**Abstract.** The firing squad synchronization problem has been studied extensively for more than forty years, and a rich variety of synchronization algorithms have been proposed. In the present paper, we examine the state transition rule sets for the famous firing squad synchronization algorithms that give a finite-state protocol for synchronizing large-scale cellular automata. We show that the first transition rule set designed by Waksman [18] includes fundamental errors which cause unsuccessful firings and that ninety-three percent of the rules are redundant. In addition, the transition rule sets reported by Balzer [1], Gerken [2] and Mazoyer [6] are found to include several redundant rules. We also present herein a survey and a comparison of the quantitative aspects of the optimum-time synchronization algorithms developed thus far for one-dimensional cellular arrays.

## 1 Introduction

In recent years, cellular automata (CA) have been used increasingly to model real phenomena occurring in fields such as biology, chemistry, ecology, economy, geology, mechanical engineering, medicine, physics, sociology, and traffic management. Cellular automata are considered to be a simple model for complex systems in which an infinite one-dimensional array of finite state machines (cells) updates itself in a synchronous manner according to a uniform local rule. Synchronizing a large scale of cellular automata has been known as the firing squad synchronization problem since its development, and the problem was originally proposed by J. Myhill in order to synchronize all parts of self-reproducing cellular automata [10]. The firing squad synchronization problem has been studied extensively for more than forty years [1-12, 14-18].

In the present paper, we examine the state transition rule sets for the famous firing squad synchronization algorithms that give a finite-state protocol for synchronizing large-scale cellular automata. We focus on the fundamental

M. Guo and L.T.Yang (Eds.): ISPA 2003, LNCS 2745, pp. 165–178, 2003.

synchronization algorithms operating in optimum steps on one-dimensional cellular arrays in which the general is located at one end. The algorithms discussed herein are the eight-state Balzer's algorithm [1], the seven-state Gerken's algorithm [2], the six-state Mazoyer's algorithm [6], the 16-state Waksman's algorithm [18] and a number of revised versions thereof. Specifically, we attempt to answer the following questions:

- First, are all previously presented transition rule sets correct?
- Do these sets contain redundant rules? If so, what is the exact rule set?
- How do the algorithms compare with each other?

In order to answer these questions, we implement all transition rule sets for the synchronization algorithms above mentioned on a computer and check whether these rule sets yield successful firing configurations at exactly $t = 2n-2$ steps for any array of length $n$ such that $2 \leq n \leq 10000$. In addition, we construct a survey of current optimum-time synchronization algorithms and compare transition rule sets with respect to the number of internal states of each finite state automaton, the number of transition rules realizing the synchronization, and the number of state-changes on the array. With the aid of a computer, the first Waksman's transition rule set is shown to include fundamental errors and the set is shown to contain a considerable number of redundancies. Approximately ninety-three percent of the rules are deleted from the original transition rule set. A number of redundant rules that are not used in the synchronization process are also found in other rule sets. We give the smallest rule set for each algorithm. Finally, we present a comparison of the quantitative aspects of the optimum-time synchronization algorithms, including Goto's and Gerken's algorithms, both having a state-change complexity of $O(n \log n)$. We indicate that the first-in-the-world optimum-time synchronization algorithm proposed by Goto [3, 4] has a state-change complexity of $O(n \log n)$.

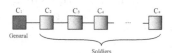

**Fig. 1.** One-dimensional cellular automaton.

# 2    Firing Squad Synchronization Problem

## 2.1    Definition of the Firing Squad Synchronization Problem

The firing squad synchronization problem is formalized in terms of the model of cellular automata. Figure 1 shows a finite one-dimensional cellular array consisting of $n$ cells, denoted by $C_i$, where $1 \leq i \leq n$. All cells (except the end cells) are identical finite state automata. The array operates in lock-step mode such that the next state of each cell (except the end cells) is determined by both its own present state and the present states of its right and left neighbors. All cells (*soldiers*), except the left end cell, are initially in the *quiescent* state at time $t = 0$ and have the property whereby the next state of a quiescent cell having quiescent neighbors is the quiescent state. At time $t = 0$ the left end cell (*general*) is in the *fire-when-ready* state, which is an initiation signal to the array. The firing squad synchronization problem is stated as follows. Given an array of $n$ identical cellular automata, including a *general* on the left end which is activated at time $t = 0$, we want to give the description (state set and next-state function) of the automata so that, *at some future time*, all of the cells will *simultaneously* and, *for the first time*, enter a special *firing* state. The set of states must be independent of $n$. Without loss of generality, we assume $n \geq 2$. The tricky part of the problem is that the same kind of soldier having a fixed number of states must be synchronized, regardless of the length $n$ of the array.

## 2.2  A Brief History of the Developments of Optimum-Time Firing Squad Synchronization Algorithms

The problem known as the *firing squad synchronization problem* was devised in 1957 by J. Myhill, and first appeared in print in a paper by E. F. Moore [10]. This problem has been widely circulated, and has attracted much attention. The firing squad synchronization problem first arose in connection with the need to simultaneously turn on all parts of a self-reproducing machine. The problem was first solved by J. McCarthy and M. Minsky who presented a $3n$-step algorithm. In 1962, the first optimum-time, i.e. $(2n - 2)$-step, synchronization algorithm was presented by Goto [3], with each cell having several thousands of states. Waksman [18] presented a 16-state optimum-time synchronization algorithm. Afterward, Balzer [1] and Gerken [2] developed an eight-state algorithm and a seven-state synchronization algorithm, respectively, thus decreasing the number of states required for the synchronization. In 1987, Mazoyer [6] developed a six-state synchronization algorithm which, at present, is the algorithm having the fewest states.

## 2.3  Complexity Measure for Optimum-Time Synchronization Algorithms

**Time.** Any solution to the firing squad synchronization problem can easily be shown to require $(2n - 2)$ steps for firing $n$ cells, since signals on the array can propagate no faster than one cell per step, and the time from the general's instruction until the firing must be at least $2n - 2$. (See Balzer [1], Mazoyer [5, 6] and Waksman [18] for a proof.) Thus, we have:

[**Theorem 1**][1, 5, 6, 18] Synchronization of $n$ cells in less than $2n - 2$ steps is impossible.

[**Theorem 2**][1–3, 6, 18] Synchronization of $n$ cells in exactly $2n - 2$ steps is possible.

**Number of internal states.** The following three distinct states: the *quiescent* state, the *general* state, and the *firing* state, are required in order to define any cellular automaton that can solve the firing squad synchronization problem. The boundary state for $C_0$ and $C_{n+1}$ is not generally counted as an internal state. Balzer [1] showed that no four-state optimum-time solution exists. In addition, there exists no five-state optimum-time solution satisfying the special conditions that Balzer [1] studied. The question that remains is: "What is the minimum number of states for an optimum-time solution of the problem?" At present, that number is five or six.

[**Theorem 3**][1] There is no four-state CA that can synchronize $n$ cells.

[**Theorem 4**][1] There is no five-state solution satisfying Balzer's special conditions.

**Number of transition rules.** Any $k$-state (excluding the boundary state) transition table for the synchronization has at most $(k-1)k^2$ entries in $(k-1)$ matrices of size $k \times k$. The number of transition rules reflects the complexity of synchronization algorithms.

**Number of state changes.** Vollmar [17] introduced state-change complexity in order to measure the efficiency of cellular algorithms and showed that $\Omega$ ($n \log n$) state changes are required for the synchronization of $n$ cells in $(2n-2)$ steps.

[**Theorem 5**][17] $\Omega$ ($n \log n$) state-change is necessary for synchronizing $n$ cells in $(2n-2)$ steps.

# 3    Transition Rule Sets for Optimum-Time Firing Squad Synchronization Algorithms

## 3.1    Waksman's 16-State Algorithm

In 1966, Waksman [18] proposed a 16-state firing squad synchronization algorithm, which, together with an unpublished algorithm by Goto [3], is referred to as the first-in-the-world optimum-time synchronization algorithm. Waksman [18] devised an efficient way to cause a cell to generate infinite signals at propagating speeds of $1/1, 1/3, 1/7, .., 1/(2^k - 1)$, where $k$ is any natural number. These signals play an important role in dividing the array into two, four, eight, ... , equal parts synchronously. The end cell in each partition takes a special prefiring state so that when the last partition occurs, all cells have a left and right neighbor in this state. Waksman presented a set of transition rules described in terms of a state transition table that is defined on the following state set $\mathcal{D}$ consisting of 16 states such that $\mathcal{D} = \{$Q, T, $P_0$, $P_1$, $B_0$, $B_1$, $R_0$, $R_1$, $A_{000}$, $A_{001}$, $A_{010}$, $A_{011}$, $A_{100}$, $A_{101}$, $A_{110}$, $A_{111}\}$, where Q is a quiescent state, T is a firing state, $P_0$ and $P_1$ are prefiring states, $B_0$ and $B_1$ are states for signals propagating at various speeds, $R_0$ and $R_1$ are trigger states which cause the $B_0$ and $B_1$ states move in the left or right direction and $A_{ijk}, i, j, k \in \{0, 1\}$ are control states which generate the state $R_0$ or $R_1$ either with a unit delay or without any delay. To describe the state transition table in a concise way, Waksman introduced a special symbol $\gamma$ that matches any state in its right and/or left neighbor. Since Waksman's table cannot be used as is on a computer , we first expand the table *automatically* according to the notation given by Waksman [18]. We thereby obtain a transition table that consists of 3208 rules. We implement these rules and examine the validity of the expanded table on a computer. The experiment revealed the following:

[**Observation 1**] For any $n$ such that $2 \leq n \leq 2000$, the expanded rule set yields successful firings only in the cases of $n = 3, 5$ or $6$.

Thus, the firing process fails in most cases.


## 3.2   USN Transition Rule Set

Umeo, Sogabe and Nomura [15] corrected all errors in Waksman's original transition table. In this subsection, we present an overview of the correction procedures described in Umeo, Sogabe and Nomura [15] and give a complete list of the transition rules which yield successful firings for any $n$. Waksman [18] presented a figure (Fig. 2 in Waksman [18]) that illustrates a firing configuration on $n = 11$. Even the configuration given by Waksman [18] can not be obtained by our computer simulation. Judging from the original figure in Waksman's paper [18], and from our numerous computer simulations, we can assume that Waksman's figure was obtained by hand simulation. Investigating the figure, Waksman appears to have forgotten to include the following two rules:

```
R1 ## B0 ## P0 -> R1;  R1 ## B0 ## P1 -> R1.
```

We have added these rules to the original list, and hereafter refer to the rule set as *Waksman's original list*. Again, we perform the computer simulation based on the rule set consisting of 3210 rules. We observed the following:

[**Observation 2**] For any $n$ such that $2 \leq n \leq 2000$, Waksman's original rule set yields successful firings only for the cases in which $n = 3, 5, 6, 11, 12, 23, 24, 47,$ $48, 95, 96, 191, 192, 383, 384, 767, 768, 1535$ or $1536$.

Thus, a problem remains in the original transition table. Cellular automata researchers have reported that errors are included in the Waksman's transition table. Our computer simulation reveals this to be true, and the original rule set includes fundamental errors. Next, we explore the transition rule set so that the resultant table yields correct firings for any $n \geq 2$. Our investigations on unsuccessful configurations revealed that the signal $A_{ijk}, i, j, k \in \{0, 1\}$ disappears in the cellular space and, as a result, synchronous divisions fail. Based on computer-assisted investigations, we altered five rules in the original list and obtained the rules shown below:

```
B0 ## Q ## P1 -> A100;  B1 ## Q ## P0 -> A000;  P0 ## Q ## B1 -> A010;
           P0 ## Q ## R1 -> A010;  P1 ## Q ## B0 -> A110.
```

All of these rules involve the transmission of the $A_{ijk}$ signals. Moreover, we added the following seven rules, which are needed for the above correction:

```
PO ## Q ## www -> P1; A010 ## Q ## R1 -> A011; A011 ## Q ## R1 -> A010;
PO ## BO ## A100 -> P1; P1 ## BO ## A100 -> P1; A110 ## BO ## PO -> P1;

                      A110 ## BO ## P1 -> P1.
```

Overall, the total number of transition rules is 3217. We herein omit the details of the process of exploring the table. The computer simulation based on the new rule set reveals the following:

[**Observation 3**] For any $n$ such that $2 \leq n \leq 10000$, the rule set consisting of 3217 rules yields successful optimum-time firings.

Our computer simulation based on the above list revealed that most of the rules are not used efficiently in the firing process. A histogram-like statistical analysis on the rule set is presented herein and the number of rules valid in the range of $2 \leq n \leq 10000$ is reduced. Figure 2(left) is our final, complete list, which consists of 202 transition rules. We refer to this list as the *USN transition rule set*. In our transition table (Fig. 2), for ease of computer simulation, the symbol "www" is used to denote the left and right boundary states.

In our correction, a ninety-three percent reduction in the number of transition rules is realized compared to Waksman's original list. The computer simulation based on the table of Fig. 2 gives the following observation. Computer simulation shows that 202 rules is the smallest set for the Waksman's optimum-time firing squad synchronization. In Fig. 2(right), we show a configuration on 25 cells.

[**Observation 4**] The set of rules given in Fig. 2 is the smallest transition rule set for Waksman's optimum-time firing squad synchronization algorithm.

### 3.3   Balzer's Eight-State Algorithm

Balzer [1] constructed an eight-state, 182-rule synchronization algorithm and the structure of which is identical to that of Waksman [18]. Our computer examination revealed no errors, however, 17 rules were found to be redundant. In Fig. 3, we give a list of transition rules for Balzer's algorithm together with a configuration on 28 cells. Deleted rules are indicated by shaded squares, where squares containing letters denote rules included in the original list. In the transition table, the symbols "M", "L", "F" and "X" represent the general, quiescent, firing and boundary states, respectively. The state-change complexity of the algorithm is $O(n^2)$.

### 3.4   Gerken's Seven-State Algorithm I

Gerken [2] reduced the number of states realizing Balzer's algorithm and constructed a seven-state, 118-rule synchronization algorithm. In our computer examination, no errors were found, however, 13 rules were found to be redundant. In Fig. 4, we give a list of the transition rules for Gerken's algorithm together with a configuration on 28 cells. The 13 deleted rules are marked by shaded squares in the table. The symbols ">", "/", "..." and "#" represent the general,

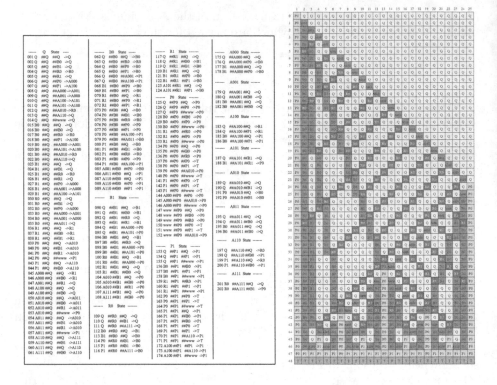

**Fig. 2.** USN transition table consisting of 202 rules that realize Waksman's synchronization algorithm(left) and a configuration of 16-state implementation of Waksman's algorithm on 25 cells(right).

quiescent, firing and boundary states, respectively. The state-change complexity of the algorithm is $O(n^2)$.

### 3.5 Mazoyer's Six-State Algorithm

Mazoyer [6] proposed a six-state, 120-rule synchronization algorithm, the structure of which differs greatly from the previous algorithms discussed above. Our computer examination revealed no errors and only one redundant rule. In Fig. 5, we give a list of transition rules for Mazoyer's algorithm together with a configuration on 28 cells. In the transition table, the letters "G", "L", "F" and "X" represent the general, quiescent, firing and boundary states, respectively. The state-change complexity of the algorithm is $O(n^2)$.

### 3.6 Goto's Algorithm

The first synchronization algorithm presented by Goto [3] was not published as a journal paper. According to Goto, the original note [3] is now unavailable, and

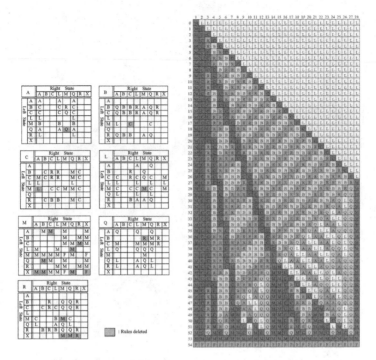

**Fig. 3.** Transition table for Balzer's algorithm (left) and a configuration of an eight-state implementation of Balzer's algorithm on 28 cells (right).

the only existing material that treats the algorithm is Goto [4]. The Goto's study presents one figure (Fig. 3.8 in Goto [4]) demonstrating how the algorithm works on 13 cells with a very short description in Japanese. Umeo [12] reconstructed the algorithm of Goto based on this figure. Mazoyer [8] also reconstructed this algorithm again based on the presentation given by Umeo [12]. The algorithm that Umeo [12] reconstructed is a non-recursive algorithm consisting of a marking phase and a $3n$-step synchronization phase. In the first phase, by printing a special marker in the cellular space, the entire cellular space is divided into subspaces, the lengths of which increase exponentially with a common ratio of two, that is $2^j$, for any integer $j$ such that $1 \leq j \leq \lfloor \log_2 n \rfloor - 1$. The marking is made from both the left and right ends. In the second phase, each subspace is synchronized using a well-known conventional $3n$-step simple synchronization algorithm. A time-space diagram of the reconstructed algorithm is shown in Fig. 6. We note that the state-change complexity of the algorithm is $O(n \log n)$.

### 3.7    Gerken's 155-State Algorithm II

Gerken [2] constructed two kinds of optimum-time synchronization algorithms. One seven-state algorithm has been discussed in the previous subsection, and the

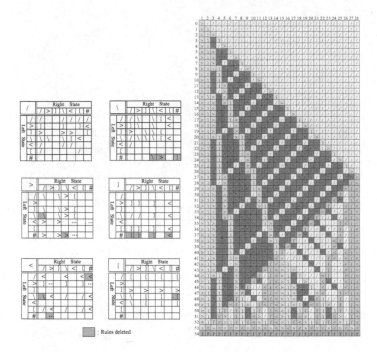

**Fig. 4.** Transition table for the seven-state Gerken's algorithm (left) and a configuration of the seven-state implementation of Gerken's algorithm on 28 cells (right). In the implementation shown at right, the letter "F" rather than "..." is used to indicates the firing state.

other is a 155-state algorithm having $O(n \log n)$ state-change complexity. The transition table given in Gerken [2] is described in terms of two-layer construction with 32 states and 347 rules. The table does not operate as is on a single-layer simulator. In order to obtain an exact transition rule set, we expand this transition table into a single-layer format and obtain a 155-state table consisting of 2371 rules. In Fig. 7 we give a configuration on 28 cells.

### 3.8 Comparison of Quantitative Aspects of Optimum-Time Synchronization Algorithms

Here, we present a table based on a quantitative comparison of optimum-time synchronization algorithms and their transition tables discussed above with respect to the number of internal states of each finite state automaton, the number of transition rules realizing the synchronization, and the number of state-changes on the array.

### 3.9 O(1)-Bit vs. 1-Bit Communication CA Model

In the study of cellular automata, the amount of bit-information exchanged at one step between neighboring cells has been assumed to be O(1)-bit data.

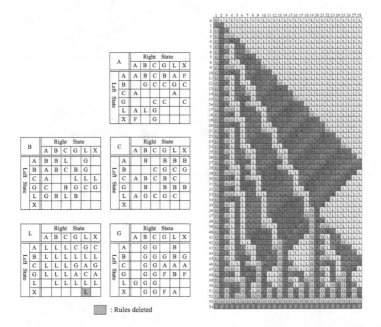

**Fig. 5.** Transition table for the six-state Mazoyer's algorithm (left) and a configuration of the six-state implementation of Mazoyer's algorithm on 28 cells (right).

**Table 1.** Comparison of transition rule sets for optimum-time firing squad synchronization algorithms. The "*" symbol in parenthesis shows the correction and reduction of transition rules made in this paper. The "**" symbol indicates the number of states and rules obtained after the expansion of the original two-layer construction.

| Algorithm | # of states | # of transition rules | # of state changes |
|---|---|---|---|
| Goto[1962] | many thousands | — | $O(n \log n)$ |
| Waksman[1966] | 16 | 3216(202*) | $O(n^2)$ |
| Balzer[1967] | 8 | 182 (165 *) | $O(n^2)$ |
| Gerken I[1987] | 7 | 118 (105*) | $O(n^2)$ |
| Mazoyer[1987] | 6 | 120 (119*) | $O(n^2)$ |
| Gerken II[1987] | 32(155**) | 347(2371**) | $O(n \log n)$ |

An O(1)-bit CA is a conventional CA in which the number of communication bits exchanged at one step between neighboring cells is assumed to be O(1)-bit, however, such inter-cell bit-information exchange has been hidden behind the definition of conventional automata-theoretic finite state description. On the other hand, the 1-bit inter-cell communication model is a new CA in which inter-cell communication is restricted to 1-bit data, referred to as the *1-bit CA* model. The number of internal states of the 1-bit CA is assumed to be finite in the usual sense. The next state of each cell is determined by the present state of that cell and two binary 1-bit inputs from its left and right neighbor cells. Thus, the 1-bit

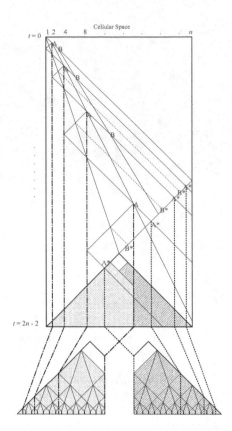

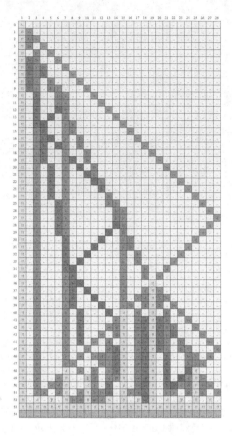

**Fig. 6.** Time-space diagram for Goto's algorithm as reconstructed by Umeo [12].

**Fig. 7.** Configuration of a 155-state implementation of Gerken's algorithm II on 28 cells.

CA can be thought of as one of the most powerless and simplest models in a variety of CA's. A precise definition of the 1-bit CA can be found in Umeo and Kamikawa [13].

Mazoyer [7] and Nishimura, Sogabe and Umeo [11] each designed an optimum-time synchronization algorithm on a 1-bit CA model, based on Balzer's algorithm and Waksman's algorithm, respectively. In Fig. 8, we show a configuration on 15 cells that is based on the 1-bit CA model of Nishimura, Sogabe and Umeo [11]. Each cell has 78 internal states and 208 transition rules. The small black right and left triangles ▶ and ◀ indicate a 1-bit signal transfer in the right or left direction, respectively, between neighboring cells. A symbol in a cell shows the internal state of the cell.

**[Theorem 6]**[7, 11, 14] There exists a 1-bit CA that can synchronize $n$ cells in optimum $2n - 2$ steps.

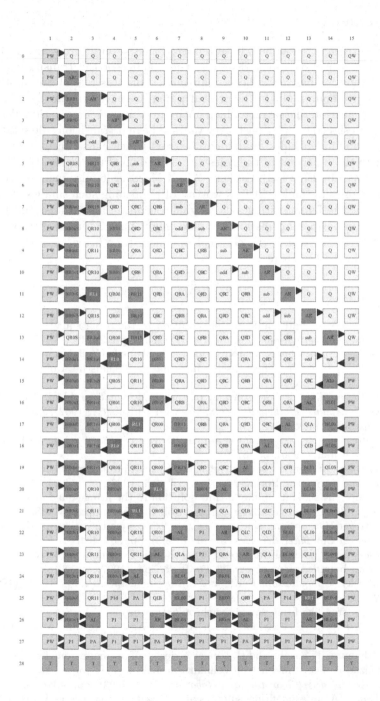

**Fig. 8.** A configuration of optimum-time synchronization algorithm with 1-bit inter-cell communication on 25 cells.

## 4    Summary

Cellular automata researchers have reported that several errors are included in Waksman's transition table. However, the validity of the transition rule sets designed thus far has never been confirmed. This was one of our motivations that we started our study. In the present paper, we have examined via computer the state transition rule sets for which optimum-time synchronization algorithms have been designed over the past forty years. The first transition rule set designed by Waksman [18] includes fundamental errors which cause unsuccessful firings and ninety-three percent of the rules are redundant. In addition, the transition rule sets given by Balzer [1], Gerken [2] and Mazoyer [6] also include redundant rules. The authors think that it is worthy of publishing such smallest transition rule sets for the famous firing squad synchronization algorithms, and they are useful and important for researchers who might have interests in those transition rule sets that realize the classical optimum-time firing algorithms quoted frequently in the literatures.

## References

1. R. Balzer: An 8-state minimal time solution to the firing squad synchronization problem. *Information and Control*, vol. 10 (1967), pp. 22–42.
2. Hans-D., Gerken: Über Synchronisations - Probleme bei Zellularautomaten. *Diplomarbeit*, Institut für Theoretische Informatik, Technische Universität Braunschweig, (1987), pp. 50.
3. E. Goto: A minimal time solution of the firing squad problem. *Dittoed course notes for Applied Mathematics* 298, Harvard University, (1962), pp. 52–59, with an illustration in color.
4. E. Goto: Some puzzles on automata. in *Toward computer sciences* (T. Kitagawa ed.), Kyouritsu, (1966), pp. 67–91.
5. J. Mazoyer: An overview of the firing squad synchronization problem. *Lecture Notes on Computer Science*, Springer-Verlag, vol. 316 (1986), pp. 82–93.
6. J. Mazoyer: A six-state minimal time solution to the firing squad synchronization problem. *Theoretical Computer Science*, vol. 50 (1987), pp. 183–238.
7. J. Mazoyer: On optimal solutions to the firing squad synchronization problem. *Theoretical Computer Science*, vol. 168 (1996), pp. 367–404.
8. J. Mazoyer: A minimal-time solution to the FSSP without recursive call to itself and with bounded slope of signals. Draft version, (1997), pp. 8.
9. M. Minsky: *Computation: Finite and infinite machines*. Prentice Hall, (1967), pp. 28–29.
10. E. F. Moore: The firing squad synchronization problem. in *Sequential Machines, Selected Papers* (E. F. Moore, ed.), Addison-Wesley, Reading MA., (1964), pp. 213–214.
11. J. Nishimura, T. Sogabe and H. Umeo: A design of optimum-time firing squad synchronization algorithm on 1-bit cellular automaton. *Proc. of the 8th International Symposium on Artificial Life and Robotics*, Vol.2 (2003), pp. 381–386.
12. H. Umeo: A note on firing squad synchronization algorithms-A reconstruction of Goto's first-in-the-world optimum-time firing squad synchronization algorithm. *Proc. of Cellular Automata Workshop*, M. Kutrib and T. Worsch (eds.), (1996), pp. 65.

13. H. Umeo and N. Kamikawa: A design of real-time non-regular sequence generation algorithms and their implementations on cellular automata with 1-bit inter-cell communications. *Fundamenta Informaticae*, 52 (2002), pp. 257–275.

14. H. Umeo, J. Nishimura and T. Sogabe: 1-bit inter-cell communication cellular algorithms (*invited lecture*). *Proc. of the Tenth Intern. Colloquium on Differential Equations*, held in Plovdiv in 1999, *International Journal of Differential Equations and Applications*, vol. 1A, no. 4 (2000), pp. 433–446.

15. H. Umeo, T. Sogabe and Y. Nomura: Correction, optimization and verification of transition rule set for Waksman's firing squad synchronization algorithm. *Proc. of the Fourth Intern. Conference on Cellular Automata for Research and Industry*, Springer, (2000), pp. 152–160.

16. R. Vollmar: *Algorithmen in Zellularautomaten*. Teubner, (1979), pp. 192.

17. R. Vollmar: Some remarks about the "Efficiency" of polyautomata. *International Journal of Theoretical Physics*, vol. 21, no. 12 (1982), pp. 1007–1015.

18. A. Waksman: An optimum solution to the firing squad synchronization problem. *Information and Control*, vol. 9 (1966), pp. 66–78.

# Impact from Mobile SPAM Mail on Mobile Internet Services

Toshihiko Yamakami

ACCESS, 2-8-16 Sarugaku-cho, Chiyoda-ku, Tokyo 101-0064, JAPAN
yam@access.co.jp

**Abstract.** Rapid penetration of internet-enabled mobile handsets is being witnessed in worldwide. It also creates some new social frictions like SPAM mail to mobile handsets. The emergence of mobile Internet services in Japan soon triggered wide spread mobile SPAM mail. It reached a certain point to attract significant social attention in April 2001. The SPAM mail impact is analyzed from the long-term transition of user mail address pattern changes. This study examines the SPAM mail impact from the viewpoint of charged mobile Internet services.

## 1 Introduction

The dramatic changes now occurring in internet-empowered information appliances have the potential to change the PC-based Internet. Extensive efforts were devoted to ensure interoperability in the non-PC Internet[1] [5]. A growing number of information appliances, like mobile handsets, private digital assistants, and game consoles set-top-boxes appear with Internet capabilities [2]. This emergence of new technologies easily triggered the new social problems like SPAM mail. In the mobile Internet, due to the difficulties of input, the user mail address is a precious resource for the content providers. The SPAM mail in the mobile Internet is rarely studied because the resource to store the SPAM mail is limited and the logs are difficult to obtain and easy to lose. In this paper, we call the Internet users who access the Internet using micro-browsers on a mobile handset as mobile Internet users. It is not accurate, however, it is natural to focus on the mobile handset based users considering the significance of mobile handset based users in the Internet users who have mobile characteristics. Japan witnesses the emergence of mobile Internet users for the first place in the world. The mobile Internet users reached 59 million at the end of 2002 after three years from the service launch. This paper examines how the SPAM mail attacks impacted the user behavior to choose mail addresses on mobile handsets.

## 2 SPAM Mail in Mobile Internet

SPAM mail is very common in PC Internet users [3] [4]. It is non-selective mail delivery, commonly advertisement mail. There are various techniques explored to catch the user mail addresses. They include the searching the Internet home

M. Guo and L.T.Yang (Eds.): ISPA 2003, LNCS 2745, pp. 179–184, 2003.

pages, identifying mail exploders, using common names. However, there is no indicator that we can control SPAM in the near future in spite of a wide variety of efforts by the mobile carriers.

In the mobile Internet, there are an emerging number of SPAM mail, however, the exploration of potential mail addresses are different. The most common method of mobile Internet SPAM mail was a brute force attack to every possible mobile Internet address. The most common format of mobile Internet addresses was a mobile phone number in the early stages. It is unique and recognizable. The limitation of the user interface prevents users from updating to the secure mail addresses. The brute force attack is to try all potential addresses including telephone numbers, and store the delivery results on a database. SPAM mail is not new. However, the unique features of the mobile Internet make the social impact different. There are two social issues in SPAM mail in mobile Internet. In many cases, the mobile carriers charges by per-packet base, which outrages the users. Second, the mobile Internet has an always-on capability, therefore, SPAM mail is more intruding for the end users These two factors impacted the end users, gradually changed the user behavior. During the mobile Internet emergence, the strong market growth attracted many Internet problems as well as many advantages. In Japan, the harms done by mobile Internet SPAM became apparent in the spring of 2001. People witnessed the forced e-mail address change because many people received more than 100 SPAM mail every month. This SPAM mail is based on a guess on mail address and brute force attacks. Gradually, end users changed their mail addresses. It is recommended to use a mixed character mail address with alphabets, numbers and special characters like a period or an underscore. In addition, it was recommended to use a longer email address that is robust against brute force attacks. The suggested length grows against stronger brute force attacks evolve. Now, the recommended length of mail address is more than 12. In a side effect, mobile Internet content providers lost a lot of customer email addresses, which are crucial in mobile e-commerce to ensure the interactions with easy-come and easy-go customers.

## 3    Email Address Transition Analysis

In this paper, the author analyzes the email address transition analysis on the commercial charged service provided for the two different carriers. The carrier A charged by per-packet base, and the carrier B did not charge on the incoming mail. The target service is a business-oriented information service listed on the mobile carrier official site. There is a news alert service, therefore, one third of the users registered their mobile handset email address. There are two logs for the mail address, one for the mail registration log, and the other from the alert sending log. In this study, the author examines the mail registration logs for the service in the carrier A from August 2000 to August 2001 and one in the carrier B from October 2000 to August 2001. In addition, the author examines the alert sending log to compare the static registration-based analysis and the dynamic active sending-based analysis. The purpose of the study includes: (a) monthly transitions of the mail address patterns, (b) comparison of the carrier A user behavior and the carrier B user behavior, and (c) comparison of the static mail address pattern analysis and the dynamic mail address pattern analysis. The author is engaged in the mobile Web side user behavior for a while [6]. This study is a long-term user behavior study on mail usage on the mobile handsets. On the transition analysis, the author performs the monthly transition over a span of time on (a) mail address length, and (b) mail address character pattern. In character patterns, the addresses are categorized in the four patterns: (a)numeric only, (b)alphabet only, (c) combination of alphabet and numeric characters, and (d) other patterns including three common punctuation characters( " ." , "_", "-").

Originally, the initial mail address was all numeric, which was identical to the user's phone number. The new system to use more robust initial mail addresses started in July 2001.

## 4   Case Studies

There are three case studies. The first one is the study for monthly logs for mail registration in the carrier A. It outlines the general trend for new mail address registration/update. The second one is the study for real use every month. The valid addresses used for the notification service is analyzed. It outlines the active user mail address behavior. The third one is the mail registration every month for another mobile carrier. It outlines the inter-carrier difference on the SPAM mail impact.

The average mail address length did not show the significant change over a san of period. The length of telephone numbers is 11. Usually, the alphabetic address is shorter than that. The average length is almost stable during the period in this observation.

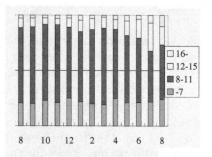
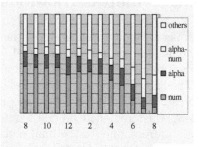

**Fig. 1.** Registration based Address Length Breakdown Transition in the carrier A case (Aug 2000 – Aug 2001)

**Fig. 2.** Registration based Address Pattern Breakdown Transition in the carrier A case (Aug 2000 – Aug 2001)

The mail address length range is slowly moving to the longer one. The numbers of the length segment, "shorter than 8", "from 8 to 11", "from 12 to 15", "longer than 15" are presented in Fig. 1. The longer addresses increase. The numbers of users in the "from 12 to 15" range increased significantly in May and June 2001. On the contrary, the "shorter than 8" range is stable.

The character patterns in mail addresses are depicted in Fig. 2. In the year 2000, the trend was stable. 80-85% of users used numeric only addresses. 10-15% of users used alphabet only addresses. This trend drastically changed in May and June 2001. Now two thirds of users use some special characters like ".", "_", and "-" in their addresses. Also, it should be noted that the initial mail address has been not in numeric only since July 2001. However, the increase showed in May 2001. Therefore, it can be observed that the user behavior to change their addresses against SPAM mail influences the trend.

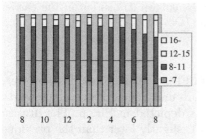
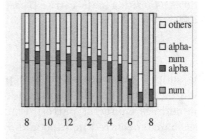

**Fig. 3.** Use based Address Length Breakdown Transition in the carrier A case (Aug 2000 – Aug 2001)

**Fig. 4.** Use based Address Pattern Breakdown Transition in the carrier A case (Aug 2000 – Aug 2001)

The registration can only partially capture the user behavior on mail address updates. The commercial service observed in this paper provides the mail notification service. It is an optional service. Users can choose it. In this service, the users can receive notification mail every time a new content with the user's registered keywords. This provides the e-mail addresses used in this notification service. It means the active mail addresses, because it is necessary to update the current mail address to enjoy the notification function. It reflects the current mail addresses, and also is influence by the active users' behavior. The registration mail addresses may be unchanged during the user's update of mail addresses to avoid SPAM mail when the user does not subscribe this particular notification service. The length ranges transition is presented in Fig. 3. The differences to Fig. 1 are minor.

Finally, the mail address patterns transition is depicted in Fig. 4. The difference with Fig. 2 is not significant.

A comparison study is done on another carrier, the carrier B. This carrier has the special charging policy that the incoming mail communication fee is free. The mail address relatively shorter addresses in the similar transition pattern.

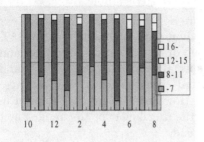

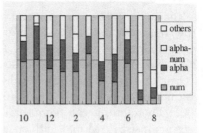

**Fig. 5.** Registration based Address Length Breakdown Transition in the carrier B case (Oct 2000 – Aug 2001)

**Fig. 6.** Registration based Address Pattern Breakdown Transition in the carrier B case (Oct 2000 – Aug 2001)

The address range transition is depicted in Fig. 5. It is not stable, however, it should be noted that the shorter addresses are unchanged or even increased.

The address character pattern transition is depicted in Fig. 6. The drastic address change occurred in June and July 2001, slightly later than the previous case studies. The different charging policy does not seem to have any impact to the user behavior.

## 5   Evaluations

### 5.1   Findings

Evaluation on the case studies are categorized in the three aspects: (a) long-term address pattern transition, (b) inter-carrier comparison on the traffic charging policy, and (c) evaluation of the mail log analysis on anti-SPAM behaviors. The mail address length is not sensitive to the mobile SPAM attacks. The 11-digit telephone number address is already too long to make it longer for end users. It is clear that users adopt special character patterns in addresses to prevent brute force attacks. The mobile handset mail characteristics may have some implications on this forced behavior. More than 50% of users use non-alphanumeric characters in their addresses. In the low SPAM context, the ratio was under 10%. The transition took two to three months. This is under influence of some social processes for further studies. About the methodology, the mail address observation captures the user behavior diffusion in mail address changes. The mail log is commonly available on most systems, therefore, it is easy to use for the first step study without intrusion to mobile users. The mail registration and real mail use are different aspects of the mobile mail services. This study shows little difference between these two factors. It is easier to analyze the mail address transition at the mail registration base when there are millions of users that are not uncommon in the top mobile content providers.

## 5.2   Limitations

To evaluate the limitations of this study, the following three aspects should be considered: (a) biases in the case study samples, (b) fairness about the inter-carrier comparisons, and (c) social processes. The first limitation is the bias in the samples. The case studies in this study focused one particular commercial mobile service due to the log availability. The second limitation is the bias in the inter-carrier comparisons. It needs more studies to make any definite comparisons.

This study examines the result of the user behavior, not the behavior itself. The social process of mobile SPAM mail is for further studies. Interesting topics include the following issues: (a) user cognitive difference between PC SPAM mail and mobile SPAM mail, (b) user mental model about changing mail addresses, and (c) social effects for mail address change behavior diffusion under SPAM attacks. The tradeoff between the SPAM attack damage and the forced mobile Internet identification update is an interesting topic.

## 6   Conclusions

The user behavior to change their mobile mail address is studies in case studies. The mail addresses in a commercial mobile service are analyzed in a long span of time. The difference between different carriers is observed. This study gives a preliminary analysis to study the mobile Internet under mobile SPAM attacks. This phenomenon is expected to prevail worldwide, however, it is rarely studied in the past literature. This study gives a first clue on the social diffusion time scale on the mail address changes on the mobile handsets. The further studies will include (a) evaluation on fairness in the case studies, (b) user perception process under SPAM attacks, and (c) social process about the mail address changes. The mental process of the forced identification change will give an interesting clue to understand the user mental cognitive process in the mobile Internet.

## References

1. Baker, M., Ishikawa, M., Matsui, S., Stark, P., Wugofsky, and T., Yamakami, T.: XHTML™ Basic, W3C Recommendation 19 December 2000 (2000) ( available at http://www.w3.org/TR/xhtml-basic )
2. Cerf, V.: Beyond the Post-PC Internet CACM, **44, 9** (2001) 34–37
3. Cranor, L. F. and LaMacchia, B. A.: Spam!, CACM, **41, 8** (1998) 74–83
4. Denning, P. J.: electronic junk, CACM, **25, 3** (1982) 163–165
5. Kamada, T.: Compact HTML for Small Information Appliances, W3C Note (1998) ( available at http://www.w3.org/TR/1998/NOTE-compactHTML-19980209 )
6. Yamakami, T.: Unique Identifier Tracking Analysis: A Methodology To Capture Wireless Internet User Behaviors IEEE ICOIN-15, Beppu, Japan (2001) 743–748

# Solving the Set-Splitting Problem in Sticker-Based Model and the Lipton-Adelmann Model

Weng-Long Chang[1], Minyi Guo[2], and Michael Ho[3]

[1,3]Department of Information Management,Southern Taiwan University of Technology,
Tainan, Taiwan 701, R.O.C.
changwl{@csie.ncku.edu.tw, @mail.stut.edu.tw}
[2]Department of Computer Software,
The University of Aizu, Aizu-Wakamatsu City, Fukushima 965-8580, Japan
minyi@u-aizu.ac.jp

**Abstract.** Adleman wrote the first paper in which it was demonstrated that DNA (*DeoxyriboNucleic Acid*) strands could be applied for dealing with solutions to an instance of the NP-complete Hamiltonian path problem (HPP). Lipton wrote the second paper in which it was shown that the Adleman techniques could also be used to solving the NP-complete satisfiability (SAT) problem (the first NP-complete problem). Adleman and his co-authors proposed *sticker* for enhancing the Adleman-Lipton model. In the paper, it is proved how to apply sticker in the sticker-based model for constructing solution space of DNA for the *set-splitting problem* and how to apply DNA operations in the Adleman-Lipton model to solve that problem from solution space of sticker.

## 1 Introduction

Nowadays, it is possible to generate roughly $10^{18}$ DNA strands that fit in a test tube through advances in molecular biology [1]. Adleman [2] wrote the first paper in which DNA strands could be applied to manipulate solutions for an instance of the NP-complete Hamiltonian path problem. Lipton [3] wrote the second paper that demonstrated that the Adleman techniques could be employed to solving the NP-complete satisfiability problem (the first NP-complete problem). Adleman and his co-authors [14] proposed *sticker* for enhancing error rate of hybridization to the Adleman-Lipton model.

In the paper, we use *sticker* in the sticker-based model to constructing solution space of DNA for the *set-splitting problem*. Simultaneously, we also use DNA operations in the Adleman-Lipton model to develop one DNA algorithm. It is proved from the main result of the proposed DNA algorithm that the *set-splitting problem* is resolved with biological operations in the Adleman-Lipton model from solution space of sticker. Furthermore, this work represents obvious evidence for the ability of DNA-based computing for resolving the NP-complete problems.

The rest of this paper is organized as follows. In Section 2, the Adleman-Lipton model is in detail introduced and the comparison of the model with other models is also

M. Guo and L.T.Yang (Eds.): ISPA 2003, LNCS 2745, pp. 185–196, 2003.

given. Section 3 introduces a DNA algorithm for solving the set-splitting problem from solution space of sticker in the Adleman-Lipton model. In Section 4, the experimental result of simulated DNA computing is also given. Conclusions are drawn in Section 5.

## 2  DNA Model of Computation

In subsection 2.1, the summary of DNA structure and the Adleman-Lipton model is in detail described. In subsection 2.2, the comparison of the Adleman-Lipton model with other models is also in detail introduced.

### 2.1  The Adleman-Lipton Model

Due to [1, 16], distinct nucleotides are detected only with their bases, which come in two sorts: *purines* and *pyrimidines*. Purines include *adenine* and *guanine*, abbreviated *A* and *G*. Pyrimidines contain *cytosine* and t*hymine*, abbreviated *C* and *T*. Because nucleotides are only distinguished from their bases, they are simply represented as *A*, *G*, *C*, or *T* nucleotides, depending upon the sort of base that they have.

The DNA operations in the Adleman-Lipton model, cited from [2, 3, 11, 12], are described below. These operations will be used for figuring out solutions of the set-splitting problem.

The Adleman-Lipton model:

A (test) tube is a set of molecules of DNA (i.e. a multi-set of finite strings over the alphabet $\{A, C, G, T\}$). Given a tube, one can perform the following operations:

1.    *Extract*. Given a tube $P$ and a short single strand of DNA, $S$, produce two tubes $+(P, S)$ and $-(P, S)$, where $+(P, S)$ is all of the molecules of DNA in $P$ which contain the strand $S$ as a sub-strand and $-(P, S)$ is all of the molecules of DNA in $P$ which do not contain the short strand $S$.

2.    *Merge*. Given tubes $P_1$ and $P_2$, yield $\cup(P_1, P_2)$, where $\cup(P_1, P_2) = P_1 \cup P_2$. This operation is to pour two tubes into one, with no change of the individual strands.

3.    *Detect*. Given a tube $P$, say 'yes' if $P$ includes at least one DNA molecule, and say 'no' if it contains none.

4.    *Discard*. Given a tube $P$, the operation will discard the tube $P$.

5.    *Read*. Given a tube $P$, the operation is used to describe a single molecule, which is contained in the tube $P$. Even if $P$ contains many different molecules each encoding a different set of bases, the operation can give an explicit description of exactly one of them.

### 2.2    The Comparison of the Adleman-Lipton Model with Other Models

Quyang et al. [4] proved that restriction enzymes could be used to solve the NP-complete clique problem (MCP). The maximum number of vertices that they can process is limited to 27 because the size of the pool with the size of the problem exponentially increases [4]. Arito et al. [5] described new molecular experimental techniques for searching a Hamiltonian path. Morimoto et al. [6] offered a solid-phase method to finding a Hamiltonian path. Narayanan et al. [7] demonstrated that the Adleman-Lipton model was extended towards solving the traveling salesman problem. Shin et al. [8] presented an encoding scheme that applies fixed-length codes for representing integer and real values. Their method could also be employed towards solving the traveling salesman problem. Amos [13] proposed parallel filtering model for resolving the Hamiltonian path problem, the sub-graph isomorphism problem, the 3-vertex-colourability problem, the clique problem and the independent-set problem. Roweis et al. [14] proposed sticker-based model to enhance the Adleman-Lipton model. Their model could be used for determining solutions to an instance of the set cover problem. Perez-Jimenez et al. [15] employed sticker-based model [14] to resolve knapsack problems. Fu [21] proposed new algorithms to resolve 3-SAT, 3-Coloring and the independent set. In our previous work, Chang et al [17, 18, 19, 20] proved how the DNA operations from solution space of *splint* in the Adleman-Lipton model could be employed for developing DNA algorithms. Those DNA algorithms could be applied for resolving the dominating-set problem, the vertex cover problem, the clique problem, the independent-set problem, the 3-dimensional matching problem and the set-packing problem. In our previous work, Chang et al [25, 26] also employed the sticker-based model and the Adleman-Lipton model to dealing with the dominating-set problem and the set-basis problem for decreasing error rate of hybridization.

## 3   Using Sticker for Solving the Set-Splitting Problem in the Adleman-Lipton Model

In subsection 3.1, the summary of the set-splitting problem is described. Applying sticker to constructing solution space of DNA sequences for the set-splitting problem is introduced in subsection 3.2. In subsection 3.3, one DNA algorithm is proposed to resolving the set-splitting problem. In subsection 3.4, the complexity of the proposed algorithm is described.

### 3.1   Definition of the Set-Splitting Problem

Assume that a finite set $S$ is $\{s_1, ..., s_d\}$, where $s_e$ is the $e^{th}$ element for $1 \le e \le d$ in $S$. $|S|$ is denoted as the number of elements in $S$ and $|S|$ is equal to $d$. Suppose that a collection $C$ is the set of subsets to a finite set $S$ and is $\{C_1, ..., C_f\}$, where $C_g$ is the $g^{th}$ element for $1 \le g \le f$ in $C$. $|C|$ is denoted as the number of subsets in $C$ and $|C|$ is equal to $f$. Mathematically, the set-splitting problem is to find whether there is a partition of $S$ into two subsets $S_1$ and $S_2$ such that no subset in $C$ is entirely contained in either $S_1$ or $S_2$ [10]. The problem has been proved to be NP-complete problem [10].

There are a finite set $S$ and a collection $C$ of subsets for $S$ in Figure 1. The finite set $S$ is $\{1, 2\}$ and the collection $C$ is $\{\{1, 2\}\}$. The two sets define such a problem. The set splitting for $S$ and $C$ in Figure 1 is $S_1 = \{1\}$ and $S_2 = \{2\}$ or $S_1 = \{2\}$ and $S_2 = \{1\}$. It is indicated from [10] that finding a set splitting is a NP-complete problem, so it can be formulated as a "search" problem.

$$S = \{1, 2\} \text{ and } C = \{\{1, 2\}\}$$

**Fig.1.** A finite set $S$ and a collection $C$ of subsets for $S$.

## 3.2  Using Sticker for Constructing Solution Space of DNA Sequence for the Set-Splitting Problem

In the Adleman-Lipton model, their main ideal is to first generate solution space of DNA sequences for those problems resolved. Then, basic biological operations are used to select legal solution and to remove illegal solution from solution space. Therefore, for a finite set $S$ with $d$ elements and a collection $C$ with $f$ elements for subsets of the finite set $S$, the first step of resolving the set-splitting problem is to produce a test tube, which includes all of the possible subsets to the finite set. Assume that a $d$-digit binary number represents each possible subset for $S$. Also suppose that $S_1$ is a subset for $S$. If the $i^{th}$ bit in a $d$-digit binary number is set to 1, then it represents that the $i^{th}$ element in $S$ is in $S_1$. If the $i^{th}$ bit in a $d$-digit binary number is set to 0, then it represents the corresponding element to be out of $S_1$. By this way, all of the possible subsets in $S$ are transformed into an ensemble of all $d$-digit binary numbers.

Hence, with the way above, Table 1 denotes the solution space of the subsets for the finite set $S$ in Figure 1. The binary number, 00, in Table 1 represents the corresponding subset to be empty. The binary numbers, 01 and 10, in Table 1 represent that those corresponding subsets, respectively, are {1} and {2}. The binary number, 11, in Table 1 represents the corresponding subset to be {2, 1}. Though there are four 2-digit binary numbers for representing four possible subsets in Table 1, not every 2-digit binary number corresponds to a *legal* solution. Hence, in next subsection, basic biological operations are used to develop an algorithm for removing illegal subsets and determining legal solutions.

**Table 1.** The solution space of the subsets for the finite $S$ in Figure 1.

| 2-digit binary number | The corresponding subset |
|:---:|:---:|
| 00 | ∅ |
| 01 | {1} |
| 10 | {2} |
| 11 | {2, 1} |

**Table 2.** Denote representation of each subset in the collection $C$ in Figure 1.

| The subset | The corresponding 2-digit binary representation |
|:---:|:---:|
| {1, 2} | 11 |

Since a collection $C$ with $f$ elements is the set of subsets to $S$, every element in each subset in $C$ comes from $S$. Hence, every subset in $C$ is represented by the same method above. Table 2 denotes representation of each subset in the collection $C$ in Figure 1. The only subset, {1, 2}, in Table 2 is represented as the 2-digit binary number, 11. To implement this way, assume that an unsigned integer $X$ is represented by a binary number $x_d, x_{d-1}, ..., x_1$, where the value of $x_i$ is 1 or 0 for $1 \le i \le d$. The integer $X$ contains $2^d$ kinds of possible values. Each possible value represents a subset for a finite set $S$. Therefore, it is very clear that an unsigned integer $X$ forms $2^d$ possible subsets. A bit $x_i$ in an unsigned integer $X$ represents the $i^{th}$ element in $S$. If the $i^{th}$ element is in a subset, then the value of $x_i$ is set to 1. If the $i^{th}$ element is out of a subset, then the value of $x_i$ is set to 0.

To represent all possible subsets to a finite set $S$ with $d$ elements for the set-splitting problem, *sticker* [14, 22] is used to construct solution space for that problem resolved. For every bit, $x_i$, to $1 \le i \le d$, two *distinct* 15 base value sequences were designed. One represents the value, 1, for $x_i$ and another represents the value, 0, to $x_i$. For the sake of convenience of presentation, assume that $x_i{}^1$ denotes the value of $x_i$ to be 1 and $x_i{}^0$ defines the value of $x_i$ to be zero. Each of the $2^d$ possible subsets was represented by a library sequence of $15*d$ bases consisting of the concatenation of one value sequence for each bit. DNA molecules with library sequences are termed library strands and a combinatorial pool containing library strands is termed a library. The probes used for separating the library strands have sequences complementary to the value sequences. Because a collection $C$ is the set of subsets for a finite set $S$, every element in every subset in $C$ comes from $S$. Therefore, the same DNA sequences above are also applied to represent every element in every subset in $C$.

It is pointed out from [14, 22] that errors in the separation of the library strands are errors in the computation. Sequences must be designed to ensure that library strands have little secondary structure that might inhibit intended probe-library hybridization. The design must also exclude sequences that might encourage unintended probe-library hybridization. To help achieve these goals, sequences were computer-generated to satisfy the following constraint [22].
1. Library sequences contain only A's, T's, and C's.
2. All library and probe sequences have no occurrence of 5 or more consecutive identical nucleotides; i.e. no runs of more than 4 A's, 4 T's, 4 C's or 4 G's occur in any library or probe sequences.
3. Every probe sequence has at least 4 mismatches with all 15 base alignment of any library sequence (except for with its matching value sequence).
4. Every 15 base subsequence of a library sequence has at least 4 mismatcheswith all 15 base alignment of itself or any other library sequence.
5. No probe sequence has a run of more than 7 matches with any 8 base alignment of any library sequence (except for with its matching value sequence).
6. No library sequence has a run of more than 7 matches with any 8 base alignment of itself or any other library sequence.
7. Every probe sequence has 4, 5, or 6 Gs in its sequence.

Constraint (1) is motivated by the assumption that library strands composed only of As, Ts, and Cs will have less secondary structure than those composed of As, Ts, Cs, and Gs [23]. Constraint (2) is motivated by two assumptions: first, that long homopolymer tracts may have unusual secondary structure and second, that the melting temperatures of probe-library hybrids will be more uniform if none of the probe-library hybrids involve long homopolymer tracts. Constraints (3) and (5) are intended to ensure that probes bind only weakly where they are not intended to bind. Constraints (4) and (6) are intended to ensure that library strands have a low affinity for themselves. Constraint (7) is intended to ensure that intended probe-library pairings have uniform melting temperatures.

The Adleman program [22] was modified for generating those DNA sequences to satisfying the constraints above. For example, for representing the two elements in the finite set $S$ in Figure 1, the DNA sequences generated were: $x_1^0$ = *AAAACTCACCCTCCT*, $x_2^0$ = *TCTAATATAATTACT*, $x_1^1$ = *TTTCAATAACACCTC* and $x_2^1$ = *ATTCACTTCTTTAAT*. Because the only subset in the collection $C$ in Figure 1 includes the first element and the second element in $S$, two 15 base DNA sequences, *ATTCACTTCTTTAAT* ($x_2^1$) and *TTTCAATAACACCTC* ($x_1^1$) are used for representing them. For every possible subset to the finite set $S$ in Figure 1, the corresponding library strand was synthesized by employing a mix-and-split combinatorial synthesis technique [24]. Similarly, for any $d$-element set, all of the library strands for representing every possible subset could be also synthesized with the same technique.

### 3.3  The DNA Algorithm for Solving the Set-Splitting Problem

The following DNA algorithm is proposed to solve the *set-splitting problem*.
**Algorithm 1:** Solving the set-splitting problem.
(1) Input ($T_0$), where the tube $T_0$ includes solution space of DNA sequences to encode all of the possible subsets for any $d$-element set, $S$, with those techniques mentioned in subsection 3.2.
(2) For $j = 1$ to $|C|$, where $|C|$ is the number of subsets in a collection $C$.
(a)    For $k = 1$ to $|C_j|$, where $|C_j|$ is the number of elements in $C_j$ in $C$. Assume that the $k^{th}$ element in $C_j$ is the $i^{th}$ element in $S$ and $x_i$ is used to represent it.
(b)    $T_0 = +(T_0, x_i^1)$ and $T_{OFF} = -(T_0, x_i^1)$.
(c)    $T_{ON} = \cup(T_{OFF}, T_{ON})$.EndFor
(d)    Discard($T_0$).
(e)    $T_0 = \cup(T_{ON}, T_0)$.EndFor
(3) For $j = 1$ to $|C|$, where $|C|$ is the number of subsets in a collection $C$.
(a) For $k = 1$ to $|C_j|$, where $|C_j|$ is the number of elements in $C_j$ in $C$. Assume that the $k^{th}$ element in $C_j$ is the $i^{th}$ element in $S$ and $x_i$ is used to represent it.
(b)    $T_0 = +(T_0, x_i^0)$ and $T_{OFF} = -(T_0, x_i^0)$.
(c)    $T_{ON} = \cup(T_{OFF}, T_{ON})$.EndFor
(d)    Discard($T_0$).
(e)    $T_0 = \cup(T_{ON}, T_0)$.EndFor
(4) If Detect($T_0$) = = "yes" then
(a) Read ($T_0$).

It is very obvious from those steps in Algorithm 1 that the set-splitting problem for any $d$-element set can be resolved.

**Proof:** Omitted. ■

The finite set $S$ and the collection $C$ in Figure 1 are used to show the power of Algorithm 1. It is pointed out from Step 1 in Algorithm 1 that the tube $T_0$ is filled with four library stands with those techniques mentioned in subsection 3.2, representing four possible subsets for the set $S$ in Figure 1. The number of the subset in $C$ in Figure 1 is one, so the number of execution to the outer loop in Step 2 of Algorithm 1 is one time. The number of the element in the only subset in the collection $C$ is two. Therefore, the number of execution for the inner loop in Step 2 of Algorithm 1 is two times.

According to the first execution of Step 2b of Algorithm 1, two tubes are generated. The first tube, $T_0$, includes those subsets: $\{1\}$ and $\{1, 2\}$ and the second tube, $T_{OFF}$, also contains those subsets: $\varnothing$ and $\{2\}$. Next, the first execution to Step 2c in Algorithm 1 pours the two tubes $T_{OFF}$ and $T_{ON}$ into the tube $T_{ON}$. Therefore, the tube $T_{ON}$ now includes those subsets: $\varnothing$ and $\{2\}$. It is very clear from the second execution of Step 2b that the two tubes are yielded. The first tube, $T_0$ contains the subset, $\{1, 2\}$. The second tube, $T_{OFF}$, consists of the subset: $\{1\}$. It is indicated from the second execution of Step 2c that the tube $T_{ON}$ contains the subsets: $\varnothing$, $\{1\}$ and $\{2\}$. In light of definition of set splitting, because the tube $T_0$ contains illegal partition, the first execution of Step 2d applies "discard" operation to discard the tube $T_0$. It is pointed out from the first execution of Step 2e that the tube $T_0$ includes the subset: $\varnothing$, $\{1\}$ and $\{2\}$.

Since the number of the subset in $C$ in Figure 1 is one, so the number of execution to the outer loop in Step 3 of Algorithm 1 is one time. The number of the element in the only subset in the collection $C$ is two. Therefore, the number of execution for the inner loop in Step 3 is two times. Due to the first execution of Step 3b, two tubes are generated. The first tube, $T_0$, includes those subsets: $\varnothing$ and $\{2\}$ and the second tube, $T_{OFF}$, also contains the subset: $\{1\}$. Next, the first execution to Step 3c pours the two tubes $T_{OFF}$ and $T_{ON}$ into the tube $T_{ON}$. Therefore, the tube $T_{ON}$ now includes those subsets: $\{1\}$. It is very clear from the second execution of Step 3b that the two tubes are yielded. The first tube, $T_0$ contains the subset $\varnothing$. The second tube, $T_{OFF}$, consists of the subset: $\{2\}$. It is indicated from the second execution of Step 3c that the tube $T_{ON}$ contains the subsets: $\{1\}$ and $\{2\}$. From definition of set splitting, since the tube $T_0$ contains illegal partition, the first execution of Step 3d applies "discard" operation to discard the tube $T_0$. It is pointed out from the first execution of Step 3e that the tube $T_0$ includes the subset: $\{1\}$ and $\{2\}$.

The first execution of Step 4a applies "detect" operation to detect the tube $T_0$. Because the tube $T_0$ is not empty, Step 4b employs "read" operation to describe 'sequence' of a molecular in the tube $T_0$. The answer for the set-splitting problem to the finite set $S$ and the collection $C$ in Figure 1 is found to be $S_1 = \{1\}$ and $S_2 = \{2\}$ or $S_1 = \{2\}$ and $S_2 = \{1\}$.

### 3.4   The Complexity of the Proposed DNA Algorithm

The following theorems describe time complexity of Algorithm 1, volume complexity of solution space in Algorithm 1, the number of the tube used in Algorithm 1 and the longest library strand in solution space in Algorithm 1.

**Theorem 3-1:** The set-splitting problem for any $d$-element set $S$ and any $f$-subset collection $C$ can be solved with $O(d * f)$ biological operations in the Adleman-Lipton model.

**Proof:** Omitted. ∎

**Theorem 3-2:** The set-splitting problem for any $d$-element set $S$ and any $f$-subset collection $C$ can be solved with sticker to construct $O(2^d)$ library strands in the Adleman-Lipton model.

**Proof:** Refer to **Theorem 3-1**. ∎

**Theorem 3-3:** The set-splitting problem for any $d$-element set $S$ and any $f$-subset collection can be solved with *three* tubes in the Adleman-Lipton model.

**Proof:** Refer to **Theorem 3-1**. ∎

**Theorem 3-4:** The set-splitting problem for any $d$-element set $S$ and any $f$-subset collection can be solved with the longest library strand, $O(15*d)$, in the Adleman-Lipton model.

**Proof:** Refer to **Theorem 3-1**. ∎

# 4   Experimental Results of Simulated DNA Computing

We finished the modification of the Adleman program [22] in a PC with one Pentium II 200 MHz CPU and 64 MB main memory. Our operating system is Window 98 and our compiler is C++ Builder 6.0. This program modified was applied to generating DNA sequences for solving the set-splitting problem for any $d$-element set $S$ and any $f$-subset collection $C$. Because the source code of the two functions *srand48()* and *drand48()* was not found in the *original* Adleman program, we used the standard function *srand()* in C++ builder 6.0 to replace the function *srand48()* and added the source code to the function *drand48()*. We also added subroutines to the Adleman program for simulating biological operations in the Adleman-Lipton model in Section 2. We added subroutines to the Adleman program to simulating Algorithm 1 in subsection 3.3. For any $d$-element set $S$ and any $f$-subset collection $C$, the size of library strands is $2^d$. Due to the limit of memory space and hard-disk space, the value of $d$ was less than or equal to 20.

The Adleman program is used to constructing each 15-base DNA sequence for each bit of the library. For each bit, the program is applied for generating two 15-base random sequences (for the '1' and the '0') and checking to see if the library strands satisfy the seven constraints in subsection 3.2 with the new DNA sequences added. If the constraints are satisfied, the new DNA sequences are 'greedily' accepted. If the constraints are not satisfied then mutations are introduced one by one into the new block until either: (A) the constraints are satisfied and the new DNA sequences are then accepted or (B) a threshold for the number of mutations is exceeded and the program has failed and so it exits, printing the sequence found so far. If $d$-bits that satisfy the constraints are found then the program has succeeded and it outputs these sequences.

Consider the finite set $S$ and the collection $C$ in Figure 1. The finite set includes {1,

2} and the collection $C$ contains $\{\{1, 2\}\}$. DNA sequences generated by the Adleman program modified were shown in Table 3. The program, respectively, took one mutation and one mutation to make new DNA sequences for the first element and the second element in $S$. With the nearest neighbor parameters, the program was used to calculate the enthalpy, entropy, and free energy for the binding of each probe to its corresponding region on a library strand. The energy was shown in Table 4. Only G really matters to the energy of each bit. For example, the delta G for the probe binding a '1' in the first bit is thus estimated to be 24.3 kcal/mol and the delta G for the probe binding a '0' is estimated to be 27.5 kcal/mol.

**Table 3.** Sequences chosen to represent the two elements in $S$ in Figure 1.

| Vertex | 5'→ 3' DNA Sequence |
|--------|---------------------|
| $x_2^0$ | TCTAATATAATTACT |
| $x_1^0$ | AAAACTCACCCTCCT |
| $x_2^1$ | ATTCACTTCTTTAAT |
| $x_1^1$ | TTTCAATAACACCTC |

**Table 4.** The energy for the binding of each probe to its corresponding region on a library strand.

| Vertex | Enthalpy energy (H) | Entropyenergy (S) | Free energy (G) |
|--------|---------------------|-------------------|-----------------|
| $x_2^0$ | 104.8 | 283.7 | 19.9 |
| $x_1^0$ | 113.7 | 288.7 | 27.5 |
| $x_2^1$ | 107.8 | 283.5 | 23 |
| $x_1^1$ | 105.6 | 271.6 | 24.3 |

The program simulated a mix-and-split combinatorial synthesis technique [24] to synthesize the library strand to every possible subset. Those library strands were shown in Table 5 and, respectively, represent four possible subsets: $\varnothing$, $\{1\}$, $\{2\}$, and $\{1, 2\}$. The program was also applied to figure out the average and standard deviation for the enthalpy, entropy and free energy over all probe/library strand interactions. The energy was shown in Table 6. The standard deviation for delta G is small because this is partially enforced by the constraint that there are 4, 5, or 6 Gs (the seventh constraint in subsection 3.2) in the probe sequences.

**Table 5.** DNA sequences chosen represent all possible subsets.

| |
|---|
| 5'-TCTAATATAATTACTAAAACTCACCCTCCT-3' |
| 3'-AGATTATATTAATGATTTTGAGTGGGAGGA-5' |
| 5'-TCTAATATAATTACTTTTCAATAACACCTC-3' |
| 3'-AGATTATATTAATGAAAAGTTATTGTGGAG-5' |
| 5'-ATTCACTTCTTTAATAAAACTCACCCTCCT-3' |
| 3'-TAAGTGAAGAAATTATTTTGAGTGGGAGGA-5' |
| 5'-ATTCACTTCTTTAATTTTCAATAACACCTC-3' |
| 3'-TAAGTGAAGAAATTAAAAGTTATTGTGGAG-5' |

**Table 6.** The energy over all probe/library strand interactions.

|  | Enthalpy energy (H) | Entropy energy (S) | Free energy (G) |
|---|---|---|---|
| Average | 107.975 | 281.875 | 23.675 |
| Standard deviation | 3.48298 | 6.28739 | 2.72615 |

The Adleman program was employed for computing the distribution of the types of potential mishybridizations. The distribution of the types of potential mishybridizations is the absolute frequency of a probe-strand match of length $k$ from 0 to the bit length 15 (for DNA sequences) where probes are not supposed to match the strands. The distribution was, subsequently, 57, 104, 110, 105, 100, 103, 59, 36, 11, 2, 1, 0, 0, 0, 0 and 0. It is pointed out from the last five zeros that there are 0 occurrences where a probe matches a strand at 11, 12, 13, 14 or 15 places. This shows that the third constraint in subsection 3.2 has been satisfied. It is very clear that the number of matches peaks at 2(110). That is to say that there are 110 occurrences where a probe matches a strand at 2 places.

It is indicated from Step 2 and Step 3 of simulation that the results were shown in Table 7 and Table 8. From Step 4 of simulation, the set splitting was shown in Table 9. That is to say that the answer of the set-splitting problem for the finite set $S$ and the collection $C$ in Figure 1 is $S_1 = \{1\}$ and $S_2 = \{2\}$ or $S_1 = \{2\}$ and $S_2 = \{1\}$.

**Table 7.** DNA sequences generated by Step 2 represent possible partitions.

| |
|---|
| 5'-TCTAATATAATTACTAAAACTCACCCTCCT-3' |
| 5'-TCTAATATAATTACTTTTCAATAACACCTC-3' |
| 5'-ATTCACTTCTTTAATAAAACTCACCCTCCT-3' |

**Table 8.** DNA sequences generated by Step 3 represent legal partitions.

| |
|---|
| 5'-TCTAATATAATTACTTTTCAATAACACCTC-3' |
| 5'-ATTCACTTCTTTAATAAAACTCACCCTCCT-3' |

**Table 9.** DNA sequences represent the answer of the set-splitting problem.

| |
|---|
| 5'-TCTAATATAATTACTTTTCAATAACACCTC-3' |
| 5'-ATTCACTTCTTTAATAAAACTCACCCTCCT-3' |

# 5   Conclusions

It is indicated from [14] that applying *splints* constructs solution space of DNA sequence for solving the NP-complete problem in the Adleman-Lipton and this causes that hybridization has higher probabilities for errors. Adleman and his co-authors [14] proposed *sticker* to decrease probabilities of errors to hybridization in the Adleman-Lipton. In the proposed algorithm, the size of solution space of sticker is exponential. Hence, this limits that we can resolve the size of the NP-complete problem. The main result of the proposed algorithm shows that the *set-splitting problem* is resolved with biological operations in the Adleman-Lipton model from solution space of sticker. Furthermore, this work represents clear evidence for the ability of DNA based computing to solve NP-complete problems.

# References

[1] R. R. Sinden. *DNA Structure and Function*. Academic Press, 1994.

[2] L. Adleman. Molecular computation of solutions to combinatorial problems. Science, 266:1021-1024, Nov. 11, 1994.

[3] R. J. Lipton. DNA solution of hard computational problems. Science, 268:542:545, 1995.

[4] Q. Quyang, P.D. Kaplan, S. Liu, and A. Libchaber. DNA solution of the maximal clique problem. Science, 278:446-449, 1997.

[5] M. Arita, A. Suyama, and M. Hagiya. A heuristic approach for Hamiltonian path problem with molecules. Proceedings of 2nd Genetic Programming (GP-97), 1997, pp. 457-462.

[6] N. Morimoto, M. Arita, and A. Suyama. Solid phase DNA solution to the Hamiltonian path problem. DIMACS (Series in Discrete Mathematics and Theoretical Computer Science), Vol. 48, 1999, pp. 93-206.

[7] A. Narayanan, and S. Zorbala. DNA algorithms for computing shortest paths. In Genetic Programming 1998: Proceedings of the Third Annual Conference, J. R. Koza et al. (Eds), 1998, pp. 718--724.

[8] S.-Y. Shin, B.-T. Zhang, and S.-S. Jun. Solving traveling salesman problems using molecular programming. Proceedings of the 1999 Congress on Evolutionary Computation (CEC99), vol. 2, pp. 994-1000, 1999.

[9] T. H. Cormen, C. E. Leiserson, and R. L. Rivest. *Introduction to algorithms*.

[10] M. R. Garey, and D. S. Johnson. *Computer and intractability*. Freeman, San Fransico, CA, 1979.

[11] D. Boneh, C. Dunworth, R. J. Lipton and J. Sgall. On the computational Power of DNA. In Discrete Applied Mathematics, Special Issue on Computational Molecular Biology, Vol. 71 (1996), pp. 79-94.

[12] L. M. Adleman. On constructing a molecular computer. DNA Based Computers, Eds. R. Lipton and E. Baum, DIMACS: series in Discrete Mathematics and Theoretical Computer Science, American Mathematical Society. 1-21 (1996)

[13] M. Amos. "DNA Computation", Ph.D. Thesis, department of computer science, the University of Warwick, 1997.

[14] S. Roweis, E. Winfree, R. Burgoyne, N. V. Chelyapov, M. F. Goodman, Paul W.K. Rothemund and L. M. Adleman. "A Sticker Based Model for DNA Computation". 2nd annual workshop on DNA Computing, Princeton University. Eds. L. Landweber and E. Baum, DIMACS: series in Discrete Mathematics and Theoretical Computer Science, American Mathematical Society. 1-29 (1999).

[15] M.J. Perez-Jimenez and F. Sancho-Caparrini. "Solving Knapsack Problems in a Sticker Based Model". 7nd annual workshop on DNA Computing, DIMACS: series in Discrete Mathematics and Theoretical Computer Science, American Mathematical Society, 2001.

[16] G. Paun, G. Rozenberg and A. Salomaa. *DNA Computing: New Computing Paradigms.* Springer-Verlag, New York, 1998. ISBN: 3-540-64196-3.

[17] W.-L. Chang and M. Guo. "Solving the Dominating-set Problem in Adleman-Lipton's Model". The Third International Conference on Parallel and Distributed Computing, Applications and Technologies, Japan, 2002, pp. 167-172.

[18] W.-L. Chang and M. Guo. " Solving the Clique Problem and the Vertex Cover Problem in Adleman-Lipton's Model". IASTED International Conference, Networks, Parallel and Distributed Processing, and Applications, Japan, 2002, pp. 431-436.

[19] W.-L. Chang, M. Guo. "Solving NP-Complete Problem in the Adleman-Lipton Model". The Proceedings of 2002 International Conference on Computer and Information Technology, Japan, 2002, pp. 157-162.

[20] W.-L. Chang and M. Guo. " Resolving the 3-Dimensional Matching Problem and the Set Packing Problem in Adleman-Lipton's Model". IASTED International Conference, Networks, Parallel and Distributed Processing, and Applications, Japan, 2002, pp. 455-460.

[21] Bin Fu. "Volume Bounded Molecular Computation". Ph.D. Thesis, Department of Computer Science, Yale University, 1997.

[22] Ravinderjit S. Braich, Clifford Johnson, Paul W.K. Rothemund, Darryl Hwang, Nickolas Chelyapov and Leonard M. Adleman. "Solution of a satisfiability problem on a gel-based DNA computer". Proceedings of the 6th International Conference on DNA Computation in the Springer-Verlag Lecture Notes in Computer Science series.

[23] Kalim Mir. "A restricted genetic alphabet for DNA computing". Eric B. Baum and Laura F. Landweber, editors. DNA Based Computers II: DIMACS Workshop, June 10-12, 1996, volume 44 of DIMACS: Series in Discrete Mathematics and Theoretical Computer Science, Providence, RI, 1998, pp. 243-246.

[24] A. R. Cukras, Dirk Faulhammer, Richard J. Lipton, and Laura F. Landweber. "Chess games: A model for RNA-based computation". In Proceedings of the 4th DIMACS Meeting on DNA Based Computers, held at the University of Pennsylvania, June 16-19, 1998, pp. 27-37.

[25] W.-L. Chang and M. Guo. "Using Sticker for Solving the Dominating-set Problem in the Adleman-Lipton Model". IEICE Transaction on Information System, 2003, accepted.

[26] W.-L. Chang and M. Guo. "Solving the Set-basis Problem in Sticker-based Model and the Adleman-Lipton Model". It was submitted to the 2003 International Conference on Parallel Processing (ICPP2003), Kaohsiung, Taiwan, Republic of China.

# Parallel MCGLS and ICGLS Methods for Least Squares Problems on Distributed Memory Architectures

Laurence Tianruo Yang[1,2] and Richard P. Brent[2]

[1] Department of Computer Science, St. Francis Xavier University
P.O. Box 5000, Antigonish, B2G 2W5, NS, Canada
lyang@stfx.ca
[2] Computing Laboratory, Oxford University
Wolfson Building, Park Road, Oxford OX1 3QD, UK

**Abstract.** In this paper we mainly study the parallelization of the CGLS method, a basic iterative method for large and sparse least squares problems in which the conjugate gradient method is applied to solve normal equations. On modern parallel architectures its parallel performance is always limited because of the global communication required for inner products, the main bottleneck of parallel performance. In this paper, we describe a modified CGLS (MCGLS) method which improve parallel performance by assembling the results of a number of inner products collectively and by creating situations where communication can be overlapped with computation. More importantly, we also propose an improved CGLS (ICGLS) method to reduce inner product's global synchronization points to half, then significantly improve the parallel performance accordingly compared with the standard CGLS method and the MCGLS method.

## 1 Introduction

Many scientific and engineering applications such as linear programming, augmented Lagrangian methods for CFD, the natural factor method in partial differential equations, tomography, seismic modelling, control theory, mechanical system and signal analysis, robotics, and structural analysis give rise to the least squares problems with a large and sparse coefficient matrix $A$. Excellent surveys of work in this area are [3,12]. Minimizing by solving the normal equations is a common and often efficient approach, because $A^T A$ is symmetric and positive definite and it can be solved by using conjugate gradient method which was developed in the early 1950's by Hestenes and Stiefel [15]. The resulting method, CGLS, is often used as the basic iterative method to solve the least squares problems. In theory, it is a straightforward extension of the standard conjugate gradient method. However, numerical unstable variants of these methods still occur in the literature. A comprehensive comparison of different implementations can be found in [4]. Here we denote the most accurate version CGLS1 as standard CGLS we described later throughout the rest of paper.

M. Guo and L.T.Yang (Eds.): ISPA 2003, LNCS 2745, pp. 197–208, 2003.
© Springer-Verlag Berlin Heidelberg 2003

On parallel architectures, the basic time-consuming computational kernels of CGLS are usually: inner products, vector updates, matrix vector products. In many situations, especially when matrix operations are well-structured, these operations are suitable for implementation on vector and share memory parallel computers [11]. But for parallel distributed memory machines, the matrices and vectors are distributed over the processors, so that even when the matrix operations can be implemented efficiently by parallel operations, we still can not avoid the global communication required for inner product computations. The detailed discussions on the communication problem on distributed memory systems can be found in [8,9,18]. In a word, these global communication costs become relatively more and more important when the number of the parallel processors is increased and thus they have the potential to affect the scalability of the whole algorithm in a negative way [7,8,9]. This aspect has received much attention and several approaches have been suggested to improve the performance of these algorithms [1,8,9,20].

In this paper, we describe a modified CGLS (MCGLS) method and an improved CGLS (ICGLS) method to reduce inner product's global synchronization points, respectively, then improve the parallel performance accordingly. In the MCGLS method, there are two ways of improvement. One is to assemble the results of a number of inner products collectively and another is to create situations where communication can be overlapped with computation. However, the improvement is still very limited. In the ICGLS method, the algorithm is derived so that global synchronization points are reduced from two to one only, then accordingly the communication time can be significantly reduced compared with the standard CGLS method and the MCGLS method.

The paper is organized as follows. In section 2 and 3, we will describe the standard CGLS method with its convergence properties. The proposed MCGLS and ICGLS approaches are described in section 4 and 5, respectively. In section 6, the parallel implementation details including data distribution and communication scheme are presented. Finally some preliminary numerical experiments carried out on a distributed memory architecture are described.

## 2   The Standard CGLS Method

There are many ways, all mathematically equivalent, in which to implement the conjugate gradient method as described in [4]. In exact arithmetic they will all generate the same sequence of approximations, but in finite precision the achieved accuracy may differ substantially.

Elfving [13] compared several implementations of the conjugate gradient method, and found CGLS1 to be the most accurate. A small variation of CGLS1 is obtained instead of $r = b - Ax$, the residual to the normal equations $s = A^T(b - Ax)$ is recurred, namely CGLS2 which is bad with regards to numerical stability. Besides these two versions of CGLS, Paige and Saunder [17] developed algorithms based on the Lanczos bidiagonalization method of Golub and Kahan [14]. There are two forms of this bidiagonalization procedure,

Bidiag1 (LSQR) and Bidiag2 (LSCG), which produce two algorithms which differ in their numerical properties. The comprehensive comparison of these different implementations has been done by Björck et al. [4]. They did a detailed analysis for the failure of CGLS2 and LSCG. In this paper, we choose the version of of CGLS1 namely standard CGLS throughout the rest as our basic method to solve the least squares problems.

When $A$ has full rank, the system of normal equations has a unique solution $\hat{x}$, and we denote by $\hat{r} = b - A\hat{x}$ the corresponding residual. For a given starting vector $x_0$ the conjugate gradient algorithm generates approximations $x_k$ in the affine subspace

$$x_k \in x_0 + \mathcal{K}_k(A^T A, s_0), \qquad s_0 = A^T(b - Ax_0), \qquad (1)$$

where $\mathcal{K}_k(A^T A, s_0)$ is the Krylov subspace

$$\text{span}\{A^T s_0, (A^T A)A^T s_0, \ldots, (A^T A)^{k-1} A^T s_0\}. \qquad (2)$$

The iterates are optimal in the sense that for each $k$, $x_k$ minimizes the error functional

$$E_\mu(x_k) = (\hat{x} - x_k)^T (A^T A)^\mu (\hat{x} - x_k). \qquad (3)$$

Only the values $\mu = 0, 1, 2$ are of practical interest. By (3), and using $A(\hat{x} - x_k) = b - \hat{r} - Ax_k = r_k - \hat{r}$,

$$E_\mu(x_k) = \begin{cases} \|\hat{x} - x_k\|, & \mu = 0; \\ \|\hat{r} - r_k\|^2 = \|r_k\|^2 - \|\hat{r}\|^2, & \mu = 1; \\ \|A^T(\hat{r} - r_k)\|^2 = \|A^T r_k\|^2, & \mu = 2. \end{cases} \qquad (4)$$

Here and in the following $\|\cdot\|$ denotes the $l_2$-norm. We consider here only the case $\mu = 1$, namely CGLS, which is of most practical interest with the best numerical accuracy. The algorithm originally given by Stiefel [19] can be formulated in Algorithm 1 as follows:

---

**Algorithm 1** The CGLS Method

---

1: Let $x_0$ be an initial approximation, set
2: $r_0 = b - Ax_0$, $s_0 = p_1 = A^T r_0$, $\gamma_0 = \|s_0\|^2$;
3: **for** k = 1, 2, 3, ... **do**
4: $\quad q_k = Ap_k$;
5: $\quad \alpha_k = \gamma_{k-1}/\|q_k\|^2$;
6: $\quad x_k = x_{k-1} + \alpha_k p_k$;
7: $\quad r_k = r_{k-1} - \alpha_k q_k$;
8: $\quad s_k = A^T r_k$;
9: $\quad \gamma_k = \|s_k\|^2$;
10: $\quad \beta_k = \gamma_k/\gamma_{k-1}$;
11: $\quad p_{k+1} = s_k + \beta_k p_k$.
12: **end for**

---

# 3  Convergence Properties of the CGLS Method

For convenience we assume that $x_0 = 0$, and hence $r_0 = b$. We also assume that exact arithmetic is used.

Based on [3], an upper bound for the rate of convergence of CGLS can be derived from the fact that $x = x_k$ minimizes the quadratic form

$$\min_{x \in \mathcal{K}_k(A^TA, A^Tb)} s^T(A^TA)^{-1}s, \qquad s = A^T(b - Ax). \tag{5}$$

For the residual vector $s_k = A^T r_k$ produced by CGLS we have

$$s_k \in T_k = \{s = A^T(b - Ax) \,|\, x \in \mathcal{K}_k\}.$$

Hence any vector $s \in T_k$ can be written

$$s_k = (I - A^T AP_{k-1}(A^T A))A^Tb = R_k(A^TA)A^Tb,$$

where $P_{k-1}$ is a polynomial of degree $k - 1$. The residual polynomial $R_k(t) = 1 - tP_{k-1}(t)$ is of degree $\leq k$, and satisfies $R_k(0) = 1$. If we let $\tilde{\Pi}_k^1$ denote the set of all such polynomial, then by the minimizing property (5)

$$\|s_k\|_{(A^TA)^{-1}} = \min_{R_k \in \tilde{\Pi}_k^1} \|R_k(A^TA)A^Tb\|_{(A^TA)^{-1}}.$$

Let $\sigma_i, u_i, v_i$ be the singular values and left and right singular vectors of $A$. Expanding $b$ along the left singular vectors we have

$$b = \sum_{i=1}^m \gamma_i u_i, \qquad A^Tb = \sum_{i=1}^n \gamma_i \hat{\sigma}_i v_i,$$

and then for CGLS we have

$$s_k = \sum_{i=1}^n \gamma_i \hat{\sigma}_i R_k(\hat{\sigma}_i^2)v_i, \qquad \|s_k\|_{(A^TA)^{-1}}^2 = \min_{R_k \in \tilde{\Pi}_k^1} \sum_{i=1}^n \gamma_i^2 R_k^2(\sigma_i^2). \tag{6}$$

An upper bound can be obtained by substituting *any* polynomial $R_k \in \tilde{\Pi}_k^1$. In particular, taking

$$R_n(\sigma_i^2) = (1 - \frac{\sigma^2}{\sigma_1^2})(1 - \frac{\sigma^2}{\sigma_2^2}) \cdots (1 - \frac{\sigma^2}{\sigma_n^2}),$$

we get $\|s_n\|_{(A^TA)^{-1}} = 0$, which proves that in exact arithmetic CGLS terminates after at most $n$ steps. Similarly, if $A$ only has $t$ distinct singular values, then CGLS converges in at most $t$ steps. Hence, CGLS is particularly effective when $A$ has low rank. If $\text{rank}(A) = p$, then $p$ steps suffices to get the exact solution.

For CGLS the residual error is reduced according to

$$\|r - r_k\|_2 < 2\Big(\frac{\kappa - 1}{\kappa + 1}\Big)^k \|r - r_0\|_2, \kappa = \sqrt{\frac{b}{a}} = \frac{\hat{\sigma}_1}{\hat{\sigma}_n}. \tag{7}$$

From this follow that an upper bound for the number of iterations $k$ to reduce the relative error by a factor of $\epsilon$ is given by

$$\frac{\|r - r_k\|_2}{\|r - r_0\|_2} \leq \epsilon \quad \Longleftrightarrow \quad k < \frac{1}{2}\kappa(A) \log \frac{2}{\epsilon}.$$

This is the same rate of convergence as for the Chebyshev semi-iterative method and the second order Richardson method. However, these methods require that accurate lower and upper bounds for the singular values of $A$ are known. For the CGLS method no such bounds are needed.

## 4    The Parallel MCGLS Method

All the operation of the CGLS method, expect for the update of $x$, must be computed in sequence. Therefore implementing CGLS for least squares problems on parallel distributed memory architectures by attempting to perform some of these statements simultaneously is bound to fail. A more promising way to parallelize the CGLS method is to exploit geometric parallelization. This means that the data will be distributed over the processors in such a way that every processor is responsible for the computations on its local data.

For the reduction in communication overhead for CGLS, in this section, we will describe the modified CGLS approach suggested by [9,10]. In this approach the operations are rescheduled to create more opportunities to overlap. The key trick is that postponing the update of $x$ one iteration does not effect the numerical stability of the algorithm. This leads to the possibility to compute the update of $x$ when the processors are communicating with each other to obtain the inner products. The modified version of CGLS, namely MCGLS, is described in Algorithm 2 as follows:

---
**Algorithm 2** The MCGLS Method

---
1:  $r_0 = b - Ax_0$, $s_0 = p_0 = A^T r_0$, $\gamma_0 = (s_0, s_0)$
2:  **for** k = 1, 2, 3, ... **do**
3:      $p_k = s_k + \beta_{k-1} p_{k-1}$;
4:      $q_k = Ap_k$;
5:      $\delta_k = (q_k, q_k)$;
6:      $x_k = x_{k-1} + \alpha_{k-1} p_{k-1}$;
7:      $\alpha_k = \gamma_k / \delta_k$;
8:      $r_{k+1} = r_k - \alpha_k q_k$;
9:      $s_{k+1} = A^T r_{k+1}$;
10:     $\gamma_k = (s_{k+1}, s_{k+1})$;
11:     $x_{k+1} = x_k + \alpha_k p_k$;
12:     $\beta_k = \gamma_{k+1} / \gamma_k$;
13: **end for**

---

Under the assumptions, MCGLS can be efficiently parallelized as follows:

-  All operations can be done in parallel. Only operation (4), (5), (9), and (10) require communication.

- The communication required for the reduction of the inner product in (5) can be overlapped with the update for $x_k$ in (6).
- Steps (3), (4), and (5) can be combined like this: the computation of a segment of $p_k$ can be followed immediately by the computation a segment of $q_k$ in (4), and this can be followed by the computation of a part of the inner product (5). This saves on load operations for segments of $p_k$ and $q_k$.
- The computation of $\beta_k$ can be done as soon as the computation in (10) has been completed. At that moment, the computation for next step (3) can be started since the required parts of $s_k$ have been completed.
- The computation of segments of $r_{k+1}$ in (8) can be followed by operation (9), which can be followed by the computation of parts of inner product in (10). This also saves on load operations.

Under the assumption of the overlap for the communication time, the communication cost for the inner products in the MCGLS iteration can be reduced.

## 5    The Parallel ICGLS Method

Although the MCGLS method can get better results on parallel performance, the improvement is still very limited because there are still two global synchronization points in (5) and (10), respectively.

The main idea of the ICGLS method is to apply the symmetric Lanczos method described in [16] to the normal equations

$$A^T A x = A^T b. \tag{8}$$

We do not need to compute the matrix $R = A^T A$, because we can compute $Rx$ as $A^T(Ax)$. To compute $A^T z$ where $z = Ax$, it is best to think of computing $(z^T A)^T$ because the elements of $A$ will be scattered across the parallel processors and we do not want to double the storage requirements by storing $A^T$ as well as $A$.

Based on the symmetric Lanczos method described in [16], since $R = A^T A$ is symmetric positive definite, $\tilde{b} = A^T b$ and $v, w$ are two vectors, then the symmetric Lanczos method [16] solves $Rx = \tilde{b}$ by iterating

$$w_i = R w_{i-1} - \sum_{j=0}^{i-1} c_{ij} w_j \quad (i > 0), \tag{9}$$

where

$$c_{ij} = \frac{w_j^T R^2 w_{i-1}}{w_j^T R w_j}, \tag{10}$$

until $w_i = 0$. If we induce $\max(i, j)$ and the symmetry of $R$, the following relation can be easily verified:

$$w_j^T R w_i = 0 \quad (i \neq j). \tag{11}$$

The vectors $w_0, w_1, \cdots, w_i$ are eventually linearly dependent, namely $\sum_{j=0}^{i} a_j w_j =0$ where $a_i \neq 0$. Pre-multiply by $w_i^T R$ and use (11) to find $a_i w_i^T R w_i = 0$. By positive definiteness, $w_i = 0$. Let $m$ denote the first value of $i$ such that $w_i = 0$.

If we define

$$x = \sum_{j=0}^{m-1} \frac{w_j^T \tilde{b}}{w_j^T R w_j} w_j, \tag{12}$$

then based on (9) and (10), $Rx - b \in \{Rw_0, Rw_1, \cdots, Rw_{m-1}, \tilde{b}\} \subseteq \{w_0, w_1, \cdots, w_{m-1}\}$. By construction, $w_j Rx = w_j^T \tilde{b}$ for $0 \leq j \leq m-1$. Hence $(Rx - \tilde{b})^T (Rx - \tilde{b}) = 0$ and $Rx = \tilde{b}$.

It can be observed that equations (9) and (10) require adding suitable multiples of all earlier $w_j$ when computing $w_i$. The terms vanish when $j < i - 2$, because of the following relation:

$$w_j^T R^2 w_{i-1} = (Rw_j)^T Rw_{i-1} = (w_{j+1} + \sum_{k=0}^{j} c_{j+1,k} w_k)^T Rw_{i-1}$$

$$= 0 \quad (j < i-2) \tag{13}$$

by equation (11). Hence equation (9) simplifies to

$$w_{i+1} = Rw_i - c_{i+1,i} w_i - c_{i+1,i-1} w_{i-1} \quad (i \geq 1), \tag{14}$$

where the coefficient $c_{i+1,i}$ and $c_{i+1,i-1}$ can be computed as follows:

$$c_{i+1,i} = \frac{(Rw_i)^T (Rw_i)}{w_i^T (Rw_i)}, \quad c_{i+1,i-1} = \frac{(Rw_{i-1})^T (Rw_i)}{w_{i-1}^T (Rw_{i-1})}. \tag{15}$$

Based on the mathematical background of the symmetric Lanczos method described above, we would go back the problem we originally aim for, namely equation (8). If we substitute $A^T A$ as $R$ into the equations described above, and define

$$\tilde{p}_i = Aw_i, \quad \tilde{q}_i = A^T \tilde{p}_i, \quad \alpha_i = \tilde{q}_i^T \tilde{q}_i, \quad \beta_i = \tilde{q}_i^T w_i, \quad \theta_i = \tilde{q}_i^T \tilde{q}_{i-1},$$

then equation (14) can be expressed as follows:

$$w_{i+1} = \tilde{q}_i - \frac{\alpha_i}{\beta_i} w_i - \frac{\theta_i}{\beta_{i-1}} w_{i-1}. \tag{16}$$

If we define $\tau_i = w_i^T \tilde{b}$ of equation (12) and $\lambda_i = \tilde{q}_i^T \tilde{b}$, we have

$$\tau_{i+1} = w_{i+1}^T \tilde{b} = \lambda_i - \frac{\alpha_i}{\beta_i} \tau_i - \frac{\theta_i}{\beta_{i-1}} \tau_{i-1}, \tag{17}$$

By substituting $\tau_i$ of (17) into equation (12), $x_i$ can be updated from the following:

$$x_i = x_{i-1} + \frac{\tau_i}{\beta_i} w_i. \tag{18}$$

**Algorithm 3** The Improved CGLS Method

1: $w_{-1} = w_0 = b$;
2: $\tilde{p}_{-1} = \tilde{p}_0 = Aw_0, \tilde{q}_{-1} = \tilde{q}_0 = A^T \tilde{p}_0$;
3: $\alpha_0 = \tilde{q}_0^T \tilde{q}_0, \beta_0 = \tilde{q}_0^T w_0 = \tilde{p}_0^T \tilde{p}_0, \theta_0 = \tilde{q}_0^T \tilde{q}_{-1}$;
4: $\tilde{b} = A^T b, \lambda_0 = \tilde{q}_0^T b, \tau_0 = w_0^T b$;
5: **for** i = 1, 2, 3, ... **do**
6:     $\tilde{p}_i = Aw_i$;
7:     $\tilde{q}_i = A^T \tilde{p}_i$;
8:     $\alpha_i = (\tilde{q}_i, \tilde{q}_i)$;
9:     $\theta_i = (\tilde{q}_i, \tilde{q}_{i-1})$;
10:     $\beta_i = (\tilde{p}_i, \tilde{p}_i)$
11:     $\lambda_i = (\tilde{q}_i, \tilde{b})$;
12:     $x_i = x_{i-1} + \frac{\tau_i}{\beta_i} w_i$;
13:     $w_{i+1} = \tilde{q}_i - \frac{\alpha_i}{\beta_i} w_i - \frac{\theta_i}{\beta_{i-1}} w_{i-1}$;
14:     $\tau_{i+1} = \lambda_i - \frac{\alpha_i}{\beta_i} \tau_i - \frac{\theta_i}{\beta_{i-1}} \tau_{i-1}$;
15: **end for**

Combining all above equations with complicated mathematical derivations with algorithm reorganization, the sketch of ICGLS method is depicted in Algorithm 3. Under the assumptions, the Improved CGLS (ICGLS) method can be efficiently parallelized as follows:

- The inner products of a single iteration step (8), (9), (10) and (11) are independent(parallel) with only one global synchronization point, instead of two.
- The vector updates (12) and (13) are independent(parallel).

Therefore, the cost of communication time, with only one global synchronization point, on parallel distributed memory computers can be significantly reduced, then parallel performance will be largely improved compared with the standard CGLS and MCGLS methods, with two global synchronization points.

## 6   Parallel Implementation

### 6.1   Data Distribution

For large and sparse matrices, if we are working on different computer system architectures or dealing with different algorithms or data, appropriately efficient storage schemes should be considered. In this paper, we use one of the most common formats called CRS format (compressed row storage). The main reason is that this type of storage scheme is very suitable for both regularly and irregularly structured large and sparse matrices. The detailed description can be found in the literature. Briefly, the non-zeros of a large and sparse matrix are stored in row-wise in three one-dimensional arrays. The values of the non-zeros are contained in array *value*. The corresponding column indices are contained in array *col_ind*. The elements of *row_ptr* point to the position of the beginning of each row in *value* and *col_ind*.

In order to efficiently parallelize the MCGLS and ICGLS methods on a distributed memory architecture, we first need to decide the data distribution of matrix and vector arrays to each processor, and then determine an efficient communication scheme by taking into account different sparsity patterns, not only for matrix-vector multiplication but also for inner products, to minimize the overall execution time. In this paper, we will mainly follow the approach has been used in [2] for data distribution and communication scheme which do not require any knowledge of the matrix sparsity pattern. The communication scheme is automatically determined by the analysis of the indices of the non-zero matrix elements.

In the following part, we will use the same notations introduced in [2] for illustration. Let $n_k$ and $e_k$ denote the number of rows and no-zeros of processor $k$, where $k = 0, \ldots, p-1$, respectively. $e$ and $n$ are the total number of corresponding numbers. $g_k$ is the index of the first row of processor $k$, and $z_i$ is the number of non-zeros of row $i$. We can get the following relations from [2]: $n = \sum_{k=0}^{p-1} n_k, e = \sum_{k=0}^{p-1} e_k, g_k = 1 + \sum_{i=0}^{k-1} n_i, e_k(g_k, n_k) = \sum_{i=gk}^{gk+nk-1} z_i$ Based on the analysis, the total costs of each iteration can be described as $c_1 \, s \, e + c_2 \, n + c_3$ where the first term corresponds to the number of operations for $s$ matrix-vector multiplications, the second term corresponds to the number of vector updates. Since we are mainly dealing with large and sparse matrices, the constants can be neglected. Now we can estimate the contribution of the operations executed on processor $k$ to the total number of operations by

$$\zeta \approx \frac{c_1 \, s \, e_k + c_2 \, n_k}{c_1 \, s \, e + c_2 \, n} = \frac{s \, e_k + \xi \, n_k}{s \, e + \xi n},$$

where $\xi = c_2/c_1$ depends on both the iterative methods and also the processor architecture. Ideally, the computational load balance should be distributed in such a way that each processor only gets $p$-th fraction for the total number of operations. Based on this, we can use the following strategy to distribute the rows of the matrix and the vector components [2]:

$$n_k = \begin{cases} \displaystyle \min_{1 \leq t \leq n - g_k + 1} \left\{ t \Big| \frac{s \, e_k(t) + \xi \, t}{s \, e + \xi \, n} \geq \frac{1}{p} \right\} & k = 0, 1, \ldots, q \\ n - \sum_{i=0}^{q} n_i & k = q+1 \\ 0 & k = q+2, \ldots, p-1 \end{cases}$$

Since our main target is large and sparse matrices and we assume $p \ll n$, the relation $q = p - 1$ or $q + 1 = p - 1$ always holds. It can be shown that for $\xi = c_2/c_1 \to 0$, each processor will get nearly the same number of non-zeros which means that the execution time of the vector updates in negligible compared to the execution of matrix-vector multiplications. It also can be shown that for $\xi = c_2/c_1 \to \infty$ each processor will get nearly the same number of rows which means that the execution time of the matrix-vector multiplications only contribute to a very small part of the total execution time.

## 6.2  Communication Schemes

After the discussion of data distribution, we also need to investigate a suitable communication scheme by preprocessing the distributed column index arrays for efficient matrix-vector multiplications, since on a distributed memory systems, its computation requires communication due to the partial vector on each processor. We will use an approach similar to that proposed in [2] for our communication schemes.

If we decide to implement the matrix vector multiplication row-wisely, components of the vector $x$ of $y = Ax$ are communicated. We firstly analyze the arrays *col_ind* on each processor to determine which elements result in access to non-local data. Then, the processors exchange information to decide which local data must be sent to which processors. Based on the above analysis, we will reorder these two arrays *col_ind* and *value* in such a way that the data that results in access to processor $l$ is collected in block $l$, called a *local block*. The motivation behind this reordering is to perform computation and communication overlapped. The elements of block $l$ succeed one another row-wise with increasing column index per row. The detailed description can be found in [2].

For the parallel implementation of this operation, each processor executes asynchronous receive-routines to receive necessary non-local data. Then all components of the vector $x$ that are needed on other processors are sent asynchronously. After the required data are available, each processor will perform operations with its local block. After that, as soon as non-local data arrive, the processor continues the matrix vector operation by accessing the elements of the corresponding blocks. This is repeated until the whole operation is completed. According to the communication scheme described, the communication and computation are overlapped, so that waiting time can be reduced.

## 7  Numerical Experiments

In this section, parallel performance of the proposed MCGLS and ICGLS methods is compared with the standard CGLS method on a parallel distributed memory computer, a SUN Cluster.

Here we mainly consider the coefficient matrix from the partial differential equation taken from [5,6]:

$$Lu = f, \qquad \text{on} \qquad \Omega = (0,1) \times (0,1),$$

with Dirichlet boundary condition $u = 0$ where

$$Lu = -\Delta u - 20 \left( x \frac{\partial u}{\partial x} + y \frac{\partial u}{\partial y} \right),$$

Basically, we discretize the above differential equation using second order centered differences on a $400 \times 400$ mesh with mesh size $1/441$, leading to a system of 193600 linear equations with an unsymmetric coefficient matrix of

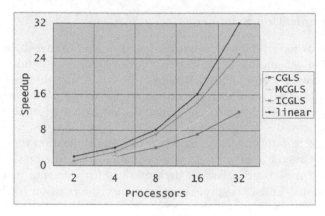

**Fig. 1.** Speed-ups for the CGLS, MCGLS and ICGLS methods

966240 nonzero entries. The right hand side vector $b$ is generated consistently with a solution vector whose components are equal to 1.

Since the vectors are distributed over the processors, inner products usually are computed in two steps. All processors start to compute in parallel the local inner products. After that, local inner products are accumulated on one central processor and broadcast. The communication time of an accumulation or a broadcast increases in proportion to the diameter of the processor grid. That means if the number of processors increases then the communication time for inner products increases as well, and hence this is a potential threat to the scalability.

The convergence and numerical behavior of the proposed MCGLS and ICGLS methods are almost the same as that of the standard CGLS method based on our preliminary numerical results. The corresponding comparison on parallel performance is given in Fig. 1 where "linear" is the theoretical linear speedup, ICGLS is the speedup of the improved CGLS method, MCGLS is the speedup of the modified CGLS method and CGLS is the speedup of the standard CGLS method. These results are based on timing measurements of a fixed number of iterations. The speedup is computed as the ratio of the parallel execution time and the execution time using one processor. From the results, we can see clearly that the MCGLS method is better than the standard one, but the improvement is very limited. Meanwhile the ICGLS method can achieve much better parallel performance with a higher scalability than the modified one and the standard one because we reduce global synchronization points to half. More detailed and extended experimental results will be conducted and reported later.

## References

1. Z. Bai, D. Hu, and L. Reichel. A newton basis GMRES implementation. Technical Report 91-03, University of Kentucky, 1991.
2. A. Basermann, B. Reichel, and C. Schelthoff. Preconditioned CG methods for sparse matrices on massively parallel machines. *Parallel Computing*, 23(3):381–398, 1997.

3. Å. Björck. *Numerical Methods for Least Squares Problems.* SIAM, Philadelphia, 1995.
4. Å. Björck, T. Elfving, and Z. Strakos. Stability of conjugate gradient-type methods for linear least squares problems. Technical Report LiTH-MAT-R-1995-26, Department of Mathematics, Linköping University, 1994.
5. H. M. Bücker and M. Sauren. A parallel version of the quasi-minimal residual method based on coupled two-term recurrences. In J. Waśniewski, J. Dongarra, K. Madsen, and D. Olesen, editors, *Proceedings of Workshop on Applied Parallel Computing in Industrial Problems and Optimization (Para96), LNCS184*, Lecture Notes in Computer Science, pages 157–165. Technical University of Denmark, Lyngby, Denmark, Springer-Verlag, August 1996.
6. H. M. Bücker and M. Sauren. Parallel biconjugate gradient methods for linear systems. In L. T. Yang, editor, *Parallel Numerical Computations with Applications*, pages 51–70. Kluwer Academic Publishers, 1999.
7. L. G. C. Crone and H. A. van der Vorst. Communication aspects of the conjugate gradient method on distributed memory machines. *Supercomputer*, X(6):4–9, 1993.
8. E. de Sturler. A parallel variant of the GMRES($m$). In *Proceedings of the 13th IMACS World Congress on Computational and Applied Mathematics.* IMACS, Criterion Press, 1991.
9. E. de Sturler and H. A. van der Vorst. Reducing the effect of the global communication in GMRES($m$) and CG on parallel distributed memory computers. Technical Report 832, Mathematical Institute, University of Utrecht, Utrecht, The Netherland, 1994.
10. J. W. Demmel, M. T. Heath, and H. A. van der Vorst. Parallel numerical algebra. *Acta Numerica*, 1993. Cambridge Press, New York.
11. J. J. Dongarra, I. S. Duff, D. C. Sorensen, and H. A. van der Vorst. *Solving Linear Systems on Vector and Shared Memory Computers.* SIAM, Philadelphia, PA, 1991.
12. I. S. Duff and J. K. Reid. A comparison of some methods for the solution of sparse over-determined system of linear equations. *Journal of the Institute of Mathematics and Its Applications*, 17(3):267–280, 1976.
13. T. Elfving. On the conjugate gradient method for solving linear least squares problems. Technical Report LiTH-MAT-R-78-3, Department of Mathematics, Linköping University, 1978.
14. G. H. Golub and W. Kahan. Calculating the singular values and pseudo-inverse of a matrix. *SIAM Journal on Numerical Analysis*, 2:205–224, 1965.
15. M. R. Hestenes and E. Stiefel. Methods of conjugate gradients for solving linear system. *Journal of Research of National Bureau of Standards*, B49:409–436, 1952.
16. P.L. Montgomery. Parallel block Lanczos. Microsoft Research, Redmond, USA, Transparencies of a talk presented at RSA-2000, January 2000.
17. C. C. Paige and M. A. Saunders. LSQR: An algorithm for sparse linear equations and sparse least squares. *ACM Transactions on Mathematical Software*, 8:43–71, 1982.
18. C. Pommerell. *Solution of large unsymmetric systems of linear equations.* PhD thesis, ETH, 1992.
19. E. Stiefel. Ausgleichung ohne aufstellung der gausschen normalgleichungen. *Wiss. Z. Technische Hochschule Dresden*, 2:441–442, 1952/1953.
20. L. T. Yang and R. P. Brent. Quantitative performance analysis of the improved quasi-minimal residual method on massively distributed memory computers. *Advances in Engineering Software*, 33:169–177, 2002.

# Faster Sorting on a Linear Array with a Reconfigurable Pipelined Bus System[*]

Ling Chen[1] and Yi Pan[2]

[1] Department of Computer Science, Yangzhou University, Yangzhou 225009, China
lchen@yzcn.net
http://www.yzu.edu.cn
[2] Department of Computer Science, Georgia State University, Atlanta, GA 30303, U.S.A.
cscyip@suez.cs.gsu.edu

**Abstract.** In this paper, we present an efficient deterministic algorithm for sorting on the LARPBS (Linear Array with a Reconfigurable Pipelined Optical Bus System) model. Our sorting algorithm sorts $n$ general keys in O($\log n$) time on a LARPBS of size $n \cdot \log n$. The previous best results can sort $n$ items in O($\log n \log \log n$) worst-case time using $n$ processors or sort $n$ items in O(($\log \log n$)$^2$)worst-case time using $n^{1+\varepsilon}$ processors. Our algorithm is also scalable to certain extent. When the system size is reduced to $n \cdot \log n / r$ for $1 \leq r \leq \log n$, the total computation time is O($r \log n$).

## 1 Introduction

Recently, arrays with reconfigurable optical bus systems [1,2] have been proposed and have drawn much attention from the researchers [3-11]. In these systems, messages can be transmitted concurrently on a bus in a pipelined fashion and the bus can be reconfigured dynamically under program control to support different algorithmic requirements. LARPBS is one such model where any processor involvement is not allowed during a bus cycle, except setting switches up at the beginning of a bus cycle. Hence, it can exploit the high bandwidth of optical buses used to connect processors there. Many algorithms have been designed for basic data movement operations, sorting and selection, computational geometry, and PRAM simulation on the LARPBS model [4-11].

Sorting is one of the most fundamental problems in computer science. A fast sorting algorithm is often used as a step in many other algorithms. The problem of sorting can be defined as follows. Given a sequence of numbers, say, $a_0, a_1, a_2, ..., a_{n-1}$, the problem of sorting is to rearrange them in nondecreasing order. Essentially, parallel sorting is a procedure of data transmission. In any fixed connection network, a single step of interprocessor communication can be thought of as a packet routing

---

[*] This research was supported in part by Chinese National Science Foundation under contract 60074013, Chinese National Foundation of High Performance Computing under contract 00219 and Science Foundation of Jiangsu Educational Commission , China.

M. Guo and L.T.Yang (Eds.): ISPA 2003, LNCS 2745, pp. 209–219, 2003.

task, which involves sending all the packets to their correct destinations as quickly as possible, and making sure that at most one packet crosses any edge at any time. Therefore, data transfer is a bottleneck of parallel sorting.  Due to the high data transmission capability of LARPBS, sorting on this model can obtain higher speed and efficiency. The first sorting algorithm on the LARPBS model, which is based on the sequential quicksort algorithm, was presented by Pan et al [8]. In an $n$ processor LARPBS, the randomized algorithm takes $O(\log n)$ expected time and $O(n)$ time in the worst case. Of course, we can improve its worst-case time complexity if we use the deterministic selection algorithm described in [1] to find the median in the current set and use it as the pivot value. In this way, we can guarantee that the set is always divided into two subarrays of equal size. Since each iteration takes $O(\log n)$ time, the algorithm sorts $n$ items in $O((\log n)^2)$ time on an $n$-processor LARPBS in the worst case [1]. It is known that $n$ elements can be sorted in $O(1)$ time on a LARPBS with $n^2$ processors[5]. This shows that the LARPBS model is stronger than any of the PRAM models. Recently, Han et al. presents a deterministic selection algorithm on an LARPBS, which can solve the selection problem in $O((\log\log n)^2/\log\log\log n)$ time [10]. Using this selection as a subroutine to find the median in the current set and use it as the pivot value, we can obtain a deterministic sorting algorithm to sort $n$ numbers in $O(\log n \cdot (\log\log n)^2/\log\log\log n)$ time. Datta et al also presented two random sorting algorithms in this model[11]. Their first algorithm sorts $n$ items in $O(\log n \cdot \log\log n)$ worst-case time using $n$ processors. The second algorithm sorts $n$ items in $O((\log\log n)^2)$ worst-case time using $n^{1+\epsilon}$ processors. Their algorithms are based on a parallel merging algorithm which can merge two sorted sequences of $n$ in $O(\log\log n)$ time on an $n$-processor LARPBS. In this paper, we present an efficient deterministic algorithm for sorting on the LARPBS model. Our sorting algorithm sorts $n$ general keys in $O(\log n)$ time on an LARPBS of size $n \log n$. As far as we know, this is the fastest deterministic sorting algorithm on this model with an increase of processor number only by a factor of $O(\log n)$. Our algorithm is based on an efficient parallel merging algorithm which can merge two sorted sequences of $n$ numbers in $O(\log\log n)$ time in a $n$-processor LARPBS. While the algorithm presented in this paper is fast, processor efficient, it is also scalable. When the system size is $n \cdot \log n/r$ for $1 \le r \le \log n$, the total computation time is $O(r \cdot \log n)$. The rest of the paper is arranged as follows. In Section 2, we explain pipelined optical buses, and linear arrays with reconfigurable bus systems. Primitive communication operations are also summarized there. In Sction3, we present an efficient deterministic merging algorithm that can merge two sorted sequences of $n$ in $O(\log\log n)$ time using $2n$ processors. In Section 4, the sorting algorithm which sorts $n$ general keys in $O(\log n)$ time on an LARPBS of size $n$ log $n$ is presented. The scalability issue is discussed in Section 5.  Section 6 concludes the paper.

## 2  Linear Arrays with Reconfigurable Pipelined Bus Systems

A pipelined optical bus system uses optical waveguides instead of electrical signals to transfer messages among processors. Besides the high propagation speed of light, optical signal transmission on an optical bus has other two important characteristics, they are unidirectional propagation and predictable propagation delay. These advantages of using waveguides enable synchronized concurrent accesses of an optical bus in a pipelined fashion. Such pipelined optical bus systems can support a massive volume of communications simultaneously and are particularly appropriate for applications that involve intensive communication operations such as broadcasting, one-to-one communication, multicasting, compression, split, and many irregular communication patterns.

It has been shown that by using the coincident pulse addressing technique, all the above primitive operations take $O(1)$ bus cycles, where the bus cycle length is the end-to-end message transmission time over a bus [14]. To avoid controversy, let us emphasize that in this paper, by "$O(f(p))$ time" we mean $O(f(p))$ bus cycles for communication plus $O(f(p))$ time for local computation.

In addition to supporting fast communications, an optical bus itself can be used as a computing device for global aggregation. It was proven in [14] that by using $n$ processors, the summation of $n$ integers or reals with bounded magnitude and precision, the prefix sums of $n$ binary values, the logical-or and logical-and of $n$ Boolean values can be calculated in constant number of bus cycles.

In addition to the tremendous communication capabilities, an LARPBS can also be partitioned into several independent subarrays. The subarrays can operate as regular linear arrays with pipelined optical bus systems, and all subarrays can be used independently for different computations without interference. Hence, this architecture is very suitable for many divide-and-conquer problems.

The above basic communication, data movement, and aggregation operations provide an algorithmic view on parallel computing using optical buses, and also allow us to develop, specify, and analyze parallel algorithms by ignoring optical and engineering details. These powerful primitives that support massive parallel communications plus the reconfigurability of optical buses make the LARPBS computing model very attractive in solving problems that are both computation and communication intensive. The reader is referred to [2,14] for more details on the LARPBS model and its basic operations.

## 3  A Merging Algorithm on LARPBS

Our sorting algorithm on the LARPBS employs an algorithm for merging two sorted arrays of length $n$ in $O(\log\log n)$ time using $2n$ processor LARPBS. In our merging algorithm, we make use of the ideas in Valiant's paper [12]. But our algorithm is not merely a simulation of Valiant's PRAM algorithm, novel features and efficient basic data movement operations on the LARPBS model are exploited to speed up the algorithm so as to obtain better time complexity than those on PRAM.

Suppose each of the two sequences $A=\{a_0, a_2, ..., a_{n-1}\}$, $B=\{b_0, b_1, ...,b_{n-1}\}$, has $n$ items and has been sorted in ascending order. In the following description, $A(i)$ represents the $i$-th subsequence while A is divided into several parts. The idea of Viliant is to partition the two sequences into $n^{1/2}$ parts $A(0)$, $A(1)$ ,..., $A(n^{1/2}-1)$ and $B(0)$, $B(1)$ ,..., $B(n^{1/2}-1)$. These parts satisfy the following condition: if $i>j$, every element in $A(i)$ is not less than every element in $A(j)$ and $B(j)$. Then we can merge the two subsequences A($i$) and B($i$) in parallel. This means our algorithm works recursively. In every level of recursion, our generic task is to set up appropriate subproblems for the next level of recursion. Since the lengths of A($i$) and B($i$) are possibly not equal, our algorithm should be extended to the case in which the sequences A and B may have different lengths.

Suppose the length of A and B are $p$, and $q$ respectively, i.e., A=$\{a_0, a_2, ..., a_{p-1}\}$, B=$\{b_0, b_1, ..., b_{q-1}\}$. Let $g= p^{1/2}$, $h= q^{1/2}$, a basic frame of the algorithm to merge A and B is described as follows.

**Algorithm Merge(A,B,$p$,$q$):**
**Begin**
1. Divide sequence A into $g=p^{1/2}$ subsequences each of which consists of $p^{1/2}$ elements. The $i$-th subsequences A($i$) =$\{a_{ig}, a_{ig+1}, ..., a_{(i+1)g-1}\}$($i$=0,1,2,...,$g$-1). Similarly, divide sequence B into $h= q^{1/2}$ subsequences each of which consists of $q^{1/2}$ elements. The $i$-th subsequences B($i$)=$\{b_{ih}, b_{ih+1}, ..., b_{(i+1)h-1}\}$($i$=0,1,2,...,$h$-1). We call the last elements of the subsequences A($i$) and B($i$), namely, $a_{ig}$ ($i$=0,1,2,...,$g$-1) and $b_{ih}$ ($i$=0,1,2,...,$h$-1) the pivot elements of the two sequences.
2. Compare each pivot element of A with all the pivot elements in B in parallel so as to know in which subsequence of B each pivot elements of A should be inserted into according to the nondecreasing order.
3. Suppose A's pivot element $a_{ig}$ will be inserted into B's subsequence B($j$), compare $a_{ig}$ with every element in B($j$) to search for the exact location of B in which $a_{ig}$ should be inserted. For $i$= 0,1,2,..,$g$-1,  these location searches can be done in parallel.
4. Suppose A's pivot element $a_{ig}$ will be inserted into B's location loc($i$), namely, be inserted between the elements $b_{loc(i)}$ and $b_{loc(i)+1}$, then B can be repartitioned into $g$ parts by the elements $b_{loc(0)}$, $b_{loc(1)}$ ,..., $b_{loc(g-1)}$ . After the repartitioning, we also denote the $i$th new subsequence of B as B($i$). Let $l_i$ be the length of B($i$), recursively call procedure Merge (A($i$),B($i$), $p^{1/2}$,$l_i$)  to merge subsequences A($i$) and B($i$). For $i$= 0,1,2,..,$g$-1,  this recursive procedure can be done in parallel. Repeat this recursive procedure until the length of A($i$) or B($i$) is one.
**End**

In the algorithm, $p+q$ processors are used. We denote the $i$th processor as PE$_i$. Each processor PE$_i$ has four registers named $c_i$, $w_i$, $x_i$, and $y_i$   respectively. At the beginning of the algorithm, elements of A are distributed in the first $p$ processors of the array, i.e., $a_i$ is stored in $c_i$ of PE$_i$ ($i$=0,1,...$p$-1). Elements of B are distributed in the last $q$ processors of the array, i.e., $b_i$ is stored in $c_{p+i}$ of PE$_{p+i}$ ($i$=0,1,...$q$-1).

In step 1 and 2 of the algorithm, we partition the first $p^{1/2} \cdot q^{1/2}$ processors of the array into $g=p^{1/2}$ groups each of which consists of $h=q^{1/2}$ processors. (Noticing that $p+q>(p \cdot q)^{1/2}$, it is possible to do such partitioning.) We denote the $i$th group as P$_i$, namely P$_i$=$\{$PE$_{ih}$, PE$_{ih+1}$,...,PE$_{(i+1)h-1}\}$. To compare the pivot elements of A and B, we multicast them to these processor groups. A's pivot element $a_{ig}$ is broadcasted to the $x$ registers in each processor of the $i$th group, namely to $x_{ih+k}$ in PE$_{ih+k}$ ($k$=0,1,2,...,$h$-1). B's pivot element $b_{ih}$ is broadcasted to the $y$ registers in the $i$th processor of each processor group, namely to $y_{kh+i}$ in PE$_{kh+i}$ ($k$=0,1,2,...,$g$-1). Therefore, pivot elements $a_{ig}$ and $b_{jh}$ are compared in the in the $j$th processor of the $i$th group, i.e. PE$_{ih+j}$.

($i$=0,1,2,...,$g$-1, $j$=0,1,2,...,$h$-1). If $a_{ig} > b_{jh}$ , we set the value of $w_{ih+j}$ to 1; else set it to 0. This can be completed in O(1) time using the primitive operation of multicasting.

To count the number of 1's in the $w$ registers in each group, we reconfigure the array into    subarrays. The $i$th group $P_i$={$PE_{ih}$, $PE_{ih+1}$,...,$PE_{(i+1)h-1}$} forms the $i$th subarray. Then we count the number of 1's of the $w$ values in the subarray using the primitive operation of binary value aggregation in O(1) time. The result, i.e., the number of 1's of the $w$ values, is stored in register $w$ of the last processor of the subarray $PE_{(i+1)h-1}$ . By comparing each pivot element of A with every pivot element in B, we know in which subsequence of B each pivot element of A could be inserted.

Suppose A's pivot element $a_{ig}$ will be inserted into B's subsequence B($j$). To search for the exact location of B in which $a_{ig}$ should be inserted, $a_{ig}$ is compared with every element of B in B($j$) in the step 3 of the algorithm. In this step, the elements of B($j$), which stored in the $c$ registers of $PE_{p+jh}$ to $PE_{p+(j+1)h-1}$ are transmitted to the $y$ registers of the $i$th group $P_i$. This data transmission can be carried out by the primitive operation of one-to-one communication (if B($j$) is send to one group of processors) or multicasting (if B($j$) is send to more than one group of processors) in O(1) time. Since A's pivot element $a_{ig}$ is stored in all $x$ registers of $P_i$, it can be compared with every element of B's subsequence B($j$) . Therefore, pivot elements $a_{ig}$ and $b_{jh+k}$ are compared in the $k$th processor of the $i$th group, i.e., $PE_{ih+k}$. ($i$=0,1,2,...,$g$-1, $k$=0,1,2,...,$h$-1). If $a_{ig} > b_{jh}$ , we set the value of $w_{ih+k}$ to 1; else set it to 0. Then we count the number of 1's of the $w$ values in the subarray. The result, i.e., the number of 1's of the $w$ values, is just the exact location in B($j$) in which $a_{ig}$ should be inserted. This result is stored in $w$ register of the last processor of the subarray $PE_{(i+1)h-1}$ .

Suppose A's pivot element $a_{ig}$ will be inserted into B's location loc($i$), namely, be inserted between the elements $b_{loc(i)}$ and $b_{loc(i)+1}$, then B can be repartitioned into $g$ parts by the elements $b_{loc(0)}$ , $b_{loc(1)}$ ,..., $b_{loc(g-1)}$ . We also denote the $i$th new subsequence of B as B($i$). In step 4, we first move the elements of A and B into the order of A(0), B(0), A(1), B(1), ...,A($g$-1), B($g$-1). To achieve this data transmission, we simply need to move A($i$) to the $c$ registers of processors from $PE_{ig+loc(i)}$ to $PE_{(i+1)g+loc(i)-1}$, and move B($i$) to the $c$ registers of processors from $PE_{(i+1)g+loc(i)}$ to $PE_{(i+1)g+loc(i+1)-1}$ ($i$=0,1,...,$g$-1). We show that the above task can be completed in O(1) time using the primitive operation of one-to-one data communication in the following way.

Each element $a_j$ in A($i$) is going to be sent to $PE_{loc(i)+j}$ . To do this data transmission, first we broadcast loc($i$) to all the processors in which elements of A($i$) are stored in the $c$ registers. Then each $a_j$ in A($i$) is sent to $PE_{loc(i)+j}$. Each element $b_j$ in B($i$) is going to be sent to $PE_{ig+j}$ . To do this data transmission, first we send $i$ to the processor $PE_{p+loc(i)}$ in which element $b_{loc(i)}$ is stored in its c register. Then we broadcast $i$ to all the contiguous processors from PE $_{p+loc(i)}$ to PE $_{p+loc(i+1)-1}$ in which elements of B($i$) are stored . At last send $b_j$ in theses processors to $PE_{ig+j}$.

After transmitting A($i$) and B($i$) to their new locations,  we reconfigure the array into $g$ subarrays and the $i$th new subarray is still denoted as $P_i$ which consists of the contiguous processors containing A($i$) and B($i$), i.e., the $g$+ $l_i$ processors from $PE_{ig+loc(i)}$ to $PE_{(i+1)g+loc(i+1)-1}$ . Let $l_i$ = loc($i$+1)-loc($i$) be the length of the new subsequence B($i$), we can recursively call procedure Merge ($A_i$,$B_i$, $g$, $l_i$) to merge subsequences A($i$) and B($i$). This can be done in the subarray $P_i$ which consists of $g$+ $l_i$ processors.   For $i$= 0,

1,2,...,g-1, these recursive procedures can be done in parallel. The total processors used for the parallel recursive procedure called in the next level is $\sum_{i=0}^{g}(g+l_i) = g \cdot g + \sum_{i=0}^{g} l_i = p^{1/2} \cdot p^{1/2} + q = p + q$. This means that $p+q$ processors are sufficient for the further recursions. Repeat this recursive procedure until the length of A($i$) or B($i$) is one.

Now we analyze the processor and time complexities of the algorithm. It can easily be seen that to merge two sorted sequences of length $p$ and $q$, the algorithm uses $p+q$ processors. In case two sorted sequences with length of $n$ are merged, the algorithm uses $2n$ processors. Regarding the time complexity, we can see that each of step 1,2 and 3 of the algorithm takes O(1) time . Therefore time complexity of the algorithm depends on the total number of recursion levels. Initially the length of sequence A is $p$, after the first recursion, the length of its subsequences is $g=p^{1/2}$. After the $2^{nd}$ recursion, the length of the subsequences is $p^{1/4}$. After the $i$-th recursion, the length of the subsequences is $p^{-2^i}$ . Since the recursive procedure will repeat until the length of A($i$) or B($i$) is one, the total number of recursions is no greater than loglog$p$. If lengths of the two-sorted sequences to be merged are both $n$, the time complexity of the algorithm is O(loglog$n$).

# 4  A Fast Sorting Algorithm on LARPBS

Given a sequence A consisting of $n$ numbers, say $a_0, a_1, a_2, ..., a_{n-1}$, the problem of sorting is to rearrange them in nondecreasing order.  The basic idea of our sorting algorithm is based on Preparata's scheme of sorting by rank enumerating [13]. Our algorithm first compares every $a_i$ with all the other elements $a_j(i \neq j)$. The number of the elements which are less than $a_i$ is its rank in the sorted sequence. (In this paper, the term "$a_i$ is less than $a_j$" means that $a_i < a_j$ or $i < j$ in case $a_i = a_j$ . )  By rearranging the elements according to their ranks, we can obtain the sorted sequence.

## 4.1  The Algorithm

Suppose $n = 2^k$, i.e., $k = \log n$. In the algorithm, $(k-1)n$ processors are used. To compare every $a_i$ with all the other elements $a_j$ ($i \neq j$), we divide A into log $n$ subsequences each of which consists of $r = n/k$ elements. The $i$th subsequence is A($i$) = {$a_{ik}, a_{ik+1}, ..., a_{(i+1)k-1}$}. We pair each A($i$) with all the other subsequences A($j$) ($i \neq j$). We define R[$i,j,h$] as the number of elements in A($j$) which is less than the $h$-th element in A($i$). Then $\sum_{j=0}^{k-1}$ R[$i,j,h$] , which is denoted as rank($i,h$), is just the rank of the $h$-th element in A($i$). To compute R[$i,j,h$], we can simply first sort the elements in A($i$) and A($j$) respectively, and then merge the two-sorted subsequences. After sorting, suppose the $h$-th element in A($i$) becomes the $h$'-th one and then becomes the $g$-th one in the merged sequence, we know R[$i,j,h$]=$g$-$h$' and R[$i,i,h$]=$h$'.

Our algorithm first sorts all the subsequences A($i$) ($i$=0,1,...,$k$-1) in parallel using this algorithm recursively. Then we pair these subsequences and merge each pair into one sequence. In this way we can obtain the R[$i,j,h$] value for every element in all the subsequences.  By summing up all the $R[i,j,h]$ values for every element, we can obtain their ranks in the whole sorted sequence. At last, the sorted sequence can be obtained by rearranging the elements according to their ranks. The algorithm consists of the following steps:

*Step 1*:   Sort each subsequence $A(i)$. To sort the subsequences in parallel, we reconfigure the processor array into $k=\log n$ groups each of which consists of $n\log n$ /$k=n$ processors. We denote the $i$th group as $P_i$, namely $P_i=\{PE_{in}, PE_{in+1},...,PE_{(i+1)\,n-1}\}$. $A(i)$ which consists of $r=n/\log n$ elements is stored and sorted in subarray $P_i$ using this algorithm recursively. Noticing that $P_i$ consists of $n=rk$ processors, later we will show $rk$ processors are sufficient for sorting $r$ elements of subsequence $A(i)$ in the next level of recursion.   The recursive procedure will end when the length of the sequence is 4. We sort this 4 elements using a sequential algorithm in constant time.

*Step 2*: To compare every element in A with all the other elements, we pair each subsequence $A(i)$ with all other subsequences $A(j)(i\neq j)$. Since there are $k$ subsequences, $k(k-1)/2$ pairs should be processed. In this step we reconfigure the first $n(k-1)$ processors into $k(k-1)/2$ groups, each of which consists of $n(k-1)/[k(k-1)/2]$ $=2n/k=2r$ processors, and can store and process one pair of A's subsequences. We also denote the $i$th group as $P_i$, namely $P_i=\{PE_{2ir}, PE_{2ir+1},...,PE_{2(i+1)r-1}\}$. We further divide $P_i$ into two parts, each of which consists of $r$ processors, and can store one subsequence of A. We denote the first $r$ processors as $PL_i$ and the last $r$ processors as $PH_i$. We distribute the sorted subsequences of A into the subarrays in the way shown in table 1 (for $k=5$).

Table 1. Distribution of A's sorted subsequences

| $i$ | 0 | 1 | 2 | 3 | 4 | 5 | 6 | 7 | 8 | 9 |
|---|---|---|---|---|---|---|---|---|---|---|
| $PL_i$ | A(0) | A(0) | A(0) | A(0) | A(1) | A(1) | A(1) | A(2) | A(2) | A(3) |
| $PH_i$ | A(1) | A(2) | A(3) | A(4) | A(2) | A(3) | A(4) | A(3) | A(4) | A(4) |

To carry out this data distribution, we should transmit these subsequences using primitive operations of multicasting according the following rule. Suppose the subsequence $A(i)$ is going to be multicaseted to the processors in contiguous subarrays $PL_{j1}$ to $PL_{j2}$, then $j1=\sum_{m=1}^{i}(k-m)=ik-i(i+1)/2$, $j2=\sum_{m=1}^{i+1}(k-m)-1=(i+1)k-$ $(i+1)(i+2)/2-1$. This means each element $a_{ik+h}$ in $A(i)$ is going to sent to $PE_{(ik-}$ $_{i(i+1)/2+j)2r+h}$ ($j=0,1,...,n-i-1$). For instance, in table 1, suppose $k=5$, $i=2$, then $j1=7$, $j2=8$, this means subsequence $A(2)$ is to be multicasted to the processors in subarrays $PL_7$ and $PL_8$.

Subsequence $A(i)$ is also multicasted to the processors in PH parts of $i$ subarrays. They are $PH_{i-1}$, $PH_{(i-1)+(k-2)}$, $PH_{(i-1)+(k-2)+(k-3)},...$, $PH_{(i-1)+(k-2)+(k-3)+...+(k-i)}$. This means each element $a_{ik+h}$ in $A(i)$ is going to send to $PE_{(i-1)2r+r+h}$, $PE_{[(i-1)+(k-2)]2r+r+h}$ ,..., $PE_{[(i-1)+(k-2)+(k-}$ $_{3)+...+(k-i)]2r+r+h}$. This data transmission can be done by sending $i+1$ selection pulses after $a_{ik+h}$ being sent. The first selection pulse $S_1$ is sent $(i-1)2r+r+h$ time slots after $a_{ik+h}$ being sent, and the second selection pulse $S_2$ is sent $(k-2)2r$ time slots after $S_1$ being sent, $S_3$ is sent $(k-3)2r$ time slots after $S_2$ being sent, .., $S_i$ is sent $(k-i)2r$ time slots after

$S_{i-1}$ being sent. For instance, in table 1, when $k=5$, $i=3$, every element in subsequence $A(3)$ is to be multicasted to the processors in subarrays $PH_2$, $PH_5$, and $PH_7$ .

*Step 3*: In every subarray $P_i$ , merge the two-sorted subsequences using the merging algorithm presented in Section 3. Since the length of each subsequence is $r=n/(\log n)$, the algorithm uses $2r$ processors of $P_i$ and takes O $(\log\log r)$ time. After merging, every element in merged pair $[A(i),A(j)]$ gets its $R[i,j,h]$ value: if the $h$-th element in the sorted subsequence $A(i)$ becomes the $g$-th element in the merged sequence $[A(i) , A(j)]$, then $R[i,j,h]=g-h$.

*Step 4*: To sum up the values $R[i,j,h]$, we should transmit every $R[i,j,h]$ value to a proper processor. The destination of $R[i,j,h]$ is the $w$ registers of the processor $PE_{in+h}$ $k+j$. After the transmission, the      $R[i,j,h]$ ($j=0,1,...,k-1$) values of the $h$-th element in $A(i)$ are stored in the $w$ registers in the contiguous processors from $PE_{in+hk}$ to $PE_{in}$ $_{+(h+1)k-1}$. This data transmission can be done by primitive operation of one-to-one communication in O(1) time.

*Step 5*: Sum up the values $R[i,j,h]$. We reconfigure the array into $n$ subarrays each of which consists of $k$ contiguous  processors. In the $(ir+h)$-th new subarray $P_{ir+h}$, which consists of contiguous $k$ processors $PE_{(ir+h)k}$ to $PE_{(ir+h+1)k-1}$ , all the values of $R[i,j,h]$ ($j=0,1,...,k-1$) are summed up using $k$ processors. The sum of $k$ integers can be computed in $O(\log k)=O(\log\log n)$ time on an LARPBS with $k$ processors using a binary tree like scheme . The sum of the values $R[i,j,h]$ ($j=0,1,...,k-1$) , which is denoted as $rank(i,h)$, is just the rank of the $h$-th element in $A(i)$, and is stored in the $w$ register of the last processor of the subarray, i.e. $PE_{(ir+h+1)k-1}$.

*Step 6*: By rearranging the elements according to their ranks, we can obtain the sorted sequence which are stored in the $c$ registers of the first $n$ processors of the array. First we can send $rank(i,h)$ to the processor where the $h$-th element in $A(i)$ is stored, and then send the $h$-th element in $A(i)$ to $PE_{rank(i,h)}$. This data transmission can be done by primitive operation of one-to-one communication in O(1) time.

## 4.2 Complexity Analysis

First we show that $n\log n$ processors are sufficient for the algorithm to sort $n$ numbers.

**Theorem 1.** For $n\geq4$, the algorithm uses at most $n\log n$ processors to sort $n$ numbers.
**Proof:** We use mathematical inductive method.

When $n=4$, it is obvious  that 8 processors are sufficient for the algorithm to sort 4 elements.

Assuming the statement is true for all $4\leq p<n$, we prove that it is also true for $n$. Let $k=\log n$ , $r=\lceil n/k\rceil$, here " $\lceil\ \rceil$ " stands for the ceiling function.  Since $n/k$ is possibly not an integer, when A is divided into $k$ subsequences, the length of the last subsequence is possibly less than $r$, it may have $n-kr$ elements. According to the assumption, $r\log r$ processors are enough for the next level of recursion in each subarray. Therefore, the total number of processors used for the next level recursion is $k\lceil r\log r\rceil+\lceil(n-kr).\log(n-kr)\rceil$. Since $n-kr$ is the remainder of $n/(\log n)$, we have $n-kr<\lceil\log n\rceil$. Therefore

$$k\lceil r\log r\rceil + \lceil (n-kr).\log(n-kr)\rceil$$
$$\leq \log n.\lceil (n/\log n)\log(n/\log n)\rceil + \lceil \log n.\log\log n\rceil$$
$$\leq \lceil n\log(n/\log n)\rceil + \lceil \log n\rceil\lceil \log\log n\rceil$$
$$= \lceil n\log n\rceil - n\lceil \log\log n\rceil + \lceil \log n\rceil\lceil \log\log n\rceil$$
$$= \lceil n\log n\rceil - \lceil \log\log n\rceil(n - \lceil \log n\rceil)$$
$$\leq n\log n \quad (\text{when } n\geq 4)$$

**Theorem 2.** Time complexity of the algorithm is O(log$n$).
**Proof:** Denote the time required for the algorithm to sort $n$ elements as t($n$) . We first analyze the time complexity of each step in the algorithm.

Step1 is a recursive procedure of the algorithm, but its size is $r = n/\log n$ instead of $n$. Hence, its time complexity is t($n/\log n$). Each of step 2, step 4 and step 6 takes O(1) time. Step 3 merges two sequence with length of $r$ using the merging algorithm described in Section 3, and takes O(loglog$r$)=O(loglog($n/\log n$))=O(loglog$n$) time. Since step 5 sums up $k$=log$n$ integers on an LARPBS with $k$ processors, it also takes O(loglog$n$) time.

Therefore, we have t($n$)=t($n/\log n$)+$c_1$loglog$n$+$c_2$ and t(4)=O(1). For constants $c_1$ and $c_2$, it is easy to see that  t($n$)=$c_1$log$n$ +O(log$n$) is the solution of the recursive equation above. Therefore, the time complexity of the algorithm is O(log$n$).

# 5   Scalability Issue

While speed is an important motivation of parallel computing, there is another issue in realistic parallel computing, namely, scalability, which measures the ability to maintain speedup linearly proportional to the number of processors. It is less practical to build an LARPBS system with $n\log n$ processors. For a system with fixed size, a large sequence should be partitioned into subsequences to fit into the fix-sized array. We say that a parallel algorithm is scalable in the range $[p_1, p_2]$, if linear speedup can be achieved for all $p_1\leq p\leq p_2$. In the other words, suppose the time complexity of a scalable parallel algorithm be presented as O(T($n$)) using $p$ processors where $n$ is the size of the problem, for some constant $r>0$, if $p/r$ processors are used, the time complexity must be O($r$·T($n$)).  Now we show that for $1\leq r \leq\log n$, our algorithm is scalable.

Suppose the system has $p=n\cdot\log n/r$ processors, we divide the sequence A into $r$ subsequences. Length of each subsequence is $n/r$. We first sort these $r$ subsequences in the array sequentially. By using the parallel sorting algorithm described above, time for sorting each  subsequence is O(log($n/r$))=O(log$n$-log$r$)=O(log$n$). Total time required for sorting the $r$ subsequences is  O($r$log$n$) and the number of processors required is $(n/r)\cdot\log(n/r) \leq(n/r)\log n = p$.

Then we pair these subsequences and merge each pair into one sequence. Since there are $r$ subsequences, $r(r-1)/2$ pairs should be processed. We divide them into $r$ groups  each of which has $(r-1)/2$ pairs. We merge these $r$ groups sequentially. Using the parallel merge algorithm presented above,  each pair needs 2$n/r$ processors, and each group requires $(2n/r)(r-1)/2=n(r-1)/r$ processors, when $r-1 \leq \log n$, $n(r-1)/r \leq n \log n/r = p$. Time for merging all pairs in each group in parallel is $O(\log\log(n/r))$ $=O(\log \log n)$. Total time for the $r$ groups is $O(r \cdot \log\log n)$.

Next, we compute $\sum_{j=1}^{r} R[i,j,h]$ for $i= 1,2,\ldots, r$, $h=1,2,..,n/r$. Since there are $r \cdot (n/r)$ $=n$ summations to compute, we divide them into $r$ groups each of which consists of $(n/r)$ summation computations. We also divide the processors into $n/r$ subarrays each of which consists of $(n\log n/r)/(n/r) = \log n$ processors. When $r \leq \log n$, the summation can be carried out in $O(\log r)$ time on $\log n$ processors. The $r$ groups of summation can be computed in $O(r \cdot \log r) \leq O(r \cdot \log\log n)$ time.

Therefore the total computation time is $O(r \log n)$ in a LARPBS with $n \cdot \log n/r$ processors for $1 \leq r \leq \log n$. Hence our algorithm is scalable in this range.


# 6   Conclusion Remarks

We have developed an efficient and fast deterministic sorting algorithm on linear arrays with reconfigurable pipelined bus systems. Our sorting algorithm sorts $n$ general keys in $O(\log n)$ time on a LARPBS of size $n\log n$ . It is based on a merge algorithm which can merge two sorted sequences of $n$ in $O(\log\log n)$ time on a $2n$-processor LARPBS. As far as we know, this is the fastest deterministic sorting algorithm on this model without using additional polynomial number of processors. While the algorithm presented in this paper is fast, processor efficient, it is also scalable . When the system size is $n \cdot \log n/r$ for $1 \leq r \leq \log n$ , the total computation time is $O(r \cdot \log n)$. Our algorithm takes advantage of many important merits of  LARPBS such as its high communication bandwidth, the versatile communication patterns it supports, and its ability of utilizing communication reconfigurability as an integral part of a parallel computation. It is shown that the LARPBS is a powerful architecture for exploiting large degree of parallelism in a computational problem that most other machine models cannot achieve. Since the time complexity of sorting $n$ numbers on the EREW and CREW PRAM models is $O(\log n)$ time using $O(n)$ processors [15], we are going to continue our work on LARPBS sorting to  further reduce the number of processors used without increasing the time complexity by fully utilizing computation ability of LARPBS architecture.


# References

1. Y. Pan "Basic data movement operations on the LARPBS model" in Parallel Computing Using Optical Interconnections, K. Li, Y. Pan and S. Q. Zheng, eds., Kluwer Academic Publishers, Boston, USA, October 1998
2. S. Pavel and S. G. Akl, "Integer sorting and routing in arrays with reconfigurable optical bus," Proc. 1996 International Conf. on Parallel Processing, Vol. III, pp. 90-94, August 1996

3.  S. Rajasekaran and S. Sahni, "Sorting, selection and routing on the arrays with reconfigurable optical buses," IEEE Transactions on Parallel and Distributed Systems, Vol. 8, No. 11, pp. 1123-1132, Nov. 1997

4.  C.H. Wu, S.-J. Horng, and H.-R. Tsai, "An Optimal Parallel Algorithm for Computing Moments on Arrays with Reconfigurable Optical Buses," Proceedings of the 2000 International Parallel and Distributed Processing Symposium, May 1-5, 2000, Cancun, Mexico, pp. 741-746

1.  Y. Pan, K. Li, and S. Q. Zheng, ``Fast nearest neighbor algorithms on a linear array with a reconfigurable pipelined bus system," Parallel Algorithms and Applications, Vol. 13, pp. 1-25, 1998

2.  J. L. Trahan, A. G. Bourgeois, Y. Pan, and R. Vaidyanathan, "An Optimal and Scalable Algorithm for Permutation Routing on Reconfigurable Linear Arrays with Optically Pipelined Buses," Journal of Parallel and Distributed Computing, Vol. 60, No. 9, Sept. 2000, pp. 1125-1136

3.  K. Li, Y. Pan, and S.-Q. Zheng, ``Efficient Deterministic and Probabilistic Simulations of PRAMs on Linear Arrays with Reconfigurable Pipelined Bus Systems," The Journal of Supercomputing, vol. 15, no. 2, pp. 163-181, February 2000

4.  Y. Pan, M. Hamdi and K. Li, "Efficient and scalable quicksort on a linear array with a reconfigurable pipelined bus system," Future Generation Computer Systems, Vol. 13, No. 6, pages 501-513, June 1998

5.  A. G. Bourgeois and J. L. Trahan, ``Relating Two-Dimensional Reconfigurable Meshes with Optically Pipelined Buses," Proceedings of the 2000 International Parallel and Distributed Processing Symposium, May 1-5, 2000, Cancun, Mexico, pp. 747-752

6.  Y. Han, Y. Pan and H. Shen, "Sublogarithmic Deterministic Selection on Arrays with a Reconfigurable Optical Bus," IEEE Transactions on Computers, Vol. 51, No. 6, pp. 702-707, June 2002

7.  A. Datta, S. Soundaralakshmi and R. Owens, "Fast sorting algorithms on a linear array with a reconfigurable pipelined bus system," IEEE Transactions on Parallel and Distributed Systems Vol. 13, No. 3, pp. 212-222, March 2002

8.  L. G.Valiant, "Parallelism in comparison problems", SIAM J. Commput., 1975, 4(3):348-355

9.  F. P. Preparata, "New parallel-sorting schemes", IEEE Trans. Computers, 1978,21(8):657-661

10. K. Li, Y. Pan and S.Q.Zheng, "Fast processor efficient parallel matrix multiplication algorithm on a linear array with a reconfigurable pipelined bus systems", IEEE Trans. Parallel and Distributed Sysytems, 1998 9(8): 705-720

11. R. Cole, "Parallel merge sort," SIAM Journal of Computing, Vol. 14, 1988, pp. 770-785

12. L. G.Valiant, "Parallelism in comparison problems", SIAM J. Commput., 1975, 4(3):348-355

13. F. P. Preparata, "New parallel-sorting schemes", IEEE Trans. Computers, 1978,21(8):657-661

14. K. Li, Y. Pan and S.Q.Zheng, "Fast processor efficient parallel matrix multiplication algorithm on a linear array with a reconfigurable pipelined bus systems", IEEE Trans. Parallel and Distributed Sysytems, 1998 9(8): 705-720

15. R. Cole, "Parallel merge sort," SIAM Journal of Computing, Vol. 14, 1988, pp. 770-785

# An Extended Star Graph: A Proposal of a New Network Topology and Its Fundamental Properties

Satoru Watanabe and Satoshi Okawa

Graduate dep ertmert of Computer system of
University of Aizu
Aizu-Wak amatsu, F ukushima-ken, 965-8580, Japan
c00watan@u-aizu.ac.jp, okawa@u-aizu.ac.jp

**Abstract.** In the past years, various netw orkarchitectures for parallel computers ha ve b eenprop osed,for instance, h yp er cub es or star graphs. These classes of net w orksare kno wnas Ca yleygraphs. In recent years, there ha ve b eensome prop osalsof new families of in terconnection net-w orks, namely, constan t degree net w orks.In this pap er, w e prop ose a new in terconnection net w orknamed extended star graphs, and we p rove the extended star graphs ha ve hyp ercub e's structure.We also prop ose routing algorithms for no de-to-node communication on extended star graphs. Based on the algorithms, w e obtain an upper b ound $2n - 1$ o n the diameter for the n-th order extended star graph.

**Keywords:** Ca yleygraphs, star graphs, degree four Ca yleygraphs, hy - p ercub es, routingalgorithm, diameter.

## 1 Introduction

Design of in terconnectionnet w orks is a v eryin tegralpart of an yparallel pro cess-ing or distributed system that has to ha ve largecomputing p ow er. Thechoice of the net w orksdepends on the typ esof the problems, the typ esof the computa-tions, the demands on sp eed or the n umb er of pro cessors.In the past researc h, various typ es of in terconnection net w orksare proposed. F or example, h yp er-cubes[10] ha ve b eenused to design v ariouscommercial multiprocessor machines.

F or the past sev eral y ears, there has b een a spurt of researc h on a class of graphs called Cayley graphs that are suitable for designing in terconnection net w orks[1][4].V arioustyp esof Cayley graphs that are based on pe rmutation groups ha vebe en proposed, and the Cayley graphs include a large n umbe r of families of graphs, suc h as star graphs, bubble sort graphs, complete transposi-tion graphs, and others. Especially , stargraphs ha ve b eenextensively studied as alternative n etworks for h yp ercubes. These graphs are symmetric, regular, and seem to share many of desirable properties like lo w diameter, lo w degree, high fault tolerance and so on.

In recent years, there ha ve b eensome proposals of new families of in tercon-nection net w orkswith constant degree, suc h as d eg ree fou r Cyley graphs[2][5],

M. Guo and L.T.Yang (Eds.): ISPA 2003, LNCS 2745, pp. 220–227, 2003.

trivalent Cayley graphs[6][7], and ShuffleExchange Permutation graphs[8]. The most attractive property of these graphs is their constant degree irrespective of the number of nodes.

Our purpose in this paper is to propose a new family of interconnection networks called extended star graphs which are defined as the combination of star graphs and degree four Cayley graphs, and to study their fundamental properties and a relation of them to hypercubes. Furthermore, we provide a routing algorithm and obtain upper bound of the diameter of extended star graphs.

## 2  Preliminary Remarks

For any integer $n \geq 3$, a sequence $\mathbf{a} = a_1 a_2 \cdots a_n$ is called a *signed permutation* if $|\mathbf{a}| = |a_1||a_2| \cdots |a_n|$ is a permutation of $n$ integers 1, 2, $\cdots$, and $n$ A negative sign is indicated by the line above an integer, that is, $-k$ is denoted by $\bar{k}$ and $\bar{\bar{k}} = k$ as usual.

The set of all signed permutation is denoted by $\mathcal{T}(n)$. Moreover, we need two subsets of $\mathcal{T}(n)$. $\mathcal{T}_S(n)$ is the set of all permutations, that is, $\mathcal{T}_S(n) = \{a_1 a_2 \cdots a_n \mid \forall a_i \geq 0\} \subset \mathcal{T}(n)$. $\mathcal{T}_D(n)$ is the set of sll signed cyclic permutations in $\mathrm{T}(n)$, that is, $\mathcal{T}_D(n) = \{a_1 a_2 \cdots a_n \mid \exists i \; |a_i||a_{i+1}| \cdots |a_n||a_1||a_2| \cdots |a_{i-1}| \text{is}$ equal to $12 \cdots n \} \subset \mathcal{T}(n)$.

Now we define mappings $s_i (2 \leq i \leq n)$, $g$ and $f$ from $\mathcal{T}(n)$ to $\mathcal{T}(n)$ as follows,

$$s_i(a_1 a_2 \cdots a_i \cdots a_n) = a_i a_2 \cdots a_1 \cdots a_n,$$
$$f(a_1 a_2 \cdots a_n) = a_2 \cdots a_n \bar{a}_1.$$
$$g(a_1 a_2 \cdots a_n) = a_2 \cdots a_n a_1,$$

Let $f^{-1}$ and $g^{-1}$ denote the inverse mappings of $f$ and $g$ respectively. For $s_i$, it is clear $s_i^{-1} = s_i$.

We introduce network topologies, $ST_n$[4], and $DF_n$[2].

**Definition 1.** *For* $n \geq 1$, $n$-th *order star graph*, $ST_n$, *is defined as* $ST_n = (V_n, E_n)$ *where* $V_n = \mathcal{T}_S(n)$ *and* $E_n = \{(\mathbf{u}, \mathbf{v}) \mid \mathbf{u}, \mathbf{v} \in V_n, \mathbf{v} = s_i(\mathbf{u}), 2 \leq i \leq n\}$.

Two nodes $\mathbf{u}$ and $\mathbf{v}$ in star graphs are joined by an (undirected) edge if and only if the permutation corresponding to the node $\mathbf{v}$ can be obtained from that of $u$ by transposing the integer at the $i$-th position ($2 \leq i \leq n$) with that at the first (leftmost) position.

**Definition 2.** *For* $n \geq 3$, $n$-th *order degree four Cayley graph*, $DF_n$, *is defined as* $DF_n = (V_n, E_n)$ *where* $V_n = \mathcal{T}_D$ *and* $E_n = \{(\mathbf{u}, \mathbf{v}) \mid \mathbf{u}, \mathbf{v} \in V_n, \mathbf{v} = h(\mathbf{u}), h \in \{f, g, f^{-1}, g^{-1}\}\}$.

Note that in this definition, the set of four generators $\{f, g, f^{-1}, g^{-1}\}$ is closed under inverse; $g$ is inverse of $g^{-1}$ and $f$ is inverse of $f^{-1}$.

In the definitions of $ST_n$ and $DF_n$, an edge generated by $s_i$ and $f$ (or $f^{-1}$), and $g$ (or $g^{-1}$) is called called $s_i$-edges, $f$-edges, and $g$-edges, respectively.

For $ST_n$, following propositions are known[4].

**Proposition 1.**
*For $n \geq 1$, $ST_n$:*

1. *has $n!$ no des;*
2. *is regular graph of degree $n - 1$;*
3. *has $\frac{(n-1)n!}{2}$ edges; and*
4. *The diameter of $ST_n$ is given by $Dia(ST_n) = \lfloor \frac{3(n-1)}{2} \rfloor$.*

For $DF_n$, following propositions are known[2].

**Proposition 2.**
*For $n \geq 3$, $DF_n$:*

1. *has $n2^n$ no des;*
2. *is regular graph of degree 4;*
3. *has $n2^{n+1}$ edges;*
4. *can be partitioned into $2^{n-1}$ f-cycles of length $2n$, where f-cycle is a cycle consisting of f-edges;*
5. *can be partitioned into $2^n$ g-cycles of length n, where g-cycle is a cycle consisting of g-edges; and*
6. *The diameter of $DF_n$ is given by $Dia(DF_n) = \lfloor \frac{3n}{2} \rfloor$.*

# 3    Exteneded Star Graphs and Their Fundamental Properties

We propose a new network topology $EST_n$ as follows.

**Definition 3.** *For $n \geq 3$, n-th order extended star graph, $EST_n$, is defined as $EST_n = (V_n, E_n)$ where $V_n = T(n)$ and $E_n = \{(u, v) \mid u, v \in V_n, v = h(u), h \in \{s_i, f, g, f^{-1}, g^{-1}\}\}$.*

In these graphs, the set of five generators $\{s_i, f, g, f^{-1}, g^{-1}\}$ is closed under inverse. These edges that are generated by $s_i$, $f$ (or $f^{-1}$), and $g$ (or $g^{-1}$) are called $s_i$-edges, $f$-edges, and $g$-edges, respectively similar to edges in $ST_n$ and $DF_n$. $EST_n$ is a combination of $ST_n$ and $DF_n$, clearly, $s_i$-edges is edges of $ST_n$, and $f$, $g$, $f^{-1}$, and $g^{-1}$ are edges of $DF_n$.

Fig.1 shows $EST_3$, as an example of $EST_n$.

Next, we give some fundamental properties of $EST_n$.

**Theorem 1.**
*For $n \geq 3$, $EST_n$:*

1. *has $n!2^n$ no des;*
2. *is regular graph of degree $n + 3$;*
3. *has $n!2^{n-1}(n + 3)$ edges;*
4. *can be devided into no de disjoint $2^n$ $ST_n$'s;*
5. *can be devided into no de disjoint $(n - 1)!$ $DF_n$'s;*
6. *has $2^{n-1}(n - 1)!$ f-cycles of length $2n$; and*

7. *has $2^n(n-1)!$ g-cycles of length $n$.*

*Proof.* First three facts 1,2, and 3 are trivial. For facts 4 and 5, we consider the equivalance relations on $\mathcal{T}(n)$, $\equiv_s$ and $\equiv_{fg}$ by $\mathbf{u} \equiv_s \mathbf{v}$ iff $\mathbf{v} = s_i(\mathbf{u})$ for some $s_i$, and $\mathbf{u} \equiv_{fg} \mathbf{v}$ iff $\mathbf{v} = h(\mathbf{u})$ for $h \in \{f, f^{-1}, g, g^{-1}\}$. Then, each class of the partition of $\mathcal{T}(n)$ by $\equiv_s$ and $\equiv_{fg}$ becomes a star graph $ST_n$ and a degree four Cayley graph $DF_n$, respectively. The size of the partitions are $2^n$ and $(n-1)!$, respectively. Therefore, facts 6 and 7 are obvious from Proposition 2 and fact 5 above.

When we think of $EST_n$ as a combination of $(n-1)!$ $DF_n$, $(n-1)!$ $DF_n$ are linked by $s_i$-edges. Then, $EST_n$ can be regarded as $ST_{n-1}$. On the other hand, when we think of $EST_n$ as a combination of $2^n$ $ST_n$, all $2^n$ $ST_n$ are linked by $f$-edges, Then, $EST_n$ can be regarded as hypercubes. (Note that $g$-edges connect a node in $ST_n$ and a node in the same $ST_n$.) We will explain this fact.

A binary sequence of length $n$, $\mathbf{b} = b_1 \cdots b_j \cdots b_n$, we define a signed permutaion $\mathbf{p_b} = p_1 \cdots p_j \cdots p_n$, where $p_j = j$ if $b_j = 0$ and $p_j = \bar{j}$ if $b_j = 1$. Then, $\mathcal{T}_{S,\mathbf{b}}(n) = \{a_1 a_2 \cdots a_n | a_1 a_2 \cdots a_n$ is permutation of $\mathbf{p_b}$ $\}$. $ST_{n,\mathbf{b}}$ is defined as $ST_{n,\mathbf{b}} = (V_{\mathbf{b}}, E_{\mathbf{b}})$, where $V_{\mathbf{b}} = \mathcal{T}_{S,\mathbf{b}}(n)$ and $E_{\mathbf{b}} = \{(\mathbf{u}, \mathbf{v}) \mid \mathbf{u}, \mathbf{v} \in V_{\mathbf{b}}, \mathbf{v} = s_i(\mathbf{u})\}$.

Now we define a graph $G_n$ as follows. $G_n = (V_n, E_n)$, where $V_n = \{ST_{n,\mathbf{b}} \mid \mathbf{b}$ is a binary sequence of length $n\}$ and $E_n = \{(ST_{n,\mathbf{b}}, ST_{n,\mathbf{b}'}) \mid \exists \mathbf{u} \in ST_{n,\mathbf{b}}, \mathbf{v} \in ST_{n,\mathbf{b}'},$ such that $\mathbf{v} = f(\mathbf{u})$ in $EST_n\}$.

**Theorem 2.** *The graph $G_n$ is isomorphic to a hypercube $Q_n$.*

*Proof.* It is clear that there is a one to one correspondence $\varphi$ between a node set $V_n$ and the set of binary sequences of length $n$. For two binary sequence $\mathbf{b}$ and $\mathbf{b}'$ with Hamming distance of them $d_H(\mathbf{b}, \mathbf{b}') = 1$, if $\mathbf{u} = u_1 u_2 \cdots u_n$ is a node of $ST_{n,\mathbf{b}}$, then a node $f(\mathbf{u}) = u_2 \cdots u_n \bar{u}_1$ is in $ST_{n,\mathbf{b}'}$. This means $(ST_{n,\mathbf{b}}, ST_{n,\mathbf{b}'})$ is an edge of $G_n$. Therefore, we can conclude $\varphi$ is an isomorphism from $G_n$ to $Q_n$.

## 4    Routing Algorithm

Since $EST_n$ is a Cayley graph, it is node symmetric[1][4]. Therefore we can always regard the distance between any two arbitrary nodes as the distance between the source node and the identity permutation $I = 1\,2\,3\cdots n$ by suitably renaming the symbols representing the permutations. For example, let $\bar{3}12$ be the source node and $23\bar{1}$ be the destination node. We can map the destination node to the identity node $123$ by renaming the symbols as $1 \mapsto \bar{3}$, $2 \mapsto 1$, $3 \mapsto 2$, $\bar{1} \mapsto 3$, $\bar{2} \mapsto \bar{1}$, and $\bar{3} \mapsto \bar{2}$. Under this mapping the source node becomes $\bar{2}\bar{3}1$. Then the paths between the original source and destination nodes become isomorphic to the paths between the node $\bar{2}\bar{3}1$ and the identity node $123$ in the graph obtained by renaming. Thus, the destination node is always assumed to be the identity node $I$ without any loss of generality. The following algorithm R that is based on the idea in [11] computes a path (a sequence of nodes) from an arbitrary node $\mathbf{v} = v_1 v_2 v_3 \cdots v_n$ in $EST_n$ to the identity node $I$.

**algorithm R**
input: $(EST_n, \mathbf{v})$
output: $p$ (path from $\mathbf{v}$ to $I$)
**method**
(initialization)
$p \longleftarrow \mathbf{v}, \mathbf{u} \longleftarrow \mathbf{v}$
(path computation)
$i \longleftarrow 1$
**repeat**
**if** $u_1 \neq i, \bar{i}$
**then**
    Find $k$ $(1 \leq k \leq n)$ such that $u_k = i$ or $\bar{i}$
**then**
    $p \longleftarrow p, s_k(\mathbf{u})$
    $\mathbf{u} \longleftarrow s_k(\mathbf{u})$
**else**
**end if**
**if** $u_1 = \bar{i}$
**then**
    $p \longleftarrow p, f(\mathbf{u})$
    $\mathbf{u} \longleftarrow f(\mathbf{u})$
**else**
    $p \longleftarrow p, g(\mathbf{u})$
    $\mathbf{u} \longleftarrow g(\mathbf{u})$
**end if**
$i \longleftarrow i + 1$
**until** $i = n$

**Theorem 3.** *The algorithm R correctly computes the path from an arbitrary node to the identity node I.*

*Proof.* In the first if sentence, the numbers from 1 to $n$ are moved to leftmost position by taking $s_k$. In the second if sentence, $i$ or $\bar{i}$ is moved to rightmost position, by taking $f$ or $g$ according to the sign of it. The numbers from 1 to $n-1$ are sorted, we obtain the path of length $\leq 2n - 2$ to the node $\mathbf{u} = n^*123\cdots n-1$ from $\mathbf{v}$, where $n^*$ means $n$ or $\bar{n}$. Finally by taking $f$ or $g$, we obtain the of length $2n - 1$ to the identity node $I$.

As a corollary to Theorem 3, an upper bound of the diameter can be obtained as follows;

**Theorem 4.** *A nupper bound on the diameter on $EST_n$ is given by*

$$Dia(EST_n) \leq 2n - 1.$$

## 5    Conclusion

In this paper, we proposed a new interconnection network called extended star graphs that is defined by the combination of star graphs and degree four Cayley graphs and examined some properties of them. The n umb er of no des degree, the number of edges, the number of no de disjoint $ST_n$ and $DF_n$, and the number of $f$-cycles and $g$-cycles are obtained, We ha v eanalyzed the relation be tween $EST_n$ and $Q_n$. We p rovided a routing algorithm, and ga v e the upper b ound of diameter of $EST_n$ . Since $EST_n$ con tains $ST_n$ as a subgraph, the diameter of $ST_n$ is a low er b ound of one of $EST_n$.

When w e regard $EST_n$ as $ST_{n-1}$ from global viewpoin t, a no de of $ST_{n-1}$ corresponds to a certain subgraph $DF_n$ in $EST_n$. Similarly, when w e regard $EST_n$ as $Q_n$ from global viewpoin t, a no de f $Q_n$ corresponds to certain subgraph $ST_n$ in $EST_n$. Therefore, almost all algorithms dev elop ed for $ST_n$, $DF_n$, an d $Q_n$ are used for $EST_n$ directly or with a few modifications of them.

Research of the $EST_n$, suc h as the optimal routing algorithm and exactly diameter, an emb edding of other graphs for instance trees and meshes etc, and a design of fault tolerant routing algorithm is exp ected in the future. F urthermore, sev eral extensions of this study are p ossible. We can consider other typ es of combinations of Cayley graphs based on p ermutation groups and constant degree net w orks F or example, w e can consider a combination of bubble sort graphs[1][4] and Degree four Cayley graphs, and a combination of complete transposition graphs[1][4] and Degree four Cayley graphs.

**Acknowledgement.**

The authers are grateful to reviewers for their comments to improv e the paper. Mr. Shinotake helps for dev eloping a routing algorithm.

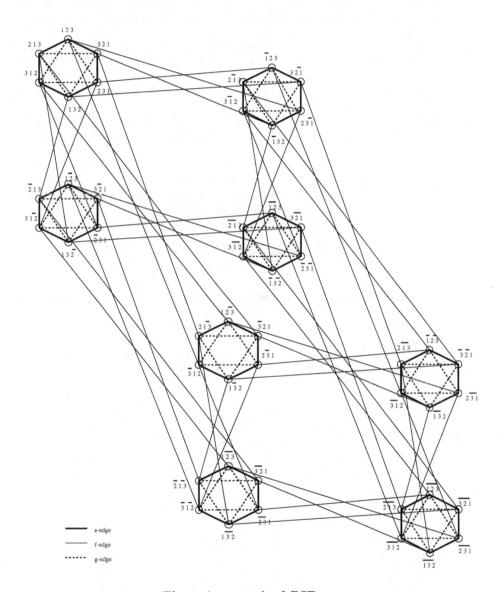

**Fig. 1.** An example of $EST_3$.

# References

1. S.Lakshmivarahan, Jung-Sing Jw oand S.K.Dhall. Symmetry in interconnection net w orksbased on Ca yleygraphs of p erm utatiorgroups: A surv ey *Par allel Computing* No.19, pp.361-407, 1993.
2. P. Vadapalli, P .K.Srimani. A new family of Ca yleygraph in terconnectionnet w orks of constan t degreefour *IEEE T ransactions on Par allel andDistributed Systems* 7 *(1) pp.26-32* 1996.
3. Mohamed Benmaiza, Abderezal T ouzene. One-to-all broadcast algorithm for constan t degree4 Ca yleygraphs *Par allel Computing*No.25, pp.249-264, 1999.
4. J.Jwo. Analysis of interconnection net w orksbased on Caley graphs related to p erm utationgroups, ph.D. Dissertation, *Scho ol of Ele ctrical Engineering and Computer Scienc e, University of Oklahoma* 1991.
5. S.Lakshmivarahan, Jung-Sing Jw oand S.K.Dhall. Emb edding of cycles and grids in star graphs. *Journal of Cir cuits,Systems, and Computers, V ol. 1*No. 1, pp43-74, 1991.
6. P. Vadapalli, P .K.Srimani. T rivalen C ayley graphs for interconnectionnet w orks. *Information Pr ocessingL etters* 54, pp329-335, 1995.
7. P. Vadapalli, P .K.Srimani. Shortest routing in trivalent C ayley graph net w ork. *Information Pr ocessingL etters*57, pp183-188, 1996.
8. S. Latifi, P .K.Srimani. A New Fixid Degree Regular Net w orkfor P arallel Processing. , 1996.
9. S. B. Ak ers,D. Harel, B. Krishnamurth y. The Star Graph: An A ttractive A lternativ e tothe n-Cube. *Pr oc.Internat. Conf. on Par allelPr oc essing*pp393-400, 1987.
10. Y. Saad, M. H. Sch ultz. T op ologicalProperties of Hypercub es.*IEEE T ransactions on computers, vol. 37* NO. 7, pp393-400, 1988.
11. M. Shinotake. New Routing Algorithms for Extended Star Graphs. *University of A izu*March, 2001.
12. S. Watanabe. A Proplsal of a new Net w orkT op ologyand Its F undamental Properties. *University of A izu*March, 2000.

# Effective Admission Control for Real-Time Anycast Flow[*]

Weijia Jia[1], Jinliang Jiao[1], and Chuanlin Zhang[2]

[1] Department of Computer Engineering and Information Technology
City University of Hong Kong, Kowloon, Hong Kong, SAR China
itjia@cityu.edu.hk
http://anyserver.cityu.edu.hk
[2] Department of Mathematics, Jinan University
Guangzhou, 510632, P.R.China

**Abstract.** This paper presents a novel admission control algorithm for anycast flow with real-time constraints. Given the time requirement, our algorithm can effective calculate the delay bound on a selected path for anycast flows. Thus our algorithms can guarantee the end-to-end deadline. Our algorithm is scalable in terms of the number of flows can be admitted through local information of the routes.

## 1 Introduction

An anycast flow is a sequence of packets that can be sent to any one of the members in a group of designated recipients. Multiple mirrored servers of the service providers, such as e-commerce companies, banks, and web-based information providers, can share a single anycast address. Applications may simply send their information flows with the anycast address in order to upload or download information from or to these multiple sites. The anycast service has been defined as a standard service in the latest version of Ipv6 in [1]. It was determined that anycast addresses are allocated from the unicast address space with any of the defined unicast address format [2]. The implication of an anycast service supported at the application layer was explored [3]. A framework for scalable global IP anycast was proposed in [4]. An anycast protocol and its integration with other routing approaches were developed [5][6][7][8][9]. Different from datagram communication, flow-oriented communication has to go through an admission process in which application makes a request with certain real-time requirement, to the network for establishing a flow between a source and an anycast group. An anycast flow can be admitted only if sufficient network resources are available so that the required real-time deadline can be adhered. The admission control plays a critical role in meeting with the real-time requirement of anycast flows. By real-time we mean that every packet of the anycast flow is delivered from its source to

[*] The work is supported by Hong Kong RGC SAR China grant nos: CityU 1055/01E, CityU 1039/02E and CityU Strategic grant nos: 7001355 and 7001446.

M. Guo and L.T.Yang (Eds.): ISPA 2003, LNCS 2745, pp. 228–238, 2003.

the same destination in a group of designated recipients within a predefined end-to-end deadline. Packets delivered beyond this end-to-end deadline are considered useless. Admission control for unicast and multicast packets has been investigated widely in many well-know systems as described in [10][11][12][13]. Distributed admission control for anycast flows with QoS requirements was developed recently in [14].

## 2  Network and Anycast Traffic Models

A network is modeled as a graph $H = N(S, E)$ of connected link servers, where S is a finite set of vertices in H, representing nodes (routers or switches) in the network concerned. E is a finite set of edges, representing the links between nodes. For the purpose of delay computation, we follow standard practice and model a router like a server, where packets can experience queuing delays. Packets are typically queued at the output buffers, where they compete for the output link. We therefore model a router as a set of output link servers. All other servers (input buffers, non-blocking switch fabric, wires etc.) can be eliminated by appropriately subtracting the constant delays incurred on them from the deadline requirements of traffic. The link servers in set S are connected through either links in the network or paths within routers, which both make up the set of edges E in the graph. We assume that all routers have N input links and all the output links with link capacity C bits per second. We use L to denote the maximal number of input edges to each server.

A stream of packets between one sender and one receiver is called a flow. An anycast flow (AF) is a sequence of packets that, in total, can be sent to any one of the members in a group of designated recipients [14]. We assume that all packets in AFs have the same length or the same supper bounds. Furthermore, we assume that anycast flows have a request on sequencing. That is, once the first packet in an AF is delivered to a member in the recipient group, all the consequent packets of the same flow should also be delivered to the same member. Anycast packets of a flow are transmitted along some (shortest) path from its source to one member in the group of designated recipients. We model a path as a list of link servers. For the incoming anycast packet, the router determines the output link by looking up its routing table and transports anycast packets to the proper output link, which, in turn, connects to the next hop. Anycast packets may exceed the capacity at the output link; thus, an anycast packet may suffer some queuing delay at the output link. This delay depends on the load of the output link and the scheduling policy adopted at the output link. In the time interval with length I, all flows (anycast or non-anycast) going through server k from input link j form a group of flows $G_{j,k}(I)$.

We define a group of anycast members as a set of servers that provide same kind of services. Therefore, a user may request any of the members for the connection of services by issue anycast connection for anycast flow. It can be seen that anycast routing gives us the room for the research of selection the destinations. We denote the anycast group as G(A). This paper deals with incomplete solution of the anycast selection for efficiency and scalability, thus we also denote the subset $\{x, y\} \subseteq G(A)$ as $\{x, y\}_A$. For simplicity, we define all the non-anycast flows obey the uniform constraint such that $f(t) \leq \sigma + \rho t$. In order to appropriately characterize traffic both at ingress router and within the network, we use a general traffic descriptor in the form of traffic functions and their time independent constraint functions as described in [14].

**Definition 1.** The source traffic of flow is constrained by a leaky bucket with parameters pair $(\sigma, \rho)$. The total amount of traffic, generated by this source during any time interval $[t, t+I]$, is bounded by $\min\{CI, \sigma + \rho I\}$, i.e. for any $t > 0$ and $I > 0$, the total amount of an traffic $f_k(t)$ at source server k in time interval $[0, t)$ satisfies the following inequality:

$$f_k(t+I) - f_k(t) \leq \min\{CI, \sigma + \rho I\} \tag{1}$$

where $\sigma$ is the burst size of source traffic for all flows, $\rho$ is the average rate of source traffic of anycast flows.

The leaky bucket appropriately characterizes the source traffic at the ingress router; this characterization is not valid within the networks for the traffic is perturbed by queuing delays at servers as it traverses the network. In general, we characterize traffic at any severs in the network by traffic functions and their time independent counterpart, traffic constraint functions as following descriptions.

**Definition 2.** The traffic function $f_{j,k}(t)$ means the amount of the traffic arriving at server k by the input link j during time interval $[0, t)$.

Traffic functions are cumbersome to handle and not of much help in admission control for they are time dependent. A time-independent traffic characterization is given by the traffic constraint function, which is defined as following:

**Definition 3.** The function $F_{j,k}(I)$ is called constraint function of traffic function $f_{j,k}(t)$ if for any $t > 0$ and $I > 0$, hold the following inequality:

$$f_{j,k}(t+I) - f_{j,k}(t) \leq F_{j,k}(I) \tag{2}$$

We define the end-to-end deadline requirement of anycast traffic (s, G) to be D, where s is the source and G is the set of recipients of the anycast flow. Suppose an anycast flow $f_A(t)$ from source s is constrained by $(\sigma_A, \rho_A)$, i.e, $f_A(t+I) - f_A(t) \leq \min\{CI, \sigma_A + \rho_A I\}$ for all time t and duration I, thus denote $f_A(t) \sim (\sigma_A, \rho_A)$. All the flows through the network are guaranteed the same delay when they pass through the same server. In this paper, we use $d_k$ to denote the local worst-case queuing delay suffered by traffic at server k, which has to pass through. In order to derive the computation formula of the local worst-case queuing delay, we first suppose that the traffic in the network system is empty before the network begins.

# 3  Calculation of Local Worst-Case Queuing Delay

Based on the description of traffic function, we may derive the output traffic through the following lemma, which is important for the calculation of the delay when the traffic is intensive.

**Lemma 1.** In time interval I, the aggregated traffic of the group of flows $G_{j,k}(I)$ where formed by all flows going through server k from input link j is constrained by

$$F_{j,k}(I) = \begin{cases} CI & I \le \tau_{j,k}(I) \\ n_{j,k}(I)[\sigma + \rho(I + Y_k)] + \sigma_A + \rho_A(I + Y_k) & I > \tau_{j,k}(I) \end{cases} \tag{3}$$

where $\tau_{j,k}(I) = \dfrac{n_{j,k}(I)[\sigma + \rho Y_k] + \sigma_A + \rho_A Y_k}{C - n_{j,k}(I)\rho - \rho_A}$, $n_{j,k}(I)$ is the maximal number of the other

flows from source s arrived at sever k from input link j in time interval with length I. $Y_k$ is the maximum of the worst-case delays experienced by all flows before arriving at server k, e.g. $Y_k = \max_{R \in S_k} \sum_{s \in R} d_s$, where $S_k$ is the set of all paths passed by packets before arriving at server k.

Proof. For flow $\chi$ in the group of flows $G_{j,k}(I)$, let $Y_k$ be the total worst-case queuing delay experienced by packets of an anycast flow $\chi$ before arriving at server k and is the source traffic function of anycast flow $\chi$, then $F_x(I) \le H_x(I + Y_k) \le \sigma + \rho(I + Y_k)$ or

$$F_x(I) \le H_x(I + Y_k) \le \sigma_A + \rho_A(I + Y_k) \qquad\qquad\qquad\text{therefore}$$

$F_{j,k}(I) \le \sum_{x \in G_{j,k}(I)} F_x(I) \le n_{j,k}(I)[\sigma + \rho(I + Y_k)] + \sigma_A + \rho_A(I + Y_k)$,  $F_{j,k}(I) \le CI$  by using these

inequality, we hold

$$G_{j,k}(I) \le F_{j,k}(I) \le \min\{ CI, n_{j,k}(I)[\sigma + \rho(I + Y_k)] + \sigma_A + \rho_A(I + Y_k)\} =$$
$$\begin{cases} CI & I \le \tau_{j,k}(I) \\ n_{j,k}(I)[\sigma + \rho(I + Y_k)] + \sigma_A + \rho_A(I + Y_k) & I > \tau_{j,k}(I) \end{cases}$$

∎

**Lemma 2.** In time interval with length I, the aggregated traffic of the group of flows $G_k(I)$ formed by all flows input to server k is constrained by

$$F_k(I) = \begin{cases} (L - i + 1)CI + \sum_{j=1}^{i-1} n_{j,k}(I)[\sigma + \rho(I + Y_k)] + i[\sigma_A + \rho_A(I + Y_k)], & \tau_{i-1,k}(I) \le I \le \tau_{i,k}(I), i = 1,2,\cdots,L \\[2mm] \sum_{j=1}^{L} n_{j,k}(I)[\sigma + \rho(I + Y_k)] + [\sigma_A + \rho_A(I + Y_k)] & I > \tau_{L,k}(I) \end{cases} \tag{4}$$

where $\tau_{1,k}(I) \le \tau_{2,k}(I) \le \cdots \le \tau_{L,k}(I)$ and L is the maximal number of input edge to each server.

Proof. By using Lemma 1, we know that

$$G_k(I) \le \sum_{j=1}^{L} F_{j,k}(I) = F_k(I) =$$

$$\begin{cases} (L-i+1)CI + \sum_{j=1}^{i-1} n_{j,k}(I)[\sigma + \rho(I+Y_k)] + i[\sigma_A + \rho_A(I+Y_k)] & n_{i-1,k}(I) \le I \le n_{i,k}(I), i = 1,2,\cdots,L \\ \sum_{j=1}^{L} n_{j,k}(I)[\sigma + \rho(I+Y_k)] + [\sigma_A + \rho_A(I+Y_k)] & I > n_{L,k}(I) \end{cases}$$

Thus, the lemma is proved.    ∎

**Lemma 3.** There exist $I_0 > 0$ such that the local worst-case queuing delay $d_k$ suffered by traffic at Server k satisfy following inequality:

$$d_k \le \frac{[\sigma_A + \rho_A Y_k] + \sum_{j=1}^{L} n_{j,k}(I_0)[\sigma + \rho Y_k]}{C - \rho_A - \sum_{j=1}^{L} n_{j,k}(I_0)\rho} \tag{5}$$

Proof. It is easy to know the following inequality: $d_k \le \dfrac{1}{C} \max_{I>0}\{F_k(I) - CI\}$, by Lemma

2, we have:

$$F_k(I) - CI = \begin{cases} (L-i)CI + \sum_{j=1}^{i-1} n_{j,k}(I)[\sigma + \rho(I+Y_k)] + i[\sigma_A + \rho_A(I+Y_k)] & \tau_{i-1,k}(I) \le I \le \tau_{i,k}(I), i = 1,2,\cdots,L \\ \sum_{j=1}^{L} n_{j,k}(I)[\sigma + \rho(I+Y_k)] - CI + [\sigma_A + \rho_A(I+Y_k)] & I > \tau_{L,k}(I) \end{cases}$$

Hence    $\exists I_0 > 0$  such  that  $\max_{I>0}\{F_k(I) - CI\} = \dfrac{[\sigma_A + Y_k] + \sum_{j=1}^{L} n_{j,k}(I_0)[\sigma + \rho Y_k]}{C - \rho_A - \sum_{j=1}^{L} n_{j,k}(I_0)\rho} C$.

Therefore, (5) is true.    ∎

**Theorem 1.** Assume that the utilization of Server k does not exceed $\alpha_k$. Thus, we have $\sum_{j=1}^{L} n_{j,k}(I)\rho + \rho_A \le \alpha_k C$ and

$$d_k \le \frac{\alpha_k}{\rho(1-\alpha_k)}[\sigma + \rho Y_k] + \frac{1}{(1-\alpha_k)C\rho}[\rho\sigma_A - \sigma\rho_A] \tag{6}$$

Proof. Note that function $f(x) = \dfrac{xY_k + \sigma_A + \frac{\alpha_k C - \rho_A}{\rho}\sigma}{C - x}$ increases along with $x$ in [0,C].

Applying Lemma 3 and the supposition, we know that:

$$d_k \le \frac{\alpha_k CY_k + \sigma_A + \frac{\alpha_k C - \rho_A}{\rho}\sigma}{C - \alpha_k C} = \frac{\alpha_k}{\rho(1-\alpha_k)}[\sigma + \rho Y_k] + \frac{1}{(1-\alpha_k)C\rho}[\rho\sigma_A - \sigma\rho_A] \quad ∎$$

It has been proved that when $\alpha_k \ge 0.62C$ for multistage and ring networks, then the delay may become unstable with the control of $(\sigma, \rho)$ regulator [15].

*Remark 1.* From Theorem 1, it is easy to know that the network is stable if
$$\rho_A + \sum_{j=1}^{L} n_{j,k}(I)\rho \le \alpha_k C.$$

We note that the upper bound of in Theorem 1 depends on $Y_k$. The value of $Y_k$, in turn, depends on the delays experienced at severs other than server k. In general, we have a circular dependency. Hence, the delay values depend on each other and must be computed simultaneously. We denote the upper bounds of delays by V-dimensional vector:
$d = [d_1, d_2, \cdots, d_V]^T$ and

$$\varphi(d) = [\varphi_1(d), \varphi_2(d), \cdots, \varphi_V(d)]^T, where \tag{7}$$

$$\varphi_k(d) = \frac{\alpha_k}{\rho(1-\alpha_k)}[\sigma + \rho Y_k] + \frac{1}{(1-\alpha_k)C\rho}[\rho\sigma_A - \sigma\rho_A], k = 1,2,\cdots,V.$$

Therefore the queuing delay bound vector can be determined by iterative methods for system of equations: $d = \varphi(d)$. Furthermore, once an anycast flow's path $r$ is selected, the end-to-end delay $d_{e2e}$ for each packet in this flow can be computed according following formula:

$$d_{e2e} = \sum_{k \in r} d_k \tag{8}$$

# 4   Efficient Admission Control Algorithms for Real-Time Anycast Flow

Let triple (s, G(A), R) denote the stream of flow requests from source s to anycast group G(A) with routes set R formed by the shortest path from source s to one destination in G(A). We assume that G(A) contains K recipients. In this section, we will present a set of efficient admission control algorithms, taking special consideration to satisfy the real-time communications for AFs. Initially, the base-line anycast algorithm will be presented and then we extend the base-line algorithm to consider the incomplete routing information for efficient and scalable admission control.

The elements in R are arranged according to their lengths in non decreasing order, e.g. R= {$r_1, r_2, ..., r_k$} with property |$r_1$|, | $r_2$|, ..., |$r_k$| where |$r_i$| denotes the static distance (number of hops) of route $r_i$. For anycast flow (s, G, R), we select destinations or route according to Biased Weight Assignment Algorithms (WD in short) as proposed in [16], e.g. the weight $W_i$ associated with destination $i$ is

$$W_i = \frac{1/|r_i|}{\sum_{j=1}^{K} 1/|r_j|} \tag{9}$$

i.e. the probability of selecting $i^{th}$ destination is $W_i$ for i = 1, 2, 3, ..., K.

Let $(s_i, a_i, r_i)$ ($i = 1, 2, ..., M$) denote the other flows in the network from source $s_i$ to destination $a_i$ through route $r_i$ and $F(A)=\{(s_i, a_i, r_i)|\ i=1, 2, ..., M\}$. Combining route selection algorithm and Theorem 1, we have the following basic admission control algorithm for real-time anycast flow:

```
Alg-1: Real-Time Admission Control for Anycast Flow

Input: The number V of nodes of the network and the set
of all flows existing in the network. Let F={(si, ai,
ui)|i=1,2,…, M} and the parameters (σ,ρ) constrain
these flows from source si. An anycast flow request
from source s to the set G of recipients by routes set
R= {r1, r2,…,rk} with constraints parameters (σA, ρA)
and deadline requirement to be D. Let the portion of
link bandwidth assigned to traffics is α and iteration
error tolerance ε. The number of input links of each
node is L. The Capacity of each node is C.

Output: whether the anycast flow can be admitted into
the network and give the destinations table for the
anycast flow when it can be admitted.
```

1. $\qquad Z_1 := 1/(1-\alpha)$; $\quad Z_2 := \dfrac{Z_1 \sigma_A}{C} + \dfrac{Z_1 \alpha \sigma}{\rho} + \dfrac{Z_1 \sigma \rho_A}{C\rho}$;

2. $\qquad$ T := 1;

3. $\qquad$ Select a destination $A_j$ in G or a route $r_j$ in R based on probability distribution $W_j$ of the corresponding route $r_j$.

4. $\qquad$ for l=1, 2, 3,…,V do $d_l := Z_2$;

5. $\qquad$ for k=1, 2, 3,…, V do

(5.1) $Y_k = \begin{cases} \displaystyle\sum_{l=1}^{m_k} d_{v_l} & r_j =< s_h, v_1, v_2, \cdots, v_{m_k}, k, \cdots, A_j > \\ 0 & k \notin r_j \end{cases}$ $\qquad$ and

$r_j =< s, v_1, v_2, ..., v_{m_j}, k..., A_j >$

(5.2) $\qquad$ for h=1,2,3,...,M do

(5.2.1) $\qquad\qquad Y_{k,h} = \begin{cases} \displaystyle\sum_{l=1}^{m_{k,h}} d_{v_l} & r_h =< s_h, v_1, v_2, \cdots, v_{m_{k,h}}, k, \cdots, D_h > \\ 0 & k \notin r_h \end{cases}$

(5.2.2) $\quad$ if $Y_k < Y_{k,h}$ then $Y_k := Y_{k,h}$

(5.3) $\qquad Z_k :=_1 \alpha Y_k + Z_2$;

6.          if $\dfrac{\sum\limits_{k=1}^{V} |Z_k - d_k|}{\sum\limits_{k=1}^{V} d_k} \leq \varepsilon$ then goto 9

7.          for k=1, 2, …, V do $d_k$:= $Z_k$;

8.          goto 5;

9.          E:= $\sum\limits_{v_i \in r_j} d_i$ ;

10.         If E > D and T < K then T:=T+1 (search another path); goto 3; else report "Reject"; stop;

11.         Report "Accept" and use path rj and destination Aj for accepting anycast flow (s, G(A), R) with deadline requirement D satisfied;

end.

The essentiality of step 3 is to transform anycast flows to unicast flows by selecting a destination or path in corresponding addresses group. The selection of destination is based on WD probability in [5]. The destination of step 4 to step 8 is iterative computation of the local delay at each nodes with taking all initial values zero under the selected route in step 3. Step 9 tests if the anycast flow arrives at one of the corresponding recipients group in pre-limited time according the selected route in step 3. When end-to-end delay of anycast flow is beyond the corresponding pre-limited time, Step 10 continues to select new route by using the multiple option of anycast communication until all possible routes combination is used up. When the results of the algorithm above give succeed information, we find route for the anycast flow requesting. Therefore, what we need to do is testing if the corresponding path $r_j$ has enough bandwidth for coming anycast requirement at source $s$ with end-to-end deadline D. This admission control is scalable.

## 5 Analysis Results

Network: The network considered in our experiments is ARPA network. Figure 2 shows the topology of the network. There are 56 nodes that are interconnected by links. Link bandwidth capacity is assumed to be 100Mbits, and 40 percent of link bandwidth is reserved for anycast flows. Every node is a router and has one host attached.

Traffic Model: We first take the ARPA network as shown in Fig.1, as an example. The network consists of 21 nodes. Assume an anycast flow's source is S={0} and corresponding recipients group G={5,9,10,13,14,15}, route set R={<0,1,5>, <0,1,5,9>, <0,2,7,10>, <0,1,5,9,14>, <0,1,5,9,14,13>, <0,2,7,10,15>}. There existing two flows from source 18 to 15 and 0 to 4, corresponding routes are <0,1,3,4> and <18,17,15 > respectively. Take $\sigma_A = \sigma = 640$, $\rho_A = \rho = 16$, $\alpha = 0.4$, $\varepsilon = 0.0000001$, D = 100, then r1=<0,1,5> is a selection of routes and the anycast is admitted.

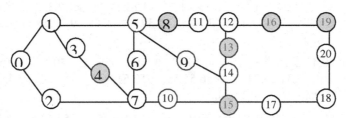

**Fig. 1.** APRA network

Our second performance is tested through 56 nodes of network as depictured in Fig. 2. We assume that the sources of anycast flows is S={1,56} and for each source, there are two anycast groups which consist 8 members. One is $G_{1,1} = G_{56,1} = \{5,9,20,23,34,35,42,53\}$, the others are $G_{1,2} = G_{56,2} = \{4,8,23,25,36,39,45,55\}$. We also assume that the route from each source to a destination is fixed. We use <p,...,q> to denote a route from node p to node q. We defined the length of a route as the number of hops (i.e. nodes) on the route.

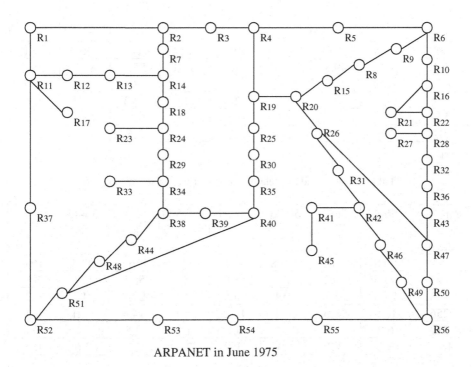

ARPANET in June 1975

**Fig. 2.**

We have tested the following paths with ns-2 simulations.

$R_{1,1}$={<1,2,3,4,5>,<1,2,3,4,5,6,9>,<1,2,3,4,19,20>,<1,2,7,14,18,24,23>,<1,2,7,1,18,24,29,34>,<1,2,3,4,19,25,30,35>,<1,11,37,52,53,54,55,56,49,46,42>,<1,11,57,52,53>}

$R_{1,2}$={<1,2,3,4>,<1,2,3,4,19,20,15,8>,<1,2,7,14,18,24,23>,<1,2,3,4,19,25>,<1,2,3,4,19,20,26,47,43,36>,<1,11,37,52,51,40,39>,<1,2,3,4,19,20,26,31,42,41,45>,<1,11,37,52,53,54,55>}

$R_{56,1}$={<56,50,47,26,20,19,4,5>,<56,50,47,26,20,15,8,9>,<56,50,47,26,20>,<56,55,54,53,52,51,40,39,38,34,29,24,23>,<56,55,54,53,52,51,40,39,38,34>,<56,55,54,53,52,51,40,35>,<56,49,46,42>,<56,55,54,53>}

$R_{56,2}$={<56,50,47,26,20,19,4>,<56,50,47,26,20,15,8>,<56,55,54,53,52,51,40,39,38,34,29,24,23>,<56,50,47,26,20,19,25>,<56,50,47,43,36>,<56,55,54,53,52,51,40,3>,<56,49,46,42,41,45>,<56,55>}

with the delay as shown in the following tables.

**Table 1.** $\sigma$=640 and the delay(s) varied with $\rho$ for source node 1

| Path Delay and Rate $\rho$ | 1-5 | 1-9 | 1-20 | 1-23 | 1-34 | 1-35 | 1-42 | 1-53 |
|---|---|---|---|---|---|---|---|---|
| 32 | 66.5 | 99.5 | 83.2 | 99.8 | 116.5 | 114.9 | 166.3 | 66.1 |
| 64 | 33.4 | 49.8 | 42.3 | 49.8 | 58.3 | 57.5 | 83.2 | 33.1 |
| 128 | 16.8 | 24.5 | 21.2 | 25.1 | 29.5 | 28.6 | 42.3 | 16.7 |
| 256 | 8.5 | 12.3 | 11.0 | 12.5 | 14.6 | 14.3 | 21.2 | 8.4 |
| 512 | 4.5 | 6.4 | 5.6 | 6.4 | 7.5 | 7.2 | 11.2 | 4.3 |
| 1024 | 2.4 | 3.3 | 2.9 | 3.3 | 3.9 | 3.5 | 5.7 | 2.3 |

**Table 2.** $\sigma$=640 and the delay(s) varied with $\rho$ for source node 56

| Pat/ Delay/ Rate $\rho$ | 56-4 | 56-8 | 56-23 | 56-25 | 56-36 | 56-39 | 56-45 | 56-55 |
|---|---|---|---|---|---|---|---|---|
| 32 | 99.8 | 101.2 | 199.8 | 99.6 | 67.4 | 116.3 | 83.4 | 16.6 |
| 64 | 49.5 | 50.2 | 101.1 | 48.6 | 33.6 | 58.2 | 41.6 | 8.3 |
| 128 | 24.9 | 25.1 | 50.1 | 24.5 | 16.7 | 29.1 | 21.1 | 4.2 |
| 256 | 12.5 | 12.6 | 25.1 | 12.2 | 8.3 | 14.9 | 11.1 | 2.1 |
| 512 | 6.2 | 6.3 | 12.6 | 6.1 | 4.2 | 7.5 | 5.1 | 1.1 |
| 1024 | 3.1 | 3.2 | 6.3 | 3.1 | 2.1 | 3.7 | 2.6 | 0.6 |

# 6  Summary and Future Work

We have studied admission control procedure for anycast flow with real-time application and presented real-time admission control algorithm for anycast flow. To the best of our knowledge, this is the first the study that addresses the issue on providing end-to-end delay analysis with real-time application for anycast flow. In our real-time admission control algorithm, we addressed scalability issue, i.e. our admission control algorithm is scalable as the number of anycast flow increases and the size of the network expands. Our approach focuses on deterministic guarantees of delay bound analysis based on network calculus [12][13]. We have tested our algorithms for 21 and 56 nodes of APAR networks and we found that indeed the end-to-end delay can be effectively calculated. However, our algorithms can be redesigned into distributed version that the delay may be evaluated by each node on the selected path. It is an interesting topic to extend the research on the stochastic cases and Differentiated Services for anycast flows and its combination with multicast flows.

# References

1.  S. Deering and R. Hinden, Internet Protocol version 6(Ipv6) specification, RFC2460, Deec.1998.
2.  R. Hinde and S.Derring, IP Version 6 Addressing Architecture, RFC 1884, Dec. 1995.
3.  S. Bhattacharjee, M. H. Ammar, E. W. Zegura, V. Shah and Z. Fei, Application-Layer Anycasting, Proceedings of IEEE INFOCOM'97, April 1997.
4.  D. Katabi and J. Wroclawski, A Framework for Scalable Global IP-Anycast (GIA), Proceeding of SIGCOMM'00, Aug. 2000.
5.  D. Xuan, W. Jia, W. Zhao and H. Zhu, A Routing Protocol for Anycast Messages, IEEE Transactions on Parallel and Distributed Systems, Vol. 11, No. 6, June 2000, pp. 571–588.
6.  W. Jia, D. Xuan and W. Zhao, Integrated Routing Algorithms for Anycast Messages, IEEE Communications Magazine, Vol. 38, No. 1, January 2000, pp. 48–53.
7.  W. Jia, G. Xu and W. Zhao, Integrated fault-tolerant multicast and anycast routing algorithms, IEE Proceeding of Computer Digital Technology, Vol. 147, No. 4, July 2000, pp. 266–274.
8.  S. Wang, D. Xuan, R. Bettati and W. Zhao, Proving Absolute Differentiated Services for Real-Time Applications in Static-Priority Scheduling Networks, IEEE INFOCOM 2001.
9.  A. Dailianas and A. Bovopoulis, Real-Time Admission Control Algorithms with Delay and Loss Guarantees in ATM networks, IEEE INFOCOM, 1994.
10. V. Firoiu, J. Kurose and D. Towsley, Efficient Admission Control for EDF Schedulers, IEEE INFOCOM, 1998.
11. B. Choi, D. Xuan, C. Li, R. Bettati and W. Zhao, Scalable QoS Guaranteed Communication Services for Real-time, Proceeding of IEEE ICDCS, 2000.
12. Rene L. Cruz, A Calculus for Network Delay, Part I, IEEE Transactions on Information Theory, Vol. 37, Jan. 1991.
13. Rene L. Cruz, A Calculus for Network Delay, Part II, IEEE Transactions on Information Theory, Vol. 37, Jan. 1991.
14. D. Xuan and W. Jia, "Distributed Admission Control for Anycast Flows with QoS Requirements", Proceedings IEEE ICDCS, Phoenix, USA, April 16-19, 2001, pp. 292–300.
15. W. Jia, H. Wang, M. Tang, and W. Zhao, "Effective Delay Control for High Rate Heterogeneous Real-time Flows", Proceedings IEEE ICDCS, May 19–22, 2003, Providence, Rhode Island, USA.

# Synergy: A Comprehensive Software Distributed Shared Memory System

Michael Hobbs, Jackie Silcock, and Andrzej Goscinski

School of Information Technology, Deakin University
Geelong, Victoria 3217, Australia.
{mick,jackie,ang}@deakin.edu.au

**Abstract.** Considerable research and development has been invested in software Distributed Shared Memory (DSM). The primary focus of this work has traditionally been on high performance and consistency protocols. Unfortunately, clusters present a number of challenges for any DSM systems not solvable through consistency protocols alone. These challenges relate to the ability of DSM systems to adjust to load fluctuations, computers being added/removed from the cluster, to deal with faults, and the ability to use DSM objects larger than the available physical memory. This paper introduces the Synergy DSM System and its integration with the virtual memory, group communication and process migration services of the Genesis Cluster Operating System.

## 1 Introduction

A cluster is an ideal alternative to a supercomputer. A dedicated cluster is generally built using commodity components: fast computers connected by fast networks. The success of this architecture for building high performance parallel machines is shown by the (increasing) number of the world's fastest computers that are built using the cluster architecture [1]. On the other hand, non-dedicated clusters based on common PCs and networks are widely available in many organisations. These clusters form a valuable and inexpensive resource that is not being taken advantage of.

DSM can be easily employed to harness the computational resources of a cluster. The area of software DSM has been the focus of considerable research for the last 10 years. Unfortunately, the primary thrust of this work has only been with the execution performance and protocols employed to maintain consistency between the shared DSM objects [2] [3]. We identified a need for addressing not only high performance but also ease of programming, ease of use and transparency and developed a software DSM system within an operating system (rather than as middleware) that offers services that satisfy these requirements [4]. A need for a more integrated approach to building DSM system was also advocated in [2].

Here we address major problems of currently available software DSM systems:
☐ DSM systems are difficult to program, use and do not support transparency;
☐ DSM processes are unable to move, leading to load imbalances;
☐ Poor (practically no) support for virtual memory;

M. Guo and L.T.Yang (Eds.): ISPA 2003, LNCS 2745, pp. 239–247, 2003.

☐ Poor support from fault tolerance services such as checkpointing; and
☐ Poor use of group communication in consistency protocols.

The culmination of these problems is that many DSM systems are inflexible in their operation. A common cause for this is that many DSM systems are implemented at the user level (library or middleware) and not fully integrated within an operating system. The goal of this paper is to present the design of the Genesis Synergy Distributed Shared Memory System, an advanced DSM system, fully integrated within an operating system, that addresses these problems.

## 2  Related Work

The well known DSM systems, Munin [3] and TreadMarks [5], have neglected ease of use, user friendliness, availability, transparency and fault tolerance. Application developers using Munin or TreadMarks must have significant understanding of both the application they are developing and the DSM system. In Munin programmers must label different variables according to the consistency protocol they require and in both systems they are required to have substantial input into the initialisation of DSM processes, by including the names as command line arguments or creating a file that contains a list of the computers that comprise the cluster [5], [3].

Many DSM systems only support the running of applications of the size that fits into the memory on a local machine. JIAJIA [6] is one of the few DSM systems that uses virtual memory to increase the size of DSM applications to larger than the size of local memory. Virtual memory is implemented in JIAJIA but the performance tests carried out are for application sizes that did not use virtual memory. The influence of virtual memory was never tested. Thus, the use of virtual memory is still open.

Research has been carried out on Network RAM [7] that uses DSM-type mechanisms to cache pages selected for replacement in the memory of remote computers rather than writing them to disk [8]. The purpose of this research was not to improve the performance of the applications but to address the problems of fault tolerance when using remote computers' memories as caches. Similarly, BFXM is a parallel file system model based on the mechanism of DSM that links the memory of all computers into a large cache reducing the need to save pages to disk [9].

Load balancing in DSM systems has been presented in [10], thread migration and loop scheduling in [11] [12], and migrating or replicating pages in [13]. In [12] the work described involves the comparison of performance between the migration of threads and data in the MCRL multithreaded DSM multiprocessor system. Many existing DSM systems allow users to create a set of DSM processes on designated computers. These processes remain on these computers until they exit [3] [6].

The need for availability, transparency and fault tolerance in DSM-based clusters has been strongly advocated in [14]. However, availability and transparency are not provided and fault tolerance is poor. Application developers experience difficulties using checkpoint systems, they must port library code and applications, there are restrictions imposed by these libraries, and their applications must be recompiled or relinked. Due to these difficulties only few developers employ checkpointing [15].

# 3  The Design of the Genesis DSM

## 3.1  Genesis Overview

Genesis is microkernel based operating system specifically designed and developed for the management of a computer cluster [16]. In this section we briefly discuss those components that are directly related to DSM, as shown in Figure 1.

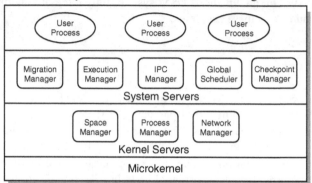

**Fig. 1.** Cluster Architecture

**Microkernel.** The microkernel is a small section of code that provides the bare minimum set of services that form a basic virtual machine. These services include handling of interrupts and exceptions, low level page management, scheduling and context switching of processes, as well as local inter-process communication. The remaining services normally provided by an operating system are provided by the kernel and system servers and form the core of Genesis.

**Kernel Servers.** The primary resources of a computer are managed and controlled in Genesis by a set of privileged, cooperating kernel server processes called managers. Those directly related to DSM include:

☐ Space Manager – a space is a region of memory, thus the role of this server is to manage the allocation, sharing and revocation of memory resources. It also supports virtual memory by mapping memory pages to disk. DSM is a component of the Space Manager.

☐ Process Manager – manages the information related to process control, execution and relationships among processes.

**System Servers.** The highest level management processes in the Genesis system are the system servers. The system servers that affect the proposed Synergy DSM (SDSM) system include:

☐ Migration Manager – coordinates the movement of an executing process from one computer to another. Process migration is an advanced service that enables dynamic load balancing as well as fault recovery (restoring checkpointed processes and moving processes of failing computers).

☐ Execution Manager – creates a process from a file (similar to the fork() and exec() combination in Unix) and duplicates a process either a heavy-weight or medium-weight (similar to fork() in Unix). In particular, it coordinates the single, multiple and group creation and duplication of processes on both local and remote computers, as directed by the Global Scheduler.

☐ IPC Manager – supports remote inter-process communication through the discovery and re-direction of messages to processes located on remote computers. It also supports group communication within sets of processes.

☐ Global Scheduler – supported by the Execution and Migration Managers is able to provide load balancing decisions at the instantiation of a process (initial placement) as well as during the execution of processes (dynamic load balancing); which are critical in spreading the computation load evenly over the cluster.

☐ Checkpoint Manager – enables checkpoints (by exploiting process duplication carried out by the Execution Manager) of processes to be taken, cooperates with other Checkpoint Managers to synchronise the building and storage of a coordinated checkpoint for the whole parallel application. In the event of a fault, the checkpoint can be restarted using services provided by the Migration Manager.

**User Processes.** User processes form the remaining entities in Genesis and access the services provided through the system servers, kernel servers (via RPCs) and the microkernel (via system calls). User applications are built to execute on the cluster as a whole and are unaware of which computer they execute on. This is achieved by making all resources uniquely identifiable over the entire distributed cluster.

## 3.2  Genesis DSM

We decided to embody DSM within the operating system in order to create a transparent, easy to use and program environment and achieve high execution performance of parallel applications [4]. Since DSM is essentially a memory management function, the Space Manager is the server into which the DSM system was integrated. This implies that the programmer is able to use the shared memory as though it were physically shared; hence, transparency is offered. Furthermore, because the DSM system is in the operating system itself and is able to use the low level operating system functions the efficiency is achieved.

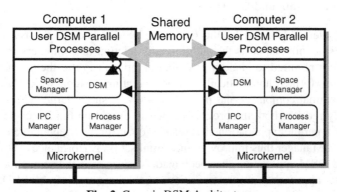

**Fig. 2.** Genesis DSM Architecture

To support memory sharing in a cluster, which employs message passing to allow processes to communicate, the DSM system is supported by the IPC Manager. This support is invisible to application programmers. Furthermore, because DSM parallel processes must be properly managed (including their creation, synchronisation when sharing a memory object, and co-ordination of their execution) the Process and Execution Managers support DSM system activities. The placement of the DSM system in Genesis and its interaction with these servers are shown in Figure 2.

When an application using DSM starts to execute, the parent process initialises the DSM system with a single primitive function. This function creates shared DSM objects and a set of processes. The latter operation is performed by the Execution Managers of remote computers, selected by the Global Scheduler.

The granularity of the shared memory object is an important issue in the design of a DSM system. As the memory unit of the Genesis Space is a page, it follows that the most appropriate object of sharing for the DSM system is a page.

The Genesis DSM system employs release consistency model (the memory is made consistent only when a critical region is exited), which is implemented using the write-update model [4]. Synchronisation of processes that share memory takes the form of semaphore type synchronisation for mutual exclusion. The semaphore is owned by the Space Manager on a particular computer which implies that gaining ownership of the semaphore is still mutually exclusive when more than one DSM process exists on the same computer. Barriers, used in Genesis to co-ordinate executing processes, are also controlled by the Space Manager but their management is centralised on one of the computers in the cluster.

# 4   Genesis Synergy DSM

We claim that the facilities provided by Genesis, such as virtual memory, process migration and process checkpointing; can be combined with the Genesis DSM facility to form an advanced DSM service called Synergy. The SDSM addresses many of the problems traditional DSM systems experience on non-dedicated clusters (Section 1).

## 4.1   Easy to Program and Use DSM

The first problem addressed by the Genesis SDSM relates to the role of the user. Genesis transparently supports the addition and deletion of computers from a cluster. The user is not required to identify available computers to run their application. This operation is performed automatically by the operating system, which hides from the user the individual computers and presents a view of single large 'virtual' computer, which greatly reduces both the programming and execution burden of the user. DSM processes of a parallel application are created concurrently on available computers by the Execution Manager thus improving the initialisation performance.

Coding of DSM applications has been made very easy as the semaphore-based mutual exclusion approach is in use to achieve synchronisation of shared DSM objects. The programmer is only required to add one statement into code of a parent and another statement into code of a child to allow the system to initialise parallel applications on a cluster.

## 4.2  DSM and Load Balancing

The second problem area addressed by the design of the Genesis SDSM is that of load imbalances between computers of the cluster which causes a reduction in the overall performance. Genesis supports process migration [17], enabling processes from over loaded computers to be moved to idle or lightly loaded computers identified by the Global Scheduler; dynamically balancing the load over the cluster.

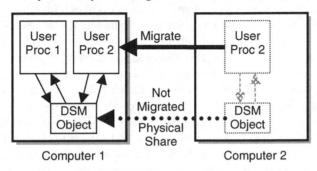

**Fig. 3.** DSM and Migration

To support the migration of processes accessing shared DSM objects, the process migration service must also support the movement of the shared DSM objects. Two issues are introduced here, the movement of a process and its DSM object to a computer that is currently not being used by another process of the DSM parallel application; and when the destination computer already has one (or more) of the processes of the DSM parallel applications and thus, already has a DSM object on that computer. In the first instance, the DSM object is simply migrated to the destination computer, updating the DSM data structures in the Space Manager to reflect this change. In the second instance, since the DSM object is a 'copy' of the same data on both computers it is not necessary to migrate the DSM object to the destination computer, just the process. The migrated process, once on the destination computer, can then physically share the original DSM object. This actually requires the migration of less data than in the first case. Figure 3 demonstrates this situation, where user process 2 is migrated to a computer already executing a process of the same parallel application.

## 4.3  DSM and Virtual Memory

It is possible for a shared DSM object to use the services of virtual memory, thus gaining the benefits of an overall improvement of memory utilisation and the use of very large DSM objects. To achieve this, the DSM system can mark a page to be flushed to disk. Before this page can be written to disk, it must be synchronised with the other DSM objects; this is a normal part of the DSM consistency operation. Once made consistent, it can be then put to disk; this status is then recorded in the DSM data structures (held within the Space Manager). This is a simple extension to the currently available consistency protocols, where a page is either owned locally, or owned remotely. Where a page is located on disk, it is as if the page is 'remote' to all of the DSM objects.

## 4.4 DSM and Fault Tolerance

As the number of computers within a cluster and the execution time of the parallel application increases, the probability that an error will occur also increases. It is not satisfactory to simply restart a parallel application in event of a fault.

Genesis uses coordinated checkpointing that requires that non-deterministic events such as process interacting with each other or with the operating system are prevented during the creation of checkpoints [18]. The messages used for the interaction are then included in the checkpoints of the sending process. The checkpointing facility provides high performance and low overhead by allowing the processes of a parallel application to continue their execution during the creation of checkpoints.

The creation of checkpoints is controlled by the Checkpoint Manager that is located on each computer of a cluster, and invokes the kernel servers to create a checkpoint of processes on the same computer. Furthermore, the coordinating Checkpoint Manager (located on the computer where the parallel application was created) coordinates the blocking of non-deterministic events, creating checkpoints for an application, and releasing the non-deterministic events. It directs the creation of checkpoints for a parallel application by sending requests to the remote Checkpoint Managers to perform operations that are relevant to the current stage of checkpointing.

Applications are recovered form faults by restoring checkpointed processes. The Migration Manager is employed to provide this service.

## 4.5 DSM and Group Communication

Genesis also supports group communication services [19], which greatly reduces the load on the network. This enables fast and efficient communication of DSM update information, as needed by the consistency protocols and checkpointing service. In Genesis, rather than to save checkpoints on a central disk, they are stored in memories of some computers of the cluster using at-least-k delivery semantics of group communication.

To track the DSM processes of a parallel application, group membership management mechanisms are used. This is achieved by creating and managing a process group on behalf of the application. The application processes are then enrolled in this process group as they are created and withdrawn when they exit.

## 5  Summary and Future Work

The design of the Genesis SDSM is an outcome of our identification and investigation of problems that are present in existing software based DSM systems. We realised that many of these problems could be addressed by integrating the existing DSM system with the services that are provided by the Genesis cluster operating system.

The Genesis SDSM system will provide a distributed shared memory system that is easy to program and use; has DSM processes that can be migrated from heavily loaded to idle or lightly loaded computers; supports the creation and use of DSM objects that are larger than the amount of physical memory available on the computers; supports the checkpointing of DSM process and recovery from faults; and possesses the ability to improve consistency protocols and execution performance of checkpointing through the use of group communication. These features combine to form a unique DSM system that is fully transparent, reliable and able to support the execution of high performance parallel applications on non-dedicated clusters.

Currently the Genesis system executes on the Sun3/50 and Intel x86 clusters. Individually, the advanced services of DSM, process migration, load balancing, virtual memory, checkpointing and group communication have all been implemented and tested [16]. We are at the stage of integrating the DSM system with the virtual memory, modifying the consistency code to utilise group communication, and to support the migration of DSM spaces.

## References

1.  Web Site. http://www.top500.org. November, 2002. Last accessed 6th December, 2002.
2.  L. Iftode and J.Singh. Shared Virtual Memory: Progress and Challenges, Shared Virtual Memory: Progress and Challenges. Proc. of the IEEE, Vol 87. No. 3, March 1999.
3.  J. Carter, J. Bennett, and W. Zwaenepoel. Techniques for Reducing Consistency-Related Communication in Distributed Shared-Memory Systems. ACM Transactions on Computer Systems, Vol. 13 No. 3, August 1995.
4.  J. Silcock and A. Goscinski. The RHODOS DSM System. Microprocessor and Microsystems, 22(3–4), 183–196, 1998.
5.  Concurrent Programming with TreadMarks, "ParallelTools", L.L.C. 1994.
6.  W. Shi and Z. Tang. Intervals to Evaluating Distributed Shared Memory Systems. IEEE TCCA Newsletter, pp 3–10, August 1998.
7.  D. Pnevmatikatos and E. P. Markatos and G. Magklis and S. Ioannidis. On Using Network {RAM} as a Non-volatile Buffer. Cluster Computing, 2(4), 295–303, 1999.
8.  E.P. Markatos and G. Dramitinos. Implementation of a Reliable Remote Memory Pager. In Proc. of the 1996 Usenix Technical Conference, pp 177–190, January 1996.
9.  Q. Li, J. Jing, and L. Xie. BFXM: A Parallel File System Model Based on the Mechanism of Distributed Shared Memory. ACM Operating Systems Review, 31(4):30–40, October 1997.
10. I. Zoraja, G. Rackl, and T. Ludwig. Towards Monitoring in Parallel and Distributed Systems. In Proc. of SoftCOM'99, pp 133–141, October 1999.

11.  W. Shi, W. Hu, Z. Tang and M. Eskicioglu. Dynamic Task Migration in Home-based Software DSM Systems. In Proc of the 8th IEEE International Symposium on High Performance Distributed Computing, Redondo Beach, California August 1999.
12.  W.C. Hsieh. Dynamic Computation Migration in Distributed Shared Memory Systems. PhD Thesis, Massachusetts Institute of Technology, Cambridge, MA, September 1995. Available as MIT/LCS/TR–665.
13.  S. Dwarkadas, N. Hardavellas, L. Kontothanassis, R. Nikhil and R. Stets. Cashmere-VLM: Remote Memory Paging for Software Distributed Shared Memory. In Proc. of IPPS'99, April 1999.
14.  C. Morin, R. Lottiaux and A.–M. Kermarrec. A Two-level Checkpoint Algorithm in a Highly-available Parallel Single Level Store System. In Proc. of the workshop on Distributed Shared Memory on Clusters (CCGrid–01), Brisbane (Australia), May 2001.
15.  A. Agbaria and J. Plank. Design, Implementation, and Performance of Checkpointing in NetSolve, In Proc. Int'l Conf. on Dependable Systems and Networks, FTCS–30 and DCCA–8. New York, New York, June 2000.
16.  A. Goscinski, M. Hobbs and J. Silcock. Genesis: An Efficient, Transparent and Easy to Use Cluster-based Operating System. Parallel Computing, 28(4), pp 557–606, 2002.
17.  D. De Paoli and A. Goscinski. The RHODOS Migration Facility. The Journal of Systems and Software, Volume 40:51–65, Elsevier Science Inc., New York, 1998.
18.  J. Rough and A. Goscinski. Exploiting Operating System Services to Efficiently Checkpoint Parallel Applications in GENESIS, Proc. 5th IEEE Inter. Conf. on Algorithms and Architectures for Parallel Processing (ICA3PP 2002), Beijing, October 2002.
19.  J. Rough and A. Goscinski. A Group Communication Facility for Reliable Computing on Clusters, Proc. ISCA International Conference on Parallel and Distributed Computing Systems (PDCS 2001), ISCA, Cary, NC, USA, 2001.

# On the Design of a Register Queue Based Processor Architecture (FaRM-rq)

Ben A. Abderazek, Soichi Shigeta, Tsutomu Yoshinaga, and Masahiro Sowa

Graduate School of Information Systems
The University of Electro-Communications
1-5-1 Chofugaoka, Chofu-shi, 182-8585 Tokyo, Japan
{ben,shigeta,yosinaga,sowa}@is.uec.ac.jp
http://www.sowa.is.uec.ac.jp

**Abstract.** We propose in this paper a processor architecture that supports multi instructions set through run time functional assignment algorithm (RUNFA). The above processor, which is named Functional Assignment Register Microprocessor (FaRM-rq) supports queue and register based instruction set architecture and functions into different modes: (1) R-mode (FRM) - when switched for register based instructions support, and (2) Q-mode (FQM) - when switched for Queue based instructions support. The entities share a common data path and may operate independently though not in parallel.

In FRM mode, the machine's shared storage unit (SSU) behaves as a conventional register file. However, in FQM mode, the system organizes the SSU access as a first-in-first-out latches, thus accesses concentrate around a small window and the addressing of registers is implicit trough the Queue head and tail pointers.

First, we present the novel aspects of the FaRM-rq[1] architecture. Then, we give the novel FQM fundamentals and the principles underlying the architecture.

## 1 Introduction

As demand for increased performance in microprocessor continues, new architectures are required to meet this demand. Implementations of existing architecture are quickly reaching their limits as increases in current superscalar Out-of-Order issue are bounded by circuit complexity[9,14,16], and performance increase, due to technology improvement, are approaching their limit.

From another hand, the motivation for the design of a new architecture generally arises from the technological development, which changed gradually the architecture parameters traditionally used in the computer architecture. With these growing changes and challenges, the computer architects are faced with answering the question what functionality has to be put on a single processor chip, giving an extra performance edge. Furthermore, as we enter into an era

---

[1] The above architecture embraces multiprogramming languages and will combine the best features of Queue , Register and Stack models of computing.

M. Guo and L.T.Yang (Eds.): ISPA 2003, LNCS 2745, pp. 248–262, 2003.
© Springer-Verlag Berlin Heidelberg 2003

of continued demand for simple, faster and compatible processors, it becomes extremely unpractical and costly to develop a separate processor for each type of application.

Queue based architectures ideas were first proposed by Sowa et al. [1,8,15, 17] and Bruno[7,11]. These processors use FIFO data structure as the underlying mechanism for results and operand manipulations; that is, at the execution stage, each instruction removes the required number of operands from the front of an operand Queue (OPQ), performs some computations and stores the result back into the tail of the OPQ. However, for several reasons, theses architectures (Queue based) did not enjoy the success of the conventional Register based (Load/Store) processors. One major reason is that, when the Queue computing model was proposed more than two decades ago, neither Stack based architecture nor Queue computing model seemed to be important paradigms in the foreseeable future. But, things have changed since then: Internet, Embedded, and home network applications are becoming very attractive nowadays.

To this end, and in order to meet the demanding requirements of compatibility and high hardware usability relative to single instruction set processor, we have decided to combine the advantages of a novel Queue based architecture with the ones of register-based (load/store) architecture[3,14].

Our proposed architecture will integrate, then, multi executions models in a single shared processor through run time assignment algorithm (RUNFA) without considerable additionel hardware complexity.

The above project, which started a couple of years ago at Sowa Laboratory[6], is named functional assignment register microprocessor (FaRM). It features simple pipeline, compact Queue based instruction set architecture, and is targeted for new class of terminals requiring small memory footprints and short programs run-times.

The rest of this paper is organized as follow: section two gives the related work. In section three, we give the FQM architecture and computing fundamental. System architecture description is given in section four. Finally, we give our concluding remarks and future work in the last section

## 2  Previous Work

Queues are well known to computer architecture designers as first-in-first-out data structures. As an attempt to improve overall processor performance, designers have used these structures as matching devices to interface two subsystems with different duty ycles[4].

Queues data structures have also a number of other interesting properties that make them useful in supporting processor design's functions efficiently. They were proposed to support instructions' operands and results manipulations in a Queue computing environment. Historically, the idea is traced back to more than two decades. Sowa [1,8,15,18] investigated the design constraints of a superscalar processor architecture based on Queue computation model. Bruno [7,11] also investigated a so called indexed Queue machine architecture that uses Queue

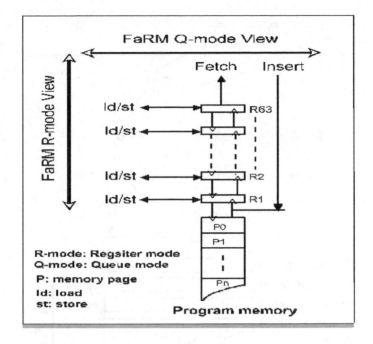

**Fig. 1.** The Shared Storage Unit as viewed by FQM and FRM modes

as the underlying mechanism for operands and results manipulations. At the execution stage of the above architecture, each instruction removes the required number of operands from the front of the Queue, performs some computations and stores the result back into the Queue at a specified offsets. A major problem with the above architecture is that it requires the relocation of a potentially large number of operands. Also there is a possiblility that the result stored by one instruction may overwrite that of an earlier one.

## 3    FQM Function Overview

The proposed FQM has operations in its instructions set which implicitly references an operand Queue (OPQ), just as SEM has operations, which implicitly references an operand stack. Each instruction removes the required number of operands from the head of the OPQ, performs some computations, and returns the result to the tail of the OPQ, which is implemented as a circular Queue. The OPQ occupies continuous storage locations and can be dynamically extended. A special register, named Queue head (QH) pointer, holds the address of the first operand in the OPQ. Operands are retrieved from the front of the OPQ by reading the location indicated by the QH pointer. Immediately after retrieving an operand, the QH pointer is automatically adjusted so that it points to the next operand. Results are returned to the tail of the OPQ indicated by a Queue tail (QT) pointer.

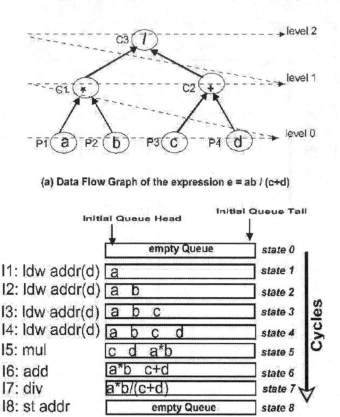

(a) Data Flow Graph of the expression e = ab / (c+d)

(b) Operand Queue Contents

**Fig. 2.** FQM Computing Fundamental. The arithmetic operations correspond to the internal nodes of the parse tree and the fetch operations correspond to the leaf node of the parse tree. Note that in FQM mode, instructions [I1,I2, I3, I4] can be first executed in parallel, then [I5, I6] can be simultaneously proceeded . This leads to about 50% speedup.

## 3.1  FQM's Queue Manipulation

The Queue manipulation is assured by a *Shared Storage Control Unit (SSCU)* and is the the backbone of the SSU unit. It performs basically the following four tasks:

1. Checks the data validity bit (DVB) for each OPQ entry
2. Controls the QH, QT and a life Queue head (LQH). The LQH is used to avoid overwriting (Queue overflow) life data within the OPQ. For each returned result , the SSCU compares the QT pointer value to the LQH pointer value and returns the comparison result to FaRM-rq's issue unit (IU). The issue unit's hardware uses the above value to issue secure instructions in parallel.
3. Handles the OPQ overflow and underflow
4. Allocates new logical Queue for each context switch.

```
ldw addr(d0)  ; assume that "d" is in the location &(addr + d0)
ldw addr(d1)  ; assume that "e" is in the location &(addr + d1)
ldw addr(d3)  ; assume that "b" is in the location &(addr + d3)
ldw addr(d2)  ; assume that "c" is in the location &(addr + d2)
add;
ldw addr(d3)  ;assume that "f" is in the location &(addr + d3)
mul
div
add
stw
```

*(a) Assembly code for h= b\*c + (d+e)/f*

```
OPQ_{s0}:--
OPQ_{s1}:d
OPQ_{s2}:d,e
OPQ_{s3}:d,e,b
OPQ_{s4}:d,e,b,c
OPQ_{s5}:b,c,d+e
OPQ_{s6}:b,c,d+e,f
OPQ_{s7}:d+e,f,b*d
OPQ_{s8}:b*c,(d+e)/f
OPQ_{s9}:b*c+(d+e)/f
OPQ_{s10}:--
```

*(b)  Queue Contents at each cycle*

**Fig. 3.** Sample Queue Instructions Sequence

## 3.2   FQM's Instructions Generation

The FQM instructions sequence generation can be obtained by traversing a given parse (binary) tree in a new traversal called level-Order-Scan-Tree (LOST)[3]. The LOST traversal is done by visiting the nodes of a parse tree from the deepest to the shallowest levels and from left to right within each level in the tree. In[3, 14] we showed that the FQM's instructions generation can be used to evaluate an arbitrary expression and the instructions sequence for an arbitrary arithmetic expression can be derived efficiently from the parse tree for that expression.

A simple example to demonstrate the basic FQM instruction generations is given in Fig. 2. The (\*) is a multiply operator, (+) is an addition operator, and (/) is a division operator.

The OPQ contents after each instruction processing is shown in Fig. 2(b). The *mul* mnemonic is a multiply operation, *add* is an addition operations and *div* is a division operations. Notice in the above example that instructions *I1, I2, I3 and I4* can be executed in parallel. Instructions *I5 and I6* can be also executed in parallel when their operands are available at the OPQ.

In FQM mode, independent instructions are dynamically detected and executed in parallel (discussed later).

## 3.3   FQM Sample Instructions Sequence

The complete mathematical theory for the FQM's instructions sequence generation can be found in[3,14]. We showed in the above mathematical theory that the FQM instructions sequence can be easily and correctly generated from a

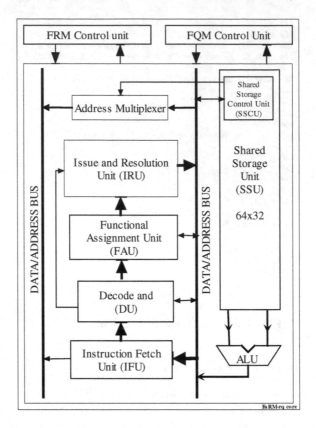

**Fig. 4.** System Architecture Basic Block Diagram

parse tree. It was also proved in that the FQM can be used to evaluate any given expression.

Consider the simple example shown in Fig. 3 (a). In this example, the instructions flow is obtained by traversing the corresponding parse tree using a new traversal called level-order-scan-tree[5]. The OPQ contents at each cycle is given in Fig. 3 (b). Note that the front of the OPQ is on the left. However, in the case of stack execution model, the top of the operand stack is on the left.

Also an important difference between the stack execution model and the FQM model is the order of operands for dyadic operators. In the stack model, the left operand of a dyadic operator is pushed first, followed by the right operand. Similarly, on the FQM mode the left operand of a dyadic operator is enqueued first followed by the right operand.

## 4  FaRM-rq Architectural Overview

As illustrated in Fig. 4, the architecture has a shared storage unit (SSU) consisting of 64 32-bit registers. The machine functions in two different modes and has five pipeline stages. During the first stage, instructions are read from the instruction memory (Instruction fetch stage). At the second stage, instructions are decoded and assignment of functional unit and storage locations is performed. Instructions are issued in the third stage (Issue). IN FQM mode, the issue hardware must check the OPQ and memory dependencies. The algorithm to check a so called *Safe-Issue* is as follow:

Assume that $I_1, I_2, \cdots, I_{n-1}, I_n$ are instructions which reside in the issue buffer within the issue unit.

Assume that: $LQH_1, LQH_2, \cdots, LQH_{n-1}, LQH_n$ are the corresponding LQH values of $I_1, I_2, \cdots, I_{n-1}, I_n$.

Assume that: $QT_1, QT_2, \cdots, QT_{n-1}, QT_n$ are the corresponding QT values of $I_1, I_2, \cdots, I_{n-1}, I_n$

if $QT_1 < all(LQH_2, \cdots, LQH_n) \Longrightarrow$ Issue

if $QT_2 < LQH_1$ and $LQH_2$ ¡ all $(LQH_3, \cdots, LQH_n) \Longrightarrow$ Issue

$\cdots$

if $QT_i < all(LQH_1, \cdots, LQH_{i-1})$ and $QT_i < all(LQH_{i+1}, \cdots, LQH_n) \Longrightarrow$ Issue

For all inverse cases $\Longrightarrow$ Wait

In the fourth stage, instructions are executed (Execute) and the sast stage, the SSU unit is updated and data memory access takes place (write Back).

## 4.1   Programming Models

The FaRM-rq system works in two different modes and with two programming models: (1) R-mode (FRM): to support conventional register based binary applications and (2) Q-mode (FQM): to support the novel Queue based binary applications. The processor has two control units, one data path, and a mode bit which keeps track of which control unit is to be in operation. The two modes communicate through the SSU unit. A schematic of the two mode views is illustrated in Fig. 1. In FQM mode, each instruction removes the required number of operands from the head of the OPQ, performs a computation and stores its result at the tail of the OPQ.

In FRM, the SSU behaves as a conventional register file. However, in FQM, the system organizes the SSU access as a FIFO latches, thus accesses concentrate around a small window and the addressing of registers is implicit trough the Queue head and tail pointers.

## 4.2   The SSU Design Considerations

In R-mode, the SSU unit is seen as a conventional register file with N registers. The program counter and other special purpose registers are included in the register file. However, in FQM mode, the SSU unit is seen as a circular Queue with $N/2$ elements as illustrated in Fig. 5.The other $N/2$ elements are used as storage registers for internal functions.

After reset, the kernel will boot in FRM mode. Upon finishing the initialization phase, it switches to FQM mode and executes the Queue programs until

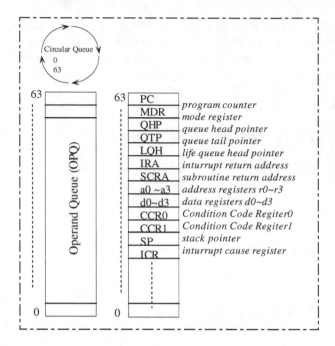

**Fig. 5.** SSU Unit when Viewed by the Queue Control Unit (QCU)

(1) an interrupt occurs, (2) an unrecognized instruction occurs or (3) the special designated Queue binary for switching to RQM mode occurs. The FaRM-rq processor continues , then, excution until a "switchover" instruction clears the mode register (MDR) defining the mode operation.

The FQM's operand Queue is implemented as a circular Queue . When the operand Queue is full, the SSCU continues to use the program memory as storage.

## 4.3   The SSU Design Trends

*Area:* The area of the SSU is the product of the number of entries (registers) R, the number of bits per entry, b, and the size of an entry cell. The layout of a register cell, given in Fig. 6 (a), shows that each cell is $(w + p)(h + p)$ girds: $(w + p)$ wire track wide, $(h + p)$ wire track high, $p$ word-line in one dimension, $p$ bit-lines in the other, and $wh$ grids for the storage cell, power, and ground. Each port requires one wire track for a *bit-line* to access the data.

*Delay:* As with a general register file, the delay of the SSU is composed of *wire-propagation delay* (WPD) and *fan propagation delay* (FPD). The WPD is the minimum time of flight across a wire, which grows linearly with distance, assuming optimally spaced repeaters. The fan-in/fan-out delay is the minimum drive delay of a lumped capacitive load using a buffer chain, which grows logarithmically with capacitance[13]. As shown in Fig. 6 (b), to access a register cell within the SSU unit, a signal must traverse a *word-line* of length $(w + p)bR^{1/2}$

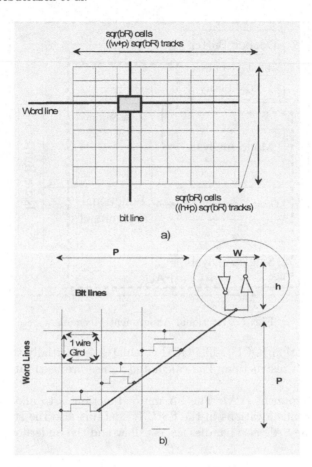

**Fig. 6.** Queue Design Trends:(a) Register Cell Access, (b) Register Cell Schematic

and then a *bit-line* of $(h + p)bR^{1/2}$, resulting in a delay that is proportional to $pR^{1/2}$. The access time is dominated by the *fan-out* of the *word-line* and the *fan-in* of the *bit-line*, which is a function of the number of entries within the SSU unit.

## 4.4    FAU Mechanism

The functional assignment unit (FAU), which is the backbone component of the FaRM-rq architecture, is shown in Fig. 7. The FAU mainly consists of the following components:

Binary File Decoder (BFD): The BFD major role is to determine the type of the file being fetched.

Mode Analysis: The mode Analysis unit's major role is set/reset the mode register (MDR) in the mode switch unit, which is responsible for switching between modes and also finding the appropriate execution model for a binary or a part of binary application.

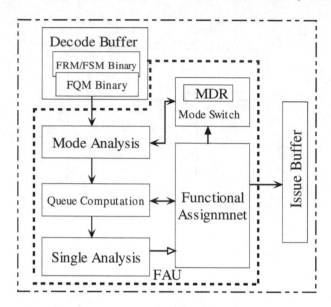

**Fig. 7.** Functional Assignment Mechanism

Queue Computation (QCU): The QCU calculates sequentially the QH and QT pointers for each instruction. The calculated values are used later by the issue unit hardware.

Functional Assignment (FA): The FA major function is to allocate functional units and operands locations in the SSU. It contains also the storage manager unit (SAU). The SAU also handles the overflow and the underflow of the OPQ.

## 5    FQM Instruction Set Architecture

All the instructions are byte addressed and provide access for bytes, half words, words, and double words. Bellow we will discuss the Instructions set design onsiderations for the FQM mode, which is our major concern in this paper.

### 5.1    Memory Type Instructions (M-Type)

The M-type, shown in Fig. 8, consists of all load and store operations. When data must be obtained from/sent to memory, the M-type instructions are needed. The *op* field is 6-bit and is used for operation coding. The *d* field is 2-bit and is used to select one of four data registers. The *addr* field is 8-bit offset.

For load instructions (i.e. lw) the contents of the *d* registers are added to the 8-bit offset to form the 32-bit address of the memory word. The word is loaded from memory to a Queue entry within the OPQ pointed by the Queue tail pointer (QT). In Fig. 9 (b), the memory instruction would be decoded as *load the 8 bit byte at memory location [contents of d0] + 0x52 into the Queue tail* pointed by the Queue tail (QT) pointer.

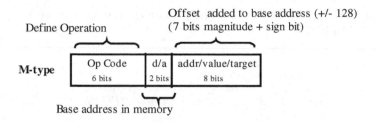

**Fig. 8.** Memory instructions (M-type) format

The store instruction has exactly the same format as load, and use the same memory calculation method to form memory addresses. However, for store instructions the data to be stored are found from the head of the operand Queue (OPQ) indicated by the Queue head (QH) pointer. In Fig. 9(a), the memory instruction would be decoded as *store the 32 bit word of the OPQ entry indicated by the QH at memory location [contents of d1] + 0x53*.

**Memory Address Extension:** In M-type instructions, the offset is only 8-bits wide; that is the address space range (from the base address) is only 128 memory slots. This may not be large enough for real applications. To cope with this address "shortage", we adopted the idea proposed by Sowa[15]. In the above idea, the compiler uses static optimizations techniques and automatically inserts (when needed) a convey instruction before each load or store instruction. The convey instruction is simply an instruction which forwards its operand (offset) to the consecutive load or store offset field. That is, when a convey instruction is inserted before a load or store instruction, the processor combines the convey instruction offset with the current load or store instruction offset and the

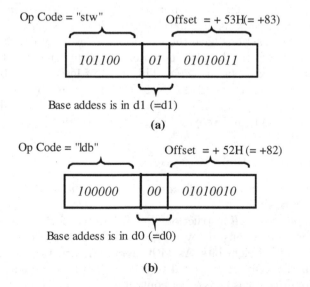

**Fig. 9.** Load and Store instructions internal coding example

data register to find the effective address. The convey instruction untilizations is illustrated in Fig. 10.

```
; address space extension
covop 25H      ; convey 25H address (offset)
ldb    12H(d0) ; load data from mem[25H(12H(d0)]
..
..
..
..
addp  4        ;
stw   24H(d1) ; store word at mem(24h(d1))
```

**Fig. 10.** Address space extention

## 5.2   Data/Address Register Instructions

The instruction set are designed with four data registers (d0~d3) and four address (a0~a4)) registers. These registers are used as base addresses for memory and control instructions respectively. The control instructions, which will be described later, consist of jump, loop, call, and interrupt instructions. The data/address registers are general purpose; that is they are visible to the programmer. These registers are 32-bits wide. Therefore, to set or reset one 32-bits address register, four instructions (sethh, sethl, setlh, setll) are needed. It may seam that the it set/reset operations are costly since four instructions are needed to set one address or data register. However, from our preliminary evaluations, operations on these registers occur not so often within a give application. Figure 11 is an example showing how data register *d0* is set with *setxx* instructions. Note that these instructions have the same format as M-type instructions. The data/address registers can be also incremented or decremented by the *inc* instruction. The syntax is: *inc a, value.* This type of instructions belongs to the I-type instructions shown in Fig. 12. Note that the range of the *value* operand is: $-8, -7, \cdots, < value ¡ +1, +2, \cdots, +8$. The I-type instruction also consists of *swi* (software interrupt) and *setr* (set register) instructions.

## 5.3   Control Instructions (C-Type)

The control instructions consist of *move, branch, jump, loop, call, interrupt, and barrier* instructions.

The *jump, loop and call* instructions have the same format as the previously defined M-type instructions. They all use *a* register as a base address register and an offset target of eight bits. As with memory instructions, target addresses of these instructions can be extended to sixteen bits by *convey* instruction. The C-type shown in Fig. 13 also has other control instruction with only one operand.

## 5.4    Transfer Instructions

The FQM supports four types of control flow (transfer) change: (1) Barrier-Branch, (2) Jump, (3) Procedure call and (4) Procedure return. As illustrated in Fig. 13, the target address (t) of these instructions is always explicitly specified in the instruction. Because the explicit target (displacement) value, which will be added to the fetch counter to find the real target address (RTA), is only 8-bits the *convey* instruction's offset can be combined with the transfer instructions' explicit target to extend the RTA space.

**Branch Instruction:** The branch instructions belong to the C-type. To avoid having too much work per instruction, the branch instruction resolution is divided into tasks (1) whether the branch in taken (with comparison instruction) and (2) the branch target address (address calculation). One of the most noticeable properties of the FQM branches is that a large number of the comparisons are simple tests, and a large number are comparison with zero. According to the type of the condition the comparison instruction compares two entries obtained from the head of the OPQ and insert the result (true/false) to a condition code

```
; set data register d0 with address A4121B45H
sethh  d0, A4H   ; set bits 23~31 of register d0
sethl  d0, 12H   ; set bits 16~24 of register d0
setlh  d0, 1BH   ; set bits 8~15 of register d0
setll  d0, 45H   ; set bits 0~7 t of register d0
; address space extension
covop 25H        ; convey 25H address (offset)
ldb     12H(d0) ; load data from mem[25H(12H(d0)]
..

..
addp  4          ;
strw   24H(d1) ; store word at mem(24h(d1))
```

**Fig. 11.** Address register setting example

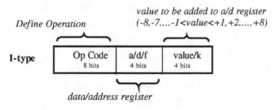

**Fig. 12.** I-type Instruction Format

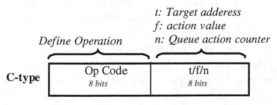

**Fig. 13.** C-type Instruction Format

(CC), which is automatically checked by the branch instruction. In our implementation, branches are also barrier instructions. That is, all instruction preceding the branch instructions should complete execution before new instructions (branch successor instructions) can be issued.

**Barrier Instructions:** This type consists of *halt, barrier, SerialOn, and SerialOff* instructions. These instructions are designed to control the execution and the process type of instructions.

*Queue Control Instruction (QCI):* The QCI consists of *stpqh (stop Queue head), stplgh (stop life Queue head autqh (automatic Queue head), and autlqh (automatic life Queue head).* These instruction are designed to control the life of data within the (OPQ).

### 5.5 Producer Order Instructions (P-Type)

This type (P-type) consists of about 70% of the total instructions in FQM execution. The P-type consists of all single and double word computing, logical, compare, and conversion instructions. The format of the P-type instruction is illustrated in the Fig. 5.5. We have to note that both integer and floating-point operations are supported.

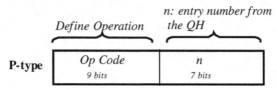

**Fig. 14.** P-type Instruction Format

## 6    Conclusions

We have proposed a hybrid processor architecture that supports Register and Queue based instructions set in a shared resources single processor core. Our hybrid architecture addresses important design challenges by featuring two programming models: (1) R-mode (when switched for register based instructions support), and (2) Q-mode (when switched for Queue based instructions support). We have also presented the novel aspects of the FaRM-rq architecture as well as the novel FQM mode architecture.

The FaRM-rq architecture is expected to increase the processor resources usability, relative to single instruction set processor and also to support the novel Queue architecture, which is targeted for a new class of terminals requiring small memory footprints and short programs run-times.

Our feature work is to investigate the parallelism exploitation and pipelining techniques within the FQM mode. In order to evaluate the real performance and the initial physical estimate of the proposed architecture, real evaluation will take place via several layers of simulation, ranging from high-level models, to logic level models.

# References

1. Okamoto S., Suzuki A., Maeda A., Sowa M.: Design of a Superscalar Processor Based on Queue Machine Computation Model. IEEE PACRIM99, (1999) 151–154
2. Sohi G.: Instructions Issue logic for high-performance, interruptible, Multiple Functional Unit, Pipelined Computer. IEEE Trans. on Computers, vol.39, No.3,(1990) 349–359
3. Abderazek B. A., Kirilka N., Sowa M.: FARM-Queue Mode: On a Practical Queue Execution model. Proc. of the Int. Conf. on Circuits and Systems, Computers and Communications, Tokushima, (2001) 939–944
4. Michael K. M., Harvey G.C.: Processor Implementations Using Queues. IEEE, Micro, (1995) 58–66
5. Philip K.: Stack Computers, the new Wave. Mountain View Press (1989)
6. Sowa Laboratory: http://www.sowa.is.uec.ac.jp
7. Bruno R., Carla V.: Data Flow on Queue Machines. 12th Int. IEEE Symposium on Computer Architecture,(1995) 342–351
8. Suzuki H., Shusuke O., Maeda A., Sowa M.: Implementation and evaluation of a Superscalar Processor Based on Queue Machine Computation Model. IPSJ SIG, Vol.99, No. 21 (1999) 91–96
9. Smith J. E., Sohi G. S.: The microarchitecture of Superscalar processors. Proceedings of the IEEE, vol. 83, (no. 12), (1995) 1609–1624
10. Silc J., Robic B., Ungerer T.: Processor Architecture: From Dataflow to Superscalar and Beyond. Springer-Verlag, Berlin, Heidelberg, New York (1999)
11. Periss B. R.: Data Flow on a Queue Machine. Doctoral thesis, Department of Electrical Engineering, University of Toronto, Toronto (1987)
12. Palacharia, Joupi N. P, Smith J.E: Complexity-Effective Superscalar Processor. Ph.D. dissertation, Univ. of Wisconsin (1998)
13. Abderazek B.A., Sowa M.: DRA: Dynamic Register Allocator Mechanism for FaRM Microprocessor. The 3rd International Workshop on Advanced Parallel Processing Technologies, IWAPPT99, (1999) 131–136
14. Abderazek B.A.: Dynamic Instructions Issue Algorithm and a Queue Execution Model Toward the Design of a Hybrid Processor Architecture. PhD. Thesis, IS Graduate School, Univ. of Electro-Communications, (2002)
15. Sowa M.: Fundamental of Queue machine. The Univ. of Electro-Communications, Sowa Laboratory, Technical Reports SLL30305, (2003)
16. Radhakrishnan R., Talla D., John L. K.: Allowing for ILP in an Embedded Java Processor. Proceedings of IEEE/ACM International Symposium on Computer Architecture, Vancouver, CA, (2000) 294–305
17. Sowa M.: Queue Processor Instruction Set Design. The Univ. of Electro-Communications, Sowa laboratory, Technical Report SLL97301, (1997)
18. Sowa M., Abderazek B.A, Shigeta S., Nikolova K., D. Yoshinaga T. Proposal and Design of a Parallel Queue Processor Architecture (PQP), 14th IASTED Int. Conf. on Parallel and Distributed Computing and System, Cambridge, USA, (2002) 554–560

# A Scheme of Interactive Data Mining Support System in Parallel and Distributed Environment

Zhen Liu[1], Shinichi Kamohara[1], and Minyi Guo[2]

[1]Faculty of Human Environment, Nagasaki Institute of Applied Science,
536 Aba-machi, Nagasaki 851-0193, Japan
Tel.: +81-95-838-4094
Fax: +81-95-839-4400,
{liuzhen,kamo}@cc.nias.ac.jp
[2]Department of Computer Software, The University of Aizu,
Aizu Wakamatsu City, Fukushima 965-8580, Japan
Tel.: +81-242-37-2557
Fax: +81-242-37-2744,
minyi@u-aizu.ac.jp

**Abstract.** In this paper, a scheme of interactive data mining support system in high performance parallel and distributed computing environment is proposed. The overall architecture and the mechanism of the system are described.

## 1 Motivation for Data Mining

Data mining extracts hidden predictive information from data warehouse or large-scale database. Data mining tools predict future trends and behaviors, allowing businesses to make proactive, knowledge-driven decisions.

The progress of data collection technology generates huge amounts of data. It has been estimated that the amount of information in the world double every 20 months. The size and number of databases probably increase even faster [1]. Enterprises store more and more data in data warehouse for decision support purposes. It is not realistic to expect all this data can be carefully analyzed by human analysts and users due to the increasing of large amount of data. The huge size of real-world databases systems brings about the following problems in data using, and creates both a need and an opportunity for an at least partially-automated form of data mining.

(1)  Data quantitative problem,
(2)  Data qualitative problem, and
(3)  Data presentation problem.

The data quantitative problem causes the decline of the processing speed having to do with a system that the accumulated amount of data becomes enormous too much. Also, there is a limit in the judgment and the ability to process. To solve this, it is necessary to develop the technique to improve processing efficiency. And the system that facilities the processing of data and judgment for the human being must be developed too.

The data qualitative problem occurs because the complicated relation exists between the attributes or the data in the large-scale databases. The near combinations

M. Guo and L.T. Yang (Eds.): ISPA 2003, LNCS 2745, pp. 263–272, 2003.

exist infinitely as the relations of data, attributes of data and the combinations of them are very complicated. As it is impossible to verify all of them, it is necessary to improve the processing efficiency.

Also, when the pattern among the detected data is too complicated, the thing that one finds some meaning from there becomes difficult. This is the data presentation problem. It is necessary to provide a complicated detection result in the form which is easy for the human being to understand to cope with this. It can expect the squeeze of further data, a new discovery and so on.

An effective way to enhance the power and flexibility of data mining in data warehouses and large-scale databases is to integrate data mining with on-line analytical processing (OLAP), visualization and interactive interface in a high performance parallel and distributed environment.

## 2  Related Technologies

### 2.1  OLAP

OLAP was introduced by E. F. Codd [2], [3], the father of relational databases in 1993. He came to the conclusion that relational databases for OLTP (On-Line Transaction Processing) had reached the maximum of their capabilities in terms of the views of the data they provided the user. The problem stemmed principally from the massive computing required when relational databases were asked to answer relatively simple SQL queries. He also came to the view that operational data are not adequate for answering managerial questions. He therefore advocated the use of multi-dimensional databases. His conversion to the DSS/EIS viewpoint gave legitimacy to the data warehouse based concepts. The basic idea in OLAP is that managers should be able to manipulate enterprise data across many dimensions to understand changes that are occurring.

As the facility of powerful multidimensional analysis for data warehouse, it is necessary to adopt on-line analytical processing technology in data warehouse and large-scale database. OLAP provides such facilities as drilling, pivoting, filtering, dicing and slicing so the user can traverse the data flexibly, define the set of relevant data, analyze data at different granularities, and visualize the results in different forms. These operations can also be applied to data mining to make it an exploratory and effective process. Together with OLAP, data mining functions can provide an overview of the discovered knowledge such that the user can investigate further on any interesting patterns or anomalies. Because with OLAP operations, the size of the data set is relatively more compact. So that, the mining integrated with OLAP technology can do insure faster response than mining in the raw data directly.

### 2.2  Parallel Processing and Distributed Technology

Parallel and distributed processing are two important components of a successful large-scale data mining application because that the computation requirements are very large, and the enormity of data or the nature of data collections often requires that the data be stored across multiple storage devices.

A distributed application can be viewed as a collection of objects (user interface, databases, application modules, users). Each object has its own attributes and has some methods which define the user behavior of the object. For example, an order can be viewed in terms of its data and the methods which create, delete, and update the order object. Interactions between the components of an application can be modeled through "messages" which invoke appropriate methods.

Parallel processing is performed by simultaneous use of more than one CPU to execute a program. Ideally, parallel processing makes a program run faster because there are more engines running it. Most computers have just one CPU, but some models have several. With single-CUP computers, it is possible to perform parallel processing by connection the computers in a network. For example, some parallel data mining researches are doing on PC/WS (Personal Computer/Work Station) clusters [7][8]. In recent years, more and more works are focused on paralleling data mining. The study field is wide-ranging from the designing of parallel processing system to the parallel realizing of various data mining algorithms [6], [7], [8], [9].

### 2.3  Visualization Technology in Data Mining

Visualization is to display data successfully in the screen of the computer for grasping the nature of the enormous data intuitively. In the past, so-called scientific visualization which deals with a great deal of numerical data such as the simulation result was to do mainstream being if saying visualization.

Numerical data are rarely comprehensive in raw forms: tables of numbers tend to confuse the content and hide the essential patterns present without the data. In addition, for many applications each data point has associated with it more attributes than can be adequately described by the standard row and column. A multi-dimensional data enables each data point to be characterized by a potentially unlimited number of patterns, visualization technology used in data mining can lead itself to slicing and pivoting among multiple dimensions to display the data in any number of forms.

Visualizing data helps user quickly determine what the data really mean; it literally transforms data into information. Visualization becomes even more powerful as the amount of raw data increase, especially if the visualization in interactive. The purpose of visualization is to transform data into information that forms a critical component within the decision making process.

## 3  Interactive Data Mining Scheme

### 3.1  Some Key Problems

In order to develop an interactive data mining support system in high performance parallel and distributed computing environment successfully, the following key problems must be considered firstly.

    (1)   On-line data mining;
    (2)   Data parallelism;
    (3)   Visual data mining; and
    (4)   Interactive interface.

Data mining and OLAP are all analytical tools, but obvious differences exist between each other. The analysis process of data mining is completed automatically. It is only needed to extract hidden patterns, and predict the future trends and behaviors without giving exact query by user. It is of benefit to finding unknown facts. While OLAP depends on user's queries and propositions to complete analysis process. It restricted the scope of queries and propositions, and affects the final results. On the other hand, to data, most OLAP systems have focused on providing access to multi-dimensional data, while data mining systems have deal with influence analysis of data along a single dimension. It is an effective way to enhance the power and flexibility of data mining in data warehouse by integrating data mining with OLAP to offset their weaknesses [10].

Data parallelism refers to the execution of the same operation or instruction on multiple large data subsets at the same time. This is in contrast to control parallelism, which refers to the key idea in data parallelism is that the whole data set is partitioned into disjoint data subsets, each of them allocated to a disjoint processor, so that each processor can apply the same operation only to its local data. From the point of view of the application programmer, automatic parallelization is an important advantage of data parallelism. In the control-parallelism paradigm the application programmer is in charge of all inter-processor communication and synchronization, which makes programming a time-consuming, error-prone activity. A major advantage of the data parallelism is machine-architecture independence.

Data parallelism should be possible to add a number of processor nodes (CPU+RAM) to the system proportional to the amount of data increase, to keep the query-response time nearly constant, although there will be some increase in query-response time due to the increase in inter-processor communication time caused by adding more processors to exploit data parallelism.

Visual data mining is different from scientific visualization and it has the following characteristic: (1) wide range of users, (2) wide choice range of the visualization techniques, and (3) important dialog function. The users of scientific visualization are scientists and engineers who can endure the difficulty in using the system for little at most. However, a visual data mining system must have the possibility that the general person uses widely and so on easily. It is almost that the simulation results are represented in 2D or 3D visualization. However, it is more ordinary that the objects are not actual one in the information visualization. Moreover, it is possible to make a completely different expression form, too. The purpose of the information visualization becomes a point with important dialogs such as repeating data more in another visualization by changing the way of seeing data and the technique of the visualization and squeezing it because it is not visualization itself and to be in the discovery of the information retrieval and the rule is many.

The idea of the interactive data mining support system is based on the following viewpoints: (1) data mining is a multi-step process, and (b) the human user must be allowed to be front and center in the mining process. In the interactive data mining support system, data mining is performed not by one-sidedly on the side of the system by the algorithms, but showing it by the visualization in the form for which it is easy to judge a temporary processing result for the human being and feeding back the judgment and the knowledge of the human being into the side of the system.

## 3.2 The Overall Architecture and Mechanism

The architecture of the interactive high performance data mining support system is suggested as shown in Figure 1.

It mainly consists of:

(1) Data Warehouse: the platform of the on-line analytical data mining;
(2) Parallel database server: a horizontal-partitioning;
(3) Data Mining Agent: performing analytical mining in data cubes aided by OLAP engine;
(4) OLAP Engine: providing fast access to summarized data along multiple dimensions;
(5) Data Cube: aggregation of data warehouse information;
(6) Meta Data: data for managing and controlling data warehouse creation and maintenance.
(7) Visualization platform: transforming multidimensional data into understandable information and providing parallel data mining visualization.
(8) Applications Programming Interface: aggregation of instructions, functions, regulations and rules for on-line data mining, supporting interactive data mining.

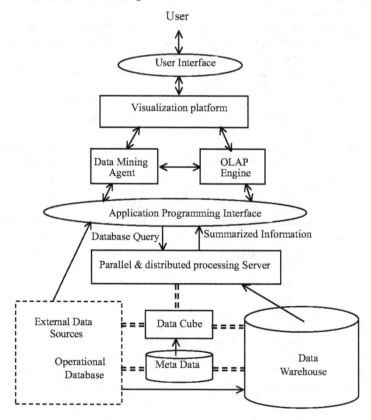

**Fig. 1.** Overall architecture of the system

The system has both of on-line data mining and parallel data mining features. Mainly components of the system is parallel database sever, API and visualization platform which will be illustrated in the following subsections.

Data cube is a core of on-line analytical data mining. It provides aggregated information that can be used to analyze the contents of databases and data warehouses. It is constructed from a subset of attributes in the databases and data warehouses. Data mining agent performs analytical mining in data cubes with the aid of OLAP engine. Data mining agent and the OLAP engine both accept user's on-line queries through the user interface and work with the data cube through the applications programming interface in the analysis. Furthermore, data mining agent may perform multiple data mining tasks, such as concept description, association, classification, prediction, clustering, time-series analysis, etc. Therefore, data mining agent is more sophisticated than the OLAP engine since it usually consists of multiple mining modules which may interact with each other for effective mining.

Since some requirements in data mining agent, such as the construction of numerical dimensions, may not be readily available in the commercial OLAP products, particular mining modules should be built in model base. Although, data mining agent analysis may often involve the analysis of a large number of dimensions the finer granularities and thus require more powerful data cube construction and accessing tools than OLAP analysis, there is no fundamental difference between the data cube required for OLAP engine and that for data mining agent. Since data mining agent is constructed either on customized data cubes which often work with relational database systems, or on top of data cubes provided by the OLAP products, it is suggested to build on-line analytical mining systems on top of the existing OLAP and relational database systems, rather than from the group up.

### 3.3 Parallel Database Server

Generally, there are two types of parallel database server, specialized hardware parallel database server and standard hardware parallel database server. The major types of the former are Intelligent Disks, Database Filters and Associative Memories. The major types of the later are Share-memory, Shared-disk, and Shared-nothing[11].

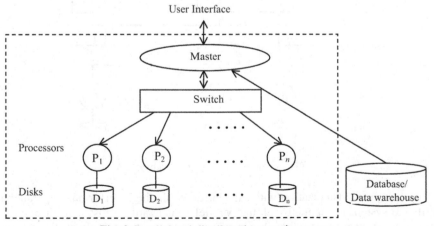

**Fig. 2.** Parallel and distributed processing server

The parallel and distributed processing server is a cluster of shared-nothing multiprocessor nodes as shown in Fig. 2. The main memory is distributed among the processors, and each processor manages its own disk. In the architecture, all processors can access their corresponding disks in parallel, minimizing the classical I/O bottleneck in database systems. Each processor can independently process its own data, and the processors communicate with each other via the Master only to send requests and receive results. This avoids the need for transmitting large amounts of data through the Master. It takes advantages of high-performance, low-cost commodity processors and memory, and it fit to be realized with PC/WS cluster.

## 3.4  Visualization Platform

Numerical simulation and analysis usually consistent of three main stages: generating computational grids, solving physical equations, and visualizing the result data. As the rapid arising of the process capability of computers, the computational grid is becoming more and more complicated, and the data amount of computational result is becoming large and large. The parallel visualization subsystem offers an effective visualization platform and an interactive exploration for various types datasets arising from parallel data mining for users. The framework of the parallel visualization subsystem is shown in Fig.3.

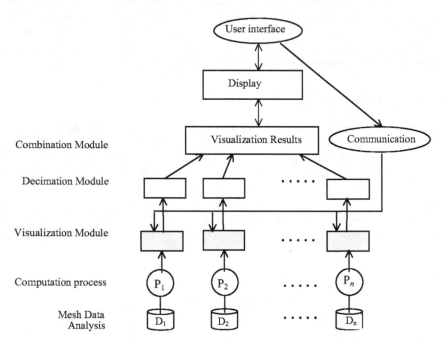

**Fig. 3.** Parallel visualization subsystem

The concurrent visualization with calculation on the high performance parallel and distributed system is supplied with the parallel visualization subsystem. It outputs to clients graphic primitives rather than resulting images. On each client, the users can set viewing, illumination, shading parameters, and so on, and display the graphic primitives.

The parallel visualization subsystem also provides the follows features for users.

(1) Data partition visualization,
(2) Dynamic communication traffic visualization, and
(3) Dynamic visual presentation of parallel data mining process.

## 3.5   Interactive Interface

Basing on parallel visualization subsystem, an interactive Application Programming Interface (API) is provided. The basic function of the API is that of a PGUI (Parallel Graphic User Interface). It includes direct operation, dynamic search, continuous operation, and reversible operation, and so on. The interactive adaptation is shown in Fig. 4.

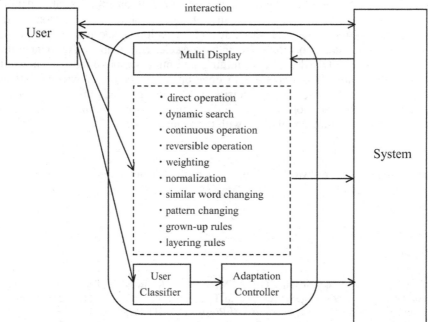

**Fig. 4.** Interactive adaptation

The interactive dialog will be realized with a GH-SOM (Growing Hierarchical Self-Organization Map) model. SOM (self-Organization Map) is an artificial neural network model that proved to be exceptionally successful for data visualization applications where the mapping from an usually very high-dimensional data space into a two-dimensional representation space is required. The GH-SOM is proposed by Dittenbach [17]. It uses a hierarchical structure of multiple layers where each layer consists of a number of independent self-organization maps. One SOM is used at the first layer of the hierarchy. For every unit in this map a SOM might be added to the next layer of the hierarchy. This principle is repeated with the third and further layers of the GH-SOM. Each layer in the hierarchy consists of a number of independent self-organizing maps which determine their size and arrangement of units also during the unsupervised training process. The GH-SOM model is especially well suited for application which have large-scale dataset. It will be applied in a high performance parallel and distributed computing environment.

## 4  Conclusion and Future Work

In this paper, a scheme of interactive data mining support system in high performance parallel and distributed computing environment is proposed. It combines the technologies of data mining, OLAP, distributed object, parallel processing and visualization to support high performance data mining.

The proposal will be realized in a PC/WS cluster environment. Some typical data mining algorithms such as association analysis, cluster analysis, classification, will be parallelized on the proposal system. Further experiments on other parallel database servers will be attempted to evaluate the efficiency in the exploitation of data parallelism on different parallel structures. To develop a successful on-line data mining system, visualization tools are indispensable. Since an OLAP data mining system will integrate OLAP and data mining and mine various kinds of knowledge from data warehouse, it is important to develop a variety of knowledge and data visualization tools. Charts, curves, decision trees, rule graphs, cube views, boxplot graphs, etc. are effective tools to describe data mining results and help users monitor the process of data mining and interact with the mining process.

**Acknowledgement.** This work is supported by The Telecommunications Advancement Foundation, Japan.

## References

1.  Frawley, W., Piatetsky-Shapiro, G., and Matheus, C, Knowledge Discovery in Databases: An Overview, Knowledge Discovery in Databases, eds. G. Piatetsky-Shapiro and W. Frawley, 1–27, Cambridge, Mass.: AAAI Press / The MIT Press, 1991.
2.  E. F. Codd, E. S. Codd and C. T. Salley, Beyond Decision Support, Computerworld, Vol.27, No.30, July 1993.
3.  Qing Chen, Mining Exceptions and Quantitative Association Rules in Olap Data Cube, IEEE Transactions on Knowledge and Data Engineering, 1999.
4.  Masato Oguchi, Masaru Kitsuregawa, Data Mining on PC Cluster connected with Storage Area Network: Its Preliminary Experimental Results, IEEE International Conference on Communications, Helsinki, Finland ,2001.
5.  Masato Oguchi and Masaru Kitsuregawa, Using Available Remote Memory Dynamically for Parallel Data Mining Application on ATM-Connected PC Cluster, Proc. of the International Parallel and Distributed Processing Symposium, IEEE Computer Society, 2000
6.  C.C. Bojarczuk, H.S. Lopes, A.A. Freitas. Genetic programming for knowledge discovery in chest pain diagnosis. IEEE Engineering in Medicine and Biology magazine – special issue on data mining and knowledge discovery, 19(4), July/Aug. 2000.

7.  Mohammed J. Zaki, Parallel Sequence Mining on Shared-Memory Machines, Journal of Parallel and Distributed Computing, 61, 2001.
8.  Diane J. Cook, Lawrence B. Holder, Gehad Galal, and Ron Maglothin, Approched to Parallel Graph-Based Knowledge Discovery, Journal of Parallel and Distributed Computing, 61, 2001.
9.  Sanjay Goil, PARSIMONY: An Infrastructure for Paralle Multidimensional Analysis and Data Mining, Journal of Parallel and Distributed Computing, 61, 2001.
10. Liu Zhen and Guo Minyi, A Proposal of Integrating Data Mining and On-Line Analytical Processing in Data Warehouse, Proceedings of 2001 International Conferences on Info-tech and Info-net, 2001
11. A.A.Freitas, Generic, Set-Oriented Primitives to Support Data-Parallel Knowledge Discovery in Relational Databases Systems, thesis of the doctoral degree, Department of Computer Science, University of Essex, 1997.
12. M. Dittenbach, D. Merkl, A. Rauber, The Growing Hierarchical Self-Organization Map, Proceeding of the international Joint Conference on Neural Networks, July, 2000.

# Parallel Algorithms for Mining Association Rules in Time Series Data

Biplab Kumer Sarker, Takaki Mori, Toshiya Hirata, and Kuniai Uehara

Graduate School of Science and Technology
Kobe University, Kobe 657-8501, Japan
{bksarker,mori,hirata,uehara}@ai.cs.scitec.kobe-u.ac.jp

**Abstract.** A tremendous growing interest in finding dependency among patterns has been developing in the domain of time series data mining. It is quite effective to find how current and past values in the streams of data are related to the future. However, these kind of data sets with high dimensionality are enormous in size results in possibly large number of mined dependencies. This strongly motivates the need of efficient parallel algorithms. In this paper, we propose two parallel algorithms to discover dependency from the large amount of time series data. We introduce the method of extracting sequence of symbols from the time series data by using segmentation and clustering processes. To reduce the search space and speed up the process we investigate the technique to group the time series data. The experimental results conducted on a shared memory multiprocessors system justifies the inevitability of using parallel techniques for mining huge amount of data in the time series domain.

**Keywords:** Time Series, Data mining, Symbols of Multi-streams, Motion Data, Association Rules, Shared Memory Multiprocessors.

## 1 Introduction

Time series analysis is fundamental to engineering and scientific endeavors. Researchers study nature as it evolves through time, hoping to develop models useful to predict and control it. Data mining is the analysis of data with the goal of uncovering hidden patterns. It encompasses a set of methods that automate the scientific discovery process. Its uniqueness is found in the types of problems addressed to those with large data sets and complex, hidden relationships such as price of stocks, intensive weather patterns, the data of a intensive care unit, data flowing from a robots sensor, human motion etc. However, these are basically a series of one-dimensional sequence of data except the human motion data [1]. Human motion data is deemed as three-dimensional data. Furthermore, it is the combination of posture of each body parts motion. So, human motion should be treated as multi-stream [4].

If we analyze the multi stream of time series data, we can find that an event on one stream is related to other events on other streams, which seems to be

M. Guo and L.T.Yang (Eds.): ISPA 2003, LNCS 2745, pp. 273–284, 2003.

independent from the former event time series patterns. The dependencies can be expressed as rules. In our case, these dependencies are called association rules.

A good number of serial and parallel algorithms have been developed for mining association rules for basket data [7-11]. Several researchers have applied data mining concepts on time series to find patterns and rules from it [1, 5, 6, 13]. Several systematic search algorithms for time series data have appeared in the literature [3, 12]. Berndt and Clifford [1] use a dynamic time warping technique taken from speech recognition. Their approach uses a dynamic programming method for aligning the time series and a predefined set of templates. Rosenstein and Cohen [12] employ the time delay embedding process to match their predefined templates. Keogh et al [6] uses a probabilistic method for matching the known templates to the time series data. However, all the above-motioned algorithms are sequential in nature.

Our approach in this paper, discovering association rules from a large amount of time series data, i.e. in our case motion data, differs from the above algorithms in two ways. First of all, we have convert the large amount of 3 dimensional motion data into symbols of multi stream to make the data into lower dimension. However, it is very expensive, time consuming and computational intensive task to discover association rules from these kinds of huge amount data represented as symbols of multi-stream. For this purpose, as a second approach we present parallel algorithms to find the association rules quickly and efficiently from the large amount of symbols of multi-stream on a Shared Memory Multiprocessor (SMP) system.

We present the segmentation and clustering procedure to convert the high dimensional multi-stream motion data into sequence of symbols of lower dimension in section 2. A parallel algorithm for mining association rules from the symbols of multi-streams has been presented in section 3. In section 4, experimental results are elaborated. Section 5 formulates another parallel algorithm as a different approach by grouping the data sets into subgroups to reduce the search space as well as speed up the process. Finally we conclude the paper by indicating the future direction of research.

## 2   Human Motion Data as Multi-stream

The motion data captured by motion capturing system consists of various information of the body parts. To get time series of 3-D motion data, we use an optical motion capture system. The system consists of six infrared cameras, 17 infrared ray reflectors, and a data processor. The cameras record the action of performing act as video images and calculate 3 dimensional locations of the markers. Thus we can obtain 3 dimensional time series stream considering various positions of various body joints. Figure 1 shows the body parts used in motion capture system that can be represented as a tree structure.

In order to find motion association rules by easy analysis with considerations of various occurrences and reduce the cost of the task, we convert the high dimensional multi-stream motion data into sequence of symbols of lower dimension.

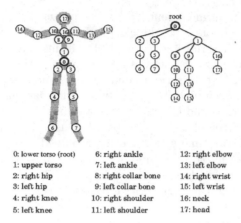

| | | |
|---|---|---|
| 0: lower torso (root) | 6: right ankle | 12: right elbow |
| 1: upper torso | 7: left ankle | 13: left elbow |
| 2: right hip | 8: right collar bone | 14: right wrist |
| 3: left hip | 9: left collar bone | 15: left wrist |
| 4: right knee | 10: right shoulder | 16: neck |
| 5: left knee | 11: left shoulder | 17: head |

**Fig. 1.** Body parts used for the experiments

That is, motion data can be converted into a small number of symbol sequences. Each symbol represents a basic content and motion data that can be expressed as the set of the primitive motions. We call this process content-based automatic symbolization [4]. For the content-based automatic symbolization, we focused on each change in the velocity of a body part that can be considered as a break point. We divide motion data into segments at those breakpoints where velocity changes. However the variations of the curve for motion data between these breakpoints are small and include noise occurred by unconscious movements, which are independent from occurrence of the changes of contents. The unconscious movements are mainly caused by the vibrations of the body parts. These are too short in time and tiny movements and contain no significant content of motion. Thus they are discarded by evaluating time scale and displacement of positions considering the 3D distances between points.

Segmented data is clustered into groups according to their similarity. However, even segmented data with same content have different time length, because nobody can perform exactly in the same manner as past. In order to find out the similarity between time series data with different lengths, we employ Dynamic Time Warping (DTW) [1], which was developed in the speech recognition domain. By applying DTW on our motion data, the best correspondence between two time series was found.

Human voice has fixed number of consistent contents, phonemes, but human motion does not have pre-defined patterns. So it is unknown that how many consistent contents exists on our motion time series data. For this reason, a simple and powerful unsupervised clustering algorithm, Nearest Neighbor (NN) algorithm [2] is used with DTW to classify an unknown pattern (content) and to choose the class of the nearest cluster by measuring the distance. Thus, motion data is converted into symbol streams based on its content by using symbol that are given to clusters (see Fig. 2). After segmenting and clustering processes, a multi-stream that represents human motion is expressed as a multiple sequence of symbols that we call the sequence of symbols of multi-stream.

The dependency on data of various operations in motion data depends on operations performed in the past that has a relation to effect on generating operations in the future. The operations that affects to generate other operations are treated as active operations. On the other hand, the operations that are influenced to be performed by the active operation are termed as passive operations. Therefore, a dependency can be established considering the group of active operations and passive operations. Such a dependency is called association rule. In order to find active motions and passive operations, we set 2 windows $W_a$ (active) and $W_p$ (passive) with the fixed interval $int$. The $int$ is the interval between the windows in order to discover the group of active operations and passive operations that appears in the fixed amount of time. It is necessary to consider simultaneous operation of each part that take places at a instance of a time to discover the association rule considering the fixed amount of time using a window.

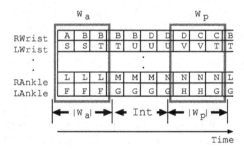

**Fig. 2.** Discovery of association rules using $W_a$ and $W_p$

We define the strength of association rules in motion data by using the frequency of occurrence for two operations. The frequency is calculated by the following function

$$f(co) = t(P_a \land P_p)/t(P_a) \tag{1}$$

where, $co$ is the identifier of motion association rules. $f(co)$ calculates the probability of occurrence for a pattern B which occurs after a pattern A in certain blocks of interval. $P_a$ and $P_p$ are the occurrence of the active and passive operations respectively. $t(P_a \land P_p)$ is the number of simultaneous occurrences of $P_a$ and $P_p$, i.e. it is performed due to active and passive operations.

In the Fig. 2, it is shown that in the symbols of multi-stream how the association rules are discovered in consideration of a fixed amount of time using active operation and passive operation as $W_a$ and $W_p$ respectively. The figure represents that in a specific condition, discovering the group of active operation and passive operation within a fixed amount of time, with the basis of $|W_a|=3$, $|W_p|=3$, and $int=4$, $\{RWrist(A, B, B)\}$ as a set of $W_a$, and $\{LAncle(F, F, F)\}$ as a set of $W_p$.

The combination is discovered from $\{RWrist(D, C, C)$ and $LAncle(H, H, G)\}$. Searching for the importance of the association rule within a fixed amount of time analysis that how many influences in certain operation can influence to generate other operation in the fixed amount of time. Therefore, from a body part of symbols, those operations are to be ignored which are not changed in the fixed amount of time to discover a dependency. It infers that discovering an association rule indicates the discovery of combination of the patterns of symbols from a symbol of multi-stream, but the symbols that are exists in $W_a$ and also exists in the $W_p$ should not be considered.

## 3    Parallel Data Mining

The symbols of multi stream data consist of the combinations of 17 body parts are very large. It requires a lot of time to find out the associations among the body parts represented as symbols employing the technique described in Sec. 2. This motivates us to introduce parallel association-mining algorithms for our time series multi stream data. To the best of the author's knowledge this is the first work of exploiting parallelism in time series data to find meaningful association rules. Our algorithm is based on the well-known *apriori* algorithm [6] in some extends. But as the experimental platform we have considered a SGI 3400 shared memory multi-processor system with 64 processors.

Basically the algorithm consists of parallel generation of candidate set of symbols and parallel determination of large set of symbols above a pre-determined minimum support and finally generate the association rules from the symbols of multistream. For candidate generation purpose let us consider a set symbols of multistream of body parts $G_k$ consists of the 17 parts of the body as shown in the Fig. 1. The naive way is to consider 2 body parts from the 17 parts of the body ($_{17}C_2$), i.e. finding the association rules between 2 parts of the body at a time. So, we compare each two parts of the body from the list $C_k$ considered as candidates of the parts list using parts ID. If the dependency is found then we apply the candidate generation step to check the dependency with the other parts upto a $k$ number ( where $k$, in our case represents upto the number of 17 as the total body parts ) with the earlier found dependency between two body parts. The candidate generation adopts in two steps.

1. In the join step, join $G_{k-1}$ with $G_{k-1}$ : insert into $C_k$, select $p.symbol_1$, $p.symbol_2$, ..., $p.symbol_{k-1}$, $q.symbol_{k-1}$. From $G_{k-1}.p$, $G_{k-1}.q$ where, $p.symbol_1 = q.symbol_1$, ..., $p.symbol_{k-2} = q.symbol_2$, $p.symbol_{k-1} < q.symbol_{k-1}$.

2. Next, in the prune step, for example, let, $G_3$ be $\{(LWrist, RWrist, LElbow), (LWrist, RWrist, RElbow), (LWrist, LElbow, RElbow), (LWrist, LElbow, LCollarBone), (RWrist, LElbow, RElbow)\}$. After the join step, $C_4$ will be $\{(LWrist, RWrist, LElbow, RElbow)$ and $(LWrist, LElbow, RElbow, LCollarBone)\}$. The prune step deletes the symbol set of $(LWrist, LElbow, RElbow, LCollarBone)$ because the symbol set of $(LWrist, RWrist, LCollarBone)$ is not in $G_3$. We then only consider the

symbol set of ($LWrist$, $RWrist$, $LElbow$, $RElbow$) in $C_4$. In Fig. 3, we present the pseudo-code of the algorithm.

---

$G_1$ ={ *Total Body parts lists* }
**for** *(k=2; $G_{k-1}$≠0; k++)* **in parallel do begin**
  // Each processor $P_i$ generates the $C_k$, another list of body parts using the complete list of body parts of $G_{k-1}$ considering parts id.
  $C_k$ = *get_learning_stream( )*;
  // Compare each two parts of the body from the $C_k$ and try to find the dependency between them as association rule. And if found join it as an itemset and compare with another part from the parts list $C_k$ to search whether there exits any dependency.
  $C_k$ = *find_rules( )*;
  // Find the rules from the parts list $C_k$ according to the given confidence and minimum support. Initially found rules are kept in the list *l*. In this function, the technique of finding association rules by using the $W_a$ and $W_p$ are performed according to the description of sec. 3.
**forall** the rules *l∈ ml* **in parallel do begin**
  $C_l$ =*integrate_rules($C_k$,l)*;
  // Copy rules from $C_l$ into *ml* and check whether it exists in the *ml*. *ml* is the superset of the all the rules found during the operation. First copy the rules exists in *l* into the *ml*. Then check whether the rules are already exists or not in *ml*. If the rules are already exists in *ml* then increase the counter for the same rule. And if not in *ml* then register it as separate rule.
**forall** rules *num_cpl∈ $C_l$* **do**
  num_cpl.count++;
**end**
  $G_k$ = {*num_cpl∈ $C_k$ | num_cpl* ≥ minimum_support}
**end**
  Answer = $\cup_k G_k$

---

**Fig. 3.** Pseudo-code of the Algorithm ($_{17}C_k$)

## 4   Experimental Evaluation

All of the experiments were performed on a 64-node SGI Origin 3400 SMP system. Each node consists of 4 MIPS R10000 processor running at 500 MHz. A node consists of 4 GB main memory and its corresponding directory memory, and a connection to a portion of the I/O subsystem. The database are stored on an attached 6 GB local disk. The system runs IRIX 7.3.

For the test data set, we consider 50 different kinds of performed motion such as walking, running, dancing, pitching etc. Each motion consists of the repetition of 2 or 3 times for one kind. Test data are about 5 to 20 seconds long and the sampling frequency is 120 times/second. The motions were performed 23 times in 6 different types, each of which lasts for about 6-12 seconds. Because of the huge amount of motion data, we convert these high dimensional multi stream motion data into sequence of symbols of lower dimension described as in Sec. 2.

In order to decrease the influence of the variation, we set the size of windows $W_a$ and $W_p$ to $|W_a|$ and $|W_p|$, and the interval of $W_a$ and $W_p$ to '*int*'. The values of $W_a$, $W_p$ and *int* may be determined flexibly. This flexibility allows the system to find $P_a$ and $P_p$ with the same interval, even if those sizes are set $|W_a|=2$, $|W_p|=2$ and *int*=2, or $|W_a|=3$, $|W_p|=3$ and *int* = 1.

For our experiment, we heuristically set $W_a = 5$, $W_p = 5$ and $int = 0$. The size of $W_a = 5(W_p = 5)$ is about 0.5 seconds long and can extract motion association rules in the scope of 0.5 +0.5 +0= 1.0 second long for the setting. In our case, 1.0 second is proper to find motion association rules using the parallel algorithm.

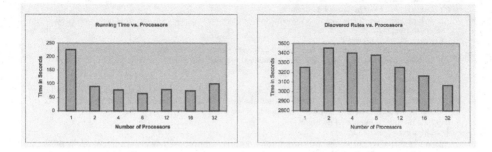

**Fig. 4.** For $_{17}C_k$ a) Running time vs. number of processors b) Discovered rules vs. number of processors

In Figure 4, it is shown that proposed algorithm takes different amounts of time by using different number of processors. It is observed that by using 8 processors the algorithm shows the best performance than all other results according to the running time to find the rules. Compared the results with the time required by 1 processor, it is found that a significant amount of improvement is achieved regarding time.

In the very few cases, human motion consists of only two parts of the body. It is obvious that while performing any kind of motion by a human, various parts of the body take part in that act. For example, while anybody performs dance, almost all the body parts such as *LAnkle, RElbow, LHip, RHips, LShoulder* etc. take part into the act. Consequently, considering the above points of view, we implement the algorithm in the several cases considering various numbers of combinations of the body parts. Figures 5(a) and 5(b) indicated below shows that the proposed algorithm is capable to discover significant number of association rules not only between two parts of the body but also among various parts of the body from the symbols of multi-stream. It is observed from the Fig. 5(b) that the algorithm can discover a number of association rules among the 3 parts of the body from the 17 parts ($_{17}C_3$), among 4 parts of the body from the 17 parts ($_{17}C_4$) and so on. As we obtained good performance by using 8 processors in the earlier experiments, so the following experiments are also conducted by using the same numbers of processors.

From the Fig. 5(a) and 5(b), it is evident that although the results shows a number of association rules has been discovered, but it outputs poor performance regarding time. By using various combinations like $_{17}C_3$, $_{17}C_4$, $_{17}C_5$ and so on, it takes too much time to discover association rules which is opposed to the objective of parallel mining of association rules. To achieve the objective of

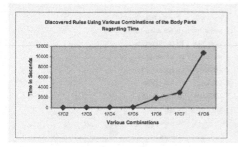 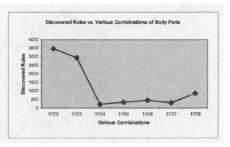

**Fig. 5.** a) Running time considering various combination using 8 processors b) Number of rules discovered using various combinations of body parts.


parallel data mining, i.e. to speed up the discovery process, we introduce another parallel algorithm in the next section.

## 5   A Different Approach of Mining Association Rules

In the earlier approach described in section 4, we considered the various combinations of 17 body parts for finding the association rules. To reduce the search space and speed up the search process, we modified our earlier approach and divide the tree structure of the body parts into 5 divisions ( $G1$ : $RightLeg$, $G2$ : $LeftLeg$, $G3$ : $RightArm$, $G4$ : $LeftArm$ and $G5$ : $Trunk$ ) as shown in the Fig. 6. The reason is due to the fact that when we think about performing motion, basically none of the two parts of body only can take part in that action. For example, if we consider two parts such as $Head$ and $LeftAnkle$, we can not perform any meaningful motion with these parts only. We need some other supporting parts like $Neck$ and $UpperTorso$ with $Head$, and $LeftHip$ and $LeftKnee$ with $LeftAnkle$ at least to perform a motion related to these parts. If we consider this point from view of using 'sensors' in every joints of body parts we can realize that the sensors placed in small gap (distance) between the two parts have small impact on the sensors placed in a comparatively long gap. So, the sensors with small gaps are considered as local part of the body and a group of those with comparatively large gaps as global part. For example, the above-said 5 groups of the 17 body parts are regarded as global for the total body tree whearas a small part as $LeftAncle$ is considered as a local part of the group $G1$. When a body moves or creates any kind of motion obviously it is rare that every parts of the body or only two of them do take part in the activity.! Hence, we divide the tree of the body in that way so that at least one of the parts of each group or several of them is included in the performed motion. Considering the above condition, we proposed another parallel algorithm that works as follows:

1) First we divide the tree structure of the body into 5 groups and with the corresponding parts ID. For example, group $G1$ consists of the body parts with parts number 6, 4 and 2 respectively. So, $G[1].ID[1]$ will be the body part with the number 6 i.e. $RAncle$ in this case. The other members of the same group

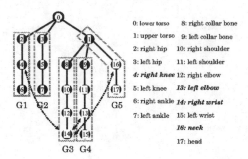

| | |
|---|---|
| 0: lower torso | 8: right collar bone |
| 1: upper torso | 9: left collar bone |
| 2: right hip | 10: right shoulder |
| 3: left hip | 11: left shoulder |
| *4: right knee* | 12: right elbow |
| 5: left knee | *13: left elbow* |
| 6: right ankle | *14: right wrist* |
| 7: left ankle | 15: left wrist |
| | *16: neck* |
| | 17: head |

**Fig. 6.** Minimum sized association rules from nodes on the body structure

$G1$ are $G[1].ID[2] = 4(RKnee)$ and $G[1].ID[3] = RHip$ respectively. The other parts of the body can also be identified in the same way with different groups as shown in Fig. 6.

2) To compare the groups with their corresponding $ID$ for finding association rules between the two parts of the body, we first compare the first part of each group according to their $ID$. If we do not find any correlation between them then we go up of the same group, and again compare between two parts whether any correlation exists. In this way, we compare each part of the group with every part of the other group. For example, consider two groups $G1$ and $G2$ to find the association rules between the parts of the body. At first, $G[1]ID[1]$ is compared with all the parts of $G[2]ID[1]$, $G[2]ID[2]$ and $G[2]ID[3]$ respectively. If no correlation is found then $G[1]ID[2]$ is compared with all the parts of $G[2]ID[1]$, $G[2]ID[2]$ and $G[2]ID[3]$ respectively as shown in the Fig. 6.

3) We assign a threshold value to determine the strength of the rules found in the above way. The rules, above the threshold value ($T_{sr}$), are considered to be strong. Otherwise, it is considered as weak rules. If the rules between the body parts are considered to be weak then search process will again continue for several pass in the same way as described above in step 2.

We implement the algorithm with the same experimental setup presented in section 4. The following results shown in the figures are obtained. It is to be mentioned that all the experiments described in this paper are carried out with support $= 10$ and confidence $= 0.5$.

The results from the Figure 8 (a) and 8 (b) presents that our algorithm ($_5C_k$) described in section 5 can efficiently discover association rules from the symbols of multi stream and a good number of associations rules has been discovered using various number of $T_{sr}$ values. The algorithm takes less time for finding association rules than the algorithm described in section 3.

It is found that by using 8 processors the algorithm shows the best performance than all other results according to the running time to find the rules. Compared the results with the time required by 1 processor, it is found that a significant amount of improvement is achieved regarding time.

$G_l =\{$ *Total Body parts lists* $\}$
*initialize ( );*
    // Initialize the structure tree of the body divided into five groups as described in section 5 according to their Group number GRP[] and Parts ID[].
**for** *(k=2; $G_{k-1}\neq 0$; k++)* **in parallel do begin**
    // Each processor $P_i$ generates the $C_k$, another list of body parts using the complete list of body parts of $G_{k-1}$ considering GRP[] and Parts ID[].
$C_k = get\_learning\_stream( );$
    // Compare each group of the body from the $C_k$ and try to find the dependency between them as association rule. And if found, join (section 3) it as an item and compare with another part from the parts list $C_k$ to search whether there exits any dependency.
$C_k = find\_rules( );$
    // Find the rules from the parts list $C_k$ according to the given confidence and minimum support. Initially found rules are kept in the list $l$. In this function, the technique of finding association rules by using the $W_a$ and $W_p$ are performed according to the description of section 2.
*rule_filter ( );*
    // find out the rules according to the prescribed threshold value as described in section 5 step (3).
*create_cpl( );*
    // strong rules found during *rule_filter( )* are kept in the list $l$ and repeat the search process of strong rules from the rules that are identified as weak according to the method described in section 5 step (3).
**forall** the rules *l∈ ml* **in parallel do begin**
  $C_l = integrate\_rules(C_k,l);$
    // Copy rules from $C_l$ into *ml* and check whether it is existed in the *ml*. *ml* is the superset of all the rules found during the operation. First copy the rules exists in $l$ into the *ml*. Then check whether the rules are already exists or not in *ml*. If the rules are already exists in *ml* then increase the counter for the same rule. And if not in *ml* then register it as separate rule.
**forall** rules *num_cpl∈ $C_l$* **do**
  num_cpl.count++;
**end**
  $G_k = \{num\_cpl\in C_k \,|\, num\_cpl \geq minimum\_support\}$
**end**
  Answer = $\cup_k G_k$

**Fig. 7.** The pseudo-code of the algorithm $(_5C_k)$

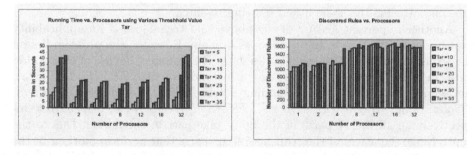

**Fig. 8.** Using different $T_{sr}$ for $_5C_k$ a) Running time vs. number of processor b) Discovered rules vs. number of processors.

By comparing the Figures 5(a, b) and 8(a, b) that represent the running time by using various combinations and $_5C_k$ respectively, it is found that by using $_5C_k$, i.e. grouping the body tree structure shows the better performance regarding running time. Basically, the 5 groups of the body consist of various parts of the body in each group. So while taking into account of $_5C_k$ combinations, in this case, we consider $k=2$ groups consisting of several parts of the body where, $k$ is number of combinations out of 5 groups. So it is evident that the results using

$_5C_k$ also achieves better performance with regards to discovery of associations rules than the results using other combinations.

## 6    Conclusion and Future Work

In this paper, we considered the problem of mining association rules for time series data on a shared memory multi-processors. We presented two parallel algorithms for this task. Both the algorithms are capable to efficiently find the association rules from the motion data, which is extracted as symbols of multi-stream due to the huge volume of data from the original motion data. The extraction technique of motion data into symbols of multi-stream has been elaborately discussed. We then presented the algorithms with their experimental results. The experimental results signify the implementation of parallel algorithms in finding association rules for the time series data. Further the parallel performances of the algorithms are analyzed.

From the analysis, it is evident that for the both of the algorithms ($_{17}C_k$ and $_5C_k$) described in Section 3 and 5, the corresponding results in the figures show that by using 8 processors present the best results among others regarding speed up and discovered rules. In our case, from the figures, it is observed that using more processors may not always output better speedup. It may cause due to the disk contention as SGI origin architecture only supports serial I/O or may be due to improper balancing of computational load etc. However, the proper balancing of the computational load to obtain the scalability requires good attention in the area of parallel data mining for shared memory multiprocessors system. We are concentrating this issue in our ongoing research.

Another important feature of the above said techniques is its applicability over the other division in the time series domain. However, the problem lies on the sequential nature of the time series data. For example, in case of the motion data, in terms of action *'walking'*, at a instances of time $T(t_1, t_2, t_3, ..., t_n)$, the sequence of body parts performing act is $LWrist$, $LLowArm$, $LUpArm$, $LCollarBone$, $RWrist$, $RLowArm$, ..., $RThigh$, $Head$, $Neck$, $UpperTorso$ respectively i.e all the 17 parts of the body take part in the action. Due to the depth (large sequence) of the sequence of the parts that perform motions of the body in the motion database, it is complex and very time swallowing matter to determine the associations among the body parts that perform any kind of motion. And, moreover, in the above said techniques, we need to specify the number of combinations before the discovery process starts. It infers that before commencing the discovery process, the algorithm is to be provided the information of the amount of combinations from which the rules can be discovered. From the data mining point of view, this problem is an important problem for time series data as the course of data is changeable in terms of time. As a result, new data are included in the data sets and the amount of data becomes more large. The other domain of time series data such as stock prices, wether patterns, earthquake signals etc. also may suffer from the same problem. So, an efficient technique needs to be investigated for this purpose.

Considering the above view as a part of our ongoing research we are paying our attention on lattice theoretic based approach for mining rules in the time series data. Recently, lattice based sequence mining has been successfully employed by the researchers using supermarket dataset. Due to its feature, the lattice based approach can be easily applicable to the problems with huge amount of time series data. It decomposes original search space into smaller pieces termed as the suffix based classes which can be processed independently in main-memory considering the advantages of the Shared Memory Multi-processors (SMP) environment. Therefore, it can be easily scalable with the enlarged search space.

# References

1. Berndt, D.J., and Clifford, J.: Finding Patterns in Time Series. A Dynamic Programming Approach. Proc. of Advances in Knowledge Discovery and Data Mining. (1996) 229–248
2. Bay, S. D.: Combining Nearest Neighbor Classifiers Through Multiple Feature Subsets. Proc. of 15th International Conference on Machine Learning. (1998) 37–45
3. Oates, T., Cohen, P.R.: Searching for Structure in Multiple Stream of Data. Proc. of 13th International Conference on Machine Learning. (1996) 346–354
4. Shimada, M., Uehara, K.: Discovery of Correlation from Multi-stream of Human Motion. Lecture Notes in Artificial Intelligence. (2000) 290–294
5. Das, G., Lin, K., Mannila, H., Renganathan, G., Smyth, P.: Rule Discovery from Time Series. Proc. of the Fourth International Conference on Knowledge Discovery and Data mining. (1998) 16–22
6. Keogh, E., Smyth, P.: A Probabilistic Approach to Fast Pattern Matching in Time Series Databases. Proc. of 3rd Int. Conf. on Knowledge Discovery and Data Mining. (1997) 24–28
7. Agrawal, R., Shafer, J.: Parallel Mining of Association Rules. IEEE Transactions on Knowledge and Data Engineering. 8 (1996) 962–969
8. Agrawal, R., Srikant R.: Fast Algorithms for Mining Associations Rules. Proc. of 20th VLDB Conference. (1994) 487–499
9. Park, J.S. Chen, M.S., Yu, P.S.: Efficient Parallel Data Mining for Association Rules. Proc. of CIKM. (1995) 31–36
10. Zaki, M.J., Parthasarathy, S., Ohigara, M., Li, W.: New Algorithms for Fast Discovery of Association Rules. Proc. of the 1997 ACM-SIGMOD Int. Conf. on Management of Data. (1997) 255–264
11. Zaki, M.J.: Effecient Enumeration of Sequential Mining. Proc. of the Int. Conf. on Information and Knowledge Management (1998) 68–75
12. Rosenstein, M.T., Cohen, P.R.: Continuous Categories for a Mobile Robot. Proc. of 16th National Conference on Artificial Intelligence. (1999) 634–640
13. Honda, R., Konishi, O.: Temporal Rule Discovery for Time Series Satellite Images and Integraion with RDB. Proc. of 5th European Conf. of PKDD (2001) 204–215

# Theory of Coevolutionary Genetic Algorithms

Lothar M. Schmitt

The University of Aizu, Aizu-Wakamatsu City, Fukushima Pref. 965-8580, Japan
lothar@u-aizu.ac.jp

**Abstract.** We discuss stochastic modeling of scaled coevolutionary genetic algorithms (COEVGA) which *converge asymptotically to global optima*. In our setting, populations contain several types of interacting creatures such that for some types (appropriately defined) globally maximal
creatures exist. These algorithms particularly demand parallel processing
in view of the nature of the fitness function. It is shown that coevolutionary arms races yielding global optima can be implemented in a procedure
similar to simulated annealing.

**Keywords:** Coevolution; convergence of genetic algorithms; simulated
annealing; parallel processing.

## Introduction

In [5], the need for theory of coevolutionary algorithms and possible convergence
theorems in regard to coevolutionary optimization ("arms races") was stated.
While there is a substantial amount of work in practical applications of coevolutionary algorithms theoretical advance seems to be limited. Work in [3] deals
theoreticly with coevolution in a general setting and presents some static aspects
related to coevolution in regard to order structures of solutions and test-sets.

The present work is a continuation and summary of work in [15,16]. We
present a theoretical framework for discrete, scaled COEVGAs that use general-
size alphabets, multi-species populations and standard genetic operators. As
*main result*, we achieve proof of a *global optimization theorem*. Furthermore,
the discussion here complements certain aspects in [15,16] in that gene-lottery
crossover is considered in detail. This also generalizes [13, Cor. 3.3.4].

Note that [12, Thm. 8.6, Rem. 8.7] solve the coevolutionary optimization
problem for competing agents of one single type (*e.g.*, game-playing programs),
if a single dominant agent exists. The results [13, Thm. 3.3.2, Cors. 3.3.3–4] and
[14, Thm. 3.4.1] extend these results, in that only a group of strictly superior
agents is required. In the present work, we shall generalize the approach taken
in [12,13,14] to an environment with several species (*e.g.*, optimization of interacting hardware and software components).

Our main result (Thm. 3.4.1) establishes strong ergodicity of the inhomogeneous Markov chain $G_t$, $t \in \mathbb{N}$, (see Sec. 3.2, line (9)) describing the scaled
COEVGA. Thus, the asymptotic limit of this procedure is a probability distribution which is independent from the initial state. In addition, convergence to
multi-uniform populations is shown. The latter results are based upon annealing

M. Guo and L.T.Yang (Eds.): ISPA 2003, LNCS 2745, pp. 285–293, 2003.

the mutation rate to zero in proper fashion (see lines (10,11)) and a contraction property of fitness selection towards uniform populations (see Prop. 2.3.2.4).

In order to obtain a global optimization theorem, we must assume that for certain species, but not necessarily all species, dominant elements exists that attain best fitness in every population they reside in (see Def. 2.3.1). The population-dependent fitness function is defined via a canonical interaction of species. For example, species could represent interacting hardware and software components of a (virtual) robot, and the interaction would measure "performance" of a particular hardware and software configuration for the robot in its environment. The population-dependent fitness function evaluates the canonical interaction for all possible settings represented in a population (see line(7)). It is quite obvious that in order for the COEVGA to be feasible, this usually large number of evaluations should be executed *in parallel* on a number of processors.

For an overview in regard to theoretical aspects of GAs, the reader is referred to the surveys [2,12,14] and to the monographs [6,18]. In this work, we shall be interested in the asymptotic behavior of scaled COEVGAs. Asymptotic behavior of GAs has been investigated by many authors (consult, *e.g.*, [12,13,14] for listing of references). However, a proof of asymptotic convergence to global optima for scaled GAs of fixed, relatively small population size using scaled proportional fitness selection has only recently been published in [12,13,14].

As in [10,11,12,13,14,15,16], the mathematical model presented in this work uses an inhomogeneous Markov chain over a finite set of pure states (populations) $\wp$ which are considered as strings of letters over the underlying alphabets. Thus, the state space $\mathcal{S}_\wp$ of the COEVGA consists of probability distributions over populations on which the stochastic matrices representing mutation, crossover and selection act. Many Markov chain models for GAs represent populations as multi-sets following [19,8,4]. As outlined in [12, Sec. 2.9], the multi-set model can be embedded into the tensor-string model considered here. The approach taken here is static in regard to length of genome and size of (sub-)populations. Work in [17] advocates a dynamic approach to coevolution where creatures are allowed to undergo "complexification". Describing a mathematical model for such coevolutionary algorithms shall be dealt with in the near future.

## 1    Notation and Preliminaries

In what follows, we shall use and slightly extend the notation of [12].

**1.1. Vectors and matrices.**    We shall assume that the reader is familiar with the canonical inner product $<i \cdot w, v> = -i \cdot <w, v>$ and the usual $\ell^1$-norm $||v||_1$ of $v, w \in \mathbb{C}^k$, $k \in \mathbb{N}$. Let $\mathcal{S}_\wp = \{v \in (\mathbb{R}^+)^k : ||v||_1 = 1\}$. $\mathcal{S}_\wp$ is the relevant state space of our model where the basis of the underlying vector space $\mathbb{C}^k$ is identified with the set of populations $\wp$.

Let $\mathbb{M}_k(\Omega)$, $k \in \mathbb{N}$, denote the set of $k \times k$ matrices with entries in a set $\Omega$. Let $\mathbb{M}_k = \mathbb{M}_k(\mathbb{C})$. $X = (X_{\kappa', \kappa}) \in \mathbb{M}_k$ will operate by matrix multiplication from the left on column vectors in $\mathbb{C}^k$. The matrix associated with the identity map $\mathbb{C}^k \to \mathbb{C}^k$ will be denoted by $\mathbf{1}$. The spectrum of $X$ will be denoted as $\mathrm{sp}(X)$. The operator norm

$$||X||_1 = \sup\{||Xv||_1 : v \in \mathbb{C}^k, ||v||_1 = 1\} = \max\{\textstyle\sum_{\kappa'} |X_{\kappa',\kappa}| : \kappa\} \tag{1}$$

with respect to the $\ell^1$-norm on $\mathbb{C}^k$ is given as, *e.g.*, in [9, p. 5: eq. (5), (7')].

**1.2. Stochastic matrices.**    $X \in \mathbb{M}_k(\mathbb{R}^+)$ is called (column-)stochastic, if each of its columns sums to 1. The next result shows the existence of a uniquely determined steady-state distribution of the stochastic matrix $G_t$ (see Sec. 3.2, line (9)) describing a single step of the scaled COEVGA considered here. For a proof, use [9, Rems. after p. 9: Prop. 2.8; p. 11: Prop. 3.4; p. 23: Cor. 2] or consult [14, Props. 1.3.4].

**1.2.1.**    Let $M \in \mathbb{M}_k(\mathbb{R}^+_*)$ and $X \in \mathbb{M}_k$ be a stochastic matrices. Then $\exists v = MXv \in (\mathbb{R}^+_*)^k \cap \mathcal{S}_\wp$ and the space of invariant vectors of $MX$ is one-dimensional. In addition, $\exists w = XMw \in \mathcal{S}_\wp$. If $M$ is invertible, then $w = M^{-1}v$ is uniquely determined as invariant eigenvector of $XM$ up to scalar multiples.    ⌋

**1.3. The alphabets.**    Let $j_* \in \mathbb{N}$, and $1 \leq j \leq j_*$. We shall assume that $j_*$ different species (types of candidate solutions, sets of creatures) $\mathcal{C}_j$ exist in the model world under consideration. The elements in $\mathcal{C}_j$ shall be encoded as words of length $\ell_j$ over disjoint alphabets $\mathcal{A}_j = \{a_j(0), a_j(1) \ldots a_j(\alpha_j{-}1)\}$ where usually $2 \leq \ell_j, \alpha_j \in \mathbb{N}$. As outlined in [12, Sec. 3.1], it may be advantageous to consider alphabet(s) representing finite, equidistant sets of real numbers in applications where real parameters are optimized in a compact domain of $\mathbb{R}^{\ell_j}$. Let $\mathcal{V}_j^{(1)}$ be the free vector space over $\mathcal{A}_j$. One has $\mathcal{V}_j^{(1)} \equiv \mathbb{C}^{\alpha_j}$. Let $\mathcal{A} = \cup_{j=1}^{j_*} \mathcal{A}_j$ be the combined set of letters considered here.

We can identify $\mathcal{A}_j$ with $\mathbb{Z}_{\alpha_j} = \mathbb{Z}/\alpha_j\mathbb{Z}$ such that $a_j(\iota) \equiv \iota, 0 \leq \iota \leq \alpha_j - 1$. This allows to define a metric $d_j : \mathcal{A}_j \times \mathcal{A}_j \to [0, \lfloor \alpha_j/2 \rfloor] \cap \mathbb{N}_0$ as follows:

$$d_j(a_j(\iota), a_j(\iota')) = d_{\mathbb{R}}(\iota + \alpha_j\mathbb{Z}, \iota' + \alpha_j\mathbb{Z}). \tag{2}$$

Let $n_j \in \mathbb{N}$ such that $n_j < \alpha_j/2$. We shall say that $a_j(\iota), a_j(\iota') \in \mathcal{A}_j$ are close neighbors, if $\iota \neq \iota'$ and $d_j(a_j(\iota), a_j(\iota')) \leq n_j$.

**1.4. Creatures and populations.**    By the discussion in Sec. 1.3, the $j_*$ disjoint sets of species satisfy $\mathcal{C}_j = \mathcal{A}_j^{\ell_j}$. Let $\hat{\ell}_j = \sum_{\iota=1}^j \ell_\iota$. Let $\mathcal{C} = \cup_{j=1}^{j_*} \mathcal{C}_j$ denote the combined set of creatures considered here. Let $\mathcal{C}_* = \mathcal{C}_1 \times \mathcal{C}_2 \times \cdots \times \mathcal{C}_{j_*}$ (see Sec. 2.3). Let $s_j \in 2\mathbb{N} \cap [4, \infty)$ be the size of the $j^{th}$ sub-population $\wp_j = \mathcal{C}_j^{s_j}$ containing elements of $\mathcal{C}_j$. Then $L_j = \ell_j \cdot s_j$ is the length of an element of $\wp_j$ as word over $\mathcal{A}_j$. Let $\hat{s}_j = \sum_{\iota=1}^j s_\iota$ and $s = \hat{s}_{j_*}$.

The set of populations, to which the COEVGA is applied, is the set $\wp = \wp_1 \times \wp_2 \times \cdots \times \wp_{j_*}$. Thus, every population is (identified with) a word of length $L = \sum_{j=1}^{j_*} L_j$ over $\mathcal{A}$. A spot in the genome is, by definition, the position of one of the letters in a word over $\mathcal{A}$ representing a creature or population.

If $p = (c_1, c_2, \ldots, c_s)$ is a population, $c_\sigma \in \mathcal{C}, 1 \leq \sigma \leq s$, then we define $\mathrm{set}(p) = \{c_\sigma : 1 \leq \sigma \leq s\}$ and $p \wedge J = (c_\sigma)_{\sigma \in J}, J \subset \mathbb{N}$. If $c \in \mathcal{C}$, then we shall write $c \in p$, if $c \in \mathrm{set}(p)$. Let $\#(c, p)$ denote the number of copies of $c$ in $p$.

The vector space $\mathcal{V}^\wp$ underlying our model for the COEVGA is the free complex vector space over $\wp$. Every population $p \in \wp$ can be identified canonically with an integer. This natural order on $\wp$ is used to index matrices acting on $\mathcal{V}^\wp$. Set $\mathcal{V}_j^\wp = \bigotimes_{\hat{\lambda}=1}^{L_j} \mathcal{V}_j^{(1)}$ which as in [12, Sec. 2.6] can be identified with the free complex vector space over $\wp_j$. Then one has up to canonical identification:

$$\mathcal{V}^\wp = \bigotimes_{j=1}^{j_*} \mathcal{V}_j^\wp, \qquad \mathcal{V}_j^\wp = \bigotimes_{\hat\lambda=1}^{L_j} \mathcal{V}_j^{(1)}. \tag{3}$$

Let $\mathcal{U}$ be the free vector space over all (multi-)uniform populations. Such populations consist of $s_1$ copies of a single creature in $\mathcal{C}_1$ in the first $s_1$ positions of the population followed by $s_2$ copies of a single creature in $\mathcal{C}_2$, etc. $\wp \cap \mathcal{U}$ shall denote the set of uniform populations. $P_\mathcal{U}$ shall denote the orthogonal projection onto $\mathcal{U}$. [12, Lemma 7.4] shows:

**1.4.1.** Let $X : \mathcal{V}^\wp \to \mathcal{V}^\wp$ be a linear map such that $Xp = p$ for every $p \in \wp \cap \mathcal{U}$. Then $X$ satisfies $XP_\mathcal{U} = P_\mathcal{U}$, and $(1 - P_\mathcal{U})X = (1 - P_\mathcal{U})X(1 - P_\mathcal{U})$.    ⌋

## 2    The Genetic Operators

**2.1. Multiple-spot mutation.**    Let $\mu_o \in [0,1]$. The spot mutation matrices $\mathbf{m}_j^{(1)}(\mu_o) \in \mathbb{M}_{\alpha_j}$ model <u>change</u> within the alphabets $\mathcal{A}_j$ at a single spot $\hat\lambda$ in the combined genome of a population, $1 < \hat\lambda < L$. Local change determined by $\mathbf{m}_j^{(1)}(\mu_o)$ is a continuous function of $\mu_o$ such that $\mu_o = 0$ corresponds to uniform change within a preferred "small set of close neighbors" of the current letter $a_j(\iota)$ at spot $\hat\lambda$ in the genome in the spirit of the simulated annealing algorithm [1] while $\mu_o = 1$ corresponds to pure random change in $\mathcal{A}_j$.

**2.1.1. Definition (spot mutation matrix $\mathbf{m}_j^{(1)}(\mu_o)$).**    Let $a_j(\iota), a_j(\iota') \in \mathcal{A}_j$ such that $\iota \neq \iota'$, $0 \leq \iota, \iota' \leq \alpha_j - 1$. Let $n_j \in [1, \alpha_j/2 - 1] \cap \mathbb{N}$ be as in Sec. 1.3. Then the stochastic matrix $\mathbf{m}_j^{(1)}(\mu_o)$ is given by:

1. $<a_j(\iota'), \mathbf{m}_j^{(1)}(\mu_o)a_j(\iota)> \ = \mu_o/(\alpha_j - 1)$, if $d_j(a_j(\iota), a_j(\iota')) > n_j$.

2. $<a_j(\iota'), \mathbf{m}_j^{(1)}(\mu_o)a_j(\iota)> \ = (1 - \mu_o)/(2n_j) + \mu_o/(\alpha_j - 1)$, otherwise.    ⌋

Based upon Def. 2.1.1, we can now define multiple-spot mutation $M_{\mu_o,\mu}$ as in [12, Sec. 3.3]: $M_{\mu_o,\mu}$ applies the $\mathbf{m}_j^{(1)}(\mu_o)$ —$j$ appropriate— with probability $\mu \in [0,1]$ (mutation rate) at every spot in the genome of the population. A straightforward check shows that $M_{\mu_o,\mu}$ enjoys the following properties:

$$M_{\mu_o,\mu} = \bigotimes_{j=1}^{j_*} \bigotimes_{\hat\lambda=1}^{L_j} ((1 - \mu)\mathbf{1} + \mu\, \mathbf{m}_j^{(1)}(\mu_o)) \tag{4}$$

in regard to line (3). In particular, $M_{\mu_o,\mu}$ is a symmetric matrix. In addition, one has for for every $p, q \in \wp$ and a constant $K_0 \in \mathbb{R}_*^+$, $\mu \in [0, 1/2]$:

$$K_0\mu^L\mu_o^L \leq \ <q, M_{\mu_o,\mu}p> . \tag{5}$$

The next result is [14, Prop. 3.1.1] and is used to show convergence to uniform populations for $\mu \to 0$. See also [12, Prop. 3.7.4] for a result similar to Prop. 2.1.2.2 which covers the case $\mu_o = 1$.

**2.1.2. Proposition (mutation flow inequality).**    Suppose $\mu \in (0,1)$. Let $C$ be a stochastic matrix and as in 1.4.1. Let $k \in \{0,1\}$. Let $v \in \mathcal{S}_\wp$. Then:

1. $\beta_\mu = \min\{||P_\mathcal{U}M_{\mu_o,\mu}p||_1 : p \in \wp \cap \mathcal{U}\} \in (0,1)$, and $\lim_{\mu\to0} \beta_\mu = 1$.

2. $||(1 - P_\mathcal{U})C^k M_{\mu_o,\mu}C^{1-k}v||_1 \leq 1 - \beta_\mu + \beta_\mu||(1 - P_\mathcal{U})v||_1$.    ⌋

**2.2. Crossover.**    The following definition of crossover allows for essentially *all* standard crossover operators. Verification of this claim is left to the reader.

**2.2.1. Definition (rational generalized crossover).**    For crossover rate $\chi \in [0,1]$, crossover $C_\chi$ is represented by a stochastic matrix $C_\chi$ that acts on $\mathcal{V}^\wp$ and satisfies:

1. $C_\chi = 1 + \chi C_o(\chi)$ where $C_o(\chi)$ has (bounded) rational entries in $\chi \in [0,1]$.

2. $C_\chi p = p$ for $p \in \wp \cap \mathcal{U}$    (*i.e.*, uniform populations are invariant).    ⌋

In what follows, we shall focus on gene-lottery crossover $C_\chi^{(\mathrm{gl})}$ as introduced in [13, Sec. 2.5]. $C_\chi^{(\mathrm{gl})}$ is a crossover operation which accelerates convergence to uniform populations by selecting letters (genes/alleles) probabilistically from the distribution of letters at corresponding spots in the creatures of the current population. Gene-lottery crossover satisfies Def. 2.2.1 and is given by:

**2.2.2. Definition (scaled, spot-wise gene-lottery crossover $C_\chi^{(\mathrm{gl})}$).**    Let $\chi \in [0,1]$. Let $p = (c_1, c_2, \ldots, c_s)$ be the current population. For $j = 1 \ldots j_*$, let $p_j = (c_{\hat{s}_{j-1}+1}, c_{\hat{s}_j})$. Let $\xi_j = (\xi_{j,\lambda})_{\lambda=1}^{\ell_j} = \mathrm{mean}_\mathbf{u}(p_j)$, *cf.* [12, Sec. 2.10]. Then:

$$\xi_{j,\lambda} = \sum_{\iota=0}^{\alpha_j - 1} \xi(j, \lambda, \iota) \cdot a_j(\iota) \in \mathcal{V}_j^{(1)}. \tag{6}$$

Now, **for** $j = 1 \ldots j_*$: $\sigma = 1 \ldots s_j$: $\lambda = 1 \ldots \ell_j$ **do** (( (STEP 1) Decide probabilistically whether or not to apply gene-lottery crossover at spot $\lambda$ in creature $c_{\hat{s}_{j-1}+\sigma}$. The decision for application of gene-lottery crossover at that spot is made positively with probability $\chi$. (STEP 2) If the decision has been made positively in step 1, then probabilistically select a letter for that spot such that $a_j(\iota) \in \mathcal{A}_j$ has probability $\xi(j, \lambda, \iota)$ of being selected, $0 \leq \iota \leq \alpha_j - 1$. ))

We shall denote the stochastic matrix associated with the scaled spot-wise gene-lottery crossover operation by $C_\chi^{(\mathrm{gl})}$ as well. The matrix $C_\chi^{(\mathrm{gl})}$ acts on $\mathcal{V}^\wp$. ⌋

**2.3. The fitness function and selection.**    The selection operation used in this work is scaled proportional fitness selection for a fitness function based upon a canonical interaction $<\cdot, \cdot, \ldots, \cdot> : \mathcal{C}_* \to \mathbb{R}$. Set the selector masks $J_j = [\hat{s}_{j-1} + 1, \hat{s}_j] \cap \mathbb{N}$ or $J_j = [\hat{s}_{j-1} + 1, \hat{s}_j] \cap 2\mathbb{N}$. The latter allows to include mixing as advocated in [18, Sec. 5.4: p. 44] into the model considered here and is only considered in that context. Fix $\varphi_j \in \{\pm 1\}$. Let $D_f = \{(c, p) : c \in p\} \subset \mathcal{C} \times \wp$. The fitness function $f : D_f \to \mathbb{R}^+$ is then given as follows: if $p = (c_1, c_2, \ldots, c_s)$ is a population, $c_\sigma \in \mathcal{C}$, $1 \leq \sigma \leq s$, then we define for $c \in \mathcal{C}_j \cap \mathrm{set}(p)$:

$$f(c, p) = \exp(\varphi_j (\sum_{\sigma_1 \in J_1} \cdots \sum_{\sigma_{j-1} \in J_{j-1}} \sum_{\sigma_{j+1} \in J_{j+1}} \cdots \sum_{\sigma_{j_*} \in J_{j_*}}$$
$$<c_{\sigma_1}, \ldots, c_{\sigma_{j-1}}, c, \ldots, c_{\sigma_{j_*}}>)). \tag{7}$$

The definition of the fitness function given in line (7) which requires many evaluations of $<\cdot, \cdot, \ldots, \cdot>$ makes it necessary to perform these evaluations in parallel in order to make the algorithm feasible after all.

One can interpret $\varphi_j = 1$ and $\varphi_{j'} = -1$ as a situation where the corresponding species $\mathcal{C}_j$ and $\mathcal{C}_{j'}$ have competing goals. For example, the case $\varphi_j = -1$ may correspond to minimizing a resource $<\cdot, \cdot, \ldots, \cdot>$ such as computation-time consumed by interacting virtual/simulated software or hardware components. Simultaneously, the case $\varphi_{j'} = 1$ may correspond to finding "tough" obstacles for other species in the virtual environment hosting the optimization process.

Besides the fitness function $f$ defined in line (7), we shall also allow species & population dependent rank based upon $f$ as <u>the</u> fitness function underlying the COEVGA considered here. Compare [12, Sec. 7.3].

**2.3.1. Definition (globally maximal elements).** Let $j_o \in [1, j_*] \cap \mathbb{N}$. We shall say that $<\cdot, \cdot, \ldots, \cdot>$ admits "globally maximal elements for $\mathcal{C}_j$ up to index $j_o$", if there exist non-empty sets $\mathcal{C}_j^{(\max)} \subset \mathcal{C}_j$ such that for every $j \in [1, j_o] \cap \mathbb{N}$:

$$\forall c \in \mathcal{C}_j \setminus \mathcal{C}_j^{(\max)} \neq \emptyset \ \forall \hat{c} \in \mathcal{C}_j^{(\max)} \ \forall p \in \wp \text{ with } c, \hat{c} \in p\colon f(c,p) < f(\hat{c},p), \text{ and}$$

$$\forall \hat{c}, \hat{c}' \in \mathcal{C}_j^{(\max)} \ \forall p \in \wp \text{ with } \hat{c}, \hat{c}' \in p\colon f(\hat{c},p) = f(\hat{c}',p). \qquad \lrcorner$$

The goal of the COEVGA discussed here is to find elements of $\mathcal{C}_{\max} = \cup_{j=1}^{j_o} \mathcal{C}_j^{(\max)}$. Let $Q_j = \{f(\hat{c},p)/f(c,p)\colon p \in \wp, \ \hat{c} \in (p \wedge J_j) \cap \mathcal{C}_{\max} \neq \emptyset, \ c \in (p \wedge J_j) \setminus \mathcal{C}_{\max} \neq \emptyset\}$, and

$$\rho_2(f) = \min \cup_{j=1}^{j_o} Q_j) > 1. \qquad (8)$$

$\rho_2(f)$ measures the "strength" of second-to-best creatures $c \in \mathcal{C}_j$ in populations $p$ containing elements $\hat{c} \in \mathcal{C}_j^{(\max)}$ where both $\hat{c}$ and $c$ are components of $p$ corresponding to indices in $J_j$. $\rho_2(f)$ is easy to determine, if $f$ is given by rank.

We define power-law scaling of the fitness function in accordance with, e.g., [6, p. 124], [12, Sec. 7.1] as follows: $f_t(c,p) = (f(c,p))^{g(t)}$, $g(t) = B \cdot \log(t+1)$ for $(c,p) \in D_f$, $B \in \mathbb{R}_*^+$ a fixed constant. Put $f_t(c,p) = 0$, if $(c,p) \in \mathcal{C} \times \wp \setminus D_f$.

Note that in view of [12, Thms. 8.2.2, 8.5], a logarithmic growth for $g$ is, essentially, the only reasonable choice.

For $j = 1 \ldots j_*$, scaled proportional fitness selection $S_t$ now selects creatures with indices in $[\hat{s}_{j-1} + 1, \hat{s}_j]$ for the next (sub-)population among the creatures with indices in $J_j$ in the current population probabilisticly proportional to their relative fitness defined by $f_t$ in accordance with [6, p. 16], [12, Sec. 7.1: eqs. 20,21]. Thus, similar to [10, Prop. 11.1/5/3/6], we obtain:

**2.3.2. Proposition.** Let $S_t$ denote the stochastic matrix acting on $\mathcal{V}^\wp$ associated with scaled proportional fitness selection. Let $\theta = 1 - \prod_{j=1}^{j_*} \#(J_j)^{-s_j}$. Let $p = (c_1, c_2, \ldots, c_s), q = (d_1, d_2, \ldots, d_s) \in \wp, c_\sigma, d_\sigma \in \mathcal{C}, 1 \leq \sigma \leq s$. Then:

1. $<q, S_t p> = \prod_{j=1}^{j_*}((\sum_{\sigma' \in J_j} f_t(c_{\sigma'},p))^{-s_j} \cdot \prod_{\sigma=1+\hat{s}_{j-1}}^{\hat{s}_j} \#(d_\sigma, p) f_t(d_\sigma, p))$.
2. If $p \in \wp \cap \mathcal{U}$, then $S_t p = p$.
3. $\|P_{\mathcal{U}} S_t p\|_1 \geq 1 - \theta$.
4. If $v \in \mathcal{S}_\wp$, then $\|(1 - P_{\mathcal{U}})S_t v\|_1 \leq \theta \cdot \|(1 - P_{\mathcal{U}})v\|_1$. $\qquad \lrcorner$

# 3   Convergence

**3.1. Genetic drift.**    Based upon Def. 2.2.1.2 and Prop. 2.3.2.4, one can apply the analysis of non-ergodic genetic drift for (scaled) genetic algorithms with zero mutation rate in [11, Sec. 6] to the present situation. In contrast to popular belief, such algorithms are not suited for optimization, cf. [12, Sec. 9].

**3.2. Ergodicity.**    The stochastic matrix representing one cycle "mixing $\to$ selection" of the scaled COEVGA considered here is given by:

$$G_t = S_t C_{\chi(t)}^{1-k} M_{\mu_o(t),\mu(t)} C_{\chi(t)}^k, \qquad k = 0,1. \qquad (9)$$

Mutation and crossover need not commute in contrast to [12, Thms. 8.5–7].

We shall assume that $\mu_o = \mu_o(t)$ and $\mu = \mu(t)$, $t \in \mathbb{N}$, are scheduled in accordance with the following two possibilities:

$$\kappa_o = 1,\ \mu_o \in (0,1] \text{ is fixed, } \mu(t) = (t+1)^{-1/L}/2. \tag{10}$$

$$\kappa_o \in (1,\infty) \text{ is fixed, } \mu_o(t) = \mu(t)^{\kappa_o-1},\ \mu(t) = (t+1)^{-1/(\kappa_o L)}/2. \tag{11}$$

Weak ergodicity of the inhomogeneous Markov chain $(G_t)_{t \in \mathbb{N}}$ as discussed in, e.g., [7, p. 142–151, p. 151: Thm. V.3.2] can then be directly obtained by applying line (5) and the technique in the proof of [12, Prop. 3.7.3]. Discussion of other, possibly slower variations of the mutation annealing schedule or different local/global mutation scalings for different species is left to the reader.

Let $m \in [1,\infty)$. Put the crossover rate to $\chi(t) = \phi\mu(t)^{1/m} \in (0,1)$ where $\phi \in (0, 2^{1/m}]$ is fixed. Strong ergodicity as discussed in [7, p. 157: Sec. V.4] follows now from the functional form of the stochastic matrices involved in the model here and weak ergodicity established above. In fact, one verifies the conditions of [7, p. 160: Thm. V.4.3] or [14, Thm. 3.3.2]. This verification uses the techniques in [12, Thm. 8.6.1, proof, pp. 53–54] to show:

$$\sum_{t=1}^{\infty} ||v_{t+1} - v_t||_1 < \infty \text{ where } v_t = G_t v_t \in \mathcal{S}_\wp, \text{ cf. [9, p. 7: Prop. 2.3]}. \tag{12}$$

$v_t$ is uniquely determined (for small $\mu < 1/2$) using 1.2.1 and line (4).

**3.3. The drive towards uniform populations.**    Let $v_\infty = \lim_{t\to\infty} v_t$ where $v_t$ is given as in line (12). In order to show that $||P_\mathcal{U} v_\infty||_1 = 1$, one applies the line of reasoning in [12, Lemma 4.4.2, Thm. 8.2.3] to the $v_t$ $(t \to \infty)$ using Prop. 2.1.2 and Prop. 2.3.2.4.

**3.4. Convergence to global optima.**    Finally, we have:

**3.4.1. Theorem.**    In addition to the settings established so far, suppose that the crossover operator $C_{\chi(t)} = C_{\chi(t)}^{(\text{gl})}$ is given by gene-lottery crossover in the sense of Def. 2.2.2. Suppose that

$$\kappa_o \hat{\ell}_{j_o} < \kappa_o LB \log(\rho_2(f)) + 1/m, \text{ and } \forall j \in [1, j_o] \cap \mathbb{N}: m\kappa_o \hat{\ell}_{j_o} < s_j.$$

Then $v_\infty$ which completely determines the asymptotic behavior of the COEVGA considered in this exposition (*cf.* [7, p. 160: Thm. V.4.3], [14, Thm. 3.3.2] ) is a probability distribution over uniform populations (*cf.* Sec. 3.3) containing only elements of $\mathcal{C}_{\max}$ in the first $\hat{s}_{j_o}$ components of populations.

PROOF: Suppose W.L.O.G. $k=1$. We shall formulate the proof for arbitrary $J_j \subset [\hat{s}_{j-1}+1, \hat{s}_j]$ to ease portability in regard to regular crossover. Let $J_o = \cup_{j=1}^{j_o} J_j$. Let $\Omega = \{p \in \wp : \text{set}(p \wedge J_o) \subset \mathcal{C}_{\max}\}$. Let $\Omega' = \wp \setminus \Omega$. Let $P_\Omega$ be the orthogonal projection onto $\text{span}_\mathbb{C}(\Omega)$. Let $P_{\Omega'}$ be the orthogonal projection onto $\text{span}_\mathbb{C}(\Omega')$. We have to only show that $||P_\Omega v_\infty||_1 = 1$. Let $\omega(t) = ||P_\Omega v_t||_1 \to ||P_\Omega v_\infty||_1$ as $t \to \infty$. Let $\Omega^+ = \{p \in \wp : \forall j \in [1, j_o] \cap \mathbb{N} : \text{set}(p \wedge J_j) \cap \mathcal{C}_{\max} \neq \emptyset\}$.

Using line (5) we have for $K_0, K_1 \in \mathbb{R}_*^+$, summations over $p \in \Omega \cap \mathcal{U}$, $q^+ \in \Omega^+$, $q' \in \Omega'$, and small $\mu, \chi$:

$$||P_\Omega G_t P_{\Omega'} v_t||_1 \geq \sum_{p,q'} <p, S_t M_{\mu_o(t),\mu(t)} C_{\chi(t)} q'> <q', v_t>$$

$$\geq \sum_{p,q^+,q'} <p, S_t q^+> <q^+, M_{\mu_o(t),\mu(t)} q'> <q', C_{\chi(t)} q'> <q', v_t>$$

$$\geq \sum_{q'} (1-\theta) K_0 \mu(t)^{\kappa_o \hat{\ell}_{j_o}} \tfrac{1}{2} <q', v_t> = K_1 \mu(t)^{\kappa_o \hat{\ell}_{j_o}} \cdot ||P_{\Omega'} v_t||_1.$$

$$\Rightarrow ||P_{\Omega'} G_t P_{\Omega'} v_t||_1 \leq ||P_{\Omega'} v_t||_1 \cdot (1 - K_1 \mu(t)^{\kappa_o \hat{\ell}_{j_o}}). \tag{13}$$

Let $q^+ = (c_1, c_2, \ldots, c_s) \in \Omega^+$. Let $\nu_{\max}^{(j)}$ denote the number of components in $q^+ \wedge J_j$ that are in $\mathcal{C}_{\max}$. The probability $\pi_{\max}^{(j)}$ for selecting an arbitrary $d \in \text{set}(q^+ \wedge J_j) \cap \mathcal{C}_{\max}$ under $S_t$ is then $\pi_{\max}^{(j)} = \nu_{\max}^{(j)} f_t(d, q^+) / (\sum_{\sigma \in J_j} f_t(c_\sigma, q^+))$. We have $\pi_{\max}^{(j)} \geq 1/(1 + (\#(J_j) - 1)(t + 1)^{-B \log(\rho_2(f))})$. Thus:

$$||P_\Omega S_t q^+||_1 \geq \prod_{j=1}^{j_o}(1 + (\#(J_j) - 1)(2\mu)^{\kappa_o LB \log(\rho_2(f))})^{-\#(J_j)} =: x_t.$$

Hence, there exists $K_2 \in \mathbb{R}_*^+$ such that for sufficiently large $t$:

$$||P_{\Omega'} S_t q^+||_1 = 1 - ||P_\Omega S_t q^+||_1 \leq 1 - x_t \leq K_2 \mu(t)^{\kappa_o LB \log(\rho_2(f))}. \tag{14}$$

We have for $K_3, K_4 \in \mathbb{R}_*^+$ and $q' \in \Omega'$, $q^c \in \wp \setminus \Omega^+$, $q^+ \in \Omega^+ \setminus \Omega$, $p \in \Omega$, and $A = \min\{\#(J_j)/m : j \in [1, j_o] \cap \mathbb{N}\}$:

$$||P_{\Omega'} G_t P_\Omega v_t||_1 = \sum_{q', q^c, p} <q', S_t q^c> <q^c, M_{\mu_o(t), \mu(t)} C_{\chi(t)} p> <p, v_t>$$
$$+ \sum_{q', q^+, p} <q', S_t q^+> <q^+, M_{\mu_o(t), \mu(t)} C_{\chi(t)} p> <p, v_t>$$
$$\leq \sum_p (1 \cdot K_3 \mu^A <p, v_t> + K_2 \mu^{\kappa_o LB \log(\rho_2(f))} \cdot K_4 \mu^{1/m} <p, v_t>). \tag{15}$$

Combining inequalities (13) and (15) yields for $K_5 \in \mathbb{R}_*^+$:

$$1 - \omega(t) = ||P_{\Omega'} v_t||_1 = ||P_{\Omega'} G_t v_t||_1 = ||P_{\Omega'} G_t P_\Omega v_t||_1 + ||P_{\Omega'} G_t P_{\Omega'} v_t||_1$$
$$\leq K_5(\mu^A + \mu^{\kappa_o LB \log(\rho_2(f)) + 1/m})\omega(t) + (1 - K_1 \mu^{\kappa_o \ell_{j_o}})(1 - \omega(t)) \tag{16}$$

Inequality (16) shows that $\lim_{t \to \infty} \omega(t) = 1$.                    Q.E.D.

A result similar to Thm. 3.4.1 can be obtained for various types of regular crossover, *cf.* [6, p. 16–17], [10, Sec. 2.2], [18, p. 41]. All these results show the remarkable effect that a larger population size allows for a more relaxed cooling schedule for crossover. Thus for larger population size, the design of data-structures (creatures), which is exploited by crossover, plays a more important role. Overall, crossover has better chance to perform its enhancement of the mixing phase of the GA, *cf.* [10, Prop. 10], [12, Thm. 6.1]. Also, an analogue of Thm. 3.4.1 for arbitrary rational generalized crossover can be obtained.

## Conclusion

The main result of this exposition, Thm. 3.4.1 extends the theory of COEVGAs to a setting where populations contain possibly several species encoded via arbitrary-size alphabets and gene-lottery crossover is used. This extends results in [12,13,15,16]. This work is inspired by [5] where theory of coevolutionary algorithms was asked for, and [4] where a theoretical framework for scaled COEVGAs similar to that of the simulated annealing algorithm [1] was proposed. In fact, the realistic, implementable algorithm presented here achieves *all* goals advocated in [4, p. 270] for a general-purpose, scaled COEVGA similar to simulated annealing. The algorithm acts in a multi-species, multi-objective setting and asymptoticly finds global optima for one or several of the species under the condition that globally optimal creatures exist at all. Explicit cooling schedules for mutation and crossover, and exponentiation schedules for fitness-selection are given. The fitness function which is induced by the interaction of creatures need not be injective. The number of creatures in populations can stay small and is independent of the problem instance, but depends upon the length of the genome of creatures and, consequently, encoding of the problem instance.

# References

1. E.H.L. Aarts, P.J.M. van Laarhoven. Simulated Annealing: An Introduction. *Statist. Neerlandica* **43** (1989) 31–52
2. H.-G. Beyer, *et al.*. How to analyse evolutionary algorithms, *Theoret. Comput. Sci.* **287** (2002) 101–130
3. A. Bucci, J.B. Pollack: A Mathematical Framework for the Study of Coevolution. In: C. Cotta, *et al.* (chairs). *Proc. of FOGA VII.* Morgan Kaufmann, San Francisco, CA, USA (2003)
4. T.E. Davis, J.C. Principe: A Markov Chain Framework for the Simple Genetic Algorithm. *Evol. Comput.* **1** (1993) 269–288
5. K. De Jong: Lecture on Coevolution. In: H.-G. Beyer, *et al.* (chairs). Seminar *"Theory of Evolutionary Computation 2002"*, Max Planck Inst. for Comput. Sci. Conf. Cent., Schloß Dagstuhl, Saarland, Germany (2002)
6. D.E. Goldberg: *Genetic Algorithms, in Search, Optimization & Machine Learning.* Addison-Wesley, Boston, MA, USA (1989)
7. D.L. Isaacson, R.W. Madsen. *Markov Chains: Theory and Applications* Prentice-Hall, Upper Saddle River, NJ, USA (1961)
8. A.E. Nix, M.D. Vose: Modeling Genetic Algorithms with Markov Chains. *Ann. Math. Artif. Intell.* **5** (1992) 79–88
9. H.H. Schaefer. *Banach Lattices and Positive Operators.* Springer Verlag, Berlin, Berlin, Germany (1974)
10. L.M. Schmitt, *et al.*. Linear Analysis of Genetic Algorithms. *Theoret. Comput. Sci.* **200** (1998) 101–134
11. L.M. Schmitt, C.L. Nehaniv: The Linear Geometry of Genetic Operators with Applications to the Analysis of Genetic Drift and Genetic Algorithms using Tournament Selection. Lect. on Math. in the Life Sci. **26**, AMS, Providence, RI, USA (1999) 147–166
12. L.M. Schmitt. Theory of Genetic Algorithms. *Theoret. Comput. Sci.* **259** (2001) 1–61
13. L.M. Schmitt: Theory of Genetic Algorithms II. —Convergence to optima for arbitrary fitness function—. Tech. Rep. 2002-2-002, Aizu Univ. (2002). To app. in *Theoret. Comput. Sci.*
14. L.M. Schmitt: Asymptotic Convergence of Scaled Genetic Algorithms to Global Optima — A gentle introduction to the theory. In: A. Menon (ed.), *Computing Horizons: The Hilbert Challenge Essays on the Frontiers of Evolutionary Computation.* (to app.). Kluwer Ser. in Evol. Comput. (D.E. Goldberg, ed.), Kluwer, Dordrecht, The Netherlands (2003)
15. L.M. Schmitt: Coevolutionary Convergence to Global Optima. Tech. Rep. 2003-2-002, Aizu Univ. (2003), 1–12. Poster in *Proc. GECCO 2003*, Lect. Notes in Comput. Sci., Springer Verlag, Berlin, Berlin, Germany (2003)
16. L.M. Schmitt: Optimization with Genetic Algorithms in Multi-Species Environments. To appear: *Proc. ICCIMA'03, Int. Conf. on Comput. Intelligence and Multimedia Appl.*, IEEE Press, New York, NY (2003)
17. K.O. Stanley, R. Miikkulainen: Continual Coevolution Through Complexification. In: W.B. Langdon, *et al.* (eds.). *Proc. GECCO 2002.* Morgan Kaufmann, San Francisco, CA, USA (2003) 113–120
18. M.D. Vose: *The Simple Genetic Algorithm: Foundations and Theory.* MIT Press, Cambridge, MA, USA (1999)
19. M.D. Vose, G.E. Liepins: Punctuated Equilibria in Genetic Search. *Complex Systems* **5** (1991) 31–44

# Predicting the Solutions of a Challenging NLP Problem with Asynchronous Parallel Evolutionary Modeling Algorithm

Yan Li[1] and Zhen Liu[2]

[1] State Key Laboratory of Software Engineering, Wuhan University, China
kang@whu.edu.cn
[2] Faculty of Human Environment, Nagasaki Institute of Applied Science, 536 Aba-machi,
Nagasaki 851-0193, Japan, Tel.: +81-95-838-4094, Fax: +81-95-839-4400,
liuzhen@cc.nias.ac.jp

**Abstract.** In this paper, the asynchronous parallel evolutionary modeling algorithm (APEMA) is used to predict the solutions of a challenging non-linear problem (NLP)–a very high dimensional BUMP problem. Numerical experiments shows that the low order ordinary differential equations (ODE) models give good results.

## 1 Introduction

Modeling the complex system and nonlinear phenomena is a hot field in the research of modeling. Some methods have proposed, such as dynamic system, fuzzy machine[1], evolutionary modeling[2] and so on. Recently, a new asynchronous parallel evolutionary algorithm (APEMA)[3] has been used to model dynamic data successfully. But there is no further research on this algorithm. In this paper, we will use APEMA to predict the solutions of a challenging problem –a very high dimensional BUMP problem, which is a difficult problem proposed by Keane[4] in 1994, up to now, the solutions of this problem is still unknown, we use APEMA to predict the solutions of this problem of any dimension, and do many experiments to analyze the efficiency of the algorithm with changing parameters.

The rest of the paper is organized as follows. Section 2 introduces the parallel algorithm for ODEs modeling problem; section 3 uses the APEMA to predict the solutions of a challenging problem; Conclusions are given in section 4. Data mining extracts hidden predictive information from data warehouse or large-scale database. Data mining tools predict future trends and behaviors, allowing businesses to make proactive, knowledge-driven decisions.

## 2 Asynchronous Parallel Evolutionary Modeling Algorithm

As we use Asynchronous Parallel Evolutionary Modeling Algorithm (APEMA) to predict the solutions of a challenging problem, let's describe the algorithm simply first.

M. Guo and L.T.Yang (Eds.): ISPA 2003, LNCS 2745, pp. 294–303, 2003.

Suppose that a series of observed data collected from one-dimensional dynamic system $x(t)$ sampling at $m+1$ time points can be written as

$$x(t_0), \ x(t_1), \ \ldots, \ x(t_m),$$  (1)

where $t_i = t_0 + i\Delta t$, $i = 0, 1, \cdots, m$, $t_0$ denotes the starting observed time and $\Delta t$ denotes the time step-size.

We want to discover a model of ordinary differential equation:

$$x^{(n)}(t) = f(t, x(t), x^{(1)}(t), \cdots, x^{(n-1)}(t)),$$

with initial condition:

$$x^{(i)}(t_0), \ i = 0, 1, \cdots, n-1.$$  (2)

Such that,

$$\min_{f \in F} \sqrt{\sum_{i=0}^{m-1} (x^*(t_i) - x(t_i))^2},$$  (3)

where F is the model space and $x^*(t)$ is the solution of problem (2). The order of the ODE usually satisfies $n \leq 4$.

Using the variable substitution:

$$y(t) = x^{(j)}(t), \qquad j = 0, 1, \cdots, n-1$$  (4)

The formula (2) can be converted into a system of first order ODEs as follows,

$$\begin{cases} \dfrac{dy_j(t)}{dt} = y_{j+1}(t), & j = 1, 2, \cdots, n-1 \\[2mm] \dfrac{dy_n(t)}{dt} = f(t, y_1, y_2, \cdots, y_n) \end{cases},$$  (5)

with initial conditions:

$$y_{j+1}(t_0) = \left. \frac{d^j x(t)}{dt^j} \right|_{t=t_0}, \quad j = 0, 1, \cdots, n-1$$  (6)

Denote $x(t_i)$ by $x_i$. Using the differences formula,

$$\Delta^{i+1} x_k = \Delta^i x_k - \Delta^i x_{k+1}, \qquad i = 0, 1, \ 2, 3,$$

we can compute the difference $\Delta x_i$, $\Delta^2 x_i$, $\Delta^3 x_i$ and $\Delta^4 x_i$..

Denote $t_{s+i} = t_i + s\Delta t$, $i \leq s \leq i+4$, the Newton-Gregory forward polynomial is:

$$x(t_{s+i}) = P_4(t_{s+i}) + error$$

$$= x_i + s\,\Delta x_i + \frac{s(s-1)}{2!}\Delta^2 x_i + \frac{s(s-1)(s-2)}{3!}\Delta^3 x_i + \frac{s(s-1)(s-2)(s-3)}{4!}\Delta^4 x_i + error$$  (7)

where

$$error = \frac{s(s-1)\cdots(s-4)}{5!}(\Delta t)^5 x^{(5)}(\xi), \ t_i \leq \xi \leq t_{i+4}$$  (8)

We have the approximate formula:

$$x^{(j)}(t_{s+i}) = \frac{d^j}{ds^j} P_4(t_{s+i}), \qquad j = 1, 2, 3$$  (9)

Using (4) and (9), we can get the following data (matrix Y):

$$Y = \begin{bmatrix} y_1(t_0) & y_2(t_0) & y_3(t_0) & y_4(t_0) \\ y_1(t_1) & y_2(t_1) & y_3(t1) & y_4(t_1) \\ \vdots & \vdots & \vdots & \vdots \\ y_1(t_m) & y_2(t_m) & y_3(t_m) & y_4(t_m) \end{bmatrix},$$

the modeling problem (1)-(3) then converts to the following modeling problem:

Given data Y, find an ODE model (5) and (6), such that,

$$\min_{f \in F} \sqrt{\sum_{i=1}^{m} \sum_{j=1}^{n} (y_j(t_i) - y_j^*(t_i))^2}, \tag{10}$$

where $F$ is the model space, $n \le 4$, and $y_j^*(t)$ is the solution of problem (5) and (6).

To make sure of the validity of models, we assume that system of ODEs implied in the observed data satisfies some degree of stability with respect to the initial conditions. Namely, the small change of the initial condition will not give rise to the great change of the solution of ODEs.

The APEMA is the asynchronous parallel form of the HEMA (hybrid evolutionary modeling algorithm) by Cao et al. [2] proposed to approach the task of automatic modeling of ODEs for dynamic system. Its main idea is to embed a genetic algorithm (GA) in genetic programming (GP) [5,6,7] where GP is employed to optimize the structure of a model, while a GA is employed to optimize the parameters of the model. It operates on two levels. One level is the evolutionary modeling process and the other one is the parameter optimization process.

Denote the population of ODEs by $P = \{p_1, p_2, \cdots, p_N\}$, where individual $p_i$ is a ordinary differential equation represented by a parse tree. We assume that a population of N individuals is assigned to each of K processors. Each processor executes the same program PROCEDURE APEMA to steer the asynchronous parallel computation.

**PROCEDURE APEMA:**
**begin}**
    $t := 0$;
    initialize the ODE model population $P(t)$;
    evaluate $P(t)$;
    **while** not (termination-criterion1) **do**
        {evolutionary modeling process begins}
        simplify $P(t)$;
        **for** $k := 1$ to MAX **do**
            {MAX is the number of models chosen to optimize}
            choose $p_k$ from $P(t)$;
            check out all the parameters contained in $p_k$;
            $s := 0$;
            initialize the parameter population $P^*(s)$;
            evaluate $P^*(s)$;
                **while** not (termination-criterion2) **do**
                    {parameter optimization process begins}

$s := s + 1;$

select $P^*(s)$ from $P^*(s-1)$;

recombine $P^*(s)$ by sing genetic operators;

evaluate $P^*(s)$;

endwhile {parameter optimization process ends}

replace the parameters of $p_k$ with the best individual in $P^*(s)$;

endfor

locate $p_{best}$ and $p_{worst}$ by sorting $P(t)$;

if $(t \equiv 0 \pmod T)$ then broadcast $p_{best}$ to $Q$ neighbors;

while (any received message probed ) do

    if ( recv individual better than $p_{best}$ )

        then $p_{best} := recv\_individual$

        else $p_{worst} := recv\_individual$;;

    locate $p_{worst}$ by sorting $P(t)$;

endwhile

$t := t + 1;$

select $P(t)$ from $P(t-1)$;

recombine $P(t)$ by using genetic operators;

handle the same class of models in $P(t)$ by sharing techniques;

evaluate $P(t)$;

endwhile {evolutionary modeling process ends}

end

Where $t \equiv 0$ *(mod T)* denotes that $t$ is congruent to zero with respect to modulus $T$.

**Remark 1**: The asynchronous communication between processors is implemented by calling **pvm-mcast( )**, **pvm-prob( )** and **pvm-nrecv( )** which are provided by PVM.

**Remark 2**: T determines the computational granularity of the algorithm, and together with $Q$, the number of neighbor processors to communicate with, control the cost of communication. That is why the granularity of the algorithm is scalable.

Once the best evolved model is obtained in one run, to check its effectiveness, we take the last line of observed data as the initial conditions, advance the solution of the ODEs model by numerical integration using some numerical methods, such as the modified Euler method or Runge-Kutta method and get the predicted values for unknown data in the next time steps.

## 3  Prediction of the Solutions of a Challenging NLP Problem

In 1994, Keane[4] proposed the BUMP problem in optimum structural design as follows:

When $n=2$, the figure of this problem is shown in fig.1., it is a multi modal function and looks like bumps, so the problem is called BUMP problem. Because this function is super-high dimensional, super-non linear, and super-multi modal, it has been regarded as Benchmark of algorithms for function optimization. Till now the solutions of BUMP problem are unknown.

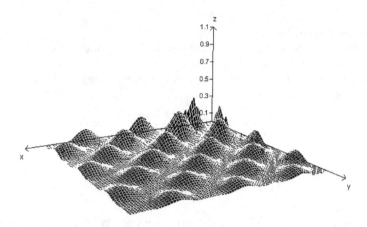

**Fig. 1.** When $n=2$, the figure of BUMP probelem(the infeasible points are appointed as $0$).

$$Maxmize\ f_n(x) \equiv \frac{\left| \sum_{i=1}^{n} \cos^4(x_i) - 2\prod_{i=1}^{n} \cos^2(x_i) \right|}{\sqrt{\sum_{i=1}^{n} i x_i^2}}$$

s. t. $0 < x_i < 10, i = 1, 2, \cdots, n,$ $\prod_{i=1}^{n} x_i \geq 0.75$ and $\sum_{i=1}^{n} x_i \leq 7.5n$ .

According to this problem, Liu proposed a challenging problem in his doctoral thesis [8] as follows:

$$\lim_{n \to \infty} Max\ f_n(x)$$

s.t. $0 \leq x_i \leq 10, 1 \leq i \leq n,$ $\prod_{i=1}^{n} x_i >= 0.75$ and $\sum_{i=1}^{n} x_i <= 7.5n$, and he got the approximate

solutions of the BUMP problem for n = 2,3,…,100,000,000.

We want to discover higher-order ODEs to model the time series:

$$f_2 , \quad f_3 , \quad f_4 , \ldots, f_{50.}$$

Denote $f_i = f(t_i)$, where $t_i = t_0 + i\Delta t$, $t_0 = 2$, and $\Delta t = 0.01$.

In our experiments, we set the function set $F = \{+, -, *, \wedge, sin, cos, exp, ln\}$ for getting good suitable models which are constructed by complex functions for the problem, $\Delta t = 0.01$, the depth of the tree $h = 3$, $max\_generation = 30$, the population size $N = 100$. Then we use different length of training data with different order to analyze this algorithm.

(1) The training number $r = 49$, the prediction number $m = 100$.

*a.* When order = 1, the best result we got is:

$$\begin{cases} \dfrac{dx}{dt} = (47.046257x - 39.370552)\ln|x| \\ x(2) = 0.364979745 \end{cases},$$

with error = 0.04710202.

So from the expression (3) and the error, we can say that the data fits very well, and the prediction is very good.

*b.* When order = 2, we use the same parameters setting as the above. And the best result we got is:

$$\begin{cases} \dfrac{d^2x}{dt^2} = (-7.290305 - \dfrac{dx}{dt})(\dfrac{dx}{dt})^2 - 6.734961\dfrac{dx}{dt} \\ x(2) = 0.364979745 \\ \dfrac{dx}{dt}\bigg|_{t=2} = 15.08058 \end{cases},$$

with error = 0.039.

So from the expression (3) and the error, we can say that both the fitting result and the prediction result are very good.

*c.* When order = 3, we use the same parameters setting as the above. And the best result we got is:

$$\begin{cases} \dfrac{d^3x}{dt^3} = 143.63081\dfrac{dx}{dt} - \dfrac{dx}{dt}(12.129137\dfrac{dx}{dt} - 556.52356) \\ x(2) = 0.364979745 \\ \dfrac{dx}{dt}\bigg|_{t=2} = 15.08058 \\ \dfrac{d^2x}{dt^2}\bigg|_{t=2} = 57.073 \end{cases},$$

with error = 0.08253098.

So from the expression (3) and the error, we can say that the data fits is not too bad, but the prediction is not so good. It shows that when order=3, it can't do long-range prediction.

(2) The training number $r = 70$, the prediction number $m = 100$.

The other parameter settings are the same with the above. Then we got the results as follows:

*a.* When order = 1, the best result we got is:

$$\begin{cases} \dfrac{dx}{dt} = (60.738609x - 50.71283)\cos x\ln|x| \\ x(2) = 0.36\cdots \end{cases},$$

with error = 0.04710202.

So from the expression (3) and the error, we can say that both the fitting result and the prediction result are very good.

*b.* When order = 2, we use the same parameters setting as the above. And the best result we got is:

$$\begin{cases} \dfrac{d^2x}{dt^2} = \dfrac{dx}{dt}*(x-5.084888) - \dfrac{dx}{dt}*14.210396 \\ x(2) = 0.364979745 \\ \dfrac{dx}{dt}\bigg|_{t=2} = 15.08058 \end{cases},$$

with error =0.042569.

So from the expression (3) and the error, we can say that both the fitting result and the prediction result are very good.

*c.* When order = 3, we use the same parameters setting as above. And the best result we got is:

$$\begin{cases} \dfrac{d^3x}{dt^3} = -31.385899 - (\dfrac{dx}{dt})^{\wedge}3 *445.088501 \\ x(2) = 0.364979745 \\ \dfrac{dx}{dt}\bigg|_{t=2} = 15.08058 \\ \dfrac{d^2x}{dt^2}\bigg|_{t=2} = 57.073 \end{cases},$$

with error = 0.351115.

(3) The training number $r = 100$, the prediction number $m = 100$.

The other parameter settings are the same with the above. Then we got the results as follows. Then we got the results as follows.

*a.* When order = 1, the best result we got is:

$$\begin{cases} \dfrac{dx}{dt} = (46.405319x - 38.824017)\ln|x| \\ x(2) = 0.364979745 \end{cases},$$

with error = 0.054357.

So from the expression (3) and the error, we can say that the data fits very well, and the prediction is very good, see fig.2.

*b.* When order = 2, we use the same parameters setting as the above. And the best result we got is:

$$\begin{cases} \dfrac{d^2x}{dt^2} = \dfrac{dx}{dt}*(-15.765037)*(t+\dfrac{dx}{dt}) \\ x(2) = 0.364979745 \\ \dfrac{dx}{dt}\bigg|_{t=2} = 15.08058 \end{cases},$$

with error = 0.044075.

So from the expression (3) and the error, we can say that both the fitting result and the prediction result are very good, see fig.3.

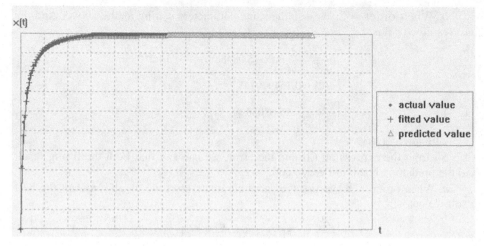

**Fig. 2.** The prediction of the BUMP when $r = 100$, $m = 100$ and order = 1.

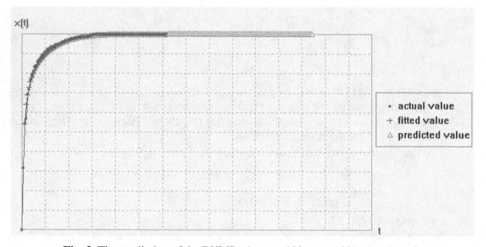

**Fig. 3.** The prediction of the BUMP when $r = 100$, $m = 100$ and order = 2.

*c.* When order = 3, we use the same parameters setting as the above. And the best result we got is:

$$
\begin{cases}
\dfrac{d^3x}{dt^3} = 3.000 * \dfrac{dx}{dt} * (-437.604706) \\
x(2) = 0.364979745 \\
\dfrac{dx}{dt}\bigg|_{t=2} = 15.08058 \\
\dfrac{d^2x}{dt^2}\bigg|_{t=2} = 57.073
\end{cases}
\quad ,
$$

with error = 0.416916, see fig.4.

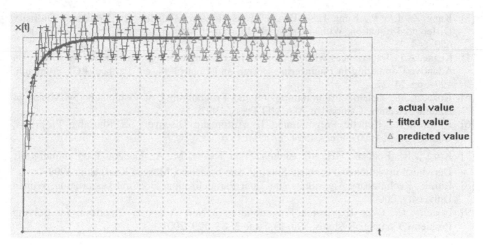

**Fig. 4.** The prediction of the BUMP when $r = 100$, $m = 100$ and order = 3.

From these numerical experiments of different order (first-order, second-order and third-order) ODE models and different length of training data (45, 70, 100), we can see that very good first-order and second-order ODE models can be got, but for the third-order ODE models, their solutions are waving, so they can't be used for prediction. And we can also see that second-order ODE models we got are better than first-order ODE models and the longer training data can get better results than shorter training data.

## 4  Conclusion

APEMA can model dynamic data very well, when we use different parameters in the algorithm, the results are not always good, it seems that APEMA needs improvement to high robustness. Recently a new method: GEP(gene expression programming) [9] proposed by Ferreira is used for symbolic regression. The authors say that this algorithm surpasses GP by more than four orders of magnitude. We plan to use GEP for searching ODE models in the future work.

**Acknowledgement.** This work was supported by National Science Foundation of China (No. 70071042 and No.40275030), National Laboratory for Parallel and Distributed Processing.

## References

[1] Fayyad U.M, Piatetsky-Shapiro, G., Smyth, P., and Uthurusamy, R. (eds.), Advances in Knowledge Discovery and Data Mining. AAAI Press/The MIT Press, 1966.
[2] Cao,H,Q., Kang,LS., Chen,Y.P.,and Yu,Z.X., "Evolutionary Modeling of Systems of Ordinary Differential Equations with Genetic Programming", Genetic Programming and Evolvable Machines, Vol.1, No.4, 2000, pp. 309–337.

[3]  Kang Z., Liu P., Kang L.S., Parallel Evolutionary Modeling for Nonlinear Ordinary Differential Equation, Wuhan University Journal of Natural Sciences, Vol.6, No.3 (2001), 659–664.
[4]  Keane, A.J., Experiences with Optimizers in Structural Design, in Proc. of the Conf. on Adaptive Computing in Engineering Design and Control 94, ed. Parmee, I.C., Plymouth, 1994, pp. 14–27.
[5]  Koza, J. R., Genetic Programming: on the Programming of Computers by Means of Natural Selection. Cambridge, MA:MIT Press, 1992.
[6]  Koza, J. R., Genetic Programming II: Automatic Discovery of Reusable Programs, Cambridge, MA:MIT Press, 1994.
[7]  Koza, J.R., Bennett, F.H, III; Andre,D. and Keane, M. A., Genetic Programming III: Darwinian Invention and Problem Solving, San Francisco, Morgan Kaufmann, 1999.
[8]  Liu, P., Evolutionary Algorithms and Their Parallelization, Doctoral Dissertation, Wuhan University, 2000.
[9]  Ferreira, C., Gene Expression Programming: a New Adaptive Algorithm for Solving Problems. Complex Systems, Vol. 13, issue 2: 87–129. 2001.

# Complete Image Partitioning on Spiral Architecture

Qiang Wu[1], Xiangjian He[1], Tom Hintz[1], and Yuhuang Ye[2]

[1] Department of Computer Systems, University of Technology, Sydney
PO Box 123, Broadway 2007, Australia
{wuq,sean,hintz}@it.uts.edu.au
[2] Department of Information and Communication Engineering
Fuzhou University, Fuzhou, Fujian, P.R.China, 350002

**Abstract.** Uniform image partitioning has been achieved on Spiral Architecture, which plays an important role in parallel image processing on many aspects such as uniform data partitioning, load balancing, zero data exchange between the processing nodes et al. However, when the number of partitions is not the power of seven like 49, each sub-image except one is split into a few fragments which are mixed together. We could not tell which fragments belong to which sub-image. It is an unacceptable flaw to parallel image processing. This paper proposes a method to resolve the problem mentioned above. From the experimental results, it is shown that the proposed method correctly identifies the fragments belonging to the same sub-image and successfully collects them together to be a complete sub-image. Then, these sub-images can be distributed into the different processing nodes for further processing.

## 1 Introduction

Computer vision and image processing is a computationally expensive field in which many operations require a large amount of computing power, especially when processing large data set such as stereo image matching and feature extraction. Naturally, parallel processing is a straightforward method to speed up the processing. In fact, a number of operations in image processing have been optimized for execution on parallel computer architecture [1].

Considering the necessary hardware and software investment, in the near-term future clusters of workstations are good alternatives for parallel processing implementation. With the advent of such platforms, the distinction between workstation clusters and real parallel machines becomes increasingly blurred. The advantages of cluster-based parallel computing are low cost and high utility. The disadvantages are high communication latency and irregular load patterns on the computing nodes [2]. Thus, performance mainly depends on the amount and the structure of communication between processing nodes.

Image partitioning is a key step in parallel processing algorithm. Divide-and-conquer policy [3] is often adopted in vision algorithms, where a complex task is divided into a number of sub-tasks and each of them is assigned to a computer or

M. Guo and L.T.Yang (Eds.): ISPA 2003, LNCS 2745, pp. 304–315, 2003.

a processor for execution. For data parallelism, many types of image partitioning are proposed in the literature [4] such as Row Partition, Column Partition and Block Partition. Except point operation, most of operations in image processing require data-exchange between the sub-tasks during the processing. Thus, though there are many coarse-grained parallel algorithms performing better than the corresponding sequential processing, fine-grained date decomposition methods require such a high communication bandwidth that execution using parallel scheme may even be slower than sequential scheme [5]. So finding high efficient data partitioning to reduce the internal communication is always an attractive topic in parallel image processing field.

In our research work, we propose a novel data partitioning method based on Spiral Architecture [6], which is inspired from anatomical considerations of the primate's vision [7]. It provides another means to achieve high efficient image partitioning for distributed processing. In this way, we can balance work load among all the processing nodes, because it partitions the input image uniformly into a number of sub-images as required. Each sub-image is a scaling down near copy of the input image, which results from a unique sampling of the input image and is mutually exclusive. However, as none of the individual light intensities have been altered in any way, the scaled image still holds all of the information contained in the original. Consequently, the computational complexity has been both reduced and nicely partitioned without giving away any information such that each sub-image will be processed independently by the individual processing node without data exchange between them. Moreover, because of data reduction the processing time is shortened dramatically on each node. Finally, uniform image partitioning is achieved by Spiral Multiplication [8] instantly without introducing the extra computation cost to the system, so it is a feasible partitioning method in fact.

However, when the number of partitions is not the power of seven like 49, each sub-image except one is split into a few fragments which are mixed together. We could not tell which fragments belong to which sub-image. It is an unacceptable flaw to parallel image processing. This paper proposes a method to resolve the problem mentioned above.

The organization of this paper is as follows. Spiral Architecture including Spiral Addition is introduced in Section 2 followed by complete uniform image partitioning on Spiral Architecture in Section 3. In Section 4, we show the experimental results. We conclude in Section 5.

## 2   Spiral Architecture

Spiral Architecture is made up of hexagonal pixels arranged in a spiral cluster. This cluster consists of the organizational units of vision. Each unit is a set of seven-hexagon compared with the traditional rectangular image architecture using a set of $3 \times 3$ vision unit as shown in Fig. 1.

In the Spiral Architecture, any pixel has only six neighbouring pixels which have the same distance to the centre hexagon of the seven-hexagon unit of vi-

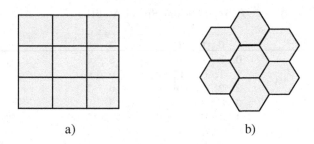

a)                                        b)

**Fig. 1.** Unit of vision in two image architectures. a)Rectangular Architecture b) Spiral Architecture

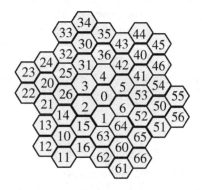

**Fig. 2.** Cluster of size 49 including spiral addresses

sion. Each pixel is identified by a designated positive number. The numbered hexagons form the cluster of size $7^n$. The hexagons tile the plane in a recursive modular manner along the spiral direction. An example of a cluster with size of $7^2$ and the corresponding addresses are shown in Fig. 2. Spiral Architecture contains very useful geometric and algebraic properties, which can be interpreted in terms of the mathematical object, Euclidean ring (refer to [9] for details). Two algebraic operations have been defined on Spiral Architecture: Spiral Addition and Spiral Multiplication. The neighbouring relation among the pixels on Spiral Architecture can be expressed uniquely by these two operations. These two operations mentioned above define two transformations on spiral address space respectively, which are image translation and image partitioning.

In this paper, Spiral Addition is the essential way to label the different partitioned area and reconstruct the complete near copies of the input image. In the following, we will briefly introduce the rules of Spiral Addition.

Spiral Addition is an arithmetic operation with closure properties defined on spiral address space so that the result of Spiral Addition will be the address in the same finite set on which the operation is performed [10]. In addition, Spiral Addition incorporates a special form of modularity. In order to proceed Spiral Addition, a scalar form of Spiral Addition is defined first as shown in Table 1. On

**Table 1.** Scalar Spiral Addition

|   | **0** | **1** | **2** | **3** | **4** | **5** | **6** |
|---|---|---|---|---|---|---|---|
| **0** | 0 | 1 | 2 | 3 | 4 | 5 | 6 |
| **1** | 1 | 63 | 15 | 2 | 0 | 6 | 64 |
| **2** | 2 | 15 | 14 | 26 | 3 | 0 | 1 |
| **3** | 3 | 2 | 26 | 25 | 31 | 4 | 0 |
| **4** | 4 | 0 | 3 | 31 | 36 | 42 | 5 |
| **5** | 5 | 6 | 0 | 4 | 42 | 41 | 53 |
| **6** | 6 | 64 | 1 | 0 | 5 | 53 | 52 |

the table, bold type stands for the scalar spiral address. Normal type stands for the results of Spiral Addition between two spiral address on the first row and the first column respectively. A procedure based on *Spiral Counting* principle [10] is defined. For the convenience of our explanation, we follow a common naming convention, i.e., any numeral $X = (X_n X_{n-1} \cdots X_1)$ for $\forall X_i \in 0, 1, \cdots, 6$, where $X_i$ is a digital component of numeral $X$. $X$ may be any character or word. Let $a$ and $b$ be two spiral addresses. Then the result of Spiral Addition is worked out as follows.

1. $scale = 1$, $result = 0$;
2. $OP1 = (a_n a_{n-1} \cdots a_1)$, $OP2 = (b_n b_{n-1} \cdots b_1)$;
3. $C = OP1 + OP2_1$. Here, carry rule is applied. Elementary Spiral Addition follows the rule as shown in Table 1.
4. $result = result + scale \times C_1$, $scale = scale \times 10$;
5. $CA = OP1$, $CB = OP2$;
6. $OP1 = (CB_n CB_{n-1} \cdots CB_2)$, $OP2 = (C_n C_{n-1} \cdots C_2)$;
7. Repeatly apply step 3 to step 6 until $OP1$ equals to zero;
8. Return $result$.

In order to guarantee that all the pixels are still located within the original image area after Spiral Addition, a modular operation is defined on spiral address space. From Fig. 2, we can see that the spiral address is a base-seven number, so modular operation based on such a number system must execute accordingly. Actually, we can convert the address number and the corresponding module number which is the maximal spiral address in the image plus one (Spiral Addition) to their decimal formats first and work out the result of modular operation by the normal way, Then, we convert the result of decimal format to its corresponding base-seven spiral address again.

In addition, an Inverse Spiral Addition exists on spiral address space. That means for any given spiral address $x$ there is a unique spiral address $\bar{x}$ in the same image area, which meets the condition that $x + \bar{x} = 0$. The procedure of computing inverse value of spiral address can be summarized briefly as follows.

The inverse values of seven basic spiral address, 0, 1, 2, 3, 4, 5 and 6, are 0, 4, 5, 6, 1, 2 and 3 respectively. So the inverse value $\bar{p}$ of any spiral address $p = (p_n p_{n-1} \cdots p_1)$ can be computed as that,

**Fig. 3.** Seven parts (near copies) image partitioning on Spiral Architecture

$$\overline{p} = (\overline{p}_n \overline{p}_{n-1} \cdots \overline{p}_1) \tag{1}$$

Furthermore, Spiral Addition meets the requirement of a bi-jective mapping. That is each pixel in the original image maps one-to-one to each pixel in the output image after Spiral Addition.

During image partitioning on Spiral Architecture using Spiral Multiplication [8], sometimes a few sub-images may be split into a few parts as what we talk in Section 1. In this paper, Spiral Addition is used to identify the different sub-image areas by comparing the neighbouring relation of spiral addresses. And the corresponding fragments are collected together to form a complete sub-image.

## 3   Complete Uniform Image Partitioning

Using the traditional data partitioning like Row Partition, Column Partition and Block Partition, the object in each sub-image contains only incomplete information of the original image, not a scaled up or down copy of the original image, so data exchange among the processing nodes is inevitable. This shortcoming results in much overhead of the network, nodes synchronization and algorithm implementation. In our work, a novel image partitioning method has been developed on Spiral Architecture, which achieves uniform image partitioing by Spiral Multiplication. For example, in order to partition an image of 16807 hexagon pixels into 7 parts we can directly multiply the original image with multiplier 10000 by Spiral Multiplication (see Fig. 3). It is shown that image partitioning is accompanied by image rotation in some degree. However, such rotation will not affect most of high-level image processing like affine invariant feature extraction [11]. To some strict and special applications which require the image to keep the original gesture, a proposed method shown in [12] was developed to fix this blemish.

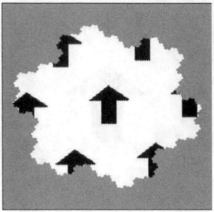

**Fig. 4.** Spiral Multiplication by a common Spiral Address, 55555

Each sub-image is a near copy of the original image, which holds all of the information contained in the original one. Consequently, for most of image processing operations, they can be executed in the local processing nodes without data-exchange with other processing nodes. That means the computational complexity has been both reduced and nicely partitioned without giving away any information for distributed processing.

In the previous work, we have developed a formula to figure out the relation between the multiplier and the number of image partitioning [8]. So such image partitioning is quantitatively measurable. Namely, we can partition the original image into proper number of copies according to the practical system capacities and the application requirements. The number of partitioning can also be determined by some adaptive methods such as Divisible Load Theory (DLT) [13].

However, in the work we found that when the number of partitioning is not the power of seven like 49, only one sub-image in the middle of the image area is a complete sub-image but other sub-images are segmented into several fragments scattering in the different positions on the original image area. For example, an image is multiplied by a common spiral address 55555 as shown in Fig. 4, which partition the original image into 4 sub-images according to [8]. Except the middle one, other three sub-images are split into two fragments respectively. This is unacceptable to distributed processing. Obviously, two problems must be resolved before distributing the data to the processing node. One is that we need to identify the corresponding fragments which belong to the same sub-image. Another problem is that we need to move all the corresponding fragments together to become a complete sub-image.

We find that the boundary of the different sub-image areas can be recognized by investigating the neighbouring relation of the spiral addresses between the reference point and its six adjacent points. Namely, the neighbouring relation of

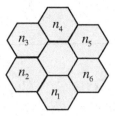

**Fig. 5.** Seven hexagons cluster with six addends for Spiral Addition along the neighbourhood

spiral addresses along the boundary is different from the neighbouring relation within the sub-image area. All the points belonging to the same sub-image area have the consistent relation. Consistency is destroyed only across the boundary between the different sub-image areas. Moreover, it is shown that such consistency can be expressed by Spiral Addition.

Fig. 5 shows a seven-hexagon cluster. There are six numbers around it, which are six addends for Spiral Addition used later. After image partitioning by Spiral Multiplication, all the points on the original image will move to the new positions on the new image. If we know a point's spiral address on the original image, its six neighbouring points' original spiral addresses will be determined by Spiral Addition with the addends as shown in Fig. 5. For example, suppose a point's spiral address on the original image is $x$ and the original address of its neighbouring point below it is $y$, which corresponds to the position labelled by $n_1$ in Fig. 5 If $y = x + n_1$, these two points are in the same sub-image. Otherwise, these two points are in the different sub-images and they both stay on the boundary of the sub-images. Here, "+" stands for Spiral Addition including modular operation if necessary. If the relation of a point's address $x$ and its six neighbouring points' addresses $y_i$ for $i \in \{1, 2, \cdots, 6\}$ meet the following condition, the point of address $x$ is defined as *inside point*, i.e. the point within a sub-image area. Otherwise it is defined as *adjoining point*, i.e. the point on the boundary between two sub-image areas. The condition is as that,

$$y_i = x + n_i, i \in \{1, 2, \cdots, 6\} \tag{2}$$

Now, the question is how to compute the addends $n_i$, $i \in \{1, 2, \cdots, 6\}$. During image partitioning, the values of addends are determined by the Spiral Multiplication which achieves the corresponding image partitioning. In other words, once the number of image partitioning is determined, the multiplier used in Spiral Multiplication is determined [8]. Then, the values of addends as shown in Fig. 5 are fixed. The relation of the original spiral addresses of the points can be figured out as mentioned above by Spiral Addition. In fact, the values of addends in Fig. 5 are the original addresses of the six points around the centre of the new image after Spiral Multiplication. We demonstrate an example below.

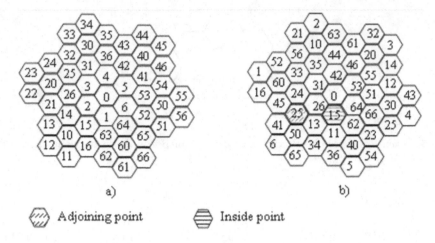

a)                                                    b)

⬡ Adjoining point          ⬡ Inside point

**Fig. 6.** Relocation of points after Spiral Multiplication with multiplier "23". a) Original image with spiral address b) New image with the original spiral address after Spiral Multiplication

Fig. 6 shows the computation results of a Spiral Multiplication with multiplier "23". As shown in the figure, all the points move to the new positions uniquely. According to what we analysis above, the addends $n_i, i \in \{1, 2, \cdots, 6\}$, are 15, 26, 31, 42, 53 and 64 respectively. Point with address "15" is an example of *inside point* because the relation between its address and its six neighbouring points' addresses meet the condition as shown in Equ. 2. But point with address "25" is an example of *adjoining point* because some of its neighbouring points cannot meet the address relation as Equ. 2. For example, its neighbouring point above it has the original address as "24". The corresponding addend used in Spiral Addition as Equ. 2 is $n_4 = 42$. According to Equ. 2 if the point of address "25" is *inside point*, the original address of the neighbouring point above it should be "30", i.e, $25+42 = 30$ (Spiral Addition) rather than "24". So the point of address "25" is *adjoining point*. Such checking procedure proceeds recursively. Then, all the points can be labelled by an area number i.e. the fragments corresponding to the same sub-image are found as shown in Fig. 7.

The last question is how to collect the corresponding fragments together to be a complete sub-image. Actually, after image partitioning on Spiral Architecture all the sub-images except the first one are incomplete partitioned images. We know that Spiral Addition with the common addend will move each point to the new position and guarantee one-to-one mapping between the input image and the output image without changing the object gesture, so it is a good means to collect fragments of sub-image. Moreover, from Fig. 7 we can observe that all the sub-images have the similar size and the sub-image in the middle area is always a complete sub-image. There is a special case that when the number of partitioning is seven or the power of seven, all the sub-images have the exactly same size. This

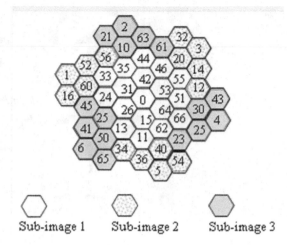

**Fig. 7.** Three identified sub-image areas after image partitioning

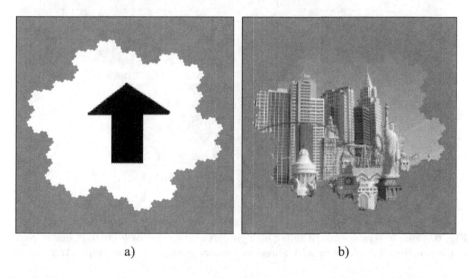

a)                                b)

**Fig. 8.** Experimental images based on Spiral Architecture. a) "Arrow" b) "New York Hotel"

fact inspires us that if we can move the pixels in an incomplete sub-image into the middle sub-image area properly, we will restore this sub-image successfully.

Since Spiral Addition is a consistent operation, if we move the point in the sub-image, which was most close to the point of spiral address "0" before image partitioning, other points will be automatically located to the corresponding positions without changing the object gesture in the image. Such movement is achieved using Spiral Addition as mentioned above. This operation is performed

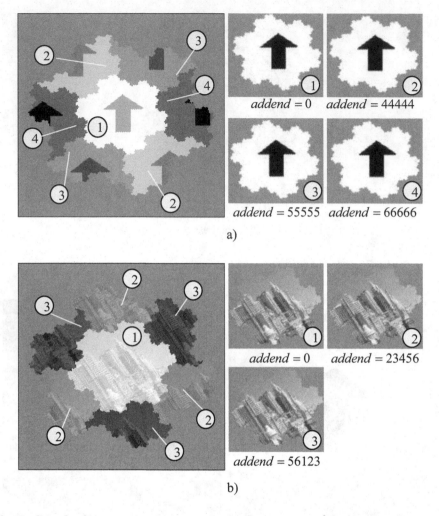

**Fig. 9.** Complete image partitioning on Spiral Architecture. a) Four-part image partitioning on Spiral Architecture b) Three-part image partitioning on Spiral Architecture

on each sub-image, which has been labelled by an area number in the previous step, and then all the incomplete sub-images will be restored one by one.

Let us call the point which was most close to the point of spiral address "0" before image partitioning as *relative centre* of the sub-image. The addend of Spiral Addition for restoring the incomplete sub-image is computed as shown in the following. Suppose the spiral address of the *relative centre* of the sub-image on the new image is $x$ after image partitioning. Then the addend of Spiral Addition for collecting the fragments of sub-images is the inverse value of $x$, i.e., $\overline{x}$, which is computed according to Equ. 1. Following this way, the *relative centre* is moved to the point of spiral address "0" and other points in the fragments are moved the corresponding positions to produce a complete sub-image.

## 4    Experimental Results

In the experiment, a synthetic image containing an up-right arrow and a photo image containing "New York Hotel" were used. There are totally 16807 hexagonal pixels in the Spiral Architecture area individually (See Fig. 8). We partitioned the synthetic image into 4 parts and partitioned the photo image into 3 parts by Spiral Multiplication with multiplier of 55555 and 56123 respectively according to [8]. The separated sub-image areas are shown in Fig. 9, which are distinguished by the different illumination and labelled by the different area number. Finally, the fragments of incomplete sub-images were collected together to produce a complete image partitioning (See Fig. 9). On each sub-image, the addend used in Spiral Addition for fragments collecting is shown. Then, such complete sub-images can be distributed to the different nodes for further processing.

## 5    Conclusions

This paper presents the further research work about image partitioning on Spiral Architecture for distributed image processing. We conquers a problem we did not resolve in our work before, i.e. incomplete image partitioning when the partitioning number is not the power of seven [8]. We develop a method based on Spiral Addition to identify the different sub-image areas including complete sub-image and incomplete sub-images. Finally, the fragments corresponding to the same sub-images are collected together to produce the complete sub-images. Such complete sub-images can be distributed to the different nodes for further processing.

It is shown that image partitioning is accompanied by image rotation in some degree. However, such rotation will not affect most of high-level image processing like affine invariant feature extraction [11]. To some strict and special applications which require the image to keep the original gesture, a proposed method as shown in [12] was developed to fix this blemish.

## References

1. Pitas, I.: Parallel Algorithm for Digital Image Processing. Computer Vision and Neural Network, John Wiley & Sons, Chichester, England (1993)
2. Squyres, J.M., Lumsdaine, A., Stevenson, R.L.: A Cluster-based Parallel Image Processing Toolkit. Proceedins of the IS&T Conference on Image and Video Processing, (San Joes, CA, 1995) 228–239
3. You, J., Zhu, W.P., Cohen, H.A., Pissaloux, E.: Fast Object Recognition by Parallel Image Matching on a Distributed System. Proceedings of the 17th IEEE Symposium on Parallel and Distributed Processing (1995) 78–85

4. Koelbel, C.H., Loveman, D.B., Schreiber, R.S., Jr., G.L.S., Zosel, M.E.: The High Performance Fortran Handbook. MIT Press, Cambridge, MA. (1994)
5. Oberhuber, M.: Distributed High-Performance Image Processing on the Internet. PhD Thesis, Graz University of Technology, Austria (1998)
6. Sheridan, P., Hintz, T., Moore, W.: Spiral Architecture in Machine Vision. Proceedings of the Australian Occam and Transputer Conference (1991)
7. Schwartz, E.: Computational Anatomy and Functional Architecture of Striate Cortex: A Spatial Mapping Approach to Perceptual Coding. Vision Research 20 (1980) 645–669
8. Wu, Q., He, X., Hintz, T.: Distributed Image Processing on Spiral Architecture. Proceedings of the 5th International Conference on Algorithm and Architectures for Parallel Processing, (Beijing, China, 2002) 84–91
9. Sheridan, P., Hintz, T., Alexander, D.: Pseudo-invariant Image Transformations on a Hexagonal Lattice. Image and Vision Computing, 18 (11)(2000). 907–917
10. Spiral Architecture for Machine Vision. PhD Thesis, University of Technology, Sydney (1996)
11. He, X., Hintz, T., Szewcow, U.: Affine Integral Invariants and Object Recognition. Proceedings of the High Performance Computing Conference, (Singapore, 1998), 419–423
12. Wu, Q., He, X., Hintz, T.: Image Rotation without Scaling on Spiral Architecture. Journal of WSCG, 10 (2)(2002) 515–520
13. Bharadwaj, V., Li., X., Ko, C.C.: Efficient Partitioning and Scheduling of Computer Vision and Image Processing Data on Bus Networks Using Divisible Load Analysis. Image and Vision Computing, 18(2000). 919–938

# Automatic Remote-Sensing Images Registration by Matching Close-Regions*

Gui Xie and Hong Shen

Graduate School of Information Science
Japan Advanced Institute of Science and Technology
Tatsunokuchi, Ishikawa 923-1292, JAPAN
{g-xie,shen}@jaist.ac.jp

**Abstract.** Remote-sensing images registration is a fundamental task in image processing, which is concerned with establishment of correspondence between two or more pictures taken, for example, at different times, from different sensors, or from different viewpoints. Because of the different gray level characters in such remote-sensing images, it's difficult to match them automatically. We usually constrain the images to some particular categories, or do the job manually. In this paper, we develop a new algorithm for remote-sensing images registration, which takes full advantage of the shape information of the close-regions bounded by contours after detecting and linking the edges in images. Based on the shape-specific points of the close-regions, we match the close-regions by evaluating their matching degrees. Using the matched pairs of the close-regions, the geometric parameters for images registration are computed and this registration task can be performed automatically and accurately. This new algorithm works well for those images where the contour information is well preserved, such as the optical images from LANDSAT and SPOT satellites. Experiments verified our algorithm, and showed that the performance of executing it sequentially depends a lot on the size of the input images. The time complexity will increase exponentially as the size of images increases. So we extend the sequential algorithm to a distributed scheme and perform the registration task more efficiently.

## 1   Introduction

Geometric registration or alignment of remote sensing images with the same target or scene accurately is a fundamental task in numerous applications in 2-D remote-sensing images processing [1,2]. For example, in the fusion of remote-sensing images [3], the accuracy of the images registration must reach the pixel or sub-pixel level; otherwise it is impossible to continue the consequent process of images fusion. Generally, images registration is to compute the parameters of geometric transformation between a pair of images, such as rotation, scaling and translation. These images with same targets are taken at different times, from different sensors, or from different viewpoints.

---

* This work is supported by Japan Society for the Promotion of Science (JSPS) Grant-in-Aid for Scientific Research (B) under Grant No.14380139.

M. Guo and L.T.Yang (Eds.): ISPA 2003, LNCS 2745, pp. 316–328, 2003.

Many different registration algorithms have been presented [4-6], which can be loosely divided into to the following classes: algorithms that use image pixel values directly, e.g. correlation methods; algorithms that use the frequency domain, e.g. FFT-based methods; algorithms that use low-level features such as edges and corners, e.g. features-based methods; and algorithms that use high-level features such as identified objects or relations between features, e.g. graph-theoretical methods. Cross-correlation is the basic statistical approach to registration, which gives a measure to evaluate the degree of similarity between an image and a template. By the convolution theory, we can use the products of Fourier transforms to compute correlation. An important reason why this metric has been widely used is that it can be implemented by using the Fast Fourier Transform (FFT). For the large input images of the same size, it can be implemented efficiently. Template matching using correlation has many variations [7]. If the allowable transformations include rotation or scale, for example, multiple templates can be used. As the number of template grows, however, the computational costs quickly become unmanageable. Moreover, using correlation has a main limitation that is its inability to deal with dissimilar images since the gray-level characteristics of images are quite different. For this reason, feature-based techniques [8-10], which match features extracted from images, are more preferable, if images are acquired under different circumstances, e.g. varying lighting or atmospheric conditions. Among them, the control-points-based mapping techniques are the primary approach currently taken to register images. The general control-points-based method consists of three stages. In the first stage, features in the image are extracted. In the second stage, feature points in the reference image, often referred to control points, are mapped with the correspondent feature points in the data image. In the last stage, the parameters of the transformation are computed by the mapped pairs of the features points in the two images. Control-points-based methods are very efficient for registration and applied widely in the registration field. However choosing appropriate feature points are very difficult for computers and mapping the feature points in two images usually needs human's help. Moreover, feature points are too sensitive to noise. Sometimes it's impossible to get valid control points. So some other features in the image, which are not sensitive to noise, are more preferred to be used in registration. Among them, contours are widely used, because they are not only insensitive to noise, but also very easy to extract.

In [11], closed boundaries are extracted and used as matching primitives. Another contour-based method for registering Spot and Seasat images is proposed in [8]. The authors in [12] present two contour-based images registration algorithms: a basic contour matching scheme and an elastic contour-matching scheme for optical-to-SAR images registration. The basic algorithm presented in [12] uses chain code correlation to match the contours between two images. It doesn't work well for image pairs in which the contour information is not well preserved. Moreover, chain code is very sensitive to noise. The computational cost on computing the chain code correlation increases rapidly as the complexity of the contours grows. As for the elastic contour-matching scheme given in [12], it just works well when optical and SAR images have been coarsely aligned.

The registration algorithm presented in this paper takes full advantage of shape information of the close-regions bounded by contours in images, which is used to register general remote-sensing images without other constraint on the image types. Moreover it can perform the registration task automatically and accurately without any manual help.

Experiments have proved the algorithm's validity. The results of experiments also showed that if we execute the registration algorithm sequentially, the performance decreases exponentially as the size of input images increases. So based on the principle of the new registration algorithm given in this paper, we extend it into a distributed computation scheme and implement the registration algorithm in parallel on a modified PRAM model.

The random access machine (RAM) [13] is the abstract model of the sequential von Neumann type of architecture. The parallel counterpart to the RAM model is the parallel random access machine (PRAM) [14], which is a theoretical model that plays a central role in studying the parallel algorithms. A PRAM is a set of synchronous processors connected to a shared memory, whose main feature is the capability for different processors to simultaneously access the shared memory. There are several variations of PRAM introduced in the literature [14,15]. The distributed computational scheme presented in this paper makes a little modification of the PRAM model and adds a controller processor into the model to supervise the progress of the registration task.

In section 2, the principle of the algorithm is introduced and also we give the method to get the close-regions in the images. The method to match the close-regions is discussed in detail in section 3. In section 4, we give the results of experiments to prove the validity of the new registration algorithm. And then we propose a distributed computation scheme to extend the algorithm in Section 5. In the last section, we conclude the paper.

## 2    The Principle of the Algorithm

Control-points-based methods can perform the registration task between images accurately, but it's very difficult to choose appropriate control points in images by computers because there is little shape information in points. The close-regions bounded by contours contain so many points that sufficient shape information can be extracted from them. Moreover, choosing and matching close-regions can be done by computers automatically without any human's help. So instead of using control points, we take full advantage of the close-regions to perform the registration task. The flow of the total algorithm is depicted in Fig. 1.

The data image is the image we want to match with the reference image. As shown in the above flow chart, firstly, the algorithm detects and links edges in the input images. Secondly, we choose the regions bounded by the closed contours, which are called as close-regions in this paper. So we get two sets of close-regions, among which one is got from the reference image $R$ and the other from the data image $I$. After getting the two sets, the following algorithm doesn't need the original input images. They can be abandoned in the following steps of the algorithm. Using the technique of matching the close-regions, which will be discussed in detail in Section 3, we can easily compute parameters of images registration such as the degree of rotation, the factor of scaling and the distances of shifting.

For detecting the edges in the input images $R$ and $I$, we can use some differential operators [16-18] such as Robert operator, Prewitt operator and Sobel operator. By these gradient operators, we get not only the magnitudes of the edges, but also the

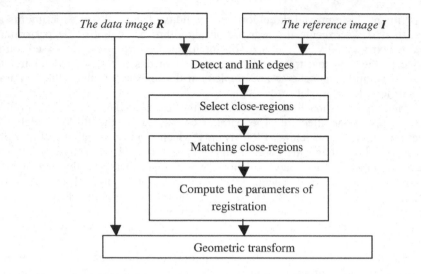

**Fig. 1.** The flow chart of the new algorithm

directions of them. So the broken edges in a contour can be linked by the following method.

Let $(x_1, y_1)$、 $(x_2, y_2)$ be the end points of two broken edges $E_1$ and $E_2$ respectively. Given the thresholds of the magnitude and the angle degree $T$ and $A$. If the following conditions are satisfied, we link $E_1$ and $E_2$ from $(x_1, y_1)$ to $(x_2, y_2)$.

$$\left| \nabla f(x_1, y_1) - \nabla f(x_2, y_2) \right| \leq T \tag{1}$$

$$\left| \varphi(x_1, y_1) - \varphi(x_2, y_2) \right| \leq A \tag{2}$$

where $f$ denotes the grayscale distribution of the remote-sensing images, $\nabla$ is the gradient operator we choose to detect edges, and $\varphi(x_i, y_i)$ denotes the angle of the gradient's direction at a given point $(x_i, y_i)$. After all the end points of broken edges have been checked by the above method, we pick up the regions encircled by closed contours into two sets of close-regions from images $R$ and $I$ respectively.

## 3    Matching the Close-Regions

We develop an efficient method to match the close-regions by shape-specific points. From the matched pairs, we can compute the parameters of image registration.

We first give the definition of shape-specific points, which plays a key role in our algorithm. Given a closed region $R$, which contains some discrete points denoted by $\left\{ (x_i, y_i) \mid i = 1, 2, ..., N \right\}$. Let T be a geometric transformation operated on $R$. Assume $R' = T(R)$, which means $R'$ is a new closed region after transforming $R$

by operator T. Given a function $f$, whose input is a set of points and output is one point. Denote two points by $p$ and $p'$, which satisfy $p = f(R), p' = f(R')$. We say $p$ is a shape-specific point if and only if $p' = T(p)$.

According to the above definition of the shape-specific points, if we let the transform T be rotation, scaling, translation or their combinations, it is easy to prove that the following points computed by following functions are shape-specific points:

a)    Center point

$$x_A = \frac{1}{N}\sum_i x_i \quad , \quad y_A = \frac{1}{N}\sum_i y_i \tag{3}$$

b)    Centroid point

$$x_B = \frac{1}{W}\sum_i \omega_i x_i \quad , \quad y_B = \frac{1}{W}\sum_i \omega_i y_i \tag{4}$$

where $\omega_i$ is the distance from the point $(x_i, y_i)$ to the center point $(x_A, y_B)$ and $W = \sum_i \omega_i$.

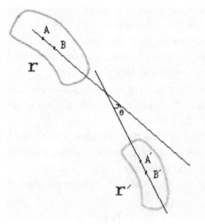

**Fig. 2.** Computing the parameters of the geometric transformation based on the shape-specific points

Then using the shape-specific points of the close-regions, we compute the parameters of the geometric transformation for a registration. The procedure is illustrated in Fig. 2. As Fig. 2 shows, let T be the combination of these operations that rotates the close-region $r$ clockwise by a degree of $\theta$, scales it $\alpha$ times and translates horizontally and vertically by the distances $\Delta x$ and $\Delta y$. We get a new region $r' = T(r)$. Let $A$, $B$, $A'$ and $B'$ be the shape-specific points of the two regions respectively, whose coordinates are $(x_A, y_A)$, $(x_B, y_B)$, $(x_{A'}, y_{A'})$ and $(x_{B'}, y_{B'})$ as illustrated in the figure. The parameters of the geometric transformation can be computed as follows:

a)    the degree of rotation

$$\theta = \arctan(\frac{y_{B'} - y_B}{x_{B'} - x_B}) \tag{5}$$

b)    the factor of scaling

$$\alpha = \frac{\sqrt{(x_{B'} - x_{A'})^2 + (y_{B'} - y_{A'})^2}}{\sqrt{(x_B - x_A)^2 + (y_B - y_A)^2}} \tag{6}$$

c)    the distances of translation

$$\begin{pmatrix} \Delta x \\ \Delta y \end{pmatrix} = \frac{1}{\alpha} \bullet \begin{pmatrix} \cos(\theta) & \sin(\theta) \\ -\sin(\theta) & \cos(\theta) \end{pmatrix} \begin{pmatrix} x_{B'} \\ y_{B'} \end{pmatrix} - \begin{pmatrix} x_B \\ y_B \end{pmatrix} \tag{7}$$

After edges are detected and linked, we get two sets of close-regions, denoted by $RS$ and $RS'$ from the two input image $R$ and $I$. If we can find a matched pair of close-regions $r \in RS_R$ and $r' \in RS_I$ satisfying $r' = T(r)$, the parameters of the geometric transformation T can be computed from the above procedure.

To find the matched pairs between two sets of close-regions, we give a method to measure the matching degree between any two close-regions. Using this measurement, we can evaluate whether two close-regions are a matched pair.

Given two close-regions $r_1$ and $r_2$, we compute the matching degree denoted by $M(r_1, r_2)$ between the two regions as following steps:

a)    Firstly, compute the parameters of a geometric transformation T between the close-regions $r_1$ and $r_2$ based on their shape-specific points as illustrated in Fig. 2.

b)    Secondly, transform $r_2$ by the operator T with the parameters we've got in the above step. Denote the outcome of the transformation by $r_3 = T(r_2)$. $r_3$ is the transformed version of $r_2$.

c)    Finally, compute the normalized matching degree between $r_1$ and $r_3$ as follows

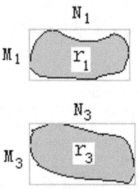

**Fig. 3.** Bounded rectangles

Suppose $r_1$ and $r_3$ are located in two bounded rectangles $M_1 \times N_1$ and $M_3 \times N_3$ as shown in Fig. 3. Let $M = \max(M_1, M_3)$ and $N = \max(N_1, N_3)$. Define two functions as

$$R_1(m,n) = \begin{cases} 1 & (m,n) \in r_1 \\ 0 & (m,n) \notin r_1 \end{cases} \tag{8}$$

$$R_3(m,n) = \begin{cases} 1 & (m,n) \in r_3 \\ 0 & (m,n) \notin r_3 \end{cases} \tag{9}$$

We let the the normalized correlation coefficient between the regions $r_1$ and $r_3$ be the matching degree $M(r_1, r_2)$ between $r_1$ and $r_2$, which is computed as

$$M(r_1, r_2) = \sqrt{\frac{\left[\sum_{n=1}^{N}\sum_{m=1}^{M} R_1(m,n)R_3(m,n)\right]^2}{\left[\sum_{n=1}^{N}\sum_{m=1}^{M} R_1^2(m,n)\right]\left[\sum_{n=1}^{N}\sum_{m=1}^{M} R_3^2(m,n)\right]}} \tag{10}$$

Obviously, $M(r_1, r_2)$ is in the range of $[0,1]$. If $(r_1, r_2)$ is a matched pair of close-regions which satisfies $r_1 = T(r_2)$, $M(r_1, r_2)$ equals 1. If they are not a matched pair, the matching degree between them is less than 1. So we can use this quantity to evaluate whether two close-regions are a matched pair.

However, in practical applications of registration, $M(r_1, r_2)$ cannot reach the idea value of 1 because of the distortion in interpolation and quantization. So we give an efficient way to do the matching work. Given a close-region $r_1 \in RS_R$, let $r_1'$ be a close-region in set $RS_I'$. We say, $(r_1, r_1')$ is a matched pair if and only if the matching degree, $M(r_1, r_1')$ is greater than any other pairs $(r_1, r_2')$, where $r_2' \in RS_I'$ and $r_2' \neq r_1'$.

After we evaluate the matching degrees between close-regions, we obtain some matched pairs of close-regions between two input images. Assume several matched pairs are got by evaluating their matching degrees. From each of them, we can compute a group of geometric parameters using the specific-points. The average of them are the registration parameters we want to compute.

## 4 Experiments

We give two experiments to verify the new registration algorithm. One is an experiment of computer simulation and the other is an experiment of registering two practical remote-sensing images.

Fig. 5 is a geometric transformed version of Fig. 4. The transformation includes rotating clockwise by $10^0$, scaling to 80% of the original size and no translation. We register Fig. 5 to Fig. 4 by the presented algorithm

Using Sobel operator to detect and link the edges in Fig. 4, after which a set of close-regions is formed. To avoid the interference of noise, we just keep large close-regions, whose sizes exceed a threshold. Similarly process Fig. 5. We get two sets of close-regions from two input images respectively. For simplicity of discussion, we assign numbers to the close-regions as illustrated in Fig.6 and Fig. 7.

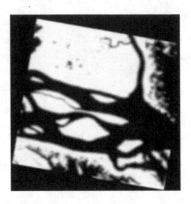

**Fig. 4.** The reference image                **Fig. 5.** The data image

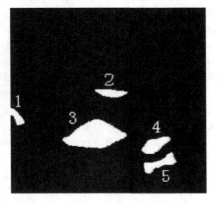
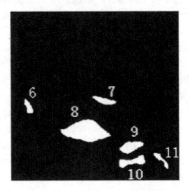

**Fig. 6.** The close-regions in the reference image   **Fig. 7.** The close-regions in the data image

By evaluating matching degrees among the close-regions, we obtain the matched pairs, which are listed in the following table. From each matched pair, we compute a group of parameters for registration as shown in the third column of Table 1.

**Table 1.** The matched pairs of the close-regions

| The matched pairs | The matching degree | The parameters of the geometric transformation | | | |
|---|---|---|---|---|---|
| | | Rotation | Scaling | H-shifting | V-shifting |
| ( 1,6 ) | 0.9052 | 10.7778 | 0.8178 | 0.0032 | 0.0008 |
| (2,7) | 0.8552 | 9.8654 | 0.8436 | 0.0056 | 0.0024 |
| (3,8) | 0.9594 | 9.5037 | 0.8031 | 0.0006 | 0.0002 |
| (4,9) | 0.9255 | 11.4381 | 0.7646 | 0.0012 | 0.0007 |

From each matched pair, we compute a group of parameters for registration as shown in the third column of Table 1. Averaging over them, we get the parameters of the geometric transformation for registering the input images as follows

a)   Rotation degree

$$\theta = \frac{1}{4}(10.7778 + 9.8654 + 9.5037 + 11.4381) \tag{11}$$

$$= 10.3963 \approx 10$$

b)   Scaling factor

$$\alpha = \frac{1}{4}(0.8178 + 0.8436 + 0.8031 + 0.7646) \tag{12}$$

$$= 0.8071 \approx 0.8$$

c)   Translation distances

$$\Delta x \approx 0 \tag{13}$$

$$\Delta y \approx 0$$

we can see, the accuracy of the new registration algorithm is excellent.

It is noteworthy that the close-regions 5 and 10 are a matched pairs, but our algorithm doesn't find them. The reason is that the two regions are circular symmetric and the two shape-specific points given in Section 3 converge into one point. For this case, we cannot evaluate the matching degree between them. But losing some matched pairs of close-regions has no effects on the outcomes of our algorithm if we get enough matched pairs. Sometimes, we can register images accurately even by one matched pair of close-regions.

The second experiment is to register two practical remote-sensing images by our algorithm. In Fig. 8 and Fig. 9 are the remote-sensing images with the same region captured by Landsat and SPOT respectively.

The parameters of the geometric transformation computed by the new algorithm are listed as follows:

a)   Rotation $\theta \approx$  -0.2183 ( clockwise )
b)   Scaling $\alpha \approx 1.2087$
c)   Translation

$$\Delta x \approx -169 \text{(horizontal shift)} \qquad \Delta y \approx 22 \text{(vertical shift )}$$

The registered image by transforming the image in Fig. 9 using the above parameters is shown in Fig. 10.

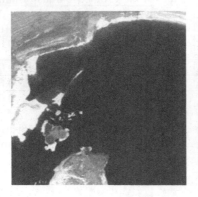
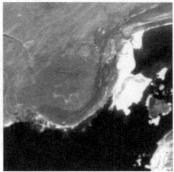

**Fig. 8.** The reference image by Landsat     **Fig. 9.** The data image by SPOT

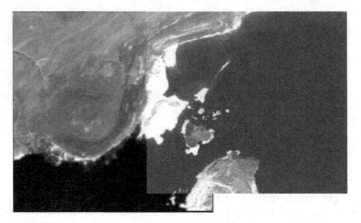

**Fig. 10.** The registered image

## 5  Parallel Execution

The time complexity depends a lot on the size of input images. Through the above experiments, we can find that 95% of the time is spent on detecting and linking edges. When the size of images exceeds 1024*1024, the performance of sequentially executing the registration algorithm is very bad, sometimes intolerable. So we design a distributed scheme to extend the registration algorithm and perform it in parallel.

We first decompose the large image into some small sub-images and assign each of them one process to detect and link edges. A controller process is used to supervise the progress of the whole scheme, which links the contours on the borders between the sub-images, form the set of close-regions after all the sub-processes finish their tasks in their correspondent sub-images, computes the parameters of the registration. The structure of the distributed scheme is illustrated in the following figures.

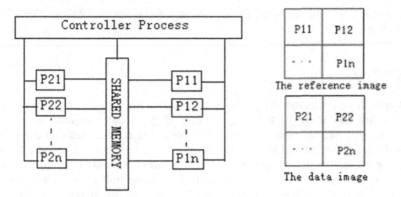

**Fig. 11.** The distribution scheme        **Fig. 12.** The decomposed images

The two input images we want to register are stored in a shared memory. As shown in Fig.12, the controller process decomposes the input two images into $n$ sub-images with same size respectively and creates a sub-process for each sub-image.

The following steps give the flow of the controller process:
1) Start all the sub-processes and wait until all of them finish their tasks and
2) When all the sub-processes stop, link the contours on the borders between the sub-images
3) Combine all the close-regions in different sub-images into two set of close-regions correspondent to two input images respectively
4) Computing the registration parameters and register the two input images

Each sub-process executes the same task as follows:
1) Detect and link the edges
2) Form the close-regions in the current sub-image

We know from experiments that the computational time denoted by $T_c$ of detecting and linking edges takes more than 95% of the total time denoted by $T_S$ of executing the original algorithm sequentially. In the extension scheme, this most time-consuming task is distributed on 2N processors. Let $T_r$ be the other part of the total time $T_S$. Denote the computational time spent on executing the distributed scheme by $T_D$, we have

$$T_S = T_c + T_r \tag{14}$$

$$T_D = \frac{T_c}{2N} + T_r \tag{15}$$

where N is the numbers of sub-images in each input image. Because $T_c \gg T_r$, we get

$$\frac{T_D}{T_S} = \frac{\dfrac{T_c}{2N} + T_r}{T_c + T_r} \approx \frac{\dfrac{T_c}{2N}}{T_c} = \frac{1}{2N} \tag{16}$$

which means the performance of the distributed scheme is about 2N times that of the sequential algorithm .

## 6 Conclusion

A new algorithm of remote-sensing images registration was presented in this paper, which takes full advantage of the shape information of close-regions in images. Without manual help, we can perform the registration task automatically and accurately. Experiments proved its validity. Moreover, we extended it to a distributed scheme and got much better performance. Our algorithm depends a lot on the well-reserved contours in images. How to efficiently detect and link edges is a important topic in the future. Also future work could be on how to incorporate the new algorithm into other existing registration schemes.

**Acknowledgement.** The author would like to thank Prof. Peng Jiaxiong for the part work in his lab of Huazhong University of Sci.&Tech. in China.

## Reference

[1]. L.Brown, "A survey of Images registration Techniques," ACM Computing Surveys, vol.24, no.4, 1992 : 325–376.

[2]. J. Le Moigne et al, "First Evaluation of Automatic Images registration Methods," IGARSS'98, July 1998.

[3]. C.Pohl, J.L. Van Genderen. Multisensor, "Image Fusion in Remote Sensing: Concepts, Methods and Applications," Intern. J. Rem. Sens., vol.19, 5, 1998.

[4]. B.J. Devereux, R.M. Fuller, L. Carter, and R.J. Parsell. "Geometric Correction of Airborne Scanner Imagery by Matching Delaunay Triangles" Int'l J. Remote Sensing, vol.11, no.12, 1990 : 2,237–2,251.

[5]. B.S. Reddy and B.N. Chatterji. "An FFT-Based Technique for Translation, Rotation, and Scale-Invariant Images registration", IEEE Trans. Image Processing, vol.3, no.8, Aug.1996 : 1,266–1,270.

[6]. J.P. Djamdji, A. Bijaoui, and R. Manjere. "Geometrical Registration of Images: The Multiresolution Approach", Photogrammetric Eng. And Remote Sensing J., vol.59, no.5, 1993 : 645–653.

[7]. W.K. Pratt, Digital Image Processing, John Wiley & Sons, Inc., NY 1978

[8]. Y. Wu and H. Maitre, "A multiresolution approach for registration of a spot image and a SAR image," in Proc. Int. Geosci. Remote Sensing Symp., May 1990, pp. 635–638.

[9]. E. Rignot et al., "Automated multisensor registration: Requirements and techniques," Photogrammetric Eng. Remote Sensing, vol. 57, pp. 1029-1038, Aug. 1991

[10]. Ventura, A. Rampini, and R. Schettini, "Images registration by recognition of corresponding structures," IEEE Trans. Geosci. Remote Sensing, vol. 28, pp.305–314, May 1990.

[11]. Goshtasby, G. Stockman, and C. Page, "A region-based approach to digital images registration with subpixel accuracy", IEEE Trans. Geosci. Remote Sensing, vol. 24, pp. 390–399, May 1986.

[12]. Hui Li, B.S. Manjunath, and Sanjit K. Mitra, "A contour-based approach to multisensor images registration", IEEE Trans. On Image Processing, vol. 4, no. 3, March 1995.

[13]. Aho, Hopcroft, et al., J. 1974, "The design and a analysis of computer algorithms", Reading, Mass.:Addison-Wesley.

[14]. Karp, R. M. and Ramachandran, V.1990, "Parallel algorithms for shared-memory machines", in Handbook of Theoretical Computer Science, ed. J. Van Leeuwen, pp. 869–941. Amsterdan:Elsevier Science Publishers.
[15]. Jaja, J. 1992. "An introduction to parallel algorithms", Reading, Mass.:Addison-Welsey.
[16]. Zhang Yujin, "Image Segmentation", ISBN-7-03-007241-3, Beijing: Science Publishing Company, 9–19, 2001.
[17]. Marr D, Hildreth E., "Theory of edge detection", Proceedings of R. Soc. London, 1980, B207:187–217.
[18]. Zhang Yujin, "Image processing and analysis", Beijing: Tsinghua Publisher,1999.

# Parallel HyperFun Polygonizer

Tsuyoshi Yamamoto and Carl Vilbrandt

The University of Aizu, Aizu-Wakamatsu City, Fukushima Prefecture 965-8580, Japan
vilb@u-aizu.ac.jp

**Abstract.** An advanced HyperFun polygonizer which produces high quality visualization from an object represented by the HyperFun geometric modeling language and a parallel HyperFun grid system which distributes the calculations of the HyperFun polygonizer over many computers through a network are presented. We show that distributing the calculation for visualization of HyperFun function represented models via a heterogeneous computer network with our parallel polygonization method can yield HyperFun polygonal models of reduced size in a shorter period of time.

## 1  Introduction

The HyperFun language (HF) [1] is a geometric modeling language, which represents objects by using mathematical functions. Such representation, generally called implicit representation, has many merits such as high accuracy and compression of data, although it is not a direct visual representation like boundary representation (B-rep). In HF, mathematical function representation (F-rep) is separated from the visual representation. F-rep allows for volume modeling of an object of mixed materials and definition of other physical properties and dimensions such as texture, time, metamorphosis and so forth. However, to visualize HF implicit models requires processing that approximates an implicit surface with a polygonal and/or other form of visual representation at a desired resolution.

The current HF polygonizer algorithm is based on the isosurface (implicit surface) piecewise analytical description method using hyperbolic arcs proposed in [6] [7]. The algorithm is free of ambiguities and heuristics essential to other algorithms of this kind, for example, [12]. Using this technique consumes much computing time and memory resources, especially in the case of high resolution and complex object rendering where a huge number of polygons are created. Because of the large number of polygons generated and the subsequent visualization processing time, the current HF polygonizer is tough to use for interactive HF modeling.

Although polygon reduction techniques exist to optimize large HF polygonal meshes, such reduction consumes a great deal of processing time.

To solve these problems, an Advanced HyperFun Polygonizer (AHP) uses a Parallel HF Grid System (PHF) to distribute calculations of polygonization or

M. Guo and L.T.Yang (Eds.): ISPA 2003, LNCS 2745, pp. 329–345, 2003.

polygon reduction over many computers through networks to realize high-speed polygonization and simplified polygonal meshes.

In the visualization of function represented object, Bloomenthal [3] describes the framework of polygonization of implicit surface and implemented implicit surface polygonizer [4]. This framework of polygonization is similar to HFP and has similar problems such as calculation cost and number of polygons.

## 2  HyperFun Project

The HyperFun Project [1] is a software development project for functionally based shape modeling, visualization and animation. The project is based on a so-called function representation (F-rep) of geometric objects and supporting software tools built around the HyperFun language.

In F-rep, geometric objects are defined by a single real continuous function of several variables like $F(x_1, x_2, x_3 \cdots) \geq 0$. The sign of the function $F(x)$ indicates if point $x$ is:

$$\begin{cases} F(x) > 0 & \text{inside the object,} \\ F(x) = 0 & \text{on the surface of the object,} \\ F(x) < 0 & \text{outside the object .} \end{cases} \qquad (1)$$

The HyperFun language (HF) is a specialized high-level language that allows for a parameterized description of functionally based multidimensional geometric shapes. HF was originally introduced for teaching and practical use of F-rep modeling. HF is a typical procedural language with branching, loops, variables, assignments, etc. HF can handle and describe complex shapes by using mathematical functions and operations. HF supports a tree structure of branched inner nodes of operations and transformations ending in leaf nodes of simple shapes or predefined primitives.

In principle, the language is self-contained and allows users to build objects from scratch, without the use of any predefined primitives. However, HF provides an "F-rep library" which is easily extendable and contains the most common primitives and transformations. There are functions implementing conventional CSG primitives (e.g. block, sphere, cylinder, cone, and torus) as well as their more general counterparts (e.g. ellipsoid, super-ellipsoid, elliptical cylinder, elliptical cone). Another group of library primitives implements popular implicits (e.g. blobby objects, soft objects, metaballs) including convolution objects with skeletons of different types (i.e. points, line segments, arcs, triangles, curves, and meshes). Primitives derived from parametric functions (i.e. Cubic spline and Bezier objects) are also implemented, and the usual primitive transformation operations are available, such as rotation, scaling, translation, twisiting, stretching, tapering, blending union/intersection, and more general operations such as non-linear space mapping driven by arbitrary control points [2].

## 2.1    HyperFun Polygonizer

There is no direct visualization of an F-rep model. To visualize the HF or F-rep model, the HF Polygonizer, a program which polygonizes and displays an object input from an HF file, is used. The HF Polygonizer has a command line interface allowing the user to define a number of options and to specify such parameters as the "Display Mode" (i.e. Wire-frame, Surface and Wire-frame, Surface with Normals - all with different lighting effects), the "Grid Density," the "Bounding Box", the "Face Color", the "Line Color", etc. Support for higher dimensional models is also available. The program makes it possible to output the results in VRML format.

## 2.2    Polygonization Method

The polygonization method of the original HF Polygonizer has two main steps, finding vertices and creating triangles. In the first step, finding vertices, vertices in order to approximate the spatial surface of HF objects ($F = 0$) are found. In the second step, creating triangles, vertices computed in the first step are connected and triangles which make up the polygonal mesh are created.

**Finding Vertices.** A spatial area is defined by an HF partition of $G_x \times G_y \times G_z$ resolution grid. The matrix $M$ is a three-dimensional array, of size $G_x \times G_y \times G_z$, filled with the value of $F$ at the location of the grid's node.

Then using the matrix $M$ makes it possible to detect a sign change between two adjacent grid nodes without any calculation. When a sign change is detected, it means that the function $F = 0$ or the spatial surface of the object lies somewhere on the segment delimited by these two nodes. In this step which detects sign changes for whole grids, if a change is detected, approximate the position of a vertex on the segment by a linear approximation of F on the segment.

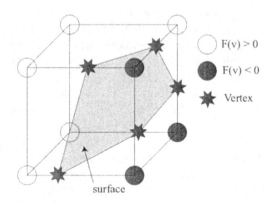

**Fig. 1.** Detected vertices with sign changes on the grid

**Creating Triangles.** The vertices, in order to approximate the spatial surface where $F = 0$, are connected and create triangles of the polygon mesh by using a connectivity graph [7] for each of the cells of the grid. To create a connectivity graph, all six faces of the cell of the grid are classified into the following cases by the number of vertices on the face.

- no vertex of a face.
- two vertices on the edges of a face.
- four vertices on the edges of a face.

A connectivity graph has twelve nodes and some edges. Each node corresponds to an edge of the sell.

In the first case, no vertex of a face, nothing is added to the connectivity graph.

In the second case face, an edge connecting two nodes is added to the connectivity graph, where these nodes correspond to two edges with vertices of the face.

In the third case face, two edges connecting two sets of nodes are created. The third case face is called "ambiguous face," because there are two possible ways of edge connections on these faces and making the wrong choice of connection causes some hole.

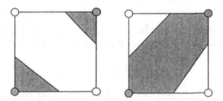

**Fig. 2.** An ambiguous face

To make the right choice of these two possible connections, HP uses the Bilinear Contours Method [6] [7] [13]. The contours of the connection can be represented locally by parts of a hyperbola. The ambiguous face occurs when both parts of the hyperbola intersect a face; therefore, the topology of the hyperbola equals the connection of the vertices. The correct choice of the connections is made by comparing the threshold with the bilinear interpolation at the crossing point of the asymptotes of the hyperbola, $F(s,t)$ as:

$$F(s,t) = \frac{P_0 P_3 - P_2 P_3}{P_0 + P_3 - P_1 - P_2} \tag{2}$$

$P_0, P_1, P_2, P_3$ : Value of $F$ on $P0, P1, P2, P3$ .

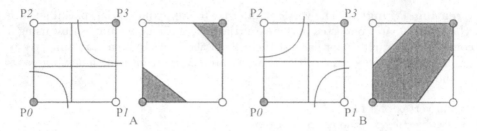

**Fig. 3.** Bilinear contours method

If the interpolation value is less than the threshold, then use orientation A, otherwise use orientation B.

Once creating the connectivity graph is finished, trace the graph to find some edge sets of closed path. In case there are more than 3 nodes on a path, create fictional edge and divide the path; then create the closed path set with 3 nodes. This set, closed path, shows triangle topology.

**Computing Normals and Triangle Orientation Normalization.** The normal of $F$ at each of the vertices is computed and the orientation of triangles are normalized, if these are required. Normals and a normalized triangle mesh representing the surface of the implicit object are needed in order to shade the surface to produce an image.

At a vertex $v$ on the surface, the normalized gradient, $\nabla F(v)$, is the surface normal. With three evaluations of the function $F$, the gradient is approximated:

$$\nabla F(v) \approx ([F(v) - F(v_x)]/\Delta, [F(v) - F(v_y)]/\Delta, [F(v) - F(v_z)]/\Delta) \quad (3)$$

$v_{x,y,z} : v$ displaced by $\Delta$ along the respective axes .

The top and wire orientations of a polygon are defined by the order of their vertices, which are clockwise or counter-clockwise. If the view is from the top side, the vertices are ordered counter-clockwise.

To normalize the orientation of triangles, calculate the face normals for each triangle by two methods; 1) an average of the normal of the vertices of the triangle; 2) compute from the vertex coordinates, $triangle(A, B, C) \Rightarrow \boldsymbol{AB} \wedge \boldsymbol{AC}$.

Check the results for orientation; the normals shpild be oriented in the same direction, and, if the results are not the same, exchange two vertices: $(A, B, C) \Rightarrow (A, C, B)$ to ensure all the triangles have the same orientation (clockwise or counter-clockwise), thus preventing problems with illumination while visualizing the mesh.

## 2.3   Problems

The above method consumes much computing resources, because it requires the sampling of a real-valued function of each of the nodes of a three dimensional

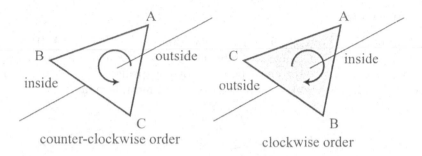

**Fig. 4.** Vertices order and polygon orientation on the $triangle(A, B, C)$

grid. The above method consumes much computer processing time, especially for large grids or complex functions.

The current method can not detect multiple vertices on the edge of the grid, and, in the case of two or more vertices on the edge, a crack, hole or warp of the surface occurs.

To prevent these shape deformations in polygonize of complex objects, the grid resolution should be set very high, although using a high resolution grid to polygonize is costly: for example, if grid resolution doubles, grid nodes where the value of $F$ is calculated increase by $2^3$ fold.

Additionally, using a high-resolution grid creates many useless polygons. In this method, the spatial area is equally divided without considering the object's shape and creates a uniform density mesh, as if there were simple surfaces. Consequently, this method consumes much memory and is inefficient in processing of the polygonal mesh, resisting easy handling of the mesh data.

These problems impede interactive modeling with the HyperFun polygonizer, especially for complex models.


## 3   Polygon Reduction in Parallel

The goal of polygon reduction on AHP is to generate low-polygon-count approximations by removing polygons which are not needed to retain the original features and shape of the objects.

Polygon reduction technique advances are being made along with LOD (Level-of-Detail) or progressive mesh [14], and the most popular method of polygon reduction is iterative edge contraction. There are several methods to reduce polygons by iteratively contracting edges [14] [15] [16] [17]. The main difference between these methods is how to choose an edge for contraction.

Therefore, these methods generally focus on the closed and uniform mesh. The meshes created by AHP are not uniform, and they are discontinuous.

## 3.1 Overview

The basic operation of the polygon simplification method used by AHP is a half edge collapse operation, the most simple method to contract edges, which is the operation to delete a vertex and 2 polygons by collapsing the edge $[v_u, v_v]$ to $v_u$. In iterating this operation, a simplified polygonal mesh is created.

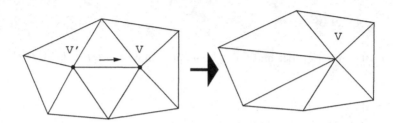

**Fig. 5.** Half edge collapse

To get a polygonal mesh which retains its original shape and has a low number of polygons, detecting the edge that can be collapsed is the salient problem for this method. This polygon reduction method estimates two parameters to find edges that can be deleted: whether the edge is contained in a feature edge path and whether the edge vertices are contained in feature vertices.

## 3.2 Feature Edge Path and Vertices

Feature edge paths are unique edge paths that feature the object shape (e.g. edge of a cube), and these edges are an important element to define the shape of an object [9].

Considering an edge path of $[v_1, v_2 \cdots v_l]$, moving $v_1$ and $v_l$, corner point of the path, means breaking the edge path and has the possibility of radically changing an object's shape. Also, collapsing the edge $[v_i, v_{out}]$ to $v_{out}$, where $v_i$ is on the edge path, has a similar possibility.

In this method, feature edges are defined as the edge angles of the normals of both side triangles on the edge if they are sharper than the angle of the border.

Feature vertices are unique vertices that feature object shape (e.g. apex of a circular cone), and these vertices are an important element to define the shape of an object. Collapsing edge $[v_f, v_{not}]$, $v_f$ is a feature vertex and $v_{not}$ is not, has the possibility of radically changing an object's shape.

In this method, feature vertices are defined as the vertices where the absolute value of $K(v)$ is larger than the border.

$$K(v) = \alpha/S \tag{4}$$

$$\alpha = 2\pi - (\text{angle around } v)$$
$$S = \text{area of triangles around } v \ . \tag{5}$$

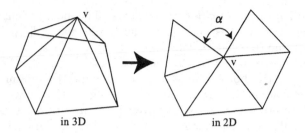

in 3D                    in 2D

**Fig. 6.** Visual image of $\alpha$

$K(v)$ approaches gaussian curvature [18] in the neighborhood of $v$ and, in the vertex, $K(v)$ is larger, if the surface curvature is more convex or concave than the feature vertex.

### 3.3   Mesh Level

One of the problems to choose an edge to collapse is that the mesh of AHP is separated into some pieces and distributed to each node. The general framework of iterative edge contraction is to estimate the edges of the mesh and delete the most worthless edges. In this way, the AHP meshes are distributed to each node at random, and the complexity of the mesh on each of the nodes is different. In deleting the most worthless edges on each node, unbalance deletion occurs.

To prevent unbalanced deletion, the idea of mesh level [5] [14] is used. The Original mesh defined $M_0$, as mesh of level 0, and is successively reduced into a series of hemimorphy mesh $M_i$ with $i < 0$. In increasing the level of mesh, as $M_i \Rightarrow M_{i+1}$ the mesh is collapsed a set of possible edges. By each node creating the same level mesh, the unbalanced deletion is prevented.

### 3.4   Mesh Simplification Method

**Estimating Vertices.** All vertices on the mesh are estimated and their value of importance $I$; if the value of $I$ is larger, the vertex is more important to retain the shape of the object.

The value of importance of vertex $v$, $I(v)$, is defined with the curvature on $v$ and the number of feature edges connected to $v$:

$$I(v) = K(v) + p_1 \times E_{corner}(v) \tag{6}$$

$$E_{corner}(v) = \begin{cases} 0 & \text{if number of feature edges connected to } v \text{ is 0 or 2,} \\ 1 & \text{otherwise .} \end{cases} \tag{7}$$
$$p_1 : \text{ parameter}$$

$I(v)$ becomes large on the feature vertices or corner point of the feature edge, which means moving these vertices has the possibility of radically changing the object's shape. $p_1$ is a pre-defined parameter which defines how much attention to pay to feature edges.

**Collecting an Independent Set of Vertices.** The independent set of vertices $M$, where their value of $I$ is lower than the border value $I_{border}$, means their vertices are possible to collapse. The collection process is shown below.

Considering the set of vertices $L \in v(v : I(v) < I_{border})$, where their value of $I$ is lower than the border value, the vertex with the minimum value of $I$ is picked up and added to $M$. If the neighboring vertices have the minimum value in $I$, these vertices are taken out from $I$. By iterating this process until $I$ becomes empty, all the independent vertices whose value $I$ are lower than $I_{border}$ is collected in $M$.

**Selecting Edges.** Edges which are connected to the vertices in $M$ and will be collapsed are selected. All sets of edges connecting to vertices in $M$ are estimated and the cost to collapse $C$ is defined. The cost of edge $e$, $C(e)$ is defined with its edge state (whether the edge is a feature edge or not) and the curvature on the vertex of the edge end.

$$C(e) = K(v) + p_2 \times F_{edge}(e) \tag{8}$$

$$F_{edge}(e) = \begin{cases} 0 & \text{if edge is feature edge,} \\ 1 & \text{otherwise .} \end{cases} \tag{9}$$
$$p_2 : \quad \text{parameter}$$

$C(e)$ becomes small on the feature vertices or the feature edge, and if so, it is possible to collapse the edges without much change in the shape. $p_2$ is a pre-defined parameter which defines how much attention to pay to feature edges.

The edges with the minimum value of $C$ in each of the sets are selected and subjected to edge collapse.

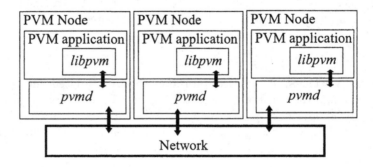

**Fig. 7.** PVM system model

**Collapsing Edges.** All edges selected are collapsed. On the edge $E(v_1, v_2)$, $v_1$ is an end vertex of the edge and $L \in v_1$; and $v_2$ is another end vertex, $v_1$ is moved to $v_2$. Edge $E$ is deleted and two polygons containing edge $E$ are deleted by this operation.

All edges are deleted; tour return to the first step and iterate these operations until no vertex with value of $I$ lower than $I_{border}$ remains or defined number of iterations are over.

In iterating these processes, vertices which are of lesser importance to retain the object's shape are deleted, and the surface is simplified while retaining the shape.

### 3.5    Boundary Part Operations

There are some problems of operations in boundary parts of cells. The meshes are discontinuous in boundary parts, and it is impossible to calculate correct curvature because of missing triangles. To calculate curvature in boundary parts, a fictional mirror copy of the mesh is reflected from the inside of the cell to outside of the cell. Using this fictional mesh, the curvature in the boundary part approach is approximated.

Another problem is the cross section curve. The edge collapse on boundary parts causes a changing of cross section curve, resulting in mismatch of the final polygon. To prevent this mismatch, additional costs are added on boundary point when estimating the vertices. The estimate function $I(v)$ is improved as:

$$I(v) = K(v) + p_1 \times E_{corner}(v) + p_3 \times B(v) \tag{10}$$

$$
\begin{aligned}
E_{corner}(v) &= \begin{cases} 0 & \text{if number of feature edges connected to } v \text{ is 0 or 2,} \\ 1 & \text{otherwise .} \end{cases} \\
B(v) &= \begin{cases} 1 & \text{if } v \text{ is in boundary part,} \\ 0 & \text{otherwise .} \end{cases} \\
p_1, p_3 &: \text{ parameter}
\end{aligned}
\tag{11}
$$

## 4    Parallel Polygonizer

The HyperFun grid is a set of computers connected by general local area networks (LANs), communicating via TCP/IP protocol, and using Parallel Virtual Machine (PVM) for message passing. It is a Distributed Memory system; each computer in the grid has independent memory, which is not sheared. The computers in the grid are called nodes. These nodes are divided into two classes of nodes, the one of master node and worker nodes. The master node controls worker nodes.

### 4.1    PVM

PVM (Parallel Virtual Machine) [8] is a free software package that enables a collection of heterogeneous computers hooked together to be used as a single large parallel computer by using message passing. Large computational problems can be solved more cost effectively by using the aggregate power and memory of many computers.

- PVM hides problems resulting from hardware / operating system differences to the user, such as little / big endian issues, size of the base type, etc.
- PVM is portable; it is available for many operating systems, machines, and architectures, and can communicate over these heterogeneous processors.

PVM consists of a console, daemons, and programming libraries. Each host in PVM runs the PVM daemon, called "pvmd." The daemon, pvmd, routes and controls messages and manages tasks under its control.

PVM applications can control tasks and send / receive messages through pvmd by using the PVM library, called "libpvm."

Everything in the virtual machine is controlled through the console, such as adding or deleting hosts, launching tasks and so on. Operations available from the console can be launched inside any application through the libpvm.

## 5    Parallel Polygonization Method

In the parallel method, two other steps are added to the current HyperFun polygonizer, the first step: distributing the processing elements to nodes, and the last step: gathering results from nodes. The calculation grid is broken into some cubic blocks, and these blocks are distributed over the nodes. Each node calculates its own blocks in the same way as the current HyperFun polygonizer and creates some parts of the polygonal mesh. Finally, the master node gathers these parts, patches them and creates a final polygonal mesh.

### 5.1    Distribute Computing Blocks

One of the important issues to parallel performance progress is load balancing. If the destribution of calculation weight is not balanced, nodes which do not calculate much finish their tasks earlier than nodes which have heavy calculation, and these lighter, early nodes must wait for the overloaded, late ones. This imbalance is a waste of computing resources and cause a decline in performance.

In case of the advanced HyperFun Polygonizer (AFP), the number of calculation elements, such as vertices or triangles, in each block is different and difficult to anticipate before calculation, and so, the AHP balances the calculation weight dynamically.

The master node of the AHP has a block pool and worker nodes make requests for new blocks to the master node, in order to avoid a worker node settiong idle.

### 5.2    Gathering Parts of the Mesh

The Advanced HyperFun Polygonizer (AHP) mesh data has a simple data structure: vertices, which have an index number; normals for each of the vertices; and triangle data, which are represented by an index of a set of three vertices, in order to reduce the cost of transporting and translating the data.

One of the problems, in gathering parts of the mesh to the master node is the numbering of the vertices index, because, before gathering, the index of vertices is local to each node and not independent of the vertices of other nodes. AHP distribute vertices on each node and changes the local index number to a global index number. Each node, $P_1, P_2, \cdots P_n$, builds an index of the array of vertices it owns a nd broadcasts this index to other nodes by turns. Each node changes its local index number to a global index number as:

$$(\text{index in } P_i \text{ array}) + \sum_{k=1}^{n-1}(\text{size of array } P_i) \qquad (12)$$

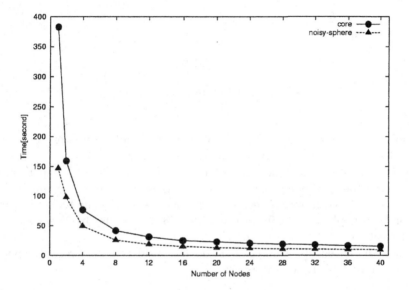

**Fig. 8.** Time result with nodes

# 6   Test Environment and Result

The Test of AHP and PHF is done on a set of 40 Sun workstations (Fujitsu GP 400S model 10) connected by Ethernet. In this test, the exact processing time is not the point of interest but rather the relative speed up.

## 6.1   AHP Speed Up Test

To make the test, two HF models, the model called "noisy-sphere" and the more complex one called "core", were polygonized with $100 \times 100 \times 100$ resolution grid

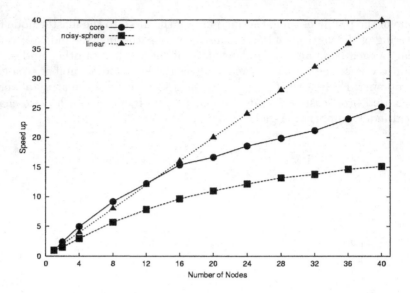

**Fig. 9.** Speed up result with nodes

and polygon reduction was not in use. The timing results graph of these objects performed on different number of nodes are shown in Fig. 8.

Using the Advanced HyperFun Polygonizer and the Parallel HyperFun Grid System, the speed of polygonization of models is increased. The time to polygonize was reduced from 147 seconds to 9 seconds (94% time reduction) in the case of "noisy-sphere," and from 6 minutes (382 seconds) to 15 seconds (96% time reduction) in the case of "core."

Then, the speed up of polygonization is considered. The relative speed up with $N$ nodes $S(N)$ is defined as:

$$S(N) = T_1/T_N$$
$$T_1 : \text{ Time with 1 node} \tag{13}$$
$$T_N : \text{ Time with } N \text{ nodes}$$

The desired speed up using $N$ nodes is $N$ times. The relative speed up graph of each model and a desired linear speed up are shown in Fig. 9

In the case of "noisy-sphere", the speed up increases as the linear ratio with the number of nodes increases. In the case of "core", the speed up increase is almost the same as desired when the number of nodes is less than 16, and when the number of nodes increasing is more than 16, the ratio of increase changes and declines but almost keeps a linear increase in speed. The speed up with 40 nodes is 15 times (37.5% of desired linear) in the case of "noisy-sphere", and 25 times (62.5% of desired linear) in the case of "core."

These results show AHP and PHF are effective to speed up the polygonization of HF models, and it is more effective if the model is complex.

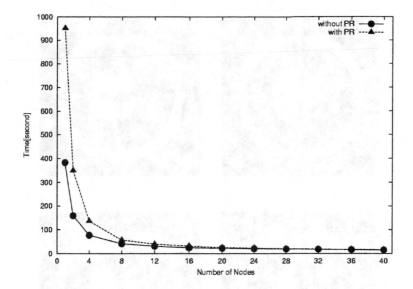

**Fig. 10.** Time result with PR and without PR

## 6.2   Polygon Reduction Speed Up Test

To make the timing test of the polygon reduction (PR), the model called "core" was polygonized with $100 \times 100 \times 100$ resolution grid and PR was used with the number of iterations being 5. The timing results graph of polygonizing "core" model with and without PR performed on different numbers of nodes is shown in Fig. 10. The timing result with PR on a single node is over twice the result without PR, 951 seconds with PR and 382 without PR, though the time difference between with and without PR is decreased with an increasing number of nodes and becomes almost the same. The timing result with 40 nodes is 16.3 seconds with PR and 15.2 seconds without PR. This result shows PR with PHF can reduce polygons with only a small timing cost.

## 6.3   Polygon Reduction Mesh Quality

The meshes of "core" in $W_0$(original), $W_3$, $W_5$ and $W_7$ are shown in Fig 11, and the number of polygons for each mesh is shown in Table 1.

**Table 1.** Numbers of triangles

| Mesh | $W_0$ | $W_3$ | $W_5$ | $W_7$ |
|---|---|---|---|---|
| # of triangle | 85537 | 45609 | 34586 | 29758 |

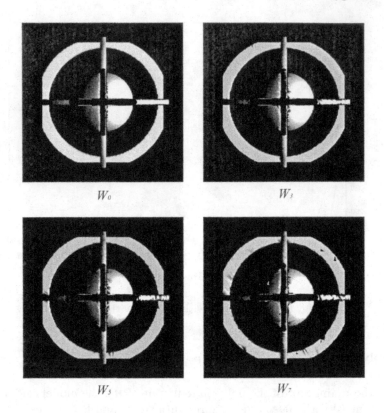

Fig. 11. Result with PR and without PR

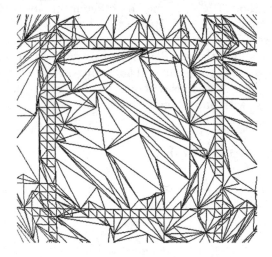

Fig. 12. Nonuniform mesh

The mesh $W_3$, in which 47% of triangles are reduced from the original mesh, still retains almost the same shape as original. The mesh $W_5$, in which 60% of triangles are reduced from the original mesh, shows some amount of degradation but still retains original shape. The mesh $W_7$, in which 66% of the triangles are reduced, still retains the shape but some holes appear at the boundary part of the mesh.

The result shows that the PR of AHP reduces the number of triangles while still retaining the original mesh shape. Note that the reducing ratio is not so high because of keeping the original shape. Additionally, the created mesh by PR has some problems, nonuniform mesh and holes. The triangle density of the created mesh is not consistent between the middle part and boundary part of grid cells and some holes appear on the boundary part.

# 7   Conclusion and Future Work

The Advanced HyperFun Polygonizer (AHP) and the Parallel HyperFun grid (PHF) realize effective speed up of the polygonization of HF models. AHP and PHF are possible solutions to facilitate the interactive shape-modeling environment with the HyperFun language for simple and complex models.

In our work, PHF is realized on a network of Sun workstations with SunOS. However, PVM is available on various environments, such as Windows, Linux, SGI and so on. Since PVM has high portability, PHF is easily realized on any environment. Additionally, there are some high performance parallel computing environments being developed, and these have the possibility to boost the performance of PHF thus improving the capabilities of the HyperFun project.

The polygon reduction in parallel needs some improvement in the quality of the mesh and the reduction ratio of polygons. To create uniform mesh or prevent some holes on boundary parts, reduced polygon information on boundary parts should be shared with their neighbors and the low cost method of sharing this data should be improved. Though the polygon reduction in parallel shows effective speed up, there is room for improvement on large polygonal meshes.

# References

1. HyperFun Project: http://www.hyperfun.org
2. Adzhiev, A., Cartwright, R. Fausett, E., Ossipov, A., Pasko, A., and Savchenko, V., "HyperFun project: Language and Software tools for F-rep Shape Modeling", Proceedings of Eurographics/ACM SIGGRAPH Workshop Implicit Surfces '99, (Bordeaux, France, September 13–15 1999), J. Hughes and C. Schlick (Eds.), pp. 59–69.
3. Bloomenthal, J., "Polygonization of Implicit Surfaces", Computer Aided Geometric Design, Vol. 5, 341–355, 1988.
4. Bloomenthal, J., "An Implicit Surface Polygonizer", Graphics Gems IV, 1994.
5. Aaron W. F. Lee, Wim Sweldens, Peter Schroder, Lawrence Cowsar, David Dobkin. "MAPS: Multiresolution Adaptive Parameterization of Surfaces", Computer Graphics Proceedings (SIGGRAPH 98), pp. 95–104, 1998.

6. Pasko A.A., Pilyugin V.V., Pokrovskiy V.V. "Geometric modeling in the analysis of trivariate functions", Communications of Joint Institute of Nuclear Research, P10-86-310, Dubna, USSR, 1986 (in Russian).
7. Pasko A.A., Pilyugin V.V., Pokrovskiy V.V. "Geometric modeling in the analysis of trivariate functions", Computers and Graphics, vol. 12, Nos. 3/4, 1988, pp. 457–465.
8. PVM : Parallel Virtual Machine: http://www.epm.ornl.gov/pvm/pvm_home.html
9. M. Hayano, T. Matsuoka, K. Ueda, "Mesh Simplification Using Edge Operation with Feature Detection", Ricoh Technical Report, 24, pp. 7–76, 1998 (Japanese).
10. I. S. Sedukhin, S. G. Sedukhin, A. A. Pasko, V. V. Savachenko, N. N. Mirenkov "Parallel Rendering of Functionally Represented Geometric Object with the Network Linda System", Technical Report 95-1-001, Department of Computer Software, The University of Aizu. 1995.
11. Sergey Ten, Andrey Savchenko, Alexander Pasko, Vladimir Savachenko "Distributed Animation of Volumetric Objects", Technical Report 95-1-016, Department of Computer Software, The University of Aizu. 1995.
12. William E. Lorensen and Harvey E. Cline, "Marching cubes: A high resolution 3D surface construction algorithm", Computer Graphics, 21(4):163–169, July 1987.
13. Gregory M. Nielson and Bernd Hamann, "The asymptotic decider: Resolving the ambiguity in the marching cubes", Proceedings Visualization '91 – sponsored by the IEEE Computer Society, pages 83–91, 1991.
14. Hugues Hoppe "Progresssive Meshes", SIGGRAPH 96 Proc., pages 99–108, 1996.
15. Hugues Hoppe, Tony DeRose, Tom Duchamp, John McDonald, and Werner Stuetzel, "Mesh optimization", SIGGRAPH 93 Proc., pages 19–26, 1993.
16. Michael Garland and Paul S. Heckbert, "Surface Simplification Using Quadric Error Metrics", SIGGRAPH 97 Proc., pages 209–216, 1997.
17. Junji Horikawa and Takashi Totsuka, "A Hierarchical Approximation for 3D Polygon Models", Proceeding of the 5th Sony Research Forum, pp. 3–7, 1995.
18. C. R. Callafine, "Gaussian curvature and shell structure", The Mathematics of Surfaces, Oxford University Press, pp. 179–196,1986.
19. HyperFun Tutorial(Japanese): http://www.hyperfun.org

# A Parallel Solver Using Block Fourier Decompositions*

Hsin-Chu Chen and Shinn-Yih Tzeng

Dept. of Computer and Information Science
Clark Atlanta University
Atlanta, GA 30314, USA
hchen@cau.edu, luistzeng@yahoo.com

**Abstract.** The block Fourier decomposition method recently proposed by the first author is a special method for decoupling any block tridiagonal matrix of the form $K = $ block-tridiag $[B, A, B]$, where $A$ and $B$ are square submatrices, into diagonal blocks. Unlike the traditional fast Poisson solver, block cyclic reductions, or the FACR algorithm, this approach does not require $A$ and $B$ be symmetric or commute. Presented in this paper is a parallel solver using this block decomposition method to solve linear systems whose coefficient matrices are of the form of $K$. We describe the computational procedure and implementation for parallel executions on distributed workstations. The performance from our numerical experiments is reported to demonstrate the usefulness of this approach.

**Keywords.** Block Fourier decomposition, orthogonal transformation, linear system, distributed and parallel computation, master-slave model, message-passing interface (MPI).

## 1  Introduction

In this paper, we present a parallel solver using the block Fourier decomposition method recently proposed in [2] for solving block tridiagonal linear systems $Kx = y$, $K \in \mathcal{R}^{pq \times pq}$, where $K = $ block-tridiag $[B, A, B]$, $A, B \in \mathcal{R}^{p \times p}$. In its partitioned form, $Kx = y$ can be written as

$$
\begin{bmatrix}
A & B & & \\
B & A & \ddots & \\
& \ddots & \ddots & B \\
& & B & A
\end{bmatrix}
\begin{bmatrix}
x_1 \\ x_2 \\ \vdots \\ x_q
\end{bmatrix}
=
\begin{bmatrix}
y_1 \\ y_2 \\ \vdots \\ y_q
\end{bmatrix}.
\tag{1}
$$

We do not impose any special structure or properties on the submatrices $A$ and $B$. The matrix $K$, however, is assumed to be nonsingular in order for the system

---

* This work was supported in part by the Army Research Laboratory under Grant No. DAAL01-98-2-D065.

M. Guo and L.T.Yang (Eds.): ISPA 2003, LNCS 2745, pp. 346–355, 2003.

to have a unique solution, although the block decomposition itself does not even require the matrix $K$ to be nonsingular.

When $A$ and $B$ are symmetric and commute, three well-known direct methods [1,4,6] are available for solving the linear system: the fast Poisson solver (FPS), block cyclic reductions, and FACR which combines the use of Fourier Analysis and Cyclic Reductions. The FPS employs a complete set of orthogonal eigenvectors common to both $A$ and $B$, which imposes the symmetry and commutability of $A$ and $B$. The approach using block cyclic reductions also requires that $A$ and $B$ commute. The FACR scheme is subject to the same constraints since it is a combination of these two. These three approaches all fail to solve the system directly when the matrices $A$ and $B$ are neither symmetric nor commuting. In such a situation the block Fourier decomposition method which employs Fourier transformations in block form becomes the method of choice because it does not impose any such constraints. The theoretical framework of this approach has been presented in [2] and will not be repeated here. The main purpose of this paper is to present the implementation of this method for solving the linear system in parallel using either multiple CPUs in a single machine or multiple computers on a single network.

In the next section, we briefly describe the block Fourier decomposition and its computational procedure for decoupling the linear system into $q$ independent subsystems so that the system can be solved not only efficiently but also in parallel. In Section 3 we present our implementation for parallel and distributed computations of this approach on workstations connected via an Ethernet local area network. In Section 4, we report the numerical experiments and performance of our implementation using the MPI (Message-Passing Interface) libraries. Conclusions are drawn in Section 5.

## 2  Block Fourier Decompositions

Before presenting our implementation of the block Fourier decomposition method for decoupling the linear system in Equation (1) into $q$ independent subsystems on a network of workstations, we briefly describe the decomposition and computational procedure in this section. Refer to [2] for a formal proof of the validity of this approach. For the sake of notational consistency, we shall follow the same notation as used in that paper.

### 2.1  Decomposition

Let $V_k \in \mathcal{R}^{pq \times p}$ and $Q \in \mathcal{R}^{pq \times pq}$ be defined as

$$V_k = \sqrt{\frac{2}{q+1}}\left[\,sin(\theta_k)I,\ sin(2\theta_k)I,\ \cdots,\ sin(q\theta_k)I\,\right]^T, k = 1, 2, \cdots, q,$$

and

$$Q = [V_1, V_2, \cdots, V_q]$$

where $\theta_k = \frac{k\pi}{q+1}$, $I$ is the identity matrix of dimension $p$, $q$ denotes the number of diagonal blocks in the matrix $K$, and $Q$ can be shown to be an orthogonal and symmetric matrix. The superscript $T$ denotes the transpose of the matrix. Using the orthogonal transformation $(Q^T K Q)Q^T x = Q^T y$, denoted as $\tilde{K}\tilde{x} = \tilde{y}$ where $\tilde{K} = Q^T K Q$, $\tilde{x} = Q^T x$, and $\tilde{y} = Q^T y$, the block Fourier decomposition method yields the following $q$ decoupled subsystems:

$$
\begin{bmatrix} \tilde{K}_1 & & & \\ & \tilde{K}_2 & & \\ & & \ddots & \\ & & & \tilde{K}_q \end{bmatrix} \begin{bmatrix} \tilde{x}_1 \\ \tilde{x}_2 \\ \vdots \\ \tilde{x}_q \end{bmatrix} = \begin{bmatrix} \tilde{y}_1 \\ \tilde{y}_2 \\ \vdots \\ \tilde{y}_q \end{bmatrix}
\tag{2}
$$

where $\tilde{K}_k = A + 2cos(\theta_k)B$ and $\tilde{y}_k = V_k^T y, k = 1, \cdots, q$.

## 2.2   Computational Procedure

The computational procedure for solving the system $Kx = y$ via $\tilde{K}\tilde{x} = \tilde{y}$ using the decomposition method just mentioned follows three well-known standard stages. The first stage involves the decomposition of the matrix $K$ into $\tilde{K}$ and the right-hand-side vector $y$ into $\tilde{y}$. Since the decoupled matrix $\tilde{K}$ and the transform matrix $Q$ (or $V_k$) are explicitly known beforehand. The decomposition at this stage is simple and straightforward. In fact, this involves only the computation of

$$
\tilde{K}_k = A + 2cos(\theta_k)B \quad \text{and} \quad \tilde{y}_k = \sqrt{\frac{2}{q+1}} \sum_{j=1}^{q} sin(j\theta_k)\, y_j
\tag{3}
$$

for $k = 1, \cdots, q$. The second stage solves the transformed system

$$
[A + 2cos(\theta_k)B]\, \tilde{x}_k = \tilde{y}_k, k = 1, \cdots, q.
\tag{4}
$$

for $\tilde{x}$, using some appropriate linear system solver. This may be a tridiagonal solver, a band solver, or a dense one, depending on the structure of the matrix $\tilde{K}$ (or that of $A$ and $B$) since no special structure has been imposed on both $A$ and $B$. Once $\tilde{x}$ has been obtained, the third stage then retrieves the final solution $x$ from $\tilde{x}$ as follows

$$
x_k = V_k^T \tilde{x} = \sqrt{\frac{2}{q+1}} \sum_{j=1}^{q} sin(j\theta_k)\tilde{x}_j, k = 1, \cdots, q
\tag{5}
$$

where we have used the fact that $Q$ is symmetric and, therefore, $x = Q\tilde{x} = Q^T \tilde{x}$, leading to $x_k = V_k^T \tilde{x}$.

## 3   Implementation for Parallel/Distributed Computations

As can easily be seen from the description in Section 2, this approach is fully parallelizable at all three stages on machines with a shared global memory. Good speedup can, therefore, be expected since all processors have access to the global memory, without the need of message passing or data transfer among processors. When implemented on a networked workstations, however, the performance of this approach using multiple workstations can be quite different, depending on the communication cost. In this section, we present an implementation of this approach on a networked distributed system. Other implementations are possible. In our implementation, we employ a master-slave computational model with one master and $q$ slaves. For programming simplicity, we make the master responsible only for transferring data to and collecting data from the slaves. All computations are performed on the slaves, one for each subsystem, although the master can also be instructed to serve as one of the slaves, in addition to serving the role as the master.

We assume that the matrices $A$ and $B$ and the right-hand-side vector $y$ are initially stored on the master. Slave $k$ is responsible for constructing $\tilde{K}_k$ and $\tilde{y}_k$, solving subsystem $\tilde{K}_k \tilde{x}_k = \tilde{y}_k$, and obtaining $x_k$. To construct $\tilde{K}_k$, slave $k$ needs to have both submatrices $A$ and $B$ ready on its memory. Since every slave will need a copy of them, this can be conveniently done through a broadcast from the master. The construction of $\tilde{y}_k$ involves the entire vector $y$ for each $k$. There are two approaches to achieving this goal. The first approach employs the following form of computation:

$$\tilde{y} = Q^T y = \begin{bmatrix} V_1^T \\ V_2^T \\ \vdots \\ V_q^T \end{bmatrix} y = \begin{bmatrix} V_1^T y \\ V_2^T y \\ \vdots \\ V_1^T y \end{bmatrix} = \begin{bmatrix} \tilde{y}_1 \\ \tilde{y}_2 \\ \vdots \\ \tilde{y}_q \end{bmatrix}$$

where the explicit form of $\tilde{y}_k$ is the same as shown in Equation (3). In this approach, one can simply ask the master to broadcast an entire copy of $y$ to all slaves, allowing each slave $k$ to independently compute $\tilde{y}_k$ without the need of communications with other slaves. Since the matrix $Q$ is symmetric, the transformation from $y$ to $\tilde{y}$ can also be expressed as

$$\tilde{y} = Q^T y = Qy = [V_1, V_2, \cdots, V_q] \begin{bmatrix} y_1 \\ y_2 \\ \vdots \\ y_q \end{bmatrix} = [V_1 y_1] + [V_2 y_2] + \cdots + [V_q y_q].$$

It is, therefore, possible to ask the master to send only subvector $y_k$ (of size $p$), instead of the entire vector $y$ (of size $pq$), to slave $k$ and let each slave $k$ independently compute $V_k y_k$ (of size $pq$), $k = 1, \cdots, q$. Note that $V_k y_k$ represents the contribution of the subvector $y_k$ to $\tilde{y}_1, \tilde{y}_2, \cdots, \tilde{y}_q$. In order to construct a complete $\tilde{y}_k$, slave $k$ needs to collect the contributions from all other subvectors $y_i, i \neq k$. Accordingly, this second approach requires an all-to-all communications among all slaves. For a distributed system connected to an Ethernet LAN, this approach is very likely to cause a great deal of transmission collisions on the shared medium. Therefore, we adapt the first approach in our implementation, which is also easier to program. Once $\tilde{K}_k$ and $\tilde{y}_k$ are computed, slave $k$ can proceed to the second stage to solve the linear subsystem $\tilde{K}_k\tilde{x}_k = \tilde{y}_k$ for $\tilde{x}_k$. This stage does not require any communication among all computers. At the third stage, slave $k$ is responsible for retrieving the final solution $x_k$ (Equation (5)). Note that retrieving $x_k$ from $\tilde{x}$ is identical to computing $\tilde{y}_k$ from $y$. However, the subvectors $\tilde{x}_k$ are distributed among all slaves and the retrieval of $x_k$ requires the entire vector $\tilde{x}$. To avoid the all-to-all communications over a shared medium at this stage, we again resort to the master to collect all $\tilde{x}_k$ to form $\tilde{x}$ and then broadcast a copy of $\tilde{x}$ back to all slaves. Upon receiving such a copy, slave $k$ then does its own share to compute $x_k$ and sends the result back to the master. The entire procedure is finished after the master has received all $x_k$ from the slaves. Figure 1 shows the computational tasks involved and communications required between the master and the slaves at the three stages, where the arrows indicate the directions of data transfer and the symbols next to each arrow represent the data to be transferred.

## 4    Numerical Experiments and Performance

To study the performance of the parallel solver using block Fourier decomposition method, we have implemented Equation (1) on distributed workstations connected by an Ethernet local area network, in which the transmission medium is shared among all workstations. The platform for our experiments includes multiple 500-MHz SunBlade-100 UltraSparc-IIe workstations connected by a 100-Mbps (100BaseT) Ethernet LAN. The programming language employed is C and the implementation for the distributed and parallel computation is done through MPICH [3], which is based on MPI Version 1.2.4. The submatrices $A$ and $B$ in $K$ are taken to be

$$
A = \begin{bmatrix} 20 & -4 & & \\ -4 & 20 & \ddots & \\ & \ddots & \ddots & -4 \\ & & -4 & 20 \end{bmatrix} \quad \text{and } B = \begin{bmatrix} -4 & -1 & & \\ -1 & -4 & \ddots & \\ & \ddots & \ddots & -1 \\ & & -1 & -4 \end{bmatrix}
$$

for the sake of convenience. Linear systems of this class can be obtained from a nine-point finite difference approximation with a uniform grid to the Poisson's equation in a rectangle subject to Dirichlet boundary conditions on all sides of the boundary [1]. See [5, Ch.10] for the derivation. Note that the matrices $A$ and $B$ used here are just a special case of those that can be decomposed using the block Fourier decomposition method. In this special case, the traditional approaches mentioned in Section 1 are also applicable since $A$ and $B$ commute and are symmetric. We use them just for the sake of convenience. This block algorithm will perform better when the bandwidth of either $A$ or $B$ becomes larger.

For our experiments, we developed two versions of the code, one for sequential execution on a single machine and the other for distributed execution based on

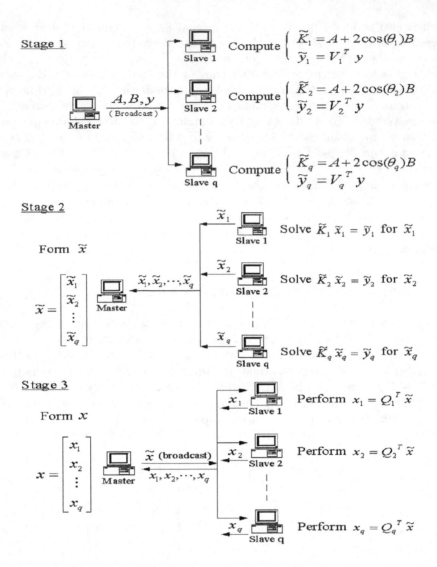

**Fig. 1.** Computation and communication using the master-salve model

**Table 1.** Best performance (wall-clock time in seconds)

| Implementation | Block Size $q$ ( $p = q$ ) | | | | | | | |
|---|---|---|---|---|---|---|---|---|
| Scheme | 128 | 256 | 384 | 512 | 640 | 768 | 896 | 1024 |
| Sequential | 1.134 | 9.056 | 30.80 | 73.53 | 143.3 | 249.0 | 395.5 | 600.4 |
| MS (2 slaves) | 0.613 | 4.824 | 16.05 | 37.98 | 73.81 | 127.6 | 202.2 | 305.9 |
| MS (4 slaves) | 0.340 | 2.626 | 8.547 | 19.49 | 38.67 | 65.47 | 103.8 | 156.5 |
| MS (8 slaves) | 0.400 | 2.214 | 5.470 | 11.71 | 21.80 | 35.92 | 56.46 | 84.12 |

the master-salve model described in the previous section using one master and multiple slaves. In both versions, the transformation matrix $Q$ is not explicitly formed and the sine functions are computed on the fly. The decomposition of the right-hand-side vector and the retrieval of the final solution are performed using straightforward multiplications. New versions that employ fast sine transforms will be developed and their performance reported later. The decoupled linear subsystems are solved using a symmetric banded direct solver with a bandwidth of 3. Table 1 shows the wall-clock time in seconds spent in all of the three stages from our current versions for various sizes of the problem. We assume that the block size $(q)$ is the same as the dimension $(p)$ of the submatrix $A$. Note that each timing presented in this table is the best one obtained from our eight repeated experiments. The best timing is used to approximate the performance that might be achieved under the condition of a dedicated execution environment, an attempt to minimize the effect of other background processes on the performance of our underlying process since the time measured is wall-clock time, instead of CPU time. As seen from this table, the use of multiple workstations greatly reduces the computational time when the problem size is large enough. Table 2 presents the speedup based on the sequential execution time for each problem size, which clearly indicates the feasibility of the master-slave implementation for this parallel solver in a distributed computing environment. The timings and speedups from Tables 1 and 2 are plotted in Figure 2 and 3, respectively.

**Table 2.** Best performance (speedup based on the sequential time)

| Implementation Scheme | Block Size $q$ ( $p = q$ ) | | | | | | | |
|---|---|---|---|---|---|---|---|---|
| | 128 | 256 | 384 | 512 | 640 | 768 | 896 | 1024 |
| Sequential | 1.00 | 1.00 | 1.00 | 1.00 | 1.00 | 1.00 | 1.00 | 1.00 |
| MS (2 slaves) | 1.85 | 1.88 | 1.92 | 1.94 | 1.94 | 1.95 | 1.96 | 1.96 |
| MS (4 slaves) | 3.34 | 3.45 | 3.60 | 3.77 | 3.71 | 3.80 | 3.81 | 3.84 |
| MS (8 slaves) | 2.84 | 4.09 | 5.63 | 6.28 | 6.57 | 6.93 | 7.00 | 7.14 |

Although each of the timings presented above was taken from the best of our repeated experiments, it deserves mentioning that the timings observed from our multiple repeated executions were very stable and close to the best timing for all cases whose block size is 256 or more. For demonstration purposes, we show the average performance of our eight repeated executions, where Table 3 and 4 represents the average timings and average speedups, which are plotted in Figure 4 and 5, respectively.

## 5   Conclusions

In this paper, we have presented a parallel solver using block Fourier decompositions for solving block tridiagonal linear systems whose coefficient matrices are

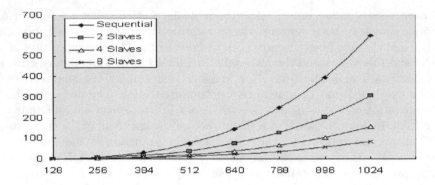

**Fig. 2.** Best wall-clock time in seconds spent in solving the linear system.

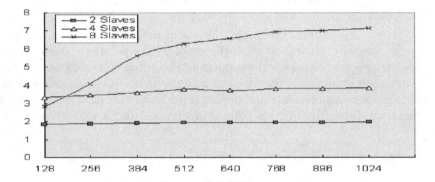

**Fig. 3.** Speedup of the master-slave implementation based on the best timing.

**Table 3.** Average performance (wall-clock time in seconds)

| Implementation Scheme | Block Size $q$ ( $p = q$ ) | | | | | | | |
|---|---|---|---|---|---|---|---|---|
| | 128 | 256 | 384 | 512 | 640 | 768 | 896 | 1024 |
| Sequential | 1.138 | 9.065 | 30.81 | 73.66 | 143.7 | 249.3 | 396.1 | 601.2 |
| MS (2 slaves) | 0.848 | 5.050 | 16.25 | 38.48 | 74.13 | 128.1 | 203.4 | 306.9 |
| MS (4 slaves) | 0.367 | 3.049 | 8.939 | 19.89 | 38.93 | 66.20 | 104.7 | 157.2 |
| MS (8 slaves) | 2.193 | 2.678 | 5.903 | 12.30 | 22.25 | 36.91 | 57.48 | 84.50 |

of the form of $K = $ block-tridiag $[B, A, B]$, where $A$ and $B$ are square matrices, in parallel on distributed workstations. The matrices $A$ and $B$ need not be symmetric; nor do they have to commute. This linear system solver is different from the traditional fast Poisson solver and can be employed where the fast Poisson solver is not applicable. The computational procedure and implementation of the solver for parallel executions on distributed workstations using the master-slave communication model have been addressed. To demonstrate the usefulness of this approach, numerical experiments using both sequential code and parallel

**Table 4.** Average performance (speedup based on the sequential time)

| Implementation Scheme | Block Size $q$ ( $p = q$ ) | | | | | | | |
|---|---|---|---|---|---|---|---|---|
| | 128 | 256 | 384 | 512 | 640 | 768 | 896 | 1024 |
| Sequential | 1.00 | 1.00 | 1.00 | 1.00 | 1.00 | 1.00 | 1.00 | 1.00 |
| MS (2 slaves) | 1.34 | 1.79 | 1.90 | 1.91 | 1.94 | 1.95 | 1.95 | 1.96 |
| MS (4 slaves) | 3.10 | 2.97 | 3.45 | 3.70 | 3.69 | 3.77 | 3.78 | 3.82 |
| MS (8 slaves) | 0.52 | 3.39 | 5.22 | 5.99 | 6.46 | 6.76 | 6.89 | 7.11 |

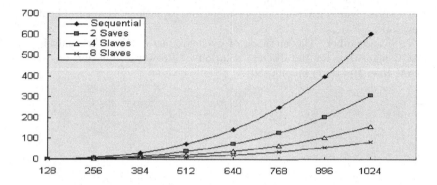

**Fig. 4.** Average wall-clock time in seconds spent in solving the linear system.

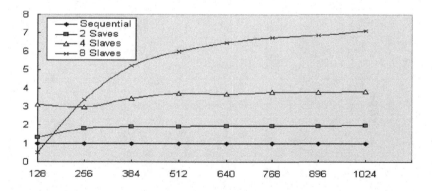

**Fig. 5.** Speedup of the master-slave implementation based on the average timing.

code have been conducted. The parallel code was implemented using MPICH. From our experiments on distributed machines connected via an Ethernet local area network, we have observed pretty decent parallel performance for large scale problems. We strongly believe this block solver will perform even better on multiprocessor machines with shared memory since in this case the communication among processors does not require direct message passing.

# References

[1] B.L. Buzbee, G.H. Golub, C.W. Nielson, On direct methods for solving Poisson's equations. SIAM J. Numer. Anal., Vol. **7**, No. 4, 1970, pp. 627–656.

[2] H.C. Chen, A block Fourier decomposition method, Lecture Notes in Computer Science 2367 (Eds.: J. Fagerholm et al.), Spring-Verlag, 2002, pp. 351–358.

[3] W. Gropp, E. Lusk and N. Doss, A high-performance, portable implementation of the MPI Message-Passing Interface standard, Parallel Computing, 22(6), 1996, pp. 789–828.

[4] R.W. Hockney, A fast direct solution of Poisson's equation using Fourier analysis, J. ACM **12** (1965) pp. 95–113.

[5] W.E. Milne, Numerical Solution of Differential Equations, Dover Publications, Inc., New York.

[6] P.N. Swarztrauber, The methods of cyclic reduction, Fourier analysis, and the FACR algorithm for the discrete solution of Poisson's equation on a rectangle, SIAM Rev. 19 (1977) pp. 490–501.

# A Parallel Algorithm for Medial Axis Transformation

Swagata Saha and Prasanta K. Jana*

Department of Computer Science and Engineering
Indian School of Mines
Dhanbad – 826004, India
pkjana@perl.ism.ac.in

**Abstract:** In this paper, we present a parallel algorithm for medial axis transformation, which is based on the parallel distance transformation presented in [1]. We first modify the parallel distance transformation as described in [1] and then apply this modified algorithm to develop a parallel algorithm for medial axis transformation. The algorithms are also simulated on two different input images.

## 1 Introduction

Skeletonization is a process for reducing foreground regions in a binary image that largely preserves the extent and connectivity of the original region while throwing away most of the original foreground pixels. The skeleton of a region may be defined by two methods. 1. Skeleton via Medial Axis Transformation (MAT) and 2. Skeleton via thinning. The terms medial axis transformation and skeletonization are often used interchangeably but there is a slight difference between them. The skeleton is simply a binary image showing the simple skeleton whereas MAT is well defined algorithm where each point on the skeleton contains both time and space information allowing original figure to be reconstructed.

In this paper, we present a parallel algorithm for medial axis transformation. There are many equivalent definition of the MAT. Here we consider the definition of MAT according to Blum as described in [9]. This definition is based on distance transformation. For different distance or metric, MAT will be different. So distance transformation takes a vital role to compute medial axis transformation of an image.

In the recent years, there have been proposed several parallel algorithms for medial axis transformation and can be found in the literatures [2], [3], [4], [6], [7], [8]. Lee [2] proposed an $O(n \log n)$ time algorithm to obtain the medial axis transformation of a planner shape with $n$ sides. Jenq and Sahni [3] proposed two $O(\log n)$ time algorithms on the CRCW PRAM model using $O(n^2)$ processors They also proposed an $O(\log n)$ time algorithm on a hypercube model using $O(n^2)$ processors. In [6], it is shown by Lee and Horng that the Chessboard distance transformation and medial axis transformation are interchangeable. They also show in their paper that the medial axis transformation of an $n \times n$ binary image can be computed in $O(\log^2 n)$ time using $n \times n$ mesh-of-trees. The same authors presented in [7] an algorithm for chessboard transformation that requires $O(\log n)$ time using $O(n^2 / \log n)$ processors on the EREW

---

* The author to be communicated.

M. Guo and L.T.Yang (Eds.): ISPA 2003, LNCS 2745, pp. 356–361, 2003.

PRAM model, $O(\log n / \log \log n)$ time using $O(n^2 \log \log n / \log n)$ processors on the CRCW PRAM model and $O (\log n)$ time on an $O(n^2)$ processors hypercube. In [4], Fujiwara et al. proposed an algorithm for MAT. They show that using this algorithm the chessboard distance transform can be computed in $O(\log n)$ time using $n^2 / \log n$ processors on the EREW PRAM, in $O(\log \log n)$ time using $n^2 / \log \log n$ processors on the common CRCW PRAM, in $O(n^2/p^2 + n)$ time on a $p \times p$ mesh and in $O( n^2/p^2 + (n \log p) / p)$ time on a $p^2$ processor hypercube, where $1 \le p \le n$. The same authors proposed in [1], an $O(\log n)$ time algorithm for computation of distance transformation using $n^2 / \log n$ processors on the EREW PRAM, in $O(\log \log n)$ time using $n^2 / \log \log n$ processors on the common CRCW PRAM, in $O(n^2/p^2 + n)$ time on a $p \times p$ mesh and in $O( n^2/p^2 + (n \log p) / p)$ time on a $p^2$ processor hypercube (for $1 \le p \le n$). They implemented their algorithm for distance transformation using nearest feature transformation.

Our parallel algorithm presented in this paper, is based on the parallel distance transformation as proposed by Fujiwara et al [1]. We first modify their parallel algorithm as follows. The nearest feature transformation (NFT) is the main operation for obtaining distance transformation (DT), which computes for each pixel, the coordinates of the nearest black pixel. For finding nearest feature transformation of a particular pixel they use prefix minima, namely UL-prefix, LL-prefix and L-prefix. However, our algorithm uses two search operations, namely RUL (reverse of UL), RLL (reverse of LL) and the L-Prefix. Next we apply this modified algorithm to develop a parallel algorithm for medial axis transformation. We also simulate our algorithm using two input images, namely H image and cup image and the results of the simulation run are shown. Thus our paper is different from that published in [1] on the following aspects.

A modified parallel algorithm for DT has been proposed

The algorithm is used to develop a parallel algorithm for MAT

The parallel algorithm for MAT is simulated using two input images

For the easy understanding and the completeness of the paper, we use the same symbols for some basic terminologies and the same steps to compute distance transform algorithm as presented in [1].

The organization of this paper is as follows. In section 2, we describe some basic terminologies. Section 3 presents the proposed parallel algorithm followed by a conclusion in section 4.

## 2  Basic Terminologies

Consider an $n \times n$ binary image denoted by $I$. Then we use $I[i, j] \in \{0, 1\}$ to denote a value for a pixel $(i, j)$ of $I$ for $0 \le i \le n - 1$ and $0 \le j \le n - 1$, where $i$ and $j$ stands for row and column index respectively. We assume that the coordinate of the pixel placed on the top left corner of the image is $(0, 0)$. We also call a pixel $(i, j)$ a black pixel if $I[i, j ]= 0$, otherwise we call the pixel a white pixel.

*Def.* 1 Distance transformation (DT): The DT of a black and white binary image is a computation that finds, for each pixel, the distance to the nearest black pixel. That is, it computes an array $DT[i, j]$ defined by $DT[i, j] = \min \{ d(p, p_B) | p_B \in \text{Black}\}$, where

$d(p, p_B)$ is the distance from the pixel $p = (i, j)$ to a pixel $p_B$ and Black is a set of all black pixels in an input image.

***Def.*** 2 Nearest feature transformation (NFT): The NFT is a computation that finds the coordinates of the nearest black pixel, for each pixel. So it computes an array NFT[$i$, $j$] given by NFT[$i$, $j$] = $(x, y)$ s.t. $d(p, p_B)$ = DT[$i$, $j$], where $p = (i, j)$ and $p_B(x, y) \in$ Black.

***Def.*** 3   Medial axis transformation (MAT): The MAT of a region $R$ with border $B$ is a process, which computes, for each point $p$ in $R$ its closest neighbor in $B$. If $p$ has more than one such neighbor, it is said to belong to medial axis of $R$.

# 3   Proposed Parallel Algorithm for Medial Axis Transformation

We now present our proposed parallel algorithm for medial axis transformation. Since our algorithm is based on the parallel distance transformation as described in [1], we use the symbols for some terms same as have been used in [1]. Further, we use the same steps for the computation of the distance transformation, i.e, phase 1 as described in [1].

For the computation of the medial axis transformation of a binary image, first the input image is divided into four sets of pixels for each pixel $(i, j)$. These four sets of pixels are denoted by $P_E(i, j)$, $P_N(i, j)$, $P_W(i, j)$ and $P_S(i, j)$ and defined by

$P_E(i, j)=\{(i + g, j + h)$ such that $\max\{- i, - h\} \le g \le \min\{n - 1- i, h\}, 0 \le h \le n - 1 - j\}$

$P_N(i, j)=\{( i - g, j + h)$ such that $0 \le g \le i, \max\{- j, - g\} \le h \le \min\{n - 1 - j, g\}\}$

$P_W(i, j)=\{(i + g, j - h)$ such that $\max\{- i,- h\} \le g \le \min\{n - 1 - i, h\}, 0 \le h \le j\}$

$P_S(i, j)=\{(i + g, j + h)$ such that $0 \le g \le n - 1 - i, \max\{- j,- g\} \le h \le \min\{n - 1 - j, g\}\}$

Phase 1: /* Compute the distance transformation */

1. Find the nearest black pixel in $P_N$ for each pixel.
2. Find the nearest black pixel in $P_S$ for each pixel.
3. Find the nearest black pixel in $P_E$ for each pixel.
4. Find the nearest black pixel in $P_W$ for each pixel.
5. Compute the nearest feature transform, i.e., select the nearest black pixel among the above four pixels for each pixel $(i, j)$ and store the coordinates to NFT[$i, j$].
6. Compute the distance transform, i.e., distance to NFT[$i, j$] for each $(i, j)$ and store the distance to DT[$i, j$].

**Computation of Nearest Feature Transformation:**  For the computation of NFT[$i$, $j$] we first calculate $NFT_E[i, j]$, $NFT_N[i, j]$, $NFT_W[i, j]$ and $NFT_S[i, j]$, the coordinates of the nearest black pixel in $P_E(i, j)$, $P_N(i, j)$, $P_W(i, j)$ and $P_S(i, j)$ respectively.

We now give an outline for computing the $NFT_E[i, j]$ followed by the detail algorithm. The other NFT[$i, j$]'s can be computed similarly. For $NFT_E[i, j]$, let DI$(i, j)$ denote the set of pixel $((P_E(i, j) - P_E(i, j +1))$ and $NFT_{ED}[i, j]$ denote coordinates of the nearest black pixel in DI$(i, j)$. Then $NFT_E$ can be computed in the follows steps.

For each pixel $(i, j)$, if $A[i, j]=1$, i.e., pixel $(i, j)$ is white, compute nearest black pixel.

Step 1: /* Compute the nearest black pixel for each $(i, j)$, in $DI_D(i, j)=\{(i + k, j + k)$ such that $(i + k, j + k) \in DI(i, j)\}$. The pixel can be computed by diagonal search operations (searching the nearest black pixel from each pixel $(i, j)$ towards boundary) on each diagonal sequence from each pixel $(i, j)$ to reverse of lower right to upper left. We call this operation RUL. */

$RUL[i, j] = [i + k, j + k]$ if $A[i + k, j + k] = 0$,
$1 \le k \le \min\{n - 1 - i, n - 1 - j\}$
for each $(i, j)$, $0 \le i \le n - 1$, $0 \le j \le n - 1$

Step 2: /* Compute the nearest black pixel, for each $(i, j)$, in $DI_U(i, j)=\{(i - k, j + k)$ such that $(i - k, j + k) \in DI(i, j)\}$ by diagonal search operations (searching the nearest black pixel from each pixel $(i, j)$ towards boundary) on each diagonal sequence from each pixel $(i, j)$ to reverse of upper right to lower left, which we call RLL */

$RLL[i, j]=[i - k, j + k]$ if $A[i-k, j + k] = 0$,
$1 \le k \le \min\{i, n - 1 - j\}$
for each $(i, j)$, $0 \le i \le n - 1$, $0 \le j \le n - 1$

Step 3: /* As $DI_D(i, j) \cup DI_U(i, j)=DI(i, j)$, so compute the nearest pixel to $(i, j)$ in $DI(i, j)$ which is one of the results of the first and the second step, i.e., nearest one of the $RUL[i,j]$ and $RLL[i, j]$, which is the nearest one to $(i, j)$ and store it in $NFT_{ED}[i, j]$. */

$$NFT_{ED}[i, j] = \left\{ \begin{array}{l} RUL[i, j] \text{ if } d((i, j), RUL[i, j]) \le d((i, j), RLL[i, j]), \\ RLL[i, j] \text{ otherwise} \end{array} \right.$$

for each $(i, j)$, $0 \le i \le n - 1$, $0 \le j \le n - 1$.

Step 4: */ Compute the $NFT_E$ among $NFT_{ED}[i, j]$, $NFT_{ED}[i, j + 1]$,..., $NFT_{ED}[i, n - 1]$ by horizontal prefix minima LP. */

For each $(i, j)$, set $B[i, j]=(d((i, j), (g, h)), g, h)$ where $(g, h)= NFT_{ED}[i, j]$.
Compute the prefix minima of B for each row from right to left by comparing the first indices, and store the result in LP, i.e., set

$LP[i, j]=B[i, j + m]=(f_m, g_m, h_m)$
such that $f_m = \min \{f_k$ such that $B[i, j + k] = (f_k, g_k, h_k)$, $0 \le k \le n - 1 - j\}$
for each $(i, j)$, $0 \le i \le n - 1$, $0 \le j \le n-1$

Set $NFT_E[i, j]=(b, c)$ such that $LP[i, j]= (a, b, c)$ for each $(i, j)$ $(0 \le i \le n - 1, 0 \le j \le n - 1)$.

Phase 2: /* Compute the medial axis transformation */

If NFT$[i, j]$ for each $(i, j)$ occur at more than one place, i.e.,
   (a) the nearest black pixel for each $(i, j)$ occur from more than one region,
       i.e., among NFT$_E[i, j]$, NFT$_N[i, j]$, NFT$_W[i, j]$ and NFT$_S[i, j]$
   (b) the nearest black pixel for each $(i, j)$ occur in one region NFT$_E[i, j]$,
       NFT$_N[i, j]$, NFT$_W[i, j]$ and NFT$_S[i, j]$ but in that region it comes at more
       than one position
then include $(i, j)$ in medial axis and store the distance to DT$[i, j]$.

**Parallel Approach:**
a. Since computation of NFT$_E[i, j]$, NFT$_N[i, j]$, NFT$_W[i, j]$ and NFT$_S[i, j]$ for each
   pixel $(i, j)$ are independent so those can be computed in parallel.
b. For each pixel $(i, j)$ NFT$[i, i]$ can be easily computed in parallel.
c. For each pixel $(i, j)$ DT$[i, j]$ can be easily computed in parallel.
d. For each pixel $(i, j)$ medial axis transformation i.e. MAT can be easily computed
   in parallel.

**Time Complexities:** The computation of NFT$_E[i, j]$ or NFT$_N[i, j]$ or NFT$_W[i, j]$ or
NFT$_S[i, j]$ dominates the whole complexity. For computing NFT$_E[i, j]$, two search
operations, namely, RUL and RLL and one prefix minima operations L-prefix are
used. The other computations require $O(1)$ time using $n^2$ processors on any PRAM
machine. The computation of medial axis transformation requires $O(1)$ time as it is
run in parallel. Now on the EREW PRAM [5], the prefix computation of $n$ data can be
computed in $O(\log n)$ using $n / \log n$ processors and on the CRCW PRAM model in
$O(\log \log n)$ time using $n / \log \log n$ processors [8]. Moreover, it requires in $O(n^2 / p^2$
$+ n)$ time on a $p \times p$ mesh and $O(n^2 / p^2 + (n \log p) / p)$ time on a $p^2$ processor
hypercube [4]. Therefore the above algorithm requires $O(\log n)$ time using $n^2 / \log n$
processors on the EREW PRAM, in $O(\log \log n)$ time using $n^2 / \log \log n$ processors
on the common CRCW PRAM, $O(n^2 / p^2 + n)$ time on a $p \times p$ mesh and in $O(n^2 / p^2 +$
$(n \log p) / p)$ time on a $p^2$ processors hypercube.

**Simulation Results:** We have simulated our parallel algorithm for medial axis
transformation by considering two input images (H and cup) as shown in Fig. 1(a) and
Fig. 1(c). The results of the simulation run on these two input images are shown in
Fig. 1(b) and Fig. 1(d) respectively.

# 4 Conclusion

A parallel algorithm for medial axis transformation has been presented. The
algorithm is based on a modified version of the parallel algorithm for distance
transformation proposed by Fujiwara et al. [1]. The algorithm is simulated using two
input images and the results of the simulation are also shown.

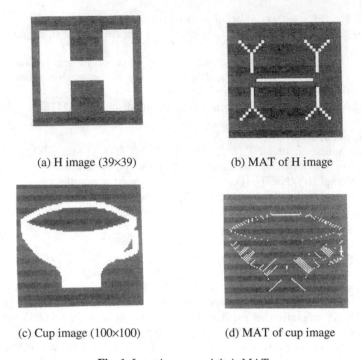

(a) H image (39×39)                    (b) MAT of H image

(c) Cup image (100×100)                (d) MAT of cup image

**Fig. 1.** Input images and their MAT

# References

[1] Akihiro Fujiwara, Michiko Inoue, T. Masuzawa, H. Fujiwara, "A cost optimal parallel algorithm for weighted distance transforms," *Parallel Computing,* Vol. 25, 1999, pp. 405–416.

[2] D.T. Lee, "Medial axis transformation of a planar shape," *IEEE Trans. On Pattern analysis and machine Intelligence,* Vol. 4, 1982, pp. 363–369.

[3] J.F. Jenq and S. Sahni, "Serial and parallel algorithms for the medial axis transform", *IEEE transactions on Pattern Analysis and Machine Intelligence, Vol.* 14, 1992, pp. 1218–1224.

[4] A. Fujiwara, M.Inoue, T. Masuzawa, H. Fujiwara, "A simple parallel algorithm for the medial axis transform of binary images," *proceedings of the IEEE second International Conference on Algorithms and Architecture for Parallel Processing,* 1996, pp. 1–8.

[5] R.E. Ladner, M.J. Fisher, "Parallel prefix computation," *Journal of ACM,* Vol. 27, 1980, pp. 831–838.

[6] Y.-H. Lee, S.-J. Horng, "The Chessboard distance transform and the medial axis transform are inter changeable," *Proceedings 10$^{th}$ International Parallel Processing symposium,* 1996, pp. 424–428.

[7] Y.-H. Lee, S.-J. Horng, "Fast parallel chessboard distance transform algorithms," *Proceedings of International Conference on Parallel and Distributed Systems,* 1996, pp. 488–493.

[8] O. Berkman, B. Schieber and U. Vishkin, "Optimal doubly parallel algorithms based on finding all nearest smaller values," *Journal of Algorithms*, Vol. 14, 1996, pp. 344–370.

[9] R.C. Gonzalez, R.E. Woods, *Digital Image Processing*, New York: Addison-Wesley, 1999.

# A Vector-Parallel FFT with a User-Specifiable Data Distribution Scheme

Yusaku Yamamoto[1], Mitsuyoshi Igai[2], and Ken Naono[1]

[1] Central Research Laboratory, Hitachi Ltd,
Kokubunji, Tokyo, 185-8601, Japan,
marula@ta2.so-net.ne.jp,
[2] Hitachi ULSI Technology Corp., Kokubunji, Tokyo, 187-8522, Japan

**Abstract.** We propose a 1-dimensional FFT routine for distributed-memory vector-parallel machines which provides the user with both high performance and flexibility in data distribution. Our routine inputs/outputs data using block cyclic data distribution, and the block sizes for input and output can be specified independently by the user. This flexibility is realized with the same amount of inter-processor communication as the widely used transpose algorithm and no additional overhead for data redistribution is necessary. We implemented our method on the Hitachi SR2201, a distributed-memory parallel machine with pseudo-vector processing nodes, and obtained 45% of the peak performance on 16 nodes when the problem size is $N = 2^{24}$. This performance was unchanged for a wide range of block sizes from 1 to 16.

## 1 Introduction

The fast Fourier transform (FFT) is one of the most widely used algorithms in the field of scientific computing. It can reduce the computational work needed to compute the Fourier transform of an $N$-point complex sequence from $O(N^2)$ to $O(N \log N)$ and has played an important role in areas as diverse as signal processing, computational fluid dynamics, solid state physics and financial engineering, etc.

The FFT has a large degree of parallelism in each stage of the computation, and accordingly, its implementations on parallel machines have been well studied. See, for example, [3] [6] [15] for implementations on shared-memory parallel machines and [2] [8] [11] [13] [15] [16] for implementations on distributed-memory parallel machines. Recently, distributed-memory machines with (pseudo-)vector processing nodes have become increasingly popular in high-end applications. The machines classified in this category include NEC SX-7, Fujitsu VPP5000 and Hitachi SR2201 and SR8000. To attain high performance on this type of machines, one has to achieve both high single-processor performance and high parallel efficiency at the same time. The former is realized by maximizing the length of the innermost loops, while the latter is realized when the volume of inter-processor communication is minimized. Implementations based on the transpose algorithm [9] [12] which satisfy both of these requirements are given in [2] [11] [16].

M. Guo and L.T.Yang (Eds.): ISPA 2003, LNCS 2745, pp. 362–374, 2003.

While there have been considerable efforts towards a high performance parallel implementation of the FFT, the problem of providing the user with more flexibility of data distribution has attracted relatively little attention. To compute the FFT in a distributed-memory environment, the user need to distribute the input data among processors in a manner specified by the FFT routine, call the routine, and receive the output data again in a manner specified by the routine. In many cases, the data distribution scheme used by the FFT routine is fixed, so if it is different from that used in other parts of the program, the user has to rearrange the data before or after calling the routine. This problem could be mitigated if data redistribution routines are provided along with the FFT routine. However, because the FFT requires only $O(N \log N)$ computation when the number of data points is $N$, the additional overhead incurred by the redistribution routines is often too costly.

To solve the problem, Dubey et al. [8] propose a general-purpose subroutine for 1-dimensional FFT. Their routine is quite flexible in the sense that it can accept general block cyclic data distributions. Here, block cyclic distribution is a data distribution in which the data is divided into blocks of equal size, say $L$, and the $i$-th block is allocated to node $\mod(i, P)$, where $P$ is the number of nodes. Their routine has a marked advantage that the amount of inter-processor communication needed for performing the FFT is independent of the block size $L$. However, it has several shortcomings. First, it is based on the binary exchange algorithm [9] [12], which requires $O((N/P) \log P)$ inter-processor communication for each node. This is much greater than the communication volume of $O(N/P)$ required by the transpose algorithm. Second, it is not self-sorting, so if one needs a sorted output, additional inter-processor communication is necessary. Finally, no consideration on vectorization has been given.

In this paper, we propose another general-purpose 1-dimensional FFT routine for distributed-memory vector-parallel machines. Our method is an extension of an FFT algorithm proposed by Takahashi [16], which is based on the transpose algorithm. His algorithm has the advantage that it requires only one global transposition, is self-sorting, and can input/output data scattered with cyclic ($L = 1$) distribution. We extend this algorithm to accept input data scattered with a block cyclic distribution of block size $L_1$ and to output the result using a block cyclic distribution of another block size, say $L_2$. $L_1$ and $L_2$ are arbitrary as long as $N$ is a multiple of $P^2 * L_1 * L_2$. This flexibility can be realized without increasing the amount of inter-processor communication, in contrast to the approaches that rely on redistribution routines.

If our method is implemented in a straightforward manner, however, the length of the innermost loops tends to become shorter as the block sizes grow, causing degradation of single-processor performance. We solve this problem by adopting the Stockham's FFT [17] suited to vector processors as the FFT kernels and employing loop merging techniques. We implemented our method on the Hitachi SR2201, a distributed-memory parallel machine with pseudo-vector processing nodes, and measured its performance using 1 to 16 nodes.

The rest of this paper is organized as follows: In section 2 we describe the conventional FFT algorithms for vector-parallel machines. Our new implementation is introduced in section 3 along with several considerations to attain high performance on vector-parallel machines. Section 4 shows the performance of our routine on the Hitachi SR2201. Conclusions are given in the final section.

## 2   Conventional FFT Algorithms for Vector-Parallel Machines

### 2.1   1-D FFT Algorithms for Vector Machines

In this section, we will explain conventional algorithms for 1-dimensional FFT on vector and vector-parallel machines following [2] [4] [16]. The discrete Fourier transform of a 1-dimensional complex sequence $\{f_0, f_1, \ldots, f_{N-1}\}$ is defined as follows:

$$c_k = \sum_{j=0}^{N-1} f_j \omega_N^{jk} \qquad (k = 0, 1, \ldots, N-1), \tag{1}$$

where $\omega_N = \exp(-2\pi i/N)$ and $i = \sqrt{-1}$.

When $N$ can be factored as $N = N_x N_y$, the indices $j$ and $k$ can be expressed in a two-dimensional form:

$$j = j_x N_y + j_y \qquad (j_x = 0, \ldots, N_x - 1, \quad j_y = 0, \ldots, N_y - 1), \tag{2}$$
$$k = k_x + k_y N_x \qquad (k_x = 0, \ldots, N_x - 1, \quad k_y = 0, \ldots, N_y - 1). \tag{3}$$

Accordingly, $\{f_j\}$ and $\{c_k\}$ can be regarded as two-dimensional arrays:

$$f_{j_x, j_y} = f_{j_x N_y + j_y}, \tag{4}$$
$$c_{k_x, k_y} = c_{k_x + k_y N_x}. \tag{5}$$

Using these notations, we can rewrite eq. (1) as follows:

$$c_{k_x, k_y} = \sum_{j_y=0}^{N_y-1} \sum_{j_x=0}^{N_x-1} f_{j_x, j_y} \omega_N^{(j_x N_y + j_y)(k_x + k_y N_x)}$$

$$= \sum_{j_y=0}^{N_y-1} \left( \left( \sum_{j_x=0}^{N_x-1} f_{j_x, j_y} \omega_{N_x}^{j_x k_x} \right) \omega_N^{j_y k_x} \right) \omega_{N_y}^{j_y k_y}. \tag{6}$$

This shows that the Fourier transform of $\{f_j\}$ can be computed by the following algorithm proposed by Bailey [4]:

[Algorithm 1]

1. Compute $c'_{k_x, j_y} = \sum_{j_x=0}^{N_x-1} f_{j_x, j_y} \omega_{N_x}^{j_x k_x}$ by repeating $N_x$-point FFT $N_y$ times.
2. Multiply $c'_{k_x, j_y}$ by $\omega_N^{j_y k_x}$.

3. Compute $c_{k_x,k_y} = \sum_{j_y=0}^{N_y-1} c'_{k_x,j_y} \omega_{N_y}^{j_y k_y}$ by repeating $N_y$-point FFT $N_x$ times.

The factor $\omega_N^{j_y k_x}$ appearing in step 2 is called *twiddle factor* and the step 2 is called *twiddle factor multiplication*. This algorithm requires about the same amount of computational effort as the FFT of $N$ data points. It is especially suited to vector machines if the loops about $j_y$ and $k_x$ are used as the innermost loops in steps 1 and 3, respectively. Then the innermost loops will have a fixed length of $N_y$ and $N_x$ and the factor $\omega$, which is a constant within these loops, can be loaded outside the loops.

## 2.2   1-D FFT Algorithms for Distributed-Memory Vector-Parallel Machines

In the algorithm explained in the previous subsection, we decompose the 1-D FFT into multiple FFTs of smaller size and use this multiplicity for vectorization. In the case of distributed-memory vector-parallel machines, we need another dimension to use for parallelization. To this end, we factor $N$ as $N = N_x N_y N_z$ and introduce a three-dimensional notation for the indices $j$ and $k$:

$$j = j_x N_y N_z + j_y N_z + j_z \tag{7}$$
$$(j_x = 0, \ldots, N_x - 1, \quad j_y = 0, \ldots, N_y - 1, \quad j_z = 0, \ldots, N_z - 1),$$
$$k = k_x + k_y N_x + k_z N_x N_y \tag{8}$$
$$(k_x = 0, \ldots, N_x - 1, \quad k_y = 0, \ldots, N_y - 1, \quad k_z = 0, \ldots, N_z - 1).$$

By regarding the input and output sequences as three-dimensional arrays $f_{j_x,j_y,j_z}$ and $c_{k_x,k_y,k_z}$, we can rewrite eq. (1) as follows:

$$
\begin{aligned}
&c_{k_x,k_y,k_z} \\
&= \sum_{j_z=0}^{N_z-1} \left( \left( \sum_{j_y=0}^{N_y-1} \left( \left( \sum_{j_x=0}^{N_x-1} f_{j_x,j_y,j_z} \omega_{N_x}^{j_x k_x} \right) \omega_{N_x N_y}^{j_y k_x} \right) \omega_{N_y}^{j_y k_y} \right) \omega_N^{j_z(k_x+k_y N_x)} \right) \omega_{N_z}^{j_z k_z}.
\end{aligned}
\tag{9}
$$

This suggests the following five-step FFT proposed by Takahashi [16]:

[Algorithm 2: Five-step FFT]

1. Compute $c'_{k_x,j_y,j_z} = \sum_{j_x=0}^{N_x-1} f_{j_x,j_y,j_z} \omega_{N_x}^{j_x k_x}$ by repeating $N_x$-point FFT $N_y N_z$ times.
2. Twiddle factor multiplication (I): multiply $c'_{k_x,j_y,j_z}$ by $\omega_{N_x N_y}^{j_y k_x}$.
3. Compute $c''_{k_x,k_y,j_z} = \sum_{j_y=0}^{N_y-1} c'_{k_x,j_y,j_z} \omega_{N_y}^{j_y k_y}$ by repeating $N_y$-point FFT $N_x N_z$ times.
4. Twiddle factor multiplication (II): multiply $c''_{k_x,k_y,j_z}$ by $\omega_N^{j_z(k_x+k_y N_x)}$.
5. Compute $c_{k_x,k_y,k_z} = \sum_{j_z=0}^{N_z-1} c''_{k_x,k_y,j_z} \omega_{N_z}^{j_z k_z}$ by repeating $N_z$-point FFT $N_x N_y$ times.

Because the operation in step 1 consists of $N_y N_z$ independent FFTs, we can, for example, use the index $j_y$ for vectorization and the index $j_z$ for parallelization. Steps 3 and 5 can be executed in a similar way.

### 2.3    Implementations Based on the Five-Step Algorithm

There are many possible ways to exploit the parallelism in Algorithm 2 for vectorization and parallelization. For example, Agarwal et al. [2] propose to scatter the three-dimensional array along the $z$-direction in steps 1 and 2, and along the $x$-direction in steps 3-5, both using block distribution. In this case, indices $j_y$, $j_z$ and $j_y$ can be used for vectorization in steps 1, 3 and 5, respectively. Takahashi [16] suggests to scatter the data along the $z$-direction in steps 1-4, and along the $x$-direction in step 5, both in a cyclic manner. In this case, vectorization can be done with respect to indices $j_y$, $j_x$ and $j_y$ in steps 1, 3 and 5, respectively. These methods are classified as the *transpose algorithms*, because all the inter-processor data transfers are done in the form of *global transposition*, i.e., redistribution of a multi-dimensional array scattered along one direction along another direction.

These methods have several advantages: first, they require only one global transposition. The volume of inter-processor communication due to this is $O(N/P)$ per node and is much smaller than $O((N/P)\log P)$, which would be required by the binary exchange algorithms [9] [12]. Second, the innermost loops have a fixed length of $N_x$, $N_y$ or $N_z$ in steps 1, 3 and 5, respectively. Takahashi also notes that it is possible to extend the length of the innermost loops to $N^{2/3}/P$ by setting $N_x = N_y = N_z = N^{1/3}$ and using loop merging techniques [16]. In addition, his implementation has a natural user interface in the sense that both the input and output data are ordered and distributed in a cyclic fashion [16].

However, some users may need more flexibility of data distribution. For example, block cyclic distribution is frequently used when solving linear simultaneous equations or eigenvalue problems on distributed-memory machines [5]. So if the user wants to connect the FFT routine with these routines, it is more convenient that the FFT routine can input/output data using block cyclic data distribution with user-specified block sizes. Note that the block sizes suitable for input and output data may not be the same, so it is more desirable if they can be specified independently. In the following section, we will propose an algorithm that satisfies these requirements.

## 3    A Vector-Parallel FFT with Flexible Data Distribution

### 3.1    Conditions on the Block Sizes

In this section, we propose a 1-D parallel FFT algorithm with the following two properties:

1. The input and output data are scattered with block cyclic distributions with user-specified block sizes $L_1$ and $L_2$, respectively.

2. Only one global transposition is needed throughout the algorithm.

And we optimize the algorithm for vector-parallel machines.

Before explaining our algorithm, we will establish a necessary and sufficient condition on $L_1$ and $L_2$ for the existence of such an algorithm. For simplicity, here we deal only with the radix-2 FFT and assume that $P$, $L_1$ and $L_2$ are powers of two.

**Proposition 1.** *A necessary and sufficient condition for the existence of a 1-D parallel FFT algorithm that satisfies the above two properties is $P^2 * L_1 * L_2 \leq N$.*

*Proof.* Here we only show that this is a necessary condition. We prove the sufficiency in the following subsections by actually constructing an algorithm.

An $N$-point radix-2 FFT consists of $p = \log_2 N$ stages. By examining its signal flow graph [17], we know that each of the intermediate quantities at the $q$-th stage $(1 \leq q \leq p)$ is computed from every $2^{p-q}$-th elements of the input data $\{f_j\}_{j=0}^{N-1}$. These elements reside on the same node if and only if $2^{p-q} \geq L_1 * P$ (assuming $P \geq 2$). This means that we need a global transposition right after the stage

$$q_1 = p - \log_2(L_1 * P) \tag{10}$$

or earlier.

On the other hand, we also know from the signal flow graph that each of the intermediate quantities at the $q$-th stage contributes to every $2^q$-th elements of the output data $\{c_k\}_{k=0}^{N-1}$. These elements reside on the same node if and only if $2^q \geq L_2 * P$. This means that we need a global transposition right before the stage

$$q_2 = \log_2(L_2 * P) \tag{11}$$

or later.

To do with only one global transposition, we need

$$q_1 \geq q_2, \tag{12}$$

which implies $P^2 * L_1 * L_2 \leq N$. □

A similar result holds when $N$ is not a power of two and we can construct an FFT algorithm with only one global transposition when $N$ is a multiple of $P^2 * L_1 * L_2$.

### 3.2    The Basic Idea of the Algorithm

To realize an FFT algorithm which has the two properties mentioned in the previous subsection, we use Algorithm 2 as a basis. Assume that $N$ is a multiple of $P^2 * L_1 * L_2$, and choose $N_x$, $N_y$ and $N_z$ so that $N_z$ and $N_x$ are divisible by $L_1 * P$ and $L_2 * P$, respectively. Now we scatter the three-dimensional array along the $z$-direction in steps 1 and 2 using block cyclic distribution of block size $L_1$, and along the $x$-direction in steps 3-5 using block cyclic distribution of block size $L_2$. Then, from eq. (7), we know that the whole input sequence of length

$N$ is scattered with a block cyclic distribution of block size $L_1$. Likewise, the whole output sequence is scattered with a block cyclic distribution of block size $L_2$. This method requires only one global transposition like the implementations discussed in the previous subsection, and leaves the room for vectorization using indices $j_y$, $j_z$ and $j_y$ in steps 1, 3 and 5, respectively.

However, a straightforward implementation of this idea may not guarantee sufficient innermost loop length to achieve high single-processor performance. This is because $N_x$ and $N_z$ need to be large enough to be multiples of $L_1 * P$ and $L_2 * P$, respectively, and therefore $N_y$, which is the length of the innermost loops in steps 1 and 5, tends to become smaller. For example, when $N = 2^{20}$, $P = 16$ and $L_1 = L_2 = 16$, $N_y$ must be less than or equal to 4. We solve this problem by adopting Stockham's algorithm [17] suited to vector processors in the FFTs in steps 1, 3 and 5, and merging as many loops as possible. We will explain the algorithm and storage scheme for our implementation in the next subsection and discuss loop merging techniques in subsection 3.4.

## 3.3   The Detailed Algorithm and the Storage Scheme

To describe our implementation, we first introduce some notations. Let $X_p^{(i)}$ denote the partial array allocated to node $p$ at step $i$. The dimension of $X_p^{(i)}$ varies depending on $i$. We also define the indices and their ranges as follows:

$$j_x = 0, \ldots, N_x, \quad j_y = 0, \ldots, N_y - 1, \quad j_z = 0, \ldots, N_z - 1, \tag{13}$$

$$k_x = 0, \ldots, N_x, \quad k_y = 0, \ldots, N_y - 1, \quad k_z = 0, \ldots, N_z - 1, \tag{14}$$

$$p = 0, \ldots, P - 1, \quad q = 0, \ldots, P - 1, \tag{15}$$

$$j_z' = 0, \ldots, N_z/(L_1 P) - 1, \quad j_z'' = 0, \ldots, L_1 - 1, \tag{16}$$

$$k_x' = 0, \ldots, N_x/(L_2 P) - 1, \quad k_x'' = 0, \ldots, L_2 - 1. \tag{17}$$

Here, $j_z'$ and $k_x'$ are local block numbers within a node and $j_z''$ and $k_x''$ are indices within a block. They are related to $j_z$ and $k_x$ in the following way:

$$j_z = j_z' L_1 P + p L_1 + j_z'', \tag{18}$$

$$k_x = k_x' L_2 P + p L_2 + k_x'', \tag{19}$$

where $p$ is the node number.

Using these notations, our FFT can be described as follows:

[Algorithm 3]

1. Data input: $X_p^{(1)}(j_y, j_z'', j_z', j_x) = f_{j_x N_y N_z + j_y N_z + j_z' L_1' P + p L_1 + j_z''}$.
2. FFT in the $x$-direction:
   $X_p^{(2)}(j_y, j_z'', j_z', k_x) = \sum_{j_x=0}^{N_x-1} X_p^{(1)}(j_y, j_z'', j_z', j_x) \omega_{N_x}^{j_x k_x}$.
3. Twiddle factor multiplication (I):
   $X_p^{(3)}(j_y, j_z'', j_z', k_x) = X_p^{(2)}(j_y, j_z'', j_z', k_x) \omega_{N_x N_y}^{j_y k_x}$.
4. Data packing for global transposition:
   $X_p^{(4)}(j_y, j_z'', j_z', k_x'', k_x', q) = X_p^{(3)}(j_y, j_z'', j_z', k_x' L_2 P + q L_2 + k_x'')$.

5. Global transposition: $X_p^{(5)}(j_y, j_z'', j_z', k_x'', k_x', q) = X_q^{(4)}(j_y, j_z'', j_z', k_x'', k_x', p)$.

6. Data unpacking:
$$X_p^{(6)}(j_z'L_1P + qL_1 + j_z'', k_x'', k_x', j_y) = X_p^{(5)}(j_y, j_z'', j_z', k_x'', k_x', q).$$

7. FFT in the $y$-direction:
$$X_p^{(7)}(j_z, k_x'', k_x', k_y) = \sum_{j_y=0}^{N_y-1} X_p^{(6)}(j_z, k_x'', k_x', j_y)\omega_{N_y}^{j_y k_y}.$$

8. Twiddle factor multiplication (II):
$$X_p^{(8)}(k_x'', k_x', k_y, j_z) = X_p^{(7)}(j_z, k_x'', k_x', k_y)\omega_N^{j_z(k_x'L_2P + pL_2 + k_x'' + k_y N_x)}.$$

9. FFT in the $z$-direction:
$$X_p^{(9)}(k_x'', k_x', k_y, k_z) = \sum_{j_z=0}^{N_z-1} X_p^{(8)}(k_x'', k_x', k_y, k_z)\omega_{N_z}^{j_z k_z}.$$

10. Data output: $c_{k_x'L_2P + pL_2 + k_x'' + k_y N_x + k_z N_x N_y} = X_p^{(9)}(k_x'', k_x', k_y, k_z)$.

In this algorithm, the most computationally intensive parts are the FFTs in steps 2, 7 and 9. The indexing scheme for array $X_p^{(i)}$ is designed so that the index with respect to which the Fourier transform is performed comes last and the loop merging techniques to be described in the next subsection can be applied easily.

## 3.4 Loop Merging Techniques for Achieving High Single-Processor Performance

From algorithm 3, it is apparent that we can merge the loops about the first three indices in the FFTs in steps 2, 7 and 9, and use the resulting loop as the innermost loop. Thus the length of the innermost loops can be extended to $N_y N_z/P$, $N_z N_x/P$ and $N_x N_y/P$ in steps 2, 7 and 9, respectively.

To further extend the innermost loop length, we use Stockham's algorithm [17] in performing these FFTs. Let $n = 2^p$ and assume we want to compute the FFT of an $n$-point sequence $Y_0(0,0), Y_0(1,0), \ldots, Y_0(n-1,0)$. This can be done with the following algorithm.

[Algorithm 4: Stockham FFT]

```
do L = 0, p − 1
   αL = 2^L
   βL = 2^(p−L−1)
   do m = 0, αL − 1
      do l = 0, βL − 1
```
$$Y_{L+1}(l, m) = Y_L(l, m) + Y_L(l + \beta_L, m)\, \omega_n^{m\beta_L}$$
$$Y_{L+1}(l, m + \alpha_L) = Y_L(l, m) - Y_L(l + \beta_L, m)\, \omega_n^{m\beta_L}$$
```
      end do
   end do
end do
```

The result is stored in $Y_p(0,0), Y_p(1,0), \ldots, Y_p(n-1,0)$.

Notice that the $\omega$ in the innermost loop does not depend on $l$. This means that if we use this algorithm to compute the $N_x$-point FFT in step 2, we can merge the loops about $j_y$, $j_z''$, $j_z'$ and $\beta_L$, thereby extending the length of the innermost loop to $N_y N_z \beta_L / P$. Because the loop of length $\beta_L$ appears $\alpha_L$ times in Stockham's algorithm, the average length of the innermost loops in step 2 is

$$\frac{N_y N_z}{P} \times \frac{\sum_{L=0}^{\log_2 N_x - 1} \alpha_L \beta_L}{\sum_{L=0}^{\log_2 N_x - 1} \alpha_L} = \frac{N_y N_z}{P} \times \frac{\frac{N_x}{2} \log_2 N_x}{N_x - 1}$$

$$\sim N_y N_z \log_2 N_x / 2P. \tag{20}$$

Hence, the loop length can be increased by a factor of $\log_2 N_x / 2$. Similarly, the innermost loop length in steps 7 and 9 can be extended to $N_x N_z \log_2 N_y / 2P$ and $N_x N_y \log_2 N_z / 2P$, respectively.

As an example, consider the case of $N = 2^{20}$, $P = 16$ and $L_1 = L_2 = 16$ which we mentioned in subsection 3.2. We can choose $N_x = N_z = 256$ and $N_y = 4$, and then the length of the innermost loops is 256, 4096 and 256 in steps 2, 7 and 9, respectively. This is enough for many vector machines to attain near-peak performance. Thus we can expect our FFT routine to attain high single-processor performance even when $L_1$ and $L_2$ are large and $N_y$ is small.

Because the FFT involves only $O(N \log N)$ operations on $N$-point data, it is also essential for higher performance to minimize memory access. This can be achieved by putting together some of the steps in Algorithm 3. For example, data packing for global transposition in step 4 can be combined with step 3. We adopt this kind of optimization techniques in the implementation described in the next section.

## 4    Experimental Results

We implemented our method on the Hitachi SR2201 [10] and evaluated its performance. The SR2201 is a distributed-memory parallel machine with pseudo-vector processing nodes. Each node consists of a RISC processor with a pseudo-vector mechanism [14], which preloads the data from pipelined main memory to on-chip special register bank at a rate of 1 word per cycle. One node has peak performance of 300MFLOPS and 256MB of main memory. The nodes are connected via a multi-dimensional crossbar network, which enables all-to-all communication among $P$ nodes to be done in $P - 1$ steps without contention [18].

Our FFT routine is written in FORTRAN and inter-processor communication is done using remote DMA, which enables data stored in the main memory of one node to be transferred directly to the main memory of another node without buffering. The FFT in the $x$, $y$ and $z$ direction in steps 2, 7 and 9 is performed using Stockham's radix 4 FFT [17], a variant of Algorithm 4 which saves both computational work and memory access by computing $Y_{L+2}$ directly from $Y_L$.

The computational steps of our implementation are illustrated in Fig. 1 for the case of $N = 512$, $P = 2$ and $L_1 = L_2 = 2$. Here, the multi-dimensional arrays in Algorithm 3 are expressed as three dimensional arrays using the relationship (18) and (19). The numbers in the first and third three-dimensional arrays correspond to the indices of input sequence $f_j$ and output sequence $c_k$, respectively. The shaded area represents elements which are allocated to node 0, and the area enclosed by a thick line represents a set of elements used to perform a single FFT in the $x$, $y$ or $z$-direction. It is apparent from the figure that (i) the FFTs in each direction can be computed within each node, (ii) there is only one global transposition, and (iii) the input and output data are scattered with a block cyclic distribution of block size 2, as required.

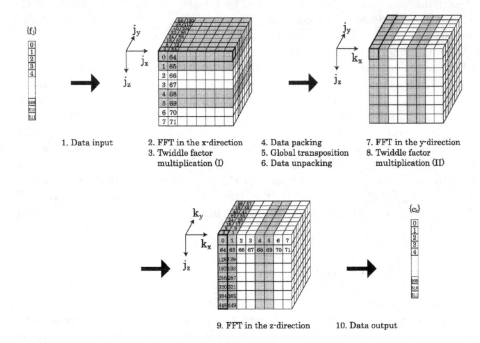

1. Data input

2. FFT in the x-direction
3. Twiddle factor
   multiplication (I)

4. Data packing
5. Global transposition
6. Data unpacking

7. FFT in the y-direction
8. Twiddle factor
   multiplication (II)

9. FFT in the z-direction      10. Data output

**Fig. 1.** Computational steps of our FFT routine

To measure the performance of our FFT routine, we varied the problem size $N$ from $2^{18}$ to $2^{24}$ and the number of nodes $P$ from 1 to 16. We set the output block size $L_2$ equal to the input block size $L_1$ to reduce the number of experiments and varied $L_1 = L_2$ from 1 to 16. $N_x$ and $N_z$ are determined so that $N_x \geq L_2 P$ and $N_z \geq L_1 P$ hold and $N_y$ is set to $N/(N_x N_z)$. The $\omega$'s used in the FFT and twiddle factor multiplication are pre-computed, so the time for computing them is not included in the execution time to be reported below.

Table 1 shows the execution time and the performance obtained when $N = 2^{20}$. We performed three experiments for each set of $L_1$ and $P$ and took the best value. From these results, we can see that (i) the performance on a single node is 130 MFLOPS, which is more than 40% of the peak performance (300 MFLOPS for one node), (ii) parallel efficiency is extremely high and is more than 94% when $P = 16$, and (iii) the performance does not change significantly with the block sizes. The last point is due to the optimization techniques we have stated in the previous subsection.

**Table 1.** Performance results for the problem of $N = 2^{20}$

| $L_1 = L_2$ | 1 node | 2 nodes | 4 nodes | 8 nodes | 16 nodes |
|---|---|---|---|---|---|
| 1 | 0.809 s | 0.414 s | 0.205 s | 0.103 s | 0.054 s |
|  | 129.5 MF | 253.3 MF | 510.7 MF | 1016.7 MF | 1920.8 MF |
| 2 | 0.809 s | 0.413 s | 0.205 s | 0.102 s | 0.054 s |
|  | 129.6 MF | 253.8 MF | 512.1 MF | 1027.9 MF | 1942.7 MF |
| 4 | 0.809 s | 0.413 s | 0.205 s | 0.102 s | 0.053 s |
|  | 129.6 MF | 253.9 MF | 512.2 MF | 1027.9 MF | 1971.2 MF |
| 8 | 0.809 s | 0.413 s | 0.206 s | 0.102 s | 0.053 s |
|  | 129.6 MF | 253.9 MF | 509.9 MF | 1028.2 MF | 1964.7 MF |
| 16 | 0.809 s | 0.413 s | 0.205 s | 0.102 s | 0.053 s |
|  | 129.6 MF | 253.8 MF | 510.7 MF | 1027.9 MF | 1965.0 MF |

The performance results when $N$ is varied is shown in Table 2 and Fig. 2. Note that we were able to perform the FFT of $N = 2^{22}$ points only when $P \geq 2$ and that of $N = 2^{24}$ points only when $P \geq 8$ because of memory limitation. The performance did not depend on the block sizes, so we showed only the results for $L_1 = L_2 = 16$. It is apparent that the performance increases as the problem size grows and reaches 2152 MFLOPS when $N = 2^{24}$ and $P = 16$, which is 45% of the peak performance (4800 MFLOPS for 16 nodes).

**Table 2.** Performance results for $L_1 = L_2 = 16$

| $N$ | 1 node | 2 nodes | 4 nodes | 8 nodes | 16 nodes |
|---|---|---|---|---|---|
| $2^{18}$ | 0.194 s | 0.099 s | 0.051 s | 0.026 s | 0.014 s |
|  | 121.7 MF | 237.5 MF | 466.2 MF | 899.9 MF | 1681.9 MF |
| $2^{20}$ | 0.809 s | 0.413 s | 0.205 s | 0.102 s | 0.053 s |
|  | 129.6 MF | 253.8 MF | 510.7 MF | 1027.9 MF | 1965.0 MF |
| $2^{22}$ |  | 1.761 s | 0.873 s | 0.441 s | 0.223 s |
|  |  | 262.0 MF | 528.3 MF | 1046.7 MF | 2070.9 MF |
| $2^{24}$ |  |  |  | 1.894 s | 0.935 s |
|  |  |  |  | 1062.8 MF | 2152.5 MF |

From these results, we can conclude that our FFT routine attains high performance on a (pseudo-)vector-parallel machine and flexibility in data distribution at the same time.

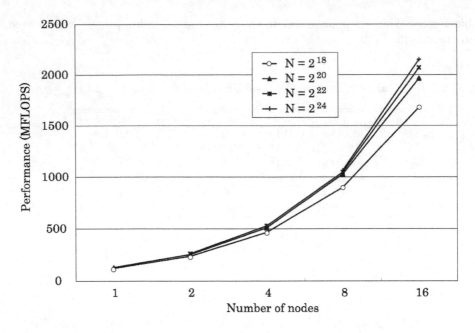

**Fig. 2.** Performance results for $L_1 = L_2 = 16$

## 5   Conclusion

In this paper, we have proposed a 1-dimensional FFT routine for distributed-memory vector-parallel machines which provides the user with both high performance and flexibility in data distribution. Our routine inputs/outputs data using block cyclic data distribution, and the block sizes for input and output can be specified independently by the user. It is based on the transpose algorithm, which requires only one global data transposition, and no additional inter-processor communication is necessary to realize this flexibility. A straightforward implementation of our method can cause a problem of short innermost loops when the block sizes are large, but we have shown how to solve this by employing loop merging techniques.

We implemented our method on the Hitachi SR2201, a distributed-memory parallel machine with pseudo-vector processing nodes, and obtained the performance of 2152 MFLOPS, or 45% of the peak performance, when transforming $2^{24}$ points data on 16 nodes. This result was unchanged for a wide range of block sizes from 1 to 16. It should be easy to adapt our method to other similar vector-parallel machines.

# References

1. R. C. Agarwal and J. W. Cooley: Vectorized Mixed Radix Discrete Fourier Transform Algorithms, *Proc. of IEEE*, Vol. 75, No. 9, pp. 1283–1292 (1987).
2. R. C. Agarwal, F. G. Gustavson and M. Zubair: A High Prformance Parallel Algorithm for 1-D FFT, *Proc. of Supercomputing '94*, pp. 34–40 (1994).
3. A. Averbuch, E. Gabber, B. Gordissky and Y. Medan: A Parallel FFT on a MIMD Machine, *Parallel Computing*, Vol. 15, pp. 61–74 (1990).
4. D. H. Bailey: FFTs in External or Hierarchical Memory, *The Journal of Supercomputing*, Vol. 4, pp. 23–35 (1990).
5. L. Blackford, J. Choi, A. Cleary, E. D'Azevedo, J. Demmel, I. Dhillon, J. Dongarra, S. Hammarling, G. Henry, A. Petitet, K. Stanley, D. Walker and R. Whaley: ScaLAPACK User's Guide, SIAM, Philadelphia, PA, 1997.
6. D. A. Carlson: Ultrahigh-Performance FFTs for the Cray-2 and Cray Y-MP Supercomputers, *Journal of Supercomputing*, Vol. 6, pp. 107–116 (1992).
7. J. W. Cooley and J. W. Tukey: An Algorithm for the Machine Calculation of Complex Fourier Series, *Mathematics of Computation*, Vol. 19, pp. 297–301 (1965).
8. A. Dubey, M. Zubair and C. E. Grosch: A General Purpose Subroutine for Fast Fourier Transform on a Distributed Memory Parallel Machine, *Parallel Computing*, Vol. 20, pp. 1697–1710 (1994).
9. G. Fox, M. Johnson, G. Lyzenga, S. Otto, J. Salmon and D. Walker: Solving Problems on Concurrent Processors, Vol. I, Prentice-Hall, Englewood Cliffs, NJ, 1988.
10. H. Fujii, Y. Yasuda, H. Akashi, Y. Inagami, M. Koga, O. Ishihara, M. Kashiyama, H. Wada and T. Sumimoto: Architecture and Performance of the Hitachi SR2201 Massively Parallel Processor System, *Proc. of IPPS '97*, pp. 233–241, 1997.
11. M. Hegland: Real and Complex Fast Fourier Transforms on the Fujitsu VPP500, *Parallel Computing*, Vol. 22, pp. 539–553 (1996).
12. V. Kumar, A. Grama, A. Gupta and G. Karypis: Introduction to Parallel Computing, The Benjamin/Cummings Publishing Company, CA, 1994.
13. S. L. Johnson and R. L. Krawitz: Cooley-Tukey FFT on the Connection Machine, *Parallel Computing*, Vol. 18, pp. 1201–1221 (1992).
14. K. Nakazawa, H. Nakamura, H. Imori and S. Kawabe: Pseudo Vector Processor Based on Register-Windowed Superscalar Pipeline, *Proc. of Supercomputing '92*, pp. 642–651 (1992).
15. P. N. Swarztrauber: Multiprocessor FFTs, *Parallel Computing*, Vol. 5, pp. 197–210 (1987).
16. D. Takahashi: Parallel FFT Algorithms for the Distributed-Memory Parallel Computer Hitachi SR8000, *Proc. of JSPP2000*, pp. 91–98, 2000 (in Japanese).
17. C. Van Loan: Computational Frameworks for the Fast Fourier Transform, SIAM Press, Philadelphia, PA (1992).
18. Y. Yasuda, H. Fujii, H. Akashi, Y. Inagami, T. Tanaka, J. Nakagoshi, H. Wada and T. Sumimoto: Deadlock-Free Fault-Tolerant Routing in the Multi-Dimensional Crossbar Network and its Implementation for the Hitachi SR2201, *Proc. of IPPS '97*, pp. 346–352, 1997.

# A Method for Sending Confidential Messages to a Group without Trusted Parties

Ren-Junn Hwang[1] and Chin-Chen Chang[2]

[1] Department of Computer Science and Information Engineering
Tamkang University, Tamshi, Taipei Hsien, Taiwan, 251, R.O.C.
`junhwang@ms35.hinet.net`
[2] Institute of Computer Science and Information Engineering,
National Chung Cheng University, Chiayi, Taiwan, 621, R.O.C.
`ccc@cs.ccu.edu.tw`

**Abstract.** A simple and efficient method to send confidential messages to a group is proposed in this paper. Firstly, we show a practical and efficient generalized secret sharing scheme based on simple operations. Next, we propose a special design concept to construct a generalized group-oriented cryptosystem (GGOC) [5]. Any group can use our design concept to construct a GGOC which provides a secure environment for a sender to send confidential messages to it. The constructed GGOC does not need the assistance of any trusted party. We also apply our design concept to construct a GGOC based on RSA, DES, and our generalized secret sharing scheme. As a result, our new GGOC is simple and easy to implement in hardware. We also show that our proposed GGOC is practical and is more efficient than Chang and Lee's GGOC.

## 1 Introduction

Cryptosystem is the efficient technique to protect confidential data from being destroyed, disclosed, or altered by unauthorized users. The conventional cryptosystems, e.g., symmetric cryptosystems and asymmetric cryptosystems, are usually only used to send confidential messages to an individual; namely, they cannot be adapted when confidential messages are intended for a group instead of an individual [6]. However, in our real world, messages are frequently addressed to a group of people, such as a board of directors. "How to transmit confidential messages to a group?" is a very important issue. The messages, which are intended for a group, are usually divided into three types by their implicit properties: *important messages*, *urgent messages* and *particular messages* [7]. The cryposystem which satisfies the preceding issues is named Group Oriented Cryptosystem (GOC) [6].

Desmedt first proposed a scheme [6] to solve the GOC problem, but, unfortunately, his scheme was impractical. However, since then, there have been many researchers proposing new $(k, n)$ threshold cryptosystems trying to solve GOC-related problems. Benaloh and Leichter [1] showed that a $(k, n)$ threshold scheme

M. Guo and L.T.Yang (Eds.): ISPA 2003, LNCS 2745, pp. 375–381, 2003.

could only handle a small fraction of the ideal secret sharing policy which we might follow. Chang and Lee [5] proposed a Generalized Group-Oriented Cryptosystem (GGOC) without a trusted party. The difference between GGOC and GOC is that GGOC can handle any secret sharing policy. As a matter of fact, Chang and Lee's GGOC can not only be implemented on any secret sharing policy but also work without the assistance of a trusted party. In most cryptographic applications, a trusted party does not exist in a group [8]. This situation becomes more common in commercial or international applications. Thus the GGOC without a trusted party is very attractive. However, Chang and Lee's scheme is neither practical nor efficient when there are many members in the recipient group. In this paper, we propose a design concept of GGOC. A GGOC constructed by our design concept does not need the assistance of any trusted party. Each group can employ our design concept to construct a secure GGOC based on a secure generalized secret sharing scheme [1], and an asymmetric cryptoscheme, and a symmetric cryptoscheme. In this paper, we also propose an efficient generalized secret sharing scheme. We use our design concept to construct a secure GGOC based on it, RSA [10], and DES. The newly proposed GGOC is practical and more efficient than Chang and Lee's GGOC.

## 2    A New Generalized Secret Sharing Scheme

Without loss of generality, we assume that a secret $K$ is shared by a set of $n$ participants $U = \{U_1, U_2, \ldots, U_n\}$. The generalized secret sharing scheme is a method which divides the secret $K$ into n shadows $K_1, K_2, \ldots, K_n$ according to the secret sharing policy. The trusted party distributes every shadow $K_i$ to a relative participant $U_i$ through a secure channel. Let $\Gamma$ be a set of subsets of participants $U$, where the subsets in $\Gamma$ are those subsets of $U$ that should be able to reconstruct the secret $K$. $\Gamma$ is named an access structure, and each element in $\Gamma$ is called a qualified subset of the secret sharing policy. By the definition of the access structure $\Gamma$, these shadows have to satisfy the following conditions: (1) if a qualified subset of participants pool their shadows, then they can reconstruct the secret $K$; (2) if an unqualified subset of participants pool their shadows, then they can reconstruct nothing about the secret $K$.

Our generalized secret sharing scheme uses a publicly accessible board where the trusted party can give away true information for all the participants to access. This board is named a bulletin board. If memory and communication are inexpensive, the trusted party can transmit the true public information to the participants instead of storing it centrally. Thus, a public bulletin board is necessary for all existing secret sharing schemes to publish the access structure $\Gamma$ and the number of participants.

With this public bulletin board mechanism, our scheme can be divided into two parts: the distribution part and the reconstruction part. In the following, we shall give a general description of our scheme according to this division, where $n$ is the number of shadows, and the access structure is $\Gamma$.

**Part 1: Distribution**

In this part, the trusted party generates and distributes the shadows to the participants as follows:

D-1. Randomly generate two distinct super-increase sets $\{a'_1, a'_2, \ldots, a'_n\}$ and $\{b'_1, b'_2, \ldots, b'_n\}$. Permute these two sets and let the new sets be $\{a_1, a_2, \ldots, a_n\}$ and $\{b_1, b_2, \ldots, b_n\}$ so that neither $< a_1, a_2, \ldots, a_n >$ nor $< b_1, b_2, \ldots, b_n >$ is an increasing or decreasing sequence.

D-2. Distribute the integer pair $(a_i, b_i)$ to the participant $U_i$ as her/his shadow through a secure channel.

D-3. For each access instance $V$ in $\Gamma$, compute $D_V$ so that

$$D_V = K - (\Sigma_{\forall U_i \in V} a_i \oplus \Sigma_{\forall U_i \in V} b_i), \tag{1}$$

where '$\oplus$' represents a bitwise exclusive-OR operation.

D-4. Publish $D_V$ on the bulletin board.

**Part 2: Reconstruction**

In this part, any qualified subset $V$ of participants can cooperate to reconstruct the secret $K$ as follows:

R-1. Pool their shadows $(a_i, b_i)$'s together.

R-2. Get the public parameter $D_V$ from the bulletin board.

R-3. Reconstruct
$$K = D_V + (\Sigma_{\forall U_i \in V} a_i \oplus \Sigma_{\forall U_i \in V} b_i). \tag{2}$$

In Equations (1) and (2), we should alter some data types. First, the results of $\sum_{\forall U_i \in V} a_i$ and $\sum_{\forall U_i \in V} b_i$ are two integers, their types should be changed to the binary form with the same bit length before performing the exclusive-OR operation. Second, the binary result of $(\sum_{\forall U_i \in V} a_i \oplus \sum_{\forall U_i \in V} b_i)$ should be changed to the integer type. Finally, we perform the subtraction and addition operations to get $K$ and $D_V$ respectively.

## 3   The Design Concept of GGOC

In this section, we shall propose a design concept of constructing GGOC. The inspiration comes from Chang and Lee's GGOC [5]. The design concept to be proposed is built on three schemes: the generalized secret sharing scheme, the asymmetric cryptoscheme, and the symmetric cryptoscheme. Each group can put any set of a generalized secret sharing scheme, an asymmetric cryptoscheme, and a symmetric cryptoscheme under our design concept to construct a GGOC. The GGOC thus constructed does not need the assistance of a trusted party. The GGOC constructed by our design concept uses the selected generalized secret sharing scheme to make sure that only the qualified subset can read the sent message. The selected asymmetric cryptoscheme is used as a channel to send some secret information and the symmetric cryptoscheme is used to encrypt the sent message. In order to illustrate our idea clearly, we make an example of constructing a GGOC based on RSA [10], DES, and our generalized secret sharing scheme.

Two roles, the sender and the recipient group, appear in a GGOC issue. The recipient group selects and publishes one asymmetric cryptoscheme, one symmetric cryptoscheme, and one generalized secret sharing scheme in the initialization phase. Each member of the recipient group generates her/his public key and secret key based on the selected asymmetric cryptoscheme and then publishes her/his public key on the public bulletin. As a generalized secret sharing scheme is all about, we also use an access structure $\Gamma$ to show which recipients can cooperate to decrypt the encrypted message in the GGOC. In our design concept, if the access structure is decided by the recipient group, then they have to publish their access structure on the public bulletin in the initialization phase. Otherwise, if the access structure of each message is dynamic and dependent on the sent message, then the access structure is decided by the sender. The sender shall send, or publish, the access structure $\Gamma$ with its corresponding message.

Let $E_k(M)/D_k(C)$ be the encryption / decryption functions of DES and $PE_{p_k}(M)/PD_{s_k}(C)$ be the encryption / decryption functions of RSA. In the initialization phase, each member $U_i$ of the recipient group selects her/his secret key $s_{k_i}$ and public key $p_{k_i}$ based on RSA. She/he also publishes her/his public key in the bulletin.

In the following paragraph, we show how to use the GGOC based on our design concept to send a message $M$ to a recipient group in three cases according to their implicit properties. We illustrate our idea by using RSA as the asymmetric cryptoscheme, DES as the symmetric cryptoscheme and our generalized secret sharing scheme proposed in Section 2 as the selected generalized secret sharing scheme. Practically, the interested reader can construct a new GGOC by replacing each scheme with another cognate scheme.

## Case 1: $M$ Is an Important Message.

The message is so important that only some specific subsets of the recipient group are authorized to decrypt it. The sender encrypts and sends this message as follows:

(1) Select a private key $K$ based on DES and compute $C = E_K(M)$.
(2) Construct the access structure $\Gamma$ to specify the qualified subsets $V$'s of the recipient group which are authorized to read this message. Alternatively, if $\Gamma$ is specified by the recipient group, she/he gets $\Gamma$ from the bulletin.
(3) Randomly generate two distinct super-increase sets $\{a'_1, a'_2, \ldots, a'_n\}$ and $\{b'_1, b'_2, \ldots, b'_n\}$. Permute these two sets and let the new sets be $\{a_1, a_2, \ldots, a_n\}$ and $\{b_1, b_2, \ldots, b_n\}$ so that neither $< a_1, a_2, \ldots, a_n >$ nor $< b_1, b_2, \ldots, b_n >$ is an increasing or decreasing sequence.
(4) Compute a pair $(A_i, B_i)$ for each member $U_i$ of the recipient group so that $A_i = PE_{p_{k_i}}(a_i)$ and $B_i = PE_{p_{k_i}}(b_i)$.
(5) Send the pair $(A_i, B_i)$ to $U_i$, or, alternatively, the sender can use the Chinese Remainder Theorem to integrate all $(A_i, B_i)$'s into an integer pair and then transmit this integer pair to the recipient group or publish it on the bulletin instead of transmitting the cipher $(A_i, B_i)$ to the member $U_i$ individually.

(6) For each access instance $V$ in the access structure $\Gamma$, compute and put a parameter $D_V$ on the bulletin board so that $D_V = K - (\sum_{\forall U_i \in V} a_i \oplus \sum_{\forall U_i \in V} b_i)$.

(7) Send the ciphertext $C$ to the recipient group.

**Table 1.** The comparison between our GGOC and Chang and Lee's GGOC

| Schemes / Types of messages | | | our scheme | Chang and Lee's scheme |
|---|---|---|---|---|
| particular message | computational operations | sender | RSA | RSA |
| | | recipient | RSA | RSA |
| | communication cost | | $|M|$ bits | $|M|$ bits |
| urgent message | computational operations | sender | RSA+DES | RSA+DES |
| | | recipient | RSA+DES | RSA+DES |
| | communication cost | | $|M| \times n + |C|$ bits | $|M| \times n + |C|$ bits |
| important message | computational operations | sender | RSA+DES+ addition + bitwise exclusive-OR | RSA + DES + multiplication + modular exponentiation |
| | | recipient | RSA+DES+ addition + bitwise exclusive-OR | RSA + DES +addition + multiplication + modular exponentiation |
| | communication cost | | $2 \times n \times |M| + |C| + |\Gamma| \times |D|$ bits | $2 \times n \times |M| + |C| + |\Gamma| \times |D|$ bits |

Any qualified subset $V$ of the recipient group can cooperate to decrypt the ciphertext $C$ as follows:

(1) Generate the shadow $(a_i, b_i)$ of each participant $U_i$ in $V$ by $a_i = PD_{s_{k_i}}(A_i)$ and $b_{n-i+1} = PD_{s_{k_i}}(B_i)$.

(2) Pool all the shadows $(a_i, b_i)$'s together.

(3) Get the public parameter $D_V$ from the bulletin board.

(4) Reconstruct $K = D_V + (\sum_{\forall U_i \in V} a_i \oplus \sum_{\forall U_i \in V} b_i)$.

(5) Read the message $M$ by $M = D_K(C)$.

**Case 2: $M$ Is an Urgent Message.**

The message $M$ is so urgent that any legal member of the recipient group is authorized to decrypt it. The sender encrypts and transmits the message $M$ as follows:

(1) Select a private key $K$ based on DES.

(2) Compute $C = E_K(M)$.

(3) Compute $S_i$ for each member $U_i$ of the recipient group so that $S_i = PE_{p_{k_i}}(K)$.

(4) Send $S_i$ to $U_i$. Or, alternatively, use the Chinese Remainder Theorem to integrate all of these ciphers $S_i$'s into one integer and then transmit this integer to the recipient group or publish it on the bulletin instead of transmitting the cipher $S_i$ to the member $U_i$ individually.

(5) Transmit the cipher $C$ to the recipient group.

Each member of the recipient group can decrypt the ciphertext $C$ as follows:

(1) Generate the private key $K$ by $K = PD_{s_{k_i}}(S_i)$.
(2) Read the message $M$ by $M = D_K(C)$.

**Case 3: $M$ Is a Particular Message.**
The sender wants to send a *particular message* $M$ to a particular member $U_i$ of the recipient group, she/he encrypts and transmits the message $M$ as follows:

(1) Retrieve the member $U_i$'s public key $p_{k_i}$ from the public bulletin.
(2) Encrypt the message $M$ by $C = PE_{p_{k_i}}(M)$.
(3) Send the ciphertext to the recipient group.

The particular member $U_i$ can read the message $M$ by $M = PD_{s_{k_i}}(C)$.

## 4    Conclusions

In this paper, we propose a design concept to construct a GGOC. This GGOC provides a secure environment for a sender to send confidential messages to a group. We also propose a secure and efficient generalized secret sharing scheme. This generalized secret sharing scheme is based on simple operations. Furthermore, we use our design concept to construct a GGOC based on our generalized secret sharing scheme, RSA, and DES. Table 1 shows the comparison of computational operations and communication cost between our GGOC and Chang and Lee's GGOC. The newly constructed GGOC is more efficient than Chang and Lee's GGOC.

## References

1. Benaloh, J. and Leichter, J. "Generalized Secret Sharing and Monotone Functions," *Advances in Cryptology: Crypto'88*, New York: Springer-Verlag, 1989, pp. 27–35.
2. Blundo, C., Santis, A. D., Crescenzo, G. D., Gaggia, A. G., and Vaccaro, U. "Multi-Secret Sharing Schemes," *Advances in Cryptology: Crypto'94*, New York: Springer-Verlag, 1995, pp. 150–163.
3. Cachin, C. "On-line Secret Sharing," *Cryptography and Coding*, Springer-Verlag, Berlin, 1994, pp. 190–198.
4. Chang, C. C. and Hwang, R. J. "An Efficient Cheater Identification Method for Threshold Schemes," *IEE Proceedings- Computers and Digital Techniques*, vol. 144, No. 1, 1997, pp. 23–27.
5. Chang, C. C. and Lee, H. C. "A New Generalized Group-Oriented Cryptoscheme Without Trusted Centers," IEEE Journal on Selected Areas in Communications, Vol. 11, No. 5, 1993, pp. 725–729.
6. Desmedt, Y. "Society and Group Oriented Cryptography: A New Concept," *Advances in Cryptology: Crypto'87*, New York: Springer-Verlag, 1988, pp. 120–127.

7. Hwang, T. "Cryptosystem for Group Oriented Cryptography," *Advances in Cryptology:Eurocrypt'90*, New York: Springer-Verlag, 1990, pp. 317–324.
8. Ingemarsson, I. and Simmons, G. L. "A Protocol to Set up Shared Secret Schemes without the Assistance of a Mutually Trusted Party," *Advances in Cryptology:Eurocrypt'90*, New York: Springer-Verlag, 1990, pp. 266–282.
9. Lai, X. *On the Design and Security of Block Ciphers*, ETH Series in Information Processing, Konstanz: Hartung-Gorre Verlag, 1992.
10. Rivest, R. L., Shamir, A. and Adleman, L. "A Method for Obtaining Digital Signatures and Public Key Cryptosystems," *Communications of ACM*, Vol. 21, No. 2, 1978, pp. 120–126.

# Key Agreement in Ad Hoc Networks

Ren-Junn Hwang and Rong-Chi Chang

Department of Computer Science and Information Engineering
Tamkang University, Tamshi, Taipei Hsien, 251, Taiwan, R.O.C.
{victor, roger}@mail.tku.edu.tw

**Abstract.** A new key agreement protocol based on a shared conference password proposed in this paper. With this protocol, it provides an efficient algorithm and takes less computation cost to construct a secret communication channel. Besides, the honest participants can use password to authenticate themselves. The proposed scheme is suitable to apply in Ad Hoc Networks. It also provides an efficient protocol to reconstruct new session key when some members join or leave the conference.

## 1 Introduction

With fast growth of the Internet and the shift of communication services to the network, group communication becomes increasingly important. Modern group-oriented applications include IP-telephony, video-conferencing and collaborative workspaces etc.,. Simultaneously, security and privacy become necessary. The security requirement of these applications can be addressed by building upon a secret key.

Group key agreement means that several parties want to create a common secret to be used in exchanging information covertly. For example, a group of people that is coming together in a closed meeting and wants to from a private wireless network with their laptop computers for duration of the ad hoc meeting. They want to share information security so that no one outside of the room can eavesdrop during their communication.

Ad hoc networks are a new wireless networking paradigm for mobile hosts. Unlike traditional mobile wireless networks, ad hoc networks are dynamic, peer-to-peer network with little or no supporting infrastructure. The members of ad hoc networks may be PDA, mobile phone or notebook and so forth. These equipments are hardware-limited lack of storage devices and due to the security problems caused by ad hoc network; we consider a small group in a closed meeting. Members in this group know each other but can not digitally identifying and authenticating each another. Group members cannot provide or access third party key management service. They need a group shared key establishment protocol to construct a secure communication channel.

In general group key management protocols come in two different flavors: contributory key agreement protocols for small groups and centralized, server-based key distribution protocols for large groups. Becker and Wille [4] analyze

M. Guo and L.T.Yang (Eds.): ISPA 2003, LNCS 2745, pp. 382–390, 2003.

the minimal communication complexity of group key distribution protocol and propose two protocols: hypercube and octopus. They proposed a method using Diffie-Hellman Key exchange protocol to construct a common group key. This protocol handles join and merge operations efficiently, but it is inefficient when the group member leave. Becker and Wille [4] proposed the hypercube protocol for the number of group member is just equal to the exponents of 2; otherwise, the efficiency to decrease. Steiner et al. [2] address dynamic membership issues of group key agreement based on the two-party Diffie-Hellman Key exchange [6]. The method named Group Diffie Hellman (GDH) protocols. GDH provides contributory authenticated key agreement and key independence. It requires one broadcast message at the end of each protocol run. The GDH protocol should be implemented on linear chain network topology where the last node has broadcast capabilities. The scheme uses a group controller and need n protocol rounds to establish a common key in a group of n members.

In this paper, we develop a key agreement protocol based on XOR operation [7]. The group members share a conference password. Each group member contributes its share to derive a common session key in a general ad hoc network environment without making additional assumptions about the availability of any support infrastructure. By the proposed method, the member generate group shared key more efficient then the previous methods.

The rest of this paper is organized as follows. In Section 2 introduces our key agreement protocols, along with novel security properties. Section 3 introduces membership events of group key agreement protocol. The protocol security discussion and complexity analysis are shown in Section 4. Finally, we make conclusions in Section 5.

## 2    Key Agreement Protocol

This section introduces our key agreement protocol. Subsection 2.1 describes a key tree structure that we construct based on the member numbers. The proposed protocol based this tree structure will be introduced in Subsection 2.2.

### 2.1    The Key Tree of the Key Agreement Protocol

We assume that there are $n$ members, $M_1$, $M_2$,...,$M_n$, want to hold a closed conference base on ad hoc network without network infrastructure. Each member of this group keeps a unique number over $[1, n]$. These members cooperate based on a *complete binary tree*. The complete binary tree is constructed based on each member unique number. Fig.1 shows an example of a key tree with 14 members. In the key tree, its root is located at level $l = 0$ and its height is $h$, where $h = 4$. Since the structure is a complete binary tree, every node is either a leaf or a parent of one or two children nodes. The nodes are denoted with each member's unique number. In this group, we assign the member $M_n$ be "*Checker*". The checker is just a group member, but with an additional role to confirm the session key correctness. The member $M_{n-1}$ is named "*Candidate*", who arranges replacement of member number after the member leave the conference meeting. For example, there are 14 members in the key tree shown Fig.1 Member number 1 is the root node. Member number 13 is the candidate and member number 14 is the checker. Besides, to simplify our subsequent protocol description, we introduce the term *key-path*, denoted as $T_i$, which is the tree path from root node to member $M_i$. In other words, every member $M_i$ (except member $M_1$ and $M_n$) along his parent node to root node can build a key-path $T_i$. For example, the key-path $T_5$ of member $M_5$ in Fig.1 is the tree path $M_5 \rightarrow M_2 \rightarrow M_1$.

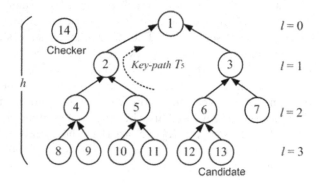

**Fig. 1.** An example of the key tree structure

## 2.2   Two Phases of the Proposed Protocol

This subsection introduces our key agreement protocol based on XOR operation. In our scenario, there are $n$ members sharing a password $P$. They can capture the existing shared context by choosing a new password and sharing it among those present in the room (e.g. by writing it on a blackboard). If this password is a sufficiently long random string, it can be used directly to set up a security session. In practice, people find it difficult to use long random strings. It is much more user-friendly if the password is a string that people recognize easily, such as a natural language phrase. But natural language phrases are weak as secrets because they are drawn from a rather limited set of possibilities; they are susceptible to dictionary attacks [5]. Therefore, we need a protocol to derive a strong shared session key from the weak shared password [1]. Our goal is that at the end of the protocol all members who know $P$ will get a shared session key $K = S_1 \oplus S_2 \oplus \cdots \oplus S_n$, where $S_i$ is contributed by $M_i$. $M_i$ selects $S_i$ randomly. The protocol is divided into two phases: the key initiation phase and the session key generation phase. In the key initiation phase, $M_1, M_2, \ldots, M_{n-1}$ cooperate to construct a subkey $\pi = S_1 \oplus S_2 \oplus \cdots \oplus S_{n-1}$ secretly. In the session key generation phase, each $M_i$ ($i = 1, 2, \ldots, n - 1$) engages in a separate exchange with $M_n$, all members have sufficient information to compute the session key $K$. He also verifies that the other members generated the same session key $K$. We introduce our method in detail as the following two phases:

**Key initiation phase.** Each member $M_i$ chooses a random quantity $S_i$, $i$ is the node number that $M_i$ located in the key tree. If the member $M_i$ locates at leaf node (*i.e.*, $2_i > n$) of the key tree, he assigns his intermediate key $K'_i$ as $S_i$. He sends intermediate key $K'_i$ and verification message, $F_i$ (generate by $f(P \parallel K'_i)$, where $f()$ is a public one-way hash function) to his parent node. The parent concatenates $K'_i$ with $P$ and generates a verification message $F'_i$ by hash function $f()$. If $F = F'$, the parent node authenticates the child note's identity and his $S_i$ because they share the same $P$. The parent node records children's intermediate keys. If the member $M_i$ locates at internal node (*i.e.*, $2_i \leq n$), he authenticates the children nodes' identities and their intermediate keys (*e.g.* $K'_{2i}$ and $K'_{2i+1}$) by using verification messages $F_{2i}$ ($= f(P \parallel K'_{2i})$) and $F_{2i+1}$ ($= f(P \parallel K'_{2i+1})$) separately. The $M_i$ randomly selects a number $S_i$ and generates intermediate key $K'_i = S_i \oplus K'_{2i} \oplus K'_{2i+1}$, where "$\oplus$" denotes the XOR operation. He also generate the verification message $F_i$ ($= f(P \parallel K'_i)$). Furthermore, he sends the intermediate key and verification message to his parent node. If the member is the root node (*i.e.*, $i = 1$), who has to collect his children nodes' intermediate keys and use his random number $S_1$ to compute the subkey $\pi$ ($= K'_1 = S_1 \oplus K'_2 \oplus K'_3$). Note that the members perform the previous simultaneously when they locate on the same level of the key tree. The key agreement algorithm is presented below:

*Algorithm 1: Key Initiation Phase of Key Agreement Protocol*
    For each *level* from the level 0 to the last shallowest level of the key tree

**Case 1** ($2i < n - 1$): $M_i$ verifies $K'_{2i}$ and $K'_{2i+1}$ by $F_{2i} = f(P \parallel K'_{2i})$ and
   ,   $F_{2i+1} = f(P \parallel K'_{2i+1})$. He selects a random number $S_i$ and computes $K'_i = K'_{2i} \oplus K'_{2i+1} \oplus S_i$. He also generates the verification message $F_i = f(P \parallel K'_i)$ for $K'_i$. He sends $F_i$ and $K'_i$ to his parent node.
**Case 2** ($2_i = n - 1$): $M_i$ verifies $K'_{2i}$ by $F_{2i} = f(P \parallel K'_{2i})$. He selects a random number $S_i$ and computes $K'_i = K'_{2i} \oplus S_i$. He also generates the verification message $F_i = f(P \parallel K'_i)$ for $K'_i$. He sends $F_i$ and $K'_i$ to his parent node.
**Case 3** ($2i > n - 1$): $M_i$ selects a random number $S_i$ and assigns $K'_i = S_i$. He also generates the verification message $F_i = f(P \parallel K'_i)$ for $K'_i$. He sends $F_i$ and $K'_i$ to his parent node.
**Case 4** ($i = 1$): $M_i$ verifies $K'_2$ and $K'_3$ by $F_2 = f(P \parallel K'_2)$ and $F_3 = f(P \parallel K'_3)$. He selects a random number $S_1$ and computes subkey $\pi = K'_1 = K'_2 \oplus K'_3 \oplus S_1$.

**Session key generation phase.** At the end of key initiation phase, the member $M_1$ generates a subkey $\pi$ ($= S_1 \oplus S_2 \oplus \cdots \oplus S_{n-1}$). In Step 1 of this phase, the member $M_1$ broadcasts subkey to each member, except the member $M_n$. In Step 2, each member $M_i$ ($i = 1, 2, \ldots, n - 1$) removes its contribution from and inserts a randomly chosen blinding factor $S'_i$. The resulting quantity, $C_i$, is equal to $\pi \oplus Si \oplus S'_i$. Each member $M_i$ ($i = 1, 2, \ldots, n - 1$) sends $C_i$ and the verification message $f(P \parallel C_i)$ to member $M_n$. $M_n$ verifies the message sent by each member. In Step 3, $M_n$ computes and sends $E_{P \oplus C_i}(C_i \oplus S_n)$ to each member $M_i$. He encrypted the message $C_i \oplus S_n$ by using the symmetric encryption function with key $P \oplus C_i$. The legal member decrypts the received messages to extract $S_n$. A this point, $M_i$ ($i = 1, 2, \ldots, n - 1$) unbinds the quantity received from $M_n$ and constructs a session key $K_i = \pi \oplus S_n$. In Step 4, each member $M_i$ (for $i = 1, 2, \ldots, n - 1$) sends the key confirmation message of $K_i$ as $E_{P \oplus S_n}(K_i)$ to member $M_n$, where $E_{P \oplus S_n}(K_i)$ denotes encrypting $K_i$ with a symmetric encryption function and key $P \oplus S_n$. In Step 5, the member $M_n$ verifies that each member generated the same session key $K$ ($= K_1 = K_2 = \cdots = K_{n-1}$). $M_n$ notifies all members the conference that the session key is established successfully. The algorithm key agreement protocol is shown as following:

*Algorithm 2: Session Key Generation Phase of Key Agreement Protocol*

(1) $M_1 \to M_i : \pi, f(P \parallel \pi)$; for $i = 2, 3, \ldots, n - 1$ and $\pi = S_1 \oplus S_2 \oplus \cdots S_{n-1}$
(2) $M_i \to M_n : C_i, f(P \parallel C_i)$; for $i = 1, 2, \ldots, n - 1$ and $C_i = \pi \oplus S_i \oplus S'_i$, $S'_i$ is a blinding factor that is randomly chosen by $M_i$
(3) $M_n \to M_i : E_{P \oplus C_i}(C_i \oplus S_n)$; for $i = 1, 2, \ldots, n - 1$
(4) $M_i \to M_n : M_i, E_{P \oplus S_n}(K_i)$; for $i = 1, 2, \ldots, n - 1$ and $K_i = (\pi \oplus S_n)$
(5) $M_n$ check session key $K$

# 3    Membership Events

In our scenario, the conference members are not always fixed. Some times there are new members joint the conference, after the session key is generated. This new member does not authorize to know the messages of this conference before he joins this conference. The conference should change their session key and the shared password. Some times there are some members leave. They do not authorize to get the messages after they leave. This conference should change the session key and the shared password, too. This section introduces two protocols to generate the new session key when the group member is adapting.

## 3.1    Member Joining Protocol

We assume that the group has $n$ members: $M_1, M_2, \cdots, M_n$. The new member $M_{n+1}$ wants to join the conference. The new member $M_{n+1}$ initiate the protocol by sending a joining request message that contains his member number. The new member will be allowed to join the conference when the members in the conference receive this message and permit it. Furthermore, the members of the conference have to change the password from $P$ to $P'$ and reconstruct the session key. We describe the reconstructing protocol in the following paragraph.

Firstly, $M_{n+1}$ sends random quantity $S_{n+1}$ encrypted with new password $P'$ to old members $M_1, M_2, \cdots, M_n$. In this conference, the old members receive and decrypt the message to extract $S_{n+1}$. Each members $M_i$ ($i = 1, 2, \ldots, n$) computes a session key $\hat{K}_i = K \oplus P \oplus S_{n+1}$. Secondly, the $M_n$ sends a quantity $K \oplus P$ encrypted with new password $P'$ (i.e., $E'_P(K \oplus P)$) to member $M_{n+1}$.

Note that $M_{n+1}$ computes the session key $\hat{K}_{n+1}$ by $\hat{K}_{n+1} = S_{n+1} \oplus (K \oplus P)$. Thirdly, $M_{n+1}$ encrypts the session key $\hat{K}_{n+1}$ with key $P' \oplus S_{n+1}$ and sends it to $M_1$. $M_1$ verifies the session key $\hat{K}_{n+1}$ that member $M_{n+1}$ generated. The algorithm member joining protocol is shown as following:

*Algorithm 3: Member Joining of Key Agreement Protocol*

(1) $M_{n+1} \to M_i : M_{n+1}, E_{P'}(S_{n+1})$; for $i = 1, 2, \ldots, n$ and $M_1, M_2, \ldots, M_n$, compute $\hat{K}_i = K \oplus P \oplus S_{n+1}$

(2) $M_n \to M_{n+1} : E_{P'}(K \oplus P)$; and $M_{n+1}$ compute $\hat{K}_{n+1} = S_{n+1} \oplus (K \oplus P)$

(3) $M_{n+1} \to M_1 : E_{P' \oplus S_{n+1}}(\hat{K}_{n+1})$; and $M_1$ verifies session key $\hat{K}_{n+1}$

## 3.2   Member Leaving Protocol

Assume that there are $n$ members in the conference room and the member $M_d$ wants to leave the conference. When a member leaved the conference, the session key should be changed and the key tree structure is altered. In order to maintain the security of conference meeting, the shared password should be changed to $P'$, too. The leaving member initiates the leave protocol by sending a leave message to all conference members. The candidate member changes his member number as the member number of leaving member. The candidate picks a new random number and sends it to his new parent node.

The reconstructing protocols are different based on the $M_d$'s location in the key tree. Generally, we divide two cases to introduce the leaving protocol.

**Case 1: $M_d$ is a leaf node.** Fig.2 shows an example of this case clearly. If $M_{11}$ leaves the conference, the candidate, $M_{13}$, (the right-most leaf node) alters his member number to 11. Moreover, the checker $M_{14}$ changes its member number to 13. $M_{12}$ is the new candidate of this conference.

The key tree is reorganized. Fig.2(b) is the new key tree structure. Firstly, each of the members, $M_i$, except the root $M_1$ on the key-path, $M_{11} \to M_5 \to M_2 \to M_1$, should select a new random number $S_i''$. The first node of this key-path, $M_{11}$, sends his new random number to his parent as $E_p'(S_{11}'')$. Secondly, the node, $M_i$, except the leaf node compute the new intermediate key $K_i'' = K_{2i}'' \oplus K_{2i+1}'' \oplus S_i''$, where $K_{2i}''$ and $K_{2i+1}''$ are intermediate keys transformed by his children. If $M_i$'s child $M_{2i}$ does not in the key-path, then $K_{2i}'' = K_{2i}'$. $M_i$ sends intermediate key $K_i''$ to his parent. The key-path that each member in it should joint previous process is from the leaving member's location to the root. Finally, $M_1$ performs the algorithm 2 in Section 2 to reconstruct and verify a new session key.

**Case 2: $M_d$ is an internal node.** Fig.3 shows an example of this case. The leaving member, $M_5$, is an internal node of this key tree. The candidate member, $M_{13}$, change his number to 5. Moreover, the checker $M_{14}$ changes its member number to 13, and the new candidate is $M_{12}$.

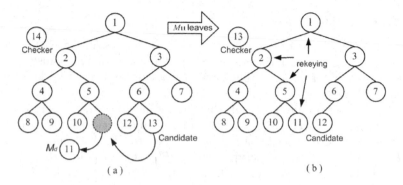

**Fig. 2.** Key tree after leaving the member $M_{11}$

The key tree is altered. Fig.3(b) is the new key tree structure. The conference has to change its session key by security considerations. Firstly, each member, $M_i$, except the root member in the key-path, $M_5 \rightarrow M_2 \rightarrow M_1$, and the two children of $M_5$ select a new random number $S_i''$. Secondly, each of the two children, $M_i$, of the first node of the key-path, sends the new random number to his parent as $E_p'(S_i'')$. Thirdly, each member $M_j$ of the key-path compute a new intermediate key as $K_j'' = K_{2j}'' \oplus K_{2j+1}'' \oplus S_j''$, where $K_{2j}''$ is a intermediate key sent by the child node $M_{2j}$. If the child $M_{2j}$ does not in the key-path then $K_{2j}'' = K_{2j}'$. The special key-path is from the altered node to the root. Finally, $M_1$ perform the algorithm 2 of Section 2 to reconstruct a new session key.

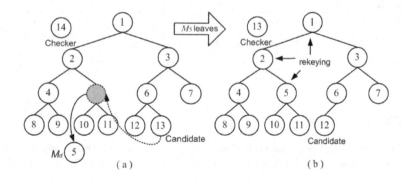

**Fig. 3.** Key tree after leaving the member $M_5$

## 4   Discussion

We discuss the security analysis and efficiency of the proposed protocols in this section. The subsection 4.1 discusses the forward and backward secrecy. We make the comparisons among the GDH.2 [2], hypercube [4], octopus protocols [4] and our method in Subsection 4.2.

## 4.1    Security Analysis

The new member of the conference cannot derive the session key before he join this conference is named backward secrecy. It is important, because that new member is legal after he joins. The session key can be derived by knowing the random number.

In the member joining protocol, the joining member $M_{n+1}$ picks a random quantity $S_{n+1}$ and encrypted it by password $P'$ and broadcasts it with its join request. The conference password $P$ is changed to $P'$. $M_n$ sends a quantity, $K \oplus P$, to $M_{n+1}$ which is encrypted with $P'$. At this point, the $M_{n+1}$ can compute the new session key $\hat{K}$, but he cannot derive old session key $K$, because the $M_{n+1}$ does not know the old password $P$. The proposed protocol provides the backward security.

A member $M_d$ leaving the conference cannot get the new session key after his leaving is named forward secrecy. In the leaving protocol, the candidate changes its share and member number to replace the leaved member location when $M_d$ leaves the conference. The members in the key-path which construct from $M_d$ to root change their shares. The leaving protocol reconstructs the session key based on these shares. The leaving member, $M_d$, cannot generate the new session key. The new session key is regenerated by new shared random number that $M_d$ does not know. The proposed protocol provides forward secrecy.

**Table 1.** Protocols comparison

| methods | GDH.2 | Hypercube | Octopus | Our method |
|---|---|---|---|---|
| Messages | $n$ | $nlog_2n$ | $3n - 4$ | $n$ |
| DH-Key Exchanges | $n$ | $\frac{nlog_2n}{2}$ | $2n - 4$ | $0$ |
| Simple Rounds | $n$ | $log_2n$ | $2\lceil\frac{n-4}{4}\rceil + 2$ | $log_2n + 1$ |
| Broadcast | Yes | No | No | Yes |

## 4.2    Efficiency Discussion

This subsection analyzes the communication and computation costs of the key agreement protocols. Table 1 shows the comparisons among GDH.2 [2], Hypercube [4], Octopus protocols [4] and our protocols. The $n$ denotes the number of member in this conference. The second row of the Table 1 shows the numbers of *DH-Key exchanges* that are sent by two members. In the third row, the *simple round* means that every member can send or receive at most one message per round. [4] In the last row, the *broadcast* means one member sends a message to each member simultaneously.

By the Table 1, it is clearly that GDH.2 and our protocol need fewer numbers of communication messages. The Octopus protocol need fewer number of 2-party DH exchanges than ours, but in our protocol all member use the XOR operation to compute the session key. The XOR operation takes less computation cost than

DH exchange operation. As Table 1 illustrates, our method need $log_2 n + 1$ times of the simple rounds. The number of simple rounds of our scheme is fewer than GDH.2 and Octopus protocols'. In generally, Table 1 shows that our protocol is more efficient than the others.

## 5    Conclusions

This paper proposes an efficient password-based key agreement protocol for the ad hoc networks. The ad hoc network does not provide additional infrastructure and physically secures communication channels. In the proposed protocol, the legal conference member use password to authenticate participants and take lower computing operations to generate the session key. The proposed protocol supports dynamic conference member events. It is more efficient than the others.

## References

1. N. Asokan and Philip Ginzboorg. "Key-agreement in ad hoc networks", *Computer Communications*, Vol. 23, No. 17, Nov. 2000, pp. 1627–1637.
2. Giuseppe Ateniese, Michael Steiner, and Gene Tsudik. "Authenticated group key agreement and friends", In *Proc. 5th ACM Conference on Computer and Communications Security*, Nov. 1998, pp. 17–26.
3. Giuseppe Ateniese, Michael Steiner, and Gene Tsudik. "New multiparty authentication services and key agreement protocols", *IEEE Journal on Selected Areas in Communications*, Vol. 8, No. 4, Apr. 2001, pp. 628–640.
4. Klaus Becker and Uta Wille. "Communication complexity of group key distribution", In *Proc. 5th ACM Conference on Computer and Communications Security*, Nov. 1998, pp. 1–6.
5. S. Bellovin and M. Merritt, "Encrypted key exchange: password-based protocols secure against dictionary attack", *IEEE Symposium on Research in Security and Privacy*, 1992, pp. 72–84.
6. W. Diffie, and M.E. Hellman, "New directions in cryptography", *IEEE Trans. On Information Theory*, Vol. IT-22, No.6, 1976, pp. 644–654.
7. Sahar M. Ghanem, Hussein Abdel-Wahab, "A simple XOR-based technique for distributing group key in secure multicasting", In Proc. *The Fifth IEEE Symposium on Computers and Communications*, pp. 166–171, 2000.
8. Y. Kim, A. Perrig, and G. Tsudik. "Simple and fault-tolerant key agreement for dynamic collaborative group", In *7th ACM conference on Computer and communications*, Nov. 2000, pp. 235–244.
9. Silja Maki, Maarit Hietalahti, and Tuomas Aura. "A survey of ad-hoc network security", Interim report of project 007- security of mobile agents and ad-hoc societies, *Helsinki University of Technology, Laboratory for Theoretical Computer Science*, Sep. 2000.
10. Michael Steiner, Gene Tsudik, and Michael Waidner. "CLIQUES: a new approach to group key agreement", In *Proc. 18th International Conference on Distributed Computing Systems* (ICDCS'98), May 1998, pp. 380–387.
11. Michael Steiner, Gene Tsudik, and Michael Waidner. "Key agreement in dynamic peer groups", *IEEE Transactions on Parallel and Distributed Systems*, Vol. 11, No. 8, Aug. 2000, pp. 769–780.

# Formalizing Active Networks Security with Seal-Calculus

Xiaojuan Zheng[1], Tao Xu[2], and Ying Jin[1]

[1] College of Computer Science and Technology, JILIN University, P.R.China, 130012
zhengxiaojuan2000@yahoo.com.cn
[2] College of Mechanism, JILIN University, P.R.China,130025

**Abstract.** Active Networks (ANs) aims at incorporating programmability into the network to achieve flexibility. However, increasing flexibility results in new security risks, which cannot be handled by existing ANs systems. In this paper, we aim at analyzing the security of ANs in language level based on the active code. First, we present the notion of active packet hierarchy. Next, we abstract the AN with Seal-calculus, and security protection is represented formally in four propositions. Finally, an example is used to address security protection. Our security protection is symmetrical, which protects a host from the untrustworthy active codes that migrate to it as well as active codes from the untrustworthy host where it migrates.

**Keywords:** ANs, active codes, security, Seal-calculus, formalization

## 1 Introduction

ANs provide a general framework within which users inject programs contained in messages into a network capable of performing computations and manipulations on behalf of users. We call these programs active codes [5].

By introducing mobile active codes into the network, the network is ensured not being destroyed and influenced, which is very important for the sharing network resource and structure. Therefore, it must, at least, be as safe, secret and sound as the present systems when the active codes migrate and execute in quite a large distributed system including many management fields [6]. It is vital to tackle security problems as our key to ANs research.

In the last couple of years, a number of process calculi have been designed to model aspects of distributed programming. Among these calculi are the $\pi$-calculus [1], the Join-calculus [2], Ambient calculus [3], and Seal–calculus [4]. The goal of seal-calculus is to explore the design space of security and mobile features. It provides strong security protection mechanisms.

Despite significant efforts devoted to security research in ANs [5,6,7], the issues of security still remain unsolved. Especially, formal description of ANs security has not yet been touched at present. This paper attempts to formally describe the security requirements in ANs with Seal-calculus. We believe that it is greatly significant to describe the security of active codes formally so as to handle the ANs security more perfectly.

In this paper, we discuss security properties of ANs in language level based on the active code. We present the notion of active packets hierarchy, in which each active

M. Guo and L.T.Yang (Eds.): ISPA 2003, LNCS 2745, pp. 391–404, 2003.

packet can be a container of other active packets. We formalize the AN in Seal-calculus. The security protections basing on the formalization above are represented formally with propositions. Finally, we address security protections with an example, which demonstrate our result. And the protection provided is symmetrical, and it protects a host from active codes that migrate to it as well as active codes from the host where it migrates

This paper is organized as follows. In Section 2, the preliminary work is introduced. The hierarchy of active packet is presented in Section 3. Next in Section 4 we give formalization of active network with Seal-calculus and its security protections. An example is presented in Section 5, and the related work is discussed in Section 6. Finally, we conclude the paper and outline future work in Section 7.

## 2   Preliminaries

### 2.1   The Security of AN

The main problem in ANs security is the security of active code. Protection mechanisms of active code security may be placed at all component boundaries with the goal to control and regulate interaction among components. Figure 1 shows the four boundaries that require security [6,7,8]:

  a.   Active packets, active extensions must be protected from being attacked by each other, which prevent a computation from disrupting another information or information gained privilege.
  b.   The computational environment (CE) must be protected from the potentially malicious active packets and active extensions.
  c.   Active packets, active extensions must be protected from the potentially malicious CE.
  d.   Protect the security from the bottom transfer network.

The remarkable thing in the case of active code security issues is the symmetry of the security concerns: both the active codes and their execution environment must be protected. The goal of this paper is to study formally how active codes can protect from each other, and how hosts can protect themselves from being attacked by active codes, and vice versa.

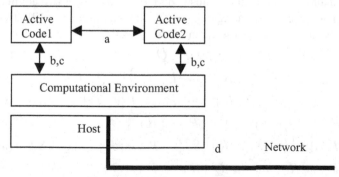

**Fig. 1.** Active Code Security Issues

## 2.2   Seal-Calculus

We adopt a calculus of mobile computations called the Seal-calculus [4,9,10] as our formal language. Here we will briefly overview its syntax and semantics.

### 2.2.1   Syntax

We assume infinite sets $N$ of names and $\overline{N}$ of co-names disjoint and in bijection via ($\bar{\ }$); We declare $\overline{\overline{x}} = x$. The set of location denotations extends names with two symbols $(*, \uparrow)$.

*Definition 1.* The set of process, ranged over by $P, Q, R, S$, is defined by following grammar:

$$P ::= 0 \mid P \mid Q \mid !P \mid (\nu x)P \mid \alpha.P \mid x[P]$$

Where $0$ denotes the inert process, $P \mid Q$ denotes parallel composition, $(\nu x)P$ is a restriction, $\alpha.P$ denotes an action $\alpha$ and a continuation $P$, and $x$ [P] denotes a seal name $x$ with body $P$.

*Definition 2.* The set of actions, ranged over by $\alpha$, is defined by:

$$\alpha ::= \overline{x}^{\eta}\langle \vec{y} \rangle \mid x^{\eta}\langle \lambda \vec{y} \rangle \mid \overline{x}^{\eta}(y) \mid x^{\eta}(\vec{y}) \mid \textbf{open}_{\eta}\, \textbf{x}$$

$$\eta ::= \text{n} \mid \uparrow \mid *$$

Where $\overline{x}^{\eta}\langle \vec{y} \rangle$ denotes a process offering $\vec{y}$ at channel $x$ located in seal $\eta$. $x^{\eta}\langle \lambda \vec{y} \rangle$ is ready to input distinct names $\vec{y}$ at $x$ in $\eta$, $\vec{y} = y_1 \cdots y_n$. $\overline{x}^{\eta}(y)$ denotes the sender process offering seal $y$ at $x$ in $\eta$. $x^{\eta}(\vec{y})$ is waiting to read a seal at $x$ in $\eta$ and start $n$ copies of it under names $y_1 \cdots y_n$. $\textbf{open}_{\eta}\, \textbf{x}$ denotes a portal is opened where $\textbf{x}$ is $x$ (the action allows the seal $\eta$ to read once the local channel $x$) or $\overline{x}$ (the action allows the seal $\eta$ to write once on the local channel $x$). Location denotations $*$, $\uparrow$ and $n$ respectively represent the current seal, parent seal, and a sub-seal bearing name $n$.

### 2.2.2   Reduction Semantics

Reduction semantics of the seal calculus is defined by means of two auxiliary notions: structural congruence and heating, the detail can be found in [12]. Here we just overview the behavior of a process given by the reduction rules in the following:

$$x^*\langle \lambda u \rangle.P \mid \overline{x}^*\langle v \rangle.Q \;\rightarrow\; P\{v/u\} \mid Q \qquad \text{(write local)}$$

$$x^y\langle \lambda u \rangle.P \mid y[\,\overline{x}^{\uparrow}\langle v \rangle.Q \mid R\,] \;\rightarrow\; P\{v/u\} \mid y[Q \mid R\,] \qquad \text{(write out)}$$

$$\overline{x}^y\langle v \rangle.P \mid y[\,x^{\uparrow}\langle \lambda u \rangle.Q \mid R\,] \;\rightarrow\; P \mid y[Q\{v/u\} \mid R\,] \qquad \text{(write in)}$$

$$x^*(u).P \mid \overline{x}^*(v)Q \mid v[B] \rightarrow P \mid u[B] \mid Q \qquad \text{(move local)}$$

$$x^y(u).P \mid y[\,\overline{x}^{\uparrow}(v)Q \mid v[R] \mid S\,] \rightarrow P \mid u[R] \mid y[Q \mid S\,] \qquad \text{(move out)}$$

$$\overline{x}^y(v).P \mid v[R] \mid y[\,x^{\uparrow}(u)Q \mid S\,] \rightarrow P \mid y[Q \mid S \mid u[R]] \qquad \text{(move in)}$$

Specific security policies are enforced directly by the Seal-calculus. The seal calculus provides protection mechanisms for the implementation of policies. This design focuses on resources. Seal-calculus incorporates a strong resource access control based on linear revocable capabilities called *portals*.

The Seal calculus provides a hierarchical protection model, in which each level can implement security policies by mediation. Mediation means that observable actions performed at a lower level in the hierarchy are scrutinized and controlled by higher levels. The hierarchical model guarantees that a policy defined at some level will not bypassed or amended at lower levels.

## 3　Hierarchies of Active Packets

The taxonomy of active codes composing of active extensions and active packets has been introduced in detail by [11], which we utilize in our formalization. The ANs system making use of active packet is basically designed as an isolated entity, which always acts and migrates independently. This is a serious limitation in the development of a large and complicated system based on active packet. The seal-calculus provides some kind of mechanism that enables active packets to be organized hierarchically and dynamically. Therefore, in order to represent the ANs in seal-calculus, we introduce hierarchy of active packets.

*Definition 3:* If an active packet $AP_1$ contains another active packet $AP_2$, we call $AP_1$ *parent* and $AP_2$ *child*. We call the active packets, which are nested by an active packet, the *descendent* active packet, and in reverse we call the active packets, which are nesting an active packet, the *ancestral* active packets.

Since the framework allows active packets to be nested, a child active packet can contain one or more active packet in the same way. A set of active packets establishes the hierarchy structure under the relationship of inclusion.

Figure 2 shows an example of an active packet migration in an active packet hierarchy. We can see that each active packet has a direct control of its descendent active packets. In contrast, each active packet has no direct control on its ancestral active packets.

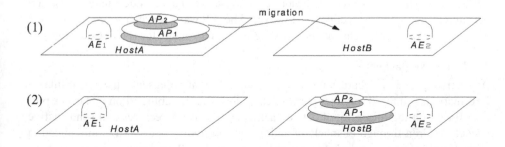

**Fig. 2.** An Example of Active packet, Active Extension Hierarchy and Migration

# 4 Formalization of ANs Security

Basing on the taxonomy of active code and hierarchy of active packets above, we present the formalization of ANs security with Seal-calculus in this section.

## 4.1 Abstraction for ANs with Seal-Calculus

### 4.1.1 Abstraction of an AN

An *AN* can be modeled by a single seal, with as many sub-seals as existing hosts in the AN. *Hosts* are designated by their IP number and for each host a process takes care of active extensions and routing active packets to be sent to other hosts on the AN. The overall configuration is therefore:

$$AN ::= Host\ ip_1 P_1\ |\ ...\ |\ Host\ ip_n P_n$$

Based on the taxonomy of active code, host is the description of three things: the actual host (a seal whose name is the host's IP number *ip*); the active packet (a seal whose name is the active packet's name *AP*); and the active extension (a seal whose name is the active extension's name *AE*).

$$Host\ ipP \stackrel{def}{=}\ !(V\ AP)\ out^{ip}(AP)$$

$$.hdr^{AP}\ \langle \lambda ipdest\ port \rangle$$

$$\overline{.\ port}^{\ ipdest}(AP)$$

$$|\ !(V\ AE)\ \overline{in}^{\ ip}(AE)$$

$$|\ ip[!\mathbf{open}_\uparrow out\ |\ !\mathbf{open}_\uparrow \overline{in}\ |\ !\mathbf{open}_\uparrow hdr\ |\ P\ ]$$

Here we represent an *AN* as parallel executing seals. The *AN* waits for the *Host ip* to send a new active packet on channel *out*, *AN* generates a new name for active packet, asks active packet on the header port *hdr* active packet's destination host and port and routes active packet there. However, The *AN* waits for the host *ip* to receive a new active extension on channel *in*, *AN* generates a new name for active extension.

### 4.1.2 Active Packets

An active packet is characterized by a seal *AP* that represents the encapsulated information, and the IP number port of destination that it published on its header port *hdr*. Based on the hierarchy of active packets, the seal *AP* receives and sends active packet children through channels *in* and *out* respectively. Request a communication with a seal *AE* on channel *chn*. In general every process *P* on a host will run a suite of protocols that listen to given ports and accordingly perform some operations.

Active packet:      $AP.P \overset{def}{=} (V\ x)\,x\,[in\,(k)$

$$\overline{.hdr}\,\langle ip\ port\rangle$$

$$\overline{.request}\,\langle AE\ chn\rangle$$

$$\overline{.out}\,(k)$$

$$|\ \textbf{open}_\uparrow\ \overline{in}\ .\textbf{open}_\uparrow hdr.\ \textbf{open}_\uparrow out\ .\textbf{open}_\uparrow request]\ .P$$

### 4.1.3   Active Extensions

An active extension is characterized by a seal $AE$ that represents the encapsulated information. The seal $AE$ receives through channels $in$. Answer a communication with a seal $AP$ on channel $chn$. In general every process $Q$ on a host will run a suite of protocols that listen to given ports and accordingly perform some operations.

Active extension:     $AE.Q \overset{def}{=} (V\ x)\,x\,[in\,(k)$

$$.request\,\langle \lambda AP\ chn\rangle$$

$$|\ \textbf{open}_\uparrow\ \overline{in}\ .\ \textbf{open}_\uparrow\ \overline{requst}\ ].Q$$

### 4.2   Security Protection

In this subsection we will first introduce some useful notations and definitions, then we will address and prove the security protection of our seal-based formalization of the AN above. This security protection is represented formally in four propositions. Following each proposition, we give its proof.

The reduction semantics defines only the internal computation of processes. However, the statements of our security properties must involve the interactions of processes within their environments. So more structure are required.

*Definition 4.* (Labels) A labeled semantics is indexed by a set of labels ranged over by $\ell$ defined by the following grammar:

$$\ell\ ::=\ \tau\ |\ x[]\ |\ \mathbf{x}^\eta\ |\ \overline{x}^\eta(y)\ |\ \textbf{open}^\eta\mathbf{x}$$

*Definition 5.* (Commitment) The commitment relation relates a process $P$, a label $\ell$ and an active packet or active extension $\omega\,Q$ and a finite set of names $A$, which can be written as:

$$A \vdash P \xrightarrow{\ell} \omega Q \qquad fn(P) \subseteq A.$$

*Definition 6.* (Wrapper) The wrapper encapsulates a single active extension or active packet. Wrapper ensures that no matter how active extension or active packet can only interact with its environment on the two channels in and out.

$$W[\_] \overset{def}{=} (V\,a)(\,a[\_]$$

$$|\,!\,in^\uparrow \langle \lambda u \rangle .\overline{in}^a \langle v \rangle$$

$$|\,!\,out^a \langle \lambda u \rangle .\overline{out}^\uparrow \langle v \rangle\,)$$

*Proposition 1.*     $(V\,x)x[P] \approx 0$, where $P$ represents a process and $x$ represents seal name.

The detail can be found in [13].

This proposition shows that **names are simple-minded capabilities**. Seal-calculus emphasizes the role of names; they are used to name seals and channels of communication. Without knowing the name on which a process wishes to interact, communication is impossible. That is to say, an arbitrary process can be completely prevented from any communication.

The semantics of the calculus guarantees that no other process than $P$ may guess $x$. If a seal is given a fresh name which isn't known by any other process, then there can be no portal open for that name (**open** $_x$ **y**), nor can there be located communication ($\mathbf{y}^x \langle ... \rangle$). It is useful as it guarantees that once a seal is in a firewall, it cannot divulge any information, nor perform any externally visible action for that matter.

*Proposition 2.*   If $A \vdash P \xrightarrow{\ell} \omega Q$ then $\ell = \overline{x}^\eta(y)$

Proof If $P \xrightarrow{\overline{x}^\eta(y)} \omega Q$ then $\omega = \epsilon$, $P \equiv (v\vec{x})(\overline{x}^\eta(y).P_1 | P_2)$, $Q \equiv (v\vec{x})(.\,P_1 | P_2)$, and $\vec{x} \cap \{x,\eta\} = \emptyset$. We have $P = \overline{x}^\eta(y)$. $Q$ and $P \xrightarrow{\overline{x}^\eta(y)} \epsilon Q$. The result is obtained by setting $P_1 = Q$, $P_2 = 0$, and $\vec{x}$ the empty vector.    $\square$

This proposition shows that **active packets are not allowed to move arbitrarily and receive freely**. Seals are not allowed to move about autonomously or arbitrarily. Migration is always under the control of a seal's environment that decides when it occurs. A host controls all external resources used by its resident active extensions. Active packets may move (enter or leave) a host only with the host's explicit permission. A seal moving action requires that a seal bearing the requested name should be presented otherwise the operation blocks. Furthermore a seal performs a receive action in order to allow a new seal to migrate from the outside and since it choose the name for the new seal it can arbitrarily isolate it from the other processes.

*Proposition 3. If* $A \vdash P \xrightarrow{\ell} \omega Q$ *then* $\ell = \mathbf{open}_\eta \, \mathbf{x}$

Proof It is the similar to the proof of proposition 2.    □

This proposition shows that **local resources are tightly controlled over**. The semantics of the calculus guarantees that all mobile computations are subject to access control, thus active packets and active extensions may only use resources to which they have been given access. Communication among active packets, active extensions and other active packets, active extensions located on the same host, or on different hosts, is also under the host's control.

The defense is using *portal*. The idea is that if a seal $A$ wants to use seal $B$'s channel $x$, then $B$ must open a portal for $A$ at $x$. A portal is best viewed as liner channel access permission. As soon as synchronization takes place, the portal is closed again. Portals are opened only for channels that are allowed by the security policy. A seal knows only the names of its direct children and can communicate with them and its parent. It means that synchronization involves at most two nested locations. A noteworthy characteristic is that it provides symmetric protection that the child active packet can protect its own resources from its parent with the same mechanism as the parent. This is the great difference from the other security policy that ANs projects have adopted. Because there is no security policy that can protect in two ways in previous ANs project. About this viewpoint we will review the related work in the section 5.

*Proposition 4. For any active packet or active extension with* $a_1 \notin fn(AP)$ *or* $a_2 \notin fn(AE)$, $\{ a_1, a_2 \} \cap fn(AE,AP) = \emptyset$ *if* $A \vdash W[AE,AP] \xrightarrow{l_1 \ldots l_k} wQ$ *then the* $l_j$ *are of the form* $\tau, \mathbf{x}^\eta, \bar{x}^\eta(y), \mathbf{open}_\eta \, \mathbf{x}$.

Proof If $N$ is a finite set of names, $a$ is a name then

$$\llbracket a; N; AE; AP \rrbracket \overset{def}{=} (\nu \, N \cup \{a\}) (AE$$

$$| \; a[AP]$$

$$| \; ! \, in^{\uparrow}\langle \lambda u \rangle . \overline{in}^{\,a}\langle v \rangle$$

$$| \; ! \, out^{\,a}\langle \lambda u \rangle . \overline{out}^{\,\uparrow}\langle v \rangle )$$

Say the 4-tuple $a, N, AE, AP$ is good if $N$, $\{a\}$, and $\{in, out\}$ pairwise disjoint, $AE$ is a parallel composition of outs of the forms: $\overline{out}^{\,a}\langle v \rangle$, $\overline{out}^{\,\uparrow}\langle v \rangle$, $\overline{in}^{\,a}\langle v \rangle$, $\bar{x}^{\bar{a}}\langle v \rangle$ where $x \notin \{out, a\}$ with $a \notin fn(v)$ in each case.    □

This proposition shows that **seal boundaries can guarantee the body process may never mix freely with the environment**. Because Seal-calculus do not allow processes located in sibling seals (and even less those located in an arbitrary seals) to communicate. So when active packet moves into host, active packet may not threat the active extension there, and vice versa.

Communication across a seal configuration must be encoded; In other words, every distributed interaction up to packet routing must be programmed. Seal boundaries are the main protection mechanism provided by the calculus; they cannot be discovered, thus guarantees that the body process may never mix freely with the environment.

## 5    An Example

In this section we demonstrate our result with an example of Figure 3, which models the behavior of the active extension and active packet hierarchy and migration in an *AN* within our formalism. The step1 configuration in Figure 3 corresponds to the expression appearing in Figure 4, where the process $P$, $P'$, $P''$ and $P'''$ denote of *stA*, active packet $AP_1$, $AP_2$ and the active extension $AE_1$. The process $Q$, $Q'$ denote of the *HostB* and active extension $AE_2$. The step2 configuration in Figure 3 corresponds to the expression appearing in Figure 5, and their alternate graphical representation is the configuration tree in the same figure. An actual implementation of the calculus would not program the AN; we only model the behavior of the *AN* within our formalism.

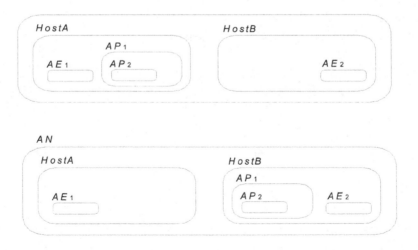

**Fig. 3.** Seal configuration

AN[HostA [P |

    AP$_1$ [P' | AP$_2$ [P"]] |

    AE$_1$ [P"'] |

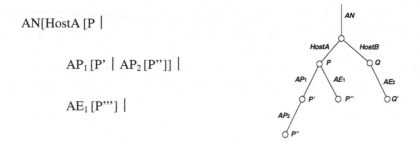

**Fig. 4.** Seal-calculus term and configuration tree. (step 1)

AN[[HostA [P$_0$ | AE$_1$ [P"']] |

    HostB [Q$_0$ |

    AP$_1$ [P' | AP$_2$ [P"]] |

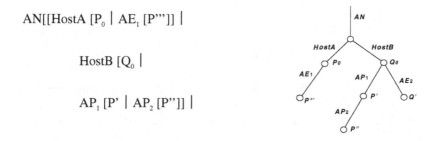

**Fig. 5.** Seal-calculus term and configuration tree. (step 2)

From Fig.3, we know that there are a few attacks when active packet $AP_1$ moves from *HostA* to *HostB*, whether active packet $AP_1$ can migrate; whether *HostB* can receive active packet $AP_1$; whether active packet $AP_1$ is allowed using the resource of *HostB* and attacks *HostB* or not if receiving the migration. On the contrary, whether *HostB* attacks active packet $AP_1$; whether active packet $AP_1$ and active extension $AE_2$ of *HostB* attacks each other or not. According to the propositions of former section, we will deal with the solutions to the attacks using Seal-calculus.

*Protection 1*: An arbitrary process $P'$ of active packet $AP_1$ can be completely prevented from any communication and is formally written

$$(V\ AP_1)\ AP_1\left[P'\right] \approx 0$$

It satisfies proposition 1. The semantics of the calculus guarantees that no other process than $P'$ may guess $AP_1$. If a seal is given a fresh name which isn't known by any other process, then there can be no portal open for that name (**open** $_{AP_1}$ **y**), nor can there be located communication ($\mathbf{y}^{AP_1} \langle ... \rangle$).

*Protection 2*: Active packet $AP_1$ can migrate, *HostB* can receive active packet $AP_1$. It satisfies proposition 2. If *HostA* allows sending active packet $AP_1$, the *HostA* sends a seal on a channel through the process $\overline{x}^* (AP_1)P$ then behave like $p$. If $AP_1$ does not exit, the processes will block. In parallel, a process must be ready to receive the mobile seal; for *HostB*, a receive action is written $x^*(z)P$ denotes a process waiting for receiving a seal along channel $x$ and naming it $z$.

*Protection 3*: Active packet $AP_1$ is allowed using the resource of *HostB* and can't attacks *HostB* if receiving the migration. On the contrary, *HostB* can't attacks active packet $AP_1$.

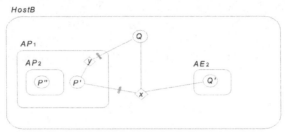

**Fig. 6.** Total mediation

It satisfies proposition 3. In figure 6 we denote after the $AP_1$ moving into *HostB*, process $P'$ of $AP_1$ interacts with process $Q$ of *HostB* via a local $x$ monitored by a portal controlled by $Q$, and via a channel in $AP_1$ and monitored y by a portal controlled by $P'$.

$$P' = \bar{x}^{\uparrow}\langle y \rangle.\, \textbf{open}_{\uparrow}\ \bar{y}.P_1 \mid y^*\langle\ \rangle.P_2$$

$$Q = \textbf{open}_{AP_1}\ \bar{x}.Q_1 \mid x^*\langle \lambda z \rangle.\bar{z}^{AP_1}\langle\ \rangle.Q_2$$

Then

$$Q \mid AP_1[P' \mid AP_2[P'']]$$

$$= \textbf{open}_{AP_1}\ \bar{x}.Q_1 \mid x^*\langle \lambda z \rangle.\bar{z}^{AP_1}\langle\ \rangle.Q_2 \mid AP_1\ [\ \bar{x}^{\uparrow}\langle y \rangle.\, \textbf{open}_{\uparrow}\ \bar{y}.P_1 \mid$$

$$y^*\langle\ \rangle.P_2 \mid$$

$$AP_2[P'']] \tag{1}$$

$$\rightarrow Q_1 \mid \bar{y}^{AP_1}\langle\ \rangle.Q_2 \mid AP_1\ [\textbf{open}_{\uparrow}\ \bar{y}.P_1 \mid y^*\langle\ \rangle.P_2 \mid AP_2[P'']] \tag{2}$$

$$\rightarrow Q_1 \mid Q_2 \mid AP_1\ [P_1 \mid P_2 \mid AP_2[P'']]$$

If the local actions in (1) and (2) had not been in parallel with the corresponding opening actions, remote interaction would have been forbidden. So *HostB* as a parent can implement total mediation. The model provides symmetric protection that the child active packet $AP_1$ can protect its own resources from its parent *HostB* with the same mechanism as the parent.

*Protection 4*: Active packet $AP_1$ and active extension $AE_2$ of *HostB* can't attack each other.

It satisfies proposition 4. When active packet $AP_1$ and $AP_2$ move into *HostB* they may not attacks the active extension $AE_2$ in *HostB*, and vice versa. Because seal boundaries can guarantee the body process may never mix freely with the environment. Seal-calculus do not allow processes located in sibling seals to communicate.

## 6   Related Works

The ANs systems making use of active packets are Smart packets [12], PLAN [13] etc, and making use of active extensions are ANTS [14], etc. More ANs systems are a hybrid system, such as ALIEN [15], SwitchWare [16].

Security of ANs is a broad area. We will mention only some of the most directly relevant work. The current existence of the ANs presents many different security means. PLAN, SNAP [17], Smart Packets, and SafetyNet [18] use type-safety, sand-boxing, and virtual machine interpreters.

SafetyNet relies on a specialized static system to guarantee various properties about programs written in it. Its type system is also able to express resource usage through the use of linear types.

ANTS relies upon the JVM's byte-code verification and sand-boxing facilities for the security. The reference to the code actually takes the form of a MD5 cryptography hash of the actual code, thus preventing code spoofing.

ALIEN provides additional safety by using module thinning to restrict their interface to a node as seen by the active packets being dynamically linked against it. SANE uses public key cryptography to establish security associations between neighboring nodes.

PLAN is strongly typed. The general recursion is disallowed, which guarantees that all PLAN programs will terminate.

SNAP takes a fairly radical approach by making it a property of the language that CPU and memory use is a linear function of the length of the packet. It does this by placing severe restrictions in the expressibility of the language.

SwitchWare security is divided into different classes from lightweight type security to authentication or to other heavyweight security mechanism.

In our formalization security is addressed by the addition of a fine-grain access control mechanism, such as wrapper, portals etc. And this protection is symmetrical, which means that it protects a host from untrustworthy active codes that migrate to it as well as active code from the untrustworthy host where it migrates. Especially, formalizing description of ANs security has not yet been touched at present. This is the great difference from the other security policy that other ANs projects have adopted. Because there is no security policy which can protect in two ways in previous ANs project.

# 7    Conclusions and Future Work

In this paper we first present packet hierarchy, then we formalize active network in the framework of the seal calculus and address its security properties. Finally an *AN* example showing an active packet migrating from *HostA* to *HostB* and its protection properties are discussed.

Seal-calculus can be viewed as a framework for exploring the design space of security and mobility features. Applying seal calculus in exploring ANs security seems a quite interesting direction. Therefore, some more suitable notions of observation, specification, and equivalence need to be defined and developed so as to provide essential theoretical foundation for design and reasoning of ANs security.

# References

1.  R. Milner, J Parrow, and D. Walker. A calculus of mobile processes, Parts I and II. Journal of Information and Computation, 100:1–77, Sept.1992.
2.  C.Fournet, G. Gonthier, J.Levy, L. Marnaget, and D.Remy, A calculus of Mobile Agents, Proceedings of CONCUR'96, LNCS, Vol.1119, pp. 406–421, Springer, 1996.
3.  L.Cardelli and A.D.Gordon, Mobile Ambients, Foundations of software Science and Computation Structures, LNCS, Vol.1378, pp. 140–155,1998.
4.  Jan Viteck and Giuseppe Castsgna. A calculus of secure mobile computations. In Proceedings of the IEEE Workshop on Internet Programming Languages, (WIPL). Chicago, I11.1998.
5.  Konstantinos Psounis. Active networks: Application, security, safety and architectures. IEEE Communication Surveys. http://www.comsoc.org.pubs/surveys. First Quarter, 1999
6.  D. Scott Alexander, william A. Arbaugh, Angelos D. Keromytis, and Jonathan M. Smith. Safety and Security of Programmable Network Infrastructures. IEEE Communications Magazine, 36(10):84–92, 1998.
7.  AN Security Working Group, "Security architecture for active nets," July 1998, available online at ftp://ftp.tislabs.com/pub/activenets/ secrarch2.ps.
8.  J. Moore. Mobile code Security Techniques. Technical Reportms-CIS-98-28, University of Pennsylvania, May 1998.
9.  J. Vitek and G. Castagna. Seal: A framework for secure mobile computation. In Internet Programming Languages, number 1686 in Lecture Notes in Computer Science. Springer, 1999.
10. G. Castagna and J. Vitek. Confinement and commitment for the seal calculus. Nov. 1998.
11. D Scott Alexander, Michael Hicks, Angelos D. Keromytis, A Taxonomy of Active Code. http://citeseer.nj.nec.com/alexander99taxonomy.html
12. Schwartz, A. Jackson, T. Strayer, W. Zhou, R. Rockwell, and C. Partridge. Smart packets for active networks. In Proceedings of the 1999 IEEE 2nd Conference on Open Architectures and Network Programming(OPENARCH'99), March 1999
13. Michael Hicks, Pankaj Kakkar, Jonathan T. Moore, Carl A. Gunter and Scott Nettles. PLAN: A packer language for active networks. In Proceedings of the 1998 ACM SIGPLAN International Conference on Functional Programming (ICFP'98), September 1998
14. David J. Wetherall, John Guttag, and David L, Tennenhouse. ANTS: A toolkit for building and dynamically deploying network protocols. In Proceedings of the 1998 IEEEConference on Open Architecture and Network Programming (OPENARCH'98), April 1998
15. Scott Alexander. ALIEN: A generalized computing model of active network.. PHD thesis University of Pennsylvania, 1998

16. Scott Alexander, William A. Arbaugh, Michael W. Hicks, Pankaj Kakkar, Angelos D. Keromytis, Jonathan T. Moore, Carl A. Gunter, Scott M. Nettles, and Jonathan M. Smith. The SwitchWare active network architecture, IEEE Network, special issue on Active and Programmable Networks, May/June 1998
17. Jonathan T. Moore. Safe and Efficient Active Packets. Technical Report MS-CIS-99-24, Department of Computer and Information Science, University of Pennsylvania, October 1999
18. Ian Wakeman. Et al., Designing a programming language for active networks. http://www.cogs.susx.ac.uk/projects/safetynet. Submitted to Hipparch special issue of Network and ISDN System, January 1999

# Research on Approaches of Iris Texture Feature Representation for Personal Identification

Yuanning Liu[1], Senmiao Yuan[1],
and Zhen Liu[2]

[1] Computer Department of Jilin University, Changchun, China, 130025
liuyn@jlu.edu.cn
[2] Faculty of Human Environment, Nagasaki Institute of Applied Science 536
Aba-machi,Nagasaki 851-0193, Japan
liuzhen@cc.nias.ac.jp

**Abstract.** Three approaches of iris texture feature representation are discussed for personal identification. After several iterative algorithms of SOR, SSOR, PSB, DFP, BFGS are presented, a new methods for feature representation of iris texture is put forward. The results of numerical examples show that these methods prove to be effective. ...

## 1 Introduction

Iris recognition technology is a kind of biometrics identification technology which it has recently received growing interests from both academia and industry. Iris is a kind of physiological biometric feature. It contains unique and stable texture and is complex enough for use in biometric signature. Furthermore, it can be non-invasive to its user. Because of its advances so much, iris recognition technology will be very promising in the future. One of the key problems to iris recognition technology lies in feature representation of iris texture. J.Daugman[1] put forward an approach of feature extraction that made use of 2-D Gabor wavelet. It applies a simple approximate quantifying and phase encoding to iris texture by use of 2-D Gabor filter. Daugman's method convolutes multi-scale 2-D Gabor filter with iris local texture, and makes iris texture phase encoding by means of the convolution results. The feature points in iris make up the iris code with 256 bytes. The pattern matching of iris code is done on statistical theory, and the Exclusive-Or operation is taken between different iris codes to compute Hamming Distance (HD). The iris recognition algorithm of Wildes[2] is different from Daugman's. It depends on image registration technology and belongs to machine visual sense field. Gauss-Laplass operator is used to take isotropy band decomposition on iris image, producing Laplass pyramid, then the decomposed image is registered. This method is complicated and depends on a set of accurate acquisition equipment of iris image, at the same, its computing task is also huge, and so it is difficult to be implemented. The researches on this field in China have recently obtained some achievements[4]. In this article, for solving the Gabor expansion coefficients better, several iterative

M. Guo and L.T.Yang (Eds.): ISPA 2003, LNCS 2745, pp. 405–410, 2003.

methods are presented based on Least-square principle. To the linear expansion systems, we describe SOR (Successive Over Relaxation) method and SSOR (Symmetric Successive Over Relaxation) method, and to the nonlinear expansion systems do with Broyden, PSB (Powell-Symetric-Broyden), DFP(Dividon-Fletcher-Powell),BFGS(Broyden-Fletcher-Goldfarb-Shanno) methods. Finally, a new method called best-fitting iris texture model is put forward for iris texture feature presentation in our practical iris recognition system. By computing NHD (Normalized Hamming Distance), this pattern matching can be finished, and a personal identification has been completed with the pattern matching system. The experiment data analysis has proved efficiency of the conclusion.

# 2    The Method for Image Analysis and Reconstruction by Use of 2-D Gabor Function Set

Let $\{G_i[x, y]\}$ be a 2-D Gabor function set, it is hoped to find a coefficient set $\{a_i\}$ to obtain a best representation of original iris image $I[x, y]$, a vector value function $H[x, y]$ is defined as:

$$H[x, y] = \sum_{i=1}^{n} a_i G_i[x, y] \tag{1}$$

where $a_i$ are expansion coefficients. When basis functions $\{G_i[x, y]\}$ forms a complete orthogonal set, representation formula (1) is exact to $I[x, y]$ and coefficients $\{a_i\}$ are easily solved and shown as following:

$$a_i = \frac{\sum\limits_{x,y} (G_i[x, y]I[x, y])}{\sum\limits_{x,y} G_i^2[x, y]}$$

However, 2-D Gabor function set may be consisted of different forms, and it wouldn't usually form a complete orthogonal basis, as a result, representation $H[x, y]$ would be approximate. When $\{G_i[x, y]\}$ form a complete (but nororthogonal) or incomplete function set, error vector function $I[x, y] - H[x, y]$ is desired as small as possible. To obtain a good expression of image $I[x, y]$, a set of coefficients $\{a_i\}$ must be determined by an optimization criterion. Thus a squared norm of the error vector function

$$E = \parallel I[x, y] - H[x, y] \parallel^2 \tag{2}$$

should be satisfied for minimum modulus principle.

Three methods are adopted to find the set of coefficients $\{a_i\}$.

## 2.1    The Method Based on Three-Layer Neural Network

The neural network method is put forward by J.Daugman to find the optimal coefficient set $\{a_i\}$.

## 2.2    The Method Based on Least Square Principle

If $\{G_i[x,y]\}$ forms a complete 2-D Gabor function set, it may be non-orthogonal, the original texture image $I[x,y]$ can be represented as

$$H[x,y] = \sum_{i=1}^{n} a_i G_i[x,y]$$

according to (1). The square of discrete difference-vector module is given:

$$E = \| I[x,y] - H[x,y] \|^2 = \| \sum_{x,y} I[x_i,y_i] - \sum_{x,y} H[x_i,y_i] \|^2 =$$

$$\| \sum_{x,y} I[x_i,y_i] - \sum_{i,j} \sum_{k=1}^{n} a_k G_k[x_i,y_j] \|^2 = E(a_1,a_2,...a_k) \qquad (3)$$

In order to make $H[x,y]$ represent the original texture image more accurately, function E should be minimized. According to the extremism theory of multivariate function, only when its partial derivatives with respect to all of n coefficients $a_1, a_2, ...a_n$ are equal to zero, that it

$$\frac{\partial E}{\partial a_i} = 0, i = 1,2,...n \qquad (4)$$

The minimum of E can be obtained by computing. In fact, equations (4) is equivalent to following expression

$$\sum_{i,j} \left( \sum_{k=1}^{n} a_k G_k[x_i,y_j] \right) G_l[x_i,y_j] = \sum_{i,j} I[x_i,y_j] G_l[x_i,y_j] \qquad (5)$$

or

$$\sum_{k=1}^{n} a_k \left( \sum_{i,j} G_k[x_i,y_j] G_l[x_i,y_j] \right) = \sum_{i,j} I[x_i,y_j] G_l[x_i,y_j], l = 1,2,...,n \qquad (6)$$

Formula (6) is linear equations of n order with unknown coefficients $a_1, a_2, ...a_n$. We may make use of SOR iterative method or SSOR iterative method to solve equations (6), and then the optimal coefficients $a_1, a_2, ...a_n$ are available. a) In SOR method, the iterative vector expression is given as following:
For $i = 1,2,...,n; k = 1,2,...$

$$x_i^{(k+1)} = x_i^{(k)} + \frac{\omega}{a_{ii}} \left( b_i - \sum_{j=1}^{i-1} a_{ij} x_j^{(k+1)} - \sum_{j=i}^{n} a_{ij} x_j^{(k)} \right) \qquad (7)$$

where $\omega$ is a relaxation factor (usually $0 < \omega < 2$). b) In SSOR method, the iterative vector expression is given as following:

For $i = 1, 2, ..., n$

$$\overline{x}_i^{(k+1)} = x_i^{(k)} + \frac{\omega}{a_{ii}} \left( b_i - \sum_{j=1}^{i-1} a_{ij} \overline{x}_j^{(k+1)} - \sum_{j=i}^{n} a_{ij} x_j^{(k)} \right) \tag{8}$$

For $i = n - 1, n - 2, ..., 1,$

$$x_i^{(k+1)} = \overline{x}_i^{(k+1)} + \frac{\omega}{a_{ii}} \left( b_i - \sum_{j=1}^{i} a_{ij} \overline{x}_j^{(k+1)} - \sum_{j=i+1}^{n} a_{ij} x_j^{(k)} \right) \tag{9}$$

## 2.3    The Method Based on Optimization Principle

If $\{G_i[x, y]\}$ forms an incomplete and non-orthogonal 2-D Gabor function set, the original texture image $I[x, y]$ can be represented as a nonlinear systems:

$$H[x, y] = F[a_1, a_2, ..., a_n; G_1, G_2, ..., G_n] \tag{10}$$

The square of discrete error-vector module may be written the form

$$E = \| I[x, y] - H[x, y] \|^2 = \| \sum_{i,j} I[x_i, y_i] - \sum_{i,j} H[x_i, y_i] \|^2 =$$

$$\| \sum_{i,j} I[x_i, y_i] - \sum_{i,j} F[a_1, a_2, ..., a_n; G_1, G_2, ..., G_n] \|^2 = E(a_1, a_2, ...a_n) \tag{11}$$

where E is still a non-negative multivariate function, but related differential equations

$$\frac{\partial E}{\partial a_i} = 0 (i = 1, 2, ...n)$$

form a nonlinear equation system.

$$M(a_1, a_2, ...a_n) = \begin{pmatrix} m_1(a_1, ..., a_n) \\ m_2(a_1, ..., a_n) \\ ... \\ m_n(a_1, ..., a_n) \end{pmatrix} = \begin{pmatrix} 0 \\ 0 \\ ... \\ 0 \end{pmatrix} \tag{12}$$

We usually use $(x_1, ..., x_n)^T$ to stand for $(a_1, ..., a_n)^T$ when we compute the equations.

If there is an estimated value of the solution $x^{(0)}$, we can directly use below Newton-Iterate method to solve equations (12):

$$M(x^{(k)}) + M'(x^{(k)})(x^{(k+1)} - x^{(k)}) = 0 \tag{13}$$

where

$$M(x^{(k)}) = \left( m_1(x^{(k)}), m_2(x^{(k)}), ..., m_n(x^{(k)}) \right)^T,$$

$$M'(x^{(k)}) = \begin{pmatrix} \frac{\partial m_1}{\partial x_1} & \frac{\partial m_1}{\partial x_2} & \cdots & \frac{\partial m_1}{\partial x_n} \\ \frac{\partial m_2}{\partial x_1} & \frac{\partial m_2}{\partial x_2} & \cdots & \frac{\partial m_2}{\partial x_n} \\ \cdots & \cdots & \cdots & \cdots \\ \frac{\partial m_n}{\partial x_1} & \frac{\partial m_n}{\partial x_2} & \cdots & \frac{\partial m_n}{\partial x_n} \end{pmatrix}_{x=x_{(k)}} ,$$

$$x^{(k)} = (a_1^{(k)}, a_2^{(k)}, ..., a_n^{(k)}) \tag{14}$$

Considering that it is difficult to compute Jacobi matrix $M'(x^{(k)})$, we could also use quasi-Newton algorithm to solve equations (13).

Quasi-Newton methods are important and effective algorithms in computing nonlinear equations and optimal computation. Broydon method is simple in computation, PSB algorithm has symmetry, and BFGS algorithm is an inverse iterative method. The other methods can also make inverse iterative expression. Feature of iris texture can be represented with the computing results by use of other algorithm formulas.

## 3   The Experiment Result and Data Analysis

An experiment has been taken with 13 samples, of which seven are from different persons and the other six are from the same person (taken at different time). The results are shown in table 1, 2. As it can be seen that from table 1 and 2, the NHD values from the same iris obviously are smaller than those from different irises. In other words, if the NHD value of decision point is set correctly, the anterior encoding and matching method can be used validly in iris recognition. It can be seen from the experiment result that the NHD value of decision point in this system is smaller than theoretical arithmetic value. The main reason is that we have not used the Gabor function set very exactly that fits for encoding the corresponded local texture from different irises. So there are some errors compared with the theoretical value. In addition, because the iris image acquisition environment of this system is simpler, it is convenient and economical on operation for uses. Although the quality of acquired image is not very accurate and this would affect the NHD value of decision point a little, it will not affect the validity of our iris recognition system.

**Table 1.** The seven images from different persons are marked as $M_i, i = 1, 2, ..., 7$ respectively. The values of NHD among the seven iris images are corresponding to the different persons.

|    | M1 | M2       | M3       | M4       | M5       | M6       | M7       |
|----|-----|----------|----------|----------|----------|----------|----------|
| M1 | 0   | 0.280723 | 0.291465 | 0.283164 | 0.298262 | 0.329023 | 0.308301 |
| M2 |     | 0        | 0.294375 | 0.305605 | 0.310234 | 0.288262 | 0.322930 |
| M3 |     |          | 0        | 0.279238 | 0.323164 | 0.290957 | 0.319766 |
| M4 |     |          |          | 0        | 0.270957 | 0.325117 | 0.303145 |
| M5 |     |          |          |          | 0        | 0.344160 | 0.321211 |
| M6 |     |          |          |          |          | 0        | 0.320723 |
| M7 |     |          |          |          |          |          | 0        |

**Table 2.** The six images from a person (taken at different time) are marked as $N_i, i = 1, 2, ..., 6$ respectively. The values of NHD among the six iris images are corresponding to the same persons.

|     | M1 | M2       | M3       | M4       | M5       | M6       |
|-----|-----|---------|----------|----------|----------|----------|
| M1  | 0  | 0.107500 | 0.072344 | 0.081113 | 0.079180 | 0.083086 |
| M2  |    | 0        | 0.118008 | 0.111895 | 0.063555 | 0.097734 |
| M3  |    |          | 0        | 0.101074 | 0.101406 | 0.078047 |
| M4  |    |          |          | 0        | 0.081621 | 0.123285 |
| M5  |    |          |          |          | 0        | 0.083320 |
| M6  |    |          |          |          |          | 0        |

# References

1. J.Daugman: "High Confidence Visual Recognition of Persons by A Test of Statistical Independence", IEEE Trans. Pattern Anal. Machine Intelligence, 1993, 15 (11),pp.1148-1161
2. Wildes R P.: "Iris Recognition: An Merging Biometric Technology", Proceeding of The IEEE, Sept.1997,Vol.85, NO.9, pp.1348-1363
3. W.W.Boles: "A Security System Based on Human Iris Identification Using Wavelet Transform", 1997 First International Conference on Knowledge-Based Intelligent Electronic System, May1997 , Australia, pp.533-541
4. Baldonado, M., Chang, C.-C.K., Gravano, L., Paepcke, A.: The Stanford Digital Library Metadata Architecture. Int. J. Digit. Libr. **1** (1997) 108–121
5. Yong Zhu, Tieniu Tan, Yunhong Wang: "Biometric Personal Identification Based on Iris Patterns", 2000IEEE, pp.801-804
6. J.Daugman: "Complete Discrete 2-D Gabor Transforms by Neural Networks for Image Analysis and Compression", IEEE, Trans. On Acoustics, Speech and Signal Processing, July1988,Vol.36,NO.7, pp.1169-1179

# A Solution for Fault-Tolerance in Replicated Database Systems

Changgui Chen and Wanlei Zhou

School of Information Technology, Deakin University
Geelong, Victoria 3217, Australia
Phone: 0061-3-52272087, Fax: 0061-3-52272028
{changgui,wanlei}@deakin.edu.au

**Abstract.** A distributed database system is subject to site failure and link failure. This paper presents a reactive system approach to achieving the fault-tolerance in such a system. The reactive system concepts are an attractive paradigm for system design, development and maintenance because it separates policies from mechanisms. In the paper we give a solution using different reactive modules to implement the fault-tolerant policies and the failure detection mechanisms. The solution shows that they can be separated without impact on each other thus the system can adapt to constant changes in user requirements.

## 1 Introduction

In a distributed computing environment, two types of failure may occur: a process/processor at a given site may fail (referred to as a site failure), and communication between two sites may fail (referred to as a link failure) [5][8]. A site failure results in fail-silent or crash failure semantics, i.e., a process/processor either works correctly or simply stops working without taking any incorrect action [10]. A link failure may result in network partitioning, which is a major threat to the reliability of distributed systems and to the availability of replicated data [11]. When these failures occur the system may generate incorrect results or may simply stop before finishing the intended computation so that the system cannot provide intended services. Therefore, it is essential to build distributed systems that can tolerate these failures.

However, the development of fault-tolerant computing systems is a very difficult task. One reason is that, in normal practice, most fault-tolerant computing policies and mechanisms are deeply embedded into application programs so that they can not cope with changes in environments and user requirements [12]. For example, in a distributed replication system, if the detection of a replica (server) failure and the strategy for dealing with this failure are put together in a program, when the detecting mechanism needs to be changed, the whole program has to be changed as well. Hence this program cannot adapt to constant changes in user requirements. Therefore, to build better fault-tolerant applications it is necessary to separate fault-tolerant computing policies and mechanisms from application programs.

M. Guo and L.T.Yang (Eds.): ISPA 2003, LNCS 2745, pp. 411–422, 2003.
© Springer-Verlag Berlin Heidelberg 2003

In this paper we use a novel approach – the reactive system approach to achieving this goal. The reactive system concepts are an attractive paradigm for system design, development and maintenance because it can separate policies from mechanisms [12]. Our previous work [3] has presented the design, implementation and evaluation of the reactive system model used in fault-tolerant computing. In this article we apply it in a replicated database system to deal with two types of failure – crash failure and network partitioning failure, for the purpose of demonstrating the potential benefits of the reactive system model.

The rest of paper is organized as follows: in the next section, we introduce the replicated database system and the failure scenarios. Section 3 addresses the reactive system approach. Fault detection and fault-tolerance based on the reactive system approach are discussed in Section 4. Finally we summarize our work in Section 5.

## 2   A Replicated Database System

In order to tolerate various failures, most fault-tolerant techniques rely on introducing extra redundant components to a system. *Replication* is such a technology making fault-tolerance possible in a distributed database system. It is the maintenance of online copies of data and other resources by using replicas, and is a key to the effectiveness of distributed systems, in which it can provide enhanced performance, high availability and fault-tolerance [7].

A distributed replication system within a wide area network (WAN) is composed of several subnets located about several or thousands miles away and connected by gateways. Replication makes database servers duplicated, i.e., it produces replicas of database servers. In a distributed replication system, there is one or more database server groups (or replica groups), which are comprised of replicas running on workstations across the network. Among one group of database servers (or replicas), there is a primary database server (called primary replica); other replicas are called non-primary replicas. The execution of a transaction must be carried out on a group of replicas. For simplicity, we only include two subnets connected by one gateway in the network configuration; each workstation has a database server and a replication manager running respectively. All database servers (or replicas) store identical information initially and each of them can accept client requests that read or update stored information independently. A replication manager can access to the local database server and other replicas through JDBC. A client connects to a replication manager and issues transaction requests through it to obtain database services. Fig. 1 depicts such two workstations located on two subnets, where RP stands for a replication manager and DB represents a database server.

The task of the replicated system is to maintain the data consistency among all the replicas throughout the whole network, even in the case of site or link failures. If a client requires a read-only operation, this request can be served by the local replication manager reading from the local database server. If a client wants to perform an update operation, the operation has to be performed in all database servers. This can be done if all the replicas are running well without faults. However, site or link failures may occur in the system, and it would be a problem to perform an update operation on the replica(s) located on a fault site or a partitioned subnet. In these cases, some strategies have to be invoked to maintain the data consistency. We discuss the failure scenarios next.

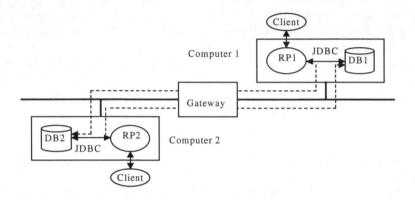

**Fig. 1.** Replication manager and database server

## 2.1  Crash Failure

Crash failures in a replicated database system include a database server failure, a replication manager failure, or a computer (workstation) failure. They may cause the data inconsistent and the system providing incorrect services. The fault-tolerant requirement is that the system should continue to work even in the case of failures. We have following strategies to deal with crash failures in the system depicted in Fig. 1:

- *A database server fails*. For example, assume DB1 on Computer 1 fails. In this case, RP1 on Computer 1 has to re-direct all requests to DB2 on Computer 2. If such a request is an update request, then RP1 has to store such an update in a stable storage (e.g. disk) and has to perform it on the failed database DB1 when it recovers. Similarly, when a client issues an update operation through RP2, RP2 has to store that operation in a stable storage and perform it on DB1 when it recovers.
- *A replication manager fails*. For example, assume RP1 on Computer 1 fails. In that case, all requests have to be submitted through RP2 on Computer 2.
- *A computer fails*. For example, assume that Computer 1 fails. In this case, all servers running on Computer 1 fail. All requests have to be submitted to RP2 on Computer 2. If there is an update operation, it has to be recorded in the stable storage and has to be performed on DB1 when Computer 1 recovers (and DB1 recovers as well).

In the case 2 and 3, a client is easy to know whether a replication manager is alive or not through the program interface. If the local replication manager fails, a client can submit his (her) requests to other replication manager. Hence it is simple to deal with a replication manager failure. In the case 1, it is essential for a replication manager to know if a database server is alive or not. How to detect and deal with a database server failure remains a problem. If the failure detecting mechanism and the failure processing policy are all embedded into a replication manager, once the detecting mechanism is changed the replication manager has to be changed as well. Thus this strategy lacks flexibility and cannot adapt to constant changes.

## 2.2 The Network Partitioning Failure

Network partitioning occurs when link failures fragment the network into isolated subnetworks called partitions, such that sites or processes within a given partition are able to communicate with one another but not with sites or processes in other partitions. If processes continue to operate in the disconnected partitions, they might perform incompatible operations and make the application data inconsistent [1] [6].

In the replicated database system we talked above, network partitioning failure happens when the gateway between two subnets fails. This leads to a situation where replication managers and server group members (replicas) distributed in different subnets cannot communicate with one another and may stop processing a client transaction request. For instance, in Fig. 1, an update operation issued by a client on Computer 1 cannot be performed on Computer 2 if a partitioning happens. Therefore, it is essential for replication managers within each subnet to know whether a partitioning happens so that they can take certain measures to process clients' requests and tolerate this kind of failure if it happens.

A number of diverse solutions have been proposed to solve the network partitioning problem. But most strategies on network partitioning require that the failure initially be recognized. They assume that the partitioning failure detection has already been done, thus they may have some restrictions due to different failure detection strategies. In this paper we attempt to use the reactive system approach to solve this problem and provide a solution for failure detection, analysis and resolving together.

## 3   The Reactive System Model

A reactive system is composed of a number of components, such as controllers, sensors, actuators, and physical objects in its environment, which may run in parallel [2]. Sensors are used to acquaint the environment information and then report them to its controllers. The controllers, we call them decision-making managers (DMMs), make certain decisions based on the predefined policies and the information received from sensors. To maintain the interaction with its environment, the system uses actuators to react to its environment by changing the states of application objects according to the decisions received from the controllers [3]. This indicates that a reactive system uses sensors and actuators to implement the mechanisms that interact with its environment or applications. Its decision-making managers (DMMs) are used to implement the policies regarding to the control of the applications. Fig. 2 depicts the architecture of such a reactive system model, which consists of three levels: *policies*, *mechanisms* and *applications*.

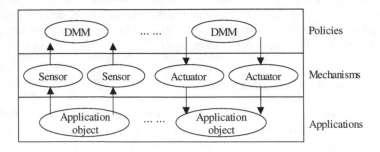

**Fig. 2.** The generic reactive system architecture

- **Policies.** The policy level deals with the system policies regarding to the control of application objects. For example, in fault-tolerant computing, it may determine what strategies are used in detecting component failures, what information is to be collected from the application programs, and what techniques are used in masking and/or tolerating component failures. These policies are implemented through DMMs. A DMM obtains information about applications via sensors and processes the information and modifies the states of applications via actuators in order to tolerate component failures.
- **Mechanisms.** The mechanism level deals with all mechanisms for implementing policies such as fault-tolerant computing strategies. For example, it deals with mechanisms used in detecting and reporting component failures, and mechanisms used in masking and recovering from component failures. These mechanisms are implemented through sensors and actuators. More specifically, the system uses sensors to monitor and report some aspects of an application's state. System entities (e.g. DMMs or other sensors) can subscribe to a sensor to receive its report. Actuators in this level provide ways for decision-making managers to control the behaviors of applications in order to tolerate component failures.
- **Applications.** This level deals with application-specific issues, i.e., issues about application objects such as database servers, replicas, network routers, etc.

This model represents a generic reactive system. The major advantage of the model is the separation of policies and mechanisms, i.e., if a policy is changed it may have no impact on related mechanisms and vice versa. For example, if a decision making condition based on two sensors was "AND" and now is changed to "OR", the sensors can still be used without any changes required, i.e., the mechanism level can remain unchanged. This advantage will lead to a better software architecture and has a great significance in developing distributed and fault-tolerant computing applications since it can separate fault-tolerant computing policies and mechanisms [12].

## 3.1  Reactive Modules

The reactive system model mainly consists of DMMs, sensors, actuators and application objects. We have designed and implemented DMMs, sensors and actuators as generic Java classes previously, which can be used in any distributed applications. They are implemented as either embedded entities or stand-alone entities. Using these generic classes, various fault-tolerant computing policies and failure detection mechanisms can be implemented.

DMMs and actuators are relatively more application-specific, i.e. they are more dependent on specific applications, since they must implement specific policies or change specific application objects. However, sensors are more general and more independent from specific applications since they only monitor events happened in applications. We have defined the following three types of sensors according to the way that a sensor performs its function:

- *Event sensor.* It reports to its subscribers immediately once a monitored event occurs.
- *Timer sensor.* It periodically sends out some message to its subscribers.
- *Polling sensor.* It periodically checks the state of an application and reports to its subscribers.

## 4  Fault Detection and Fault Tolerance

We can use the Java reactive system modules introduced above to deal with crash failures and network partitioning failures occurred in the replicated database system. We use sensors to detect the possible failures of various system objects and DMMs to implement various fault-tolerant policies.

### 4.1  Fault Detection

#### 4.1.1  Crash Failure

As discussed earlier, a replication manager crash or a computer crash is simple to deal with. We only discuss a database server failure here. When a database server crashes, it is essential for replication managers to know it so that they can take certain measures to further process client requests. To achieve this, we run a Java DMM, a Java sensor and a Java actuator on each computer respectively. Each DMM will subscribe to all sensors and actuators running on all computers. Due to different types of reactive module we can have several choices:

- *Using stand-alone DMMs*: Stand-alone DMMs can run independently on each host and operate concurrently with other objects. Actuators are embedded into replication managers for transmitting decisions from DMMs to the replication managers. To detect a database server failure, we also have two options of using sensors: polling sensors and event sensors.

1. *Using polling sensors.* A polling sensor can be run on each computer independently to check the status (liveliness) of the database server periodically and then report to the DMMs subscribing to it, as depicted in Fig. 3, where we only include two workstations located on two subnets. Once a database server fails, the polling sensor monitoring it will report to both DMMs. In this case, DMMs and polling sensors are running independently on Computer 1 and 2, while actuators are embedded into RPs.

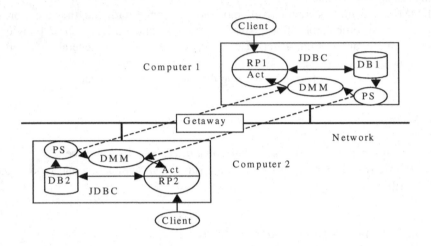

**Fig. 3.** Using polling sensors – (PS: polling sensor; Act: actuator)

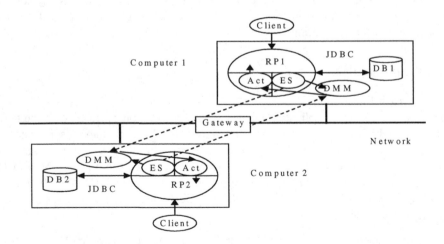

**Fig. 4.** Using event sensors – (ES: event sensor; Act: actuator)

2. *Using event sensors.* We may want to know the failures of database servers immediately once they occur. In this case we can use event sensors instead of polling sensors running on each computer. The DMMs and actuators are same as

above, but two event sensors are attached to RP1 and RP2 respectively to report the failure of the connection between RP1 and DB1 or between RP2 and DB2, as depicted in Fig. 4. If a database server fails the connection between this replica and the relevant replication manager fails as well. Thus the corresponding event sensor will catch this event and report to both DMMs immediately.

- *Using embedded DMMs*: We can also use embedded DMMs to implement the above functions. In this case, an embedded DMM is embedded into the replication manager on each computer, thus we do not need actuators since the DMMs can instruct the replication managers directly. Sensors in this case are polling sensors which run independently on each computer. Once a database server fails, the polling sensor monitoring it will report to both DMMs.

In all cases above, both DMMs will receive the reports from the sensors about the failures of database servers if occurred. Then they will make certain decisions (as described earlier) and use the actuators to instruct RP1 and RP2 to process clients' requests promptly.

**Detecting strategy**

Let S be a sensor. We use $S_r$ to denote the sensor report about the state of a replica r that S monitors, or the connection state between a replica r and a replication manager. For a polling sensor, if $S_r$ is true, that means the replica r is alive; whereas for an event sensor, if $S_r$ is true, that means a connection failure between the replica r and the related replication manager occurs. We use "$\neg$" to denote no event occurred. Hence we have

$$\text{if } \neg S_r, \text{ then r is faulty, where S is a polling sensor} \tag{1}$$

and

$$\text{if } S_r, \text{ then r is faulty, where S is an event sensor} \tag{2}$$

The time interval for evaluating "$\neg$" in (1) is set to be greater than the polling time interval of S. Formula (1) and (2) are the strategies used by DMMs to detect the fault existence.

### 4.1.2 Network Partitioning Failure

To detect and analyze partitioning failures, we add a dedicated decision making manager (DMM) as a server group component in each subnet for failure handling and help in transaction processing. Each of these DMMs will subscribe to multiple sensors/actuators attached to each server member on different subnets to find out the partition existence. The idea of detecting a partitioning failure is described as follows. A DMM in one subnet regularly receives reports from sensors attached to all server members some of which may not be reachable if a partitioning occurs. If the DMM does not receive the reports from some sensors within a maximum time frame, the DMM decides that the gateway might be down by noticing those unreachable members are all located in the same subnet. To confirm the partitioning happened, the DMM sends a message to the other DMM in that subnet to see if they are reachable. If it does not receive the replied message within a maximum time from another DMM, the gateway between the two DMMs is assumed down, which leads to the two subnets being partitioned from each other.

Similarly, we can have several choices in terms of using different sensors/actuators, or different DMMs to do that. Here we give two options, one using polling sensor and the other using timer sensor, to demonstrate our method.

- *Using polling sensor.* We run a polling sensor on each host across the whole network to periodically report the connection state of the host it monitors to the DMMs subscribing to it, as depicted in Fig. 5. Each polling sensor runs on a host independently and is subscribed by all DMMs located on different subnets. Actuators are embedded into each replication manager on a host and used to instruct them to process clients' requests according to decisions made by the DMMs.

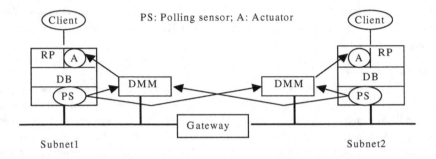

**Fig. 5.** Using polling sensors for network partitioning problem

- *Using timer sensor.* We can also use timer sensors to report each host's state. In this case, a timer sensor is attached to a host by being embedded into the replication manager to monitor the connection state of this host to the network, as depicted in Fig. 6, where the DMMs and actuators are same as above. Once a connection failure occurs the timer sensor will report it to the DMMs subscribing to it.

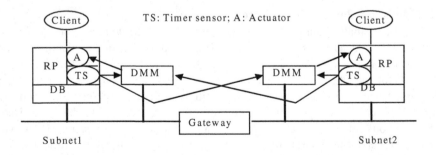

**Fig. 6.** Using timer sensors for partition-tolerant applications

In both cases, the DMMs will decide whether a partition happens according to the reports received from the sensors and then make decisions to instruct the RPs how to process clients' transactions using the actuators. In this solution, the RPs deal with transaction processing while the DMMs deal with failure handling.

**Partition detecting and notifying**

Assume that there are $m$ subnets in the network environment and the maximum number of replicas on each subnet is $n$. We use $S_{ij}$ ( $i=1, 2, ..., m; j=1, 2, ..., n$) to denote the sensor attached to the $j^{th}$ replica in the $i^{th}$ subnet; $D_k$ ($k=1, 2, ..., m$) denotes the DMM in the $k^{th}$ subnet. $S_{ij}$ will report to all $D_k$ periodically about the connection state (or liveliness) of the replica it is attached to. Hence, if $\neg\, S_{ij} . D_k,\ i \neq k$, then the $j^{th}$ replica in the $i^{th}$ subnet is faulty to $D_k$, i.e., faulty to the $k^{th}$ subnet. Therefore we have, $\forall k, \exists i, i \neq k$, for all $j$ (=1, 2, ..., n)

$$\text{if } \neg\, S_{ij} . D_k, \text{ then the } i^{th} \text{ subnet may be partitioned with the } k^{th} \text{ subnet} \qquad (3)$$

To confirm the partitioning happened, two DMMs located in the partitioned subnets send a message to each other to see if they are reachable, i.e., for $i, k$ in (3)

$$\text{if } \neg\, D_k . D_i, \text{ then the } i^{th} \text{ subnet must be partitioned with the } k^{th} \text{ subnet} \qquad (4)$$

The time interval for " $\neg$ " is set to be greater than the bigger time interval of polling $S$ and timer $S$. Formula (3) and (4) are the strategies for each DMM located in a subnet to detect a partition existence. Once a network partitioning has been detected, one of the DMMs from two subnets will use actuators to notify all the server groups about the partition situation to save unnecessary network communication overheads caused by some server members trying to contact the other partitioned subnet. The DMM is also responsible to notify all parties once the crashed gateway is up and the partition no longer exists.

## 4.2   Fault Tolerance

Once a database server crash failure has been detected, the fault tolerance is simple. The policy for a replication manager to process a client's requests in the case of the failure has been described in Section 2.1. We discuss partitioning tolerance in the following.

In this paper we use a relatively centralized method with the Primary/Non-Primary replication control protocol [9] to deal with the network partitioning problem. The method is described as follows. A client transaction request can consist of different sub-transactions each of which is to be served by a group of servers or replicas. Replication managers which receive requests from clients divide the transactions into sub-transactions and pass them onto different replicas. Among one group of replicas, a Primary Replica leads other Non-primary Replicas. The transaction processing policy for the system is to treat the Primary Replica for every sub-transaction, or service, as the checkpoint for fully commit mode. Any replica can execute a service freely but a partial commit mode is returned if it is a Non-primary Replica. Only those transactions checked by Primary Replicas will be finalized by either being upgraded to a fully commit mode or downgraded to an abort if conflict exists. Coordination among replica groups is carried out by replication managers to finalize transactions after collecting results from different service executions [4].

During network partitioning, the main problem is that a client could issue a transaction request which involves server members in different partitioned subnets so that the continued transaction processing could result in data in different replicas inconsistent. To solve this problem, we assume that all the Primary sites for one such transaction locate in the same subnet, which is the common case for most transactions. Hence, network partitioning could happen in two cases:

- One is when a P site sends a transaction to a NP site in the partitioned subnet.
- The other is when a NP site sends a transaction to a P site in the partitioned subnet for checking and finalizing it from a partial commit mode.

Our solution is that, in either case, a DMM is running on each subnet respectively and each DMM will decide whether a partitioning happens according to the formula (3) and (4). If a transaction is sent to the partitioned subnet, the replication manager on the P/NP site will send it to the relevant DMM located on the same subnet for recording and further processing. When a DMM receives a transaction record during the partitioning, it identifies its type, whether initialized by the P or NP site, and then stores it in different object lists. After the partitioning is repaired, these DMMs exchange their knowledge of transactions and then send their transaction lists to the relevant replication managers on the same subnet. A DMM will then use actuators to instruct the replication managers to perform these transactions.

For the transactions from P sites for compulsory execution, the replication managers execute them and then check the result to ensure whether it conflicts with the present state. If the conflict exists, the replication managers notify the DMM to invoke certain conflict resolving program such as a backout strategy. For the transactions from NP sites for checking and finalizing, the replication managers check them to see whether they can be executed. If they can, the replication managers will check the result to see if it conflicts with the present state. If the conflict does exist, a notification should be made to the DMM and it will abort these transactions and notify the original NP sites to roll back. If no conflicts, the DMM will contact the original NP to finalize the transactions. This is the primary first policy which guarantees the primary site interest. The detailed algorithms used by DMMs and replication managers for partition detection and transaction execution can be found in [4].

In the case where network partitioning results in that different P sites involving in one transaction locate in different partitions, the replication managers in the P sites cannot fully execute the whole transaction. We propose two options: one is to let the client abort the transaction and the other is to store the transaction and re-execute it after the network partitioning is recovered.

# 5  Conclusion

This paper presented a fault-tolerance solution to deal with crash failures and network partitioning failures in a replicated database system using the reactive system approach. The main advantage of this approach is the separation of mechanisms and policies in software development. Compared with other fault-tolerant strategies, our method has the flexible system architecture which can adapt to constant changes in environments and user requirements. In the solution, we use different DMMs and sensors to implement the fault-tolerant policies and the failure detection mechanisms, and separate them, i.e., the DMMs stay the same no matter what sensors and actuators are or what changes they have, and vice versa. This separation makes the system maintenance easier, and provides a flexible system architecture.

However, one may argue that a relatively centralized DMM used in each subnet for the network partitioning problem is fault prone. This situation could be very rare by placing DMMs in stable sites. While the possibility does exist, transactions recorded by DMMs should be backed up in non-lost devices when they are sent by other P/NP sites.

# References

1.  Kenneth P. Birman. Building Secure and Reliable Network Applications, Chapter 13, *Guaranteeing Behavior in Distributed Systems*. Manning Publications Co., 1996.
2.  M. Boasson. Control Systems Software. *IEEE Transactions on Automatic Control*, vol. 38, nr. 7, 1094–1107, 1993.
3.  C. Chen and W. Zhou. Building Distributed Applications Using the Reactive Approach. In *Proc. of the 11th Australasian Conference on Information System (ACIS-2000)*, Brisbane, Australia, Dec. 2000.
4.  C. Chen and W. Zhou. An Architecture for Resolving Network Partitioning. *Pro. of the ISCA 15$^{th}$ Int'l Conf. for Computers and Their Applications (CATA-2000)*, 84-87, New Orleans, USA, March 2000.
5.  Flaviu Cristian. Understanding Fault-tolerant Distributed Systems. *Communications of the ACM*, pp. 56-78, February 1991.
6.  Susan B. Davidson. Consistency in Partitioned Networks. *ACM Computer Surveys* 17(3) 341-370, Sept. 1985.
7.  Abdelsalam A. Helal et al. *Replication Techniques in Distributed Systems*. Kluwer Academic Publishers, 1996.
8.  Pankaj Jalote. *Fault Tolerance in Distributed Systems*. Prentice Hall, 1994.
9.  Jehan-Francois Paris. Using Volatile Witnesses to Extend the Applicability of Availability Copy Protocols. *Proc. 2nd Workshop on the Management of Replicated Data*, 1992, pp 30–33.
10. R. D. Schlichting and F.B. Schneider. Fail-stop Processors: An Approach to Designing Fault-Tolerant Computing Systems. *ACM Transactions on Computer Systems*, 1(3):222–238, 1983.
11. A. Tanenbaum. *Computer Networks*, 3$^{rd}$ Ed., Printice-Hall, 1996.
12. W. Zhou. Detecting and Tolerating Failures in a Loosely Integrated Heterogenerous Database System. *Computer Communications*, 22, 1056-1067, 1999.

# Information Hiding System StegoWaveK for Improving Capacity

Young-Shil Kim[1], Young-Mi Kim[2], Jin-Yong Choi[2], and Doo-Kwon Baik[3]

[1] Dept of Computer Science & Information, Daelim College
526-7 Bisan Dong, Dongan-gu, Anyang-si, Kyungki-do, Korea
pewkys@daelim.ac.kr
[2] Dept of R&D, CEST .LTD
Hyocheon B/D, 1425-10,
Secho-Dong, Secho-Gu, Seoul,Korea
rose@cest.co.kr,cjng96@hanmail.net
[3] College of Information & Communication, Korea University
5 Ga, Anam-Dong, Sungbuk-Gu, Seoul, Korea
baik@software.korea.ac.kr

**Abstract.** Steganography was designed to get users harder to find out the data through hiding data in forms of various materials such as text, image, video, and audio. The most generalized Audio Steganography technique is Lowbit Encoding which insert one bit of message to the last bit. Attacker has the disadvantage where attack was able to do the message which was easily concealed in case of Lowbit Encoding. Also capacity of stego-data is low. To improve low capacity, we embed more than one bit in every sixteen bit. But the attacker easily filters message when inserted bit is equally bits in every sixteen bits, it is proposed that the message should be inserted in forms of sign curve with changing the number of bits.

## 1   Introduction

Steganography was designed to get average users(not specialized ones) harder to find out the data through hidden data in forms of various materials such as text, image, MPEG, and audio. If some secret message were encrypted, the security level could go higher. Though some attacker might find out the coded secret data, the attacker had to decoding the data. According to the size of message, the size of cover-data should be decided. Therefore message must be condensed to be hidden in the cover-data. At present the most highly developed Steganography is the one with using image technique; the most heated Steganography is the one with using audio technique. In the audio steganography, data is generally hidden where the listener actually does not listen to. Therefore, listeners are not aware that data is actually hidden. Besides, since the Stego-data size is almost similar to the Cover-data size, most listeners cannot tell the difference. For better stability, some methods are used in the copyrights field such as the digital watermarking technique. On the other hand, for higher capacity to hide data,

M. Guo and L.T.Yang (Eds.): ISPA 2003, LNCS 2745, pp. 423–436, 2003.

most commercialized steganography softwares adopt Lowbit encoding method. According to [23], the audio steganography is used to hide data off line. Unlike encoding, the steganography does not require any additional memory for the secret message and can hide data without affecting the size of the audio file. Based on the techniques explained above, this study suggests StegoWaveK system improving the existing methods to provide higher capacity and to survive visual attack without allowing loss of hidden data and compromising the sound quality, and describes how to design and implement StegoWaveK system.

## 2    File Encryption Algorithm

Encryption algorithm is divided into two algorithms, Private-key encryption and Public-key encryption algorithm. Private-key encryption algorithm is called Symmetry key encryption algorithm, too. This algorithm is the same as session key used for encryption and decryption. For creating session key, random number generator is generally used or user could create the needed key by himself. A way to using a random number generator will make it difficult to infer session key though has a strong in a dictionary attack method. On the contrary, it is easy remember the way which a user creates a key to want directly but it is weak in a dictionary attack. DES one of Symmenty key algorithm is faster than RSA one of Public-key algorithm approximately $1000 \sim 10000$ times in hardware process speed and about 100 times if implemented with software comparatively[5][6]. We propose improved file encryption algorithm that can improve the problem that showed a specific pattern in addition to encrypt of a file to raise a level of security. The proposed method is composed of following steps. First is the applying stage which employs AES algorithm to enhance over one step level of encryption. AES has variable key length of 128 bits, 192 bits, 256 bits at a variable length block of 128 bits, 192 bits, 256 bits. Therefore, safety of data is improved. Second is hiding the structure and form of encrypted Ciphertext for removing some particular patterns which could be appeared in encrypted Ciphertext. And it is applied to the MBE(Modified Block Encryption) which encrypts Ciphertext using the key based on this after generating random number of Ciphertext blocks.

## 3    Steganography

Steganography means "Covered Writing" coming from Greek language. This is to hide some secret message between sender and receiver who are two subjects in telecommunication. This method aims at concealing the fact that an ordinary message has some secret contents by a third person[8][9]. Currently disputable Steganography techniques are ones developed being based upon digital environment.

## 3.1  Difference of Steganography and Watermarking

It is a purpose that data conceal hidden fact as for the Steganography but watermarking is a purpose to do in order to be able to give no transformation to the data that it is not a purpose to hide data. Because Watermarking is the give proof of ownership of digital data by embedding copyright statements[2]. But it is limited which degree size of the data can embed in a wave file of approximately 4 minutes play quantity to work in case of Watermarking. Therefore, it cannot embed data of large size. A purpose of Steganography is not recognize the fact which has hidden data in stego-data. So Steganography is that actual attacker can embed data of large size within the range that data do not know embedded fact. And Steganogrphy is usually not robust against modification of the data, or has only limited robustness but Watermarking is not.

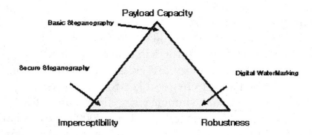

**Fig. 1.** Steganography and Digital Watermarking[3]

## 3.2  Audio Steganography

Audio Steganography is developed upon the theory secret data would be easily transported if message could be hidden in audio files. Low-Bit Encoding, Phase Encoding, Spread Spectrum, and Echo Data Hiding are all the methods that make it possible to do audio Steganography[4][11][12]. Lowbit Encoding method is the simplest one to insert data into different data structure. This method is to substitute the secret data with the last bit of sampling one by binary stream. The phase coding method works by substituting the phase of an initial audio segment with a reference phase that represents the data. Spread Spectrum is that most communication channels try to concentrate audio data in as narrow a region of the frequency spectrum as possible in order to conserve bandwidth and power. When using a spread spectrum technique, however, the encoded data is spread across as much of the frequency spectrum as possible Echo data hiding embeds data into a host signal by introducing an echo. The data are embedded by varying three parameters of the echo: initial amplitude, decay rate, and offset, or delay. The Capacities of Lowbit Encoding, Echo Hiding, Phase Coding, Spread Spectrum, and Ceptral Hiding are 44100 bps, 16 bps, 20 bps, 4 bps, and 20 bps. Assuming music is played for 1 minute, users can store 846000 bits using lowbit encoding, 960 bits using echo hiding, 1200 bits using phase coding, 240 bits using spread spectrum, or 1200 bits using ceptral hiding. In other words, all techniques suggested except Lwbit Encoding are strong against attacks such as compression, but can store only small amount of data and have to support synchronization to reproduce signals. Also, to insert and extract hidden data as in the original status before the message was hidden, additional techniques must be used [21][22]. These techniques are not appropriate to hide general documents, but instead, they are mostly used for copyrights protection. Therefore, a technique that does not have good stability but has high capacity must be selected to hide and extract data without any loss.

## 4    StegoWaveK Model

StegoWaveK is a model that uses the 2-Tier file encryption in order to raise a security level of the data which are going to embed the audio Steganography system that can hide message of various banishments and encoded. Commercialized Audio Steganography software has greatly two problems. First, is taking the Low-Bit Encoding way that is the simplest application way of audio Steganography. By listening to a wave file or watching wavelength type simply, users or listeners did not know that information is embedded, but there is the important thing that information embedded by attacker has a problem for a filtering to be able to easily work. Second, we need the cover-data of 16 times for message file arithmetically. It makes difficulties for choice of the cover-data. Therefore, development of the technology that can embed of large size message is necessary.

### 4.1    Design of StegoWaveK Model

In order to solve a problem that is able to have been easily analyzed structure and a characteristic of a file because general file encryption algorithm shows a specific pattern and that a filtering can easily work in attacker, and capacity was low because commercialized audio steganography lets the last 1 bit of 16 bit hide data, this paper proposes StegoWaveK. Figure 3 is a StegoWaveK model to be composed of a level to insert secrete message in cover-data by compression, encryption and embedding

### 4.2    2-Tier File Encryption

2-Tier file encryption is the file encryption that can improve the problem that showed a specific pattern in addition to encrypt of a file to raise a level of security. 1-Tier is the applying stage which employs AES algorithm to enhance over one step level of encryption. AES has variable key length of 128 bits, 192 bits, 256 bits at a variable length block of 128 bits, 192 bits, 256 bits. Therefore, safety of data is improved

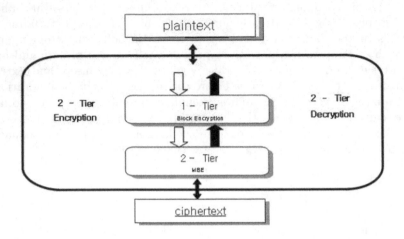

**Fig. 2.** Flowchart of Message Encryption in StegoWaveK

2-Tier hides structure and form of secondly encrypted Ciphertext for removing some particular patterns which could be appeared in encrypted Ciphertext. And it is applied to the MBE(Modified Block Encryption) which encrypts Ciphertext using the key based on this after generating random number of Ciphertext blocks. MBE algorithm circulates 255 keys which it has sequential created from image key and carries out each block and XOR operation.

### 4.3    Message Embedding Algorithm

The most generalized audio Steganography technique is Low-Bit Encoding which insert one bit of message to the last bit. In the Commercialized system, it embeds message only to the most right digit from the 16 bit of wave file. But the most reliable Steganography technique is the Cepstral Hiding, it's storing capacity is very low. It is very hard to embed all different size of message. The proposed algorithm in this paper is revised Low-Bit Encoding method, and improves the two types of problems, which is low capacity and easy filtering in Commercialized Audio Steganography. First, in order to insert bigger size of message to the limited size of cover-data, we embed more than one bit in every sixteen bit. (Fig.3) shows result from opinion of 100 students listening stego-data hiding as 1 bit, 2 bit, 4 bit, and 6 bit. The student listened to music using a speaker. All students were not able to distinguish between stego-data and cover-data. Therefore, we used headphones for a precision analysis. Most of student do not feel the difference of cover-data and stego-data. But if we increase the number of bit to insert unconditionally, then there is significant difference of the two data. Since cover-data is injured, listener is aware of information embedding. Thus we know how about the damage of cover-data is reduced as to 1 bit, 2 bit, 4 bit, and 6 bit, and how about difference in the these stego-data and cover-data is showed by file structure aspect. (Fig.4) shows the discrepancy of values of weighted bit between stego-data and cover-data.

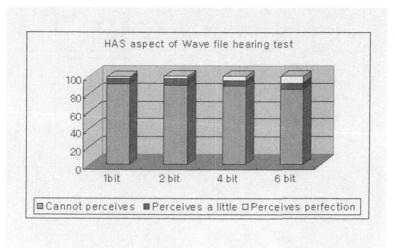

**Fig. 3.** Flowchart of Message Encryption in StegoWaveK

In (Fig.4), the difference of the bit-value which is inserted to message bit from 1 bit to 4 bit to stego-data is not significant. However, for the data inserted more than six bit, we get the information that there are significant difference of the bit value. From this fact, we could conclude that the ideal number of insertion bit is from 1 bit to 4 bit in order to minimize changing between cover-data and stego-data, and evaluate the efficiency of capacity.

In order to prove no meaningful difference between cover-data and stego-data inserted by 1 bit, 2 bit, 4 bit, and 6 bit, we use cover-data having format of 16 bit PCM Wave file. We transfer 16 bit segment to decimal number and select three thousand of decimal values to analyze. The correlation analysis is performed to know what difference is between cover-data and stego-data. In the analysis result, since correlation coefficient of relation between stego-data and cover-data is close to 1, we know the fact that stego-data obtains properties of cover-data. But in the case of 6 bit stego-data, correlation coefficient is 0.9996 and thus some properties of cover-data is dropped. The Attacker easily filters message when inserted bit is equally 2 bit, 3 bit, or 4 bit. To improve this problem, we propose the method that bits of message is inserted in forms of sign curve with changing the number of bits, not inserted by regular rate per 16 bit of cover-data. As a result of correlation analysis for cover-data and 1 bit stego-data, we can know that high correlation relationship appears between stego-data with a 1 bit sign curve and cover-data. In insertion of message, we use sign curve and can keep a characteristic of cover-data. In the Dynamic Message Embedding (DME)

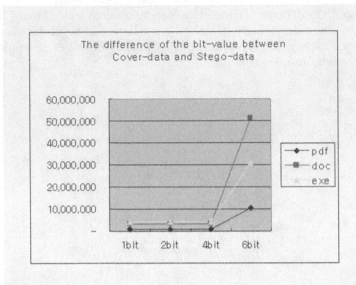

**Fig. 4.** The difference of the bit-value

module, the secret message is inserted into a certain critical value, not the lowbit as long as characteristics of the cover-data are maintained. For the critical value, features of the cover-data and the secrete message are analyzed and processed. Also, the most suitable algorithm is selected to insert the secret message from the algorithm that hides one bit and the algorithm that improves capacity by the sine curve form.

In the pre-processing, the sound volume of the cover-data that is a wave file is analyzed and distribution of the sound volume of the wave file is studied. Then, referring to the ratio with the next secret message, the critical value to hide the secret message is decided. After the location to hide the secrete message is decided, the message embedding algorithm is decided Basically, Fmt chunk (the header of the wave file) size is 18 bytes. Last 2 bytes of these 18 bytes describe the size of extension information. However, if extension information is not included, remaining 16 bytes is designed as Fmt chunk. Actually, in most cases, Fmt chunk is designed to be 16 bytes. In the commercialized audio steganography software, only the wave file with the data chunk identifier in 4 bytes from the 37th byte (the location defined assuming that Fmt chunk of the wave file is 16 bytes) is recognized as a wave file. In other words, the commercialized audio steganography software does not recognize 18 byte wave files. Especially, when MP3 music files are converted into wave files, mostly they have 18 byte or 14 byte Fmt chunk, which is not supported by the commercialized audio steganography software. To solve this problem, the Chunk Unit Read (CUR) module processing according to the chunk of the wave file has been designed. In the CUR module, data characteristics are not judged by reading fixed location values, but instead, the wave file is processed according to the chunk. Therefore, not only the wave

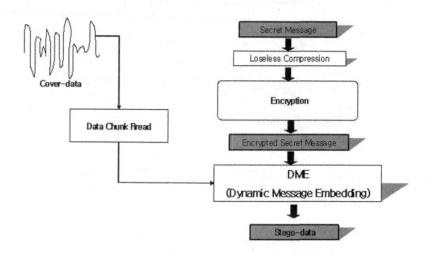

**Fig. 5.** Flowchart of Message Encryption in StegoWaveK

file with 18 byte Fmt chunk (the basic format) but also wave files with 16 byte and 14 byte Fmt chucks can be used as the cover-data.

## 5    Performance Evaluation of StegoWaveK

In this section, StegoWaveK that has been implemented by VC++.Net is compared with Invisible Secretes 2002 (hereinafter to be referred to as "CS I") and Steganos Security Suite 4 (hereinafter to be referred to as "CS II") that have been commercialized and in use now. According to [36], in steganography analysis, visual, audible, structural, and statistical techniques are used. Therefore, the comparison and the analysis in this study were based on criteria of the Human Visible System (HVS), Human Auditory System (HAS), Statistical Analysis (SA), and Audio Measurement (AM). Since the HAS can be relatively subjective, audio measurement analysis was added to more objectively analyze and compare the stego-data and the cover-data. For comparison and analysis data, PopSong by Kim Min Song was used. In experiments with other genre music, similar results were gained.

### 5.1    Human Visible System (HVS) Criteria

According to the waveform analysis result of the stego-data created by Invisible Secrets 2002 and StegoWaveK using an audio editor, CoolEditor, it is hard to visually tell the difference due to HVS characteristics. (Fig.7) shows waveform of the stego-data captured by CoolEditor and (Fig.8) shows hexa-decimal code values of cover-data and stego-data.

**Fig. 6.** Example of First Step in StegoWaveK

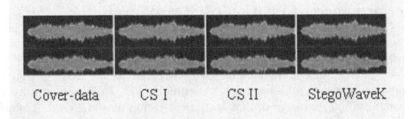

**Fig. 7.** Hexa-decimal values of cover-data and stego-data

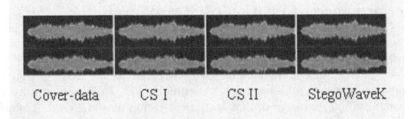

Cover-data          CS I          CS II          StegoWaveK

**Fig. 8.** Waveform of the stego-data

## 5.2   Human Auditory System (HAS) Criteria

To analyze and compare the suggested system with the existing system on criteria of the Human Auditory System (HAS), 13 messages with different sizes and 4 wave files were selected as cover-data. We played the stego-data where the message is hidden through CS I and CS II using lowbit encoding and the stego-data where the message is hidden through StegoWaveK system to 100 students. Although it could be subjective, most students could not tell the difference between the cover-data and the stego-data. Following (Fig.9) shows the experiment result

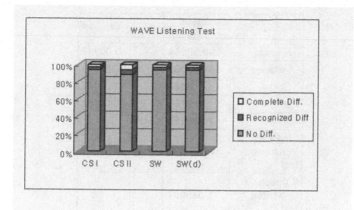

**Fig. 9.** Hearing results of many stego-data

## 5.3   Statistical Analysis (SA) Criteria

In the following, correlations between the cover-data and the stego-data created by the CS I, and between the cover-data and the stego-data where the secret message was hidden through StegoWaveK are analyzed by extracting characteristics from stego-data. In the result, we can find the stego-data have similar characteristics to the cover-data in both cases.

|  | Cover-data | CS I |
|---|---|---|
| Average | 0.00964 | 0.00965 |
| Variance | 0.223003 | 0.222976 |
| Obs. | 9143 | 9143 |
| DF | 9143 | 9142 |
| F ratio | 1.00012 | |
| P(F<=f) one-tailed test | 0.497721 | |
| F threshold: one-tailed test | 1.35007 | |

**Fig. 10.** Results of one-way analysis of variance

| | Cover-data | StegoWaveK |
|---|---|---|
| Average | -0.00964 | -0.00988 |
| Variance | 0.223003 | 0.221045 |
| Obs. | 9143 | 9143 |
| DF | 9143 | 9142 |
| F ratio | 1.008857 | |
| P(F<=f) one-tailed test | 0.336674 | |
| F threshold: one-tailed test | 1.035007 | |

**Fig. 11.** F-Test StegoWaveK and cover-data

| Treatments | Obs. | Sum | mean | Variance |
|---|---|---|---|---|
| Cover-data | 9143 | -88.177 | -0.00964 | 0.223003 |
| CS I | 9143 | -88.218 | -0.00965 | 0.222976 |
| StegoWaveK | 9143 | -90.315 | -0.00988 | 0.221045 |

Analysis of variance

| Source | Sum of square | DF | Mean square | F ratio | P-value | F threshold |
|---|---|---|---|---|---|---|
| Treatments | 0.00037 | 3 | 0.000123 | 0.000555 | 0.999982 | 2.605148 |
| Error | 8136.622 | 36568 | 0.222507 | | | |
| Total | 8136.623 | 36571 | | | | |

**Fig. 12.** Results of one-way analysis of variance

## 5.4   Audio Measurements (AM) Criteria

Audio measurement and analysis includes frequency response, gain or loss, harmonic distortion, intermodulation distortion, noise level, phase response, and transient response. These parameters include the signal level or phase and the frequency. For example, the Signal to Noise Ratio (SNR) is a level measurement method represented by dB or ratio. The quality of the stego-data where the message is hidden was measured using SNR. SNR represents ratios of relative values [15][16] The following graph shows SNRs between the cover data and the stego-data created by the CS I, the CS II, and StegoWaveK. The SNR of the stego-data created by the suggested system is not significantly different from that of the stego-data created by the CS I. However, the SNR of the stego-data created by the CS II is relatively different from that of the stego-data created by the suggested system.

| Variable | N | Average | Standard Deviation | Sum |
|----------|---|---------|--------------------|-----|
| Origin | 9144 | -0.00949 | 0.47221 | -86.77300 |
| CS I | 9144 | -0.00964 | 0.47221 | -88.17800 |
| StegoWaveK | 9144 | -0.00965 | 0.47218 | -90.21500 |

Simple Statistics

| Variable | Min | Max |
|----------|-----|-----|
| Origin | -1.37000 | 2.10600 |
| CS I | -1.37000 | 2.10600 |
| StegoWaveK | -1.37000 | 2.10600 |

Pearson Correlation Coefficient  N=9144

| | CS I | StegoWaveK |
|--------|------|------------|
| Origin | 0.99952 | 0.99952 |
| | <0.0001 | <0.0001 |

**Fig. 13.** Correlation Analysis of cover-data and stego-data

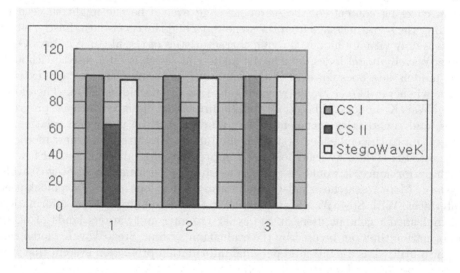

**Fig. 14.** Comparison of SNR(dB) between cover-data and stego-data

# 6    Conclusion

The audio steganography that hides data uses the wave file as cover-data; the cover-data has the same size as the size of the stego-data file in the suggested system; and most listeners and users do not tell any difference in the sound quality. Therefore, they cannot recognize that data is hidden in stego-data. Also, none of the HVS system or the HAS system can analyze the wavelength that had been analyzed through a simple audio editing tool in an intuitive way. Therefore, it can be useful to send secret data. The commercialized steganography software uses only certain types of wave files as the cover-data. As one bit of the secret message is inserted into the Lowbit of the cover-data, the cover data can be easily filtered. Also, as one bit is inserted to hide the secrete message, the cover-data size increases. StegoWaveK model suggested in this study has been specially designed for Korean users to improve problems of existing commercial audio steganography softwares have. Firstly, to solve the problem that the secret message can be hidden only in the wave file of which Fmt Chuck is composed of 16 bytes, StegoWaveK model processes the wave file by Chunk. Secondly, to improve the capacity of the cover-data and to prevent the attacker from filtering the cover-data, the writer designed and implemented DME module and applied it. With DME module, users can decide the critical value and the insertion algorithm to hide the secret message based on the cover-data and characteristics of the secret message. This will make it difficult to tell whether there is hidden data as in the case of the open key steganography, although the suggested model uses the private key steganography. Thirdly, in StegoWaveK model, encoding is performed to prevent the attacker from visually checking characteristics of the secret message before the secret message was hidden and to prevent the attacker from checking contents of the secret message even if he/she might succeed in gaining the secret message from the stego-data and the cover-data. Lastly, while data is only visually hidden through characteristics of the file in Windows O/S, StegoWaveK model hides data in the audio data that is often used. Although the hidden data does not exist in the computer any longer, the user can extract data whenever he/she wants without any loss of the hidden data. Therefore, StegoWaveK model can be useful to hide important design drawings, program files, and confidential documents. More studies shall be performed relating to migration to the embedded system in the future. By introducing new methods suggested in [37], or by using loss-free compression programs such as TIFF with high performance, it would be possible to improve performance of StegoWaveK system. More researches shall be made also to develope more convenient user interfaces. With StegoWaveK system, it is possible to hide personal information of multimedia content users at the cyber training and various kinds of other information that can be used by the evaluation system. StegoWaveK model can be also utilized as a multi-level personal information protection system that can protect personal information at several levels.

# References

1. J.Zollner, H.Federrath, H.Klimant, A.Pfitzmann, R.Piotraschke, A.Westfeld, G.Wicke, G.Wolf: Modeling the security of steganographoc systems 2nd Workshop on Information Hiding, Portland, LNCS 1525, Springer-Cerlag, pp. 345–355, (1998)
2. Stegan Katzenbeisser, Fabien A.P Petitcilas : Information Hiding Technique For Steganography and Digital Watermarking Artech House, pp. 97–98, (2000)

3. http://www.crazytrain.com/monkeyboy/mde_johnson_gmu2001_stegob.pdf
4. http://www.cbcis.wustl.edu/ãdpol/courses/cs502/project/report/node1htm
5. Raymond G. Kammer : DATA ENCRYPTION STANDARD Federal Information Processing Standards Publication (1999)
6. http://www.securitytechnet.com.
7. http://www.softforum.co.kr/learningcenter/learningcenter_04.html
8. A Study on the Information Hiding Techniques and Standardization for the Protection of Intellectual Property Right, Korea National Computerization Agency, pp. 19–41, (2000).
9. Ross J. Anderson, and Fabieb A.P. Petitcolas, On The Limits of Steganography, IEEE Journal of Selected Areas in Communication, 16(4):474–481, (1998)
10. G. J. Simmoms, The Prisoners' Problem and the Subliminal Channel, Proceeding of CRYPTO '83, Plenum Press, pp. 51–68, (1984)
11. http://www.cs.uct.ac.za/courses/CS400W/NIS/papers99/dsellars/stego.html
12. S.K. Pal, P.K. Saxena, and S.K. Muttoo, "The Future of Audio Steganography".
13. http://www-ccrma.stanford.edu/CCRMA/Courses/422/projects/WaveFormat
14. http://www.wisdom.weizmann.ac.il/ĩtsik/RC4/rc4.html
15. http://burtleburtle.net/bob/rand/isaac.html
16. Dr. Richard C. Cabot, P.E., Bruce Hofer, and Robert Metzler, Chapter 13.1 Audio Measurement and Analysis,
17. http://www.tvhandbook.com/support/pdf_files/audio/Chapter13_1.pdf
18. http://211.38.132.225/new_b24.htm
19. J.D.Gordy and L.T.Bruton Performance Evaluation of Digital Audio Watermarking Algorithms IEEE MWSCAS (2000)
20. Stefan Katzenbeisser, and Fabien A.P.Petitcolas Information hiding techniques for steganography and digital watermarking Artech House Publishers, (2000)
21. BenZamin Arazi, A Commonsense Approach to the Theory of Error Correcting Codes, MIT Press (1986).
22. http://debut.cis.nctu.edu.tw/ỹklee/Reaserch/Steganography/Qalter_Bender/IHW96.pdf
23. Peter Wayner, Disappearing cryptography Information Hiding : Steganography & Watermarking, second edition, chapter 17, Morgan Kauffman, (2002)

# Multimedia Parallel Programming Tool for Cellular Automata Systems

Mahmoud Saber and Nikolay Mirenkov

Graduate Department of Information Systems
The University of Aizu
Aizu-Wakamatsu City, Fukushima, 965-8580, Japan
{d8032101,nikmir}@u-aizu.ac.jp

**Abstract.** The Active Knowledge Studio group at the University of Aizu is studying, designing, and developing multimedia programming tools for various domains. These special purpose tools are developed within the frame-work of a more general environment (Active Knowledge Studio) and based on common design and implementation approaches. However, because of the orientation to different domains, each tool possesses its own features represented through specific multimedia objects and interface panels. In this paper, we provide an outline of our approach to programming cellular automata systems with one of our multimedia tools. We also provide a brief explanation of a user interface subsystem and discuss concepts and features of a program generator subsystem in this tool. We pay special attention to the parallel template programs supporting the automatic generation of executable codes from the multimedia specifications.

## 1 Introduction

Cellular automata systems have long needed a way to understand their essential features and global behaviors during all phases of the life cycle. We designed and implemented a new multimedia tool that can be used to specify, present, and execute computational algorithms from the field of cellular automata (CA) systems. The Active Knowledge Studio (AKS) group at the University of Aizu is studying, designing, and developing multimedia programming tools for various domains; see, for example, [1]-[5]. These special purpose tools are developed within the framework of a global environment and based on common design and implementation approaches. However, because of the orientation to different domains, each tool possesses its own features represented through specific multimedia objects and interface panels. In this paper, a tool oriented to programming CA systems where global behavior arises from the collective effect of many locally interacting, simple components is presented.

The multimedia programming tool is based on *self-explanatory components approach* [6]. Self-explanatory components constitute a framework for visual representation and specification of objects/processes, based on the idea of multiple views and algorithmic multimedia skeletons. A series of multimedia frames represents a set of algorithm features in a film format. In this format, computational algorithms become

M. Guo and L.T. Yang (Eds.): ISPA 2003, LNCS 2745, pp. 437–448, 2003.

components that are accessed and manipulated through a number of views related to its dynamic, static, and hierarchical features [7].

"Film" is used as a new type of abstraction to represent computational algorithms by combining mathematical and physical concepts [6]. Mathematical concepts are used to convey the arithmetic/logic aspects of algorithmic activities. Physical concepts are used mainly to convey the spatial and temporal aspects of computation. A film is a series of multimedia frames (stills.) One frame represents a view (aspect) of an algorithm; many frames represent many algorithmic aspects.

Frame views are arranged into six special groups. The first three groups visualize 1) computational steps and data structures, 2) variables attached to the structures and formulas used in space-time points of algorithm activity, and 3) input/output operations. The fourth group consists of frames of an integrated view where important features from previous groups are presented altogether. Groups 5 and 6 are auxiliary views related to the film title, authorship, registration date, and links to other algorithms, additional explanations, statistics of the usage, etc. Films as pieces of "active" knowledge are acquired in a film database. The film frames are watchable and editable in a non-linear order according to the user's demands. Therefore, the conventional animation (movie) is a mere partial case of our film concept. We also consider our films as self-explanatory components, because multiple views are an excellent basis for bridging the gap between "syntax and semantics" and understanding the component meaning.

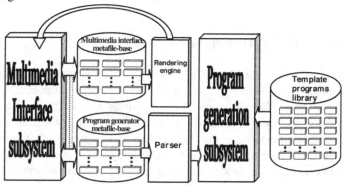

**Fig. 1.** The architecture of the multimedia parallel programming tool.

An overall architecture of the multimedia tool comprises a multimedia interface subsystem, a program generation subsystem, a rendering engine, a parser, a template programs library, and metafiles bases (Figure 1). We will explain main parts of the tool's architecture in Sections 3-5.

The work presented here is situated in the context of several research areas like pixel rewriters, pixel-level computation, and fine grain parallel computation. Some of them include software visualization techniques. Pixel rewriters are used to explore the variety of interesting computations on, and manipulation of, shape directly in the pixels [8]. These are close to Furnas's BITPICT system [9], a pixel rewriting system proposed as a possible model for "purely graphical" reasoning. A work of the same area is Yamamoto's VISULAN system [10]. It is an extension of Furnas's pixel rewrite programming language.

Pixel-level computations are used extensively in the early stages of processing and parsing images in the area of computer vision. Filters highlight edges by enhancing brightness gradients in the pixel array [11]. In morphological analysis [12], noisy edges are healed by first dilation. Image processing is central to photo manipulation applications of Photoshop type, using pixel operations like blurring, sharpening, and color substitution.

WinALT [13],[14] is a simulating system of fine grain algorithms and structures that have a recognizable and intuitively clear interface which eases the learning of the system. Graphics is used to represent the intermediate and resulting data visually.

However, these systems usually focus on computational and performance issues, and provide a rather "conventional" view of the algorithm description. They pay not enough attention to the human abilities, and reserve the graphics and colors to represent the intermediate and final results only, while the algorithm structures and steps of computation are described in a pure textual form.

The rest of this paper is organized as follows. In Section 2, we reconsider the modeling of CA systems and in Section 3, the multimedia interfaces subsystem is briefly explained. In Sections 4 the program generator subsystem is described. In Section 5, the features of the parallel template programs are shown, and in Section 6, the conclusion is presented.

## 2  Modeling Cellular Automata Systems

Most entities that exhibit life-like behavior are complex systems made up of many elements simultaneously interacting with each other. One way to understand the global behavior of a complex system is to model that behavior with a simple system of equations that describe how global variables interact. By contrast, the characteristic approach followed in artificial life is to construct lower-level models that *themselves are* complex systems and then to iterate the models and observe the resulting global behavior. Such lower-level models are sometimes called agent- or individual-based models, because the whole system's behavior is represented only indirectly and arises merely out of the interactions of a collection of directly represented parts (agents or individuals).

As complex system changes over time, each element changes according to its state and the state of those neighbors with which it interacts. Complex systems typically lack any central control, though they may have boundary conditions. The elements of a complex system are often simple compared to the whole system, and the rules by which the elements interact are also often simple. The behavior of a complex system is simply the aggregate of the changes over time of all of the system's elements. In rare cases the behavior of a complex system may actually be derived from the rules governing the elements' behavior, but typically, a complex system's behavior cannot be discerned short of empirically observing the emergent behavior of its constituent parts. The elements of a complex system may be connected in a regular way, e.g. on an

Euclidean lattice, or in an irregular way, e.g. on a random network. Interactions between elements may also be without a fixed pattern, as in molecular dynamics of a chemical soup or interaction of autonomous agents. When adaptation is part of a complex system's dynamics, it is sometimes described as a complex adaptive system.

For long time it has been very difficult to study the behavior of complex systems because the formal models describing them were so hard that the main computational modality, represented by the integration of differential equations, was intractable even using powerful parallel computers.

The development of computer science in the latest years considerably enlarged its application boundaries because of the continuous rise of computing power. At the same time research in parallel computing showed evidence of the significant potential of parallel computing models, such as cellular automata and neural networks, in representing a valid alternative to differential calculus in the description of complex phenomena [15]. This occurs especially when differential equations cannot efficiently be solved because of their complexity or when is very difficult to model the problem being solved in terms of differential equations.

Cellular automata (CA) are very effective in modeling complex systems because they can capture the essential features of systems in which the global behaviour arises from the collective effect of large numbers of locally interacting simple components. CAs are decentralized spatially extended systems consisting of large numbers of simple identical components with local connectivity. Such systems have the potential to perform complex computations with a high degree of efficiency and robustness, as well as to model the behavior of complex systems in nature. For these reasons, CAs and related architectures have been studied extensively in the natural sciences, mathematics, and in computer science. They have been used as models of physical and biological systems, such as fluid flow, galaxy formation, earthquakes, and biological pattern formation. They have been considered as mathematical objects about which formal properties can be proved. They have been used as parallel computing devices, both for the high-speed simulation of scientific models and for computational tasks such as image processing. In addition, CAs have been used as abstract models for studying emergent cooperative or collective behavior in CA systems [16]-[18]. Many programming languages and systems were developed to implement cellular automata (CA) based algorithms (see, for example [19]-[21].)

After a study of the interesting features of the CA model, we had the motivation to create a new multimedia representation of the CA model that can be manipulated with user-oriented visual interfaces, and translated to efficient parallel programs, as we are going to explain in the following sections.

## 3 Multimedia Interface Subsystem

In the case of a conventional language, a source program is input as a text with some support of a text editor. In our case of the film language, a source program can be input as collection of icons, colored shapes, in addition to text whenever it is more expressive than other media. Figure 2 depicts the contents of the multimedia interface subsystem. A special module to perform searching and opening operations for films, scenes, and frames is considered as a multimedia navigator that helps the users to get their needs from the film-base in a user-friendly few steps. The users can create there own films from scratch based on their own experience or with the help of an interactive wizard. After these operations, the user can watch a film or its parts and perform editing and composing manipulation. Editing mode allows the specification of cellular models. The power of a specification method is mainly related to its flexibility, generality, and capability to customize visualizations [22].

While watching a film is close to algorithm animation field, an algorithm animation visualizes the behavior of an algorithm by producing an abstraction of both data and the operations of the algorithm (for a comprehensive view of the field, see [23].)

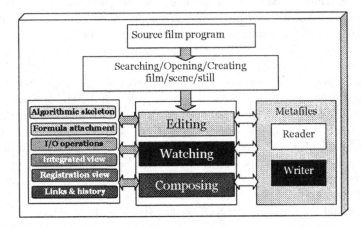

**Fig. 2.** The multimedia interface subsystem

These manipulations are divided into six groups depending on algorithmic film features (as we have mentioned in the Introduction, these features are directly represented by six groups of film frames). As a result, the editing/watching/composing module is created as six sub-modules. Each sub-module is a multimedia interface to edit, watch, and compose frames of a corresponding group. A metafile reader/writer module is responsible for storing the specifications of the manipulated films in the metafile-bases, and fetching them to the interfaces modules whenever they are requested.

The multimedia interface subsystem is developed in JAVA. Figure 3 shows some of the panels (editing, watching, and, formula attaching panels) developed and used for the CA domain. See [24]-[25], for more details about the design and implementation of this subsystem.

In the film format, a CA is specified by a series of stills (computational steps) and repetitive constructs on sub-series of these stills. Each step is defined by a set of substitution rules and a partial order to apply on the rules. In its turn, each substitution rule is specified as a parallel operation of "find & replace" type applied on all CA cells. Each *still* shows a view (some features) of an algorithmic step. The stills can be watched in either static or dynamic (animated) views. To represent contents of stills

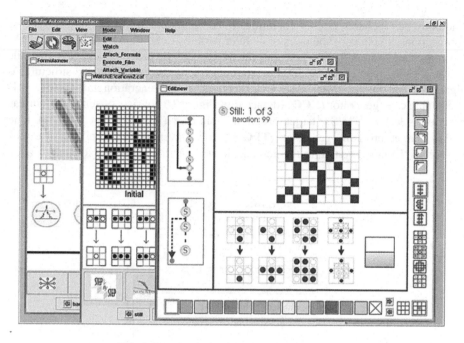

**Fig. 3.** Panels of Multimedia interfaces subsystem

and orders of their execution, a special icon language has been developed. A still contains a sample grid, and pairs of micro-icons that represent substitution rules applied on the grid, control micro-icons that represent an iteration scheme applied on a set of stills, and micro-icons for introducing some irregularity and priority conditions applied on the rules and iteration schemes.

## 4 Program Generator Subsystem

After watching the film specification from different points of view, and performing new editing/composing operations, a metafile writer module generates a program generator metafile. The writer module is considered as a multimedia scanner that analyzes film sections (scene by scene, still by still, etc.), then writes their description in a metafile used in later stages of the program generation. The program generator metafiles have a common outline that consists of a header and body parts. The header part stores global information about the film; it consists of the following records:

- A system (source) grid of cells,
- The size of the grid,
- Variables declared on the grid,
- Still transformations,
- Types of iterations, irregularity of iterations, grid boundaries, and cell neighborhood.

The body part includes priority conditions to be applied to still substitutions, types of substitutions, and data of the pairs of cellular patterns to be found and replaced. Next, a parsing unit (system parser) performs the analysis of the program generator metafile, that is a global type checking. This parsing unit recognizes the syntactic structures of algorithmic skeletons. After that, an executable code generation takes place. The executable code generator (**ECG**) (depicted in Figure 4 ) consists of semantic template program selector (**STPS**), target program composer (**TPC**), target program tuner (**TPT**), target program generator (**TPGs**), and conventional compilers. The final product of **ECG** subsystem is a target machine (sequential/parallel) executable code.

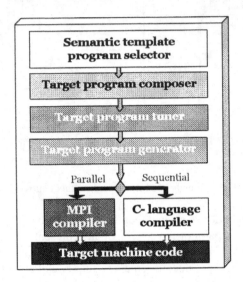

**Fig. 4.** The program generator subsystem

ECG has a read-only access to the template program library which will be discussed later in this section. **STPS** defines hand-coded template programs to be called for representing corresponding computational schemes. **STPS** selects templates based on a type of the grid (1D, 2D, 3D, etc.), a size of the grid (small, medium, big, huge), the number of expected operations on each cell of the grid, in addition to, types of boundaries (close/open), neighborhood, iterations, and overlapping solving schemes. **TPC** adjusts the selected template programs to be parts of one program. In other words, it creates a program of template programs by adjusting them from a whole program view. **TPT** uses the declarations of variables, formulas, etc. related to the above mentioned syntactic structures to tune the composed program on an "indivisual" basis. The tuner output is used by a program generator to create either a sequential or parallel C-program which is compiled by a conventional compiler to obtain a target machine code. During the program generation phase, the template programs library (**TPL**) is accessed frequently, so, it is important to mention a few features related to **TPL**. Like any library of programs, the contents must be high-tech pieces of code written by expert developpers in order to be used by users of various levels of skills and experiences. **TPL** consists of three major modules: searchable index, a sequential template programs pool, and a parallel template programs pool. The searchable index is an interface between the entire library and outsiders. It faciltate the process of finding the most suitable templates in a short time. **TPL** uses adaptive searching techniques that accumulate its experience over time to improve the searching process. Sequential template programs pool is a collection of light-load computational codes to be used on a single processor architecture. Meanwhile, parallel template programs pool is a collection of heavy-load computational codes which are used on a parallel architecture. In the following section, we will talk in details about parallel template programs.

# 5  Parallel Template Programs

In this section, we provide some details of parallel template programs (**PTP**): background, classification of parallel template programs, and a look inside a parallel template program.

## 5.1  Target Machines and Parallel Model

At the University of Aizu, we use MPICH [26] implementation of Message Passing Interface (**MPI**) [27], on a network of  Fujitsu GP400 S machines with " Sun UltraS-PARC-Iii" processors. A parallel program can be executed over a variable number of machines reaches 96 machines connected by 100 Mbps network. **MPI** parallel computational model (Figure 5) posits a set of processes that have only local memory but are able to communicate with other processes by sending and receiving messages. It is a defining feature of the message-passing model that data transfer from the local memory of one process to the local memory of another requires operations to be performed by both processes. Message-passing model has become widely used for many reasons like universality, expressivity, ease of debugging, and providing high performance computation. Two levels of parallelism are supported: (1) coarse grain and (2) fine grain parallelism. The coarse grain parallelism is especially valid for the strategies of parallelism like master-worker and macro-pipelines, where the communication activity is relatively small in comparison with the computation performed. In the fine grain parallelism, there is a relatively large amount of communication in comparison with the computation done.

## 5.2  Classification of Parallel Template Programs

It is too difficult to create a single parallel program that enjoy every feature of the parallel computational model because of the complex nature of parallelism. We clas sify **PTP** into several categories that are expandable over time to satisfy user needs and cover the recent technologies and programming techniques. **PTP**s are selected

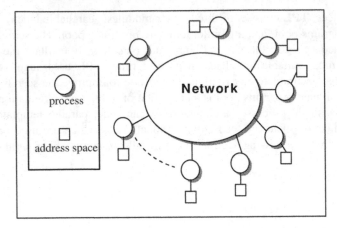

**Fig. 5.** The message passing model

based on this classification to generate executable codes. **PTP** are classified according
to:
- Granularity of tasks (coarse grain/fine grain)
- Parallelism model (data/functional)
- Task assignment (static/semi static/dynamic)

### 5.3  Inside Parallel Template Program

A generic parallel template program (Figure 6) consists of non-changeable and
changeable parts. The non-changeable part is prepared as a ready-made program to
implement a computational scheme written in C&MPI. It is usually a set of nested
loops with formal parameters, variables, and bodies of formal operations. The changeable part including the formal parameters, variables, bodies of formal operations, and
positions to be filled out by real parameters, variables, and operation bodies, which are
specified by user's operations performed through the multimedia interfaces.
For CA models, the **PTP**s have common functions to process the cellular grid; the first
basic function is the pattern discovery, which is responsible for finding all instances of
the specified patterns in the grid. Two approaches to search the cellular grid are implemented. The first approach directly searches the whole grid for each pattern in turn.
This means if there are $N$ patterns related to different substitutions, the grid is searched
$N$ times. The second approach is to compose $N$ patterns into a single larger pattern,
and to search the grid for that pattern. Selecting the proper searching approach is based
on the nature of the CA system. The second function is the overlapping detection. Its
main task is to analyze the discovered instances of patterns; if an overlapping occurs
among them, this function selects one of the overlapped patterns to be replaced and
discard all others. This decision is taken based on a priority condition specified by
the user in earlier stages. The third function is pattern replacement. Its task is to apply
the substitution rules to the processed grid after solving all overlaps by the previous
function.

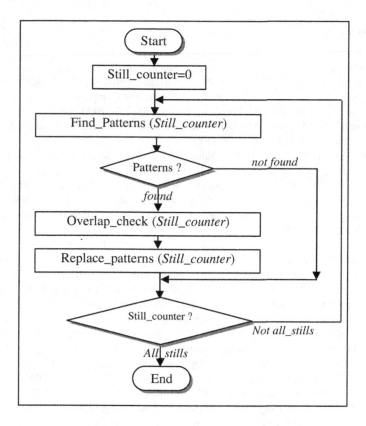

**Fig. 6.** A generic template program chart

## 6  Conclusion

In this paper, we overviewed the modeling of cellular automata systems, briefly explained multimedia interfaces, described the program generation, and showed the features of the parallel template programs.

We demonstrated how in designing our multimedia tool, we abstract the knowledge as much as possible from the underlying computational infrastructure. We also presented our approach to provide higher level tools that allow the users to effectively manage their knowledge, experience, and abilities, as well as, their computational resources and domain tools.

As a future work, we are working on empirical study to measure the self-explanatory factors of our multimedia tool. The feedback will be used in improving our work. In addition, we will run experiments to measure the improvement of performance of our parallel template programs.

# References

1.  R. Yoshioka, N. Mirenkov: Visual Computing within Environment of Self-explanatory components, Soft Computing, Vol. 7, No. 1, Springer-Verlag, p. 20–32 (2002)
2.  T. Ebihara, N. Mirenkov: Self-explanatory Ssoftware Components for Computation on Pyramids, J. Three Dimensional Images, 14, 4, p. 158–163 (2000)
3.  T. Hirotomi, N. Mirenkov: Multimedia Representation of Computation on Trees, J. Three Dimensional Images, 13, p. 146–151 (1999)
4.  A. Vazhenin, N. Mirenkov, D. Vazhenin: Multimedia Representation of Matrix Computations and Data, Information Sciences, 141, Elsevier Science, p. 97–122 (2002)
5.  N. Mirenkov, Oleg Monakov, R. Yoshioka: Self-explanatory Components: Visualization of Graph Algorithms, , In the Proceedings of Visual Computing (VC'02), published in The Proceedings of the Eighth International Conference on Distributed Multimedia Systems (DMS2002), p. 562–567 (2002)
6.  N.Mirenkov, A. Vazhenin, R. Yoshioka, T. Ebihara, T. Hirotomi, T. Mirenkova: Self-explanatory Components: A New Programming Paradigm, International Journal of Software and Knowledge Engineering, Vol. 11, No. 1, World Scientific, p. 5–36 (2001)
7.  R. Yoshioka, N. Mirenkov: A Multimedia System to Render and Edit Self-explanatory Components, Journal of Internet Technology, Vol. 3, No.1 ( 2002)
8.  Furnas, George W. and Qu, Yan: Shape Manipulation Using Pixel Rewrites. In the Proceedings of Visual Computing (VC'02), published in The Proceedings of the Eighth International Conference on Distributed Multimedia Systems (DMS2002), p. 630–639 (2002)
9.  Furnas, G.W.: New Graphical Reasoning Models for Understanding Graphical Interfaces. Proc. of CHI '91 Conf. on Hum. Factors in Comp. Sys. 1991, p. 71–78 (1991)
10. Yamamoto, Kakuya: Visulan: A Visual Programming Language for Self-Changing Bitmap. *Proc. of International Conference on Visual Information Systems,* Victoria Univ. of Tech. cooperation with IEEE (Melbourne, Australia), p. 88–96 (1996)
11. Russ, John C.: The Image Processing Handbook 3rd Ed, Boca Raton, FL: CRC Press (1998)
12. Serra, Jean: Image Analysis and Mathematical Morphology, New York: Academic Press (1982)
13. D.Beletkov, M. Ostapkevich, S. Piskunov, I. Zhileev: WinALT, a Software Tool for Fine-grain Algorithms and Structures Synthesis and Simulation, lecture notes in computer science. 1662, p. 491–496 (1999)
14. M.B. Ostapkevich, S.V. Shashkov: Basic Constructions of Models in WinALT, Bulletin of the Novosibirsk computer center, issue 14 (2001)
15. T. Toffoli: Cellular Automata as an Alternative to (Rather than an Approximation of) Differential Equations in Modeling Physics", Physica 10D, pp. 117–127 (1984)
16. M. Resnick: Turtles, Termites, and Traffic Jams, MIT Press, Cambridge, Mass. (1994)
17. B. Chopard and M. Droz: Cellular Automata Modeling of Physical Systems, Cambridge Univ. press, Cambridge, England (1998)
18. D. Talia and P.Sloot, eds., Future Generation Computer Systems, Dec.1999.
19. M. Sipper, The Emergence of Cellular Computing, IEEE Computer society, COMPUTER magazine, Vol. 32, No. 7, July (1999), p. 18–26
20. G. Spezzano and D. Talia, CARPET: a Programming Language for Parallel Cellular Processing. In proc. 2$^{nd}$ European school on parallel programming tools (ESPPE'96), p. 71–74, Alpe d'Huez,April (1996)

21. Di Napoli, C., Giordano, M., Mango Furnari, M., Mele, F., and Napolitano, R.: CANL: a Language for Cellular Automata Network Modeling. In R. Vllmar, W. Erhard, and V. Jossifov, editors, Parcella '96, number 96 in Mathematical research, p. 101–111, Berlin. Akademie Verlag, (1996)
22. C. Demetrescu, I. Finocchi, and Stasko J.: Specifying Algorithm Visualizations, Lecture notes in computer science ; 2269, Springer, p. 16–29 (2002)
23. Kerren A., and Stasko J.: Introduction to Algorithm Animation, chapter 1, Lecture notes in computer science ; 2269, Springer, p. 1–15 (2002)
24. M. Saber, N. Mirenkov: Filmification of Methods: Cellular Programming Approach, Journal of Three Dimensional Images, Vol.15, No. 1, 3D Forum, p. 110–115 (2001)
25. M. Saber, N. Mirenkov: Visual Cellular Programming Based on Self-Explanatory Components Technology, In the proceedings of the Second International Workshop on Intelligent Multimedia Computing and Networking (IMMCN'2002), published in The proceedings of the Sixth Joint Conference on Information Sciences (JCIS'2002), p. 931–935
26. MPICH-A Portable Implementation of MPI
    http://www.unix.mcs.anl.gov/mpi/ mpich/index.html
27. William Gropp, Ewing Lusk, and Anthony Skjellum: Using MPI: Portable Parallel Programming with the Message Passing Interface, 2nd edition, MIT Press, Cambridge, MA (1999)

# Author Index